AMNESTY INTERNATIONAL
REPORT 2001

UNITED STATES OF AMERICA
CANADA
ICELAND
UNITED STATES OF AMERICA
MEXICO
BAHAMAS
CUBA
HAITI
DOMINICAN REP.
BELIZE
JAMAICA
GUATEMALA
HONDURAS
EL SALVADOR
NICARAGUA
SAINT KITTS AND NEVIS
ANTIGUA AND BARBUDA
DOMINICA
SAINT VINCENT AND THE GRENADINES
SAINT LUCIA
BARBADOS
GRENADA
TRINIDAD AND TOBAGO
COSTA RICA
PANAMA
VENEZUELA
GUYANA
SURINAME
COLOMBIA
ECUADOR
PERU
BRAZIL
BOLIVIA
PARAGUAY
URUGUAY
CHILE
ARGENTINA
KIRIBATI
PACIFIC OCEAN
SAMOA
TONGA
ATLANTIC OCEAN
PORTUGAL
MOROCCO
WESTERN SAHARA
MAURITANIA
CAPE VERDE
SENEGAL
GAMBIA
GUINEA-BISSAU
GUINEA
SIERRA LEONE
LIBERIA

RUSSIAN FEDERATION
FINLAND
NORWAY
SWEDEN
ESTONIA
LATVIA
LITHUANIA
BELARUS
POLAND
UKRAINE
GERMANY
CZECH REP.
SLOVAKIA
AUSTRIA
HUNGARY
ROMANIA
MOLDOVA
YUGOSLAVIA
CROATIA
BULGARIA
ITALY
GREECE
ALBANIA
MACEDONIA
BOSNIA-HERZEGOVINA
TUNISIA
TURKEY
GEORGIA
ARMENIA
AZERBAIJAN
KAZAKSTAN
MONGOLIA
UZBEKISTAN
KYRGYZSTAN
TAJIKISTAN
TURKMENISTAN
AFGHANISTAN
CHINA
KOREA (DEM. REP.)
KOREA (REP.)
JAPAN
PACIFIC OCEAN
SYRIA
CYPRUS
LEBANON
ISRAEL
OT/PA
JORDAN
IRAQ
IRAN
PAKISTAN
NEPAL
BHUTAN
BANGLADESH
TAIWAN
HONG KONG
MACAO
KUWAIT
BAHRAIN
QATAR
UNITED ARAB EMIRATES
SAUDI ARABIA
OMAN
INDIA
MYANMAR
LAOS
THAILAND
CAMBODIA
VIET NAM
PHILIPPINES
LIBYA
EGYPT
YEMEN
ERITREA
DJIBOUTI
NIGER
CHAD
SUDAN
ETHIOPIA
SOMALIA
NIGERIA
CAMEROON
CENTRAL AFRICAN REP.
EQUATORIAL GUINEA
GABON
CONGO (REP.)
CONGO (DEM. REP.)
UGANDA
KENYA
RWANDA
BURUNDI
TANZANIA
SRI LANKA
MALDIVES
SINGAPORE
MALAYSIA
BRUNEI
MARSHALL ISLANDS
PALAU
MICRONESIA
NAURU
SEYCHELLES
INDONESIA
PAPUA-NEW GUINEA
COMOROS
ANGOLA
ZAMBIA
MALAWI
INDIAN OCEAN
EAST TIMOR
SOLOMON ISLANDS
TUVALU
MOZAMBIQUE
ZIMBABWE
NAMIBIA
BOTSWANA
MADAGASCAR
MAURITIUS
SOUTH AFRICA
SWAZILAND
LESOTHO
VANUATU
FIJI
AUSTRALIA
NEW ZEALAND

First published in 2001 by
Amnesty International
322 Eighth Avenue
New York, NY 10001

www.amnestyusa.org

© Copyright
Amnesty International Publications 2001
ISBN: 1 - 887204 - 27 - x
AI index: POL 10/001/2001
Original language: English

Printed by:
Globe Lithographing Co., Inc.
Ridgefield Park, New Jersey
USA

Cover design by Synergy

All rights reserved. No part of this publication may be reproduced, stored in a retrieval system, or transmitted, in any form or by any means, electronic, mechanical, photocopying, recording and/or otherwise without the prior permission of the publishers.

AMNESTY INTERNATIONAL
REPORT 2001

This report covers the period January to December 2000

CONTENTS

Preface/1
AI's appeals for action/2

PART 1
Foreword by Pierre Sané/5
Introduction/11

PART 2
Afghanistan/25
Albania/26
Algeria/28
Angola/30
Argentina/32
Armenia/34
Australia/35
Austria/36
Azerbaijan/38
Bahamas/40
Bahrain/41
Bangladesh/43
Belarus/44
Belgium/45
Belize/47
Bhutan/48
Bolivia/49
Bosnia-Herzegovina/51
Brazil/54
Bulgaria/56
Burkina Faso/58
Burundi/60
Cambodia/62
Cameroon/64
Canada/66
Chad/67
Chile/68
China/69
Colombia/73
Congo (Democratic Republic of the)/77
Congo (Republic of the)/80
Côte d'Ivoire/81
Croatia/83
Cuba/85
Czech Republic/87
Dominican Republic/88
East Timor/89
Ecuador/90
Egypt/92
El Salvador/94
Equatorial Guinea/96
Eritrea/97

Ethiopia/98
Fiji/100
Finland/102
France/103
Gambia/105
Georgia/107
Germany/108
Ghana/110
Greece/111
Guatemala/113
Guinea/115
Guinea-Bissau/116
Guyana/118
Haiti/119
Honduras/121
Hungary/123
India/124
Indonesia/126
Iran/129
Iraq/131
Ireland/134
Israel and the Occupied Territories/135
Italy/137
Jamaica/140
Japan/141
Jordan/143
Kazakstan/144
Kenya/145
Korea (Democratic People's Republic of)/148
Korea (Republic of)/149
Kuwait/150
Kyrgyzstan/151
Laos/153
Latvia/154
Lebanon/154
Lesotho/157
Liberia/158
Libya/160
Macedonia/162
Malawi/163
Malaysia/164
Maldives/165
Mali/166
Mauritania/167
Mexico/168
Moldova/170
Morocco/Western Sahara/171
Mozambique/173
Myanmar/175
Namibia/177

CONTENTS

Nepal/178
New Zealand/180
Nicaragua/180
Niger/181
Nigeria/182
Pakistan/184
Palestinian Authority/186
Paraguay/188
Peru/190
Philippines/192
Poland/193
Portugal/194
Qatar/196
Romania/196
Russian Federation/198
Rwanda/202
Saint Lucia/204
Samoa/205
Saudi Arabia/206
Senegal/208
Sierra Leone/209
Singapore/213
Slovakia/214
Slovenia/215
Solomon Islands/216
Somalia/217
South Africa/219
Spain/222
Sri Lanka/224
Sudan/226
Suriname/228
Swaziland/229
Sweden/230

Switzerland/231
Syria/233
Taiwan/235
Tajikistan/236
Tanzania/237
Thailand/239
Togo/240
Trinidad and Tobago/243
Tunisia/244
Turkey/247
Turkmenistan/250
Uganda/251
Ukraine/253
United Arab Emirates/254
United Kingdom/255
United States of America/258
Uruguay/261
Uzbekistan/262
Venezuela/264
Viet Nam/266
Yemen/267
Yugoslavia (Federal Republic of)/269
Zambia/272
Zimbabwe/273

PART 3
What is AI?/279
AI in action/283
International and regional organizations/290
Selected international human rights treaties/295
Selected regional human rights treaties/299

PREFACE

Amnesty International (AI) is a worldwide movement of people who campaign for human rights. AI's work is based on careful research and on the standards agreed by the international community. AI is independent of any government, political ideology, economic interest or religion. It does not support or oppose any government or political system, nor does it support or oppose the views of the victims whose rights it seeks to protect. It is concerned solely with the impartial protection of human rights.

AI mobilizes volunteer activists in more than 140 countries and territories in every part of the world. There are more than 1,000,000 AI members and subscribers from many different backgrounds, with widely different political and religious beliefs, united by a determination to work for a world where everyone enjoys human rights.

AI works independently and impartially to promote respect for all the human rights set out in the Universal Declaration of Human Rights. The main focus of its campaigning is to:
- free all prisoners of conscience. According to AI's Statute, these are people detained for their political, religious or other conscientiously held beliefs or because of their ethnic origin, sex, colour, language, national or social origin, economic status, birth or other status — who have not used or advocated violence;
- ensure fair and prompt trials for all political prisoners;
- abolish the death penalty, torture and other ill-treatment of prisoners;
- end political killings and "disappearances";
- ensure that governments refrain from unlawful killings in armed conflict.

AI also works to:
- oppose abuses by armed political groups such as the detention of prisoners of conscience, hostage-taking, torture and unlawful killings;
- assist asylum-seekers who are at risk of being returned to a country where they might suffer violations of their fundamental human rights;
- cooperate with other non-governmental organizations, the UN and regional inter-governmental organizations to further human rights;
- ensure control of international military, security and police relations in order to protect human rights;
- organize human rights education and awareness raising programs.

AI is a democratic, self-governing movement. Major policy decisions are taken by an International Council made up of representatives from all national sections.

AI's national sections and local volunteer groups are primarily responsible for funding the movement. No funds are sought or accepted from governments for AI's work investigating and campaigning against human rights violations.

Amnesty International Report 2001

This report documents human rights issues of concern to AI during the year 2000. It also reflects the activities AI has undertaken during the year to promote human rights and to campaign against specific human rights abuses.

The core of this report is made up of entries on individual countries and territories, listed alphabetically. Each of these entries gives a summary of the human rights situation in the country or territory and describes AI's specific human rights concerns there. The absence of an entry on a particular country or territory does not imply that no human rights abuses of concern to AI took place there during the year. Nor is the length of individual entries any basis for a comparison of the extent and depth of AI's concerns.

A world map has been included in this report to indicate the location of countries and territories, and each individual country entry begins with some basic information about the country during 2000. Neither the map nor the country information may be interpreted as AI's view on questions such as the status of disputed territory, population size or language. AI takes no position on issues other than human rights concerns which fall within its mandate.

The later sections of the report contain some information about AI and its work during the year. The final section focuses on AI's work with intergovernmental organizations and includes information about which states are bound by key international and regional human rights treaties.

Internet addresses

Reports published during the year are listed at the end of country entries. These are available on the AI website. The AI Index given in this report can be used to locate a document as follows: AI Index: ABC 63/004/2000
http://www.web.amnesty.org/ai.nsf/index/ABC630042000

Abbreviations for treaties

The following abbreviations have been used:
- **UN Convention against Torture** refers to the Convention against Torture and Other Cruel, Inhuman or Degrading Treatment or Punishment.
- **UN Women's Convention** refers to the Convention on the Elimination of All Forms of Discrimination against Women.
- **UN Children's Convention** refers to the Convention on the Rights of the Child.
- **UN Convention against Racism** refers to the International Convention on the Elimination of All Forms of Racial Discrimination.
- **UN Refugee Convention** refers to the Convention relating to the Status of Refugees.
- **European Convention on Human Rights** refers to the (European) Convention for the Protection of Human Rights and Fundamental Freedoms.

Torture Free Zone tape

This report is published during AI's worldwide campaign to eradicate torture. Torture Free Zone tape is used as a visual link with the campaign in many country entries where torture was a significant concern in 2000. However, the absence of the tape in a country entry does not indicate that AI did not have concerns about torture or ill-treatment in that country.

AI'S APPEALS FOR ACTION

The country entries in this report include numerous examples of human rights abuses that AI is dedicated to oppose under its mandate. In response to these human rights abuses, AI urges those in authority in all countries where violations occur to take the steps recommended below. More detailed additional recommendations relevant to particular situations are included where necessary in the specific country entry.

Recommendations to governments
Prisoners of conscience
AI calls for the immediate and unconditional release of all prisoners of conscience. According to AI's Statute, prisoners of conscience are people detained anywhere for their political, religious or other conscientiously held beliefs or because of their ethnic origin, sex, colour, language, national or social origin, economic status, birth or other status — who have not used or advocated violence.

Political prisoners
AI calls for all prisoners whose cases have a political aspect to be given a prompt and fair trial on recognizably criminal charges, or released.

AI calls for trials to meet minimum international standards of fairness. These include, for example, the right to a fair hearing before a competent, independent and impartial tribunal, the right to have adequate time and facilities to prepare a defence, and the right to appeal to a higher tribunal.

Torture and ill-treatment
AI calls on governments to take steps to prevent torture and ill-treatment. Such steps include initiating impartial, prompt and effective investigations into all allegations of torture and bringing to justice those responsible for torture.

Further safeguards against torture and ill-treatment which AI promotes include:
- clear policies that torture and ill-treatment will not be tolerated;
- an end to incommunicado detention, including giving detainees access to independent medical examination and legal counsel;
- outlawing the use of confessions extracted under torture as evidence in courts of law;
- independent inspection of places of detention;
- informing detainees of their rights;
- human rights training for law enforcement personnel;
- compensation for the victims of torture;
- medical treatment and rehabilitation for the victims of torture.

Prison conditions
AI calls on governments to ensure that prison conditions do not amount to cruel, inhuman or degrading treatment or punishment, in line with international human rights standards for the treatment of prisoners.

Death penalty
AI calls on governments to abolish the death penalty in law and practice.

Pending abolition, AI calls on governments to commute death sentences, to introduce a moratorium on executions, to respect international standards restricting the scope of the death penalty and to ensure the most rigorous standards for fair trial in capital cases.

Political killings and 'disappearances'
AI calls on governments to end extrajudicial executions and "disappearances". It calls for prompt, independent and effective investigations into such violations and for those responsible to be brought to justice.

AI calls on governments to:
- demonstrate their total opposition to extrajudicial executions and "disappearances" and make clear to security forces that these abuses will not be tolerated in any circumstances;
- end secret or incommunicado detention and introduce measures to locate and protect prisoners;
- provide effective protection to anyone in danger of extrajudicial execution or "disappearance", including those who have received threats;
- ensure that law enforcement officials use force only when strictly required and to the minimum extent necessary — lethal force should be used only when unavoidable to protect life;
- ensure strict chain-of-command control of all security forces;
- ban "death squads", private armies and paramilitary forces acting outside the official chain of command.

Unlawful killings in armed conflict
AI calls on governments engaged in armed conflict to adhere to provisions of international humanitarian law, including the prohibition of direct attacks on civilians and of indiscriminate attacks.

Asylum-seekers
AI calls on governments to ensure that no asylum-seekers are returned to a country where they might suffer violations of their fundamental human rights.

AI calls on governments to ensure that all asylum-seekers have access to a fair and impartial individual asylum determination, and to ensure that they are not arbitrarily detained or otherwise put under undue pressure.

Promote and respect human rights
AI calls on states to ratify international and regional human rights instruments without reservations, and calls on all governments to respect and promote the provisions of these instruments.

Recommendations to armed political groups
AI calls on armed political groups to respect fundamental standards of human rights and international humanitarian law, and to halt abuses such as the detention of prisoners of conscience, hostage-taking, torture and unlawful killings.

AI REPORT 2001
PART 1

FOREWORD

by Pierre Sané, Secretary General

This is AI's 40th anniversary year. Back in 1961 a British lawyer heard the story of two Portuguese students who had been imprisoned for drinking a toast to freedom. He launched a newspaper appeal, and from this individual initiative grew a worldwide movement in which millions of people have taken part. In its 40 years of work, AI's volunteer activists and their supporters have worked tirelessly to free the unjustly imprisoned, protect those at risk of torture and obtain justice for victims. More than a million AI members are involved in mobilizing their communities, putting pressure on governments and supporting victims and their families. Usually it is impossible to measure the impact of our endeavours, and we are generally part of a far wider effort, but we do know that we have saved lives, we have stimulated action and we have contributed to lasting improvements.

Anniversaries invite reflection not only on past achievements, but also on how the world has changed. This year, the first of a new century, is an opportune moment to look back over the recent past in order to prepare for the challenges ahead. For me personally, it is equally a time of reflection, as I leave the post of Secretary General of AI after nearly 10 years. The past decade – the years since the fall of the Berlin Wall – has seen massive political, social and economic changes. The human rights movement has grown in strength and numbers, and consciousness of human rights is undoubtedly greater than ever. Yet repression, poverty and war devastate the lives of much of humanity. The optimism we enjoyed in 1990 has been replaced by well-founded fears, and human rights activism is needed today more than ever.

1. GLOBALIZATION

The end of the Cold War was hailed by many as the start of a new world order that would bring freedom and prosperity for all. But for millions the reality has proved very different. Globalization – the spread of the free market economy, multi-party political systems and technological change – has been accompanied by growing wealth for some, but destitution and despair for many.

Globalization did not start in the 1990s but its effects have intensified and become clearer over the past 10 years. Capital has always been mobile; what has changed is that the reliance of corporations on national states has become less and less important. Parallel with the concentration of wealth in the hands of multinational corporations has been the growing power of global economic institutions such as the International Monetary Fund (IMF), World Bank and World Trade Organization (WTO).

Globalization has undoubtedly led to enormous economic expansion. The world is richer than it has ever been and technology is advancing faster and faster. There is unprecedented potential to eradicate poverty and fulfil the aspirations of the Universal Declaration of Human Rights – freedom from fear and freedom from want. But globalization has also brought economic volatility and instability. The 1997 financial crisis in Asia led to massive unemployment and the displacement of millions of migrant workers. The effects included reduced welfare spending in apparently unconnected countries in Latin America, and a sudden rise in the cost of vital imports into Africa.

Globalization has been accompanied by debt and poverty. More than 80 countries had a lower per capita income in 2000 than they had in 1990. At least 1.3 billion people struggle to survive on less than a dollar a day. Deregulation, privatization and the dismantling of social welfare provision have led to widening inequalities in many countries. In large parts of the world, corruption has increased, and personal, social and political insecurity has spread. The predictable and almost inevitable consequence of this growth in poverty has been a parallel escalation in violations of all human rights. The Berlin Wall may have crumbled, but the walls of poverty, intolerance and hypocrisy still stand.

The new human rights challenges arising from globalization have stimulated AI to take on new areas of work, namely socio-economic rights and economic actors.

AI and socio-economic rights

In a 1997 policy decision, AI members reaffirmed their determination to promote *all* human rights. At its forthcoming International Council Meeting, AI members will debate ways of further intensifying the work of the organization in the fields of social, economic and cultural rights. AI has acknowledged the relative neglect of economic, social and cultural rights by the international human rights movement, and has taken steps to address these rights more directly in its own work.

The 50th anniversary of the Universal Declaration of Human Rights in 1998 allowed AI to reiterate the importance and the indivisibility of the human rights which are fundamental to the dignity and development of every human being. These range from economic rights, such as the right to work and to an adequate standard of living, to political rights, such as freedom of opinion, expression and association. They include civil rights, such as equality before the law, and social and cultural rights, such as the right to education and to participate in the cultural life of the community. AI's campaign to promote awareness of the Universal Declaration involved entering into a dialogue with millions of people around the world. The campaign also aimed to put pressure on states to ensure that all the rights in the Universal Declaration, including social and economic rights, moved beyond paper promises to become a reality for everyone.

AI and economic actors

The Universal Declaration not only addresses governments but also calls upon "every individual and every organ of society" to promote respect for these rights and freedoms and to secure their observance. By

FOREWORD

In the past decade AI has run major campaigns taking up these themes. In 1992, the 500th anniversary of the arrival of Europeans in the Americas, we campaigned against the widespread human rights violations suffered by indigenous peoples in the Americas. In the run-up to the Beijing World Conference on Women's Rights we launched worldwide action around the slogan *Women's Rights are Human Rights*. Faced with growing efforts by governments to avoid their obligations to refugees, and rising intolerance towards asylum-seekers, we organized a worldwide campaign for refugee rights. We took a dual approach: to show that every refugee is a human being with a story of persecution, not a statistic; and to press governments to fulfil their commitments to refugee protection. Above all, we stressed that states should work to end the human rights crises that force people to leave home in search of safety.

Discrimination can take many different forms. In the Israeli-occupied West Bank, for example, thousands of Palestinians live in fear that their homes may be demolished without warning by the Israeli authorities. Palestinians living in the West Bank have no chance of getting a building permit from the authorities, which means their home is effectively illegal even if built on land that has belonged to their family for generations. In 1999 AI published a report which clearly revealed how planning laws are interpreted according to two policies: one for the Palestinians and one for the Israelis.

Our campaign against human rights abuses in the USA — *Rights for All* — highlighted racism in the criminal justice system. Pointing to the disproportionate number of black people in prison and on death row, and systematic police brutality against blacks and Latinos, we called on the USA to deliver rights for all its people. This work fed into our efforts to contribute to the 2001 World Conference against Racism.

Discrimination is also one of the three main messages of the current campaign against torture, which is built around the need to prevent torture, to combat discrimination and to end impunity. Discrimination paves the way for torture by allowing the victim to be seen not as human but as an object, who can, therefore, be treated inhumanely. Institutionalized discrimination also means that the victims are less likely to receive protection and support from the authorities. The campaign has focused special attention on racism and torture, on torture of women, on torture of children, and on torture and sexual identity.

One of the debates among anti-torture activists is the extent to which states are responsible for acts of violence committed not by police officers or soldiers, but by private individuals — "non-state actors". Domestic violence, racist attacks by skinhead gangs and "cleansing campaigns" against street children are examples where AI holds that the state can be held accountable if it does not take the basic steps necessary to prevent the abuses and bring those responsible to justice.

AI and human rights defenders

One of the most dramatic changes in the 40 years since AI was created has been the growth and development of human rights groups at the local and national level. Their constant vigilance and dedication are often the only defence against injustice and the abuse of power.

Human rights defenders work to protect the weak and hold the powerful to account. For this they are often victimized. Some have "disappeared" after making inquiries about the "disappeared". Some have been assassinated for protesting against state violence. Some have been put behind bars for demanding prisoners' rights. For AI, supporting and protecting human rights defenders at risk, making sure that their voices can be heard, is a vital part of its strategy.

From its inception, AI has worked to protect human rights defenders through campaigning, government lobbying, urgent actions and so on. AI has also worked with other human rights organizations pressing for the adoption of a UN declaration on human rights defenders and the creation of the UN Special Representative on human rights defenders, both of which have become a reality after years of hard work.

The late 1990s saw a real increase in AI's work on behalf of, and with, human rights defenders. It began in 1996 with the International Conference on the Protection of Human Rights Defenders in Latin America and the Caribbean (the Bogotá Conference), held in Colombia. This was followed in November 1998 with the All-Africa Conference on Human Rights Defenders held in Johannesburg, South Africa, and ended with the Paris Summit in December 1998 which brought together more than 300 defenders from all over the world.

Human rights defenders are playing an ever more crucial role in the defence of the rights of groups who have been marginalized and silenced. Without their tireless work, those who face discrimination and human rights abuses would have little or no protection.

Fragmentation – the challenge for AI

AI was born at a time of widespread global radicalization and drew its strength from people determined to express solidarity with the victims of government repression. In the 1960s the peoples of Africa were struggling to free themselves from colonial domination, and people living under authoritarian regimes in Spain, Portugal or the USSR were fighting to assert their right to dissent. AI said, "let opinions flow freely", and we organized to unlock the cells of the dissenters.

When, in the 1970s and 1980s, military juntas used torture to break the opposition in Latin America, we campaigned to secure an international convention against torture and to close down the torture chambers. When political repression moved out of the prisons to the streets in the form of "disappearances" and extrajudicial executions, we took on these new violations. AI responded to the proliferation of armed conflicts in the 1990s by adjusting its mandate to address all the combatants, not just governments.

The challenge facing AI now is to enlarge its focus beyond freedom of opinion to encompass identity-based abuses. We have to work not only for people who are targeted because of what they think, but for those who are at risk because of who they are. This is not a turn away from our roots: the Universal Declaration of

Human Rights was a product of revulsion against the Holocaust — and genocide is the ultimate identity-based human rights violation.

This is no easy process. We need new methods of research. We need new campaigning techniques. Above all we need to find new ways of building international solidarity. It has proved in many ways harder to mobilize the public around identity-based abuses. For example, while the torture of anti-apartheid leaders was the subject of worldwide condemnation and popular protest, the torture of criminal suspects in South Africa's police stations today barely registers. While many of the political dissidents around the world that AI campaigned for in the early days were well-connected, middle class intellectuals, the victims of identity-based abuses are often poor and uneducated. Many are unpopular within their own countries. Some people have turned against human rights organizations, regarding their work as little more than the protection of criminals. They have accepted the killing of young suspects, provided it was not their own sons killed by mistake. AI must find new ways to generate compassion, solidarity and action.

3. ASSAULT ON THE NATION STATE

States are being squeezed between the twin pressures of globalization and fragmentation. The nation state can neither control global trends, nor easily accommodate the demands of different groups living within its borders. Some states have collapsed completely under the pressure of competing demands. In others, state control over parts of the national territory is minimal or non-existent. Many states have been weakened, and some have lost legitimacy in the eyes of those they are supposed to represent.

Virtually all governments have adopted the rhetoric of liberal democracy and of human rights. Few have delivered this as a reality. Many states claim they have been forced to adopt economic policies which undermine social, economic and cultural rights. While it is true that no national economy can survive in isolation from globalized markets, it is not true that national governments are totally lacking in powers to defend their people against the arbitrary actions of multinational corporations or the pressures of intergovernmental financial institutions. There is much that governments can and should do.

They can ensure that workers are protected from the worst forms of exploitation. They can tackle official corruption. They can stop attacking human rights defenders. They can, and must, live up to their human rights obligations, national and international.

How to hold states accountable for their conduct? That is the central question that AI tackles on a daily basis. The answer is as varied as the situations we face. The traditional techniques of generating publicity and appealing directly to the responsible authorities through letters, faxes and e-mails are still important. However, AI has moved towards a more strategic approach by identifying in each instance who can influence those with the power to stop abuses, how to mobilize them to take action, and what steps need to be taken to prevent further human rights violations. Companies and other governments can use their economic and diplomatic links to press for improvements. Non-governmental organizations, AI members and local human rights defenders all have a role to play and all have particular strengths to bring to the defence of human rights.

Sometimes an international campaign mobilizing as many people as possible all around the world is the best way to achieve change. In the past 10 years AI members have organized worldwide campaigns against human rights violations in countries including China, Saudi Arabia, Sudan, Turkey and the USA. These campaigns motivated and inspired thousands of people and achieved measurable improvements, from raising the profile of human rights issues to the introduction of legislative safeguards. Looking back over these campaigns, one of the most striking developments is the way in which AI has joined forces with other human rights organizations, operating as part of the wider human rights network. The strategy for the USA campaign, for example, was discussed openly with coalitions of US human rights and civil liberties groups.

Increasingly, work to support and strengthen local human rights organizations is an integral part of AI's international campaign strategies. One element is the use of high-profile delegations visiting the country, engaging in discussions with local non-governmental organizations, confronting government officials directly and generating publicity in the local news media. I myself have led more than 50 such high-level missions and they have provided valuable opportunities to speak directly to new audiences and to present AI's message in our own words. Often we have helped give new confidence to the local human rights community and, by making clear what kind of organization we are, what our demands are and how we work, we have given a real boost to our own members. Sometimes the tangible results have exceeded our expectations.

To give just one example, in February 2000 I led an AI delegation which visited Nepal at a time of escalating violence in the "people's war" between the government and the Communist Party of Nepal (Maoist). Our packed schedule included talks with a large number of government officials; meetings with human rights defenders, refugees and victims; a human rights defenders' workshop; a human rights training workshop for police officers; and media work. For most of that week, we were front page news. We raised our concerns about political killings, torture, arbitrary detention and an emerging pattern of "disappearances". The highlight of the visit was the release of two "disappeared" prisoners — Suresh Ale Magar and Pawan Shrestha — whose cases the AI delegation had brought to the attention of the authorities throughout the week.

AI holds states accountable not only for their actions, but for their inaction. When states pay lip-service to women's and children's rights but fail to train their police in how to deal with domestic violence and child abuse, they have not lived up to their responsibilities and therefore share the blame. Similarly AI holds states accountable not only for their actions at home, but also for the harm they do in other parts of the world. The failure to regulate international transfers of arms,

FOREWORD

security equipment and expertise used to abuse human rights has equipped torturers, propped up repressive regimes and fuelled conflicts.

The horror of crimes committed in these conflicts has finally prompted the international community to take serious steps towards ending impunity. The attempt to bring former Chilean leader Augusto Pinochet to justice in Europe showed just how far the world's understanding of international justice had come. Although Augusto Pinochet was eventually allowed to return to Chile, his arrest in London transformed the human rights landscape. The principle of universal jurisdiction – that there can be no hiding place for those who commit torture and other terrible crimes – is at the heart of international efforts to establish the International Criminal Court. Pinochet may have escaped justice in Europe, but he now faces trial in Chile. At long last.

Regionalization

Regional groupings of states – such as the European Union, Economic Community of West African States (ECOWAS), the North Atlantic Treaty Organization (NATO) and the Asia-Pacific Economic Co-operation (APEC) – are playing an increasingly prominent role on the world stage. Some of these bodies, for example the Council of Europe and the Organization of American States (OAS), have provided valuable human rights machinery. However, too often states have hidden behind regional bodies to deflect criticism from their own actions. In addition, the perception that decision-making is moving further and further away from ordinary people has in some instances reinforced a reactionary and nationalistic response to human rights initiatives by these bodies. For example, politicians in English-speaking Caribbean countries have stoked support for the death penalty by arguing, among other things, that the OAS was interfering in internal affairs.

AI has worked to further its human rights concerns on the agendas of these regional bodies. AI's office in Brussels seeks to influence the evolution of the European Union's human rights mandate and to monitor its actions. Most recently AI has focused on issues surrounding foreign policy, refugees and asylum, the death penalty, torture and the arms trade. ECOWAS, the West African regional grouping, has deployed peace-keeping troops in several countries. AI has lobbied ECOWAS, seeking to ensure that its peace-keeping troops respect human rights. In the aftermath of the Asian economic crisis, AI highlighted its impact on freedom of association and expression in APEC member states, and urged APEC to guarantee basic human rights and labour standards. In 1999 NATO launched a bombing campaign against the Federal Republic of Yugoslavia, with the declared aim of ending human rights violations against ethnic Albanians in Kosovo. NATO claimed that its air campaign was the "most precise and lowest-collateral damage air campaign in history". However, after careful analysis of a number of incidents in which civilians were bombed, AI publicly stated its belief that NATO forces had committed serious violations of the laws of war, leading in a number of cases to the unlawful killings of civilians. AI called for redress for the victims, and reforms to the command structure and decision-making processes of NATO.

The nation state: the challenge for AI

The pressures of globalization and fragmentation are indisputable. However, despite the growing powers of multinational corporations and international institutions, the challenge for AI remains above all to hold states accountable. Recentring the debate to focus on the powers and obligations of governments does not mean ignoring the responsibilities of others. It does mean insisting that states are bound by international human rights law and have no alternative but to uphold it. It does mean confronting their cowardice, their cover-ups and their efforts to shirk their responsibilities. It does mean stressing that they have the power, despite external constraints, to deliver on human rights if they have the political will to do so. In short, we need to bring the state back in.

When AI calls on states to be strong in defence of human rights, it is not calling for the use of repression or strong-arm tactics. States often claim that they have to use force to control the irretrievable slide into division. But the use of violence in the face of internal dissent and fragmentation is not a sign of strong governance. Strong governance depends on transparency, inclusion and respect. Governance does not mean mere government. It means the framework of rules, institutions and established practices that set limits and give incentives for the conduct of individuals, organizations and companies. National and global governance have to be reinvented with human rights at their core.

In the name of the victim

AI never loses sight of the fact that these principles are important because of their impact on the real lives and personal tragedies of the victims of human rights violations. The victim is always at the heart of the battles we fight. The first battle is the battle to preserve the individual identity of the victim. A victim is not a statistic or a sociological category. A victim is a human being. And every human being has the right to the elemental human dignity of being named. The second battle is the battle against forgetting. The suffering of victims must be acknowledged and given its due importance. There can be no justice while the perpetrators are allowed to ignore or deny what they have done. The third battle is the battle for compassion for all victims of human rights violations. Human rights are the birthright of all, not just the popular, the articulate and the well-connected. But to build international solidarity on behalf of the socially excluded requires new ways of organizing and reaching people. It requires a new inclusiveness.

I am confident that new audiences will find a home in a multifaceted mass human rights movement, and that together we will rise to these challenges. The forces ranged against us may be formidable. However, the outrage at injustice that led to the founding of AI 40 years ago continues to inspire and motivate millions of people determined to build a better world.

Happy anniversary to all AI members, supporters and staff.

INTRODUCTION

"When I got out I was amazed to hear that Amnesty International had somehow heard about me and had been campaigning for me. For me, Amnesty International means a lot. It is because of the people who care enough about other people to contribute to the work of Amnesty International that people like me all over the world are still alive and are what they are now."

Sylvestre Gahungu, a survivor of human rights violations in Burundi, now an AI member living in New Zealand.

For the past 40 years AI has fought to defend victims of human rights violations. During that time, AI members have steadfastly refused to be daunted by the scale of the task. Whether faced with apparently impregnable totalitarian regimes or the chaos and devastation of war, AI members have found ways to campaign on behalf of prisoners of conscience and victims of other human rights violations, including torture, "disappearances", political killings and executions. Since AI's creation in 1961, AI members have worked on more than 45,000 cases. Some of these cases were on behalf of individuals, others involved whole families or groups. Since the first urgent action appeal was issued in 1973, AI has initiated some 16,600 urgent appeals on behalf of men, women and children in immediate danger. In about one third of new urgent action appeal cases, AI learns of some improvement in the situation of the person or people named in the appeal.

During 2000, in addition to its continuing work monitoring and exposing human rights violations wherever they occur, AI launched a concerted new effort to eradicate torture around the world.

This Amnesty International Report summarizes human rights issues of concern to the organization during 2000. The individual entries which make up the bulk of the report look at these concerns within individual countries and territories. This introductory chapter aims to highlight major campaigning initiatives undertaken by AI members during the year and to reflect some of the major human rights developments worldwide.

Campaign against torture

Few people today would defend the use of torture, yet every year thousands of people beat, rape and electrocute other human beings. AI's renewed campaign to eradicate torture, launched in October 2000, affirms that torture is always indefensible, and that it can be stopped. The message is not new. However, what is new is that more people, in more countries, are taking part in a greater variety of activities to promote this message than ever before.

In Nepal, for example, members organized a motorbike rally involving more than 80 riders. They set out from Kathmandu in two groups — heading for the eastern and western extremes of the country. On their way the riders went into every police station trying to persuade police officers to declare their police stations torture free zones and to show their commitment by displaying "Torture Free Zone tape". The day after the launch of the anti-torture campaign, 14 of the country's 15 newspapers carried reports about the campaign, many on the front page. As well as imaginative and effective public events, members organized a workshop for lawyers on the shortcomings of Nepal's Torture Compensation Act and participated in human rights training for more than 700 police personnel.

In countries around the world AI members are seeking to reach out beyond AI's traditional partner organizations and forge links not only with local human rights groups, but also with other organizations willing to become involved, such as women's groups and trade unions. These new networks are able to draw on complementary capacities and expertise to develop a

A Peruvian theatre group taking part in a "Marathon for Life, Against Torture", part of AI Peru's activities for the launch of AI's worldwide campaign against torture. More than 2,000 people took part, old and young, including TV personalities and members of Congress.

Amnesty International Report 2001

INTRODUCTION

collective strategy for action, appropriate to their specific country or locality.

The campaign has local roots, but global reach. On 18 October the campaign was launched by human rights activists not only in London, but also in Beirut, Buenos Aires, Nairobi and Tokyo. "Torture Free Zone tape" was wrapped around embassies, police stations and courts of justice. In Argentina, speakers at AI's heavily attended press conference included Isabel Allende, a Chilean Deputy, and Argentinian Deputy Dr Alfredo Bravo, a survivor of torture adopted by AI as a prisoner of conscience in the 1970s. In Lebanon, Marcel Khalife, a renowned Lebanese singer and poet, and over 100 AI members held a press conference at the Press Syndicate where solidarity messages from other celebrities were read out. In Japan the launch press conference was attended by torture victims from Tibet, Myanmar, South Korea and Indonesia. Yenny Rosa Damayanati, an Indonesian human rights activist and torture victim, paid tribute in front of the Indonesian embassy to those who died as a result of torture. In Kenya speakers at the launch included Joseph Etima, Uganda's Commissioner for Prisons; Elvis Thodi, Malawi's Assistant Commissioner of Police; and Anisia Achieng, Coordinator of Sudanese Women's Voice for Peace and Human Rights.

The painstaking planning and tireless efforts of those involved set a new benchmark for the level of media coverage and attention that a human rights campaign can and should achieve.

Campaigning against torture online

Working to prevent or stop the torture of individuals at risk has always been at the heart of AI's work. The methods of the torturers have changed over the decades, and so have the methods of the anti-torture campaigners. This campaign is using the Internet to try to extend the protection of international scrutiny to an ever greater number of potential victims. The www.stoptorture.org website has led to individuals in 188 countries registering to get involved and add their voice to the clamour for justice and freedom from torture.

One of the first urgent actions posted on this website was on behalf of Trabun Ibrahim Laku, a Sudanese asylum-seeker detained in Lebanon. There were fears that he and other asylum-seekers were being tortured to force them to drop their asylum claims. Twelve hours into the campaign, 1,300 people had sent expressions of concern for Trabun Ibrahim Laku from the website. The Lebanese government asked AI "to please stop the e-mail messages which are still arriving at a rate of 2 every minute".

Take a step to stamp out torture

At the start of the campaign AI published *Take a step to stamp out torture*, drawing on recent reports of torture and ill-treatment from more than 150 countries. Torture continues to be used as an instrument of political repression. In many parts of the world, those who challenge the prevailing order, whether non-violently or by taking up arms, are still likely targets of torture and ill-treatment.

However, AI's global survey into patterns of torture revealed that the most common victims of torture and ill-treatment are convicted criminals and criminal suspects. In some countries, beatings of criminal suspects are so routine that they are not recognized as torture, even by the victims themselves. Criminal suspects often come from the poorest or most marginalized sectors of society. Discrimination against

© Gilles Peress/Magnum Photos

Cambodia: a woman looks at pictures of people tortured by the Khmer Rouge in the late 1970s. This photograph appears in a book produced by AI Italy to promote the anti-torture campaign.

INTRODUCTION

Imen Derouiche, a former prisoner of conscience from Tunisia, speaks of her experience of torture and why she is backing AI's campaign, Take a step to stamp out torture. She was one of a group of students at the University of Tunis who were held in incommunicado detention, beaten, threatened and denied essential medical treatment in 1998 and 1999.

such groups often contributes to the lack of action against their torture or ill-treatment.

AI's increased emphasis on working against abuses based on identity – especially women and children – is at the heart of the torture campaign. For many people torture is what happens to political prisoners under brutal dictatorships. This is true. But it is also what happens in liberal democracies, especially to members of groups which have been silenced or marginalized by wider social discrimination. The link between discrimination against women, children, members of ethnic minorities and lesbian, gay, bisexual and transgendered people is key to the campaign.

Children and torture

"He had a pair of pliers in his hand. He kept asking where the mobile [phone] was. I told him I had not seen it... He got hold of my thumb and placed it between the pliers. He pressed it hard and crushed my thumb. I do not remember what happened next."

This description would be shocking no matter who the victim was. What makes it particularly abhorrent is that these are the words of a nine-year-old boy tortured by police in Bangladesh.

As part of the anti-torture campaign, AI published a report which highlighted the horrific violence and abuse to which children are subjected throughout the world. Every day children are tortured in police stations, by rival armies and in their homes. Most children suffer in silence, their stories never told, their tormentors never called to account. AI's campaign seeks to expose the hidden scandal of the torture of children and to end it. (*Hidden scandal, secret shame – Torture and ill-treatment of children*, AI Index: ACT 40/038/2000)

Women and torture

"She was crying when she came back. She told us she had been raped by three or four soldiers. She cried for a long time. She asked why we were lying about it because she said she knew it had happened to us too."

A woman from Suva Reka, Kosovo, Federal Republic of Yugoslavia, 1999

The kind of torture that women are subjected to is decisively influenced by their gender. Rape and other sexual violence have been inflicted on women in all the armed conflicts investigated by AI in recent years.

Women in custody have been subjected to many forms of torture. Prominent among them is sexual violence, including rape, by police and prison guards. Yet in most countries women's greatest risk of violence comes not from police officers or soldiers, but from people they know. Whatever the setting, whoever the perpetrator, most women victims of violence have to contend not only with the abuse itself, but also with official silence or indifference.

Although governments have a duty to prevent, investigate and punish abuses against women, in reality women often face inadequate preventive measures, police indifference, a failure to define abuses as criminal offences and gender bias in the court system. In Italy, in February 1999, the Supreme Court overturned an appeal court verdict which had found a male driving instructor guilty of raping his 18-year-old student, commenting: "It is common knowledge... that jeans cannot even be partly removed without the active cooperation of the person wearing them... and it is impossible if the victim is struggling with all her force". The court concluded that rape was not proved and referred the case back for retrial.

As part of the anti-torture campaign, AI is seeking to hold states accountable for all acts of torture, including those committed by private individuals.

Sexual identity and torture

The torture of lesbian, gay, bisexual and transgendered people around the world is concealed behind a veil of secrecy and taboo. It is a worldwide problem – AI has documented numerous cases from every continent – but one that is greatly under-reported. The stigma surrounding homosexuality in many cultures means that those speaking out are often ignored, further marginalized or abused. While some governments seek to deny that such torture takes place – or even that homosexuals exist in their countries – others openly justify it in the name of morality, religion or ideology. Either way, the effect is that torture goes unchallenged.

Laws criminalizing homosexuality not only deprive a sector of the population of basic human rights, they may also act as a licence to torture or ill-treat. However, torture is not limited to countries where homosexuality is illegal. Institutionalized prejudice means that lesbians, bisexuals, gay men and

Amnesty International Report 2001

INTRODUCTION

transgendered people who come into contact with the law for other reasons may be targeted for abuse, in particular rape and other sexual violence. AI campaigns against laws that criminalize homosexuality. As part of this campaign AI is highlighting the links between discriminatory laws and practices and torture.

Racism and torture

The recent resurgence in racist ill-treatment and torture is nourished by increasingly xenophobic responses to immigration, discrimination in the criminal justice system, and the proliferation of armed conflicts with an ethnic dimension.

According to AI's research, many if not most of the victims of police brutality in Europe and the USA are black or members of other ethnic minorities. In the Americas, torture and ill-treatment of indigenous people, especially in the context of land rights disputes, is a continuing legacy of centuries of subjugation. Rape, mutilation and other torture have been used as weapons of war in recent conflicts with an ethnic dimension in Africa, Asia and Eastern Europe.

The link between racism and torture is a key theme of the anti-torture campaign, and the 2001 UN World Conference on Racism provides a welcome opportunity to cast the spotlight on patterns of racist abuse.

Take a step to stamp out torture

- Join AI's campaign against torture
- Join AI and other local and international human rights organizations which fight torture
- Make a donation to support AI's work
- Tell friends and family about the campaign and ask them to join too
- Register to take action against torture at www.stoptorture.org and campaign online. Visitors to the website will be able to appeal on behalf of individuals at risk of torture

Campaign against the death penalty

"The death penalty is disgusting, particularly if it condemns an innocent. But it remains an injustice even when it falls on someone who is guilty of a crime."
Giuliano Amato, Prime Minister of Italy, 14 September 2000, commenting on a scheduled execution in Virginia, USA

A permanent end to all executions in the year 2000 — that was the challenge to governments that went out from AI and other abolitionist organizations. It was a challenge that was directed to all governments, but above all to the handful of states responsible for the vast majority of executions — China, Iran, Iraq, Saudi Arabia, and the USA. At the end of 2000 more than half the countries in the world had abolished the death penalty in law or practice.

An 11-year-old boy holds up a sign protesting against the scheduled execution of Bettie Lou Beets in Texas, USA, February 2000. The 62-year-old woman was later put to death by lethal injection for a murder committed in 1983.

More than three countries a year on average have abolished the death penalty for all crimes in the past decade. Once abolished, the death penalty is seldom reintroduced. Since 1985, more than 40 countries have abolished the death penalty in law or, having previously abolished it for ordinary crimes, have gone on to abolish it for all crimes. During the same period only four abolitionist countries reintroduced the death penalty.

In March Malta became the first country to abolish the death penalty for all crimes in the new century. Côte d'Ivoire followed in July when a new Constitution which stipulates that "all penalties resulting in the deprivation of human life are prohibited" was adopted by referendum.

In the USA a recent survey has shown a majority in favour of a moratorium on executions until a study is carried out on the fairness of how the death penalty is used. In January, the Governor of Illinois declared a moratorium on executions in his state owing to its "shameful" record of wrongful convictions in capital cases. His decision fuelled calls for executions to be

By the end of 2000, 75 countries and territories had abolished the death penalty for all crimes. A further 13 countries had abolished it for all but exceptional crimes such as wartime crimes. At least 20 countries were abolitionist in practice: they had not carried out any executions for the past 10 years or more and were believed to have an established practice of not carrying out executions.

INTRODUCTION

> In 2000 at least 1,457 people were executed in 28 countries. At least 3,058 people were sentenced to death in 65 countries. These figures include only cases known to AI; the true figures were certainly higher.
>
> The vast majority of executions worldwide are carried out in a tiny handful of countries. In 2000, 88 per cent of all known executions took place in China, Iran, Saudi Arabia and the USA.
> - In China, preliminary figures indicated that at least 1,000 people were executed, although the true number was believed to be much higher.
> - At least 75 executions were carried out in Iran.
> - Eighty-five people were executed in the USA.
> - In Saudi Arabia, 123 executions were reported, but the total may have been much higher.
> - In Iraq, hundreds of executions were reported, but many of them may have been extrajudicial.

halted elsewhere in the country. Despite this, the death penalty continued to be widely used. Four juvenile offenders were executed; the highest number since 1993. In Texas alone, 40 people were executed, a record in any one year; in December, the 150th prisoner was executed under the five-year governorship of George W. Bush. The USA continued to violate international standards by using the death penalty against the mentally impaired, individuals who were under 18 at the time of the crime, and defendants who received inadequate legal representation. Studies continued to show that the death penalty is applied in the USA in an arbitrary and unfair manner, prone to bias on grounds of race and class.

Although the worldwide abolition of the death penalty has come closer over the past four decades, much still remains to be done, especially in the handful of countries where judicial killing by the state is most entrenched.

Worldwide actions

AI members around the world took special action during 2000 in response to situations in a number of specific countries where the scale or long-term nature of human rights abuses were the cause of acute concern. This was in addition to their continuing work on behalf of individuals, and their efforts to persuade governments to improve their human rights policies and practices.

Sierra Leone

The internal armed conflict in Sierra Leone has been marked by terrible atrocities against unarmed civilians, including mutilations and sexual violence, ever since its outbreak in 1991. In early May 2000 there was a serious deterioration in the political and security situation, precipitated by the capture of some 500 UN peace-keeping troops by rebel forces of the Revolutionary United Front. This crisis showed clearly the link between impunity and continued human rights abuses – the Lomé peace agreement of 1999 included a blanket amnesty for crimes committed in the conflict, which provided no deterrent to a resurgence in the violence.

Although the captured UN forces were released by mid-July 2000, through the mediation of President Charles Taylor of Liberia, the situation remained volatile, with shifting alliances and continuing hostilities between a number of armed forces. Large parts of the north and east of the country, including the key diamond-producing areas, remained under the control of rebel forces, and the illicit trade in diamonds continued to finance the provision of arms and ammunition to rebel forces. Both rebel forces and government-allied forces committed abuses.

AI responded to this crisis by mobilizing its members worldwide to protest at gross human rights abuses against civilians – including killings, mutilation and rape – and to call for the protection of refugees and internally displaced people. AI members highlighted the widespread use of child soldiers in the conflict and the need to prevent the illicit trade in diamonds from Sierra Leone being used to finance arms purchases by rebel forces. AI members around the world called on their governments to enforce effectively an embargo on arms sales to rebel forces, and to ensure that transfers of arms and services to government forces did not facilitate human rights violations.

AI's strategy on Sierra Leone sought to maintain human rights concerns high on the agenda of influential actors, in particular the UN Security Council, the Economic Community of West African States

Internally displaced people in Sierra Leone. Thousands of people fled to Freetown in May 2000 to escape rebel attacks.

© Yannis Behrakis/Reuters

Amnesty International Report 2001

INTRODUCTION

(ECOWAS) and key governments. AI pressed the UN Mission in Sierra Leone (UNAMSIL) to fulfil its mandate to protect civilians, while urging the international community to ensure that the UNAMSIL human rights section received adequate resources and political support.

AI called for an effective international mechanism for investigating human rights abuses and bringing perpetrators to justice. In August 2000 the UN Security Council agreed to establish an independent Special Court for Sierra Leone to try crimes against humanity, war crimes and other serious violations of international humanitarian law. AI called for the Special Court to have the power to prosecute those most responsible for atrocities throughout the conflict and anyone who recruited children under the age of 15 into armed forces or groups, whether such recruitment was forced or voluntary. It also called for the Special Court to receive adequate and sustained funding and for priority to be given to the speediest possible reconstruction of the national judicial system so that it can eventually assume responsibility for bringing to justice perpetrators of human rights abuses not tried by the Special Court.

AI also lobbied the international diamond trading community, as well as major diamond trading centres, to implement UN restrictions on diamonds from Sierra Leone. AI addressed meetings of the International Diamond Manufacturers Association and the World Federation of Diamond Bourses in Antwerp. As a result of ground-breaking work on diamonds and arms, AI was able to involve its grassroots members in taking action on issues concerning economic relations to a greater extent than ever before and to develop expertise in sustaining such activities in countries around the world. Working together with other non-governmental organizations, AI had an impact in that the industry acknowledged the need for regulation and worked towards a tamper-proof certification scheme for diamonds from Sierra Leone.

AI sees its work with the Sierra Leone human rights movement as crucial. Although Sierra Leonean non-governmental human rights organizations have consolidated their work by forming a National Forum for Human Rights and cooperating with the UNAMSIL human rights section and international human rights and humanitarian organizations, they still require training and logistical support. The partnership between AI and the Sierra Leone human rights movement was greatly strengthened during 2000.

Israel and the Occupied Territories

On 29 September, Israeli soldiers shot and killed five Palestinians and injured more than 200 others in East Jerusalem. The shooting took place after stones were thrown over the Western Wall following Friday prayers at the al-Aqsa Mosque. Demonstrations which followed were in protest at these killings, and became even more widespread after television viewers saw the prolonged agony ending in the death of a 12-year-old boy, Muhammad al-Dura, shot at Netzarim Junction on 30 September in the Gaza Strip by Israeli security forces, while his father tried to protect him. In the following days, demonstrations, which often developed into violent clashes between Palestinians and Israeli security forces, took place — sometimes daily — in cities and villages in the West Bank and the Gaza Strip. Demonstrations also took place in Palestinian towns and villages within Israel. In the four days that followed more than 50 Palestinians were killed — 13 in Israel and at least 40 in the West Bank and Gaza — by soldiers using rubber-coated metal bullets and live ammunition, including high-velocity bullets.

By the end of 2000, Israeli security forces had killed at least 300 and wounded more than 10,000 Palestinians, many of whom were children under 18. The Israel Airforce and the navy used heavy weaponry, including helicopter gunships, tanks and naval vessels, to shell randomly Palestinian areas from where armed Palestinians had opened fire. Armed Palestinians, including paramilitary groups linked to the Palestine Liberation Organization (PLO) and opposition groups such as Islamic *Jihad*, carried out attacks, killing 16 Israeli civilians.

AI's overriding concern was the excessive use of lethal force by the Israeli security forces. AI members around the world called for the killings to stop. They

A Palestinian schoolboy face to face with an Israeli soldier. In the last three months of 2000, Israeli security services killed at least 300 Palestinians, many of whom were children. AI used this photograph on a poster with the slogan "Stop the Killing".

© Reinhard Krause/Reuters

INTRODUCTION

demanded that killings, on both sides, be investigated. By the end of the year, not a single killing had been properly investigated and few autopsies had been conducted by either side to determine how individuals had been killed.

AI publicly called for the immediate suspension of all transfers of attack helicopters from the USA to Israel, including a pending upgrade of Apache helicopter gunships.

AI reiterated its urgent call for an independent international investigation by the UN into serious human rights abuses in Israel and the Occupied Territories, including the areas under the jurisdiction of the Palestinian Authority. In October, a special session of the UN Commission on Human Rights set up a Commission of Inquiry into the violations of human rights in Israel and the Occupied Territories. AI asked that it cooperate with all other ongoing investigations, that it be given access to all persons, documents and places and that it report publicly.

A key focus of the action was to generate the maximum impact through public events, as well as more traditional lobbying and letter-writing activities aimed at those with the power to influence the situation. AI members faced particular challenges in addressing the human rights crisis in Israel and the Occupied Territories. In a situation where inaccurate information and disinformation were common currency, AI's sustained presence and accurate reporting from the field were crucial to the effectiveness of our campaigning, as was our work together with Israeli and Palestinian non-governmental organizations.

AI members in Washington DC, USA, protest against human rights abuses in Saudi Arabia, September 2000. Human rights activists all over the world took part in AI's campaign, End Secrecy, End Suffering in Saudi Arabia.

Saudi Arabia

AI's campaign on human rights violations in Saudi Arabia was launched in March with the slogan "End Secrecy, End Suffering". The launch report, *A Secret State of Suffering* (AI Index: MDE 23/001/2000), highlighted the secrecy and fear permeating every aspect of the criminal justice system in Saudi Arabia. This secrecy facilitates human rights violations including arbitrary arrest and indefinite detention, the imprisonment of prisoners of conscience, torture, secret and summary trials, cruel judicial punishments and executions. AI's campaign also drew attention to the fact that responsibility for human rights violations in Saudi Arabia lies not just with the government but also with the international community, which has largely been reluctant to speak out against human rights violations in the country.

The campaign provoked unprecedented debate within Saudi Arabia about fundamental human rights. A number of Saudi Arabian newspapers reported AI's arguments and the reaction of the authorities. Newspapers carried articles about the criminal justice system and other human rights issues. Live debates and interviews on human rights in Saudi Arabia were broadcast by TV and radio stations to viewers and listeners throughout the Middle East.

In an unprecedented move, the Saudi Arabian government publicly stated its belief in the universality and indivisibility of human rights and announced measures to promote and protect such rights. During the March/April 2000 session of the UN Commission on Human Rights, Saudi Arabia's Deputy Foreign Minister stated that "...human rights are a non-negotiable objective for the achievement of which we must all strive together", and that Saudi Arabia was committed to "...the protection and promotion of human rights through carefully studied measures within the context of a comprehensive human rights strategy." In September, days before AI launched its report Saudi Arabia: Gross human rights abuses against women (AI Index: MDE 23/057/2000), Saudi Arabia acceded to the UN Women's Convention.

AI's campaign has been successful in drawing attention to the grave human rights violations which have persisted for so long in the country. It has broken through the wall of secrecy; the challenge now is to end the suffering.

Impunity

Impunity — the failure to bring to justice those responsible for human rights violations — feeds the cycle of violence, encourages further abuses and denies the victims justice. Tackling impunity is a vital step in building a vigilant society where human rights are respected and protected, where routine abusive practices cannot persist and where isolated cases, should they occur, are dealt with promptly and effectively.

AI, therefore, opposes any measures which grant amnesties to perpetrators of human rights crimes before the truth has been established. The failure to acknowledge the truth prolongs the original harm by

Amnesty International Report 2001

INTRODUCTION

seeking to deny that it ever took place – a further affront to the dignity and humanity of the victim.

States have a duty to investigate human rights violations, to identify those responsible, to impose the appropriate penalties and to ensure the victim receives adequate reparation. Yet in countries all around the world, evidence is concealed, investigations are inept or corrupt, and the system conspires to protect the perpetrators rather than the victims.

States also have responsibilities that extend beyond their borders. According to the principle of universal jurisdiction, states should bring to justice those presumed responsible for crimes against humanity, war crimes and genocide, regardless of where the crimes were committed, the nationality of the person responsible, or the nationality of the victim. All states are obliged to cooperate in this process.

Augusto Pinochet

The case of the former Chilean military leader, Augusto Pinochet, continued to attract immense international interest, both because it broke new ground in the practical application of the principle of universal jurisdiction and because the scale and ferocity of the repression in Chile after the 1973 military coup reverberated throughout the world. This case continued to have an unprecedented impact in terms of spreading awareness of universal jurisdiction and sending a clear message of warning to perpetrators of gross human rights abuses in all parts of the world.

Developments in the case in 2000 highlighted some of the limitations and the possibilities of universal jurisdiction in the struggle against impunity.

Despite criminal investigations or proceedings against him in Spain, the United Kingdom, Belgium, France, Switzerland and the USA, Augusto Pinochet was allowed to return home in March on grounds of ill health. By then, however, the publicity surrounding his arrest had punctured his apparent invincibility and given renewed impetus to the calls for justice within Chile itself.

In June, the Santiago Appeals Court ruled that Augusto Pinochet's parliamentary immunity should be lifted. In December, Judge Juan Guzmán ordered that Augusto Pinochet be placed under house arrest as author of the kidnapping and/or murder of 75 people during an October 1973 military operation known as the "Caravan of Death" ("*Caravana de la Muerte*"). Subsequently, the Supreme Court overturned the order, ruling that the judge had failed to interrogate Augusto Pinochet before issuing the order, and that mental and physical tests should be carried out to determine his fitness to stand trial before the interrogation could take place. At the end of 2000 Augusto Pinochet's name appeared in 202 lawsuits which were pending before Chilean courts in connection with human rights violations committed under his military government.

Hissein Habré

The case of Hissein Habré, former president of Chad, demonstrates that at both the national and international levels, overcoming impunity requires political will on the part of the authorities. Although Senegal had ratified the UN Convention against Torture, it had failed to incorporate all of its provisions into national legislation. In particular, the authorities failed to incorporate the provision which would explicitly allow Senegalese courts to try a foreign national for acts of torture committed abroad. In July, the Senegalese court investigating charges of complicity in acts of torture against Hissein Habré dismissed the charges on the grounds that it could not prosecute crimes committed in Chad. An appeal against this verdict was pending at the end of the year.

Hissein Habré had been indicted following a criminal complaint filed in January by Chadian victims and a coalition of non-governmental organizations. The legal action accused Hissein Habré of crimes against humanity and acts of torture. The lesser charge of complicity in acts of torture was retained by the investigating judge and Hissein Habré was placed under house arrest while investigations into the charges against him began. However, the defence lodged a motion to dismiss the case on the grounds that Senegal has no jurisdiction over crimes committed in Chad and that the prosecution is barred by the 10-year statute of limitations.

No one has been brought to justice in Chad for their part in the abuses committed under the former government of Hissein Habré.

A Chinese police officer about to arrest a follower of the spiritual group *Falun Gong* in Tiananmen Square, Beijing, April 2000. Many thousands of *Falun Gong* adherents were held in detention during 2000.

© Andrew Wong/Reuters

INTRODUCTION

A student in Aceh, Indonesia, tries to push back riot police during clashes between protesters and the security forces in March 1999. Police and military operations against separatist rebels continued throughout 2000. Hundreds of people were extrajudicially executed. Some were tortured before being killed. Many of the victims were ordinary civilians, including aid workers, human rights defenders and political activists.

No justice, no peace

In Algeria, more than 100,000 people have been killed by the security forces, state armed militias and armed groups since the current conflict began in 1992. Thousands "disappeared" after being seized by the security forces. Despite the scale of this long-drawn-out tragedy, there have been no independent, impartial investigations. The authorities have stated that they want to close this sad chapter in Algeria's history, but are seeking to do so by granting immunity to those who may have committed gross human rights crimes. The immunity from prosecution previously enjoyed by members of the security forces and their allied militias has been extended to members of armed opposition groups. Meanwhile, the violence continues, albeit at a much reduced level; since early 1999 about 200 people have been killed every month.

In the year after the Indonesian security forces and allied militias unleashed a wave of violence against the people of East Timor which shocked the international community into taking action, Indonesia continued its path towards democratic reform. Addressing and making amends for its repressive past and establishing accountability before the law are important elements of this process. Credible prosecutions for past human rights violations in Indonesia are a crucial test of the government's commitment to reform. However, political resistance and the weakness of legal and judicial institutions continued to be an obstacle to successful investigations and trials of perpetrators of human rights violations.

New legislation was introduced providing for the establishment of human rights courts to try gross violations of human rights. It was expected that those suspected of committing crimes, including crimes against humanity, in East Timor in 1999 would be brought to trial under this legislation. However, progress in these cases was slow. Although the Indonesian authorities completed investigations into five cases in October, no human rights court had been established by the end of 2000 to hear the cases. There were also fears that a constitutional amendment adopted in August which bans the retroactive application of legislation might be used to try to prevent suspected perpetrators of human rights violations from being brought to justice under the new legislation.

Mothers' groups protest against violence, militarism and human rights violations, September 1999, Jakarta, Indonesia. During 2000 there was a marked deterioration in the human rights situation in parts of Indonesia, including Aceh and Papua.

Amnesty International Report 2001

INTRODUCTION

An opposition supporter lights a torch during a rally outside the federal parliament building in Belgrade, Federal Republic of Yugoslavia, 6 October 2000. One day earlier, some protesters had stormed the building as part of a popular revolt against President Slobodan Milošević, demanding that he step down in favour of Vojislav Koštunica who had won the elections.

Investigations into events in East Timor during 1999 were also carried out by the UN Transitional Administration in East Timor (UNTAET), but progress was also slow. Indictments were served, but trials had not begun by the end of the year. In the meantime, hundreds of extrajudicial killings and incidents of torture, including rape, committed by the Indonesian security forces and their allied militias were not even investigated.

In Aceh, Indonesia, one civilian and 24 members of the military were found guilty in April of killing a Muslim cleric and over 50 of his followers. However, the trial, which took place in a joint civilian-military tribunal, fell short of international standards for fair trial. Other scheduled trials in Aceh failed to take place and the climate of impunity shielded the perpetrators of human rights abuses in Aceh and Papua where repression of pro-independence supporters intensified.

Women's march for peace, Harare, Zimbabwe, May 2000.

In Zimbabwe, widespread state-sponsored violence started in March and persisted throughout the year, particularly during the months leading up to the June parliamentary elections. The governing Zimbabwe African National Union-Patriotic Front (ZANU-PF) party used genuine grievances over land distribution and racial inequalities to foment violence, including killings and torture. These politically motivated violations of human rights and the complete lack of accountability of those responsible took place against a background of decades of impunity.

Serious violations and abuses of human rights during the war of independence (1972 to 1980), especially by the government led by Ian Smith, were covered up by the blanket amnesty that accompanied independence. Zimbabwe was soon after gripped by a new wave of violence as operations by the Zimbabwe National Army 5th Brigade in Matabeleland resulted in thousands of executions, "disappearances" and torture. These atrocities were themselves subject to an amnesty in 1988.

This same pattern of impunity was repeated in October 2000 when President Robert Mugabe issued a clemency order granting a blanket amnesty for all those suspected of politically motivated crimes committed between 1 January 2000 and 31 July 2000. Although the order made exceptions for some grave crimes, the amnesty protects many perpetrators of grave human rights abuses including those responsible for torture and ill-treatment.

In the aftermath of NATO's bombing campaign from late March to early June 1999, reports of human rights violations in the Federal Republic of Yugoslavia against opposition activists, non-governmental organizations and independent journalists increased in frequency

INTRODUCTION

and severity. In October 2000, however, the Federal presidential and parliamentary elections, accompanied by mass public protests, brought about the fall of Slobodan Milošević and a significant decrease in the incidence and range of human rights violations. By the end of the year, the new government of Vojislav Koštunica had failed to cooperate with the International Criminal Tribunal for the former Yugoslavia by arresting and transferring indicted suspects, including Slobodan Milošević, to the custody of the Tribunal.

In Kosovo delays in establishing a functioning police force and a multi-ethnic, independent and impartial judiciary enabled widespread human rights abuses, particularly against members of minority communities, to be committed with virtual impunity. Early in the year, members of the judiciary were subjected to threats and intimidation, while delays in the establishment of a functioning judiciary led to suspects being held in pre-trial detention for periods exceeding international standards. Other concerns were also expressed about human rights violations perpetrated by the international community – including KFOR (Kosovo Force) and the international police – and about the failure of the UN Interim Mission in Kosovo (UNMIK) to protect and promote human rights.

In Colombia the long-running conflict between government forces, illegal paramilitary groups which have the tacit and active support of important sectors of the armed forces, and armed opposition groups, continued to escalate. The conflict has been characterized by a blatant disregard for human rights and international humanitarian law. At least 4,000 people were killed in political violence in 2000 alone. Hundreds of thousands of civilians, mostly poor peasant farmers from remote rural areas, have been forced to flee their homes.

In July US President Bill Clinton signed a law granting US$1.3 billion in aid to Colombia, the bulk of it for the Colombian military. According to US law, certain human rights conditions have to be met before military assistance can be given to Colombia, such as civilian trials for armed forces personnel accused of gross human rights violations. AI, together with two US-based non-governmental organizations, presented evidence that these conditions had not been met. President Clinton responded by waiving the human rights conditions on grounds of US national security interests.

One of the cornerstones of impunity in Colombia, and indeed elsewhere, is the failure to try military personnel before civilian courts. Even Colombian military officers have admitted that military tribunals are unfair, cover up crimes and shield high-ranking officers. Many cases never even reach the courts; hundreds of outstanding arrest warrants for known paramilitaries have never been carried out. Known killers continue to walk the streets freely in Colombia.

It can sometimes take many years for the truth about human rights violations to emerge or to be publicly acknowledged. In France, two army generals admitted their direct involvement in torture and extrajudicial executions during the Algerian war of independence (1954 to 1962). Their admission followed growing public pressure on the authorities to acknowledge and condemn torture during the war. There were also

A "regroupment" camp in Burundi, February 2000. In September 1999, the government of Burundi forced more than 290,000 mainly Hutu civilians to leave their homes and enter "regroupment" camps. Conditions in the camps were appalling. Following international condemnation, the camps were closed by September 2000, but no provision was made for people returning to their homes, many of which had been destroyed.

© AI

INTRODUCTION

moves to make the Paris police grant access to its archives on the October 1961 massacre of Algerians by police officers during a peaceful demonstration in Paris. Disagreement persisted about the number of demonstrators killed, figures varying between 32 and 200. In November AI called for those responsible for war crimes and crimes against humanity during the war to be brought to justice. In AI's view the lack of political will by successive French governments to confront this issue had helped to present torture, summary executions and "disappearances" as a "necessary evil".

Hidden victims

In 2000, as in other years, while some human rights tragedies captured the public imagination and generated anger and action, many others went virtually unnoticed.

In Burundi the civilian population paid the price of the civil war which continued despite the signing of a peace agreement in August. Hundreds of civilians were killed in cold blood by government armed forces and armed opposition groups. In China there was no sign of any relaxation of the 1999 crack-down on fundamental freedoms. Thousands of people were arbitrarily detained for peacefully exercising their rights to freedom of expression, association or religion. Torture and ill-treatment of prisoners continued to be widespread and thousands of people were sentenced to death. In the Democratic Republic of the Congo the continuing armed conflict was used as a pretext to justify widespread repression of peaceful dissent, as the government and armed opposition used imprisonment and torture to silence their critics. In Iraq, air strikes by US and UK forces continued, resulting in further civilian deaths. According to Iraqi government figures around 300 people have been killed since the air strikes began in December 1998. In Russia, the fading of international attention on the conflict in Chechnya did not mean that human rights violations in the conflict had decreased, just that they could be committed without even the most minimal level of international scrutiny.

For 40 years AI members have struggled to give a voice to the forgotten prisoner, to shine a light on the secret world of the torturer, and to give a name to the anonymous victim. This struggle goes on. While the challenges we face are greater than ever, so are the forces marshalled in support of human rights. The international human rights movement, of which AI is proud to be a part, is growing, diversifying and gaining strength. We urge you to join it.

© Reuters

A Chechen boy looks from a tent window in the Sputnik refugee camp in Ingushetia, October 2000. The conflict in Chechnya caused mass displacement. Russian forces were responsible for gross human rights violations against Chechen civilians. Thousands were killed in indiscriminate attacks and there were widespread reports of torture, incommunicado detention, and summary executions.

AI REPORT 2001
PART 2

AFGHANISTAN

TALEBAN'S ISLAMIC EMIRATE OF AFGHANISTAN,
headed by Mullah Mohammad Omar, recognized as a government by three countries
ANTI-TALEBAN ALLIANCE's ISLAMIC STATE OF AFGHANISTAN,
headed by Burhanuddin Rabbani, recognized as a government by other governments and the UN
Capital: Kabul
Population: 23.7 million
Official languages: Dari, Pushtu
Death penalty: retentionist

Human rights abuses, including arbitrary detention and torture, continued to be reported in the context of the ongoing conflict between warring factions. The *Taleban* continued to impose harsh restrictions on personal conduct and behaviour as a means of enforcing their particular interpretation of Islamic law. Fighting in the northern provinces intensified during the second half of the year as the *Taleban* and anti-*Taleban* forces fought for control of territory. Forced displacement of the civilian population was used by the *Taleban* to gain control of territory in areas north of Kabul, creating a severe humanitarian crisis.

Background

War and drought resulted in a serious threat to the food supply in many areas. A peaceful resolution to the armed conflict remained a remote prospect; UN efforts to bring the warring factions to the negotiating table were again unsuccessful. Other peace efforts, including an initiative by the former Afghan king, Zahir Shah, to establish a government representative of all ethnic groups and factions through a traditional *Loya Jirga* (Grand Assembly), did not receive support from the *Taleban*.

The *Taleban* continued to assert that it represented the majority of people in the country, despite the absence of any independently verifiable evidence to support this claim. As in previous years, the civilian population was denied the opportunity to formally express its wishes regarding the kind of government it wanted.

In December the UN Security Council imposed new sanctions, stating that unless the *Taleban* "cease the provision of sanctuary and training for international terrorists and their organizations... turn over Osama bin Laden to appropriate authorities in a country where he has been indicted, or to appropriate authorities in a country where he will be returned to such a country, or to appropriate authorities in a country where he will be arrested and effectively brought to justice... act swiftly to close all camps where terrorists are trained within the territory under its control", all states would prevent the sale and transfer of military supplies, including technical advice, assistance, or training, to areas of Afghanistan under *Taleban* control, and close *Taleban* offices and deny *Taleban* officials entry in their territory.

Forced displacement

More than 70,000 people were reported to have fled intensified fighting in the northern province of Takhar to the neighbouring province of Badakhshan. Tens of thousands more were reported to have fled not only drought-stricken rural areas but also a deteriorating security situation in the northern and central regions of the country. The International Committee of the Red Cross (ICRC) warned of health risks and lack of preparation for the winter months and nutritional surveys by the relief organization *Médecins sans Frontières* showed a substantial increase in levels of malnutrition in the northern region.

The bulk of this massive displacement was a direct consequence of the pressure exerted by *Taleban* guards on the local population to flee their homes. The *Taleban* initially denied that mass displacement had taken place, but later reportedly criticized the UN and other aid agencies for not providing food and shelter to the displaced people.

◻ On 11 September, after *Taleban* forces reportedly declared Taliqan town and its surrounding villages military zones, some 18,000 people living in the villages of Ganj Ali Beg, Sarai Sang, Khatayan, Qazaq, Ahan Dara, and Shurab were forced to abandon their homes in search of safety.

Refugees

During the year Iran, Pakistan and Tajikistan closed their borders to tens of thousands of Afghan refugees fleeing the war and the drought.

In May, the Iranian parliament voted to close, in principle, Iran's border with Afghanistan, supposedly to prevent drug smuggling. The Tajik government closed its border with Afghanistan in mid-September, preventing tens of thousands of Afghans fleeing the fighting from entering Tajikistan. Pakistan closed its North West Frontier Province and Balochistan border to Afghan refugees without valid travel documents in early November while *Taleban* guards stopped Afghan refugees at checkpoints on the road from Jalalabad to the Torkham border crossing with Pakistan, reportedly beating many of them. Restrictions were particularly applied to family groups including women.

From April onwards, Iran repatriated tens of thousands of Afghan refugees under a program jointly implemented with the UN High Commissioner for Refugees (UNHCR). However, aid workers monitoring the repatriation process said many refugees cited pressure from the Iran government as their reason for returning to Afghanistan. In December, *Médecins sans Frontières* withdrew from the repatriation program on the grounds that the safety and well-being of Afghan refugees who were returned could not be guaranteed.

Women

Despite statements by some *Taleban* officials that the ban on women's right to education, employment and

Cabinda

The armed conflict continued between the government and two armed factions of the *Frente para a Libertação do Enclave de Cabinda* (FLEC), Front for the Liberation of the Cabinda Enclave. Government soldiers carried out military activities against civilians, often in retaliation for FLEC military actions. They also arrested and beat people suspected of supporting FLEC.

In November, 60-year-old Silvana Domingos; her husband, Janúario Bingu; their son, José Pascoal Bingu; and João Baptista Cebola, a neighbour, were beaten by several members of the Rapid Intervention Police, apparently because a member of the family was married to a FLEC soldier. José Pascoal Bingu was arrested after being beaten and taken to the Rapid Intervention Police headquarters in Cabinda city were he was held incommunicado.

In May, one of the FLEC armed factions, FLEC-Cabindan Armed Forces, took hostage three Portuguese employees of a construction firm and refused to release them unless Portugal recognized the struggle for independence of the enclave. The hostages had not been released by the end of the year.

AI country reports and visits

Reports
- Angola and Namibia: Human rights abuses in the border area (AI Index: AFR 03/001/2000)
- Angola: Freedom of expression on trial (AI Index: AFR 12/008/2000)

Visits
AI delegates visited northern Namibia in January and February to assess the human rights situation in the border area.

ARGENTINA

ARGENTINE REPUBLIC
Head of state and government: Fernando de la Rúa
Capital: Buenos Aires
Population: 37 million
Official language: Spanish
Death penalty: abolitionist for ordinary crimes
2000 treaty ratifications/signatures: Optional Protocol to the UN Children's Convention on the involvement of children in armed conflict; Optional Protocol to the UN Women's Convention

Reports of killings by police and of ill-treatment and torture of detainees in police stations continued. A transvestite died, allegedly as a result of torture. Two "disappearances" were reported. Lawyers working on human rights cases were subjected to death threats and harassment. Courts abroad continued investigations into past human rights violations.

Background

Throughout 2000 there were strikes and demonstrations against government economic policies, unemployment and lack of social welfare; some were violent. Scores of demonstrators were detained for short periods and several were injured in clashes with the police. In November, Anibal Verón was shot dead, allegedly by the police in the province of Salta, during the clearing of roadblocks set up by demonstrators on a national highway near the town of General Mosconi.

Torture/ill-treatment

There were continued reports of violence by provincial police. More than 80 people were reportedly killed by police in circumstances suggesting excessive or disproportionate use of force. There were reports of torture and ill-treatment of criminal suspects and detainees by police officers. Although a number of police officers were charged, the outcome of the majority of the complaints was unknown.

In June, two university students — Marcelo Burchinski and José Luis Gherardi — were arrested in the streets of Posadas, Misiones Province, by a provincial police patrol. They were reportedly beaten and taken to the 4th police station where they were subjected to further beatings, stripped naked and drenched with buckets of cold water. They were subsequently released.

Vanessa Lorena Ledesma, a transvestite activist, was arrested in a bar in Córdoba in February. She was held in the police station *Precinto 18* where she was segregated from the other detainees, apparently because she was HIV-positive. Five days later she was dead. A police report recorded that she had died as a result of a "cardiac arrest". However, an autopsy reportedly indicated that her body showed strong evidence of torture. An investigation initiated by the Control Court No. 3 was subsequently closed. The president of the *Asociación Travestis Unidas de Córdoba*, United Transvestites Association of Córdoba, was threatened and harassed by police after pressing for an investigation into the death.

Prison conditions
There were credible reports of harsh prison conditions, overcrowding and ill-treatment of detainees by prison guards. There was a spate of riots in protest at conditions.

☐ Following a violent riot in March by prisoners at the Mendoza Provincial jail prisoners were subjected to beatings, intimidation and restrictions on their use of lavatories. Lawyers were not allowed to see the prisoners for four days. A diabetic prisoner, Raúl Eduardo Cobo Espinosa, died, allegedly as a result of a lack of medical attention. The authorities announced improvements in conditions and investigations into complaints.

'Disappearances'
☐ José Segundo Zambrano and Pablo Marcelo Rodríguez "disappeared" in March in Mendoza city, Mendoza Province, after one of them had allegedly arranged to meet a member of the Mendoza Investigations police. According to the habeas corpus writ filed by the lawyers acting for the men's families, José Zambrano had been subjected to death threats by a member of the local police. The bodies of the two men were found in July. An investigation was initiated into this case. Carlos Varela and Diego Lavado, human rights lawyers representing the "disappeared" men's relatives, faced a campaign of intimidation and harassment.

Past human rights violations
Judicial proceedings and investigations in Italy, Spain and Germany continued during the year in relation to human rights violations committed under the military government (1976-1983). Requests for extradition were submitted in a number of countries against former members of the Argentine armed forces. In Argentina, human rights violations committed under the military government are covered by the Full Stop and Due Obedience laws.

Italy
In September, Jorge Olivera, a former member of the Argentine armed forces was released and allowed to return to Argentina after the Rome Appeal Court applied the statute of limitations to the crimes of which he was accused. He had been detained in Italy in August, after an international arrest warrant was filed by France, for the abduction and torture of French citizen Marie Anne Erize Tisseau who "disappeared" in 1976 in the Argentine province of San Juan.

In December an Italian court sentenced seven former Argentine military officers to prison terms ranging from 24 years to life. The trial *in absentia*, initiated in Rome, related to the abduction and murder of seven Italian citizens and the kidnapping of the child of one of them in Argentina under the military government.

Mexico
In August, Ricardo Miguel Cavallo, a former Argentine Navy officer was arrested in Cancun. A Spanish judge subsequently requested his extradition to Spain in connection with accusations of torture in the context of investigations initiated in 1996 by the Spanish National Court into human rights violations committed by the military government in Argentina. A French judge also filed an official request to interrogate Ricardo Miguel Cavallo in connection with human rights violations committed against 15 French citizens including the "disappearance" in 1977 of two French nuns.

Argentina
In October, a court in Buenos Aires requested the extradition of Augusto Pinochet and six former members of the Chilean secret police for their alleged involvement in the killing in Buenos Aires in 1974 of the former head of the Chilean army, Carlos Prats, and his wife. In November in the same case the court found Enrique Arancibia Clavel, a former member of the Chilean secret police, guilty of double homicide and sentenced him to life imprisonment.

La Tablada case
Members of the *Movimiento Todos por la Patria* (MTP), All for the Fatherland Movement, serving sentences ranging from 20 years to life imprisonment imposed in previous years, staged two hunger strikes in May and September to protest at the failure of the Argentine government to comply with the recommendations made in 1997 by the Inter-American Commission on Human Rights, regarding the prisoners' right of appeal. The prisoners, including prisoner of conscience Fray Antonio Puigjane, were tried under the Defence of Democracy Law, which denies the right of appeal. Although two draft bills were submitted to Congress to modify the Law, by the end of the year neither bill had been debated in parliament. In December, the prisoners ended the hunger strike after the life sentences of 11 prisoners were reduced by presidential decree.

Intergovernmental organizations
In October the UN Human Rights Committee examined Argentina's third periodic report on its implementation of the International Covenant on Civil and Political Rights. In its concluding observations the Committee recommended that measures be taken to ensure that military personnel involved in past human rights violations "are removed from military or public service". It included its concern at allegations of widespread practice of torture and ill-treatment by police, and requested information on remedies available to complainants, the outcome of such complaints and the sanctions imposed as well as the specific responsibilities of federal and provincial authorities.

AI country reports and visit
Public statements
- Argentina: Bringing the law into line with international obligations – a challenge for the legislators (AI Index: AMR 13/012/2000)

- Argentina: Transvestite dies in detention (AI Index: AMR 13/004/2000)
- Argentina: Cases of "disappeared" facing judicial closure in Germany (AMR 13/003/2000)

Visit
In December an AI delegate observed the trial of a provincial judge accused of malpractice in cases of human rights violations in Mendoza.

ARMENIA

REPUBLIC OF ARMENIA
Head of state: Robert Kocharian
Head of government: Andranik Makarian (replaced Aram Sarkisian in May)
Capital: Yerevan
Population: 3.5 million
Official language: Armenian
Death penalty: retentionist

Reports of torture and ill-treatment continued, amid allegations that the authorities were often reluctant to investigate them thoroughly and impartially. Among those who complained of torture were a number of political prisoners who also reported other violations of their right to a fair trial. The authorities continued to imprison conscientious objectors to military service. At least two death sentences were passed during 2000, and around 30 men were under sentence of death at the end of the year, although the moratorium on executions continued.

Background
The political situation remained volatile, in the wake of the October 1999 assassinations of the Prime Minister and the Speaker of Parliament. In May President Kocharian dismissed the prime minister, appointing Andranik Makarian in his place, and made other ministerial changes. In October the Constitutional Court reinstated the parliamentary speaker, following disputes over a parliamentary vote on his resignation the previous month.

Torture/ill-treatment
Reports of torture and ill-treatment in custody continued, together with complaints about brutal treatment, known as "hazing", of army conscripts. As in previous years, there were persistent allegations that law enforcement officials subjected people to torture and ill-treatment in order to obtain confessions and coerce testimony, and that in some cases the authorities appeared reluctant to conduct prompt and comprehensive investigations, or to initiate proceedings against those alleged to be responsible.

Among those alleging torture were several men detained in connection with an armed attack in the Armenian parliament in October 1999, which left eight men dead. Journalist Nairi Badalian, for example, reported that he had been subjected to sustained torture and ill-treatment at the hands of law enforcement officials in the Nurabashen investigation-isolation prison in Yerevan. He said he had been made to stand outside in freezing temperatures in the winter without warm clothing; doused with water; chained to a metal chair while some 10 people beat him, knocking out some of his teeth; and made to stand against a wall for extended periods of time without sleep. He also reported that officials had threatened to rape his wife and sister. He was eventually released on 3 June, and all charges against him were dropped.

Nairi Unanian, the alleged leader of the attack, also stated that he had been tortured. In May he withdrew his testimony, including that which implicated some of the other accused, on the grounds that it had been extracted under duress. Charges against him included some which carry a maximum sentence of death.

UN Committee on the Rights of the Child
In January the UN Committee on the Rights of the Child reviewed Armenia's initial report on the steps the authorities had taken to implement the UN Children's Convention, to which Armenia became a party in 1993. Among the Committee's main concerns was Armenia's failure to acknowledge and address domestic violence. The Committee expressed its concern at the ill-treatment of children, including sexual abuse, within the family as well as in schools and institutions. The Committee was further concerned at the limited access to complaints mechanisms and the insufficient rehabilitation measures for children in such situations. It recommended that Armenia ensure that all forms of physical and mental violence are prohibited, including corporal punishment and sexual abuse against children in the family, schools and care institutions, and that mechanisms be established to receive complaints, as well as to monitor, investigate and prosecute instances of ill-treatment.

UN Committee against Torture
In November the Committee reviewed Armenia's second periodic report under the UN Convention against Torture. AI had submitted its own report to the Committee, detailing its concerns. The Committee's recommendations included: detainees should be guaranteed immediate access to their lawyer, family members and a doctor of their choice; Armenia should establish an effective and genuinely independent system of inspection of all places of detention; and officials should carry out prompt, independent investigations into allegations of hazing in the army (and institute proceedings when such allegations are upheld). The Committee welcomed the stated willingness of Armenia to establish an ombudsperson, and the moratorium on the death penalty. However, the Committee noted that the uncertain situation of those currently on death row pending abolition appeared to amount to cruel and inhuman treatment.

Membership of the Council of Europe

Armenia's application to join the Council of Europe was reviewed in June. Membership was recommended provided Armenia fulfilled a number of commitments. These included ratifying the European Convention on Human Rights and the European Convention for the Prevention of Torture and Inhuman or Degrading Treatment or Punishment within a year of accession; adopting the draft Criminal Code within a year of accession, thus abolishing the death penalty and decriminalizing consensual homosexual relations between adult males; and adopting, within three years of accession, a law on an alternative to compulsory military service in compliance with European standards. In the meantime, Armenia pledged to pardon all imprisoned conscientious objectors. A formal invitation of membership was issued in November, with Armenia expected to join early in 2001.

Prisoners of conscience

There was no sign during 2000 of Armenia acting in the spirit of its Council of Europe commitments with regard to conscientious objectors to compulsory military service. At least 16 young men were reportedly sentenced to prison terms for refusing to perform military service on religious grounds. They included one man sent to serve a second prison term on these grounds, and at least 12 sentenced after the recommendations on Council of Europe membership had been issued in June.

▫ Vitaly Usupov, a Jehovah's Witness, refused his call-up papers on religious grounds but was forcibly conscripted into a military unit. He continued to refuse to perform military service, and as a result was reportedly beaten by military personnel in the unit. He was sentenced by a court in Vanadzor on 17 March to four-and-a-half years' imprisonment, for "evading military service" under Article 257a of the Armenian Criminal Code. It was further alleged that Vitaly Usupov, an ethnic Kurd, was not provided with an interpreter during his trial as specified under Armenian law.

The death penalty

By the end of 2000 the draft new criminal code, under which the death penalty would be replaced by a maximum sentence of life imprisonment, had still not finally passed into law, although it had had its first parliamentary reading in April 1997. At least two death sentences were passed during the year. Armen Ter-Sahakian and Alik Grigorian were sentenced to death in June by a court in Yerevan. They were convicted of involvement in murdering a number of people regarded as opponents of those in power at the time. There were no executions.

AI country report

- Armenia: Torture and ill-treatment – Comments on the forthcoming review by the United Nations Committee against Torture (AI Index: EUR 54/002/2000)

AUSTRALIA

AUSTRALIA
Head of state: Queen Elizabeth II, represented by William Deane
Head of government: John Howard
Capital: Canberra
Population: 18.5 million
Official language: English
Death penalty: abolitionist for all crimes

The government's rejection of international human rights scrutiny and policies on asylum-seekers were major human rights issues. The arbitrary detention of at least 3,000 refugee applicants and "boat people" triggered riots, mass breakouts and complaints of ill-treatment by guards. The government announced legislation to ratify the Rome Statute of the International Criminal Court.

Background

Human rights advocates called for a Bill of Rights to safeguard the rights provided in international human rights treaties to which Australia is party. Their concerns were echoed by the UN Human Rights Committee (HRC), which monitors implementation of the International Covenant on Civil and Political Rights (ICCPR), and by the UN Committee on Economic, Social and Cultural Rights. They found that treaty rights have no legal status in Australia and cannot be invoked in domestic courts, leaving gaps in Australia's human rights system and impeding the recognition and applicability of treaty provisions.

In May, the Prime Minister failed to participate in public events to recognize past human rights violations against indigenous peoples and indicated his opposition to proposals for reconciliation and racial tolerance developed over 10 years by the government-funded Council for Aboriginal Reconciliation.

Refugees and asylum-seekers

The Minister for Immigration and Multicultural Affairs sought revisions of international refugee standards to deter irregular movements of asylum-seekers. More than 2,940 "boat people", including 500 children, were automatically detained under the Migration Act, which prohibited courts from ordering their release. Hundreds were held in tents and other improvised detention facilities in remote areas. The national Human Rights and Equal Opportunity Commission investigated allegations that guards ill-treated immigrant detainees and neglected medical care. In September the UN Working Group on Arbitrary Detention had to cancel plans to investigate the immigration detention regime, after the government failed to allow it to visit.

▫ In May, the family of a three-year-old Chinese boy, detained all his life at Port Hedland detention centre, was released following a High Court decision that he should not be denied protection from persecution in China because his parents were unsuccessful refugee applicants.

In January, a 32-year-old Algerian asylum-seeker was deported despite a written request by the UN Committee against Torture not to remove him from Australia, so that the Committee could consider his case. The government argued it had "no obligation" to act on such requests.

International obligations
A Senate committee report in June addressed the government's failure to grant protection to unsuccessful asylum applicants in accordance with Australia's obligations under the UN Convention against Torture, the ICCPR and the UN Children's Convention. The report criticized continuing procedural flaws that had led to the deportation in 1999 of a Chinese woman more than eight months pregnant who underwent an abortion on arrival in China. It recommended that certain government officials should not be members of the tribunal which decides on unsuccessful refugee applications.

Three UN treaty bodies published observations on Australia's obligations towards asylum-seekers. The Committee on the Elimination of Racial Discrimination (CERD) recommended the "faithful" implementation of international refugee law. The HRC recommended policy changes on mandatory detention under the Migration Act. The Committee against Torture found "an apparent lack of appropriate review mechanisms for ministerial decisions" on people who may face torture if deported.

Deaths in custody and imprisonment of Aborigines
Aborigines continued to die in custody in disproportionate numbers, sometimes in disputed circumstances.

In January, the controversial death in custody of a 15-year-old Aboriginal boy in Darwin heightened public interest in a Senate inquiry into mandatory imprisonment schemes for juveniles. The inquiry found that the schemes violated the UN Children's Convention and recommended the passing of draft federal legislation overriding such schemes. The Prime Minister prevented the passing of the draft legislation. In March, the CERD recommended changes to the schemes which "appear to target offences that are committed disproportionately by indigenous Australians, especially in the case of juveniles". The HRC observed in July that such schemes raised a "serious issue of compliance" with the ICCPR. In November, the Committee against Torture recommended measures to prevent such schemes violating international standards. The Committee also expressed concerns about reported ill-treatment of prisoners, including the use of unnecessarily painful and humiliating restraint instruments.

In June, a Coroner's inquest in Tasmania found that prison authorities had failed in their duty of care to prisoners at risk of suicide, following repeated inquest recommendations since 1991 to improve safety at Risdon prison, Hobart. The Tasmania state government introduced extensive prison reforms, including in prison health services, to halt a spate of prison deaths.

Withdrawal from UN scrutiny
Following a review triggered by the CERD observations, in August the government announced major limitations on Australia's future cooperation with UN human rights bodies. It decided to agree to UN treaty body visits and requests for information only in "compelling" cases, to report to UN treaty monitoring bodies on a selective basis and to reject "unwarranted requests from treaty committees to delay removal of unsuccessful asylum-seekers from Australia".

AI action
In September, AI sent an open letter to Prime Minister Howard, asking his government to reconsider the above measures, which AI said constituted an attack on the UN human rights protection system and set a bad example internationally. Australia's selective approach to reporting to treaty bodies would be in breach of the binding obligations it undertook when becoming party to human rights treaties, and its reluctance to cooperate with the UN's special human rights mechanisms created the impression it had something to hide. In a written reply, the Prime Minister's office failed to respond to any of the serious concerns expressed by AI.

AUSTRIA

REPUBLIC OF AUSTRIA
Head of state: Thomas Klestil
Head of government: Wolfgang Schüssel (replaced Viktor Klima in February)
Capital: Vienna
Population: 8.2 million
Official language: German
Death penalty: abolitionist for all crimes
2000 treaty ratifications/signatures: Optional Protocol to the UN Children's Convention on the involvement of children in armed conflict; Optional Protocol to the UN Women's Convention; Rome Statute of the International Criminal Court

There were continued allegations that police officers had ill-treated detainees and used excessive force. People who complained about or witnessed police ill-treatment risked being threatened with police counter-charges. One man was shot dead by police in controversial circumstances. The investigation into the death in May 1999 of Marcus Omofuma during deportation was not concluded. There were concerns about restraint techniques reportedly used in prisons.

Background
The traditional coalition between the Social Democratic Party and the Austrian People's Party collapsed after elections in October 1999 and a new government was formed in February which included the People's Party and the main party of the far right, the Austrian Freedom Party.

Allegations of police ill-treatment
Allegations that police ill-treated detainees and used excessive force continued.

▫ Around 130 police officers raided a building used to house asylum-seekers in Traiskirchen, Lower Austria, on the evening of 17 January, searching for drugs. Around 80 residents were confined to certain areas of the building, such as their bedrooms and kitchens. Many reportedly had their hands bound with plastic ties while they were systematically searched for drugs. Some detainees were reportedly subjected to internal body searches in front of other residents as well as police officers. A number of detainees were allegedly searched internally by officers using the same pairs of latex gloves. Police officers allegedly acted towards the detainees in a disparaging manner, laughing at those who suffered pain while being searched internally, and using degrading language. The police raid reportedly lasted for approximately four hours, during which 80 asylum-seekers were temporarily deprived of their liberty, but only 15 people were eventually arrested, reportedly for possessing small amounts of drugs. In May the Ministry of the Interior stated that an investigation had been launched into the allegations of ill-treatment. On 10 July the Lower Austrian Independent Administrative Tribunal in St. Pölten heard the first of a series of testimonies about the police raid from detainees, who brought complaints against the police. The investigation had not concluded by the end of the year.

Excessive use of force
The Special Criminal Deployment Group appeared to have violated the principle of proportionality of force during another police operation in Vienna in the early hours of 3 March. Two masked police officers in civilian clothes, who were reportedly not identifiable as police officers, brandished guns and dragged two men out of a car and on to the ground. The two men reportedly belonged to a left-wing protest group and had participated in an anti-government demonstration the previous evening. The men were later charged only with the relatively minor offence of resisting state authority.

Police counter-complaints
Complainants and witnesses of alleged police ill-treatment risked being threatened with criminal counter-charges such as resisting state authority or defamation of the arresting police officers.

▫ Two police officers accused of ill-treating and racially abusing a French citizen of African origin in March 1999 at the Schottenring underground station in Vienna attempted to sue privately two of the five eyewitnesses for defamation of character. An initial court hearing in late August was adjourned for technical reasons.

Death during deportation
The investigation into the death of 25-year-old Marcus Omofuma, a Nigerian citizen who died in May 1999 after being gagged and bound during his forced deportation from Vienna to Nigeria, had not come to a close nearly 20 months after the incident. The three police officers who effected the deportation faced charges of ill-treating a prisoner with death as a consequence. Their trial was expected to start in 2001.

Dangerous restraint techniques
In April AI learned that inmates in Austria's largest penal institution, the Josefstadt prison in Vienna, were being restrained by being placed in cage-beds, beds enclosed in a 1.2m-high metal cage. Reports suggested that in some instances prisoners had been confined inside cage-beds for up to 48 hours. AI expressed concern that the use of cage-beds might represent a cruel, inhuman and degrading method of restraint and asked to be informed of the regulations governing their use.

Police shooting
An unarmed man, referred to in the Austrian news media as Imre B., was shot dead by a police officer of the Special Criminal Deployment Group on 19 May in Vienna. It transpired that the weapon was the police officer's own firearm and not a service revolver. Two suspects under observation in a vehicle were about to drive away when two police officers approached the vehicle brandishing revolvers. As one police officer reportedly attempted to open the door of the vehicle, he fired his gun, killing the driver, Imre B. The Special Criminal Deployment Group was reportedly disbanded in July.

Unequal age of consent
A man was convicted in Vienna and sentenced to a fine in July for having sexual relations with his 16-year-old boyfriend in September 1999. He was 19 years old at the time of the incident. The age of consent for heterosexuals and lesbians is set at 14 years of age, but 18 for gay men. AI welcomed the decision of the court not to sentence the man to a term of imprisonment, but expressed concern that other men may still face up to five years' imprisonment.

AI country report
- Austria before the UN Committee against Torture: Allegations of police ill-treatment (AI Index: EUR 13/001/2000)

AZERBAIJAN

REPUBLIC OF AZERBAIJAN
Head of state: Heydar Aliyev
Head of government: Artur Rasizadeh
Capital: Baku
Population: 7.7 million
Official language: Azeri
Death penalty: abolitionist for all crimes
2000 treaty ratifications/signatures: Optional Protocol to the UN Children's Convention on the involvement of children in armed conflict, Optional Protocol to the UN Women's Convention

Several people active in the political opposition were detained for short periods. Reports of torture and ill-treatment in custody continued to be received. In the disputed Karabakh region, one prisoner of conscience received a suspended sentence; other political detainees were reportedly ill-treated; and two death sentences were commuted.

Background
Opposition political parties continued to report harassment and intimidation, especially outside the capital and in the run-up to the November parliamentary elections. International pressure helped reverse a decision which would have prevented some parties from taking part in the elections. The ruling New Azerbaijan party won the elections which were described as falling short of international standards. A joint observer mission by the Organization for Security and Co-operation in Europe and the Council of Europe reported that the elections were "marred by numerous instances of serious irregularities, in particular a completely flawed counting process. Observers reported ballot stuffing, manipulated turnout results, pre-marked ballots, and production of either false protocols or no protocols at all. Additionally, party proxies frequently suffered intimidation, harassment and sometimes even arrest whilst carrying out their legitimate activities." Protesters at various demonstrations around the country following the elections also aired grievances at poor socio-economic conditions.

The Presidents of Armenia and Azerbaijan continued their one-to-one meetings regarding the disputed region of Karabakh, but no major progress was reported in attempts to achieve a political settlement. In March a failed assassination attempt on the region's leader prompted a wave of arrests.

Torture/ill-treatment
Positive moves
In March the Supreme Court issued instructions to lower courts specifying, among other things, that the term "torture" should be understood in accordance with the definition in the UN Convention against Torture; reminding courts of their obligations to initiate investigations whenever defendants allege torture or ill-treatment; reiterating that evidence obtained in violation of the law is inadmissible; and repeating the 1999 decision of the Constitutional Court that those detained under administrative procedures are entitled to a lawyer. The UN Special Rapporteur on torture visited the country in May at the invitation of the government. In June an agreement was finally concluded allowing access by the International Committee of the Red Cross (ICRC) to all places of detention and all detainees within its mandate.

Continuing allegations
In spite of these positive moves, however, there were continuing reports of ill-treatment during 2000.

In April there were allegations that police used excessive force in Baku when dispersing opposition party supporters trying to hold an unauthorized demonstration in connection with the parliamentary elections. According to reports a number of journalists were assaulted while covering the events, during which 34 police officers were officially reported to have been injured and a number of leading opposition figures were allegedly ill-treated.

Vajif Hadjibeyli, chairman of the *Ehrar* (Peasants) Party, was reportedly severely beaten by police while being detained. He was then taken to the local police station suffering from concussion for which he allegedly did not receive prompt, appropriate medical attention. He was not allowed to see his lawyer or telephone his family and was sentenced to 10 days' administrative detention for resisting the lawful demands of a police officer. Before the end of this term he was transferred from the Main Police Directorate to Bailov investigation isolation prison No. 1, after being charged with resisting a police officer. He was subsequently released on bail but no trial had taken place by the end of the year.

Council of Europe
In June Azerbaijan's application to join the Council of Europe was reviewed by the Council's Parliamentary Assembly, which recommended membership on the understanding that Azerbaijan would fulfil a number of commitments within a stated time frame. These included ratifying the European Convention on Human Rights and the European Convention for the Prevention of Torture and Inhuman or Degrading Treatment or Punishment within a year of accession; adopting a law on an ombudsperson within a year of accession; and adopting, within two years of accession, a law on an alternative to compulsory military service, in compliance with European standards. Among other things, Azerbaijan also undertook to allow unrestricted access to prisoners by the ICRC; to release or grant a new trial to political prisoners; and to prosecute members of law enforcement bodies suspected of human rights violations, in particular torture. A formal invitation of membership was issued in November, although additional conditions were set in connection with the instances of fraud and irregularities reported during the November parliamentary elections.

Possible prisoners of conscience

Several people active in the political opposition were detained for short periods, and were possible prisoners of conscience.

☐ Rauf Arifoglu, editor-in-chief of the opposition newspaper *Yeni Musavat*, was arrested on 22 August at his home in Baku after police claimed to have found an illegally held pistol in the apartment.

Events leading to Rauf Arifoglu's arrest began on 18 August, when a man attempted to hijack an aircraft carrying more than 100 passengers. Before being overpowered, the hijacker telephoned Rauf Arifoglu and listed a number of political demands regarding the parliamentary elections. Rauf Arifoglu stated that immediately after the call he rang the Minister of National Security and the press services of the Interior Ministry and the General Procurator's Office.

The following day, two employees of the district procurator's office and three police officers arrived at the *Yeni Musavat* offices with a search warrant, stating that they were looking for a tape recording of the telephone conversation with the hijacker. Rauf Arifoglu was taken to Sabail police department where he gave oral and written testimony, and the cassette tape was taken from him. He was then released.

Three days later, police arrived at Rauf Arifoglu's apartment and started to conduct a search. Rauf Arifoglu rang journalist colleagues and they gathered outside his apartment. Police did not allow either the journalists or Rauf Arifoglu's lawyer to enter the apartment while the search was conducted. When the pistol was found, Rauf Arifoglu shouted down to his colleagues that it had been planted, and refused to sign the police protocol of the search. He was arrested on a charge of illegally possessing a weapon, and later charged with other serious offences, including treason, in connection with the hijack. Rauf Arifoglu was released on bail on 5 October after widespread national and international pressure. Charges against him were still pending at the end of the year.

Decriminalization of homosexuality

Consensual homosexual relations between adult males, previously punishable by up to three years' imprisonment, were decriminalized when a new criminal code came into force in September. The new code sets a general age of consent at 16 and punishes only forcible sexual acts.

Karabakh

In the early hours of 22 March gunmen attempted to assassinate Arkady Ghukasian, "President" of the Nagorno-Karabakh Republic (elections in the disputed region are not regarded as legitimate by the Azerbaijani authorities).

Samvel Babaian

The assassination attempt was immediately followed by a wave of arrests centring on the former Defence Minister of the region, Samvel Babaian, and his associates. A number of those detained, including Samvel Babaian, were said to have been severely ill-treated in detention. Specific details were difficult to obtain, however; most of those detained reportedly had no access to their families and, in some cases, inadequate access to a defence lawyer. In May, for example, Sasun Aghajanian's lawyer reported that they had met only twice since his client's arrest some two months earlier — once in private for a meeting that lasted around 10 minutes and once during an interrogation on 27 April, which was reportedly stopped by the lawyer when his client lost consciousness. There were also allegations that those detained in connection with the assassination attempt were denied food parcels from their relatives, and that some had no opportunity to take daily exercise.

AI urged the procurator general in Karabakh to ensure that all necessary procedures for a fair trial were observed for all defendants at each stage of the criminal proceedings, including the requirement that public authorities, particularly prosecutors and the police, not make public statements about the guilt or innocence of the accused before the outcome of the trial which could prejudice the presumption of innocence.

The trial opened in September, but was adjourned several times over the question of whether Sasun Aghajanian was mentally fit to stand trial. It had not concluded by the end of 2000.

Vagram Aghajanian

Journalist Vagram Aghajanian was among those arrested following the March assassination attempt. He had been critical of the Karabakh authorities and was regarded as close to opposition figures such as Samvel Babaian. Vagram Aghajanian was detained on 28 March after officers searched his home, reportedly without presenting a warrant. Vagram Aghajanian was subsequently found guilty of "hampering the implementation of martial law" by publishing articles regarded by the authorities as "contributing to internal tension", and sentenced to 10 days' administrative detention.

In April Vagram Aghajanian was sentenced to one year's imprisonment for libel. The criminal case had originally been opened in December 1999 following an article in which Vagram Aghajanian had criticized what he regarded as insufficient aid being made available to those who wished to resettle in some areas of Karabakh. The article quoted several people who claimed that the Prime Minister told them there was no money available in the budget for such help.

The Prime Minister is said to have denied that he had met the people quoted. It was reported that both Vagram Aghajanian and the newspaper editor had offered to publish a retraction of the report that such a meeting had taken place, but that this was rejected in favour of a criminal prosecution. There were allegations that Vagram Aghajanian's friends and colleagues were given very little notice of the impending trial, hampering their attempts to find him a defence lawyer. As a consequence the lawyer was said to have had only a few hours to acquaint himself with the case before the trial began. In April the appeal court changed the custodial sentence to a suspended one.

The death penalty

The death penalty was retained in the Karabakh region. In January Arkady Ghukasian commuted two death sentences to periods of 15 years' imprisonment. No executions were reported.

AI country report

- Concerns in Europe, January-June 2000: Azerbaijan (AI Index: EUR 01/003/2000)

BAHAMAS

COMMONWEALTH OF THE BAHAMAS
Head of State: Queen Elizabeth II, represented by Orville Turnquest
Head of government: Hubert Alexander Ingraham
Capital: Nassau
Population: 0.3 million
Official language: English
Death penalty: retentionist
2000 treaty ratifications/signatures: Rome Statute of the International Criminal Court

One person was hanged despite having international appeals pending and three people were scheduled to be executed. Asylum-seekers were detained, in violation of international standards, and forcibly repatriated to Haiti and Cuba. Several deaths were reported in Fox Hill Prison amid continuing reports of brutality and cruel, inhuman and degrading conditions of detention. A new Code of Conduct and Complaints Division for the Royal Bahamas Police Force was introduced. However, there were continuing reports of unjustifiable use of force and arbitrary detention by police officers. A prisoner of conscience was released after four days, following a national and international campaign.

Death penalty

Twenty-five prisoners remained on death row at the end of 2000, according to official figures. One person was hanged.

A ruling by the Judicial Committee of the Privy Council (JCPC) in the United Kingdom — the final court of appeal of the Bahamas — in the case of Neville Lewis and others in Jamaica, commuting the death sentences of six prisoners, had implications for the administration of the death penalty in the Bahamas (see Jamaica entry). However, during a debate in parliament in December, the Attorney General called for the death penalty to be extended to cover selling or giving drugs to children.

David Mitchell was executed in January despite the fact that the Inter-American Commission on Human Rights was due to hear his petition, alleging violations under the American Declaration of the Rights and Duties of Man, in February 2000.

John Higgs died in prison two days before his scheduled execution on 6 January. His petition to the Inter-American Commission on Human Rights was also due to be heard in February. A coroner's inquest was convened in January to investigate the cause of death, suspected to be suicide. It had yet to release its findings at the end of the year.

Corporal punishment

Corporal punishment remained available under the law but no new sentences were imposed or carried out. Individuals remain under sentence of corporal punishment pending legal appeals.

Prisons

There were continuing reports of brutality and of prison conditions which failed to meet international minimum standards for the treatment of prisoners at Fox Hill Prison; several deaths were reported during 2000. Prisoners were routinely denied medical attention and exercise and were held in insanitary conditions. Remanded and convicted prisoners were held together in the section of the prison reserved for those under sentence of death.

In September Sidney Winston McKenzie was found dead in his cell. His body reportedly showed evidence of severe beating. Family members were denied access to view his body. A coroner's inquest was convened but it had not released its findings by the end of the year.

Refugees

Asylum-seekers from Haiti and Cuba continued to be forcibly returned without prior access to a full and fair determination procedure, in violation of international law. In May, the Inter-American Commission on Human Rights requested that the government halt forcible returns. Following hearings in October, the Commission agreed to negotiate a "friendly settlement" with the government.

Adult and children asylum-seekers were still detained at Fox Hill Prison in conditions amounting to cruel, inhuman and degrading treatment and in violation of the UN Refugee Convention. Asylum-seekers were held in incommunicado detention and denied visits, phone calls or mail from lawyers and relatives. Children were denied access to other relatives in prison. There were reports that some asylum-seekers were beaten and denied medical attention. Following an attempted escape in May a number of Cuban asylum-seekers were reportedly put on a diet of bread and water.

Torture/ill-treatment

There were reports of arbitrary detention and ill-treatment, possibly amounting to torture, of criminal suspects by police. Children were reportedly held together with adults in some police lock-ups.

In January, a number of men were allegedly arrested and detained for several hours in Central Police Station without charge before being transported elections in October, frequently complained about the conditions of detention. AI has also expressed concern about conditions in prisons and pre-trial detention centres which fall well below international standards and amount to cruel, inhuman and degrading treatment.

◻ On 30 March Vyacheslav Sivchik, deputy chairman of the Belarusian Popular Front, received a 10-day prison sentence for his part in organizing a demonstration several days previously. After his release from the Okrestina detention centre he reportedly stated that he was deliberately placed in a cell with a broken window while the weather was very cold. He alleged that fellow inmates with a severe form of tuberculosis were kept together with other prisoners. In addition, on the last day of his imprisonment, guards allegedly spread disinfectant all over the cell while the prisoners were still in it.

Detention of protesters

During its third periodic review of Belarus in November, the UN Committee against Torture expressed concern about "persistent abrogations of the right to freedom of expression, such as limitations of the independence of the press, and of the right to peaceful assembly". During 2000 AI continued to receive numerous reports of people who were arrested for exercising these rights.

◻ In the run-up to the elections in October, protesters in various cities and towns, including Minsk, Bobruysk and Vitebsk, were reportedly detained by police because of their attempts to organize a boycott of the elections. A number were reportedly fined, and their leaflets and other materials confiscated.

◻ In November over 100 young protesters, many of them minors, were detained by police in Minsk after staging an unauthorized demonstration. The police reportedly used considerable force to herd them onto police buses and into police vans.

Police ill-treatment

During an unauthorized demonstration in Minsk on 25 March, between 400 and 500 demonstrators were reportedly detained for several hours by the police. At least 30 journalists covering the demonstration were also targeted by the authorities. There were reports that police officers used unnecessary force to detain some protesters. A number of people complained of being knocked to the ground, beaten with truncheons, kicked by police officers and verbally abused.

◻ Yury Belenki, deputy chairman of the Conservative Christian Party of the Belarusian Popular Front, alleged that he and his companions were attacked by a group of police officers on Yakub Kolas Square in Minsk on 25 March. He stated that he was hit in the face with a truncheon, knocked off his feet and repeatedly punched and kicked. He was then arrested and held in detention for three days. The relevant prosecutor's office in Minsk reportedly refused to investigate his allegations of police ill-treatment.

Conscientious objection

Belarusian legislation does not allow conscientious objectors to military service to undertake an alternative civilian service. Military conscription is compulsory for men aged between 18 and 27 and lasts 18 months, except for university graduates, who serve 12 months.

◻ On 23 March Valentin Gulai, a 21-year-old Jehovah's Witness, was given a suspended 18-month prison sentence by Rechitsa regional court for refusing to perform military service. The sentence was conditional and required him to spend 18 months working on state construction projects. Gomel regional court later reduced the sentence to a one-year suspended sentence.

AI country reports and visit

Reports
- Possible "disappearances" in Belarus (AI Index: EUR 49/003/2000)
- Belarus: Conscientious objector Valentin Gulai (AI Index: EUR 49/012/2000)
- Belarus: Dissent and Impunity (AI Index: EUR 49/014/2000)

Visit
AI delegates visited Minsk in March to take part in a human rights conference, to monitor a demonstration and trial and to meet lawyers and non-governmental organizations.

BELGIUM

KINGDOM OF BELGIUM
Head of state: King Albert II
Head of government: Guy Verhhofstadt
Capital: Brussels
Population: 10.2 million
Official languages: Dutch, French, German
Death penalty: abolitionist for all crimes
2000 treaty ratifications/signatures: Optional Protocol to the UN Children's Convention on the involvement of children in armed conflict; Rome Statute of the International Criminal Court

There were further allegations that criminal suspects were ill-treated by law enforcement officers and that asylum-seekers were ill-treated during forcible deportations and in detention centres for aliens. Criminal investigations were opened or continued into many such incidents. By the end of 2000 nobody had been brought to justice in connection with the death in 1998 of an asylum-seeker asphyxiated after gendarmes pressed a cushion over her face during forcible deportation. There was concern that, although a proposed government reform of asylum procedures, announced in November, would introduce welcome and substantial simplification of

▫ Robert Hill was sentenced to death on 10 April. However, the Court of Appeal ordered a retrial following a successful appeal against the sentence.
▫ The appeal against the sentence of Patrick Reyes, convicted of murder in 1999, was dismissed by the Belize Court of Appeal on 28 March.
▫ In June Estevan Sho, who was convicted of murder and sentenced to death on 2 December 1999, had his sentence commuted to 25 years' imprisonment on appeal.

Torture/ill-treatment
Reports of torture by police, and of excessive use of force, continued. Human rights organizations, lawyers and journalists reported that ill-treatment and torture by the security forces were widespread but often remained unreported because of victims' fear of retaliation.
▫ Police officers allegedly beat Charlie Slusher and Norman "Tilliman" Núñez in August, in Belmopan, as they made their way to a party in the Orange Walk district. Following a police investigation, the Commissioner of Police reportedly removed an Inspector and Assistant Inspector from active duty pending disciplinary proceedings. Two police constables were also under further investigation.
▫ Randolph Miller was allegedly beaten in July and had his hand broken by an officer at the Department of Corrections in the presence of another officer, after he was recaptured by police after his escape from Hattieville prison. An investigation was carried out by the Ombudsman.

Police shootings
Reports of police shootings in disputed circumstances continued.
▫ Leslie "Mobley" Smith was reportedly killed by police on 19 August after they tried to arrest him. Police reports indicated that he was armed with a knife, but other witnesses apparently contested this. The Internal Affairs Desk of the Belize Police Force conducted an investigation and announced that it would pass the file to the Director of Police Prosecutions.

Prison conditions
Conditions in Hattieville Rehabilitation Centre, the main penal institution in Belize, were reported to be very poor. The main concerns included poor sanitation, lack of water and toilet facilities, and lack of facilities for prisoners to have confidential consultations with their lawyers. The prison was severely overcrowded, holding more than twice the 500 inmates it was designed for. There were reports of prisoners being beaten by other inmates. There was a riot in March in which one inmate died and three others were shot.
▫ Jason Flowers was found hanging in his cell on 7 November. His mother and other relatives rejected the presumption of suicide and alleged that he was murdered by inmates.

A government minister stated that measures to improve conditions had been taken in 2000, including the introduction of a clinic with three nurses and a doctor and the opening of a female facility in August. Officials also stated that foreign prisoners would be deported to their countries of origin to ease overcrowding, giving rise to concern that some might be at risk of human rights violations on their return.

Corporal punishment
Corporal punishment was reinstituted in prisons in February as a punishment for mutiny, incitement to mutiny, or gross personal violence to an officer. It was used retrospectively as a punishment for crimes committed before it was introduced. In addition, from 1 July, the offences for which corporal punishment could be used were extended to include possession of weapons or attempted escape from prison.
▫ In March Nehru Smith received 12 lashes with a tamarind whip and Bert Elijio received six, both for allegedly stabbing fellow inmates.

AI country report
- Belize: Government commitments and human rights (AI Index: AMR 16/003/2000)

BHUTAN

KINGDOM OF BHUTAN
Head of state: King Jigme Singye Wangchuck
Head of government: Yeshi Zimba (replaced Sangay Ngedup in August)
Capital: Thimphu
Population: 0.6 million
Official language: Dzongkha
Death penalty: abolitionist in practice

Amid increased international attention, there was a breakthrough in negotiations between Bhutan and Nepal on the right of almost 100,000 Nepali-speaking people in refugee camps in eastern Nepal to return to Bhutan. Torture by police was reported. Leaders of political parties in exile were reportedly arrested on their return.

Background
Finance Minister Yeshi Zimba took office as Chairman to the Council of Ministers in August. A new system of "security clearance certificates", issued by the Royal Bhutan Police, replaced "no objection certificates" and "police clearance certificates". However, there were continuing concerns that members of the Nepali-speaking community would continue to face discrimination when applying for such certificates in order to be able to obtain work, promotion or business licences or to travel abroad, on the basis that they had

contacts with "anti-nationals" in refugee camps in Nepal. As part of strengthening the country's legal framework, new charge-sheets were introduced on which police must enter the sections of the law under which a person is to be charged.

Nepali-speaking refugees
Several high-level delegations visited the country to discuss with the authorities the plight of people living in refugee camps in Nepal since the early 1990s. Among them were US State Department officials who visited in January and December.

After her visit in April, the UN High Commissioner for Refugees reported that Bhutan was ready to proceed with joint verification of people living in the camps to determine their eligibility for inclusion in a future voluntary repatriation program. However, in May the ninth round of ministerial talks between Bhutan and Nepal failed to reach agreement. Bhutan's position was that individuals over the age of 18 should be verified individually while Nepal wanted the unit of verification to be the head of the family. A compromise formula, put forward by the High Commissioner was initially rejected by Bhutan. In late December, Nepal and Bhutan finally reached an agreement on the mechanisms and unit of verification. A joint verification team — consisting of five officials from each government — was mandated to first validate the family units and then proceed to verify heads of families and individual units.

In September the European Parliament passed a resolution calling on "the Governments of Bhutan and Nepal, in cooperation with all parties involved, to reach an agreement which will allow the early and voluntary repatriation of the refugees to their country of origin".

Torture
Torture by police was reported.

☐ Tul Man Tamang, a 30-year-old construction worker, was arrested on 27 June on suspicion of organizing political activities. He was taken to the police station at Chimakothi in Chhukha district where he was allegedly kicked and beaten with a cane, leather belt and rifle butt on his back, legs and buttocks. He was reportedly held incommunicado in a dark cell for three days before being taken to the police station at Phuntsholing on the border with India. He was forced to sign a statement saying he was leaving the country of his own free will and was forcibly exiled to India.

Arrests of politicians
Several leaders of political parties in exile who returned to Bhutan were arrested. Some remained held at the end of the year.

☐ N.L. Katwal, a central committee member of the Bhutan Gorkha National Liberation Front, was reportedly among more than 50 people arrested during a demonstration in Phuntsholing in April.

☐ Ugyen Tenzing, a member of the Druk-Yul Peoples Democratic Party, was reportedly arrested in Samtse district in June and taken to Thimphu police headquarters.

AI country report
- Bhutan: Nationality, Expulsion, Statelessness and the Right to Return (AI Index: ASA 14/001/2000)

BOLIVIA

REPUBLIC OF BOLIVIA
Head of state and government: Hugo Bánzer Suárez
Capital: La Paz
Population: 8.3 million
Official language: Spanish
Death penalty: Abolitionist for ordinary crimes
2000 treaty ratifications/signatures: Optional Protocol to the UN Women's Convention

Human rights violations were reported in Cochabamba Department in the context of a state of siege. Scores of people were arbitrarily detained and human rights activists and journalists were harassed and intimidated. Conditions in prisons and detention centres constituted cruel, inhuman or degrading treatment. Human rights violations were reported in El Chapare region.

Background
A state of siege was declared on 8 April following demonstrations against a government waterworks project in the city of Cochabamba, Department of Cochabamba. Scores of union and community leaders were arrested; most were held in incommunicado detention and sent into internal exile. Five people, including an army officer and a minor, were reportedly killed during violent confrontations between protesters and the military. A media blackout was imposed and local radio stations were forced off the air. The state of siege was lifted on 20 April after the government reached an agreement with peasant and trade union organizations. All those arrested were released without charge.

Police brutality
Demonstrations called in January and February by the *Coordinadora Departamental de Defensa del Agua y la Vida*, Coordinating Committee for the Defence of Water and Life, in Cochabamba, were met with excessive use of force by the police and the military. The security forces indiscriminately fired tear gas, rubber bullets and pellets into the crowds. There were also reports of disproportionate use of force by the security forces against demonstrators in April. Scores of people were injured and four died, including a minor.

☐ In February, 14-year-old Wanderley Siñani Cardoso was doused with tear gas and sustained a fractured coccyx as a result of a beating by members of the security forces. A few days later he collapsed at school and had to be taken to hospital where it was confirmed that he had suffered a brain haemorrhage.

◻ In April, 17-year-old Hugo Daza was shot dead in Cochabamba at the time that an army officer in civilian clothing was seen firing into the crowd during a demonstration. Investigations were reportedly initiated by the army into the incident.

Torture/ill-treatment
Scores of people were detained in February; all were reportedly beaten by the security forces.

Hours before the state of siege was declared in April, hooded police officers raided the homes of union leaders and members of the Coordinating Committee for the Defence of Water and Life in Cochabamba, arresting the leaders, beating members of their families, stealing household goods, and shooting at neighbours with pellets. There were also reports that people, including minors, were detained in La Paz Department and tortured to coerce them into incriminating community or union leaders. No investigations were initiated into these incidents. The government denied that minors had been ill-treated.

◻ Sixteen-year-old Pedro Alejandro testified that in February he had been subjected to electric shocks on his testicles while he was under arrest at a police station.

◻ Sixteen-year-old David Goitía Benito was arrested in April in Cochabamba by police and taken to the offices of the *Grupo Especial de Seguridad*, Security Special Group, where he was badly beaten with a chain and hose. His nose was broken and his torso badly bruised. He managed to escape a few hours later.

Freedom of expression
Several journalists and human rights activists who were perceived as critical of the government or who had publicly criticized the authorities' actions in Cochabamba were threatened and intimidated.

◻ Journalists Osvaldo Rioja and Jhenny Osinaga received anonymous death threats after their television network broadcast footage of an army officer in civilian clothing firing at the crowd during a demonstration in Cochabamba in April.

◻ Sacha Llorenti, Legal Affairs Secretary of the *Asamblea Permanente de Derechos Humanos*, Permanent Human rights Assembly, received anonymous death threats in August. The threats were believed to be linked to his role in filing judicial complaints and calling for independent investigations covering human rights violations committed during the state of siege.

Prison conditions
Conditions in prisons and pre-trial detention centres fell well below international minimum standards and amounted in most cases to cruel, degrading or inhuman treatment. Most prisoners and detainees received inadequate medical care and were housed in poorly heated and ventilated, squalid and insanitary conditions. Many were forced to sleep on the floor in overcrowded communal rooms, halls and open yards. Access to washing facilities was limited and the quality of food and water was very poor. Detainees at the high security prison of San Pedro de Chonchocoro in La Paz were reportedly tortured and ill-treated; AI delegates interviewed two inmates who had been tortured the day before their visit to the prison. No investigation was known to have been initiated into their allegations.

El Chapare
Reports of human rights violations in the context of the eradication of coca leaf crops in El Chapare increased in the second half of the year. In September and October security forces reportedly used excessive and arbitrary force against groups of demonstrators who had been blockading the main roads in the El Chapare area in protest at government policies. Ten people died and more than 100 were injured.

AI country reports and visit
Reports
- Bolivia: A shameful prison system (AI Index: AMR 18/006/2000)
- Bolivia: The state of siege is no excuse for human rights violations (AI Index: AMR 18/002/2000)
- Bolivia: There can be no justification for human rights violations (AI Index: AMR 18/011/2000)

Visit
AI delegates visited Bolivia between June and July and interviewed prisoners and detainees in nine prisons and detention centres in La Paz, Santa Cruz, Cochabamba and El Chapare. The delegates held meetings at ministerial and local authority level.

BOSNIA-HERZEGOVINA

BOSNIA AND HERZEGOVINA
Head of state: three-member rotating presidency – Alija Izetbegović, Živko Radišić and Ante Jelavić
President of the Muslim/Croat Federation of Bosnia-Herzegovina: Ejup Ganić
President of Republika Srpska: vacant until December
Heads of national government: rotating premiership – Spasoje Tuševljak, Martin Raguz,
Capital: Sarajevo
Population: 3.97 million
Official languages: Bosnian, Croatian, Serbian
Death penalty: abolitionist for ordinary crimes
2000 treaty ratifications/signatures: Second Optional Protocol to the International Covenant on Civil and Political Rights, aiming at the abolition of the death penalty; Optional Protocol to the UN Children's Convention on the involvement of children in armed conflict; Optional Protocol to the UN Women's Convention; Rome Statute of the International Criminal Court

Overwhelming international involvement in political and administrative matters in Bosnia-Herzegovina continued to contribute to the stabilization and normalization of the country during 2000. There was a substantial increase in the number of refugees and displaced persons returning to their pre-war communities, now administered and mostly inhabited by members of another ethnic group (minority returns) – such returns had been disappointingly few in past years despite considerable efforts by the international community. However, there remained serious concerns about the overall human rights situation, in particular the lack of genuine commitment by local authorities to protect human rights and address past violations. Most perpetrators of the massive and grave abuses of human rights committed during and in the wake of the civil war continued to enjoy impunity. Tens of thousands of people remained unaccounted for; many had "disappeared" during the war. Trials of political prisoners often failed to meet internationally recognized standards of fairness. Ill-treatment of people in police custody persisted, especially of socially marginalized groups such as the Roma.

Background

Bosnia-Herzegovina consists of two entities – the Federation of Bosnia-Herzegovina (Federation) and the Republika Srpska (RS) – and the autonomous multi-ethnic district of Brčko. Both entities and the Brčko district have their own government, legislature, judicial system, police and armed forces. The central government, composed of representatives of the three constituent peoples – Serbs, Croats and Bosniacs – was too weak and internally divided to carry out its functions effectively. A political and governmental crisis continued in the RS for a second year; there was no president and the caretaker government was subjected to repeated no-confidence votes by the RS parliament.

Municipal elections took place in March, which resulted in a general consolidation of the power of the main nationalist parties, although the opposition Social Democratic Party (SDP) made considerable gains in some urban areas in the Federation. In November, general elections took place, as well as presidential elections in the RS, in which results reflected the outcome of the municipal elections. Mirko Šarović was elected president of the RS.

In July the Constitutional Court of Bosnia-Herzegovina — comprising four judges from the Federation, two judges from the RS, and three international jurists — ruled that the Bosniac, Serb and Croatian peoples were entitled to enjoy equal rights throughout the country. The ruling meant that the Constitutions of the Federation and the RS needed to be amended, as neither recognized the equal rights of all three nationalities. However, by the end of the year no such amendments had been made. In February the RS parliament adopted a law establishing a multi-ethnic ombudsperson institution. In June a new Criminal Code was passed by the RS parliament which no longer provided for the death penalty.

Minority returns

According to figures published by the UN High Commissioner for Refugees (UNHCR), more than 60,000 registered minority returns took place during 2000. Following a comprehensive registration exercise in the Federation and RS, the number of internally displaced people and refugees at the end of 2000 was placed at around 500,000 and 700,000 respectively, as compared to around 830,000 and 60,000 at the end of 1999.

This significant increase in the number of returns was primarily caused by the massive and spontaneous return of displaced people to destroyed housing, mostly outside urban areas. International monitors remained concerned that returns to town and city centres were proceeding slowly, if at all, primarily as a result of the failure to implement property legislation. Statistics on the implementation of property legislation compiled by various international organizations on the basis of information provided by local authorities, showed that by the end of 2000, 50 per cent of claims in the Federation had been resolved but in only 21 per cent of cases had the property been repossessed by the pre-war owner or occupant. Statistics for the RS were even worse: only 24 per cent of claims had been resolved and only nine per cent had resulted in repossession. In September, the High Representative, appointed by the UN Security Council to oversee the civilian implementation of the Dayton Peace Agreement, removed 15 government officials from office for their obstruction to the return process.

Many of the spontaneous returns proved unsustainable because of a lack of funding for the reconstruction of housing and infrastructure.

In addition to social and economic obstacles, returnees also continued to face violence in many areas of the country.

☐ In Bijeljina and Janja municipalities in the RS, Bosniac returnees and residents had explosives and stones thrown at their houses and were subjected to physical assaults in February and June. Police reportedly failed to protect them and although investigations against suspected perpetrators were launched, international observers noted that these were not conducted diligently or thoroughly and that the charges which were eventually brought did not reflect the seriousness of the attacks. Further attacks took place in October and November.

☐ In Srebrenica, also in the RS, several houses of Bosniac returnees were set on fire in May, June and July.

☐ A very tense situation developed in Brčko town in October, after a demonstration by Serb secondary school students protesting against sharing education facilities with Bosniac students turned violent. Bosniac houses and shops in the town were reportedly vandalized following the demonstrations which then led to counter-demonstrations by Bosniac students. District police officers allegedly did not take appropriate action to prevent and respond to the violence, which to a large degree appeared to be organized.

Prosecutions for war crimes
International Criminal Tribunal for the former Yugoslavia

A number of trials before the International Criminal Tribunal for the former Yugoslavia (Tribunal) were concluded.

☐ In January, five Bosnian Croats were convicted of crimes against humanity in connection with the killing of over 100 Bosniac civilians in the central Bosnian village of Ahmići in 1993. They received sentences ranging from six to 25 years' imprisonment.

☐ In March, another Bosnian Croat, General Tihomir Blaškić, the highest-ranking army commander tried by the Tribunal to date, was found guilty of war crimes and crimes against humanity committed in the Lašva River valley in central Bosnia. He was sentenced to 45 years' imprisonment, the longest sentence handed down so far.

A number of trials before the Tribunal were continuing at the end of the year.

☐ In March Bosnian Serb General Radislav Krstić — accused of planning and ordering the killing of thousands of Bosniac men and boys after the fall of the former UN protected enclave of Srebrenica — became the first person to go on trial before the Tribunal on charges of genocide.

☐ Also in March the trial began of three Bosnian Serb paramilitary commanders accused of crimes against humanity in Foča (now renamed Srbinje and in the RS). This trial was expected to set legal precedents in prosecutions for sexual crimes against women. Dragoljub Kunarac, Radomir Kovač and Zoran Vuković were accused, along with five other Bosnian Serbs, of the rape and sexual enslavement of Bosniac women and girls who were held in detention in Foča or nearby towns.

☐ In October Bosnian Serb Milorad Krnojelac went on trial on charges of war crimes committed in Foča prison.

☐ The trial of Bosnian Croats Dario Kordić and Mario Ćerkez continued for a second year. Both stand accused of war crimes against the Bosniac population in the Lašva River valley and were originally included in a larger indictment together with Tihomir Blaškić and Zlatko Aleksovski, who eventually went on trial separately.

Arrests

Stabilization Forces (SFOR) arrested four war crimes suspects during the year, including the former RS presidency member Momčilo Krajišnik, who had been secretly indicted for genocide, crimes against humanity and war crimes committed in a large number of municipalities throughout Bosnia-Herzegovina. The arrest of Bosnian Serb Mitar Vasiljević in January in Višegrad in the eastern RS revealed the existence of a previously sealed indictment for crimes under international law committed in that town. In November the Tribunal's Prosecutor revealed that two other Bosnian Serbs, Milan and Sredoje Lukić, were included in the same indictment.

A fifth arrest attempt by SFOR in October in Foča/Srbinje resulted in the death of Janko Janjić, who, after SFOR soldiers had entered his flat, reportedly detonated a hand grenade and killed himself. He had been charged jointly with Dragoljub Kunarac, Radomir Kovač and Zoran Vuković.

In March, Croatia transferred Mladen Naletilić, a Bosnian Croat indicted for war crimes in Mostar, to the Tribunal's custody, following lengthy judicial proceedings to establish his fitness to travel.

Domestic prosecutions

In the Federation there were a number of domestic criminal proceedings against people accused of war crimes, following clearance to proceed from the Tribunal's Prosecutor under the "Rules of the Road" procedure which was established to ensure that domestic prosecutions would not be brought on an arbitrary basis. Some of these trials posed significant challenges for local courts which were required to impartially and independently prosecute members of their own ethnic group for crimes committed during the war.

☐ In January, the public prosecutor for Herzegovina-Neretva Canton indicted five Bosnian Croats for war crimes including the "disappearances" of Bosniac soldiers in 1993. However, even though the Office of the High Representative had urged the arrest of the five suspects, who reportedly appeared in public in Mostar regularly, the police failed to arrest them. In August and October, three of them gave themselves up to the police. In November trial proceedings began, with two of the accused being tried *in absentia*.

Other criminal trials revealed that the authorities were aware of human rights violations committed by groups under their control but failed to investigate them adequately or to prosecute the perpetrators.

☐ In October and November appeal hearings were conducted in the case of Edin Garaplija, a former officer in the Bosnian secret police. In November he was convicted after the charges against him were changed to ill-treatment in the course of duty and his sentence was reduced to seven years' imprisonment. He had been sentenced in 1997 to 13 years' imprisonment for abduction and attempted murder of another police officer. In 1996 Edin Garaplija had been ordered by his superior officer to detain and question a member of a paramilitary unit known as the *Ševe*. After several days of questioning the suspect made an attempt to escape during which Edin Garaplija reportedly shot and wounded him. During subsequent investigations and trial proceedings into the incident in 1997, Edin Garaplija claimed that he was instructed by his superiors to remain silent about his investigation or he would lose his life. He had not been allowed to be present when his appeal was heard by the Federation Supreme Court in 1998, in breach of international fair trial standards.

The Human Rights Chamber — which together with the Ombudsperson's Office forms the national Commission on Human Rights, created under the Dayton Peace Agreement — ruled in July 2000 that appeal proceedings in the case of Edin Garaplija should be renewed so he could present new evidence to the Supreme Court in person. During appeal hearings in October and November Edin Garaplija presented the Supreme Court with a detailed account of the findings of his investigations in 1996, which implicated various former members of the *Ševe* and serving government officials in criminal activities, including human rights violations. However, no criminal investigations had been launched into these allegations by the end of 2000.

Attacks on the independent media

Journalists critical of the government and leading political officials or those connected with them were attacked, threatened with death and prosecuted for libel. The Organization for Security and Co-operation in Europe (OSCE) reported in April that since the end of 1999, 65 cases had been registered where journalists' civil rights had been violated, many in March and April during the period running up to municipal elections. By August an OSCE helpline, established in May for journalists subjected to such persecution, was reported to have registered some 39 new incidents in both the Federation and the RS.

⌕ In June Edin Avdić, a reporter for the Sarajevo-based independent weekly *Slobodna Bosna*, was beaten by two unidentified men in front of his house in Sarajevo. Edin Avdić had been threatened a week earlier by a local businessman affiliated with the governing Bosniac political party, the Party of Democratic Action, because he had criticized the cultural policies of that party. The assailants reportedly repeated the earlier message and also delivered a death threat. A police investigation into the attacks was launched immediately but had not been concluded by the end of the year.

⌕ In June RS police arrested five men thought to have been involved in the attack on Željko Kopanja, editor of the Bosnian Serb independent newspaper *Nezavisne novine*, who lost both legs in a car bomb attack in October 1999. All five were released within days without charge.

'Disappearances'

According to the International Committee of the Red Cross (ICRC) more than 17,500 people remained unaccounted for, including 280 detained prisoners registered by ICRC during the war who subsequently "disappeared".

Exhumations continued by both Federation and RS government commissions on missing persons, especially in eastern RS. The Federation commission exhumed more than 4,000 remains, half of whom were identified. The RS exhumed several hundred bodies. Serious problems persisted with the identification and storage of bodies and as a result the RS authorities buried more than 400 unidentified bodies in October.

Some local authorities actively obstructed the preservation of sites thought to contain mass graves.

⌕ In Sultanovići, eastern RS, a plot of land holding four mass graves and containing 360 bodies was used by nearby Zvornik municipality as a rubbish dump for more than six months. Although the authorities eventually stopped dumping their rubbish there, they failed to clear up the waste already accumulated, which had reportedly seeped into the soil and damaged the bodies buried there.

AI country report and visits
Report
- Bosnia-Herzegovina: Waiting on the doorstep — minority returns to eastern Republika Srpska (AI Index: EUR 63/007/2000)

Visits
AI visited Bosnia-Herzegovina in March and April to carry out research into minority returns.

BRAZIL

FEDERATIVE REPUBLIC OF BRAZIL
Head of state and government: Fernando Henríque Cardoso
Capital: Brasília
Population: 170 million
Official language: Portuguese
Death penalty: abolitionist for ordinary crimes
2000 treaty ratifications/signatures: Optional Protocol to the UN Children's Convention on the involvement of children in armed conflict; Rome Statute of the International Criminal Court

The systematic use of torture and ill-treatment continued in police stations, prisons and juvenile detention centres. There were no reported convictions for torture. Conditions for common criminal prisoners and juvenile detainees constituted ill-treatment. Deaths in custody were rarely, if ever, investigated or documented. Killings by police and "death squads" linked to the security forces increased, especially in urban centres. Land reform activists and indigenous people involved in land disputes were harassed, assaulted and killed both by military police and by gunmen hired by local landowners, with the apparent acquiescence of the police and the authorities. Human rights defenders were threatened and attacked.

Torture/ill-treatment

Torture and ill-treatment were routinely inflicted by both military police during arrests and by civil police in overcrowded police stations. Beatings as a means of extracting confessions, extortion or maintaining control were regularly reported, and electro-shock torture, the so-called "parrot's perch" and other forms of torture were used with impunity. Prison guards used beatings and intimidation to control long-term detainees. Few allegations of torture were investigated, and many injuries were attributed to "resisting arrest". Many police suspected of practising torture were transferred to other postings and very few were prosecuted under the anti-torture law. By the end of 2000 there had been no reported convictions under this law.

On 28 July, a prison inspection in the Public Jail in the city of Sorocaba, São Paulo state, discovered that a number of prisoners had knives hidden in their cells. The prisoners were forced to walk, in their underpants, between two rows of policemen, while being beaten with sticks, broom handles and electricity cables, punched and kicked. Sixteen of the prisoners were found on later medical inspection to have suffered severe injuries. Unusually, the public prosecutor's office charged 25 civil policemen and prison guards under the anti-torture law. However, the police and prison guards remained in active service within the same prison, where they reportedly continued to beat the prisoners. Public prosecutors working on the case received several telephoned threats, warning them to abandon the prosecution.

In April, AI delegates visited the Lemos Brito prison in Salvador, Bahia state. They were unable to complete the visit as the director and prison guards refused to let them speak to the prisoners alone, and military police insisted on filming all conversations, claiming this was for the delegates' security. When delegates asked the reason for stashes of iron bars and sticks at the guards' desk, the director said they were purely to uncover potential escape tunnels hidden behind posters in the prisoners' cells.

Deaths in custody

There were numerous deaths in custody. Some resulted from excessive use of force by guards and military and civil police officers, who were often poorly trained and outnumbered during prison riots and disturbances. Other prisoners died as a result of inadequate medical care and inadequate protection against violence from other inmates.

On 11 February 2000 Adroaldo Araújo was arrested in São Félix do Xingu, Pará state, following a knife fight. He was detained by the military police and taken to the local police station, where his injuries were inspected by a male nurse, who authorized his continued detention. Adroaldo Araújo was left in his cell, and was found dead the next morning, having bled to death. The case was investigated by military police from the same jurisdiction. No criminal charges were brought, although one police sergeant and the nurse were found culpable of professional negligence.

Children in detention

The 10th anniversary of the Children and Adolescents Statute (ECA) was marked by the continued deterioration of the juvenile detention system. Reports of widespread torture, ill-treatment, intimidation and deaths in custody were compounded by the use of excessive force by military police and prison guards during riots and disturbances.

Juvenile detainees in detention units run by the Foundation for the Well-Being of Minors (FEBEM) in São Paulo state continued to suffer cruel, inhuman and degrading treatment; large-capacity units were extremely overcrowded and had poor sanitation and little or no educational facilities. A rebellion on 10 November in Paralheiros FEBEM Unit was the 28th such uprising during 2000 in FEBEM units in the state. Two juvenile detainees were tortured after they met the UN Special Rapporteur on torture during his visit to the Franco da Rocha unit on 23 August. In July AI released a report on the juvenile detention system in the state of São Paulo, documenting not only abuses suffered by detainees, but also the legal battle waged by the state authorities against attempts to force them to bring FEBEM up to the minimum standards required by the ECA.

Extrajudicial executions and 'death squads'

Deaths resulting from excessive use of force by police, or in circumstances suggesting extrajudicial executions, continued. "Death squads", acting with the participation or collusion of the police, continued to operate in a number of states, including Acre, Bahia, Espírito Santo, Goiás, Rio de Janeiro and Rio Grande do Norte. Moves to reform Rio de Janeiro's notorious police forces were undermined when political support was withdrawn, reportedly after hard-line elements within the police exerted pressure on the state authorities.

▫ In Rio de Janeiro, two survivors of the 1993 Candelária massacre, when eight street children were killed by a "death squad", suffered violent deaths. On 12 June, Sandro do Nascimento hijacked a bus in Rio de Janeiro and held a number of people hostage, at gunpoint, for several hours. Police shot and injured him, then took him to hospital in a police car. He was found dead on arrival, as a result of strangulation. Five police officers accused of involvement in his killing had preventive detention orders revoked by a judge, but the state public prosecutor's office appealed against that ruling and sought to bring them to trial.

Elizabeth Cristina de Oliveira Maia was shot dead outside her home on 26 September, just before giving evidence at the appeal hearing of one of the military police accused of involvement in the Candelária massacre. Her murder suggested the involvement of a "death squad", and increased the fears of other witnesses in "death squad" trials.

▫ The office of São Paulo's police Ombudsman published a study on the use of lethal force by the police in the state during 1999. The study showed, among other things, that 56 per cent of those killed had no previous criminal record, 51 per cent were shot in the back and 54 per cent were black.

▫ João Elizio Lima Pessoa was driving to his home in Aguas Lindas, Goiás state, on 7 February. The road was blocked by rocks and when he tried to clear them he was shot dead. His wife was also shot, but survived. João Elizio Lima Pessoa had been working with the Public Security Community Council, investigating "death squad" killings in the region. The authorities brought in police from other areas to investigate the killing, but AI continued to receive information about "death squad" activities.

Human rights defenders

Human rights defenders continued to suffer harassment, death threats, public defamation and killings. Those working in rural areas were especially vulnerable to attacks from gunmen hired by landowners, often with the acquiescence of the police.

Offices of police Ombudsmen, recently set up in a number of states, also came under increasing pressure, as moves were made to weaken their mandate in several states.

The implementation of a new federal witness program in July 1999 gave little security to those prepared to testify against police or local officials as it lacked the necessary financial support and political backing. Few places were offered to witnesses, and some potential witnesses were killed, especially those testifying in high profile cases such as the Federal Parliamentary Commission of Inquiry into drug trafficking.

▫ Valdênia Aparecida Paulino, a human rights lawyer working in São Paulo, received several anonymous threats after she took up the cases of José Nunes da Silva and Ednaldo Gomes, reportedly killed by military police in São Paulo on 31 March 1999. Márcio Celestino da Silva, who witnessed the shooting of the two men, was detained by police in June 1999 and held for four months. He was beaten, subjected to electric shock torture, and ordered to withdraw his testimony. He was forced to go into hiding as he continued to receive threats.

▫ In Belem, Pará state, police Ombudswoman Rosa Marga Roth was taken to court by a police chief who was the main suspect in a torture case. The police chief accused her of crimes including libel and tampering with a witness. At the end of 2000 she faced two court cases.

Violence over land rights

Conflict over land rights continued to generate violence, as land activists were harassed, threatened and killed by military police carrying out evictions, or policing demonstrations. They were also attacked by gunmen hired by landowners, with the apparent acquiescence of the police authorities.

▫ On 9 September Sandoval Alves de Lima was shot dead in the street, in the municipality of Sapé, Paraíba state. He was one of the leaders of a land occupation at the *Fazenda Antas* estate in the neighbouring municipality of Sobardo. The gunman shouted out as he escaped on horseback that there were several more names on his death list. The gunman was identified by several witnesses as being an employee of a local businessman with close links to the owner of the *Fazenda Antas* estate.

Eldorado de Carajás massacre

▫ The 1999 trial of 153 Pará state military police officers, charged with aggravated homicide for killing 19 landless peasants in Eldorado de Carajás in April 1996, was closed by the state appeals court in April. The presiding judge stepped down and a retrial was set to begin in early 2001. AI delegates met survivors of the massacre in April and were told that of 69 wounded survivors, 20 were severely injured and some still had bullets in their bodies. Two survivors died during 2000, one from a bullet lodged in his head.

Corumbiara massacre

▫ In September, 12 military police and two land activists were tried for the killing of 10 land activists and two military police officers, in Corumbiara, Rondonia state, in August 1995. All but three of the military police were acquitted for lack of evidence. Other people, including a local landowner, reportedly implicated in the crimes were never brought to trial. The two land activists were convicted of the murder of two military police officers, despite the apparent absence of any evidence proving their individual criminal responsibility. The paucity of the police investigation and the apparent prejudice of the public prosecutor's office raised doubts as to the validity of the verdicts. Appeals against all the verdicts were lodged.

Indigenous peoples

Indigenous peoples protesting over land rights suffered threats, harassment and assaults by gunmen hired by local landowners, working with the acquiescence of the police and local authorities. Many indigenous peoples also suffered injuries as a result of excessive force used by military police during public demonstrations.

On 13 January up to 50 heavily armed gunmen (*pistoleiros*) in military uniforms converged on the village of Potrero Guaçu, Paranhos municipality, burning most of the 35 houses and many of the villagers' belongings. They reportedly raped several women and beat other villagers including a two-year-old child. Thirty of the villagers, members of the Guarani-Nhandeva indigenous community, were reportedly forced onto a truck and taken away, in an attempt to clear them off the land. Although the villagers returned to their land with the help of the Federal Police, they continued to receive threats.

On 22 April, the 500th anniversary of the Portuguese arrival in Brazil, the Bahia state military police reportedly used excessive force to prevent protesters reaching Porto Seguro, where official celebrations were taking place. The police used tear gas, rubber bullets and baton charges to break up two peaceful marches, injuring 34 protesters and temporarily detaining over 140 others.

AI country reports and visits
Reports
- Brazil: A waste of lives, FEBEM juvenile detention centres, São Paulo — A human rights crisis, not a public security issue (AI Index: AMR 19/014/2000)
- Brazil: Police violence and the 500th anniversary (AI Index: AMR 19/029/2000)

Visits
AI delegates visited Brazil in March and April, and again in November. During these visits they covered six different states, visiting prisons, police stations and women's detention centres. They took part in a meeting of over 100 indigenous peoples, prior to the 500th anniversary celebrations. Delegates also observed a trial and met politicians, non-governmental organizations and victims of torture.

BULGARIA

REPUBLIC OF BULGARIA
Head of state: Petar Stoyanov
Head of government: Ivan Kostov
Capital: Sofia
Population: 8.2 million
Official language: Bulgarian
Death penalty: abolitionist for all crimes
2000 treaty ratifications: Optional Protocol to the UN Women's Convention

There were numerous reports of ill-treatment and torture by law enforcement officials. Members of the Romani community, who suffered widespread discrimination, were frequently the target of such human rights violations, which were committed with virtual impunity. Law enforcement officials continued to use firearms in circumstances prohibited by international standards, resulting in deaths and injuries. Conditions in some institutions for mentally handicapped children amounted to cruel, inhuman or degrading treatment. Restrictions on the right to freedom of expression continued to be imposed.

Torture/ill-treatment

Ill-treatment and torture by the police continued to be widespread. Most incidents occurred during police investigations into complaints, when criminal suspects were apprehended or within the first few hours of custody.

In January a police officer beat Gencho Tonchev, a local businessman, and his son Tihomir in Dimitrovgrad police station. Gencho Tonchev suffered two broken ribs.

In March, a group of armed border police and immigration officers boarded the ship *Olga J.* which had been impounded and held in Burgas harbour for two years. The officers beat nine seamen from Ghana with truncheons and kicked them.

Investigations
The authorities did not provide AI with reports of investigations into cases of torture and ill-treatment, casting doubt on their conduct.

The authorities have still not made public the autopsy report on Zaharie Aleksandrov Stefanov, who died in detention in suspicious circumstances in June 1993.

Impunity
Changes to the Penal Procedure Code came into force at the beginning of 2000 which included the possibility of judicial review of refusals by prosecutors to initiate investigations, and an open court process for termination of criminal investigations by prosecutors.

The European Court of Human Rights ruled in May that Bulgaria had violated the European Convention on Human Rights in the case of Anya Velikova. Anya Velikova's husband, Slavcho Tsonchev, died of internal bleeding after being beaten in police detention in Pleven on 25 September 1994, 12 hours after his arrest on suspicion of theft. In December 1994 the Pleven military prosecutor decided not to indict any police officers. The European Court found that the Bulgarian authorities had violated the right to life, and that they had failed to provide Anya Velikova with an effective judicial remedy by failing to conduct an effective investigation.

Discrimination against Roma

Incidents of police brutality against Roma were reported against a background of extreme poverty for many Romani communities, as well as rising social tensions frequently incited by racist discrimination. In the village of Mechka near Pleven, the murder in early April of an ethnic Bulgarian man prompted a campaign by ethnic Bulgarian villagers to expel all the Romani inhabitants. The village mayor instituted a ban on Roma being served in village shops or grazing their animals on village land. Police officers acted to prevent threatened acts of violence, yet they were reported to be randomly detaining several Romani men each day for 24-hour periods. In September, in the village of Bukovets, Vidin region, a group of around 20 villagers severely beat four young Romani men who were suspected of stealing corn.

☐ Tsvetalin Perov, a 16-year-old Romani boy, sustained severe burns in Vidin police headquarters in April. The boy, who suffers from epilepsy and learning difficulties, was well known to the police. He alleged that he was beaten unconscious by a police officer and, when the pain of the fire brought him round, the same officer was standing over him. Police officers claimed that Tsvetalin Perov set himself alight with a cigarette lighter, but no cigarette lighter was found at the scene and his clothes disappeared before they could be forensically examined. The severity of the burns makes it likely that an accelerant such as petrol or lighter fuel had been used.

Use of firearms by police

No attempts were made to reform the Law on National Police which permits the use of firearms in circumstances prohibited by international standards. Investigations into police shootings were usually terminated as a result of police actions being deemed lawful. The authorities failed to provide information on investigations into most of the cases previously raised by AI.

☐ In July in Sofia a police patrol arrested 19-year-old Traicho Dimitrov Lyubomirov in a friend's house. He was reportedly handcuffed and taken away. Several hours later his body was taken to the morgue with a bullet wound to his head. A police source reportedly claimed that the young Rom had been apprehended while attempting to steal a car, that he had attacked a police officer and tried to take away his gun, and that the officer had fired the gun inadvertently.

☐ In May Atanas Djambazov, a 14-year-old Romani boy, climbed into a wine factory in Sliven with three friends in order to steal wooden pallets for firewood. A police office guarding the factory shot Atanas Djambazov twice as he tried to climb back over the wall. He was hit in the face and the right arm, and collapsed. The police officer allegedly failed to help him or to report the incident. Atanas Djambazov's friends took him home and he was hospitalized.

Conditions in homes for handicapped children

Virtually all the handicapped children in permanent care in state institutions, who numbered at least 2,200, lived in conditions of extreme neglect. They were frequently deprived of food and basic care, as well as lacking attention to medical and educational needs. Such conditions amount to cruel, inhuman or degrading treatment. Research conducted by the Bulgarian Helsinki Committee, a local human rights organization, revealed that the state budget for these institutions was so inadequate that the children could only be fed with the help of charitable donations. The conditions in the home for handicapped children in Fakia, in the Burgas region, were described by both its administrator and independent monitors as life-threatening. In August, three children died of dysentery in the home for handicapped children in Medven. An inquiry by independent monitors established serious deficiencies in hygiene, administration and medical services.

Restrictions on freedom of expression

In March the National Assembly amended the Penal Code and abolished imprisonment for defamation, although it increased the fines available as punishment and maintained special protection for public officials. AI had urged the authorities to amend the Penal Code, after numerous prosecutions of journalists for criticizing public officials. Other provisions of the Penal Code continued to be used to detain people exercising their right to freedom of expression.

☐ In July, in Pleven, police detained Alexander Kandjov, a local political activist, for four days. He had collected signatures on a petition calling for the resignation of the Minister of Justice, and describing him as "the top idiot of the judiciary". Alexander Kandjov was charged with aggravated hooliganism. His trial opened but had not concluded by the end of 2000.

Forcible exile

In January, six foreign nationals, who were reportedly Islamic clerics, were expelled from the country for preaching without a licence, under a legal provision which had been pronounced invalid by the Constitutional Court in 1992. In August the authorities deported to Jordan Ahmad Naim Mohammed Musa, a director of an Islamic charity, for endangering "the security and the interests of the country". Ahmad Musa had spent most of the past 16 years in Bulgaria, and his wife and three children all have Bulgarian citizenship. AI considered that Ahmed Musa was forcibly exiled, apparently because of his religious beliefs, in violation of international standards.

International organizations

In January the Council of Europe's Parliamentary Assembly closed the procedure monitoring Bulgaria's fulfilment of the commitments it made upon joining the

Council of Europe. However, rapporteurs noted as an outstanding concern "continuing police brutality, particularly as regards Roma". They also urged the government to take a number of steps including the provision of better guarantees for the independence of the judiciary and the media. They called for special attention to be given to the recruitment policy, training and motivation of police officers, codes of conduct, psychological counselling of field officers and their awareness of human rights issues.

AI country reports
- Bulgaria: The shooting of Atanas Djambazov, a 14-year-old Roma boy (AI Index: EUR 15/001/2000);
- Bulgaria: Tsvetalin Perov, a 16-year-old Roma boy severely burned in police detention (AI Index: EUR 15/003/2000)

BURKINA FASO

BURKINA FASO
Head of state: Blaise Compaoré
Head of government: Ernest Yonli (replaced Kadré Désiré Ouédraogo in November)
Capital: Ouagadougou
Population: 10.9 million
Official language: French
Death penalty: abolitionist in practice

Pressure from all sectors of society on the government to end impunity for past human rights violations led to the arrest of dozens of people, some of whom were ill-treated. Three presidential security officials were convicted in connection with the death in January 1998 of David Ouédraogo. Charges against the President's brother in connection with the death were dropped. There was no progress in bringing to justice those responsible for the killing in December 1998 of Norbert Zongo and his three companions.

Background
In September the ruling party of President Blaise Compaoré, the *Congrès pour la démocratie et le progrès*, Congress for Democracy and Progress, won an overwhelming majority in much delayed local government elections. The elections were boycotted by the more significant opposition parties who felt that political reforms, including the introduction of proportional representation, had not addressed the overriding need to strengthen democracy.

In April a three-day general strike was called to protest against the use of force by police which had left 30 demonstrators injured. The strike led to the arrest of several prominent leaders of the *Collectif d'organisations démocratiques de masse et de partis politiques* (*Collectif*), a coalition of opposition political parties, human rights organizations, trade unions, and journalists' and students' organizations. The *Collectif*, which called the strike, had been formed to campaign for those responsible for the death in December 1998 of independent journalist Norbert Zongo to be brought to justice. Other strikes and protests, which largely focused on demands for ending impunity, took place throughout the year. Talks between the government and the *Collectif* broke down in June.

Following the death in December of Flavien Nébié, a 12-year-old student, when the security forces opened fire on a small demonstration in Boussé, all public demonstrations were banned. Events planned to commemorate the death of Norbert Zongo, including the International Festival on Freedom of the Press and Expression in West Africa, were also banned and more than 50 festival participants travelling from Ghana were prevented from entering the country. Those who tried to visit Norbert Zongo's grave were dispersed by the security forces using tear gas.

Impunity
Civil society, including human rights groups and the political opposition, continued to demand an end to impunity for past human rights violations.
Norbert Zongo
No one was arrested or charged in connection with the deaths of Norbert Zongo and three others in December 1998, despite the recommendation of an Independent Commission of Inquiry in May 1999 that judicial proceedings be instituted against six named suspects, and the appointment of a judge to investigate the case. The Commission had concluded that Norbert Zongo had been killed for purely political reasons, including his investigation into the death of David Ouédraogo.
David Ouédraogo
Five people were finally brought to trial in August for the death in custody, as a result of torture, of David Ouédraogo in January 1998. David Ouédraogo, chauffeur of François Compaoré, presidential adviser and brother of the President, had been arrested with two other employees, accused of having stolen a large amount of money from their employer. François Compaoré was charged in January 1999 with the murder of David Ouédraogo and with harbouring the body. In 1999 the Criminal Appeal Court in Ouagadougou had ruled that it was not competent to hear the case against him and referred it to a military court. The charges were subsequently dropped.

In August, five members of the *Régiment de la sécurité présidentielle*, the presidential security force, were tried by the military court in Ouagadougou on charges of assault occasioning death. One of the defendants was reported to have admitted that he had ill-treated David Ouédraogo, but sought to justify this by stating that he was seeking information about an alleged coup plot. François Compaoré testified in court, but his statement was challenged by defence lawyers because dates he gave conflicted with those confirmed by other witnesses. The President's personal chief of staff, Colonel Gilbert Diendéré, sought forgiveness before the court for what happened, but refused to accept responsibility.

Three of the defendants were convicted — two were sentenced to 20 years' imprisonment and one received a 10-year sentence — and the other two were acquitted. The three defendants who were convicted and one of those acquitted were among the six suspects in the murder of Norbert Zongo named by the Independent Commission of Inquiry.

In May, the magistrate investigating the separate legal case concerning the theft in which David Ouédraogo was implicated alleged that statements presented to the court had been fabricated and named Warrant Officer Abdoulaye Semdé as among those responsible. One month later, Abdoulaye Semdé died, apparently as a result of a sudden illness. The lack of autopsy or other investigation into his death led to suspicion that he may have been killed to prevent him revealing evidence.

Other cases
The widow of former President Thomas Sankara lodged a complaint against persons unknown before the Criminal Appeal Court concerning her husband's death. Thomas Sankara and at least 12 others were killed during the coup in 1987 which brought President Compaoré to power. In January, the Court rejected the case saying that it was a military matter. The family intended to pursue the case before the Supreme Court.

Other deaths in custody or in suspicious circumstances, including those of university teacher Guillaume Sessouma in 1989 and opposition leader Clément Ouédraogo in 1991, remained unresolved.

The trial of a gendarme, who was accused of responsibility for the deaths of two school students in Garango in 1995, opened in December. The trial was adjourned because the legal dossier was incomplete; the gendarme, who had never been arrested, remained at liberty.

Mamadou Kéré
On 10 June, the *Naabe Tigré* of Tenkodogo, a powerful traditional chief, ordered the punishment by beating of Mamadou Kéré and reportedly did not intervene to prevent his death. Mamadou Kéré had apparently criticized the inactivity of the ruling party. His criticism was perceived as disrespectful because the *Naabe Tigré*'s son was the elected parliamentary representative. The chief was charged with not helping a person in danger, held only briefly, but remained free pending trial. Some 20 people accused of causing the death were imprisoned at the *Maison d'arrêt et de correction de Ouagadougou* (MACO) awaiting trial.

Arrests and ill-treatment of political opponents
Six leading members of the *Collectif* were arrested and ill-treated in April including Halidou Ouédraogo, President of the *Collectif* and also of the *Mouvement burkinabè des droits de l'homme et des peuples*, Burkinabè Movement for Human and Peoples' Rights; Tolé Sagnon, Vice-President of the *Collectif*; Pierre Bidima; and Etienne Traoré. All were held at the *Direction de la compagnie d'intervention rapide* (DCIR), the police rapid deployment force headquarters, denied visits and had their heads shaved. All six were subsequently released without charge.

Following the death of Flavien Nébié on 6 December, 15 local members of the *Collectif* were arrested. The school student died when the security forces opened fire on a crowd who reportedly began to throw stones when their attempt to present a petition critical of proposed educational reforms to the local government representative was met with a closed door. The authorities accused the *Collectif* of being responsible for the unrest which resulted in the security forces' intervention, and even claimed that the *Collectif* was therefore responsible for Flavien Nébié's death. *Collectif* members were taken to the gendarmerie in Ouagadougou where they were held without charge or trial for up to 21 days; the last four were released on 27 December. The authorities have stated that an investigation has been started to establish responsibility for the death of Flavien Nébié.

During December other attacks against the *Collectif* were carried out by local militia. In Koudougou, Mohamed Sawadogo, the local president of the *Collectif*, was reportedly briefly detained and interrogated by armed supporters of Hermann Yaméogo, leader of a political party, because he suspected the *Collectif* of destroying some of his property. In Fada N'Gourma, Etienne Convolbo, a local representative of the teachers' union and member of the *Collectif*, was detained, beaten and expelled from his home town by armed supporters of the mayor. Some member organizations of the *Collectif* publicly complained that the security forces had seemed unwilling to intervene to protect their members.

Students
In response to five months of strikes which also focused on calls for an end to impunity, the authorities closed the university in Ouagadougou on 6 October. The *Association nationale des étudiants burkinabè* (ANEB), National Association of Burkinabè Students, demanded its reopening and arranged a meeting with school pupils to gather support for their action. As a result, around 50 students, including Souleymane Kologo, ANEB's President, were arrested and held at the DCIR. They were held for four days and had their heads shaved before being released without charge. Some 10 other students were arrested for seeking permission to hold a student meeting in a school and taken to the gendarmerie on 23 October. They were all released without charge during November.

AI country statement
- Burkina Faso: Cruel, inhuman and degrading treatment/Prisoners of conscience (AI Index: AFR 60/001/2000)

BURUNDI

REPUBLIC OF BURUNDI
Head of state and government: Pierre Buyoya
Capital: Bujumbura
Population: 6.6 million
Official languages: Kirundi, French
Death penalty: retentionist

Civil war continued throughout 2000, despite the signing of a peace agreement in August. Hundreds of unarmed civilians were killed by government armed forces and armed opposition groups. Scores of others were arrested and tortured. Several people "disappeared" while in custody. Hundreds of thousands of people remained forcibly displaced around the capital, mostly in appalling conditions, until August. Thousands of people remained in detention without trial, some since 1993. At least 99 death sentences were passed and two soldiers were executed.

Background

From late 1999 the level of violence and human rights abuses escalated sharply. Both government forces and armed opposition groups continued to derive support from their allies in the regional conflict in the Democratic Republic of the Congo (DRC). In August, following intense international pressure, an Agreement for Peace and Reconciliation in Burundi was signed in Arusha, Tanzania. As the date for the signature of the agreement approached, violence intensified throughout Burundi. By the end of 2000, the agreement had not yet been implemented and two major armed opposition groups had yet to join it.

Possible reform of the Tutsi-dominated army generated political tension. Some Tutsi-dominated political organizations insisted that an army reformed on ethnic lines could not protect them from the threat of genocide, and they sought to undermine the peace process. *PA Amasekanya*, a Tutsi "self-defence" movement, and other groups with similar political views, incited violent disturbances in Bujumbura around the signature of the agreement. Members of *PA Amasekanya* were also reported to have been behind an ambush in May near Gatumba, Rural Bujumbura, in which at least three members of the opposition political party *Front pour la Démocratie au Burundi* (FRODEBU), Front for Democracy in Burundi, all Hutu, were killed.

Hundreds of civilians killed

The armed forces and armed opposition groups continued to show complete disregard for human life, acting with little or no accountability. On numerous occasions, the armed opposition killed unarmed civilians in reprisal for alleged collaboration with the government or for failing to support them. Scores of civilians were killed in ambushes. Humanitarian workers were also attacked.

One armed opposition group, the *Forces nationales de libération* (FNL), National Liberation Forces, concentrated on attacking Bujumbura and consolidating positions around the city. A second group, the *Conseil National pour la Défense de la Démocratie-Forces pour la Défense de la Démocratie* (CNDD-FDD), National Council for the Defence of Democracy-Forces for the Defence of Democracy, increased its activity in the central, eastern and southern border provinces, subjecting the local population to a campaign of terror and intimidation through killing, rape, kidnapping and theft.

On 1 October, members of an armed opposition group, presumed to be the FNL, attacked the Cibitoke and Mutakura districts of Bujumbura. Eleven people were killed, mostly Hutu, including one woman and her four sons. The victims were singled out in what appeared to be reprisal killings for supposed collaboration with the government or because they had refused to give money during the attack.

Hundreds of civilians, many of them elderly, women or children, were killed by government armed forces.

Between 25 and 28 June, at least 44 unarmed civilians were extrajudicially executed by soldiers in Itaba commune, Gitega province, in reprisal for military losses following clashes with the armed opposition. Most were killed with bayonets. Much of the local population had already fled the area; it appears that those who remained were considered to be members of the armed opposition and killed.

'Disappearances'

Detainees, particularly those in military custody, continued to be vulnerable to "disappearance". A number of new cases were reported.

One man, Bigirimana, "disappeared" following his arrest at Kavumu regroupment camp, Rural Bujumbura, by soldiers on 7 May. He was accused of throwing stones during a disturbance at the camp after an army search operation degenerated into a looting spree by soldiers. Bigirimana was taken to a nearby military position, where he was reportedly seriously beaten. Soldiers later denied that he had ever been held. Several people who tried to stop the soldiers looting were arrested and charged with collaboration with armed opposition groups. At least four others were reportedly beaten to death.

Torture/ill-treatment

Torture remained a serious problem particularly in the early stages of detention, and several people died as a result.

Diomède Buyoya, a domestic worker, died in February at the *Brigade spéciale de recherche* (BSR), a gendarmerie special investigation detention centre, in Bujumbura. He was detained by a BSR investigating officer who allegedly tortured him to death after he had insulted the officer's wife. The officer was arrested and detained in Mpimba Central Prison, Bujumbura. However, one month later all charges against the officer were dropped on the instructions of the Military Prosecutor's Department and the officer returned to work in a different unit. No further investigation took place.

Refugees and internally displaced
Approximately 70,000 Burundians fled to Tanzania. Mines laid on the border by the Burundian armed forces prevented others from crossing the border. By the end of 2000, around 330,000 people were internally displaced within Burundi. Another 500,000, most of whom had been forcibly displaced in late 1999, had left camps but were still vulnerable to hunger and disease.

Forcible 'regroupment'
In September 1999, following repeated attacks on Bujumbura by the armed opposition, the government forced more than 290,000 mainly Hutu civilians to leave their homes in Rural Bujumbura province and enter "regroupment" camps. Conditions in the camps were appalling.

Following international condemnation of the regroupment policy, in early June the government announced that all "regroupment" camps would be closed by the end of July. In the following days, three camps close to Bujumbura were cleared by the security forces within a matter of hours. Approximately 40,000 people were ordered abruptly to return to homes which in many cases had been destroyed by the warring factions. No provision was made for the basic needs of the returning population. By September, all camps had been officially closed.

Refoulement from Burundi
In February, Janvier Rugema, Innocent Byabagamba and François Rukeba were arrested and forcibly returned from Burundi to Rwanda, where they were at risk of torture and unfair trial. They had fled Rwanda because they were suspected of having helped the former speaker of the Rwandese National Assembly to flee the country.

Political trials
Trials related to the political violence and massacres of Tutsi which followed the 1993 assassination of President Melchior Ndadaye continued. The subsequent reprisal killings of Hutu have not been investigated. Several thousand people remained in detention awaiting trial, some since 1993. The fairness of trials continued to be undermined by inadequate time for the preparation of defence arguments, constant deferrals and the denial of the right to a full appeal.

In August, after more than three years' detention, the verdict was announced in a trial of political opponents linked to the *Parti pour le redressement national* (PARENA), National Recovery Party, and *Solidarité jeunesse pour la défense des droits des minorités* (SOJEDEM), Youth Solidarity for the Defence of Minority Rights. The defendants had been accused of involvement in a plot to assassinate President Buyoya. Many were tortured. Six defendants received sentences of 10 years' imprisonment and two were acquitted. Another detainee who had been charged with a lesser offence had already been released. Just weeks after the verdict, all but one of the convicted prisoners, Emmanuel Manzi, a Rwandese national, were conditionally released.

The verdict in another trial of 25 people linked to PARENA and SOJEDEM was announced in January. The majority of defendants received sentences of between 10 and 15 years' imprisonment after being convicted of plotting to threaten state security by forming an armed group to overthrow the government. During the trial, a witness, Onésphore Mdayitwayeko, alleged that the case had been fabricated by the *Documentation nationale*, National Intelligence Agency, which is directly responsible to the Presidency, and that he had been offered money to make incriminating allegations. An attempt to arrest him the day before he appeared in court was foiled. However, he was arrested immediately after testifying in court and held at the *Documentation nationale*, which has no legal power to hold detainees, for one month before being unconditionally released.

In November 1999, a grenade exploded in Bujumbura's main market, killing at least two people and injuring many more. The attack was attributed to the FNL and in the weeks that followed scores of people were arrested by the armed forces and gendarmerie. The majority were eventually released, but it was feared that a number may have died in detention or "disappeared". At least three of those arrested and tortured during this period were on trial at the end of the year, accused of collaboration with the FNL. Testimony extracted under torture formed part of the prosecution's case.

Children
Children have been particularly vulnerable to the economic and social consequences of the war in Burundi. Hundreds of children reportedly died of malnutrition and preventable diseases in the "regroupment" camps. Both government and opposition armed forces recruited children as combatants. Over 100 children, some of them accused of collaboration with armed opposition groups, were in detention during 2000, and were at risk of sexual abuse from other inmates. Some children have been held for years without trial, including Antoine Hatungimana, who was arrested in 1998 when he was approximately 12 and accused of collaboration with armed opposition groups.

Death penalty
During 2000, at least 97 people were sentenced to death by civilian courts, mostly on charges related to political violence and killings in 1993. Two soldiers were sentenced to death by military court and executed. More than 350 people have been sentenced to death since 1996, many after unfair trials and years in detention. Nine people have been executed since 1997. Military jurisdictions continued to show blatant disregard for the rule of law.

☐ Napoléon Manirakiza, an army deserter, and Sergeant René Rukemanganizi were executed by firing squad on 19 October, just hours after being sentenced to death by Gitega military court. Both had been convicted of murders committed earlier in the month. They were denied legal representation and were not allowed to appeal against their sentence.

In July 2000, the decision was finally taken to close the isolation cells of Mpimba central prison. Until then, all prisoners under sentence of death in Mpimba were held in three tiny cells in appalling conditions, under a punitive regime.

Intergovernmental organizations

The Representative of the UN Secretary-General for Internally Displaced Persons visited Burundi in February. The UN Special Rapporteur on Burundi also visited the country from 27 June to 7 July. In her subsequent interim report she condemned violations of the right to life by state forces and armed opposition groups, and the frequent use of torture. The Special Rapporteur was also highly critical of the policy of "regroupment". She drew attention to violations of children's rights, in particular those of girls.

The UN Committee on the Rights of the Child considered the initial report of Burundi in September. Although it noted efforts to bring domestic legislation into line with the UN Children's Convention, it expressed strong concern at abuses of children's rights particularly in relation to the conflict, through killings, "regroupment", torture and use by both government and opposition forces of child soldiers.

In May, Burundi ratified the African Charter on the Rights and Welfare of the Child.

In November, the African Commission on Human and Peoples' Rights passed a resolution calling for compliance with and the immediate implementation of the Arusha Peace Agreement.

AI country reports and visits

Reports
- Burundi: Protecting human rights – an intrinsic part of the search for peace (AI Index: AFR 16/001/2000)
- Great Lakes Region: Refugees denied protection (AI Index: AFR 02/002/2000)
- Burundi: Conditions in "regroupment" camps – an update (AI Index: AFR 16/013/2000)

Visits
An AI delegate visited Burundi in February to collaborate with two human rights groups, the *Association burundaise pour la défense des droits des prisonniers*, Burundian Association for the Defence of Prisoners Rights, and the *Ligue ITEKA*, Burundian Human Rights League, in the production of a video promoting their work – *Burundi: Caught in the crossfire*. In February and March AI delegates visited Arusha, Tanzania, to lobby delegates and others involved in the peace process on human rights protection and promotion in this context. AI delegates visited Burundi in August primarily for research purposes.

CAMBODIA

KINGDOM OF CAMBODIA
Head of state: King Norodom Sihanouk
Head of government: Hun Sen
Capital: Phnom Penh
Population: 11.1 million
Official language: Khmer
Death penalty: abolitionist for all crimes
2000 treaty ratifications/signatures: Optional Protocol to the UN Children's Convention on the involvement of children in armed conflict; Rome Statute of the International Criminal Court

As in previous years, the main human rights problem in Cambodia was impunity for human rights violators, compounded by a weak and corrupt judicial system. The UN and the government reached agreement over the formation of a tribunal to bring to justice those suspected of responsibility for gross human rights violations during the period of Khmer Rouge rule (17 April 1975 to 7 January 1979). Debate on a bill allowing for the establishment of the tribunal began in the National Assembly at the end of 2000. Meanwhile, two Khmer Rouge suspects arrested in 1999 remained in pre-trial detention throughout the year. Torture in police custody was reported, and the police were complicit in vigilante killings of alleged criminals. Human rights workers were threatened and intimidated during the course of their work. Scores of people were arrested at the end of November after an attack in the capital by an armed group.

Impunity

The problem of impunity continued to have an adverse effect on the lives of Cambodians. Lack of confidence in the judicial system and the police led to an increase in vigilante killings. There were numerous reports by human rights monitors and in the local press, documenting mob killings of alleged criminals. Police officers often made no attempt to intervene and protect the individuals and in a number of cases actually handed over alleged thieves to crowds of angry people. In October, King Norodom Sihanouk appealed for an end to the killings. However, no steps were taken to investigate these killings or to bring those responsible to justice.

◻ In January Chhouk Rin, a former Khmer Rouge soldier, was arrested on charges of involvement in the murder of three Western hostages in 1994. In 1999 he had given evidence at the trial of Nuon Paet, a former Khmer Rouge commander accused of ordering the murder of the hostages. Chhouk Rin was brought to trial in July, but was controversially acquitted on the basis of a 1994 law providing amnesty to Khmer Rouge forces who surrendered within a given time-frame, although the offence occurred after the law was passed. Nuon Paet appealed against his life sentence, a penalty which is not actually prescribed in Cambodia's Penal Code, but the sentence was upheld by the Appeals Court in October.

Khmer Rouge cases
Negotiations continued between the government and the UN over the establishment of a tribunal to bring to justice those suspected of responsibility for the gross human rights violations during the period of Khmer Rouge rule. After the rejection by the Cambodian side in 1999 of an international tribunal, a new compromise solution of a trial under Cambodian law with international participation was put forward by the USA. Senior UN delegations visited Cambodia in March and July for talks with the Cambodian negotiating team. By the end of the July visit, there was a draft Memorandum of Understanding between the two sides, which was not signed. The Cambodian side stated that the National Assembly would have to pass the required legislation in order to move forward. Debate on the draft law to establish a domestic tribunal began in the National Assembly at the end of December. The law raised serious human rights concerns, and fell short of international standards for fairness. Cambodian and international human rights groups expressed their concern throughout the year about the proposed tribunal and the need for an independent, impartial tribunal which would be able to conduct trials in accordance with international standards.

Two Khmer Rouge suspects who were arrested in 1999 remained in detention in Phnom Penh's military detention facility throughout the year. In November, the new Special Representative of the UN Secretary-General on Human Rights in Cambodia was allowed to visit the two men in detention, the first independent human rights monitor to be given access to them.

Case developments
Kong Bun Hean and Mong Davuth, opposition party activists who had been arrested in September 1999 and detained in the Military Detention Facility were released in March. The President of the Military Court announced that investigations into their cases were ongoing and that they could be summoned to appear at any time. The two men fled the country to seek asylum.

Following the Prime Minister's December 1999 order to rearrest individuals previously released by the courts, dozens of people were detained without warrants, and without legal basis; more than 30 were still in detention at the end of 2000. In a related development, the chief of the Phnom Penh Municipal Court and the prosecutor were dismissed from their posts, accused of corruption.

Extrajudicial executions
Evidence emerged in August of the apparent extrajudicial executions of at least five men in Kratie and Kampong Cham provinces. Three of the men had allegedly been members of an armed group known as the *Khmer Serei* (Free Khmer) who then defected to become members of the Royal Cambodian Armed Forces, based in Snoul district, Kratie province. Their bodies were found in Snoul district blindfolded and with their hands tied behind their backs. At least 20 other defectors from the group were reported missing.

The bodies of two men were found in Kampong Cham province. They had allegedly been executed after being taken into military custody. Cambodian human rights groups launched an investigation and called for an independent inquiry into the killings. The Ministry of Defence issued a statement which threatened to bring court action against the human rights workers, some of whom subsequently went into hiding.

Situation of minorities
People of ethnic Vietnamese descent remained at risk of human rights violations. Vietnamese refugees in Cambodia were vulnerable to arrest, detention and *refoulement* (forcible return).

In March, a group of Vietnamese nationals were found to be working illegally at a factory in Phnom Penh. They had been trafficked into Cambodia to work, but were then arrested during a raid on the factory. Workers with non-governmental organizations who tried to assist the trafficked women prior to their forcible return to Viet Nam were threatened and harassed by the authorities and accused of trying to help the women to escape.

Mass arrests
In November, there was an attack in Phnom Penh, allegedly by a group called the Cambodian Freedom Fighters, the key target of which was the Ministry of Defence. Members of the Royal Cambodian Armed Forces were engaged in a gun battle, which left at least eight people dead. In the aftermath, scores of people were arrested in Phnom Penh, and in the provinces, including Sihanoukville, Pursat, Kampong Cham, Kampong Thom and Stung Treng. Those arrested in Phnom Penh were given immediate access to lawyers and to human rights monitors. Some of those arrested in the provinces were transferred to Phnom Penh, others remained in detention at the place of arrest. Dozens of people were released after a short period in detention, but dozens of others remained in detention at the end of the year, apparently facing charges of terrorism and organized crime. Some cases were placed under the jurisdiction of the Military Court while others appeared to be under that of the Municipal Court. The authorities issued arrest warrants for the alleged leaders of the Cambodian Freedom Fighters believed to be living abroad.

Intergovernmental organizations
The new Special Representative of the UN Secretary-General on Human Rights in Cambodia made his first visit to the country in November and met the Prime Minister. Reports were presented to the UN Commission on Human Rights and the UN General Assembly, both of which adopted resolutions requesting that reports should be submitted to their next sessions.

AI country report and visit
Report
- Kingdom of Cambodia: Law and order – without the law (AI Index: ASA 23/001/2000)

Visit
An AI delegate visited Cambodia in March.

CAMEROON

REPUBLIC OF CAMEROON
Head of state: Paul Biya
Head of government: Peter Mafany Musonge
Capital: Yaoundé
Population: 15 million
Official languages: French, English
Death penalty: retentionist

Several hundred extrajudicial executions were reported by the security forces in combating crime. There were no independent investigations into these or previous such killings. Torture, ill-treatment and life-threatening prison conditions persisted. The UN Special Rapporteur on torture confirmed that torture was widespread and systematic. Members of political opposition groups and journalists were detained without charge or trial. Prisoners convicted after unfair trials in 1999 remained in prison. Some long-standing political detainees were released.

Background
The government refused to accede to renewed calls by opposition parties for an independent electoral commission. In 1997 international observers recommended an independent body after legislative elections were marred by irregularities and intimidation, and opposition parties boycotted presidential elections.

A 1990 law ending a state monopoly on broadcasting was enacted in April and resulted in an increase in the number of private and regional radio stations.

A crack-down on crime raised public concerns about a continuing high level of killings of criminal suspects by the security forces.

Controversy continued around the project to build an oil pipeline from Chad through Cameroon, with local rights activists campaigning for environmental and minority rights to be respected.

In October there were reports of incursions by gendarmes into the coastal Bakassi region resulting in loss of life and property. The area, believed to be rich in oil, has been the subject of international legal dispute between Cameroon and Nigeria for several years.

Extrajudicial executions
Hundreds of criminal suspects were reportedly killed in and around Douala, the economic capital, and in northern Cameroon in circumstances suggesting that they may have been extrajudicially executed by the security forces. There has been no independent investigation into these killings or similar large-scale killings which have occurred in previous years.

In its final conclusions following consideration of Cameroon's periodic report in November, the UN Committee against Torture called for special security units accused of gross human rights violations, including extrajudicial executions, to be disbanded.

Douala
In February a special security unit, known as the *Commandement opérationnel* (CO), the Operational Command, was set up to combat street crime in Douala and Yaoundé, the capital. It was reportedly responsible for killing scores of criminal suspects, as well as for carrying out beatings, rapes and other ill-treatment of detainees.

On 9 April the mutilated body of Alain Dikala was found in Douala with bullet wounds to the head. He had been arrested by the unit on 18 March and, four days before his death, transferred to the naval base in Douala.

In May the bodies of nine people reportedly killed by CO officers were found in Petit Dibamba, a village near Douala.

In June Cardinal Christian Tumi, Catholic Archbishop of Douala, complained to the Minister of the Interior about the killings of more than 500 people by the security forces. In early September a local human rights organization named 29 of those killed. In November a mass grave containing at least 36 bodies was discovered in a Douala cemetery, and there were concerns that they included victims of extrajudicial execution. An eyewitness and others have cast doubt on the government's statement that these were authorized burials. The eyewitness subsequently received anonymous threats. The government promised an inquiry but no information was available on its progress by the end of 2000.

Northern Cameroon
A joint army and gendarmerie anti-robbery unit, known as the *brigade anti-gang*, which has been responsible for extrajudicial executions of criminal suspects in recent years, reportedly carried out further killings. In early December, 13 detainees held without charge or trial were alleged to have been executed shortly after the *brigade anti-gang* received an order from the Ministry of Defence to release 77 detainees from its detention centre in Maroua, Far-North Province. The fate of two nationals from neighbouring Chad, Toki Soromoukou and Adam Yahya, detained since their arrest in Garoua, North-Province, in September 1998, remained unknown.

Photographer Aminou Aliou was released without charge by the *brigade anti-gang* in September. He had been feared killed or secretly detained following his arrest and subsequent "disappearance" in October

1998 after he distributed photographs of victims of extrajudicial executions.

Torture/ill-treatment

Cases of torture and ill-treatment in police, gendarmerie and prison cells continued to be reported throughout the country. Prison conditions remained so harsh as to amount to cruel, inhuman and degrading treatment. Political prisoners were held incommunicado and denied access to health care, resulting in a high level of illness and death.

In February the UN Special Rapporteur on torture published a report in which he described the practice of torture in Cameroon as "systematic and widespread". During his visit to the country in May 1999 he had been refused access to the detention centre of the *brigade anti-gang* in Maroua, Far-North Province. In November 2000 the UN Committee against Torture confirmed the Special Rapporteur's assessment and called for "energetic investigations into all allegations of human rights violations and torture" and "a publicly accessible register of detainees".

☐ In late January Mboua Massok, a leading member of the political party *Programme social pour la liberté et la démocratie*, Social Program for Liberty and Democracy, and student leader Guy Simon Ngakam were arrested and reportedly beaten by police. Their arrests followed student protests in Douala about education policy. They were released uncharged after a few days.

☐ On 14 September Mathew Titiahonjo Mboh died in Bafoussam prison, West Province, after being denied access to medical treatment. He was a member of the Southern Cameroons National Council (SCNC), a group supporting independence for the English-speaking North-West and South-West Provinces. He had been arrested in May with nine other SCNC supporters in Ndop, North-West Province, and held without charge or trial. The other detainees were subsequently released on bail.

Prisoners held for political reasons

Political opponents, journalists and others were detained on charges which were apparently politically motivated.

Members of the political opposition

Opposition leaders from English-speaking areas of Cameroon were arrested as suspected secessionists and detained without charge or trial.

☐ From a group of 36 prisoners convicted in October 1999, 18 remained in prison, all held at the Central Prison, Nkondengui, in Yaoundé. The charges against them, including murder and robbery, were in connection with armed attacks in North-West Province in March 1997 in which 10 people died. The authorities blamed the attacks on the SCNC, although no evidence substantiating this accusation was produced in court. Their trial by military tribunal was unfair and they had no right of appeal to a higher or independent court. Several were seriously ill as a result of medical neglect. In May Philip Tete had a stroke and was left partly paralyzed after being denied timely hospital treatment. In December student Julius Ngu Ndi was reportedly close to losing his sight from being detained in unhygienic conditions and almost permanently in the dark.

☐ Following the radio broadcast of a declaration of independence for the Southern Cameroons in the early hours of 31 December 1999, as many as 36 members and supporters of the SCNC and its youth branch, the Southern Cameroons Youth League (SCYL), were reportedly arrested between January and May in the South-West, West and North-West Provinces. They included Justice Frederick Ebong Alobwede, a High Court judge, Chief Ayamba Etta and James Sam Sabum. At least 11 detainees had not been charged or tried by the end of 2000.

☐ Three more SCYL supporters – Richard Lukong, George Yuvenyu and Mevanga Weikam – were arrested in Nkwen in early November and remained in detention in Bamenda, North-West Province, at the end of 2000.

Journalists

Journalists were detained, beaten and sentenced to terms of imprisonment after they published criticisms of government policy and officials. Their concerns included human rights violations by the security forces and corruption by government officials.

☐ In February Chris Oben, Jean-Mathias Kouemeko and Thérèse Forbin, journalists with *Radio Buea*, were briefly detained for interrogation by police after they broadcast interviews with exiles who accused the government of human rights violations against English-speaking Cameroonians.

☐ In April Michel Pekoua, publisher of the newspaper *Ouest-Echos*, was sentenced to six months in prison on charges of defamation for publishing allegations of embezzlement at the state-owned fuel company, the *Société nationale des hydrocarbures* (SNH).

☐ In July journalists Daniel Atangana and Thierry Mbouza from the journal *Dikalo* were sentenced to six months' imprisonment for defamation. Célestin Biaka Difana, the editor, received a suspended six-month prison sentence. They had published accusations of corruption against the head of the *Syndicat camerounais des transporteurs routiers*, Cameroonian Road Transport Union.

☐ In November Richard Touma of *Le Messager* newspaper was beaten by the security forces during a demonstration in Yaoundé by members of the opposition Social Democratic Front party to press for an independent electoral commission.

Releases

Nana Koulagna, a former National Assembly deputy for the opposition party, the *Union nationale pour la démocratie et le progrès*, National Union for Democracy and Progress, was released in early September. Arrested in 1997 by a private militia of the *Lamido* of Rey Bouba, head of a traditional area in North Province, he had been detained without charge or trial as a prisoner of conscience at the Central Prison in Garoua, North Province.

Five members of the SCNC arrested as suspected secessionists in 1995 and 1997 were released in

November after several years' detention without charge or trial.

AI reports
- Cameroon: Fear of "disappearance" or extrajudicial execution of Maurice Tchambou (AI Index: AFR 17/001/2000)
- Cameroon: Fear of torture and ill-treatment of members of the Southern Cameroons National Council (AI Index: AFR 17/002/2000)
- Cameroon: United Nations expert confirms that torture is "widespread and systematic" (AI Index: AFR 17/004/2000)
- Cameroon: Impunity in face of large-scale extrajudicial executions in the Douala area (AI Index: AFR 17/005/2000)

CANADA

CANADA
Head of state: Queen Elizabeth II, represented by Adrienne Clarkson
Head of government: Jean Chrétien
Capital: Ottawa
Population: 31.1 million
Official languages: English, French
Death penalty: abolitionist for all crimes
2000 treaty ratifications/signatures: Optional Protocol to the UN Children's Convention on the involvement of children in armed conflict; Rome Statute of the International Criminal Court

There were sporadic reports of the use of excessive force by police officers. At least two people faced extradition to the USA where they faced a possible death sentence.

Background
General elections were held in November. The ruling Liberal Party won a third term in office with an increased majority.

Police brutality
There were allegations of patterns of police abuse against First Nation (Aboriginal) men in Saskatoon, Saskatchewan. There were reports that members of Saskatoon City Police had for a number of years had an unofficial policy of abandoning intoxicated or "troublesome" members of the indigenous community away from the population centre of Saskatoon, thereby placing them at great risk of dying of hypothermia during the winter months.

First Nation member Darrell Night claimed that in January two Saskatoon police constables handcuffed him, drove him outside the city and abandoned him in freezing conditions. He only survived because he was able to get help from the nightwatchman of a nearby power station. The two police officers were reportedly suspended from duty and were under investigation in connection with the incident at the end of the year.

The bodies of First Nation members Rodney Naistus and Lawrence Wegner were discovered near a power station on the outskirts of Saskatoon on 29 January and 3 February respectively. Both bodies were without jackets and the men appeared to have frozen to death.

In August, 55-year-old Otto Vass died after reportedly being beaten by police officers outside a shop in Toronto. The police had removed him from the shop following an argument. According to witnesses, the officers "pummelled" Otto Vass with batons for approximately four minutes. Following an investigation by the civilian Special Investigations Unit, four police officers were charged in October with manslaughter in connection with the death of Otto Vass. No trial had taken place by the end of the year.

Canadian federal and Ontario authorities failed to hold a public inquiry into the death in 1995 of Dudley George, despite calls to do so from the Ombudsman of Ontario, churches, trade unions, relatives of Dudley George, AI, the media, and the UN Human Rights Committee. Dudley George, an indigenous protester, was shot dead by a police marksman during demonstrations at Ipperwash Park. In 1997 an Ontario provincial police officer was tried in connection with the case and given a two-year conditional sentence for "criminal negligence". During the trial, the officer testified that he fired his weapon because he believed Dudley George was armed and threatening other officers. However, the judge concluded that the officer had knowingly shot an unarmed man.

Death penalty
In May, the Supreme Court of Canada heard the case of Sebastian Burns and Atif Rafay, two Canadian citizens facing extradition to the State of Washington, USA, on capital murder charges. In 1997, the British Columbia Court of Appeals ruled that the extradition of Canadian citizens without satisfactory assurances against the death penalty, violated rights protected under the Canadian Charter of Rights and Freedoms. The Canadian government appealed against this ruling to the Supreme Court, which had not issued a decision by the end of the year.

In June 1999 – minutes after the execution of Canadian citizen Joseph Stanley Faulder in Texas, USA – the Canadian government had issued a statement noting that Canada "deeply regrets that Texas authorities did not accept its request for executive clemency... the Government of Canada will continue its efforts to ensure that the rights of Canadians in such circumstances are fully respected in accordance with the law."

Refugees
Some asylum-seekers continued to be detained for prolonged periods before being deported. The Canadian

authorities examined criteria for eligibility before hearing the evidence of the need for protection in the individual case. This had the effect of rendering certain groups of people ineligible to make a refugee claim. Asylum-seekers whose applications were turned down by the Immigration and Refugee Board did not have access to a meaningful appeal on the merits of their case. At least one refugee was at risk of forcible return.

☐ Manickavagsagam Suresh, who had been recognized as a refugee by Canadian authorities in 1991, faced possible forcible return to Sri Lanka because of his alleged links to the Liberation Tigers of Tamil Eelam. The Canadian government took the position that the UN Convention against Torture allows for the forcible return of individuals alleged to be security risks, even though they may be at risk of torture on their return. An appeal against the decision was before the Supreme Court of Canada at the end of the year.

CHAD

REPUBLIC OF CHAD
Head of state: Idriss Déby
Head of government: Nagoum Yamassoum
Capital: N'Djaména
Population: 7.6 million
Official languages: French, Arabic
Death penalty: retentionist
2000 treaty ratifications/signatures: African Charter on the Rights and Welfare of the Child

Despite moves towards negotiation, the armed conflict in northern Chad continued to threaten the government of Idriss Déby. Independent information on human rights abuses in the area was difficult to obtain. However, there were several reports of the use of forcibly recruited child soldiers. A brief resurgence of armed conflict in southern Chad led to a serious increase in human rights abuses in the region, in particular a number of reported cases of extrajudicial execution and ill-treatment.

Impunity
No one has been brought to justice for serious human rights violations, including thousands of extrajudicial executions, which occurred under the government of Hissein Habré (1982-1990). In 1992 a government Commission of Inquiry identified the *Direction de la documentation et de la sécurité* (DDS), Directorate for Documentation and Security, which was directly responsible to Hissein Habré, as one of the main units responsible for violations. In October 2000, a coalition of national and international human rights groups assisted in filing 17 cases against members of the DDS for crimes of torture, murder and "disappearances" under Hissein Habré. Further cases were filed subsequently calling for investigations and compensation. In November, the investigating judge ruled that he did not have jurisdiction to try the cases because a special court to try Hissein Habré and his collaborators, provided for in a 1993 law, had never been established. An appeal against this ruling was lodged. Hissein Habré himself was charged with complicity in acts of torture in Senegal, but the charges were later ruled to be inadmissible (see Senegal entry).

Torture and extrajudicial executions
Torture continued to be routine during interrogation and as a form of intimidation.

☐ Ali Hadji Garondé Djarma was badly beaten by members of the judicial police after his arrest in November. He was charged with defamation following publication in the independent newspaper *N'Djaména Hebdo* of his opinion piece criticizing relations between the Chadian and Libyan governments. He was convicted of the lesser offence of "insult" and received a two-year suspended sentence and a fine. He had also alleged that the serving Libyan ambassador to Chad was responsible for the "disappearance" in 1984 of a Chadian national. The director of *N'Djaména Hebdo*, Oulatar Bégoto, was acquitted of "complicity to defame through the press".

In March, two prisoners who were reportedly attempting to escape from Abéché prison were shot and killed, although their feet were chained and they posed no threat. On 3 April a soldier, Yogeurna, was shot shortly after his arrest by police officers in Koumra, Moyen Chari region. Yogeurna had apparently been arrested for trying to steal branches from a mango tree. On 15 May, Sylvain Laohoye was extrajudicially executed in gendarmerie detention in Bessao, Logone oriental region.

Human rights abuses in the south
The *Comité national du salut pour la paix et la démocratie* (CNSPD), National Salvation Committee for Peace and Democracy, which had been brought into the government in 1994, took up arms again in April after its leader, Moïse Kette, lost his position as director of national intelligence. The re-emergence of the CNSPD prompted a large military counter-insurgency and intelligence-gathering operation in the south. The military operation and fears of a return to conflict caused large population displacements. Extrajudicial executions and ill-treatment of people suspected of supporting Moïse Kette were documented by Chadian human rights groups. A number of women were allegedly raped.

☐ On 13 August Raphaël Mbeurdé and Robtol Nadji, a village chief, were arrested by soldiers in Bendho, taken to a neighbouring village, and shot. The killings followed fighting between government forces and the CNSPD in the area.

☐ Paul Mbaitidem, Joseph Nadjiadoumdom and Martin Djimta, all relatives of Moïse Kette, were reportedly extrajudicially executed by soldiers in the Béboto region in August.

Amnesty International Report 2001

☐ Adolphe Soulabé was arrested in Moundou in September and transferred to Béboto where he was executed. His wife was also arrested. Her fate was not known.

Moïse Kette himself was killed in September. According to official sources he was killed in a clash with government soldiers. However, other evidence, including a photograph which appeared to show that his throat had been cut, suggested that he may have been summarily executed after capture.

In May, villagers from Békoura, Béboto and Manga were ill-treated by soldiers who believed they had information on the whereabouts of Moïse Kette.

Some CNSPD combatants also reportedly ill-treated civilians. In July, a vehicle was ambushed and six people were injured in the Goré area by armed men reportedly belonging to the CNSPD. In August, the CNSPD reportedly kidnapped Justin Nadjibeye, whom they suspected of passing information to the government. His fate was not known.

Human rights defenders
Human rights defenders continued to be at risk.
☐ Tiglao Mbayki, of the Ligue tchadienne des droits de l'homme (LTDH), Chadian Human Rights League, was briefly detained and beaten in Pala. Other members of the LTDH were threatened in Kélo. In September, the house of Dobian Assingar, president of the LTDH, was attacked by four men in military uniform. He had been attacked before, and had received death threats.

The Chad/Cameroon pipeline
In June the World Bank agreed to finance the Chad/Cameroon oil development and pipeline project. Human rights organizations in Chad and international environmental organizations have criticized the pipeline on environmental, social and economic grounds. Representatives of civil society bodies, including human rights groups, were included in a government body to monitor the project. In 1999 a number of civil society members who had spoken out against the pipeline or who had sought to raise awareness of the rights issues involved were intimidated or detained. President Idriss Déby acknowledged in October 2000 that part of the international finance received for the project had been allocated to the defence budget. Military equipment including helicopters and jeeps used in counter-insurgency operations were reported to have been purchased.

Intergovernmental organizations
In January, the UN Committee on the Rights of the Child considered Chad's initial report. Questions were raised on the measures taken by the government to prevent gender discrimination and to protect girls from rape, and on juvenile justice. The government acknowledged that rape and other abuses had occurred in conflict areas, but denied that such violations were systematic. It also acknowledged that street children were victims of police brutality, but denied that minors were used in the armed forces. It acknowledged, however, that there was no age limit on recruitment to the government armed forces and that rehabilitation programs for child combatants from former armed opposition groups were inadequate. A project to support human rights through technical cooperation between the UN Development Programme, the UN High Commissioner for Human Rights and the government began in February.

CHILE

REPUBLIC OF CHILE
Head of state and government: Ricardo Lagos (replaced Eduardo Frei Ruiz-Tagle in March)
Capital: Santiago
Population: 15.2 million
Official language: Spanish
Death penalty: retentionist

There were reports that detainees were tortured and ill-treated by police. Legal proceedings in connection with past human rights violations continued in Chile and abroad.

Background
In January Ricardo Lagos of the Concertación de Partidos por la Democracia, Coalition for Democracy Party, was elected President in January and inaugurated in March.

The political and human rights debate in 2000 were dominated by the return to Chile of Augusto Pinochet, following his release from detention in the United Kingdom (UK) on health grounds.

Members of the Mesa de Diálogo, a dialogue set up in 1999 to deal with the issue of "disappearances" during the years of military rule between 1973 and 1990, signed a Declaration in June. This initiative was rejected by some human rights groups, including relatives of the "disappeared". The Declaration recognized the grave human rights violations committed under the military government. It registered, among other things, that the armed forces and Carabineros (uniformed police) had no information on the "disappeared", but established their commitment to cooperate in obtaining it. It set a timetable of six months, which can be extended for a further six months by the President, to gather information, and called for new legislation to grant anonymity to those who came forward with information on the location of the remains of the "disappeared". New legislation for this purpose was passed by Congress and became law in July.

A bill abolishing the death penalty for ordinary crimes and increasing the minimum term to be served under a life sentence from 20 to 40 years was passed by the Senate in December. By the end of the year the bill had not become law.

Past human rights violations
Augusto Pinochet
In March, after protracted legal procedures, the UK authorities decided not to order the extradition of Augusto Pinochet to Spain or to allow legal proceedings in respect of extradition requests from Switzerland, Belgium and France on grounds that Augusto Pinochet was unfit to stand trial. Augusto Pinochet left the UK for Chile the same day.

In Chile, more than 70 criminal complaints involving nearly 2,000 individual cases of human rights violations had been filed against Augusto Pinochet by the time he returned to the country. Seven Chilean human rights lawyers filed a legal request before the Santiago Appeals Court to lift Augusto Pinochet's parliamentary immunity from prosecution as a senator for life.

The Chilean Council for Defence of the State, which represents the legal interests of the state, joined the complaint against Augusto Pinochet and other members of the armed forces for their responsibility for the "disappearance" of 19 people during a military operation in October 1973 known as the "Caravan of Death".

In June, the Santiago Appeals Court ruled by 13 votes to nine to lift Augusto Pinochet's parliamentary immunity. An appeal against the ruling was lodged before the Supreme Court. In August, the Supreme Court announced its decision to uphold the decision to lift parliamentary immunity, opening the way for a criminal investigation of Augusto Pinochet's involvement in the "Caravan of Death" "disappearances".

In December, the Supreme Court overturned on appeal an order for the house arrest of Augusto Pinochet for the kidnapping and/or murder of 75 victims of the "Caravan of Death" issued by the judge in charge earlier the same month. The Supreme Court ruled that the judge had failed to interrogate Augusto Pinochet before issuing the order and subsequently ruled that, before the interrogation could take place, mental and physical medical tests should be carried out to determine Augusto Pinochet's fitness to stand trial. By the end of 2000, a total of 202 criminal complaints had been filed against Augusto Pinochet in Chile.

Three other former high-ranking officers were charged in connection with the "Caravan of Death". During the year criminal proceedings were also opened against over 80 former members of the security forces in connection with a number of past human rights violations.

In Argentina in October, a Buenos Aires court requested the extradition of Augusto Pinochet and six former members of the Chilean secret police for their alleged involvement in the killing of Carlos Prats, former head of the Chilean army, and his wife, in Buenos Aires in 1974 (see Argentina entry).

Torture/ill-treatment
There were continued reports of torture and ill-treatment of criminal suspects detained by members of the *Carabineros*. A number of victims required hospital treatment for their injuries and several others lodged official complaints.

A report compiled by the Chilean non-governmental human rights organization, *Corporación de Promoción y Defensa de los Derechos del Pueblo*, Committee for the Defence of the Rights of the People, containing 33 complaints of torture or ill-treatment during 1999 and the first half of 2000 and affecting over 141 individuals, was submitted to the Chilean authorities by an AI delegation in October.

Government authorities continued to deny all reports of torture or ill-treatment.

AI report and visits
Report
- Memorandum to the Government of the Republic of Chile – AI's Secretary General on mission to Chile, 1-6 October 2000 (AI Index AMR 22/022/2000)

Visits
In July an AI delegate observed the Supreme Court's hearings on the lifting of Augusto Pinochet's parliamentary immunity. In October an AI delegation led by Pierre Sané, AI's Secretary General, visited Chile to hold talks with government officials, representatives of human rights organizations, victims of human rights violations and other members of civil society. During a meeting with President Ricardo Lagos, AI submitted a memorandum on its concerns in Chile and called for the implementation of a National Action Plan on Human Rights.

CHINA

PEOPLE'S REPUBLIC OF CHINA
Head of state: Jiang Zemin
Head of government: Zhu Rongji
Capital: Beijing
Population: 1.2 billion
Official language: Standard Chinese or Mandarin
Death penalty: retentionist

2000 saw continued repression of peaceful dissent throughout the country. There was no sign of any relaxation of the 1999 crack-down on fundamental freedoms. Thousands of people were arbitrarily detained for peacefully exercising their rights to freedom of expression, association or religion. Some were sentenced to long prison terms after unfair trials under national security legislation; others were detained without trial and assigned to up to three years' "re-education through labour". Torture and ill-treatment of prisoners continued to be widespread. The limited and incomplete records available showed that at least 1,511 people were sentenced to death and 1,000 executed; the true figures were believed to be far higher. In the autonomous regions of Xinjiang and Tibet, religious freedom continued to be severely restricted and people suspected of nationalist activities or sympathies were subjected to particularly harsh repression.

Background

The government's campaign of repression against those it deemed a threat to political stability and public order continued against a background of growing public criticism of official corruption. The government intensified its anti-corruption campaign and several high-ranking officials were convicted of corruption following highly publicized trials; some were sentenced to death.

Although implementation of the law continued to be arbitrary in many cases, the government renewed efforts to encourage implementation of 1997 legal changes, including some aimed at improving the fairness of trials. Further legal reform was debated with reference to international human rights treaties which China had signed but not yet ratified. In November, the government signed a Memorandum of Understanding with the UN High Commissioner for Human Rights, designed to set up a program of technical cooperation in the field of human rights.

At the UN Commission on Human Rights, China again blocked debate on a draft resolution by using a procedural motion "not to take action". In May, the UN Committee against Torture recommended that China adopt a definition of the crime of torture consistent with the UN Convention against Torture and abolish all forms of administrative detention.

In September survivors of the 1989 massacre which followed pro-democracy protests in Tiananmen Square filed a civil lawsuit in New York, USA, against Li Peng, the then Chinese Premier, for human rights violations including crimes against humanity and torture.

Labour unrest and repression

The enormous social costs of economic restructuring continued to provoke social unrest during 2000. The absence of effective social welfare provisions left many of the millions of workers who had lost their jobs in recent years facing acute poverty. A severe drought also brought hardship and disquiet among the country's rural population. Tens of thousands of demonstrations were believed to have taken place during the year, although most were not reported by China's tightly controlled official media. China's expected entry into the World Trade Organization was set to increase economic and social challenges.

▢ In May, nearly 50 people were reportedly injured when several hundred police dispersed a demonstration of up to 5,000 steel workers from the Liaoyang Perroalloy Factory, Liaoning province. Workers were protesting that some had not been paid since 1998 and that 2,000 workers who had been laid off and 1,000 retired workers had not received their benefits for up to six months.

▢ Peasants from eight rural towns in Shaanxi province were beaten and illegally detained for refusing to pay excessive taxes imposed by local Communist Party officials. Ma Xiaoming, a journalist investigating the story, was detained for several hours by police in August. The peasants were campaigning for the release of Ma Wenlin, a paralegal who was imprisoned for five years in 1999 after lodging a formal complaint against the taxes with the central government.

Repression of spiritual and religious groups

Followers of the *Falun Gong* spiritual group faced detention, unfair trials, torture and imprisonment as part of the government's continuing crack-down on groups it considered to be "heretical organizations". Legislation was used retroactively to convict alleged leaders of the *Falun Gong* on politically driven charges and new regulations were introduced to further restrict fundamental freedoms. Since the *Falun Gong* was banned in July 1999, at least 93 adherents were believed to have died in police custody. Some of the deaths were a result of suicide or injuries inflicted during forcible feeding, but most were reported to have died as a result of torture. New arrests and detentions were reported daily throughout 2000. Thousands, possibly tens of thousands, of practitioners were believed to remain in detention at the end of the year. Many were assigned without trial to "re-education through labour" and some were detained in psychiatric hospitals.

The clamp-down on "heretical organizations" increasingly encompassed other *Qi Gong* and religious groups. Evangelical Protestants and Roman Catholics who worshipped outside the official "patriotic" churches were the victims of a continuing pattern of arrests, fines and harassment. Scores arrested in recent years remained in prison or labour camps.

▢ In August, 130 evangelical Christians were detained in Henan province. All were members of the *Fangcheng* Church, one of many Protestant "house churches" which are not recognized by the authorities. According to reports, 85 of those detained were subsequently charged with joining an "heretical organization". However, in September official sources claimed that all those detained had been "re-educated and sent back to where they came from".

▢ In September, 24 Roman Catholics, including a priest and 20 nuns, were detained in Fujian province when police found them holding church services in a mushroom-processing factory. According to reports, Father Liu Shaozhang was so severely beaten by police during arrest that he vomited blood. Two of the nuns were allegedly released the following day after parishioners paid a large sum of money to the police; the whereabouts of the other 22 detainees remained unknown at the end of the year.

Repression of Internet users

People continued to be arrested and charged with serious offences for using the Internet to spread information about human rights or other politically sensitive issues. Attempts by the authorities to control access and use of the Internet in China included the closure in August of what was described as the first ever pro-democracy website. In October and November, the government issued regulations to control news sites and chat-rooms and combat "internet crimes", including the expression of views deemed "harmful to the state".

◻ Huang Qi was arrested in the southwestern city of Chengdu in June for publishing information on the Internet about the 1989 crack-down on pro-democracy protests. He was charged with "subverting state power", but was not known to have been tried by the end of the year.

Repression of reformers and dissidents

People continued to be detained and sentenced to terms of imprisonment or "re-education through labour" for peacefully promoting reforms. These included political dissidents, such as members of the banned China Democratic Party, and anti-corruption and environmental campaigners.

◻ In September dissident writer Qi Yanchen was sentenced to four years' imprisonment for "subversion" by a court in Hebei province. He was one of the founders of an environmental movement, the China Development Union, which was banned in 1998. His imprisonment was believed to be connected with his writings, in particular his book, *China's Collapse*, which argues that China must introduce political reforms if it wants to avoid widespread social unrest.

◻ In April, An Jun, an anti-corruption campaigner, was sentenced to four years' imprisonment for "anti-government activities" by a court in Xinyang, Henan province. The evidence against him was reportedly based on four essays he had written but never published. Prior to his arrest in July 1999, An Jun had formed an independent anti-corruption group which claimed to have uncovered over 100 cases of corruption.

Tiananmen Square anniversary

The authorities once again suppressed all attempts to mark the anniversary of the June 1989 crack-down on pro-democracy activists when hundreds of civilians were massacred and tens of thousands of others were injured or arrested. Every year since 1989, the anniversary has sparked further arrests and detentions of those seeking justice for the victims and their families.

Eleven years on, no public inquiry had been instituted into the events and no compensation had been granted to the families of the victims. At the end of 2000 more than 200 people were believed to remain in prison for their activities in connection with the 1989 protests.

Torture/ill-treatment

Torture and ill-treatment of detainees remained widespread. Victims included both political detainees and criminal suspects. Incidents were reported in police stations, detention centres, prisons, labour camps, repatriation centres and drug rehabilitation centres. There were also frequent reports of the use of torture during non-custodial control measures such as "residential supervision" and during the "special isolation" of officials being investigated for alleged corruption.

Torture during interrogation was perpetrated against all types of detainees and was a component part of some high-profile anti-crime or political campaigns such as the crack-down on the *Falun Gong*.

The extent of deaths in custody as a result of torture remained largely unacknowledged by the authorities. In many cases, particularly those involving political prisoners or perceived enemies of the government, officials simply denied responsibility and no proper investigation was undertaken.

◻ Chen Zixiu, a 60-year-old *Falun Gong* practitioner, reportedly died under torture in February while held by police in Weifang, Shandong province. Fellow detainees testified in detail about how she was tortured. According to her daughter, when the family came to fetch Chen Zixiu's body, it was covered in bruises, her teeth were broken and blood was coming out of her ears. Local police reportedly later claimed that she had "died of a heart attack".

Prison conditions remained harsh and the routine denial of medical care posed a serious threat to many prisoners.

◻ Zhang Shanguang, a former teacher and labour rights activist held in Hunan Province No. 1 Prison, was forced to continue doing heavy physical work in fetters despite suffering from a serious lung illness. When he tried to stop working, he was reportedly beaten. He had been detained in July 1998 and one of the charges against him was based on an interview he gave to a US-funded radio station in which he spoke, among other things, about peasant demonstrations in Hunan province. He was sentenced to 10 years' imprisonment and five years' deprivation of political rights following a trial behind closed doors that lasted just over two hours. By the end of the year, Zhang Shanguang had reportedly been held for four months in solitary confinement as punishment for "refusing to confess his crimes". He had also reportedly been denied family visits.

Denial of due process and unfair trials

The authorities continued to flout the Criminal Procedure Law in many cases. Political defendants were routinely denied their right to due process and their lawyers were often subjected to pressure by the authorities.

◻ Li Xiaobing and Li Xiaomei, two sisters from Beijing, were tried in secret in Beijing in January and sentenced to seven and six years' imprisonment respectively. The sisters were convicted of "illegal trading" in connection with the sale of *Falun Gong* publications. However, they were arrested on 20 July 1999 — two days before the *Falun Gong*, and therefore its literature, were banned. The two women were held for more than three months without charge, in violation of Chinese law, and denied access to their family. In August 1999, before formal charges had been laid, the official *Xinhua* news agency published accusations against them, showing clearly that they were already considered guilty. According to unofficial sources, their lawyer was put under pressure not to present a plea of "not guilty" at their trial.

Death penalty

The death penalty continued to be used extensively and arbitrarily. Political interference was common. Often mass executions were carried out before major events or public holidays as a warning to others. Execution was by shooting or lethal injection and sometimes took place within hours of sentencing. The limited and incomplete records available to AI at the end of the year showed that at least 1,511 death sentences had been passed and at least 1,000 executions carried out in 2000. These were believed to be only a fraction of the true figures as death penalty statistics remained a state secret in China. Many cases were reported in which death sentences were passed on the basis of contentious evidence, including confessions extracted under torture.

☐ Zhuo Xiaojun was sentenced to death on 14 January after a blatantly unfair trial. He had been detained in December 1989 and sentenced to death. However, the conviction was overturned on appeal and a retrial ordered. This began in January 1993 but was adjourned for seven years. The latest trial in January 2000 lasted only a few hours. No witnesses were called; no new evidence was reportedly presented; and a confession — which Zhuo Xiaojun testified was extracted under torture and which had been undermined by forensic evidence — was central to the prosecution's case. No visits by Zhuo Xiaojun's family had ever been permitted. He was reported to suffer from hepatitis, a bleeding stomach and ulcerating skin. Both while under the initial and the second death sentences, he was reported to be held with hands and feet shackled together at all times. Zhuo Xiaojun's appeal was heard on 28 November. No decision had been reported by the end of the year.

Xinjiang Uighur Autonomous Region (XUAR)

Executions of Uighur political prisoners labelled as "separatists" or "terrorists" by the authorities continued. Most were passed after secret or summary trials where convictions were based on confessions extracted under torture. The XUAR was the only region of China where political prisoners were known to have been executed in recent years. The pattern of gross human rights violations reported from the XUAR included prolonged arbitrary incommunicado detention, torture and ill-treatment and unfair trials. The targets of abuses were mainly Uighurs, the majority ethnic group among the predominantly Muslim local population. There was an increase in religious persecution by the authorities. Islamic groups and prominent individuals in the Muslim community were subjected to repressive and often brutal measures. Thousands remained imprisoned.

☐ Rebiya Kadeer, an Uighur businesswoman and mother of 10, was sentenced to eight years' imprisonment after a secret trial in March. She was charged with "providing secret information across the border" for sending copies of publicly available newspapers to her husband, a former political prisoner living abroad. Rebiya Kadeer, a prominent campaigner promoting Uighur women's rights, had been detained in August 1999 in Urumqi, capital of the XUAR, while on her way to meet a visitor from the US Congressional Research Service. Her appeal against her sentence was rejected in November by the XUAR High People's Court, following which she was transferred to the Baijiahu prison in Urumqi. She was reported to be in poor health.

Tibet Autonomous Region (TAR)

In January the 17th Karmapa — the highest profile religious leader to leave the TAR in recent years — escaped into exile. Repression of religious activities in the TAR intensified during 2000. Hundreds of Buddhist monks and nuns were believed to remain in prison at the end of the year. Many prisoners were forced to work long hours in harsh conditions. Inadequate and poor quality food combined with insanitary conditions caused health problems for many inmates. Few escaped torture and ill-treatment, particularly during the early stages of custody.

☐ Ngawang Choephel, a Tibetan ethno-musicologist, continued to serve an 18-year prison sentence. He had been convicted in 1996 of "espionage and counter-revolutionary activities". At the time of his detention he had been gathering material for the production of a documentary film about traditional Tibetan performing arts. Ngawang Choephel was held in Powo Tramo prison and was reported to be in poor health, suffering from "bronchitis, hepatitis and respiratory infections". In August, his mother was given permission by the Chinese authorities to travel from India to Tibet to visit her imprisoned son for the first time since his arrest in 1995.

Asylum-seekers

In April some 50 North Korean nationals were forcibly returned by the Chinese authorities to North Korea (Democratic People's Republic of Korea) where they were feared to be at serious risk of human rights violations. They were among thousands of others reportedly returned to North Korea in previous months without being granted access to any asylum procedure.

Hong Kong Special Administrative Region

Continuing litigation over the right of abode stipulated in the Basic Law fuelled debate over the role and autonomy of Hong Kong courts when interpreting constitutional rights under the "One Country Two Systems" model.

Freedom of expression and the right to peaceful assembly

Frequent demonstrations were held against a wide range of government policies.

☐ In May, activist Leung Kwok-hung was sentenced to 14 days' imprisonment for "contempt" after shouting a slogan during an October 1999 legislative council meeting.

☐ In August and September, 16 demonstrators, including seven student leaders, were arrested under the controversial 1997 Public Order ordinance for failing to give seven days' notice prior to a demonstration in June. Participants had formally complained of excessive use of force by police who had used pepper spray and punched and kicked protesters.

The arrests triggered large unauthorized solidarity marches and renewed public scrutiny of the ordinance. In October, the charges were dropped.

◻ A public investigation which substantiated allegations of official interference in academic freedom at the University of Hong Kong led to the resignation of the vice-chancellor and pro-vice-chancellor in September.

◻ Staff of the Central Government Liaison Office (formerly the New China News Agency or *Xinhua*) told the Hong Kong media not to report the views of pro-independence Taiwanese, and warned Hong Kong businesses of the risks of choosing such trading partners.

Alleged illegal immigrants and asylum-seekers
Two officials and an interpreter were charged with perverting the course of justice after several people were wrongfully detained for immigration offences after allegedly being pressurized or misled into making false confessions. They included a teenage girl and a female tourist from Viet Nam. A severely mentally disabled boy went missing in mainland China after immigration officials allowed him to cross the border alone without papers and then blocked his attempts to return.

In January, the jury at a coroner's inquest into the August 1999 death of Prince Evis Ose in a fire in his cell in Victoria Prison called for "serious action" across government departments. The prison was used to detain alleged overstayers, illegal immigrants and asylum-seekers under the Immigration Ordinance, potentially without trial and for an unlimited period. The inquest heard that recommendations made in 1987 to install fire-fighting equipment and remove flammable fittings had been largely ignored by officials because they considered prisons had no public access.

In May the UN Committee against Torture recommended that Hong Kong's laws and practices to outlaw torture and to protect refugees be brought into conformity with the UN Convention against Torture.

Macao Special Administrative Region (MSAR)
Rising unemployment undermined high expectations of economic recovery and government reform under the Chinese regime. Unemployed workers staged several large marches, culminating in a violent confrontation on 2 July when police used tear gas to disperse stone-throwing demonstrators and arrested several alleged organizers.

The police reported a significant decrease in triad-gang related violence. Several defendants complained they had been falsely charged and denied any right to bail under wide-ranging 1999 legislation against organized crime. Severe overcrowding was reported at the MSAR's one prison.

In December, on the eve of President Jiang Zemin's visit to celebrate the first anniversary of the MSAR, police occupied the home of *Falun Gong* organizer Lam Yatming, claiming they were searching for banned items, and detained democracy activist Lee Kinyuen. Peaceful *Falun Gong* gatherings were forcibly dispersed, and many local and foreign practitioners were detained. The Chief Executive promised to investigate allegations that police had beaten practitioners while removing them from the MSAR. President Jiang Zemin urged Macao to take concrete measures to defend Beijing's authority and prohibit activities against the central government.

AI country reports
- Women's Rights are Human Rights — China: Arbitrary detention of Rebiya Kadeer — a women's human rights defender and prisoner of conscience (AI Index: ASA 17/004/2000)
- People's Republic of China: The crack-down on *Falun Gong* and other so-called "heretical organizations" (AI Index: ASA 17/011/2000)
- People's Republic of China: Tiananmen — 11 years on and still no government inquiry: "forgotten prisoners" (AI Index: ASA 17/017/2000)
- People's Republic of China: Death Penalty Log 1999 (AI Index: ASA 17/049/2000)

COLOMBIA

REPUBLIC OF COLOMBIA
Head of state and government: Andrés Pastrana Arango
Capital: Santafé de Bogotá
Population: 42.3 million
Official language: Spanish
Death penalty: abolitionist for all crimes
2000 treaty ratifications/signatures: Optional Protocol to the UN Children's Convention on the involvement of children in armed conflict

The human rights crisis continued to deepen against a background of a spiralling armed conflict. The parties to the conflict intensified their military actions throughout the country in campaigns characterized by gross and systematic violations of human rights and international humanitarian law. The principal victims of political violence were civilians, particularly peasant farmers living in areas disputed between government forces and allied paramilitaries, and armed opposition groups. Human rights defenders, journalists, judicial officials, teachers, trade unionists and leaders of Afro-Colombian and indigenous communities were among those targeted. More than 4,000 people were victims of political killings, over 300 "disappeared", and an estimated 300,000 people were internally displaced. At least 1,500 people were kidnapped by armed opposition groups and paramilitary organizations; mass kidnaps of civilians continued. Torture — often involving mutilation – remained widespread, particularly as a prelude to murder by paramilitary groups. "Death squad"-style killings continued in urban areas. Children suffered serious human rights violations particularly in the context of the armed conflict. New evidence emerged of continuing collusion between the armed forces and illegal paramilitary groups. Progress continued in a limited number of judicial investigations, but impunity for human rights abuses remained the norm.

Escalating conflict

Few areas of the country remained unaffected by the escalating conflict. The number and intensity of direct confrontations between the parties to the conflict increased. The principal victims continued to be civilians. The majority of killings were carried out by illegal paramilitary groups operating with the tacit or active support of the Colombian armed forces. All parties to the conflict, including the Colombian armed forces, routinely breached their obligation to allow and facilitate access by humanitarian organizations to conflict areas to aid civilian communities under attack or caught in the crossfire, and to assist wounded combatants. In separate incidents, wounded combatants under the protection of the International Committee of the Red Cross were summarily executed by the *Autodefensas Unidas de Colombia* (AUC), United Self-Defence Groups of Colombia, and the *Fuerzas Armadas Revolucionarias de Colombia* (FARC), Revolutionary Armed Forces of Colombia.

Peace process

Peace talks which began in 1999 between the government and the FARC continued in the demilitarized zone for much of the year, but no substantive agreement was reached. In November the FARC indefinitely suspended talks demanding that the government demonstrate greater and clearer efforts to combat paramilitary groups.

Despite the suspension of talks, in December the government extended until the end of January 2001 the demilitarization of five municipalities in Meta and Caquetá departments which remained under the *de facto* control of the FARC.

The fragility of the peace process was further underlined by the government's failure to implement peace proposals in the face of opposition from sectors of the armed forces and paramilitary groups. Efforts to begin peace talks with the *Ejército de Liberación Nacional* (ELN), National Liberation Army, were systematically blocked by paramilitary-backed protests in the three municipalities in the central Magdalena Medio region which the government had agreed in April to demilitarize in order to facilitate talks. The designated area had not been demilitarized and formal talks had not begun by the end of the year.

Paramilitaries

Despite repeated government promises to dismantle paramilitary forces, no effective action was taken to curtail, much less to end, their widespread and systematic atrocities. In contrast to their declared aim to combat guerrilla forces, paramilitary actions continued to target the civilian population through massacres, torture, the destruction of communities and the displacement of the population.

▫ In February, 200 paramilitary gunmen raided the village of El Salado, Bolívar department, killing 36 people, including a six-year-old child. Many victims were tied to a table in the village sports field and subjected to torture, including rape, before being stabbed or shot dead. Others were killed in the village church. During the three-day attack, military and police units stationed nearby made no effort to intervene. Instead, a Navy Infantry unit reportedly set up a roadblock on the access road to El Salado, thus preventing humanitarian organizations from reaching the village. Arrest warrants were issued against 11 paramilitary members, including AUC leader Carlos Castaño, in connection with the massacre. Marine Colonel Rodrigo Quiñones, commander of the Navy's 1st Brigade, was promoted to General while investigations into the possible criminal responsibility in connection with the massacre of troops under his command were still under way. Government investigations had previously linked General Quiñones to the murders of more than 50 people in Barrancabermeja, Santander department, in 1991 and 1992. However, the military justice system, which claimed jurisdiction in the case, dropped the charges.

▫ Over 40 people were killed in November during an AUC attack on several fishing villages in the municipality of La Ciénaga, Magdalena department. A further 30 people reportedly "disappeared".

The government again failed to set up the specialist military units to combat paramilitary groups which it had repeatedly promised. The armed forces failed to attack or dismantle paramilitary bases, the majority of which were located in close proximity to army and police bases.

Armed forces

▫ Six children aged between six and 15 on a school outing were shot dead by the army in August. Several others were seriously injured. An army patrol opened fire on the school party in Pueblorrico, Antioquia department, allegedly in the belief that they were guerrilla fighters. Fourteen soldiers were under investigation by a military court at the end of the year. None was arrested.

Collusion between the Colombian security forces, particularly the army, and paramilitary groups continued and, indeed, strengthened. Instances of collaboration included the sharing of intelligence information, the transfer of prisoners, the provision of ammunition by the armed forces to the paramilitary, and joint patrols and military operations in which serious human rights violations were committed.

▫ A wide-ranging pattern of collusion between the national police, the army and paramilitary forces in the area of Puerto Asís, Putumayo department, was revealed to the authorities by a member of the national police and the local human rights ombudsman. According to their sworn testimonies, paramilitary groups consorted openly with army personnel and police in the town of Puerto Asís. On the outskirts of the town they maintained a base, where people who had been abducted were taken to be tortured and killed. The base was only a few hundred metres from the headquarters of the army's 24th Brigade and a base of the 25th Battalion. Army officers held regular meetings with paramilitary leaders in the base.

In September, President Pastrana, by decree law, delegated to the armed forces command discretionary presidential powers to dismiss offending armed forces personnel. This paved the way for the dismissal in October of 89 officers and 299 lower-ranking members of the armed forces. No details were released of the names of those dismissed or the causes. However, it was believed that fewer than 50 involved human rights offences. None of those dismissed was brought to justice and senior members of the armed forces implicated in human rights violations, by action or omission, continued in service. In December, the Minister of Defence acknowledged that 50 of the dismissed army officers had joined the AUC.

Armed opposition groups

Violations of international humanitarian law by armed opposition groups increased significantly. Several hundred people, including scores of civilians, were deliberately and arbitrarily killed by armed opposition groups. In many cases the killings appeared to be reprisal or punishment killings of alleged military or paramilitary collaborators. Those killed included judicial officials, local politicians and journalists who were targeted because they were investigating guerrilla abuses or opposed their policies.

▫ Eighteen-year-old Irish national Tristan James Murray was killed with his Colombian friend, Javier Nova, by FARC urban militia in July. The two youths were beheaded after being captured in the town of Icononzo, Tolima department.

The FARC and the ELN carried out numerous disproportionate and indiscriminate attacks on military targets which caused significant civilian casualties. Police and military bases in scores of towns and villages were attacked, frequently with loss of civilian life. Some communities were attacked successively by paramilitary and armed opposition groups. FARC combatants reportedly summarily executed seriously wounded soldiers and police.

Further reports emerged of serious violations of international humanitarian law by the FARC in the demilitarized area. There were also credible reports that people, including children, kidnapped by the FARC had been taken to the demilitarized area.

▫ In July the Attorney General said he had evidence that three-year-old Andrés Felipe Suarez was being held in the FARC-controlled demilitarized zone. Andrés Felipe Suarez had been kidnapped in April. Although a senior FARC commander pledged to investigate the allegation, the whereabouts of the child remained unknown at the end of the year. No independent investigation of the allegations of abuses within the demilitarized area was permitted by the FARC.

Children as young as 13 continued to be recruited by the FARC.

Kidnapping

Kidnapping and hostage-taking reached unprecedented levels. Of a reported 3,000 cases, more than half were believed to have been carried out by armed opposition groups and paramilitary organizations. Children accounted for 200 of the victims.

▫ In September the ELN abducted more than 50 people from roadside restaurants outside the southern city of Cali. While most were eventually released, two hostages died as a result of injuries they sustained in captivity and one died because of lack of adequate medical treatment for an ulcer.

▫ In October, AUC paramilitary forces abducted six congressional representatives to protest about the debate in Congress of a government proposal to exchange FARC political prisoners for soldiers and police held captive by the FARC. The representatives were released following a meeting — described by the government as "humanitarian" — between AUC commanders and the Interior Minister.

Plan Colombia

A controversial aid package, known as Plan Colombia, was presented by the Colombian government to the international community. The Plan, originally designed to seek aid to support the peace process, was transformed into a predominantly military plan ostensibly aimed at combating illicit drug cultivation. In July the Plan received the backing of the US government which approved a US$1.3 billion, principally military, aid package. In approving the aid, the US Congress added human rights conditions and a requirement that the US government periodically certify that the Colombian armed forces were acting to punish human rights violators and to sever their ties to the paramilitary. In August, US President Bill Clinton waived most of the human rights conditions on the grounds of US national security interests. AI opposed the military aid program which it believed would escalate the human rights crisis and the armed conflict and deplored the decision to waive human rights conditions.

Other members of the international community, including the European Union, pledged support for the peace process, human rights and development programs, but made clear that such support was independent of Plan Colombia.

Putumayo

Although the military component of Plan Colombia was not due to come into effect until early 2001, its impact was immediate. In response to the US military aid package, the FARC launched a series of attacks throughout the country. The southern department of Putumayo, the principal focus of Plan Colombia, was particularly affected by an upsurge in violence. Civilians were caught in the crossfire as the FARC and army-backed paramilitary forces fought for control of the region.

Persecution of human rights defenders
Protection programs set up by the Colombian government proved insufficient to counter the continuing campaign of intimidation, harassment and attacks against human rights defenders. At least two human rights defenders were killed and three "disappeared". Many others received persistent death threats. Defenders in Barrancabermeja, Santander department, and in Medellín, Antioquia department, were particularly at risk.

☐ Jesús Ramiro Zapata Hoyos, founding member of the *Comité de Derechos Humanos del Nordeste Antioqueño*, North East Antioquia Human Rights Committee, was shot dead in May in Segovia, Antioquia department. He had received repeated death threats from paramilitary forces.

☐ Angel Quintero and Claudia Monsalve, members of the *Asociación de Familiares de Detenidos-Desaparecidos* (ASFADDES), Association of Families of the Detained Disappeared, were abducted by unidentified gunmen in Medellín in October. Their whereabouts remained unknown at the end of the year. Angel Quintero had faced continuous threats and harassment as a result of his work with ASFADDES. Several members of his family had "disappeared" in previous years.

Journalists investigating and publishing reports about human rights and political violence were also targeted. Eight journalists were killed, mainly by paramilitary forces, and many more received death threats or were kidnapped.

☐ In May, Jineth Bedoya Lima, a journalist with the daily *El Espectador* newspaper, was abducted in Bogotá by paramilitary gunmen and subjected to physical and psychological torture before being released 12 hours later. During her ordeal, her abductors threatened to kill her and four of her colleagues who also reported on human rights issues.

Increasing numbers of judicial officials investigating human rights abuses were threatened, attacked and kidnapped by army-backed paramilitary forces and guerrilla organizations.

☐ Seven judicial investigators "disappeared" following their abduction by paramilitary forces in Cesar department in March. Six judicial officials were killed.

☐ In April, Margarita Pulgarín, a Medellín-based prosecutor who specialized in investigating links between the military and paramilitary groups, was shot dead outside her home.

Justice and impunity
The Attorney General's Human Rights Unit investigated over 900 cases of violations of human rights and international humanitarian law. Significant progress was made in a number of cases.

☐ In June, six members of the National Police were remanded in custody on charges of colluding with paramilitary forces in a massacre in the town of Tibú, North Santander department, in July 1999. Several army officers were also under investigation in connection with the massacre.

☐ Two members of the FARC were formally charged *in absentia* with the murder of three US indigenous rights activists abducted and murdered in February 1999.

☐ Four paramilitary gunmen were convicted of the murder in May 1997 of human rights and environmental activists Mario Calderón and Elsa Alvarado, and Elsa's father, Carlos Alvarado.

However, the vast majority of perpetrators of violations of human rights and international humanitarian law continued to evade accountability. Despite numerous outstanding arrest warrants, no attempt was made by the armed and security forces to capture paramilitary leaders responsible for widespread human rights violations. Paramilitary leaders arrested by civilian judicial investigators, routinely escaped from police or military detention.

In defiance of the Constitutional Court, the military justice system continued to claim jurisdiction in cases in which senior armed forces officers were implicated.

Legislation
In July, after six previous attempts had failed, a law was enacted making "disappearances", genocide and forced displacement criminal offences punishable with prison terms of up to 60 years. The law, however, omitted a clause, opposed by President Pastrana, that would have provided that all heinous crimes would be tried by civilian courts.

A reformed Military Penal Code came into effect in August. The Code introduced important modifications, including allowing civilians to act as plaintiffs in military penal proceedings and prohibiting commanding officers from sitting as judges in cases involving military personnel under their command. However, the new law failed to give civilian courts exclusive jurisdiction over human rights violations.

Intergovernmental organizations
In a statement from the Chair, the UN Commission on Human Rights condemned the persistent grave human rights violations and abuses perpetrated by paramilitary forces and armed opposition groups and called on the government to ensure that members of state forces involved in human rights violations, or collusion with paramilitary groups, were suspended and brought to trial. The Commission expressed particular concern about the increase in the number of internally displaced people, the continuing attacks on human rights defenders and the persistence of impunity, particularly in the military jurisdiction.

During a visit to Colombia in December, the UN High Commissioner for Human Rights said the human rights situation was "extremely critical".

AI country reports and visits
Reports
- Colombia: Protection of human rights defenders – One step forward, three steps back (AI Index: AMR 23/022/2000)

- Colombia: Return to Hope – Forcibly Displaced Communities of Urabá and Medio Atrato (AI Index: AMR 23/023/2000)
- Colombia: Human Rights and USA Military Aid to Colombia (AI Index: AMR 23/065/2000), published jointly with Human Rights Watch and the Washington Office on Latin America

Visits
AI delegates visited Colombia on six occasions and, during a meeting with the Vice-President in September, reiterated AI's call to the government to end human rights violations.

CONGO
(DEMOCRATIC REPUBLIC OF THE)

DEMOCRATIC REPUBLIC OF THE CONGO
Head of state and government: Laurent-Désiré Kabila
Capital: Kinshasa
Population: 51.6 million
Official languages: French, Kikongo, Kiswahili, Lingala, Tshiluba
Death penalty: retentionist
2000 treaty ratifications/signatures: Optional Protocol to the UN Children's Convention on the involvement of children in armed conflict; Rome Statute of the International Criminal Court

War continued to ravage the Democratic Republic of the Congo (DRC). Thousands of civilians were unlawfully killed and tens of thousands more, displaced from their homes and cut off from humanitarian aid within the DRC, were facing starvation by the end of 2000. Tens of thousands fled to neighbouring countries. Torture, including rape, was widespread. All sides used the war to justify the repression of political dissent and the imprisonment of opponents was routine. At least 35 executions were carried out by the DRC government. The armed opposition also carried out executions.

Background
At least six foreign countries continued to be directly involved in the war in the DRC, which continued despite the signing of the Lusaka cease-fire agreement in mid-1999. DRC government troops were supported by Angolan, Namibian and Zimbabwean forces. The armed opposition — composed of the Goma-based faction of the *Rassemblement congolais pour la démocratie* (RCD-Goma), Congolese Rally for Democracy, the *RCD-Mouvement de Libération* (RCD-ML), RCD-Movement of Liberation, and the *Mouvement pour la libération du Congo* (MLC), Movement for the Liberation of Congo — received support from Burundi, Rwanda and Uganda.

There appeared to be a lack of genuine political will to reach a settlement, with belligerents on all sides reportedly exploiting the DRC's vast natural resources. The proposed deployment of UN troops to monitor the cease-fire was prevented by insecurity and lack of cooperation from the warring parties, particularly the DRC government. Diplomatic initiatives included the signing of a disengagement plan in Kampala in April and a meeting in Kenya in June between DRC President Laurent-Désiré Kabila and President Paul Kagame of Rwanda. Rwanda and Uganda continued to invoke the security threat posed by armed opposition groups based within the DRC to justify their involvement in the conflict. Burundi continued to deny any involvement.

Heavy fighting was reported throughout much of 2000 in the northwestern province of Equateur between DRC government troops and the MLC, led by Jean-Pierre Bemba. The DRC government was accused of indiscriminate bombing in the region which resulted in civilian casualties. The fighting forced tens of thousands of civilians to flee to neighbouring countries (see Republic of the Congo entry). There was also heavy fighting in the southeastern province of Katanga, where the RCD-Goma and its allies took the town of Pweto in December. Thousands fled across the border to Zambia.

In August Ugandan forces and the RCD-ML forcibly recruited over 100 child soldiers in Bunia and transferred them to Uganda for military training. In November and December the RCD-Goma engaged in a mass recruitment drive in the Kivu region in which hundreds of people, including children, were reportedly recruited, many by force.

Deliberate reprisals against the civilian population were a common reaction by all sides to military setbacks and many unarmed civilians were extrajudicially executed in revenge attacks. There were also many rapes. By the end of 2000 as many as two million civilians were internally displaced and unable to support themselves. Many were facing starvation.

Areas under government control
Political prisoners
A law passed in 1999, which effectively amounted to a ban on opposition parties, led to the imprisonment of prisoners of conscience and the repression of political activity. A presidential amnesty for political prisoners announced in February led to the release of some 300 detainees from Kinshasa's central prison, the *Centre pénitentiaire et de rééducation de Kinshasa* (CPRK). However, some individuals who should have benefited remained in detention. Others were rearrested soon after their release and other politically motivated arrests continued throughout 2000.

☐ On 19 July, 10 members of the *Union pour la démocratie et le progrès social* (UDPS), Union for Democracy and Social Progress, a major opposition party, were arrested in Kinshasa for allegedly holding a political meeting. Several were ill-treated and threatened with death during their initial police interrogation. For the next month all 10 were detained together in a tiny police cell, where they were allowed no visits or medical treatment. They then spent three days in an unventilated underground cell before being transferred to the CPRK on 19 August.

◻ Catherine Nzuzi wa Mbombo, president of the *Mouvement Populaire de la Révolution* (MPR), Popular Revolution Movement, was arrested on 22 July and subjected to five days' interrogation by the security services during which she was ill-treated. She was charged with endangering state security, apparently on the basis of radio interviews she had given to *Radio France Internationale*. She was kept under house arrest until 8 December, when she was provisionally released.

◻ On 15 November Eugène Diomi Ndongala Nzomambu, the coordinator of the *Front pour la Survie de la Démocratie* (FSD), an umbrella group of about 15 small parties, was arrested by the security services and held incommunicado for over two weeks before being transferred to the CPRK. Charged with endangering state security, he was provisionally released on 8 December.

◻ On 8 December Jonas Mukamba Kadiata, a former director of a national mining company, and pastor Placide Tshisumpa, president of a prisoner support organization, were released after nearly six months' detention without trial. They were charged in November with endangering state security. As a result of their detention, both men had to be hospitalized. Pastor Tshisumpa was in particularly poor health with a heart condition. He was nevertheless briefly returned to the CPRK in November until fellow prisoners protested to the prison authorities and secured his return to the clinic.

Crack-down on alleged coup conspirators

From late October onwards, the government arrested soldiers and civilians from the eastern provinces of North-Kivu and South-Kivu, after uncovering an alleged coup plot. Anselme Masasu Nindaga, formerly a leading figure in the armed group which brought President Kabila to power in 1997, was among the first to be arrested. In November he was transferred to Katanga where he was reportedly held incommunicado, awaiting probable court martial. Such court martials have not in the past met international fair trial standards. There were unconfirmed reports that some of those arrested in connection with the alleged coup plot were extrajudicially executed.

Scores of others were held incommunicado and without charge in various detention centres in Kinshasa. They included Jeanine Mukanirwa, a women's rights activist from South-Kivu, who was arrested on 12 December. Several "disappeared", including Aimée Ntabarusha Mungu, a civil servant, who was arrested with her three-month-old son on 13 November, apparently because she had a lodger from Kivu suspected of involvement in the alleged coup plot. She was held at a security service detention centre known as the *Groupe Litho Moboti* (GLM) building until 23 November, when she was reportedly taken away in a truck with several other detainees. She had not been seen again by the end of the year.

Death penalty

Despite repeated assurances given to both AI and the UN High Commissioner for Human Rights that the government was committed to a moratorium on executions, at least 35 people were executed during 2000. The majority of death sentences were handed down by the *Cour d'ordre militaire* (COM), Military Order Court, a court which does not meet international fair trial standards. There is no appeal against the decisions of the Court.

In late January and early February, 19 people were executed. Most had been convicted of murder or armed robbery. In September, five soldiers and three civilians were taken from the CPRK and reportedly executed. On 12 December a further eight prisoners, including three civilians, were executed by firing squad. Among them was a police officer, Kabangi Ngoy, who had been sentenced by the COM the previous day for a murder committed on 8 December.

At the end of 2000 up to 60 people were on death row at the CPRK. Some had been convicted of economic or political crimes. They included Ngimbi Nkiama and Bukasa Musenga, who were convicted in 1999 of stealing fuel from the military.

Torture/ill-treatment

Torture and ill-treatment continued to be widespread in unofficial detention centres run by the security services, where detainees were almost invariably held incommunicado. Beatings, including whippings administered with *cordelettes* (belts), were particularly common. Psychological torture was also frequent, with many detainees being threatened with death and some subjected to mock executions.

Conditions in many detention centres were appalling and constituted cruel, inhuman and degrading treatment. Detainees were routinely refused medical care. Some detainees died as a result of torture.

◻ On 13 October Kikuni Masudi, a former member of the security services, died in security service custody in Lubumbashi. He had reportedly been continuously tortured since his arrest on 7 October by agents from the *Agence nationale de renseignements* (ANR), National Intelligence Agency. He had reportedly been whipped, burned and his feet had been crushed by hammer blows. There was apparently no investigation of his death.

◻ On 25 May Isaac Akili, a former soldier, was detained by security service agents in Kinshasa and interrogated for three hours, during which he was beaten around the head with rifle butts and tortured with electric shocks. He was also shown a hole that had been dug in the ground and told that it was going to be his grave. He was later transferred to the CPRK where he remained at the end of 2000, accused of endangering state security.

◻ On 16 November, 12 students, including Vital Ntaboba Badheka, were arrested by the army after a disturbance on a college campus in Kinshasa. They were taken to Kokolo military barracks where they were stripped naked, whipped and threatened with death. They were detained overnight, naked and many with open wounds, in a filthy cell awash with excrement. They were released the following morning. No action was taken against the soldiers responsible.

Human rights defenders
Several human rights activists were harassed, threatened or briefly detained. Some, including members of *La Voix des Sans Voix*, The Voice of the Voiceless, and of the *Association africaine de défense des droits de l'homme* (ASADHO), African Association for the Defence of Human Rights, were temporarily forced into hiding to avoid arrest.

⌑ On 17 October André Tshowa Mbuisha, a member of *Journaliste en danger* (JED), Journalist in Danger, was arrested in Kinshasa while distributing a report on press freedom. He was taken to an unofficial detention centre where he was whipped and subjected to a mock execution. He was released a few hours later but in December was asked to report to the COM for questioning on unspecified charges.

Journalists
Press freedom remained tightly controlled. In September freedom of expression was further curtailed when the government announced that it was bringing some of the main privately owned television and radio stations under state control. A number of journalists were prisoners of conscience.

⌑ On 19 May Freddy Loseke, editor of *La Libre Afrique*, was sentenced to three years' imprisonment by the COM for allegedly insulting the army.

⌑ On 12 September, two newspaper editors, Emile-Aimé Kakese Vinalu and Jean-Pierre Mukuna Ekanga, were sentenced to two years' imprisonment by the COM on contrived charges of endangering state security. Jean-Pierre Mukuna Ekanga had gone to court that day to act as a trial witness. Emile-Aimé Kakese Vinalu had been detained since 23 June and was tortured. His newspaper's equipment, including two computers and a printer, was confiscated.

⌑ Feu d'Or Bonsange, a journalist with the weekly newspaper *L'Alarme*, was arrested on 11 November and detained incommunicado by the security services. He was released without charge on 11 December but *L'Alarme* was forced to cease publishing.

Unlawful killings
Unarmed civilians were reportedly killed by government forces as a result either of direct attacks or of indiscriminate bombings. However, it was often difficult to obtain independent confirmation of incidents in conflict zones.

⌑ On 29 December DRC government airplanes bombed the port of Boyele on the Oubangui river in neighbouring Republic of the Congo, reportedly killing eight people and injuring dozens.

Areas controlled by opposition groups and foreign forces
The RCD factions and their foreign allies were responsible for widespread abuses in eastern DRC, in particular the unlawful killing of civilians, arbitrary arrests, unlawful detention and torture, including rape (see Rwanda and Uganda entries). Such abuses were often committed in response to attacks by armed groups opposed to the RCD-Goma, which included the Rwandese *interahamwe* and *ex-FAR* (former Rwandese government army), Congolese armed groups known as the *mayi-mayi*, and Burundian, mainly Hutu, armed groups. All of these groups were responsible for grave human rights abuses.

Unlawful killings
⌑ Ugandan forces and RCD-ML troops were implicated in the killing of dozens of unarmed members of the Lendu ethnic group in the northeastern province of Kibali-Ituri. On 20 April at least 15 were killed in Rethy and a further six were killed at Buba two days later. Tens of thousands of Lendu fled from their homes to surrounding forests, where many died of starvation and disease.

⌑ On 14-15 May, some 30 civilians were reportedly killed by RCD-Goma troops at the village of Katogota, south of Bukavu, apparently in reprisal for the killing of a senior RCD commander during clashes between the RCD-Goma and a Burundian armed opposition group. The RCD-Goma announced an investigation.

⌑ Between 5 and 10 June, at least 700 civilians were killed when fighting broke out between Rwandese and Ugandan troops in Kisangani. Some people were shot dead; many others were killed in indiscriminate shelling. Some captured soldiers were also extrajudicially executed – Rwandese soldiers reportedly executed at least 10 captured Ugandan soldiers on 11 and 12 June after the fighting had stopped.

⌑ On 9 July *interahamwe* forces attacked a camp for the internally displaced at Sake, west of Goma, reportedly killing 40 people.

⌑ On 28 August as many as 12 people were reportedly killed at the village of Kirima, west of Butembo, in an attack on a local restaurant by Ugandan soldiers. They included the couple who ran the restaurant and a schoolboy named Muhindo.

Persecution of human rights defenders
The RCD continued to be hostile towards human rights activists and dozens were detained during 2000. Some were tortured.

⌑ On 2 February Jean-Pierre Masumbuko, a member of the Goma-based non-governmental organization (NGO) APREDECI, was arrested by RCD soldiers and taken to the *Chien Méchant* detention centre in Goma where soldiers reportedly took turns at beating him. He was apparently accused of passing information to international human rights groups, including sending photographs to AI. He escaped on 5 February.

⌑ In February Archbishop Emmanuel Kataliko was banished by the RCD from Bukavu and sent to Butembo, after he criticized the presence of foreign powers in the DRC. Priests who voiced support for the archbishop were themselves threatened. He was allowed to return to Bukavu in September, shortly before his death during a visit to Italy.

⌑ On 29 August, four men who had recently been appointed to a new transitional assembly announced by President Kabila were detained in Bukavu by the RCD-Goma and held for a month. They included Paulin Bapolisi and Gervais Chirhalwira Nkunzimana, both lecturers.

⌑ On 9 October, 13 activists from various NGOs were arrested by Rwandese soldiers at the offices of the NGO *Groupe Jérémie*. They had gathered to discuss the visit of the UN High Commissioner for Human Rights to

Goma on 3 October. The 13 were taken to a military camp at Saio on the border with Rwanda, where they were reportedly tortured. They were released later the same day. Some later fled the country.

Torture/ill-treatment
There was widespread torture, including rape, of detainees held in RCD-Goma custody.

Karume Chisirikaa, a former teacher, was arrested by RCD-Goma in Bukavu on 28 September for his alleged role in a grenade attack in the town in August. He was reportedly beaten with an iron bar and told that he would be killed if he did not sign a confession. He was still detained at the end of 2000.

Willy Kabala, Félicité and Françoise Nzibera were beaten and detained for several hours on 16 January by RCD-Goma members, after failing to reveal the whereabouts of human rights activists.

AI country reports and visits
Reports
- Democratic Republic of Congo: Government terrorizes critics (AI Index: AFR 62/001/2000)
- Democratic Republic of Congo: Killing human decency (AI Index: AFR 62/007/2000)
- AI urges the Presidents of Uganda and Rwanda to stop killings (AI Index: AFR 62/015/2000)

Visits
In October AI delegates visited parts of eastern DRC controlled by the armed opposition, including Goma, Bukavu and Bunia. In late October and early November AI visited the Republic of the Congo and the Central African Republic to interview refugees from the DRC. From late November to early December AI visited Kinshasa.

CONGO
(REPUBLIC OF THE)

REPUBLIC OF THE CONGO
Head of state and government: Denis Sassou Nguesso
Capital: Brazzaville
Population: 2.6 million
Official language: French
Death penalty: abolitionist in practice

A measure of stability returned to the country after cease-fire agreements between warring militia were signed at the end of 1999. Around half those militia were estimated to have been demobilized during 2000, with many being reintegrated into the army. However, a proposed national dialogue involving all sides to the conflict did not take place. Although most of those who had been internally displaced by the fighting were able to return to their homes, the country was hit by a new refugee crisis in the north as tens of thousands of civilians fled the war in neighbouring Democratic Republic of the Congo (DRC). Conditions of detention were harsh; 13 people died in police custody.

Demobilization of militia
Following the signing of two cease-fire agreements in November and December 1999, the process of demobilizing an estimated total of 25,000 militia fighters began. These included members of the *Cocoyes* (loyal to former President Pascal Lissouba), the *Cobras* (loyal to President Dennis Sassou Nguesso), and the *Ninjas* (loyal to former Prime Minister Bernard Kolélas). All those who surrendered and handed in their weapons were guaranteed an amnesty by the government, including those responsible for serious human rights abuses during the armed conflict.

In April in the northern town of Owando, 700 weapons were reportedly handed in by the militia known as the *Faucons* (Falcons), loyal to former Prime Minister Joachim Yhombi Opango. In July, 800 members of the *Cocoyes* were reportedly demobilized in the western town of Mossendjo. In December the follow-up committee responsible for overseeing the implementation of the cease-fire announced that 13,000 weapons had been handed in and that 12,000 militia fighters had been demobilized during 2000.

However, some groups reportedly refused to demobilize, including militia in the Niari region, traditionally a stronghold of the *Cocoyes*. Many of those who had been demobilized found themselves homeless and without the means to support themselves properly. In October the government announced a reintegration program, part-funded by the UN, aimed at reintegrating 5,000 former militia members into civil society.

In March Lieutenant Jean-Claude Bayoulath, a former member of the *Cocoyes*, was reportedly killed in the town of Nkayi following a dispute with a former member of the Cobras. Both had recently been reintegrated into the army. It was not known if anyone was brought to justice for the killing.

National dialogue delayed
The cease-fire agreements provided for an inclusive national dialogue on ways forward for the country, and the year began positively with the release in Impfondo in January of 17 political prisoners linked to Bernard Kolélas. They had been detained since late 1997. However, the proposed national dialogue had still not taken place by the end of 2000 and it remained unlikely that some of the main opposition leaders in exile, who were excluded from the amnesty, would take part.

On 4 May Bernard Kolélas and former Minister of the Interior Philippe Bikinkita were convicted *in absentia* of torture during the 1997 conflict. They were sentenced to death after a trial lasting three days. In late 1999 Pascal Lissouba had been sentenced *in absentia* to 20 years' imprisonment for plotting to kill President Nguesso. All three remained in exile at the end of 2000.

A preliminary draft of a new constitution was approved by the government in November but criticized by opposition groups, which claimed that it concentrated too much power in the hands of the President. The government announced that elections would take place in 2001.

Refugees and the internally displaced
Almost all the estimated 800,000 people who were internally displaced by the armed conflicts of 1997 and 1998 were reported to have returned to their homes by the end of 2000. Many were in poor health after being forced to live in forests where food was scarce and medical care virtually non-existent. The homes of many had been looted in their absence.

Heavy fighting between DRC government forces and the armed opposition in neighbouring DRC forced tens of thousands to seek safety in northern Congo. Some claimed to have been fleeing forcible recruitment by DRC government forces. On 29 December, DRC government planes bombed the port of Boyele on the Oubangui river, reportedly killing eight people and injuring dozens. By the end of 2000 at least 100,000 refugees from the DRC were estimated to be living in the northern province of Likouala. There were serious food shortages. In September the UN High Commissioner for Refugees (UNHCR) estimated that as many as 28,000 refugees were inaccessible and cut off from humanitarian aid, but by the end of 2000 UNHCR had managed to gain access to most areas.

AI delegates attempting to visit refugee camps around Bétou in November were refused permission to enter the camps by the Congolese authorities.

Deaths in custody
On 12 November, 13 detainees died, reportedly of suffocation, in a police cell in the coastal town of Pointe-Noire. Three others were admitted to hospital in a critical state. They had been held in a small cell for several days, reportedly without charge. In December, five police officers went on trial, accused of causing the deaths of the 13 through negligence.

Prison conditions were generally poor, with reports that in several prisons, including those in Pointe-Noire and in the northern town of Ouesso, detainees were deprived of food for several days at a time. Medical care was often unavailable.

Freedom of expression
On 15 July Crepin Casino Mbeto, a journalist for the pro-government newspaper *Le Choc*, was arrested at his home in Ouesso, apparently for having reported on a recent clash in the town between members of the police and the gendarmerie. He was held for several days without charge.

AI country visit
In November AI delegates visited Bétou in the northern Congolese province of Likouala in order to interview refugees from the DRC.

CÔTE D'IVOIRE

REPUBLIC OF CÔTE D'IVOIRE
Head of state: Laurent Gbagbo (replaced General Robert Gueï in October)
Head of government: Affi N'Guessan
Capital: Yamoussoukro
Population: 14.7 million
Official language: French
Death penalty: abolitionist in practice

During 2000 the security forces committed some of the most serious human rights violations to take place in Côte d'Ivoire in three decades. Killings and torture were carried out with total impunity. At least 57 opposition supporters, whose bodies were found in a mass grave in Youpougon in October, were reported to be victims of extrajudicial execution. An inquiry was set up to investigate the massacre but no information about its nature or progress was available by the end of the year, and no arrests or investigation were known to have been initiated.

Background
After the government of President Henri Konan Bédié was overthrown by a military coup on 24 December 1999, General Robert Gueï headed a transitional government which included representatives of the main political parties. In July the military government introduced a new Constitution which was approved by a public referendum. It stipulated that presidential candidates must be born of Ivorian parents and have never held another nationality. This provision focused

public debate on the nationality of Alassane Ouattara, leader of the opposition party, the *Rassemblement des Républicains* (RDR), Republican Assembly. The Supreme Court ruled that he was ineligible to run in the October presidential elections and the December legislative elections on grounds relating to his nationality.

The presidential election was won by Laurent Gbagbo of the *Front populaire Ivoirien* (FPI), Ivorian Popular Front. General Gueï, who was also a candidate in the elections, tried forcibly to reject the results. However, after two days of mass demonstrations in Abidjan, the economic capital, in which several people were killed, he handed over power. In December protesters clashed with the security forces over the exclusion of Alassane Ouattara's candidacy in the legislative elections. President Gbagbo declared a state of emergency. The elections went ahead despite a boycott by RDR supporters and widespread calls for a postponement, and were won by the FPI. Voting did not take place in many northern constituencies because of the boycott and elections there had not been held by the end of the year.

Parallel military units

During the first half of the year military personnel, including unofficial gangs of soldiers known as the *Camora* or the Red Brigades, committed a wide range of human rights violations. They killed suspected offenders, sometimes in public, and arrested, ill-treated and threatened others, including critics of the government. Sometimes abuses took place in public or at the *Primature*, the Head of State's offices.

☐ Several times in the first three months of the year officers raided Douakro, the birthplace of former President Konan Bédié, assaulted his relatives and seized money and valuables that the new government considered had been obtained fraudulently.

☐ In May Thomas N'Dri, a lawyer, was forcibly taken by soldiers from his office and detained for several hours at a military camp in Akouedo, near Abidjan, apparently in an attempt to extort money from him.

☐ Also in May soldiers detained and beat several journalists from *La Référence* newspaper.

Excessive use of force and extrajudicial executions

The security forces reportedly killed protesters and extrajudicially executed political opponents.

☐ In Abidjan, on 24 October, General Gueï's presidential guard fired on hundreds of peaceful demonstrators who were calling on the military government to respect the results of the presidential election two days previously. The security forces also fired at demonstrators who had fled into a lagoon at Carena, in Abidjan. The bodies of more than 20 men and women were subsequently retrieved from the lagoon, some of them with bullet wounds.

☐ On 25 and 26 October dozens of suspected sympathizers of the RDR were arrested, some at their homes, by the gendarmerie. Subsequently, 57 bodies were found in a mass grave in Youpougon, in north Abidjan. Two survivors reported that the detainees had been taken to a gendarmerie commando camp at Abobo, in north Abidjan, where most of them were killed. The few surviving detainees were forced to load the bodies onto a lorry to be taken to an area of wasteland at Youpougon. Before they were buried, the security forces reportedly fired further shots to kill any who were still alive. When the mass grave was discovered shortly afterwards, the new civilian government announced that an inquiry would investigate the killings. However, by the end of the year no information had been made available about the nature or progress of the inquiry, and no arrests or investigation of alleged perpetrators had been carried out despite compelling evidence.

Torture/ill-treatment

Torture and ill-treatment of detainees, resulting in at least three deaths, was also reported.

☐ In September, three armed forces officers, including Staff Sergeant Souleymane Diomandé, reportedly died as a result of torture. They were among about 30 officers detained at the Akouedo military camp in Abidjan who were alleged to have attacked General Gueï's residence on 18 September. Members of General Gueï's presidential guard reportedly tied them down onto barbed wire and trampled on them in the presence of senior military justice officials. An internal inquiry was opened into the deaths but no information about its progress was made public by the end of 2000.

☐ In December scores of detainees reported being beaten, burned or raped. On 4 and 5 December hundreds of people were arrested after they protested at the blocking of Alassane Ouattara's candidacy in the legislative elections. AI considered some of those arrested to be prisoners of conscience, arrested solely because of their suspected support for the RDR or their ethnic origin, since the RDR receives much of its support from Muslim northerners. In December an AI delegation visited detainees held at the Police Academy in Abidjan. Most bore visible traces of injuries and burns, and many said they had been thrown on a fire or beaten with belts and clubs. Some women detainees said that, after their arrest, police had handed them over to RDR opponents who had raped them. Many people had witnessed these rapes. After AI published its concerns, President Gbagbo ordered an inquiry which concluded that the rapes had occurred. The President said that the perpetrators would be punished.

AI country report and visits

Report
- Côte d'Ivoire: Some military personnel believe they have impunity above the law (AI Index: AFR 31/003/2000)

Visits
In May AI sent a delegation to Côte d'Ivoire, led by its Secretary General, Pierre Sané, which met General Gueï and carried out research. A further research visit was carried out in November.

CROATIA

REPUBLIC OF CROATIA
Head of state: Stjepan Mesić
Head of government: Ivica Račan
Capital: Zagreb
Population: 4.8 million
Official language: Croatian
Death penalty: abolitionist for all crimes
2000 treaty ratifications/signatures: Optional Protocol to the UN Women's Convention

Returns of Serb refugees to Croatia increased, although concern about their sustainable reintegration into their pre-war communities remained. The new authorities made considerable efforts to increase cooperation with the International Criminal Tribunal for the former Yugoslavia (Tribunal). A number of Croat and Bosnian Croat military and paramilitary leaders were arrested on suspicion of having committed war crimes in Croatia and Croat-held areas of Bosnia-Herzegovina; scores of Croatian Serb returnees were also arrested on outstanding war crimes charges.

Background

General elections were held in January 2000 and resulted in a landslide victory for a coalition of six opposition parties over the governing *Hrvatska demokratska zajednica* (HDZ), Croatian Democratic Union. Presidential elections, held in February, were similarly won by an opposition politician, Stjepan Mesić. The new government announced its intention to improve Croatia's human rights record, in particular its willingness to enable all Serb refugees to return to their country freely. In November the lower house of Parliament adopted a number of amendments to the Constitution, which limited the powers of the President and established wider-ranging control by Parliament over the government.

In September the Parliamentary Assembly of the Council of Europe closed its monitoring procedure, as it considered that Croatia had mostly honoured the commitments regarding democratization and human rights which it had undertaken when joining the Council of Europe in 1996 and had implemented the provisions of the Dayton and Erdut peace agreements. In November negotiations started between the government and the European Commission on the establishment of a stabilization and association agreement as a first step towards future European Union membership.

In May Croatia joined the North Atlantic Treaty Organization (NATO) Partnership for Peace.

Refugee returns

According to statistics of the UN High Commissioner for Refugees (UNHCR), during 2000 more than 18,000 Croatian Serbs returned to the country under the Return Programme, a decree adopted by the Croatian Parliament in 1998. It was estimated that thousands of others returned spontaneously. The increase in returns appeared to be a result of the new government's announced resolve to accelerate the return process and to remove legal and political obstacles that had hampered returns in previous years.

A number of new or amended laws regulating return and reintegration were passed. For instance in June an amended reconstruction law was adopted by Parliament, which removed discriminatory regulations included in the previous version. However, the law was subsequently further amended, giving rise to concern that it might still discriminate against Croatian Serbs in its system for setting priorities.

The inaction of many local housing committees, tasked under the Return Programme to process returnees' applications for the return of private property, continued throughout 2000. By the end of the year, in about 30 per cent of these cases, repossession had taken place. This inaction arose partly from the lack of clarity in how various provisions of the Return Programme should be implemented, as well as legal inconsistencies in the Return Programme. In some parts of the country — primarily eastern Slavonia — the legal situation was confusing as entirely different property laws were applied to enable the return of Croatians.

However, in many cases political obstruction appeared to underlie the failure to reinstate Serbs in their property. For instance, in September, the UNHCR and Organization for Security and Co-operation in Europe (OSCE) missions presented the government with a list of 88 cases of illegal double occupancy of returnees' houses, asking it to urgently resolve these as a first step. By the end of 2000, only seven households had reportedly been reinstated as a result of this initiative. In the Knin area, where 25 cases of double occupancy had been reported to the authorities, only two cases were resolved.

Prosecutions for war crimes

The new government made immediate and significant efforts to ensure fuller cooperation with the Tribunal.

In March the authorities surrendered a Bosnian Croat, Mladen Naletilić, to the custody of the Tribunal. He had been indicted for war crimes in Mostar in Bosnia-Herzegovina, and the Tribunal had repeatedly requested his transfer from Croatia, where he was imprisoned pending trial for other crimes.

In April the Croatian Parliament adopted a declaration on cooperation with the Tribunal, pledging to hand over all documents in the government's possession that could be used as evidence by the prosecution or the defence. In addition, the declaration confirmed the Tribunal's jurisdiction over crimes under international law committed during and after the armed conflict. Previously, the Croatian authorities had disputed such jurisdiction for crimes committed after Operations Flash and Storm in 1995. In April, Tribunal investigators were allowed for the first time to exhume a mass grave site near Gospić, thought to contain bodies of Serb civilians executed in 1991. Nevertheless, in November the Tribunal's Prosecutor told the UN Security Council that several requests for information from the Croatian government were still outstanding, including some for access to witnesses and documents in connection with Operation Storm.

In August unidentified perpetrators killed former special policeman Milan Levar, apparently in retaliation for his widely publicized statements implicating local Croatian military and police officers in the killings of Serbs in Gospić in 1991, and his open cooperation with Tribunal investigators. Despite the fact that the Tribunal had expressed concern about Milan Levar's safety in a letter to the Croatian Minister of the Interior in 1998, it appeared that the Gospić police had never been formally instructed to protect him. The killing met with official condemnation and a police investigation was opened immediately, although nobody had been charged by the end of 2000.

In September, five Croatian Army officers were arrested in Gospić and an investigation into their suspected involvement in war crimes in 1991 was conducted by the Rijeka County investigative judge. Based on evidence given by these suspects, another mass grave site near Udbina — west of Gospić — was identified in December. The bodies of 18 people, presumed to be Serb civilians, were exhumed.

Also in September, police arrested two former officers of the Bosnian Croat intelligence services who were suspected of having participated in the killing of over 100 Bosniac (Bosnian Muslim) civilians in the village of Ahmići in central Bosnia in 1993. These men had apparently been in hiding in the town of Zadar since 1998. Two local Croatian police officers were charged with providing them with false identity papers and driving licences, but were acquitted in November for lack of evidence.

Police also arrested scores of Croatian Serbs for alleged war crimes. Many of those arrested had returned under the Return Programme and some had apparently previously received confirmation from the Interior Ministry that they had no outstanding criminal records or had been granted amnesty. AI was concerned that in several cases the arrests were reportedly based on indictments brought during the armed conflict in which large groups of individuals were charged together, and that some of the charges might have been arbitrarily defined.

▫ Jovanka Nenadović, a 67-year-old Croatian Serb woman, was arrested in Pakrac in October for allegedly participating in war crimes against Croatian civilians in that area. Before her arrest she had been a refugee in the Republika Srpska in Bosnia-Herzegovina, but she had visited her home in Pakrac several times. An indictment against her, which was issued in 1999, appeared to be solely based on hearsay evidence given by a local witness, now deceased. Because of her poor health Jovanka Nenadović was transferred to the Zagreb prison hospital pending trial.

▫ In July the Osijek County Court acquitted five Croatian Serbs of war crimes after a second retrial. The men, all from the eastern Slavonian village of Šodolovci, had been charged in 1994 with the indiscriminate shelling of surrounding villages. Both their original trial and their first retrial were flawed by violations of international fair trial standards and of domestic criminal procedure.

▫ In June the retrial of Croatian Serb Mirko Graorac ended with his renewed conviction. He received a reduced sentence of 15 years' imprisonment. AI had criticized the original trial proceedings, which were held in 1996, for serious violations of his right to a fair trial. The renewed conviction appeared to be solely based on evidence given by prosecution witnesses, several of whom had identified the accused in flawed identification procedures held during the original investigation and trial proceedings. In addition, no investigation was ever conducted into allegations that Mirko Graorac had been tortured after his arrest in 1995.

Unresolved 'disappearances'

The fate and whereabouts of thousands of people who "disappeared" during the war years remained unknown. Despite large-scale exhumations, mostly of mass graves in eastern Slavonia, more than 1,500 Croats were still unaccounted for. Some 600 Croatian Serbs were still missing since Operations Flash and Storm in 1995. The slowness with which cases were resolved was to a large degree due to the lack of progress in negotiations between the government commissions on missing persons of the Federal Republic of Yugoslavia (FRY) and Croatia, which met twice during 2000.

In November AI called on newly elected FRY President Vojislav Koštunica to transfer three indicted men who remained on FRY territory to the Tribunal. The three, who were officers in the then Yugoslav People's Army, were allegedly responsible for the abduction of some 260 men from the hospital in Vukovar, after the town fell in November 1991, and their subsequent execution. The bodies of scores of victims were never found.

CUBA

REPUBLIC OF CUBA
Head of state and government: Fidel Castro Ruz
Capital: Havana
Population: 11.2 million
Official language: Spanish
Death penalty: retentionist
2000 treaty ratifications/signatures: Optional Protocol to the UN Children's Convention on the involvement of children in armed conflict; Optional Protocol to the UN Women's Convention

Individuals and groups peacefully exercising their rights to freedom of expression, association and assembly continued to face repression. Some conditional releases of prisoners of conscience gave rise to hopes that the attitude of the Cuban government towards dissidents might be thawing, but new sentences and a serious escalation in repression during the closing months of 2000 discouraged such optimism. Journalists, political opponents and human rights defenders were subjected to severe harassment. Several hundred people, at least 13 of whom were prisoners of conscience, remained imprisoned for political offences. The authorities continued to use short term detention, house arrest, threats and harassment to stifle and discourage political dissent. The courts continued to apply the death penalty.

Background

In Cuba, repression of dissent is legitimized by the Constitution and the Penal Code. Some offences against state security, such as "enemy propaganda", as well as offences against authority, such as "disrespect", have been widely applied to silence critics. Others, like "dangerousness", are ill-defined and open to politically motivated misuse. At times, dissidents have been convicted of criminal offences believed to have been fabricated in order to discredit them or their organization or in retaliation for peaceful expression of their beliefs. Detained dissidents have on occasion been held for long periods without trial, or convicted after procedures that did not meet international standards for fair trial.

The US embargo against Cuba continued. The Cuban government has traditionally argued that it is justified in depriving dissidents of fundamental freedoms of expression, association and assembly in order to maintain the unity of the country against hostile forces abroad. Although AI's mandate does not permit it to take a position on the US embargo against Cuba or any other type of sanction, AI recognizes that the embargo has increased hardship within Cuba and has contributed, for example, to poor prison conditions. However, AI maintains that all states, irrespective of any external threat, are obliged to fulfil the duties laid out in the Universal Declaration of Human Rights, including the duty to respect fundamental freedoms.

Prisoners of conscience

At least 13 identified prisoners of conscience were held at the end of 2000. AI was also investigating the cases of numerous possible prisoners of conscience, including a further 13 individuals arrested during the escalation in repression at the end of the year.

☐ Angel Moya Acosta and Julia Cecilia Delgado were convicted of "disrespect" and sentenced to a year's imprisonment each after being detained in mass arrests that took place in the days leading up to the anniversary of the Universal Declaration of Human Rights in December (see below).

☐ Víctor Rolando Arroyo Carmona, a journalist, was sentenced to six months' imprisonment in January for collecting toys which he planned to give away to children. He was convicted of hoarding. His conviction appeared to be motivated by his work for the independent press agency *Unión de Periodistas y Escritores Cubanos Independientes*, Union of Cuban Independent Journalists and Writers, and his reported links with exile groups in Miami, USA, opposed to the government. His arrest in January took place during a period of clamp-down on dissidents, in the aftermath of the Ibero-American Summit in Havana. He was released in July after serving his sentence.

☐ In July Nestor Rodríguez Lobaina, president of the unofficial *Movimiento de Jóvenes Cubanos por la Democracia*, Cuban Youth Movement for Democracy, was convicted of "disrespect", "public disorder", and "damages". Eddy Alfredo Mena y González, another member of the movement, stood trial with him on the same charges. Nestor Rodríguez was sentenced to six years and two months' imprisonment, while Eddy Alfredo Mena was sentenced to five years and one month.

☐ Dr Oscar Elías Biscet González, president of the *Fundación Lawton de Derechos Humanos,* Lawton Foundation for Human Rights, a humanitarian organization considered illegal by the Cuban authorities, was sentenced to three years' imprisonment on 25 February. He was initially arrested on 3 November 1999 and charged with "insult to the symbols of the homeland", which carries a maximum sentence of one year's imprisonment. The charge was reportedly brought against him because he hung a Cuban flag sideways on his balcony during a press conference at his home on 28 October 1999. The prosecutor's petition against him, issued in February 2000, included two further charges – "public disorder" and "instigation to commit a crime".

Releases

Several prisoners of conscience were conditionally released.

☐ Marta Beatriz Roque, Felix Bonne Carcasés and René Gómez Manzano, three of the so-called "Group of Four", were conditionally released in May. The four members of the *Grupo de Trabajo de la Disidencia Interna para el Análisis de la Situación Socio-Económica Cubana*, Internal Dissidents' Working Group for the Analysis of the Cuban Socio-Economic Situation, had been held in custody since July 1997. They were sentenced in 1999 to between three-and-a-half and five years' imprisonment on a charge of sedition, under state security legislation. The fourth member of the group, Vladimiro Roca Antúnez, remained in prison.

☐ Orestes Rodríguez Horruitiner, sentenced to four years' imprisonment in 1997 for "enemy propaganda" was conditionally released in April after serving part of his sentence. He was prosecuted after publications considered by the authorities to be counter-revolutionary were found at his home.

Dissidents detained without trial

A number of members and supporters of opposition groups were detained without trial. More than 100 were rounded up and held briefly in the days around 10 December.

☐ Maritza Lugo Fernández, vice-president of the unauthorized *Partido Democrático 30 de Noviembre "Frank País"*, "Frank País" 30 November Democratic Party, was arrested on 23 December 1999. She planned to participate in a religious procession to celebrate Christmas but was detained along with six others, all of whom were released within a few days. She went on hunger strike twice in protest against her arrest and continued detention without charge. She was eventually charged with "public disorder", but was not tried. She was released on 1 June, more than five months after her arrest. Maritza Lugo Fernández was rearrested on 15 December and remained in detention at the end of the year.

☐ Angel Moya Acosta and brothers Guido and Ariel Sigler Amaya, all members of the illegal *Movimiento Opción Alternativa*, Alternative Option Movement, were detained on 15 December 1999 after participating in a peaceful demonstration five days earlier in Pedro Betancourt village, Matanzas province, to celebrate the 51st anniversary of the Universal Declaration of Human Rights. Although they were charged with "resistance", "public disorder", and "instigation to commit a crime", no trial ever took place. Guido Sigler Amaya was transferred from prison to house arrest in June, and was freed in July. Ariel Sigler Amaya and Angel Moya Acosta were freed on 7 August. Angel Moya Acosta was rearrested in December and sentenced to one year's imprisonment for "disrespect" (see above).

Death penalty

Cuba maintains the death penalty for a large number of offences. At least eight people were sentenced to death by firing squad in 2000, and at least 20 people were under sentence of death at the end of the year. Concern about the death penalty is exacerbated by the authorities' failure to uphold their own guarantees of fair trial, particularly the right to adequate defence. It is difficult for AI to monitor application of the death penalty in Cuba as sentences and executions are rarely made public.

☐ Jorge Luis Rodríguez Mir, who has consistently maintained his innocence, was sentenced to death for the murder of a policeman in November 1999. Jorge Luis Rodríguez Mir reportedly suffers from schizophrenia and epilepsy and while in prison mutilated his own hands so badly that they had to be amputated.

According to reports, although his medical condition was considered at trial, the authorities decided not to take this into account when giving their verdict, in contravention of international standards.

☐ Osmany Brito Cartaya, Alberto Díaz Pérez, Julio Alberto Morales Montero, Morlaix Nodal Pozo, Reidel Rodríguez Reyes and Héctor Santana Vega were all tried and sentenced to death in February 2000, following a December 1999 escape attempt from the Ciego de Avila Provincial Prison during which five prison guards died. The six men exercised their automatic right of appeal to the People's Supreme Court, which upheld the convictions and the cases then went before the Cuban Council of State. The men were held in Cuba's most secure prison, the National Special Regime Prison in Camaguey province.

☐ Edimir Torres Sifonte was sentenced to death on 25 January for the rape and murder of a young woman. He appealed in May against his conviction, which was reportedly upheld.

☐ José Hassán Rojas was sentenced to death for murder in July. His appeal was before the People's Supreme Court at the end of the year.

Prison conditions

Prison conditions reportedly continued to be poor and in some cases constituted cruel, inhuman or degrading treatment. Many prisoners were said to be in poor health as a result of insanitary conditions and inadequate medical attention.

AI country reports and visits
Reports
- Cuba : Short term detention and harassment of dissidents (AI Index: AMR 25/004/2000)
- Cuba: Prisoners of conscience – New convictions overshadow releases (AI Index: AMR 25/021/2000)

Visits
AI last visited Cuba in 1988. Since then the government has not responded to the organization's requests to be allowed into the country.

CZECH REPUBLIC

CZECH REPUBLIC
Head of state: Václav Havel
Head of government: Miloš Zeman
Capital: Prague
Population: 10 million
Official language: Czech
Death penalty: abolitionist for all crimes
2000 treaty ratifications/signatures: Optional Protocol to the UN Children's Convention on the involvement of children in armed conflict

Police arbitrarily detained and ill-treated dozens of people suspected of participating in protests against the World Bank and the International Monetary Fund (IMF) in September. A number of Roma who were subjected to racist violence were inadequately protected by police officers. Poor conditions in prisons led to widespread peaceful protests.

Arbitrary detention and ill-treatment

Around 850 people were detained in Prague following protests organized to coincide with the annual meeting of the World Bank and the IMF. The demonstrations attracted between 10,000 and 12,000 activists from around the world. Violence erupted when 400 people attempted to break through a police cordon guarding the conference centre where the meeting was being held. Sporadic acts of violence continued into the evening as dozens of activists smashed shop windows in Wenceslas Square. However, the vast majority of those detained had engaged in non-violent protests. A number of those detained were not involved in any unauthorized protest activity and a smaller number were simply incidentally present at the scene of the police action to apprehend protesters. The decision to detain them appears to have been arbitrary.

Many detainees complained about police ill-treatment and submitted medical evidence of injuries caused by the beatings. The police apparently systematically refused detainees the rights to inform a member of their family or a third person of their whereabouts, to be informed about the charges in a language which they could understand, and to contact a lawyer. Detainees were not medically examined after being apprehended and there were reports that some were denied adequate medical care. The vast majority of detainees also appeared to have been detained in the first 24 to 48 hours in overcrowded conditions, without receiving adequate food or water. In several police stations detainees were forced to pass between two lines of police officers who hit many of them.

Roma

A new law on the residence of aliens, which came into force in January, was severely criticized for giving police arbitrary powers. Article 5 lists documents which the police, at their discretion, can demand of an alien applying for residence; it was feared that the power to demand a full list of documents would be used in a discriminatory manner, especially against Roma. In addition, Article 65 gives foreign spouses of Czech nationals the right to permanent residence, but denies this right to spouses of foreigners with permanent residence. Since many benefits and basic social services are linked to permanent residence, many families of foreigners could be denied social benefit or the right to work. Many Roma who were denied Czech citizenship in 1993 when the Czechoslovak Federation was dissolved, and have not acquired it since, were particularly affected by the legislation.

There were reports of racist violence against Roma and allegations that the authorities apparently failed to investigate some incidents effectively.

In February in a bar in Náchod, around 15 skinheads shouted racist insults and attacked five Roma and one other man who was punched in the head, breaking one of his teeth. Gabriela Farkašová, Romani Advisor to the District Government Office and a witness to the attack, managed to leave the bar and call the police. Although the Romani victims identified some of the attackers, the police allegedly failed to detain or even properly register their identities at that time. Subsequently, all of the victims were questioned about the incident and helped to identify one of the attackers from the documentation concerning local skinheads. However, the majority of the skinheads were not local and the police did not show the victims photos of any skinheads from outside the locality. Apparently the police treated the incident as a bar brawl rather than a racist attack.

In August the UN Committee on the Elimination of Racial Discrimination expressed concern about the increasing number of racially motivated attacks against minority groups, particularly Roma, and noted that many such attacks may not even be reported. The Committee also expressed concern about the lack of effectiveness of and confidence in the criminal justice system in preventing and combating racial crimes and the ineffective implementation of existing legislation to prosecute perpetrators of incitement to racial hatred. Concern was also expressed about the degrading treatment minority groups were subjected to by members of the police force. The Committee recommended that the Czech government strengthen measures to improve the enforcement of criminal laws against racially motivated crimes, and continue and strengthen training programs for police and officials in charge of implementing the law on issues related to racially motivated crime.

Prison conditions

In January around 6,000 inmates of several Czech prisons, including Kuřim, Rýnovice, Vinařice, Ostrava-Heřmanice, Valdice, and Pardubice prisons, were involved in hunger strikes and other protests over prison conditions. Their complaints focused on serious overcrowding; some facilities were holding almost twice as many prisoners as they should. This had

DOMINICAN REPUBLIC

DOMINICAN REPUBLIC
Head of state and government: Hipólito Mejía (replaced Leonel Fernández Reyna in May)
Capital: Santo Domingo
Population: 8.4 million
Official language: Spanish
Death penalty: abolitionist for all crimes
2000 treaty ratifications/signatures: Optional Protocol to the UN Women's Convention; Rome Statute of the International Criminal Court

A pattern of unlawful killings by police and military continued in 2000. In many cases, the authorities alleged that the victims were killed in exchanges of gunfire with criminal suspects, but this version was disputed by witness testimony and other evidence. Such cases were normally heard before police or military, rather than civilian, courts. There were also reports of ill-treatment of criminal suspects in police stations, and prisons were extremely overcrowded.

Background
The presidential elections held in May were won by Hipólito Mejía of the *Partido Revolucionario Dominicano*, Revolutionary Dominican Party. The elections were declared free and fair by international observers. Human rights initiatives announced by Hipólito Mejía following his inauguration included the creation of a Commission for the Reform and Modernization of the Armed Forces and the Police and a Military Institute for Human Rights.

Killings by security forces
Killings in disputed circumstances by police and military continued. Some appeared to be extrajudicial executions. In May, the US government halted nearly US$1 million in aid to the Dominican police because of inaction on killings by police.

On 18 June in Guayubín, Monte Cristi province, soldiers pursued and opened fire on a covered truck after it failed to stop at a checkpoint some distance from the border with Haiti. After a chase of several kilometres, the truck crashed. Six Haitians and one Dominican were killed, all but one by multiple gunshot wounds. Numerous other occupants of the vehicle were wounded. A military commission was created to investigate. AI called for the soldiers to be tried before civilian courts, but the case remained within the military justice system, and virtually no information about the proceedings was made public.

Two police officers accused of killing Padre José Antonio Tineo outside his church in August 1998 were, exceptionally, tried in civilian courts following public pressure. One of the officers was sentenced to 15 years' imprisonment for the killing, while the second was acquitted.

Torture/ill-treatment
Reports of beatings of detainees continued. In May, 12 prisoners in Rafey prison in Santiago were said to have been badly beaten by guards. The guards were sent before a police court, and the chief of police announced the formation of a commission to investigate claims of ill-treatment of pre-trial detainees.

There were several reports of killings of detainees by military or police guards, generally in the context of escape attempts.

In Najayo prison on 19 August, three prisoners were shot dead after being taken into custody following an escape attempt. Although an investigation by the Attorney General and Chief of the National Police concluded that excessive force had been used, there was no public information on whether the officers involved had been disciplined or prosecuted.

Harsh conditions
In November, AI assessed conditions in seven of the country's 34 prisons. All the facilities were extremely overcrowded (containing between two and a half and four times their maximum capacity) and in each the conditions constituted cruel, inhuman or degrading treatment. Extreme overcrowding contributed to the deaths of 14 inmates in a fire in La Victoria prison in June.

Skin diseases were rampant and contagious diseases such as tuberculosis were of major concern. Medical care was inadequate. Water and sanitary conditions were also sub-standard in many prisons, contributing to intestinal and other health problems.

Overcoming impunity
There was a breakthrough on impunity issues in 2000, when four men, including two high-ranking military officers, were brought to trial for the 1975 killing of journalist Orlando Martínez Howley. The four were sentenced to 30 years' imprisonment and fined. However, other important cases remained pending, including that of Narciso Gonzalez, who "disappeared" in 1994.

Treatment of Haitians
In August the Inter-American Court of Human Rights considered a request for provisional measures to prohibit mass expulsions of suspected Haitians. Dominican human rights activists who appeared before the Court were subjected to acts of intimidation

and threats by nationalist figures. The Court's resolution was considered only a partial victory by human rights advocates, in that it failed to address the practice of mass expulsions; these continued at the end of the year. The Dominican Republic failed to comply with protection mechanisms ordered by the Court on behalf of the individuals involved.

AI country report and visit
Report
- Dominican Republic: Killings by security forces (AI Index: AMR 27/001/2000)

Visit
- In November, AI representatives visited the Dominican Republic and met government officials, other authorities and members of different sectors of civil society.

EAST TIMOR

EAST TIMOR
Capital: Dili
Population: 0.8 million
Death penalty: abolitionist for all crimes

The legacy of the massive human rights violations and widespread destruction of infrastructure and property by the Indonesian security forces and pro-Indonesian militia in September 1999 continued to impact heavily on East Timor. Under the UN Transitional Administration in East Timor (UNTAET), the process of reconstruction and the establishment of institutions of government and administration proceeded, although delays in some areas contributed to the emergence of new human rights problems. A Special Crimes Unit was established to investigate the hundreds of extrajudicial executions and other human rights violations which took place during 1999. However, progress was slow and although some suspects were indicted, trials had not begun by the end of 2000. Approximately 174,000 East Timorese who fled or who had been forcibly expelled in September 1999 returned to East Timor, although some 100,000 remained in West Timor, Indonesia.

UNTAET
Basic structures of government and administration were established during the year. UNTAET responded to criticism of lack of East Timorese participation in government with a number of measures including the appointment of a joint UNTAET/East Timorese Cabinet and an extension of the legislative body, the National Council, from 15 to 36 members. However, there continued to be concern about insufficient direct participation and consultation with the East Timorese in decision-making, including decisions on new legislation and institutions.

An Ombudsperson with responsibility for investigating complaints against UNTAET officials was appointed, but legislation had not been passed by the end of 2000 and the institution was not operational, giving rise to criticism regarding a lack of accountability for UN officials.

Criminal justice system
Providing access to a fair legal system was recognized as a priority by UNTAET, but progress in establishing a fully functioning criminal justice system was patchy. During 2000, the first East Timorese judges and prosecutors were recruited and received training. Provision was made for four District Courts to be set up, but they were not functioning fully by the end of 2000.

Responsibility for law enforcement lay with the UN Civilian Police (Civpol) Force. A police training academy was opened in March to train a local East Timorese police force to replace Civpol eventually. By the end of 2000, about 100 East Timorese police officers had completed the 12-week training course. A program to refurbish prison facilities was under way and three facilities with a joint capacity of 460 inmates were open by the end of 2000.

Indonesian law, when it conformed with international standards, remained applicable. A new Code of Criminal Procedure was adopted in September but the Indonesian Criminal Procedure Code continued to be applied when provisions in the new Code proved inadequate.

A lack of resources, facilities and trained police and judicial officials contributed to the appearance of new human rights problems. In particular, the partial law and order vacuum led to the emergence of vigilante groups which were in some cases associated with political parties. There were cases of unauthorized detentions, beatings and intimidation of individuals suspected of belonging to pro-Indonesian militias. Relatives of militia members were also harassed and intimidated and, in at least one case, tortured. Returning refugees and members of minority groups such as Muslims or ethnic Chinese were at particular risk. Human rights defenders who publicly criticized the activities of vigilante groups were threatened and harassed.

The lack of capacity of the judicial system to process cases expeditiously gave rise to the risk that the right to fair trial might be contravened, including the right to be tried within a reasonable time or be released. In some cases detainees did not have access to public defenders for weeks after their arrest. In other cases the rights of detainees were contravened because of confusion regarding arrest and detention procedures.

Investigations into past violations
The legal and institutional framework for investigating and prosecuting serious crimes was introduced by UNTAET. Jurisdiction over serious crimes under international law including war crimes, crimes against humanity, torture and sexual offences was established.

A Special Crimes Unit was established to investigate the massive human rights violations which were perpetrated by pro-Indonesian militia and the Indonesian security forces in 1999. However, lack of support and resources contributed to the slow pace of investigations. Only five cases were actively investigated by the Special Crimes Unit. Twelve indictments were issued in relation to these cases in November and December, but by the end of 2000 no one had been brought to justice for crimes committed during 1999.

Some of those charged had been detained for over a year without trial, raising concerns about prolonged periods of pre-trial detention. Suspects in other cases had to be released because lack of capacity prevented the Special Crimes Unit from actively pursuing investigations into their cases.

On the basis of a Memorandum of Understanding on legal cooperation signed with Indonesia in April, UNTAET provided assistance to Indonesia in its investigations into crimes committed in East Timor during 1999. Members of an Indonesian investigation team visited East Timor in July 2000 to collect evidence on five cases. (See Indonesia entry.) A request to Indonesia by UNTAET for the extradition of a militia leader detained in Indonesia was turned down.

AI country report and visit
Report
- East Timor: Building a new country based on human rights (AI Index: ASA 57/005/2000)

Visit
An AI delegation visited East Timor in April and met representatives of UNTAET and East Timorese human rights organizations.

ECUADOR

REPUBLIC OF ECUADOR
Head of state and government: Gustavo Noboa Bejarano (replaced Jamil Mahuad Witt in January)
Capital: Quito
Population: 11.9 million
Official language: Spanish
Death penalty: abolitionist for all crimes
2000 treaty ratifications/signatures: Optional Protocol to the UN Children's Convention on the involvement of children in armed conflict; Inter-American Convention on Forced Disappearance of Persons

Torture and ill-treatment remained a concern. Threats against lawyers and witnesses of human rights violations were frequent. Impunity remained institutionalized. There were reports of possible "disappearances". Transvestites were arbitrarily detained.

Background
In January indigenous groups, trade unions, and grassroots organizations staged mass demonstrations and protests against the government's economic policy, which included making the US dollar, rather than the sucre, the official currency. On 21 January protesters forced President Jamil Mahuad Witt to resign. A National Salvation Junta was formed, which was dissolved almost immediately, and Vice-President Gustavo Noboa Bejarano, backed by the Chief of the Joint Command of the Armed Forces, was appointed to the presidency.

More than 15 army officers were detained because of their role in the ousting of President Jamil Mahuad Witt. The officers were charged with rebellion and detained in army barracks for over four months. By June all had been granted amnesty and released.

The newly appointed President continued with the previous government's economic policy. The US dollar became the official currency and an extensive program of privatization of state-owned enterprises was implemented.

An influx of refugees from the Colombian Putumayo region led to concerns about the future impact the US-backed military aid package, known as *Plan Colombia*, would have on Ecuador once it was implemented in early 2001. (See Colombia entry.)

Human rights during the January uprising
There were serious concerns for the safety of hundreds of people who were arbitrarily detained during the January demonstrations and protests. Among those detained were trade union leaders and leaders of opposition parties. All were released without charge a few days after their detention.

Impunity
Cases of human rights violations involving members of the security forces were not resolved. Many of these

cases were brought before police courts where the vast majority of those responsible for human rights violations were never punished. Disputes of jurisdictional competence between the police and civilian courts delayed the course of legal proceedings and resulted in victims of human rights violations having to wait for years to have access to justice.

⬜ Anibal Alonso Aguas Acosta died in police custody in March 1997. The Constitutional Tribunal ruled that the case fell within the jurisdiction of the police courts. By the end of 2000 the trial of those charged with his death had not yet finished, and there were concerns that delays in the judicial proceedings showed a lack of will to bring those responsible to justice.

⬜ In the case of the attempted extrajudicial execution of Pedro Geovanny Baque Tuárez and the extrajudicial execution of brothers Carlos and Pedro Jaramillo in February 1999, the Supreme Court of Justice decided in July that it should be judged by a civilian court. However, by the end of 2000 no judge had yet been designated to the case in a civilian court.

Unresolved killings
Two Congressmen — Jaime Hurtado González and Pablo Vincente Tapia — as well as Jaime Hurtado's assistant, Wellington Borja Nazareno, were shot dead in February 1999. Their killing remained unresolved. Three men detained in connection with the killings soon after the murder were convicted of illicit association. One of them, Serguey Merino, sentenced to six years on illicit association charges, was reported to be innocent. Serguey Merino was also charged with terrorism and illegal possession of firearms, but the courts shelved the case in relation to these two charges for lack of evidence. Serguey Merino and the other two suspects still faced a trial for murder. There were credible allegations that the actual authors of the crime were linked to authorities whom Congressman Jaime Hurtado González was investigating for alleged money laundering and drug trafficking.

Torture/ill-treatment
Torture and ill-treatment remained widespread. Methods of torture and ill-treatment reported included kicking in the face, stamping on feet, burning, and electric shocks on genitals, tongue and chest, as well as beatings.

⬜ Wilfrido Jaramillo Mera, brother of Carlos and Pedro Jaramillo who were extrajudicially executed in 1999 (see above), was detained in November on suspicion of robbery in the town of Manta, Manabí province. During the police interrogation he was blindfolded and was given electric shocks on the genitals and close to the heart.

Possible extrajudicial executions
There was serious concern at the number of possible extrajudicial executions in the city of Guayaquil during 2000. One human rights organization alone documented 18 cases of people whose bodies were found in the city's outskirts and who had been shot dead in circumstances which suggested they might have been extrajudicially executed. The majority had a criminal record and many showed signs of torture.

Prison conditions
In March an AI delegation visited the Provisional Detention Centre in the city of Guayaquil. The Centre holds detainees under investigation by the police who by law should be released or charged within 24 hours. AI found the conditions in which these detainees were held to be cruel, inhuman and degrading. The Centre had two cells for women but no female guards. The main cell is approximately 15m x 10m. At the time of the delegation's visit there were approximately 120 people detained in the main cell. Many had spent more than two months in the Centre.

Harassment of lawyers and witnesses
There were continued reports of threats and harassment of those working on human rights cases.

⬜ Julio Edison Román Muñoz was detained in February by two officers against whom he had filed a complaint for having tortured him. The two officers threatened him in detention before releasing him without charge.

⬜ The relatives and lawyers of Pedro Baque and the Jaramillo brothers (see above) were constantly threatened throughout 2000. By September, three of the lawyers had been granted military protection by the Attorney General.

Arbitrary detention of transvestites
Nine transvestite sex workers were detained for over three weeks in July on charges which are not punishable with imprisonment. AI considered that they were detained solely because they were transvestites and called for their immediate and unconditional release. According to reports, many transvestites in Ecuador are subjected to persecution by the police and are targeted for imprisonment, simply on the ground of their sexual orientation. In November 1997 homosexual acts between consenting adults were decriminalized in Ecuador.

Possible 'disappearances'
Elias Elint López Pita was detained by policemen in November in the town of Ambato and was not seen after that. The police denied knowledge of the arrest. Luis Alberto Shining Laso, who testified that he had been held in the same cell as Elias Elint López at the police Provisional Detention Centre in Ambato, was abducted a few days after he gave evidence before the prosecutor investigating the possible "disappearance". By the end of 2000 the whereabouts of Elias Elint López and Luis Alberto Shining Laso remained unknown.

AI country reports and visit
Reports
- Ecuador: Impunity — The long road to justice (AI Index: AMR 28/007/2000)
- Ecuador: Pedro Baque Tuárez and the Jaramillo brothers — Another case of human rights impunity (AI Index: AMR 28/013/2000)
- Ecuador: Arbitrary detention of transvestites (AI Index: AMR 28/014/2000)

Visit
An AI delegation visited Ecuador in March. The delegation met Ecuadorian officials as well as human rights organizations and victims of human rights abuses.

EGYPT

ARAB REPUBLIC OF EGYPT
Head of state: Muhammad Hosni Mubarak
Head of government: 'Atif Muhammad 'Ubayd
Capital: Cairo
Population: 68.4 million
Official language: Arabic
Death penalty: retentionist
2000 treaty ratifications/signatures: Rome Statute of the International Criminal Court

Thirty prisoners of conscience were sentenced to between six months' and five years' imprisonment; 20 remained held at the end of the year. Eight prisoners of conscience sentenced in 1999 remained in detention at the end of 2000. While hundreds of suspected supporters of banned Islamist groups were released, thousands of others, including possible prisoners of conscience, remained held without charge or trial. Others served sentences imposed after grossly unfair trials before military courts. Torture and ill-treatment of detainees continued to be widespread; the majority of cases occurred in police stations. Prison conditions amounting to cruel, inhuman or degrading treatment were reported. At least 79 people were sentenced to death and at least 22 people were executed.

Background
Hundreds of supporters of the opposition were detained during the months leading up to parliamentary elections which were held between mid-October and mid-November. The vast majority of the detainees were alleged members of the banned Muslim Brothers organization. A ruling of the Supreme Constitutional Court in July led to legislation being amended to require judicial supervision of the election process inside the polling stations.

During the elections excessive use of force by the security forces resulted in civilians being killed and injured during demonstrations protesting at restricted access to polling stations. An AI delegate was beaten and kicked in front of a polling station in the Shubra al-Khaima district of Cairo. He was assaulted by several men who were acting under the orders of or in collusion with the security forces. Several journalists covering the elections were ill-treated in similar circumstances. Candidates of the ruling National Democratic Party gained an overwhelming majority of seats in parliament. In May the state of emergency, declared in 1981, was extended for a further three-year period.

In January sectarian violence in al-Kushh, a village in Upper Egypt, left 20 Coptic Christians and one Muslim dead. The trial of 96 men charged in connection with the killings began in June and was continuing at the end of the year. All detained defendants were released without bail in December.

Freedom of expression and association
Hundreds of possible prisoners of conscience — including members of non-governmental organizations (NGOs) and political activists — were held for weeks in so-called preventive detention; the majority of them were released without being formally charged.

Civil institutions such as political parties, NGOs, professional associations and trade unions, and the news media, continued to face legal restrictions and government control. In June the Supreme Constitutional Court found that the NGO law of 1999 was unconstitutional on procedural grounds. In July, the authorities informed the Egyptian Organization for Human Rights (EOHR) that its registration as an NGO had been postponed for "security reasons".

The Political Party Committee, a governmental body, decided in May to freeze the activities of the Islamist *Hizb al-'Amal* (Labour Party) and to suspend the publication of its newspaper *al-Sha'ab* (The People). In September the Supreme Administrative Court ruled that the ban on the newspaper had to be lifted. However, publication of *al-Sha'ab* had not resumed by the end of the year.

Human rights defenders
Human rights defenders continued to be targeted.

◻ In February the Public Prosecution Office announced that the case against Hafez Abu Sa'ada, General Secretary of the EOHR, would be referred to trial before the Emergency Supreme State Security Court. However, Hafez Abu Sa'ada subsequently received oral assurances that his case would not be pursued. Investigations against Hafez Abu Sa'ada began in November 1998 following an EOHR report on human rights violations in the predominantly Coptic Christian village of al-Kushh and led to his detention for several days.

◻ In June human rights defender Dr Sa'ad Eddin Ibrahim, Director of the Ibn Khaldun Center for Development Studies and lecturer at the American University in Cairo, was arrested at his home in Cairo. Several of the Ibn Khaldun Center's staff, including the finance director Nadia 'Abd al-Nur, and people affiliated with the institution were also arrested and detained without being formally charged until their release in August. In November the trial of 28 people charged with offences including disseminating false information abroad, unauthorized funding, forgery and bribery opened before the Supreme State Security Court. The charges related to the conduct of projects promoting participation in elections.

Prisoners of conscience

Prisoners of conscience, including political activists, journalists and members of religious groups, were sentenced to up to five years' imprisonment, in some cases following unfair trials that did not allow for appeals.

▫ In November the Supreme Military Court sentenced 15 alleged Muslim Brothers to between three and five years' imprisonment; five others were acquitted. The 20 doctors, lawyers and other professionals, most of whom held leading positions in professional bodies, had been detained since October 1999. The Supreme Military Court had been due to deliver its verdict in July, but this was postponed until November in an obvious attempt to prevent the defendants from participating in the parliamentary elections.

▫ In April an appeal court upheld the sentences of two years' imprisonment of Magdi Hussein and Salah Badawi, in a criminal libel case brought against journalists of *al-Sha'ab* by a government minister. Both were released in an amnesty in December.

▫ In July the Sohag Criminal Court sentenced Sourial Gayed Ishaq, a 37-year-old Coptic Christian, to three years' imprisonment for publicly insulting Islam.

▫ In September, the Emergency State Security Court for Misdemeanours sentenced Manal Wahid Mana', the alleged leader of a religious group, and 12 of her followers to prison terms of between six months and five years. Accusations against the group included attributing divine status to a late Sufi religious leader.

Detention under emergency legislation

Hundreds of political detainees were released and hardly any new cases of administrative detention under emergency legislation were reported. However, thousands of suspected members or supporters of banned Islamist groups arrested in previous years, including possible prisoners of conscience, remained administratively detained without charge or trial. Some had been held for more than a decade. Others were acquitted by military or (Emergency) Supreme State Security Courts, but remained in detention.

▫ Mahmoud Mubarak Ahmad, a doctor, had been arrested in January 1995 by officers of the State Security Intelligence (SSI) and accused of membership of an illegal Islamist organization. A court had ordered his release, but instead of being released he was issued with a new detention order and remained in prison. In 1999 the UN Working Group on Arbitrary Detention judged his administrative detention to be arbitrary and in conflict with Egypt's international obligations.

Prison conditions

In September the Ministry of the Interior announced that flogging as a punishment in prisons would be outlawed.

Thousands of detainees continued to be held in prisons where conditions amounted to cruel, inhuman or degrading treatment. Several prisoners reportedly died as a result of diseases for which they received little or no treatment.

Scores of Islamist activists in administrative detention were reportedly held in overcrowded conditions with inadequate sanitation and health care and poor quality food. As a result illnesses including tuberculosis and skin diseases were common. Several prisoners reportedly died as a result of diseases which received little or no treatment.

Hundreds of political detainees continued to be denied the right to visits by lawyers and family members. A ban on any visits imposed for more than five years remained in force in three prisons holding political detainees.

Torture/ill-treatment

Torture in police stations continued to be widespread. The decrease in arrests of alleged members of armed Islamist groups was reflected in a significant reduction in reports of systematic torture of political suspects. The most common torture methods reported were electric shocks, beatings, suspension by the wrists or ankles and various forms of psychological torture, including death threats and threats of rape or sexual abuse of the detainee or a female relative.

▫ In March Salha Sayid Qasim was detained at Giza Police Headquarters in connection with a criminal investigation. She reported that in detention she was blindfolded, beaten, whipped, suspended by her arms and subjected to electric shocks.

Deaths in custody

Several people died in custody in circumstances suggesting that torture or ill-treatment may have caused or contributed to their deaths.

▫ In February the Public Prosecution Office announced the referral of five police officers to a criminal court in connection with the killing of Ahmad Muhammad 'Issa in Wadi Natroun Prison in February. Torture was reported to have caused or contributed to his death. The outcome of the trial was not known at the end of the year.

Harassment of victims and relatives

Victims of torture and their relatives who made complaints continued to report harassment.

▫ Relatives of Ahmed Mohammad Mahmud Tamam, a 19-year-old student who died in police custody in July 1999 in circumstances suggesting that torture had caused or contributed to his death, alleged that during 2000 they had been threatened in an attempt to force them to withdraw their complaint.

Inadequate investigation

Despite the fact that hundreds of victims of torture had filed complaints with the authorities over the past decade, no prompt and impartial investigations which met international standards had been carried out by the end of 2000.

▫ By the end of the year the Alexandria prosecution office had not yet decided how to proceed in the case of Muhammad Badr al-Din Gom'a Isma'il, who had been tortured and forced to make a false confession in 1996 and 1997.

Excessive use of force

Excessive use of force by the security forces resulted in civilians being injured and killed in the context of demonstrations. Mass demonstrations in Cairo, consisting mostly of students, took place in May in protest at the publication of a novel and in October in solidarity with the Palestinian people. Several people, including young people, were killed in demonstrations protesting at the security forces restricting access to several polling stations during the parliamentary elections.

◻ On 14 November, three people were killed in clashes between demonstrators and the security forces in al-'Amara village in Qalyubiya province.

Forcible return
There were reports of the forcible return of Egyptian nationals suspected of being affiliated to armed Islamist groups.

◻ In May, Ayman Kamal al-Din was reportedly forcibly returned from Lebanon to Egypt where he was feared to be at risk of human rights violations.

Death penalty
The death penalty continued to be used extensively. At least seven women and 72 men were sentenced to death by criminal courts during 2000, the majority of them on charges of murder. At least six women and 16 men were executed, including two men who had been sentenced following unfair trials *in absentia*.

Armed groups
In October, two members of an armed Islamist group were killed when members of the security forces raided a flat in Aswan. The circumstances surrounding the deaths suggested that the two men may have been extrajudicially executed. No further incidents of clashes between security forces and armed Islamist groups were reported. The leadership of the main armed Islamist group, *al-Gama'a al-Islamiya*, Islamic Group, maintained that it had halted its armed operations.

Islamist groups failed to publicly revoke death threats issued in previous years against civilians whom they considered political and ideological enemies, including the writer Naguib Mahfuz and university professor Nasr Hamed Abu Zeid.

AI country report and visits
Report
• Egypt: Muzzling civil society (AI Index: MDE 12/021/2000)
Visits
In March and November AI delegates visited Egypt and met victims of human rights violations, representatives of human rights organizations and other members of civil society. They also met government officials and raised concerns about the lack of proper investigations of and preventive measures against human rights violations. AI delegates observed trials before the Supreme Military Court and the Supreme State Security Court.

EL SALVADOR

REPUBLIC OF EL SALVADOR
Head of state and government: Francisco Flores
Capital: San Salvador
Population: 6.2 million
Official language: Spanish
Death penalty: abolitionist for ordinary crimes
2000 treaty ratifications/signatures: Optional Protocol to the UN Children's Convention on the involvement of children in armed conflict

Efforts to end impunity for past human rights violations suffered a serious setback when the Supreme Court of Justice declared the General Amnesty Law to be constitutional. Work by a non-governmental organization on behalf of children who "disappeared" during the armed conflict (1980 to 1992) did not receive official support. The *Policía Nacional Civil* (PNC), National Civil Police, were responsible for human rights violations including killings of civilians and ill-treatment of demonstrators.

Background
The main opposition party, the *Frente Farabundo Martí de Liberación Nacional*, Farabundo Martí National Liberation Front, won the largest number of seats in parliamentary elections in March.

More than 1,000 members of the PNC faced investigation and there was official confirmation that members of the PNC were involved in criminal activities such as kidnapping and robbery. Lack of confidence in the police and fear of reprisals meant that victims did not always report violations.

The judicial system was also the subject of review, leading to recommendations that some judges should be removed from their posts. Serious concerns about the performance of the Office of the Procurator for Human Rights persisted throughout 2000 (see below).

Impunity
Impunity for past human rights violations continued to be a serious concern. The judicial authorities failed to implement the recommendations of international bodies.

◻ In March the Inter-American Commission on Human Rights (IACHR) concluded that the state had violated the rights to life, to justice and to judicial protection enshrined in the American Convention on Human Rights in the case of Archbishop Oscar Arnulfo Romero, who was assassinated in March 1980. The Commission recommended that the state should thoroughly and effectively investigate the murder of Monsignor Romero; bring those responsible to justice in a fair and impartial trial; implement reparations; and bring national legislation into line with the Convention, which would involve annulling the 1993 General Amnesty Law.

The authorities dismissed the decision, stating that "the decisions of the Commission are not binding, they are recommendations", and took no steps to implement the recommendations.

☐ The authorities failed to implement any of the recommendations made by the Inter-American Commission on Human Rights in December 1999 in the case of the extrajudicial execution of six Jesuits, a domestic helper and her daughter by military personnel in 1989. They also resisted appeals from the *Compañía de Jesús*, Society of Jesus, (Jesuits) to bring to justice those involved in planning and ordering the murders, among them a former President of El Salvador. Military personnel who carried out the murders were tried and sentenced to prison terms in 1991, but were released in 1993 when the General Amnesty Law was approved.

The decision on the General Amnesty Law (see below) opened the door for proceedings to move ahead and the Attorney General made some attempts to take action on the case. These did not prosper because, for example, the wrong procedure was invoked. In December the Attorney General's Office was reported to have conducted a study which concluded that it could proceed to seek the definitive dismissal of the charges against the suspects because a period exceeding 10 years had elapsed since the crime was committed and no evidence had been brought against them. The Attorney General then requested the Third Magistrate's Court of San Salvador to effect this dismissal. The judge ruled that those alleged to have been the intellectual authors of the killings would not face charges because the event had happened over 10 years earlier and therefore, according to national law, criminal responsibility had lapsed. The judge did, however, recognize that the amnesty law did not apply to the suspects, following the October ruling of the Supreme Court.

The General Amnesty Law

On 3 October the Supreme Court of Justice issued a decision on a petition to declare the 1993 General Amnesty Law unconstitutional. The Court ruled that the law was constitutional but that in cases involving military personnel or civil servants involved in crimes which contravened the Constitution and had been committed between 1989 and 1994, it should be judicial officials who decide whether to prosecute or not. Although the decision would allow some cases to be prosecuted, the majority of human rights violations committed during the armed conflict, including massacres in which hundreds of civilians were killed, took place before 1989.

The Inter-American Commission on Human Rights had made it clear in a number of decisions that amnesty laws "remove the most effective measure for enforcing human rights, i.e., the prosecution and punishment of the violators" and were incompatible with the American Convention on Human Rights.

Office of the Human Rights Procurator

The crisis in the Office of the Human Rights Procurator continued. After a long drawn out process, which included petitions from civil society organizations to remove him and an investigation by the Legislative Assembly, Procurator Eduardo Peñate resigned in January. The Deputy Procurator assumed the post in an acting capacity while a replacement was found. Although a process to elect a new Procurator formally started in July, an appointment had not been made by the end of the year. The election of the new Procurator was the cause of considerable concern as there were clear indications that, contrary to the spirit in which the Office had been created, the process and the post had been thoroughly politicized.

National Civil Police

Members of the police force were responsible for human rights violations including abuse of authority, torture and ill-treatment, and killings of unarmed civilians. In some cases investigations were initiated and charges brought against police officers. However, the sentences imposed often did not reflect the gravity of the violation. The PNC was also responsible for injuring health workers taking part in peaceful demonstrations against the privatization of health care. A journalist covering the demonstration was shot in the legs with rubber bullets and needed hospital treatment. Many people, including patients in neighbouring hospitals, suffered from the effects of tear gas used by the police.

Human rights defenders

Although reports of attacks, death threats or intimidation against human rights defenders were greatly reduced compared to previous years, the authorities continued to accuse human rights defenders and organizations of seeking to damage the institutions of the state or the peace of the country, or of defending delinquents.

Children

The non-governmental *Asociación Pro-Búsqueda de Niñas y Niños Desaparecidos* (*Pro-Búsqueda*), Association *Pro-Búsqueda* for the Search for Disappeared Children, located more children during the year. Its work suffered a setback in September when its proposal that the Legislative Assembly create a commission to investigate the whereabouts of children who "disappeared" during the armed conflict was rejected. The army, which had initially expressed its willingness to participate, changed its position. The commission would have had power to call people to provide information and would have had access to archives which were not open to *Pro-Búsqueda*.

Updates

☐ William Hernández, executive director of the non-governmental organization *Asociación Salvadoreña de Desarrollo Integral para Minorías Sexuales, Entre Amigos*, Salvadoran Association for the Integral Development of Sexual Minorities, Among Friends, was granted police protection following death threats received in 1999. There were further instances of attacks on the organization, including break-ins at their offices during which membership lists were taken.

AI country report and visit
Report
- El Salvador: The Supreme Court ruling is an affront to victims (AI Index: AMR 29/005/2000)

Visit
AI delegates visited El Salvador between September and October to carry out research into human rights violations.

EQUATORIAL GUINEA

REPUBLIC OF EQUATORIAL GUINEA
Head of state: Teodoro Obiang Nguema Mbasogo
Head of government: Angel Serafin Seriche Dougan
Capital: Malabo
Population: 0.4 million
Official languages: Spanish, French
Death penalty: retentionist

Harassment of peaceful political opponents, which has been common for many years, continued throughout 2000. Some prisoners of conscience continued to be held and peaceful political opponents or individuals exercising their right to freedom of expression were arrested and faced ill-treatment by government officials.

Background
The two main opposition parties — *Convergencia para la Democracia Social* (CPDS), Convergence for Social Democracy, and *Unión Popular*, Popular Union — found it increasingly difficult to mobilize their supporters, especially in the continental part of the country where government control is more intense. Against this background, municipal elections in May were marked by very low voter turn-out following a call by three opposition parties to boycott what they called an "electoral farce". This boycott led to a landslide victory for the ruling *Partido Democrático de Guinea Ecuatorial* (PDGE), Equatorial Guinea Democratic Party.

UN Commission on Human Rights
In April the UN Commission on Human Rights examined the report of the UN Special Representative on Equatorial Guinea who had visited the country in November 1999. The Commission urged the government to respect freedom of movement, association and expression. It called on the authorities to adhere to the UN Convention against Torture and to ensure that military jurisdiction (which has frequently been applied to civilians) is strictly limited to military offences committed by military personnel. After this, the authorities appeared to be reluctant to allow the UN Special Representative access to the country and failed to respond to several requests for a visa.

Treatment of Bubi prisoners
In March, some 40 prisoners from the Bubi ethnic group who were convicted after an unfair military trial in 1998 were transferred from the main prison of the capital Malabo, on Bioko Island, to Evinayong, some 500km east of Malabo. This made it very difficult for their families to bring them medicine and food and provide support. AI launched an appeal expressing concern that as the prisoners had to buy their own food, and not all had money to do so, many could soon be nearing starvation. Most of these prisoners had been tortured in pre-trial detention and they had been held for two years in extremely harsh conditions. Many appeared to be prisoners of conscience, arrested solely on account of their ethnic origin.

Conditions for this group of prisoners improved slowly. Their families were given access to them, although the distance and cost made visits rare. The prisoners were allowed to work outside the prison and to meet people from the town. In December the President issued a decree in which he pardoned 14 of these prisoners, including Milagrosa Cheba, the only woman in the group.

Prisoners of conscience
Two members of the *Fuerza Demócrata Republicana* (FDR), Democratic Republican Force, an opposition political party which has been refused official recognition, were held for most of 2000. Mariano Oyono Ndong was sentenced in December 1999 to three years' imprisonment. He was accused of possession of "material of dubious provenance" after the security forces found a two-year-old AI appeal in his home. Antonio Engonga Bibang was also convicted in December 1999 on charges of "insults against the government and the Armed Forces". These two prisoners were pardoned by the President in December.

Four FDR members were arrested in May and reportedly tortured in Malabo. They remained detained without trial until December, when they were confined to their villages in the district of Mongomo.

Torture/ill-treatment
Augusto Mba-Sa Oyana, a businessman with joint Guinean/Spanish nationality, was reportedly tortured in Black Beach prison in Malabo. He was arrested in July on his arrival at Malabo Airport, from Yaoundé, Cameroon, where he resided. It appeared that he was suspected of having links with political opponents living abroad. Augusto Oyana escaped from prison in August but one of his friends, Jesús Miguel Ondó, was arrested, accused of helping him to escape, and reportedly tortured. Jesús Miguel Ondó was released without charge in December.

Threats to freedom of expression
The authorities ill-treated individuals seeking to exercise their right to freedom of expression.

Pedro Nolasko, a journalist, was reported to have been physically assaulted in March by the Secretary General of the Ministry of the Interior after publishing an interview with the leader of an opposition party. In April a newspaper vendor who was trying to sell issues of *La Opinión* — the newspaper published by Pedro Nolasko — inside the building of the General Secretariat of the Government was reported to have been assaulted by the Minister Delegate of the Interior. There was apparently no investigation into these two incidents.

AI country report
- Equatorial Guinea: No free flow of information (AI Index: AFR 24/004/2000)

ERITREA

ERITREA
Head of state and government: Issayas Afewerki
Capital: Asmara
Population: 3.8 million
Official languages: English, Arabic, Tigrinya
Death penalty: retentionist
2000 treaty ratifications/signatures: African Charter on the Rights and Welfare of the Child

A cease-fire in June followed by a peace treaty in December ended the border war with Ethiopia. The UN began to supervise the return to Eritrea of southern areas captured by Ethiopia in heavy new fighting in May. Eritrean troops pulled out of Ethiopian areas they had occupied in May 1998. Each side accused the other of human rights abuses during these occupations, but many of the allegations were difficult to substantiate. Eritrea interned many Ethiopian nationals in make-shift camps. There were reports of detentions and extrajudicial executions of political opponents, which were difficult to verify.

Background
The war with Ethiopia
The border war with Ethiopia resumed in May after a year's tense confrontation along the 1,000-kilometre border. Both sides had continued to expand their forces and to buy weapons. Eritrea continued to conscript nationals for military service, allegedly recruiting some children under 18 years old. Some people tried to evade military service by fleeing the country and several Jehovah's Witnesses were detained when they refused to serve in the armed forces. There was no provision for conscientious objection.

In May Ethiopia attacked and captured large parts of southwestern Eritrea, forcing Eritrean troops out of areas they had occupied since the war began in May 1998. The UN Security Council called for a cease-fire and imposed an arms embargo on both sides. After three weeks of fighting with heavy casualties, a cease-fire was signed in June under the auspices of the Organization of African Unity (OAU). Ethiopian troops withdrew to a buffer zone 25 kilometres from the border. Some 60,000 Eritrean civilians and hundreds of soldiers had fled to Sudan and about 370,000 civilians were internally displaced by the fighting. Despite mutual recriminations and accusations, the cease-fire held and there was no further fighting. Refugees and internally displaced civilians began to return. Almost half the population was at risk of famine.

A formal peace treaty was signed in December in Algeria in the presence of the UN Secretary-General. This provided for UN supervision of the withdrawal of Ethiopian troops and temporary UN administration of the buffer zone, neutral demarcation of the border, and examination of claims by both sides for compensation. The UN Secretary-General promised international help to both sides to recover from the destruction caused by the conflict. In December the UN Mission in Ethiopia and Eritrea (UNMEE) began deploying troops and human rights observers into the Ethiopian-occupied zone.

Ratification of the Geneva Conventions
Eritrea finally signed the Geneva Conventions in July and allowed the International Committee of the Red Cross (ICRC) access to prisoners of war. In December an exchange of prisoners of war and civilian internees began under the auspices of the ICRC, which had previously registered 2,600 Eritrean prisoners of war in Ethiopia and 1,000 Ethiopian prisoners of war in Eritrea.

Constitutional process
In October the National Assembly announced that elections would be held in December 2001 and that an Assembly Committee would draft regulations for the formation of political parties. The only permitted party was the ruling People's Front for Democracy and Justice. Shortly before this announcement, a group of Eritrean intellectuals, mostly living abroad and not attached to opposition groups, had called on the government for more democracy, the abolition of the Special Court, and the fair trial or release of detainees.

Internal armed opposition
Both Eritrea and Ethiopia continued to support opposition groups, both political and armed, in the other country. Information on the activities in Eritrea of the Ethiopian-supported Alliance of National Eritrean Forces, which included the Eritrean Liberation Front-Revolutionary Council and the Sudan-supported Eritrean Islamic Salvation Movement, was difficult to obtain. Allegations by these groups and by the Ethiopian government of killings, torture and detentions of their supporters were impossible to verify with independent evidence.

ETHIOPIA

FEDERAL DEMOCRATIC REPUBLIC OF ETHIOPIA
Head of state: Negasso Gidada
Head of government: Meles Zenawi
Capital: Addis Ababa
Population: 58.8 million
Official language: Amharic
Death penalty: retentionist

The border war with Eritrea resumed in May. Heavy fighting stopped with a cease-fire in June and a peace treaty was signed in December. Each side accused the other of committing human rights abuses against its own nationals. Armed conflict continued within Ethiopia between government forces and Oromo and Somali opponents, with many human rights violations and abuses reported. Suspected rebel supporters were detained, tortured or sometimes extrajudicially executed. Several thousand remained in detention, some having been held for years without charge or trial. Journalists, demonstrators and other critics of the government were arrested, most of whom were held without trial, although some received unfair trials. During preparations for elections in May, several opposition party supporters in the south were shot dead by police and scores were detained. The trials of officials of the former Dergue government proceeded slowly on charges including genocide and extrajudicial executions. Several death sentences were imposed but no executions were reported.

Background
War with Eritrea

The border war with Eritrea erupted again in May after a year's tense confrontation along the 1,000-kilometre border. Both sides had continued to expand their forces and to buy weapons. Forced recruitment was reported in southern Ethiopia, with some children allegedly recruited.

In May Ethiopia attacked and captured large parts of southwestern Eritrea, forcing Eritrean troops out of areas they had occupied since the war began in May 1998. The UN Security Council urged a cease-fire and imposed an arms embargo on both sides. After three weeks of fighting with heavy casualties, a cease-fire was signed in June under the auspices of the Organization of African Unity. Ethiopian troops withdrew to a buffer zone 25 kilometres inside Eritrea, administered by a UN Mission in Ethiopia and Eritrea (UNMEE). Recriminations and allegations of human rights abuses by each side against the other's nationals in their country continued. More than 300,000 Ethiopians were displaced by the fighting.

A formal peace treaty was signed in December in Algeria in the presence of the UN Secretary-General. This provided for UN supervision of the withdrawal of Ethiopian troops and temporary UN administration of

Ethiopian nationals in Eritrea

Immediately after the outbreak of fighting in May, the security forces interned thousands of Ethiopians throughout Eritrea. Some 3,000 were interned in makeshift camps near Asmara without adequate provision of food, shelter, water, medical facilities or hygiene. Following international criticism, the authorities improved conditions, allowed access and after a few weeks released most of the internees. Others were detained on suspicion of helping the Ethiopian attacks and many were still held without charge or trial throughout 2000. The authorities claimed that others were held for their own protection in displacement camps, having been evacuated during the fighting.

The Ethiopian government's claims of widespread killings, torture, detentions and forcible expulsions of Ethiopian nationals in Eritrea were difficult to verify. Some members of the Kunama ethnic group (or nationality), for example, were allegedly killed for supporting the Ethiopian military advance. Some abuses did occur, and there were incidents of Eritrean civilians targeting Ethiopians for reprisals after the Ethiopian attacks, leading to some deaths reported in Barentu in May. But there was no evidence of any official government policy of systematic abuses or forcible expulsion. Hundreds of destitute Ethiopians voluntarily returned to Ethiopia in November and December under ICRC auspices.

Detention without trial

There were continuing allegations that the authorities held many Eritreans, as well as thousands of Ethiopian nationals, without charge or trial for political reasons, particularly for suspected links with armed Eritrean opposition groups. "Disappearances" and cases of incommunicado detention were reported in 2000, as they had been in previous years, but were denied by the government. Hundreds of people remained in detention throughout 2000 for possible trial by the Special Court, where international fair trial standards are not followed. Some Special Court detainees were released in early 2000 after several years in detention without having been charged or tried.

In October, six journalists from the new private media were arrested, allegedly on account of articles critical of the government. Four were released after a few days but the other two were detained for longer periods. The government said the arrests were connected to national service requirements.

Updates

As many as 100 Eritrean officials of the former Ethiopian government in Eritrea continued to serve prison sentences, imposed without fair trial, for human rights abuses.

There were conflicting reports about whether some "disappeared" members of the Eritrean Liberation Front-Revolutionary Council abducted from Sudan in 1992 might still be alive in detention. The government had never satisfactorily accounted for them.

the buffer zone, neutral demarcation of the border, and examination of claims by both sides for compensation. The UN Secretary-General promised international help to both sides to recover from the destruction caused by the conflict.

In December UNMEE began deploying troops and human rights observers into the Ethiopian-occupied zone. An exchange of prisoners of war and civilian internees began under the auspices of the International Committee of the Red Cross, which had previously registered 2,600 Eritrean prisoners of war in Ethiopia and 1,000 Ethiopian prisoners of war in Eritrea. Over 1,200 Eritrean civilians were also held by Ethiopia, most of whom had been detained without charge or trial since May 1998. The future remained uncertain for the substantial long-standing community of Eritreans in Ethiopia, who had been stripped of their Ethiopian citizenship when the war broke out.

Human Rights Commission and Ombudsman
In July the Human Rights Commission and the Office of Ombudsman were formally established, but members had not been appointed by the end of 2000.

Internal and regional armed conflicts

The government continued to face long-running armed opposition in the Oromo region from the Oromo Liberation Front (OLF), and in the Somali region from the Ogaden National Liberation Front (ONLF) and *Al-Itihad*, an Islamist group allied to the ONLF with ties to Islamist groups in Somalia. Many human rights abuses were reported in these two conflicts, particularly by government troops against civilians suspected of supporting the rebels. International and national humanitarian staff were at risk of attacks and kidnapping by Somali rebels.

Ethiopian troops remained in Somalia's Gedo, Bay and Bakol regions, supporting particular local Somali factions. Ethiopia was involved in the Somali peace talks held in Djibouti which led to the formation of the new interim Somali government.

Elections

Elections for the national and regional parliaments were held in May. More than 50 political parties took part, including 23 opposition parties. The government barred international election observers but allowed over 1,500 national observers, including those from the Ethiopian Human Rights Council, which was finally granted legal registration. There were numerous complaints by opposition parties of repression and intimidation during voter registration and campaigning, particularly in the southern region. The All-Amhara People's Organization and several southern opposition parties, including the Southern Peoples' Democratic Front Coalition, the Hadiya National Democratic Coalition and the Gambela People's Democratic Congress, complained of supporters being beaten and detained, offices closed, candidates prevented from registering and supporters dismissed from government employment. In Hadiya zone in March, police reportedly shot dead two demonstrators and detained scores of people. Five people were allegedly killed by government forces on election day in Hadiya zone. Following complaints, the election was re-run there in June. Elections in the Somali region were postponed to August because of drought and insecurity.

The ruling Ethiopian Revolutionary Democratic Front (EPRDF) coalition led by Prime Minister Meles Zenawi's Tigray People's Liberation Front won more than 90 per cent of seats. In October a new government headed again by Meles Zenawi was sworn in.

Political imprisonment

Hundreds of people were arrested for political reasons, most of whom were detained without charge or trial, some in secret. Some were prisoners of conscience, and others might also have been prisoners of conscience although supposedly detained on suspicion of having links with armed opposition groups.

Detentions were particularly frequent in the Oromo and Somali regions, where some thousands of detainees arrested over the previous eight years continued to be detained without charge or trial.

Journalists
Police arrested journalists from the private media on the grounds that articles criticizing the government were false or a threat to security. Arrests continued despite the government's unexpected decision in March to allow the Ethiopian Free Press Journalists Association to be registered, alongside the Ethiopian Journalists Association which mostly represented the pro-government and state media. Dozens of journalists were taken for questioning and released on bail with charges pending, and several fled the country after repeated court appearances and police summonses. The Press Law (1992) allows courts to imprison journalists for publishing false information or for allegedly inciting ethnic conflict. At the end of 2000, eight journalists were in prison as prisoners of conscience.

◻ In January Tessalegne Mengesha of *Mabruk* magazine was jailed for a year and Tewodros Kassa of *Etiop* magazine was sentenced to one year's imprisonment in June. The charges were dubious, and their trials unfair.

◻ Mairegu Bezabih, a veteran journalist and the European Union's Information Officer in Ethiopia, was arrested in March in unclear circumstances — the authorities accused him of involvement in human rights violations 13 years previously.

Election-related arrests
In certain southern constituencies, particularly Hadiya, Kambata and Gambela zones, members of opposition parties were detained during the election process.

◻ Abula Obang, an education official, and 17 others who formed the Gambela People's Democratic Congress and were arrested in early 1999 remained in detention without charge or trial as prisoners of conscience throughout the election period.

Oromo demonstrations
In March there were widespread demonstrations by Oromos in Addis Ababa, Ambo, Nekemte and several other towns in western Oromia. The demonstrators

accused the authorities of failing to take sufficient action to stop a huge forest fire in southern Oromia. Hundreds of demonstrators, notably schoolteachers and students, were arrested and held for several weeks without charge or trial. At least one person, Diribe Jifara, was reportedly shot dead by police. Most detainees were non-violent protesters and were prisoners of conscience. There were further demonstrations and short-term arrests of Oromos in October and November on account of the government's decision to move the Oromia regional capital from Addis Ababa (where there is a large Oromo community) to Nazareth in the southeast. In late December up to 200 students were arrested at Addis Ababa University after a dispute over an Oromo political issue. After some days in custody, where they were ill-treated and forced to do harsh exercises, most were released but 18 Oromo students were taken to court and remanded in custody.

Eritrean detainees
In March and April, when war was again imminent, nine Eritreans were sentenced to between one and 15 years' imprisonment on charges of spying for or collaborating with the Eritrean armed forces. More than 1,200 other Eritreans were still detained without charge or trial after mass round-ups in 1998 and 1999.

Political trials
The group trial in Addis Ababa of more than 60 Oromos for armed conspiracy with the OLF entered its third year. The defendants faced a variety of mostly separate charges. Among these prisoners were seven human rights defenders who had founded the Human Rights League to protect Oromos against human rights violations, and two journalists. They were prisoners of conscience.

Taye Wolde-Semayat, president of the Ethiopian Teachers Association and a former university professor, lodged an appeal against his 15-year prison sentence imposed in 1999 for alleged armed conspiracy. A prominent critic of the government, he was a prisoner of conscience, convicted in an unfair trial.

Dergue trials
The trial of 46 members of the former military government of Mengistu Haile-Mariam (which was known as the Dergue) entered its sixth year. They were charged with genocide, war crimes and other crimes against humanity. Some trials began of more than 2,200 other former officials, most of whom had been held since 1991 and were facing lesser charges. A few trials were completed. Several people were convicted and sentenced to prison terms, a few were acquitted, and at least one was sentenced to death in his absence. The majority of trials, however, had not yet started and many detainees, including Mammo Wolde, the former Olympic athlete, remained in prison with little chance of an early opportunity to defend themselves.

Torture/ ill-treatment
Reports continued to be received of a persistent pattern of torture of political prisoners. Torture took place during unlawful and incommunicado detention in official and unofficial places of custody. Judges did not investigate complaints of torture made when prisoners were brought to court. Torture was particularly common in certain police stations and security centres in Addis Ababa and in zones of armed conflict or intense political conflict, such as Oromia, the Somali region and parts of the south. Prison conditions were generally harsh and medical treatment was inadequate.

Extrajudicial executions
There were reports of suspected rebel supporters being extrajudicially executed by government forces, but these proved difficult to verify.

Death penalty
Several people were sentenced to death for murder but no executions were reported. Up to 100 prisoners were under sentence of death.

FIJI

REPUBLIC OF THE FIJI ISLANDS
Head of state: Ratu Josefa Iloilo (replaced Ratu Sir Kamisese Mara in July)
Head of government: Laisenia Qarase (replaced Frank Bainimarama in July who replaced Mahendra Chaudhry in May)
Capital: Suva
Population: 0.77 million
Official language: English
Death penalty: retentionist

A violent coup attempt in May led to widespread human rights abuses and a flagrant disregard for the rule of law. Scores of civilians, police and army officers were injured; some were killed. Thousands of Fijians of Indian ethnic origin were forced to leave their homes as a result of racist or opportunistic attacks and fear of violence. Decrees issued under martial law allowed for racial discrimination but preserved other basic human rights. These rights were, however, frequently violated during operations against suspected rebels. As many as six suspected rebels were reportedly beaten to death by soldiers following an attempted mutiny in November. Investigations into alleged human rights violations were hampered by fears of retaliation; no findings were made public.

Political instability
On 19 May an indigenous Fijian nationalist movement led anti-government demonstrations in the capital. During the demonstrations, members of the military's

elite Counter Revolutionary Warfare Unit (CRWU) led by George Speight, a civilian, stormed parliament, and took Prime Minister Mahendra Chaudhry, his son and most government members of parliament hostage; the hostages were held for up to 56 days. The rebels declared the 1997 Constitution abrogated and "appointed" a president and government that ensured indigenous supremacy. The 1997 Constitution had removed previous guarantees, imposed after two military coups in 1987, of political dominance by indigenous Fijians.

President Ratu Sir Kamisese Mara declared a state of emergency after coup supporters rioted, looted and burned down shops and houses, the majority belonging to Indo-Fijians. Police allowed hundreds of coup supporters and the media to freely enter and leave the parliamentary complex. Coup leaders incited racist attacks against Indo-Fijians which masked indigenous power struggles behind the coup. Mobs terrorized towns and villages, took scores of people hostage, killed an unarmed policeman, shot several army officers and a cameraman, and ransacked a television station. Following threats against his life, President Mara dismissed the government and fled the capital on 29 May. The military commander, Commodore Voreqe Bainimarama, took power, declared martial law and published emergency decrees, drafted by the Chief Justice, to replace the Constitution and abolish the Supreme Court. A decree on fundamental rights and freedoms largely preserved Fiji's Bill of Rights but allowed for racial discrimination. Military leaders and the ethnic Fijian Great Council of Chiefs negotiated with the rebels on the release of the hostages, the conditions for an amnesty and the composition of a new administration.

After all hostages were released in July, the military regime arranged the appointment of Laisenia Qarase as interim Prime Minister who formed a civilian, predominantly indigenous Fijian, administration. He appointed a committee to review the 1997 Constitution with the aim of replacing it with one that guarantees political supremacy and economic advancement for indigenous Fijians. Coup supporters welcomed the moves as effectively implementing their objectives.

In November, eight soldiers died and dozens were injured during an attempted mutiny by CRWU members suspected of seeking to remove the military commander and to free coup leaders not released on bail.

In November the High Court upheld the 1997 Constitution, rejected the dilution of human rights in decrees and declared that Ratu Sir Kamisese Mara remained President and should appoint a Prime Minister. An appeal against the ruling by the interim administration was pending at the end of the year.

Hostage crisis

Indo-Fijian and indigenous Fijian cabinet members held hostage by the rebels were detained in separate buildings within the parliamentary complex. Coup supporters beat the Prime Minister and his son, and there were reports that hostages were temporarily denied food and medical attention. George Speight publicly threatened to kill the Prime Minister. After the release of all hostages in July, the hostage-takers failed to comply with agreed conditions for an amnesty by not handing in all their weapons. Following further violence by coup supporters, the army and police arrested some 400 of them, a number of whom were ill-treated in custody. A majority were initially charged with minor offences and later released from detention. Many suspected coup leaders were later charged with treason and other serious crimes but most were conditionally released owing to insufficient evidence. Eight remained in detention awaiting trial at the end of the year. At least 1,500 ethnic Fijians were arrested for minor offences, and some reportedly retaliated against their Indo-Fijian victims after being released on bail.

Abuses against Indo-Fijians

During and after the hostage crisis, hundreds of Indo-Fijian homes and businesses were burned down or looted. In some rural areas, coup supporters terrorized Indo-Fijian farmers and robbed them of crops, cattle and valuables, often in order to feed the hostage-takers. There were reports of police complicity in some attacks and of widespread beatings, rapes and hostage-taking by indigenous Fijians. The authorities subsequently failed to cooperate with the new Fiji Human Rights Commission which investigated more than 120 complaints received following the coup attempt.

At least 1,000 Indo-Fijians were internally displaced or made homeless as a result of the violence and thousands were forced to leave leased properties. Up to 350 found shelter in the town of Lautoka, where the non-governmental Fiji Human Rights Group organized a refuge. Members of the group and other human rights activists became the target of political intimidation and criminal investigations by police on suspicion of threatening national security.

By November, all indigenous Fijians arrested for violence against Indo-Fijians had been released. By the end of the year, no one was known to have been convicted of any coup-related human rights violations.

Torture/ill-treatment by the security forces

There were reports that many of those arrested during operations against suspected rebels were severely beaten and bore visible injuries when they appeared in court. The interim Minister of Home Affairs stated that alleged brutality by members of the security forces against coup supporters would be investigated and disciplinary action taken. No such investigation was known to have taken place by the end of the year. In November, soldiers beat up to 39 CRWU members during arrest for their suspected involvement in an attempted mutiny and denied them visits by family members for at least a week. They faced military tribunals in 2001 on charges which carry the death penalty.

Possible extrajudicial executions

During an attempted mutiny at the Queen Elizabeth Barracks in the capital in November, members of the

CRWU who had recently been released from military custody took other soldiers hostage and reportedly killed three soldiers. Armed forces loyal to the government launched a counter-attack to free hostages and regained control of the barracks. Up to five CRWU soldiers arrested after the mutiny were reportedly beaten to death by members of the armed forces. On the night of their arrest, two of the dead CRWU officers were seen uninjured in custody at a police station before they were driven away by regular troops. The findings of autopsies on the two soldiers were not made public.

An escaped convict who had engaged in rebel activities was killed by members of the army in November.

Freedom of expression
Felix Anthony, Secretary of the Fiji Trade Unions Congress, and other trade unionists were reportedly subjected to repeated short-term arrests and harassment. Fiji Broadcasting Commission staff were detained by the military and questioned for several hours about the source of a news item they had broadcast.

AI country reports
- Fiji: Human rights under the Interim Military Government (AI Index: ASA 18/004/2000)
- Fiji: Human rights at risk (AI Index: ASA 18/009/2000)

FINLAND

REPUBLIC OF FINLAND
Head of state: Tarja Halonen
Head of government: Paavo Lipponen
Capital: Helsinki
Population: 5.1 million
Official languages: Finnish, Swedish
Death penalty: abolitionist for all crimes
2000 treaty ratifications/signatures: Optional Protocol to the UN Children's Convention on the involvement of children in armed conflict; Optional Protocol to the UN Women's Convention; Rome Statute of the International Criminal Court

Sixteen conscientious objectors were adopted as prisoners of conscience. A draft bill to amend the Non-Military Service Act failed to address concerns about the punitive length of alternative civilian service. The government's follow-up response to the report of the European Committee for the Prevention of Torture and Inhuman or Degrading Treatment or Punishment (ECPT) on its visit to Finland in June 1998 was published in September.

Conscientious objectors
During the year AI adopted 16 conscientious objectors as prisoners of conscience. Because of the punitive length of alternative civilian service — more than 50 per cent of recruits serve 180 days of military service while all conscientious objectors have to perform 395 days of alternative civilian service — AI regards conscientious objectors in Finland as prisoners of conscience.

A review of the alternative civilian service initiated by the government, published in December 1999, proposed that alternative civilian service be reduced to 330 days. However, in October the Minister of Labour confirmed that, despite his department's proposal, the government would put forward a bill proposing a reduction in the length of alternative civilian service to 362 days. In December, Parliament rejected the government's proposal to reduce the length of alternative civilian service.

Ill-treatment
The government published a follow-up report to its response of November 1999 to the findings of the ECPT on its visit to Finland in June 1998. In the follow-up report the government stated that the term of the working group set up to study the detention of people on the basis of the Aliens Act had been extended until December 2000 and that the Aliens Act needed amendment with regard to detention facilities. In response to the ECPT's concern about long-term prisoners spending most of the day in their cells, it reported that there had been amendments in accordance with the recommendations of the ECPT.

AI country report
- Finland: AI adopts Finnish conscientious objectors as prisoners of conscience and calls for their immediate release (AI Index: EUR 20/001/2000)

FRANCE

FRENCH REPUBLIC
Head of state: Jacques Chirac
Head of government: Lionel Jospin
Capital: Paris
Population: 59 million
Official language: French
Death penalty: abolitionist for all crimes
2000 treaty ratifications/signatures: Optional Protocol to the UN Children's Convention on the involvement of children in armed conflict; Optional Protocol to the UN Women's Convention; Rome Statute of the International Criminal Court

Allegations of police brutality, notably involving asylum-seekers and others of non-European origin, persisted. Police shootings, some fatal, occurred in disputed circumstances. Some courts continued to play a part in perpetuating a situation of effective impunity, notably in regard to deaths in custody. Conditions in holding areas for asylum-seekers were described as inhuman and degrading. A book by a prison doctor reinvigorated debate about prison conditions. Refugees continued to be subject to a form of prolonged administrative detention. Two French generals were among others who publicly admitted that, during the Algerian war of independence, they had committed torture and extrajudicial executions.

Background

New laws affecting human rights concerns were approved or announced. In June Parliament approved a law on the "protection of the presumption of innocence and rights of victims". New measures included an appeal structure for assize courts and legal assistance for detainees in the first hour of police custody — although not in the case of terrorism-related crimes or drug-trafficking offences. Video recording of police interrogation of minors was expected to help prevent brutality in police custody. However, a plan to introduce similar safeguards for adults was postponed in the face of fierce police opposition.

In June Parliament also approved a law creating a commission to oversee the working and implementation of codes of practice governing law enforcement officers.

Two commissions of inquiry into the state of prisons published critical reports following the appearance of a book by the then chief doctor at Paris-La Santé Prison, Dr Véronique Vasseur, about inhuman and degrading conditions at the prison. In October the Minister of Justice announced that she was preparing a comprehensive law on the penitentiary system. In November a law providing legal representation for prisoners during disciplinary hearings came into force.

In December, following the "Matignon Agreement" on the future status of Corsica, the Assembly of Corsica approved a draft law aimed at transferring a range of regulatory and legislative powers to the island.

Acts of violence were attributed to Breton, Basque and Corsican nationalist groups and there was political unrest and rioting in the overseas department of French Guiana. In September and October the representatives of 18 independence and autonomist movements from metropolitan France and from the overseas departments and territories met in Paris to discuss joint steps towards self-determination.

Torture and killings of Algerians

Pressure grew on the Paris police authorities to grant access to its archives on the October 1961 massacre by police officers of Algerians at a peaceful demonstration in Paris during the Algerian war of independence (1954-1962). There was still disagreement about the number of demonstrators who had been killed and figures varied between 32 and 200. In June the newspaper *Le Monde* published testimony by Louisette Ighilahriz. She was a member of the Algerian National Liberation Front (FLN) who had been tortured by French parachutists in 1957. Her testimony elicited regret about torture from General Jacques Massu.

In October, 12 public figures appealed to the authorities to acknowledge and condemn torture committed during the war. Generals Massu and Paul Aussaresses both admitted their direct involvement in torture and extrajudicial executions. Torture — which had also been committed by French police before the outbreak of war — included administration of severe electric shocks, suspension by the arms and legs and use of the "*baignoire*" ("bathtub"). In November AI called for those responsible for crimes against humanity during the Algerian war of independence to be brought to justice. AI stated that the lack of political will by successive governments to confront this issue had helped to present torture, summary executions and "disappearances" as a "necessary evil".

Police shootings

A disturbing pattern of use of excessive and sometimes lethal force continued. Such incidents have often occurred during police investigations of car thefts in the urban conglomerations and depressed suburbs where many young people of North African origin live. In April and September rioting broke out respectively in southern Lille and in two areas of Seine-et-Marne after two such killings.

◻ Three nights of rioting followed the killing in Lille in April of Riad Hamlaoui, a French resident of Algerian origin. Riad Hamlaoui, the passenger in a reportedly stolen car, was shot dead by a police officer. The bullet was fired at close range, piercing his neck. Both he and the driver were unarmed. The driver had got out of the car but Riad Hamlaoui, still inside, was said to have made a "sudden movement" which, combined with the darkness of the night and condensation on the windows, had caused the officer to fear for his life. The officer was detained for investigation in connection with a charge of "voluntary homicide". Two reconstructions took place and in July the officer was provisionally released.

Ill-treatment in police custody
Police brutality was widely reported. Most allegations were of beatings with truncheons or fists. Victims included asylum-seekers of African and Cuban origin and several women of non-European origin resident in France who alleged that they had been physically assaulted and racially abused.

A number of allegations related to ill-treatment and harassment by police at the Ibis Hotel and other holding areas at Roissy-Charles de Gaulle Airport. In February AI brought some of these allegations to the attention of the Minister of the Interior and expressed concern that the tense situation there, created by poor and inadequate facilities, could help to fuel confrontation between asylum-seekers and police officers. No response was received.

In September magistrates in Seine-Saint-Denis alleged that police had ill-treated minors suspected of delinquency in several incidents over the last few years, including one in which a minor was subjected to "Russian roulette" and another in which five black children were used as "punchbags".

Shekuna Sumanu, from Sierra Leone, was among a group of Sierra Leonean nationals who claimed that they had been ill-treated and racially insulted by drunken police officers at the Ibis Hotel at Roissy-Charles de Gaulle Airport on the night of New Year's Eve when they emerged into a corridor to pray and sing as part of their religious rituals. Shekuna Sumanu was reportedly beaten across his thighs with a truncheon and required medical treatment.

Cornélie Chappuis, of Congolese (Zairian) origin, claimed that in January she was ill-treated by police officers from Roubaix (Nord), who removed her from her house during a dispute with her husband and held her overnight at Roubaix police station. In transit to the station Cornélie Chappuis was reportedly handcuffed, thrown to the police van floor, pulled by the hair and told that if she did not stop protesting she would meet the same fate as Semira Adamu, a Nigerian national who died in 1998 during deportation by Belgian gendarmes. Later Cornélie Chappuis was reportedly forced to strip while officers made lewd remarks, one referring to her as a "nigger". Her family doctor subsequently recorded injuries on her body which had not been recorded in a medical report of the previous evening. Cornélie Chappuis was not charged.

'Islamist network' trials
In May Isabelle Coutant-Peyre, one of the lawyers who, during the 1998 "Chalabi" trial, had defended alleged members of support networks for Algerian armed opposition groups, was fined by a Paris court for defaming the national police. She had publicly described mass arrests preceding the trial in 1994 and 1995 as "raids worthy of the methods of the Gestapo and Militia, at all hours of the day and night, against whole families, including children." The court concluded that she had impugned the honour of the police.

The methods of France's specialized "anti-terrorism" investigating judges and of the 14th section of the Paris prosecution service continued to be brought into question by a number of court decisions, particularly with regard to the abusive use of provisional detention and to a catch-all conspiracy charge, "criminal association with a terrorist enterprise".

The appeal of 33 "Chalabi" defendants who had been convicted in 1999 was heard in January. In March the Paris appeal court found four of them not guilty. This brought the number acquitted of the conspiracy charge to 55 out of 138. Proceedings against another 35 had been dropped before the opening of the trial. In 1998 AI had criticized the entire judicial proceedings for falling short of international fair trial standards on a number of grounds. In November a compensation commission awarded to 20 of those acquitted a total sum of almost two million francs, on account of the long periods they had spent in provisional detention.

In December the Correctional Court of Paris acquitted 16 out of 24 suspected members of another "Islamist" network of the charge of "criminal association with a terrorist enterprise". They were accused of preparing attacks during the 1998 World Cup.

Administrative detention
Several refugees, asylum-seekers and former prisoners (who had completed sentences served in France in connection with the above-mentioned conspiracy charge) were held under a form of administrative detention (*assignation à résidence*) instead of being expelled. This form of detention restricts the detainee's movements to a specific and extremely limited geographical area. They had no recourse to a court of law to contest the detention order. They included North Africans and Basques.

In February AI renewed its appeal to the Minister of the Interior, first made in 1998, to review the case of Tunisian refugee Salah Ben Hédi Hassen Karker, who had been subjected to such administrative detention, far from his wife and child, for more than six years. AI reiterated that Salah Karker had never been given an effective opportunity to contest either the expulsion or administrative detention orders against him and considered it "intolerable to hold Salah Karker indefinitely under such a form of confinement". No response was received.

Impunity
The effective impunity granted by some courts to police officers or gendarmes, notably with regard to deaths in custody, continued to cause concern.

In January the Court of Cassation annulled an appeal court verdict against a gendarme who, in 1993, had shot dead Franck Moret when he tried to escape a road checkpoint. The court refused the family leave to appeal. In July 1998 the Court of Appeal of Grenoble (Isère) had sentenced the gendarme to a suspended 18-month prison term, finding that, although the gendarme was entitled to fire to stop the car, the fatal shot had been fired in a "particularly imprudent and clumsy way". AI has expressed concern over the continuing application of a decree law which grants particular latitude to the gendarmerie with regard to the use of firearms. This concern was shared by the UN Human Rights Committee and by the UN Committee against Torture.

◻ In July, two Anti-Crime Brigade (BAC) officers were sentenced by the Correctional Court of Lille to a nominal suspended seven-month prison term for "involuntary homicide" in connection with the death in custody of Zairian-born Sydney Manoka Nzeza. Three other officers were acquitted of failing to provide help. The family's lawyer stated that an appeal would be lodged against the light sentences. In 1998 Sydney Manoka Nzeza was apprehended by a number of police officers during an argument with a car driver. He was pinned to the ground and held under restraint, shackled by his arms and feet and taken to the police station, where he died. An autopsy established that death was caused by thoracic compression.

◻ In October a judge ordered that a charge of "voluntary and involuntary homicide" against police officers involved in the death of Mohamed Ali Saoud be dropped. In the course of a violent struggle in 1998, Mohamed Ali Saoud, who was suffering from a mental disability and needed urgent medical attention, was shot with rubber bullets and allegedly repeatedly beaten before and while being held under heavy restraint. The judge concluded that the officers had found themselves in a dangerous situation and had not acted criminally. An appeal was lodged against the decision.

AI country reports and visits
Report
- Concerns in Europe, January-June 2000: France (AI Index: EUR 01/003/00)

Visits
An AI delegate visited France in March and April to gather information.

GAMBIA

REPUBLIC OF THE GAMBIA
Head of state and government: Yahya Jammeh
Capital: Banjul
Population: 1.2 million
Official language: English
Death penalty: abolitionist in practice
2000 treaty ratifications/signatures: Optional Protocol to the UN Children's Convention on the involvement of children in armed conflict

At least 14 people were killed and dozens injured in April when security forces used excessive and indiscriminate force to break up student demonstrations. Members of the opposition faced harassment and arrest. Civilians and soldiers suspected of plotting against the government were arrested and held incommunicado for long periods without charge or trial. Arbitrary detentions, ill-treatment and torture by the security forces were frequently reported.

Background
Political tension remained high throughout 2000. The government claimed to have foiled two coup plots in January and in June. Harassment and repression of political opponents continued unabated. In July President Jammeh was reported to have stated publicly that "anyone bent on disturbing the peace and stability of the nation would be buried six feet deep".

In December, the UN Panel of Experts investigating the trade in arms and diamonds in Sierra Leone identified Gambia as a transit country for conflict diamonds from Sierra Leone and called for an immediate embargo "on trade in all so-called Gambian diamonds". The Gambian authorities, accused by the UN experts of not cooperating with the investigation, reportedly denied any lack of cooperation and any involvement in diamond trafficking.

Excessive and indiscriminate use of force
On 10 and 11 April, at least 14 people were killed and dozens injured, some severely, when security forces used excessive and indiscriminate force to break up demonstrations. Several of the dead were less than 18 years old. The unauthorized demonstrations were organized by the Gambian Students Union in Banjul, Brikama and other towns. They were called in protest at two incidents in March: the death, allegedly after torture, of a student, Ebrima Barry, and the rape of a 13-year-old schoolgirl, Binta Manneh, by a police officer. The demonstration in Banjul on 10 April became violent after the security forces tried to disperse crowds, including by using tear gas, batons and rubber bullets. It appeared that some demonstrators threw stones at security forces, burned tyres and set fire to buildings, including fire stations and police stations. The security forces reportedly fired into the crowd and autopsies

apparently confirmed that live ammunition was used. Omar Barrow, a journalist and Gambia Red Cross volunteer, wearing Red Cross insignia, was among those killed as he went to help injured demonstrators.

Neither the findings of a Commission of Inquiry subsequently set up by the government nor those of the inquiry carried out by the Coroner were made public by the end of 2000. In September, the Chair of the Commission of Inquiry was reported to have publicly acknowledged that security force officers were found to be largely responsible for the deaths and injuries of the students.

Torture/ill-treatment

Torture and ill-treatment were frequently reported. Many of the students arrested during and after the mid-April demonstrations were tortured and ill-treated in custody by members of the security forces, including the National Intelligence Agency.

☐ On 9 March, Ebrima Barry, a 19-year-old student, died in hospital allegedly after torture by Brikama Fire Service personnel. Officers suspected of responsibility for his death were arrested. Their trial had not concluded by the end of 2000.

The practice of female genital mutilation reportedly remained widespread, especially in rural areas.

Arrests of opponents

On 18 June, Ousainou Darboe, Secretary General of the opposition United Democratic Party (UDP), was arrested with scores of UDP members in the Basse region, east of Banjul, while campaigning for local elections. He was released on bail after being charged together with 24 others, including members of the National Assembly, with the murder of a supporter of the ruling Alliance for Patriotic Reorientation and Construction (APRC). Ousainou Darboe's arrest followed what appeared to be an ambush of his convoy by members of a pro-government militia, the "22 July Movement". Although officially disbanded in 1999, the militia reportedly continued to operate.

At the end of 2000 the murder charges were dropped against all but five people, including Ousainou Darboe and other prominent UDP members. It appeared that this prosecution was intended to silence the UDP and prevent Ousainou Darboe from standing in presidential elections in 2001, as no credible evidence was reported to have emerged against the five. On 18 July, the European Union urged the Gambian authorities to respect fully the independence of the courts in the proceedings against Ousainou Darboe and members of his party.

Unlawful detention of suspected plotters

Civilians and members of the military arrested in January and in June on suspicion of plotting a coup were held incommunicado for long periods without being charged.

☐ Lieutenant Landing Sanneh was arrested in January on suspicion of plotting to overthrow the government. He was held incommunicado for several months and charged in June with treason. It appeared that at least one of his confessions was obtained after a death threat. Landing Sanneh was detained at State Central Prison (Mile II) awaiting trial before the High Court. However, in early December the authorities announced that he would be tried by the Court Martial.

☐ Momodou Ousman Saho and five others— Lieutenant Lato Jaiteh, Lieutenant Omar Darbo, Ebrima Barrow, Momodou Marena and Ebrima Yarbo— were arrested at the end of June and held incommunicado for more than four months. For at least three weeks the authorities denied to their families that they were being detained. The six were charged in mid-July by a magistrates' court which did not have jurisdiction to hear the case. Their lawyers were not present in court. Three others were charged *in absentia*. At the end of 2000, the six were being held at Mile II prison, where detention conditions were reportedly harsh.

Intimidation of journalists

Journalists continued to face arbitrary detentions and threats of violence by the security forces. Decrees 70 and 71, which unduly restrict freedom of expression, remained in force. Proposed legislation on the National Media Commission, which would have imposed further restrictions on the news media, was not passed by the National Assembly during 2000.

☐ In July, Baba Galleh Jallow and Alhagie Mbye of the *Independent* were arrested, briefly detained and released on bail after being charged with libel for reporting on a prison hunger strike.

Death penalty

Appeals against death sentences passed by the High Court for treason had not been decided by the end of 2000. They related to four political prisoners sentenced to death in 1997 after an armed attack on Farafenni military camp in 1996, and to three others sentenced in 1999 after an armed attack on Kartong military post in 1997.

AI country report

- Gambia: Fourteen people killed and at least 28 injured (AI Index: AFR 27/001/2000)

GEORGIA

GEORGIA
Head of state and government: Eduard Shevardnadze
Capital: Tbilisi
Population: 4.9 million
Official language: Georgian
Death penalty: abolitionist for all crimes
2000 treaty ratifications/signatures: Protocol No. 6 to the European Convention on Human Rights concerning the abolition of the death penalty

Reports of torture and ill-treatment in custody continued in 2000. Among the victims were children and members of non-traditional religious groups. At least one man was reported to have died in custody as a result of police ill-treatment. In the disputed region of Abkhazia, at least one man was sentenced to death; no executions were reported. Ethnic Georgians displaced by the conflict continued to face obstacles to their return.

Background

President Eduard Shevardnadze won a second term of office in elections held in April. Also in April, parliament adopted a program of national reconciliation aimed at healing divisions dating back to the armed ousting of former President Zviad Gamsakhurdia in 1992. Scores of his imprisoned supporters were subsequently pardoned and released. In July parliament appointed Nana Devdariani as the second Public Defender (Ombudsperson) of Georgia, a post that had been vacant since the previous September. Rising concern at widespread corruption led the authorities to set up a special commission to combat the practice. There was little progress in talks aimed at regulating the status of the disputed regions of Abkhazia and South Ossetia, which remained outside the control of the Georgian authorities.

Torture/ill-treatment

As in previous years there were persistent allegations of torture and ill-treatment by law enforcement officials, and reports that many official investigations instigated in such cases were not pursued impartially and with vigour.

There were also continuing complaints that officials obstructed access to defence lawyers and to an independent forensic medical expert seeking to examine prisoners who had made allegations of torture. This expert reported in September that she had been routinely denied permission to visit prisoners while they were held in police custody. When access was granted, after a prisoner had been transferred to a remand facility under the control of the Ministry of Justice, it was often weeks after the initial allegations had been made and correspondingly much more difficult to determine the nature and cause of any injury sustained.

Elene Tevdoradze, the chairwoman of the parliamentary Human Rights Committee, was among those who reported extremely poor prison conditions, including cases in which officials attempted to extort bribes before transferring a sick prisoner to appropriate medical facilities.

☐ An 11-year-old boy was reportedly beaten while kept for three days in a juvenile holding facility. Sergey (not his real name) was detained by police in Tbilisi on 18 August while trying to sell a sheet of aluminium, and taken to the city's facility for holding juveniles while officials trace their parents or guardians. He reported that one of his teeth was knocked out during a beating by officials on the second day of his stay there, and that he saw other children, boys and girls, also being ill-treated, including by being punched around the head and shoulders and hit with a bunch of keys. It is also alleged that Sergey's parents more than once rang the local police station after their son failed to return home the first day, but that the police failed to reveal his location in the hopes of extorting a bribe from the family. Sergey was released the evening of his third day in detention after his parents and neighbours held a protest demonstration.

☐ Jehovah's Witness communities around the country were subjected to a number of attacks throughout the year by supporters of an unfrocked Georgian Orthodox priest, Father Basil Mkalavishvili, violently opposed to non-traditional religions. In most cases the attackers were said to have been allowed to act with impunity by the police, and in at least one instance police officers were alleged to have joined in the assault.

On 16 September a number of buses carrying Jehovah's Witnesses were reportedly stoned and passengers assaulted outside of the town of Marnueli. The Jehovah's Witnesses had planned to hold a convention there that day. However, police at roadblocks set up that morning were said to have turned back all vehicles carrying Jehovah's Witnesses, while giving free passage and a police escort to busloads of Father Mkalavishvili's supporters. In the light of this, the convention was cancelled, and delegates on buses were told to return home. At one roadblock, however, some buses returning to Tbilisi were reportedly attacked by a stone-throwing crowd. Windows were broken, and one woman passenger was said to have been struck on the head by a rock. According to the Jehovah's Witnesses, Orthodox supporters also stopped another bus, dragged out three male passengers and beat them. The attackers also entered the bus, shouted insults, and robbed passengers. Police at the scene were said to have supported and participated in the beatings, and also to have joined in the looting and destruction of the site of the cancelled convention.

Death in custody

As in previous years, there were allegations that torture in police custody led to the death of a detainee.

☐ Mamuka Rizhamadze was detained by police on 24 May in Tkibuli, and transferred the following day to preliminary detention facilities in Kutaisi. On 31 May he was found hanged in his cell by a noose made from a blanket. A post-mortem carried out by the state forensic service concluded that he had committed suicide. However, an independent forensic expert carried out a second post-mortem at the request of the family on 5 June. She found two wounds to Mamuka Rizhamadze's head, inflicted in her opinion while he was still alive and caused by a blunt heavy object. She concluded that these injuries were the cause of death. Investigation of the skin on Mamuka Rizhamadze's neck also indicated to her that he was dead before the noose was applied. It was not known whether any investigation had been initiated into the death following the post-mortem.

▭ Criminal proceedings began against a traffic police officer in connection with the 1999 death of Davit Vashaqmadze. Davit Vashaqmadze had been stopped by officers in November 1999 in Tbilisi and reportedly beaten so severely by them that he died in hospital two days later. In July the officer was convicted of "exceeding his authority" and sentenced to two years' imprisonment.

Abkhazia

The situation in Abkhazia remained relatively calm although unstable, especially in the southern district of Gali. Widespread, organized crime along the cease-fire line and the lack of effective law enforcement on both sides were major contributors to the poor security situation, hampering the return of refugees and displaced people. In November the UN Security Council called on both sides to take concrete steps to guarantee the security of those wishing to return, and to address urgently the undefined and insecure status of those who had returned spontaneously.

During the year the UN Human Rights Office in Abkhazia reported that it had raised cases of human rights violations with the *de facto* authorities, including incidents of harassment on ethnic and gender grounds, and the monitoring of places of detention.

Prisoners of conscience

According to reports at least two men were imprisoned for refusing on religious grounds to perform compulsory military service. No civilian alternatives to military service were available during 2000, although a draft law providing for such alternative service was reportedly under consideration by the Abkhaz authorities.

▭ In October, 18-year-old Elgudzha Tsulaya was sentenced to four years' imprisonment by the Military Court. He had been charged with desertion, reportedly in connection with the steps he had taken earlier in the year to avoid forcible conscription on the grounds that military service was incompatible with his religious beliefs. His appeal was turned down by the Supreme Court in November.

Zurab Achba

Zurab Achba, a legal assistant to the UN Human Rights Office in Abkhazia, a human rights defender and a leading opposition figure, was shot and killed in Sukhumi in August. Despite assurances from the Abkhaz authorities, the UN was not kept informed of developments in the investigation into the killing.

Death penalty

In October the Abkhaz Supreme Court sentenced Albert Tarba to death for the 1995 murder of Abkhaz Deputy Prime Minister Yury Voronov. Press reports stated that Albert Tarba, who had been in hiding, had been seized in March in the Krasnodar Territory of Russia, but it was not clear by whom or through which channels he had been transferred to Abkhazia. A second man, Sayed Itslayev, from the Chechen Republic in the Russian Federation, had been sentenced to death in Abkhazia in 1997 for his role in the murder.

At least 15 death sentences were believed to have been passed in Abkhazia since it declared independence; no judicial executions had been reported.

AI country report and visit
Reports
- Georgia: Continuing allegations of torture and ill-treatment (AI Index: EUR 56/001/2000)

Visit
AI delegates visited Georgia in September and met various officials.

GERMANY

FEDERAL REPUBLIC OF GERMANY
Head of state: Johannes Rau
Head of government: Gerhard Schröder
Capital: Berlin
Population: 82.2 million
Official language: German
Death penalty: abolitionist for all crimes
2000 treaty ratifications/signatures: Optional Protocol to the UN Children's Convention on the involvement of children in armed conflict; Rome Statute of the International Criminal Court

There were reports of police ill-treatment of detainees, and of abusive use of restraints. A mentally disabled man was shot dead by police. No criminal proceedings were taken against police officers who shot dead a man in controversial circumstances in 1999. An asylum-seeker committed suicide at Frankfurt-am-Main airport, where conditions of detention had previously been criticized by the European Committee for the Prevention of Torture and Inhuman or Degrading Treatment or Punishment. No developments were reported in the investigation of the death of Aamir Ageeb in May 1999 during his forced deportation.

Allegations of police ill-treatment

There were continued allegations of ill-treatment of detainees by police officers. Complainants reported that they were subjected to repeated kicks, punches and blows from the knee. In some instances non-Caucasian and foreign nationals alleged they were abused with racist language. It sometimes took an unduly long time to bring offending police officers to justice.

◻ Three police officers in Cologne were suspended from duty for allegedly attacking a taxi driver of Tunisian origin in the early hours of 21 September. According to reports, the three police officers, who were off-duty and intoxicated at the time of the incident, physically assaulted the 48-year-old taxi driver after he refused to transport them and their two companions. He was reportedly knocked to the ground and repeatedly kicked and punched, resulting in bruising to his head and chest. Eyewitnesses stated that before the attack one of the police officers verbally abused the taxi driver with racist language.

◻ On 16 February a court in Frankfurt found two police officers guilty of ill-treating a detainee, referred to as C., more than three years earlier. C. was physically ill-treated by police officers at Frankfurt's main railway station during the night of 3 November 1996. The court sentenced the two police officers to conditional prison sentences of six months and fines.

Restraint techniques

◻ A 20-year-old pregnant woman, originally from Togo, was arrested in June after she reportedly refused to leave a babycare shop in the town of Geldern in North Rhine-Westphalia. The woman and her husband alleged that during the arrest she was rolled onto her front although she was obviously pregnant, and she was subsequently handcuffed. The detainee, who had to undergo a gynaecological examination at St. Clemens hospital in Geldern to ensure that her unborn baby had not been injured, stated that police officers refused to remove her handcuffs. A gynaecologist at the hospital reportedly initially refused to examine her because she was in handcuffs. AI called for a prompt and impartial investigation into the allegations and asked to be informed why police officers refused to remove the handcuffs of the pregnant woman when she required medical treatment and a gynaecological examination.

◻ Thomas Müller, a 56-year-old man, who was being held in pre-trial detention for alleged fraud in Koblenz, was shackled to a hospital bed for three days, reportedly on grounds of security, while undergoing medical treatment at Kemperhof hospital in Koblenz in late June. An additional chain was reportedly linked around the shackles and attached to the hospital bed. In addition to the shackles and the chain, two prison officials were present in the hospital room. AI urged the authorities to review current practices regarding the prolonged shackling of detainees in hospital in order to ensure that the treatment of detainees does not constitute or lead to cruel, inhuman or degrading treatment.

Police shootings

◻ A 28-year-old mentally disabled man of Vietnamese origin, referred to as Mr B. in the German media, who was in possession of a plastic toy gun, was shot dead by two police officers on 20 September in a wooded area near the town of Ulm. The man, who was a long-term resident of a home for the mentally disabled, had been reported missing earlier in the afternoon. The two police officers, who had been called to the area after receiving a report of a man roaming through the woods with a gun, reportedly shot at the man 21 times, hitting him eight times. AI expressed concern that the police officers appeared to have used little restraint in discharging their firearms in apprehending a suspect who had not returned fire.

◻ AI received a response from the Ministry of the Interior of Thuringia in March about the controversial fatal shooting of a 62-year-old man from Cologne in a hotel in Heldrungen in Thuringia in June 1999 by two plainclothes police officers. The letter stated that criminal proceedings against the police officers for manslaughter through culpable negligence had been terminated by the investigating state prosecutor on the basis that the officers had not acted in a culpable manner. The widow of the deceased reportedly lodged an appeal.

Death during forced deportation

By the end of 2000, there were no developments reported in the investigation into the death of 30-year-old Aamir Ageeb, a Sudanese national who died in late May 1999 during his forced deportation from Frankfurt-am-Main airport to Khartoum via Cairo, Egypt. AI had originally expressed concern that the federal border police may have contributed to his death by using restraint techniques which impeded breathing.

Conditions of detention

An Algerian asylum-seeker committed suicide in the transit area holding facility of Frankfurt-am-Main airport on 6 May. The conditions of detention at Frankfurt-am-Main airport had previously been criticized in a report published in May 1999 by the European Committee for the Prevention of Torture and Inhuman or Degrading Treatment or Punishment (ECPT), which had visited the airport in May 1998. AI expressed concern that the conditions of detention at the airport, and the prolonged periods for which certain asylum-seekers were held there, might adversely affect both their physical and mental health. AI called on the German authorities, following the recommendations of the ECPT report of 1999, to improve conditions and to reconsider the practice of detaining asylum-seekers in the transit area holding facility for prolonged periods.

AI country reports

- Concerns in Europe, January – June 2000: Germany (AI Index: EUR 01/003/2000)

GHANA

REPUBLIC OF GHANA
Head of state and government: J.J. Rawlings
Capital: Accra
Population: 20.2 million
Official language: English
Death penalty: retentionist
2000 treaty ratifications/signatures: International Covenant on Civil and Political Rights; Optional Protocol to the International Covenant on Civil and Political Rights; International Covenant on Economic, Social and Cultural Rights; UN Convention against Torture; Optional Protocol to the UN Women's Convention

Journalists and others were briefly detained or imprisoned for criticizing government officials or protesting at human rights violations. A number of detainees were reportedly assaulted in military custody. There was no progress in the trial, re-trial or appeal in three continuing treason cases. At least one death sentence was passed; no executions were carried out.

Background

The winner of presidential elections in December was John Kufuor, leader of the opposition New Patriotic Party (NPP). President J.J. Rawlings, head of state and government since coming to power in a coup in 1981, served his second and final term of office as an elected President since the return to civilian rule in 1993.

The NPP won a majority of seats in the National Assembly in general elections in December. Seven people were killed in clashes between party supporters over the conduct of the elections in the town of Bawku, northern Ghana. The armed forces briefly closed down a regional radio station after an NPP candidate allegedly incited violence; charges were subsequently brought against him. Both government and opposition made repeated calls for the elections to be peaceful.

Prisoners of conscience and freedom of expression

Freedom of expression continued to be inhibited in Ghana by the imprisonment of journalists under the laws on defamation and contempt of court. Individuals were subjected to lengthy interrogation, brief detention and in some cases assault for publicly raising concerns about human rights violations, offending members of the government or being associated with the opposition.

In January Stephen Owusu, editor of the *Free Press* newspaper, was fined and sentenced to one day's imprisonment by the High Court in Accra. He was found to be in contempt of court for publishing an article commenting on a civil suit before the Court.

In May John Kufuor, leader of the NPP, and three visiting Italian politicians from the *Forza Italia* party were detained overnight at police headquarters. The authorities said that they were suspected of breaching immigration regulations. The victims said they were arrested as they were leaving the country, held for 15 hours without food or drink, and questioned in detail about their activities in Ghana. The NPP said that the government was seeking to deter its legitimate contacts with foreign political leaders and businessmen.

In November the security police detained two journalists for questioning before releasing them on bail. Felix Odartey-Wellington, a television presenter, was charged with insulting behaviour for making critical remarks about the President on television. Kofi Coomson, editor-in-chief of the *Ghanaian Chronicle* newspaper, was charged with receiving stolen goods after publishing allegations that the then ruling National Democratic Congress party was proposing election fraud.

Treason trials

By the end of 2000 the Supreme Court, which has appellate jurisdiction in treason cases, had not yet heard the appeal of four men sentenced to death in February 1999 following a long-running treason trial. Sylvester Addai-Dwomoh, Kwame Alexander Ofei, Kwame Ofori-Appiah and John Kwadwo Owusu-Boakye had been imprisoned since their arrest in September 1994 and convicted of plotting to overthrow the government. The special High Court trying the case had ruled admissible statements allegedly made under duress despite evidence that the defendants and some soldiers who later testified for the prosecution had been beaten following their arrest.

The trial did not commence of alleged co-conspirator James William Owu who was detained in Sierra Leone in early 1999, taken to Ghana by the Ghanaian armed forces without formal extradition proceedings, and charged with treason.

The retrial on treason charges of Karim Salifu Adam, an NPP member imprisoned since May 1994, did not proceed.

Releases of political prisoners

Two long-standing political prisoners were among more than 1,000 prisoners released under a presidential amnesty in April: former Captain Adjei Edward Ampofo, sentenced to death in 1983 after being convicted *in absentia* of involvement in an attempted coup in 1983; and former Sergeant Oduro Frimpong, who was sentenced to death in 1985 after a trial *in camera* for involvement in an alleged coup plot in 1984. In 1997 their death sentences had been commuted under a previous clemency measure.

Detentions and alleged assaults by the military

Arrests and detentions were reported to have been carried out by the military. Some detainees were assaulted; others were unlawfully detained without access to lawyers or recourse to the courts in places such as the Castle, Osu — the presidential office and residence in Accra — and at Military Headquarters, Burma Camp in Accra. In some cases, the reason for the arrest was political — criticism of the military or offence to the President or his family.

◻ In January Kabral Blay Amihere, publisher of the *Independent* newspaper, was arrested at gunpoint by military police late at night in his car and detained overnight for questioning after his newspaper published an article deemed critical of the military.

◻ In January Selassie O'Sullivan-Djentuh, aged 23, and two employees of his mother — William Katey and James Narh — were seized by armed men. Because of previous threats by members of the presidential guard, his parents sought information at the Castle which was refused. His father was detained overnight for questioning by the military after appealing on national radio for information about their son. The three men were released from detention after three days at the Castle, where they were reportedly assaulted and threatened and held in a dark and overcrowded cell in which there was no room to lie down. After further threats, attacks in the state-controlled news media against the family, and the demolition by armed police of family property, Selassie O'Sullivan-Djentuh left the country in fear of his life. His parents were charged with, and in August convicted of, assaulting a member of the presidential guard and offensive conduct. A Circuit Tribunal in Accra ordered their imprisonment for two weeks to await sentencing. After widespread protests, the court bound them to keep the peace or risk reimprisonment.

◻ In July Paul Poku, a US citizen of Ghanaian origin, was detained for two weeks at Military Headquarters, Burma Camp in Accra, after being arrested at night by armed soldiers. He was reportedly severely beaten and ill-treated, apparently in an attempt to force him to pay money in connection with a civil lawsuit.

◻ In September military police arrested for questioning Sedi Bansah, a journalist on the *Crusading Guide* newspaper, at the instigation of a government minister, after the journalist telephoned the minister to check a report of the minister's involvement in a shooting incident. Shortly afterwards, unidentified assailants smeared the newspaper's offices with human excrement, a form of harassment previously used against other privately owned newspapers which criticized the government.

◻ In October armed officers from the Second Infantry Brigade in Kumasi were alleged to have taken five girls, all hairdressing apprentices, to an army barracks where they were assaulted and then to a police station where two were held overnight. The soldiers reportedly stripped and beat the girls' employer, Gifty Brown Davis, at her hairdressing salon and drove her, naked, to the military barracks where she was reportedly again beaten before a senior officer. The soldiers were said to have been acting at the request of the landlady, who had already been served with a court order restraining her from harassment.

Impunity

The government continued not to respond to calls for investigations into human rights violations committed before and after the return to civilian rule in 1993. The military continued to act with impunity and were not held accountable for instances in which they reportedly detained or assaulted people. In August the police denied knowledge of an unofficial "police station" at Military Headquarters, Burma Camp, where soldiers reportedly detained and assaulted a number of civilians.

During the election campaign, John Kufuor promised an investigation into human rights violations if he was elected.

Death penalty

In July the High Court sentenced to death Ebenezer Quaynor, an armed forces officer, following his conviction for murder. No executions were carried out.

In August AI's Ghanaian Section and other local human rights groups launched an action in Accra as part of a worldwide campaign seeking a moratorium on the use of the death penalty as the first step towards its abolition in countries where executions had not been carried out for several years.

AI country report

- Ghana: Briefing on the death penalty (AI Index: AFR 28/001/2000)

GREECE

HELLENIC REPUBLIC
Head of state: Konstandinos Stephanopoulos
Head of government: Konstandinos Simitis
Capital: Athens
Population: 10.6 million
Official language: Greek
Death penalty: abolitionist for all crimes
2000 treaty ratifications/signatures: Optional Protocol to the UN Children's Convention on the involvement of children in armed conflict

Fourteen people faced legal proceedings for peacefully exercising their right to freedom of expression or religion. Conscientious objectors who refused to perform alternative civilian service of punitive length continued to face trial. There were further allegations of ill-treatment by law enforcement officials. Inadequate investigations into past human rights abuses raised serious concerns about impunity.

Freedom of expression and religion

Fourteen people faced legal proceedings for peacefully exercising their right to freedom of expression or religion.

◻ Legal proceedings continued against Mehmet Emin Aga for peacefully exercising his right to freedom of religion and expression. He was tried in June and November in Lamia and Serres on five separate counts for the same offence of "usurpation of the function of a Minister of a known religion". At an appeal hearing in Lamia the sentences were reduced to seven months' imprisonment. In November the Appeal Court in Serres confirmed another seven-month sentence against him on the same charges. Mehmet Emin Aga had been sentenced to a total of 28 months' imprisonment on the same charges in previous years, but had been allowed to pay a sum of money in lieu of terms of imprisonment. AI takes no position on the procedures to be followed for choosing religious leaders or their legitimacy. AI's concern in this case is based solely on its belief that Mehmet Emin Aga was tried for exercising his right to freedom of religion and expression and that, if imprisoned, he would be a prisoner of conscience.

In June, Hara Kalomiri was sentenced to two months' imprisonment, suspended for three years, for operating a place of worship without a state licence between September 1994 and March 1995. The charges related to her role as administrator of the Karma Rik Drol-Ling Center of Practical Philosophy and Psychology in Trapezi, Halkidiki. The court considered this to be a "temple of Buddhist cult" because residents "engaged in Buddhist acts of cult, concretely...in meditation". She had initially been sentenced to three months' imprisonment in 1996, but this was reduced on appeal to two months in 1997. In March 1998, the Supreme Court had overturned this decision and sent the case back to the Appeal Court.

In June, 12 teachers from the ethnic Turkish minority were acquitted on appeal in Patras. In June 1997 they had been sentenced to eight months' imprisonment, suspended for three years, for participating in the Union of Turkish Teachers in Western Thrace. The organization was declared illegal because it had the word "Turkish" in its title. They were charged with inciting mutual hatred between Christians and Muslims in the area by speaking about "Turkish" rather than "Muslim" teachers, and for urging teachers and pupils to boycott classes.

Conscientious objectors

Provisions of the law on conscription continued to fall short of international standards. For example, the length of alternative civilian service remained punitive and its application discriminatory. In September the Parliamentary Committee in charge of reviewing the Constitution made a proposal to amend the current Constitution, which states that "[e]very Greek capable of bearing arms is obliged to contribute to the defence of the Fatherland as provided by law", and to introduce, for the first time, full recognition of the right to conscientious objection. Under existing legislation, those deemed not to have conscientious objector status and to have refused to perform military service can be sentenced to up to four years' imprisonment.

In June Nikos Karanikas, a conscientious objector on philosophical and political grounds, was acquitted by a Thessaloniki court following a successful appeal against his conviction in October 1995 for "insubordination in a period of general mobilization". He had been sentenced to four years' imprisonment, subsequently reduced on appeal to one year's imprisonment, suspended for three years.

Ill-treatment

There were further allegations of ill-treatment by law enforcement officials. Many reports involved beatings by police officers at the time of arrest. There were also reports of ill-treatment of asylum-seekers during forced deportation.

Despite repeated appeals, the authorities failed to investigate adequately allegations of ill-treatment of Roma by police or to bring those responsible to justice. Impunity for past human rights violations remained a concern.

In March the authorities confirmed that no disciplinary measures were being taken against police officers suspected of involvement in the shooting and killing of Angelos Celal in Partheni in April 1998. An appeal against this decision was lodged with the Supreme Court. Little or no progress had been made in the investigation initiated in June 1998 into the killing and there were reports that members of Angelos Celal's family had been repeatedly harassed by police officers prior to his death.

AI country visit

AI visited Greece in June to observe trials and carry out research.

GUATEMALA

REPUBLIC OF GUATEMALA
Head of state and government: Alfonso Portillo (replaced Álvaro Arzú Irigoyen in January)
Capital: Guatemala City
Population: 11.2 million
Official language: Spanish
Death penalty: retentionist
2000 treaty ratifications/signatures: Optional Protocol to the International Covenant on Civil and Political Rights; Optional Protocol to the UN Children's Convention on the involvement of children in armed conflict; Optional Protocol to the UN Women's Convention; Inter-American Convention on Forced Disappearance of Persons

Implementation of the 1996 Peace Accords continued to be slow. The recommendations of two recent human rights reports were not acted on and impunity continued to prevail for most human rights violations perpetrated during the civil conflict. Those attempting to investigate and bring to justice the perpetrators continued to face legal obstructions, harassment, intimidation and an escalating level of attacks, including several apparent "disappearances" and extrajudicial executions. Several demonstrators protesting over social and economic issues were killed. Lynchings of criminal suspects increased, allegedly provoked on occasion by local leaders. The death penalty continued to be imposed: two prisoners were executed by botched lethal injections.

Background

In January Alfonso Portillo assumed the presidency and promised that the Peace Accords, which formally ended Guatemala's civil conflict in 1996, would become state policy. He pledged to implement the recommendations of the 1998 report of the Guatemalan church's Recuperation of the Historical Memory (REMHI) project, and of the UN-sponsored Historical Clarification Commission (CEH) which reported in 1999. He stated that shadowy "parallel" structures interfering with the administration of justice would be dismantled and that the murder of Bishop Juan José Gerardi would be clarified within six months. Bishop Gerardi, the head of the Archbishop's Human Rights Office (ODHAG) and leader of the REMHI project, was murdered in April 1998, just two days after the official presentation of REMHI's report.

President Portillo failed to fulfil these promises, and observers noted the increasing power of General Efraín Ríos Montt, former President, founder of President Portillo's political party, and now President of Congress. General Ríos Montt was Head of State and Commander of the Armed Forces during a period when the army killed tens of thousands of indigenous peasants, apparently assisted by unofficial security units and by civil patrols. These patrols had acted as auxiliaries to the military during the conflict and were officially disbanded after the Accords, but were allegedly operating again.

The government did not implement the CEH's recommendation to establish a program to exhume the bodies of those killed in the conflict. Similarly, little progress was made in establishing a witness protection program. The government also failed to implement CEH recommendations to establish special commissions to assess the conduct of military officials during the conflict, and to establish the fate of the "disappeared", including an estimated 444 children.

It was announced that the Presidential Chiefs of Staff Unit (EMP), frequently implicated in abuses including Bishop Gerardi's murder, was to be disbanded. However, EMP staff were to be "recycled" into other government security bodies. A new unit announced in September, mandated to prevent threats to internal security and combat crime, was challenged by the Constitutional Court as it had been created by decree rather than Congressional vote, and would report to the Minister of the Interior, rather than to Congress. The government rescinded the decree and proposed a new unit of special military police to assist the civil police. A similar unit had been disbanded following the Peace Accords.

In May, a database of 650,428 names, apparently compiled by military intelligence during the 1980s, was made public by a government official. Guatemalan analysts believed the coded number against each name contained information on their fate.

Allegations of government incompetence and corruption created repeated rumours of an impending coup and heightened tensions. In April protests in the capital over proposed public transport price rises resulted in four deaths, including that of a prominent journalist. The discovery that General Ríos Montt and members of his party had altered a liquor tax law after passage by Congress sparked further demonstrations later in the year. One demonstrator was killed.

Efforts to combat impunity

Efforts to combat impunity in individual cases or with respect to specific past massacres made very slow progress through the courts.

Depositions were finally taken in March 2000 from two former special forces soldiers (*kaibiles*) who testified in exchange for safe passage abroad regarding the 1982 massacre at Dos Erres, El Petén, when the army killed more than 350 indigenous villagers. Almost immediately, the government announced "friendly settlements" with the Inter-American Commission on Human Rights in several cases, including Dos Erres. The settlements involved some compensation for the survivors, and official recognition that government forces had been responsible, but no prospect of legal proceedings. They were not accepted by all the families concerned. The military objected to arrest orders issued against a number of soldiers in connection with the massacre, arguing that the pre-trial testimony of the former *kaibiles* violated the presumption of innocence and due process. By the end of 2000, the soldiers had not been arrested.

In a new departure, in May the Centre for Legal Action in Human Rights (CALDH) assisted survivors from 10 massacres to file genocide charges before the Guatemalan courts against former Head of State General Romeo Lucas García (1978-1982) and several officials from his administration. The CEH had concluded that genocide had been committed against indigenous peoples in four specific areas.

A suit filed before the Spanish High Court in December 1999 by the Rigoberta Menchú Foundation, based on the concept of universal jurisdiction, charged a number of former officials, including General Ríos Montt, with human rights crimes including genocide. The suit was joined by several individual victims, survivors and non-governmental organizations. In December the High Court ruled that it did not currently have jurisdiction to judge the crimes. The plaintiffs immediately appealed against the decision; judgment on their appeal was pending at the end of the year.

▭ In August, two men with petty criminal records charged with the May 1999 kidnapping and murder of businessman Edgar Ordóñez Porta were acquitted. The court found that the Public Ministry had allowed an unofficial "parallel" agency to carry out its own "investigation". Proceedings were left open against military officials charged by relatives with carrying out and covering up the murder.

Bishop Gerardi's murder

Obstructions continued in the case of Bishop Gerardi, who was murdered in 1998. In May, two members of the ODHAG investigating team received death threats after the case judge, who has herself received threats and been followed, ruled that three high-ranking military officers should stand trial for the murder, along with the priest who shared Bishop Gerardi's residence, and their housekeeper. By the end of 2000, no date had been set for the trial. Earlier, several others involved in the case were forced to flee the country after threats.

In October, a long-promised report on the case was made public by President Portillo, but provided no new information.

Attacks on human rights defenders

Human rights defenders and journalists were subjected to an escalating wave of abuses. Victims included members of the Guatemalan Forensic Anthropology Association, active in exhuming mass graves; the Students Association of the state University of San Carlos; members of a shanty-town dwellers' association; indigenous and women's rights activists; staff and directors of the news agency *CERIGUA* which regularly covers human rights issues; staff of human rights organizations including the Rigoberta Menchú Foundation; and officials of the Human Rights Procurator's Office.

▭ In one typical incident in August, Celso Balán, a CALDH worker, was detained, robbed, drugged and left unconscious in Chimaltenango by two men. They appeared to be paramilitaries acting under the orders of those responsible for the 1982 army massacre in Chipastor, San Martín Jilotepeque, Chimaltenango, currently under investigation by CALDH. Celso Balán required treatment for neurological, physical, psychological and emotional damage.

▭ In September, heavily armed men raided offices shared by two human rights groups: Families of the Detained and "Disappeared" of Guatemala, FAMDEGUA, and HIJOS, children of the "disappeared" who want their parents' fate clarified. The armed men forced their victims to the floor, held pistols to their heads, and threatened to kill them. Male victims were forced to strip. Office equipment and case records, including some concerning Dos Erres, were stolen.

'Disappeared' children and illegal adoptions

In August an ODHAG study reported that it had located eight children out of 86 "disappeared" children's cases it had investigated. It stated that Guatemala's lucrative trade in illegal adoptions began during the conflict, when military or paramilitary families took in children found wandering after massacres.

People who tried to investigate illegal adoptions faced threats and intimidation. Staff of a human rights and economic migrants organization on the Guatemalan-Mexican border were threatened, apparently because they provided information regarding illegal transfers of children across the border to the UN Special Rapporteur on the sale of children, child prostitution and child pornography.

▭ University professor Mayra Angelina Gutiérrez, missing since April, was reportedly targeted because she submitted information about illegal adoptions to the Special Rapporteur. Her name was found on the military database released in May, supporting the hypothesis that her "disappearance" was politically motivated.

Women and sexual minorities

In October, Guatemalan women's rights activists reported the failure to implement Peace Accord provisions regarding women to the UN Security Council.

▭ In June and July, two transvestite sex workers were killed in Guatemala City. Guatemalan gay groups have alleged the existence of an orchestrated program of "social cleansing" carried out with police acquiescence, support, and possible direct involvement.

Death penalty

Concern over crime rates contributed to widespread support for the judicial death penalty. By the end of 2000 about 40 people were under sentence of death. In May Congress annulled legislation providing for executive clemency, a right recognized under international law. However, President Portillo considered clemency appeals already filed, and in May granted clemency to a mentally disturbed indigenous man, deemed fit to stand trial after psychological testing carried out in Spanish, which he did not speak, and then convicted at a trial also held in Spanish. In November, the Constitutional Court revoked five death sentences on the grounds that according to the Guatemalan Constitution, international law prevailed over national law in human rights matters.

◻ Tomás Cerrate Hernández and Luis Amílcar Cetino Pérez were convicted in 1998 of the kidnapping and murder of a wealthy woman. They were executed by lethal injection in June 2000, and the executions were televised. Tomás Cerrate Hernández took seven minutes to die and Luis Amílcar Cetino Pérez eight to nine minutes, after the machine malfunctioned.

◻ In January, five lawyers who appealed against death sentences passed on alleged kidnappers received death threats, apparently from death penalty supporters. Fearful for their lives, the lawyers resigned.

AI country reports and visits
Reports
- Guatemala: Women's rights defender missing – Mayra Angelina Gutiérrez (AI Index: AMR 34/016/2000)
- Guatemala: Breaking the wall of impunity – Prosecution for crimes against humanity (AI Index: AMR 34/020/2000)
- Guatemala: Further executions loom (AI Index: AMR 34/022/2000)
- Guatemala: HIJOS – Justice for the new generation (AI Index: AMR 34/042/2000)

Visits
An AI research delegation visited Guatemala in April and May and helped make public the CALDH genocide suit. AI's Guatemala Trial Observers Project monitored proceedings related to the killing of Edgar Ordóñez Porta and the 1982 massacres at Dos Erres and Tululché, El Quiché.

GUINEA

REPUBLIC OF GUINEA
Head of state: Lansanna Conté
Head of government: Lamine Sidimé
Capital: Conakry
Population: 7.4 million
Official language: French
Death penalty: retentionist
2000 treaty ratifications/signatures: Rome Statute of the International Criminal Court; African Charter on the Rights and Welfare of the Child

There were reports of human rights abuses in border areas, in the context of cross-border incursions by armed groups from neighbouring countries. Several prisoners of conscience, including prominent opposition leader Alpha Condé, were sentenced to prison terms after an unfair trial by the State Security Court. Torture of detainees to extract confessions or intimidate suspects continued to be reported on a regular basis.

Background
Armed clashes between the security forces and armed groups from neighbouring countries intensified from September onwards in the southern border areas. The Guinean authorities accused the Sierra Leonean opposition force, the Revolutionary United Front (RUF), and the Liberian authorities of backing the cross-border attackers, who included Guinean army deserters. Liberia accused Guinea of harbouring dissidents who had been fighting government troops in northern Liberia since early July. (See Liberia entry.)

The fighting forced thousands of people to flee from the area. In December, the heads of state of the Economic Community of West African States (ECOWAS), meeting in Mali, decided to send an intervention force to police the borders of Guinea. The ECOWAS summit also recommended an "urgent meeting" between the leaders of the three countries (Guinea, Liberia and Sierra Leone) under the auspices of ECOWAS and the Organization of African Unity (OAU).

Municipal elections were held in June, but were marred by violence and allegations of vote-rigging. Official sources confirmed that five people were killed and others wounded when they protested against delays in announcing the elections results. The elections were won by the ruling *Parti de l'unité et du progrès*, Party of Unity and Progress. The opposition alleged that the results were invalid. Parliamentary elections originally scheduled for June 1999 were postponed and had not been held by the end of 2000.

Prisoners of conscience
In April Alpha Condé, president of the *Rassemblement du peuple de Guinée* (RPG), Guinean People's Rally, and 47 others were tried on charges of threatening the security of the state. Their trial before the State Security Court did not meet international standards for fair trial. In September Alpha Condé was sentenced to five years' imprisonment and 10 other defendants were given sentences ranging from a suspended one-year prison term to three years' imprisonment. Four others were convicted *in absentia*.

AI sent an observer to the early hearings of this trial, which lasted from April to September. AI concluded that all those convicted who were still in detention were prisoners of conscience, held solely because of their political affiliations, without any evidence of involvement in or advocacy of violence. AI was particularly concerned by the fact that the defendants were detained incommunicado for months and that most of them were tortured in order to extract confessions. These confessions were accepted by the Court, despite evidence of torture. The right to a fair hearing was not respected during the investigation phase. Lawyers did not have access to their clients' files until five days before the trial started, and during the trial one defence lawyer was subjected to serious intimidation by the Minister of Justice.

The State Security Court, a special court, was composed of magistrates appointed directly by the President, even though Alpha Condé was a leading opposition figure and a former presidential candidate.

GUI

Furthermore, contrary to international standards, the verdict of this special court was not open to appeal. The only possible appeal, the *pourvoi en cassation* (appeal on points of law), prohibited any re-examination of the facts. AI called, therefore, not only for the immediate and unconditional release of the prisoners of conscience, but also for the abolition of the State Security Court if its procedures were not brought in line with international standards for fair trial.

Torture/ill-treatment

Torture of detainees to extract confessions or intimidate suspects continued to be reported on a regular basis. The majority of those tried with Alpha Condé were subjected to ill-treatment or torture at the time of their arrest in 1999, to extract confessions or to make them sign statements incriminating the RPG leader. During a fact-finding mission in April 2000, AI delegates collected testimony from a number of them. They described torture techniques used by the security forces, including: blows all over the body; slaps, punches and kicks; suffocation under water at sea; starvation; and death threats. The victims stated that people close to the Presidency were present when they were tortured.

There were also reports of arbitrary arrests followed by torture and ill-treatment, and of women accused of supporting the opposition being subjected to sexual violence while in detention in 1998.

Death in custody

At least one person died in custody as a result of torture.

▢ Sergeant Guey Keita died during the night of 15 January, after reportedly having been starved for eight days. The evening before his death, he was tortured in an attempt to make him admit that he had received money from Alpha Condé.

Reprisal attacks against refugees.

In September, following incursions by armed groups from Liberia and Sierra Leone, the President of Guinea called on the security forces to search everywhere so that suspects could be arrested. He urged the international community to "rid" Guinea of its thousands of refugees from these two countries and called on Guinean "civilians and members of the armed forces" to "crush the invaders". After this statement, several hundred refugees from Sierra Leone and Liberia were arbitrarily arrested in Conakry. AI publicly appealed to the government to protect the fundamental rights of refugees.

In mid-September, following an attack on Macenta, a town on the border with Liberia, Mensah Kpognon, a member of the UN High Commissioner for Refugees (UNHCR), was killed. Laurence Djeya, another member of UNHCR, was abducted. She managed to escape and reached Côte d'Ivoire a fortnight later.

AI country report and visits
Report
- Guinea: The Alpha Condé affair – A mockery of a trial (AI Index: AFR 29/002/2000F)

Visits
AI delegates visited Guinea in April to conduct research and to hold talks with the government. It was not possible for any government official to meet the delegation.

AI sent an observer to the trial of Alpha Condé and 47 others before the State Security Court in April.

GUINEA-BISSAU

REPUBLIC OF GUINEA-BISSAU
Head of state: Kumba Ialá
Head of government: Caetano N'Tchama
Capital: Bissau
Population: 1.2 million
Official language: Portuguese
Death penalty: abolitionist for all crimes
2000 treaty ratifications/signatures: International Covenant on Civil and Political Rights and its two Optional Protocols; UN Convention against Racism; UN Convention against Torture; Optional Protocol to the UN Children's Convention on the involvement of children in armed conflict; Optional Protocol to the UN Women's Convention; Rome Statute of the International Criminal Court

Following elections in November 1999 a coalition government was appointed which announced its commitment to human rights protection and to ending impunity. Security officers were convicted of human rights violations committed during the armed conflict of 1998-1999 and sentenced to prison terms. Political prisoners were released, some pending trial. Seven political leaders and about 200 soldiers were arrested following an army rebellion. There were reports of human rights abuses by soldiers. The mandate of the UN Peace-building Support Office in Guinea-Bissau (UNOGBIS) was extended for one year.

Background

Kumba Ialá, president of the *Partido da Renovação Social* (PRS), Social Renewal Party, won the second round of presidential elections in January, and in February he was sworn in as President. Caetano N'Tchama of the PRS became Prime Minister and formed a coalition government with the second largest party, the *Resistência da Guiné-Bissau-Movimento Bafatá* (RGB-MB), Guinea-Bissau Resistance-Bafatá Movement. The new government stated that its priorities were to promote reconciliation following the 1998-1999 civil war, to strengthen democracy, the rule of law, good governance and respect for human rights, and to combat corruption and poverty. It also announced plans to depoliticize the armed forces and to demobilize 6,000 soldiers by the end of 2001. The salary of soldiers was increased but about 50 soldiers arrested at the end of 1999 in connection with a strike over salaries remained in prison without charge.

There was tension between civil and military authorities and the government was increasingly confronted with indiscipline by senior military officers. Efforts were under way to redefine the role of the military in the new democratic Guinea-Bissau. Negotiations between the new government and the former Junta Militar, Military Junta, were led by a group of mediators from civil society, with assistance from the Special Representative of the UN Secretary-General in Guinea-Bissau. In February, the leader of the former Military Junta, General Ansumane Mané, turned down President Kumba Ialá's offer of the post of special defence adviser to the government, stating that the army had pledged political neutrality. However, the military continued to maintain a high public profile and to perform police functions, as police were constrained by lack of resources and appropriate training. Tension increased in April when Lamine Sanha, the navy commander, was dismissed but refused to leave his post, arguing that he was accountable only to General Ansumane Mané. The case was resolved after negotiations involving the goodwill commission of religious and community leaders set up during the conflict. Tension was further heightened in November after General Ansumane Mané rejected the government's promotion of army officers. Fighting briefly erupted in Bissau between army factions loyal to the government and supporters of General Ansumane Mané, who proclaimed himself chief of staff of the armed forces after placing the then chief of staff under arrest.

After a few days at large, General Ansumane Mané was captured and killed, reportedly in a shoot-out with soldiers loyal to the government, in Quinhamel, some 30 kilometres north of Bissau. Some reports, however, suggested that he had been captured alive, tortured and then shot. By the end of 2000 no investigation into his death had been carried out.

At least 200 soldiers who supported General Ansumane Mané were arrested and accused of attempting to overthrow the government. None had been tried or formally charged by the end of 2000.

In March the mandate of UNOGBIS, which had helped with the transition process, was extended for another year. UNOGBIS monitored prison conditions and releases of political prisoners. It provided support to the Supreme Court by training a further 20 magistrates, including in human rights issues.

In August the International Committee of the Red Cross ran a seminar on humanitarian law which was attended by 370 soldiers and officers. The *Liga Guineense de Direitos Humanos* (LGDH), Guinean (Bissau) Human Rights League, held several seminars on human rights for 50 police officers and judicial officials.

Relations between Senegal and Guinea-Bissau were strained. In April Guinea-Bissau accused Senegal of bombing its territory while it denied accusations that its territory was being used by rebels of the *Mouvement des forces démocratiques de Casamance* (MFDC), Democratic Forces of Casamance Movement, to attack Senegal. Relations deteriorated in August when, following attacks by armed groups, Senegalese villagers closed the border between the countries, causing shortages of food and fuel in Guinea-Bissau.

Steps to end impunity

The new government repeatedly stated its commitment to overcome impunity and important steps were taken to that end.

In August, three security officers were tried on charges of human rights violations committed during the armed conflict, including arbitrary arrest, torture and extrajudicial executions. They were convicted and sentenced to prison terms ranging from seven to 15 years and ordered to pay large sums in compensation to the victims and their families. One was convicted of killing Lai António Lopes Pereira, who was shot dead at his home in July 1998, and of the arbitrary arrest and torture of Bitchofola Na Fafé and Ansumane Fati. He was sentenced to 15 years' imprisonment and ordered to compensate the victims and their families.

Human rights defenders

In May, Inácio Tavares, president of the LGDH, was threatened with reprisals after denouncing the beating by soldiers of electricity company workers following a power cut at a military air base. General Ansumane Mané reportedly ordered the arrest of a radio journalist who reported the beatings, alleging that the story was false. In another incident in May, television news reader Issufe Queta and news editor Paula Melo were detained for 48 hours after reading a press statement by Fernando Gomes, president of the *Aliança Socialista Guineense* (ASG), Socialist Alliance of Guinea (Bissau), who was himself detained for 36 hours. He had criticized the political situation in the country. The three were released on bail and faced charges of slander and defamation. They had not been tried by the end of 2000. Fernando Gomes was arrested again in November and detained for over a week, accused of supporting the military rebellion. He was severely beaten at the time of the arrest.

Arrests of political opponents

Several leading members of opposition political parties were arrested in the wake of the military rebellion. Among them were several members of the *União para Mudança* (UM), Union for Change, including Aminé Saad, former Procurator General, Caramba Turé, a member of parliament, who was held for two days, and Agnelo Regalla, the director of *Bombolón Radio*. Also arrested were Fernando Gomes (see above) and Francisco Benante, president of the *Partido Africano para a Independência da Guiné e Cabo Verde* (PAIGC), African Party for the Independence of Guinea (Bissau). Those arrested were held for over a week at the main police station and placed under house arrest where they remained, uncharged, at the end of 2000.

Abuses by soldiers
Soldiers continued to abuse their power and to ill-treat civilians. None was brought to justice. Most of the incidents involved General Ansumane Mané's bodyguards.

◻ In May, bodyguards of General Ansumane Mané detained and beat human rights activist Marcelino Víctor. He had gone to the General's house to get his niece and two other girls who had been detained there for several hours after they dumped rubbish outside the house. He was detained there overnight and beaten. He complained to the authorities but no action was taken.

Political trials
Most of the 270 people still in detention at the beginning of 2000 in connection with crimes committed during the conflict were released, some pending trial. Others had the charges against them dropped. Seven were in prison at the end of the year, three serving sentences (see above) and four awaiting trial.

◻ Avito da Silva and Manuel dos Santos "Manecas", two civilian former ministers in the government of ousted President João Bernardo Vieira, were acquitted in February of charges of treason, giving financial support to the former President, incitement to war and collaboration with foreign troops. The prosecution failed to present evidence to sustain the charges. Their acquittal led to the dismissal of the Attorney General in March.

GUYANA

REPUBLIC OF GUYANA
Head of state: Bharrat Jagdeo
Head of government: Samuel Hinds
Capital: Georgetown
Population: 0.8 million
Official language: English
Death penalty: retentionist
2000 treaty ratifications/signatures: Rome Statute of the International Criminal Court

There were reports of torture and ill-treatment by the police, and of police shootings in disputed circumstances. There were 23 people under sentence of death at the end of 2000. Prison conditions amounted to cruel, inhuman and degrading treatment.

Background
The Constitution Reform Committee, a parliamentary body, received proposals for the amendment of the 1985 Constitution. The Guyana Defence Force proposed that the Constitution should outline the criteria for the deployment of troops in maintaining law and order.

Torture/ill-treatment
There were reports of torture and ill-treatment, including sexual assault, by the police. Victims included criminal suspects and their relatives. Individuals were arrested and detained arbitrarily, and were held in incommunicado detention by the police in conditions falling well below international standards.

In January, the Guyana Police Force reported that 40 officers had been disciplined or charged with a criminal offence as a result of complaints made during 1999. A further 15 were charged in June following complaints made in 2000.

◻ In September Mohammed Shafeek, aged 47, died in Brickdam police lock-up. An autopsy reportedly revealed multiple injuries, including fractures, cuts and bruises. Police failed to inform his family of his death. Initial police reports stating that he had been killed by fellow inmates conflicted with eyewitness reports which maintained that he had been injured by the police and was subsequently denied medical attention.

Police shootings
There were several police shootings in disputed circumstances, some of which appeared to be possible extrajudicial executions. Inquests had still not reportedly taken place into many killings by police, including the cases of Bonitus Winter and Shawn Nedd.

◻ On 7 January, Dexter Randolph was fatally shot by police officers in Tiger Bay in disputed circumstances. Eyewitnesses alleged that he was dragged from under a police vehicle and shot. The police asserted that he was armed.

◻ On 14 April, an inquest jury concluded that no one could be held criminally responsible for the death of Victor Bourne, who was fatally shot by police in June 1998 at his home in Rasville. AI called for the findings of the inquest to be published in full.

Death penalty
Twenty-three people were under sentence of death at the end of 2000, including two women. Death sentences continued to be handed down, and some defendants in death penalty cases did not have adequate legal representation.

The executions of Ravindra Deo, Oral Hendricks, Ganga Deolall and Lawrence Chan were scheduled for 7 and 8 February 2000. All four men were granted stays of execution, to allow the courts to consider further legal applications.

◻ Lawyers acting for Abdool Saleem Yasseen and Noel Thomas, two death row prisoners, argued that the Court of Appeal had shown bias, since its three judges had publicly stated their support for capital punishment in comments on their cases. The outcome of the two men's appeals were still pending at the end of 2000.

Prison conditions
There were reports of ill-treatment in prison and of conditions which amounted to cruel, inhuman or

degrading treatment. Severe overcrowding, aggravated by long delays in the judicial system, contributed to outbreaks of infectious diseases including tuberculosis. Children continued to be held alongside adult prisoners, and human rights organizations were denied access to prisoners.

International organizations

In March AI attended a hearing on Guyana of the UN Human Rights Committee in New York, USA, and in April AI urged the government to implement in full the Committee's recommendations, in particular those concerning the use of excessive force by law enforcement officials, the obligation to treat those deprived of their liberty with humanity and the need to stop detaining children with adults.

Guyana failed to comply with its international reporting obligations under the UN Convention against Torture.

In April the Inter-American Commission on Human Rights (IACHR) wrote to the government regarding the "disappearance" of Franz Britton, who has not been seen since he was detained in police custody in January 1999. The government failed to respond.

Following a hearing in October on the situation in Guyana by the IACHR in Washington, USA, the IACHR agreed to send a delegation to investigate human rights abuses.

AI visit

In February AI delegates visited Guyana to conduct research, and met government officials including the Minister for Home Affairs and the Minister for Foreign Affairs.

HAITI

HAITI
Head of state: René Préval
Head of government: Jacques Edouard Alexis
Capital: Port-au-Prince
Population: 8.2 million
Official languages: French, Creole
Death penalty: abolitionist for all crimes

The human rights situation deteriorated sharply, despite some positive steps towards accounting for past human rights violations. The electoral period was marred by assassinations of public figures and by violent attacks by political partisans, most often self-described supporters of the *Fanmi Lavalas* (FL) party. Illegal security forces acting under the auspices of newly-elected local and regional officials emerged. Haiti also became more isolated from the international community, with the UN announcing its intention to end its field mission there.

Background

In January 1999, President René Préval failed to extend the mandates of Haitian parliamentarians. The terms of local officials expired as well, with the result that until the third quarter of 2000 there were practically no sitting officials in Haiti, and the president ruled by decree. Local and legislative elections were eventually held in May 2000, with a reported 29,000 candidates running for 7,500 posts. Turnout, estimated at 60 per cent, was the highest since 1990. The vote was declared generally peaceful by observers, with consensus that FL candidates had won the majority of contests.

However, dissension arose over the method used by electoral officials to determine whether a second round was necessary. International and some national observers declared the method used at the central level to tally votes and to determine whether run-offs were necessary in any given race to be fraudulent and biased in favour of FL candidates. Léon Manus, head of the Provisional Electoral Council, eventually fled the country for the USA, where he denounced President Préval for pressurizing him to tabulate results in favour of the FL party. The Organization of American States pulled out its election observers before the second round in July in protest. A modified Electoral Council oversaw the November presidential elections, despite some domestic criticism and lack of international support. The international community declined to support or monitor the presidential race and suspended much-needed aid.

Following a wave of pre-election violence, including anonymous bomb and grenade attacks that killed two children and wounded a reported 16 people, turnout was lower than for earlier contests. However, former President Jean-Bertrand Aristide was elected overwhelmingly. His inauguration was set for February 2001.

HAI

The UN field mission, *Mission Civile Internationale d'Appui en Haïti* (MICAH), began work on 15 March. Its human rights advisers, already reduced in number from the previous level, were not deployed for several months owing to funding constraints. In November, UN Secretary-General Kofi Annan announced that the mission, which had been present in various forms since 1993, would not be renewed the following year, stating that the UN contribution would be reduced to technical aid only. AI believed that this was due to funding or other constraints, rather than to consideration of the needs of the situation in Haiti. AI expressed great concern at the discontinuation of a human rights monitoring presence in the field when the human rights situation in Haiti was more serious than at any time since the 1994 return to democracy.

Violence in the electoral context

A number of electoral candidates, party members and their relatives were killed during 2000, most by unidentified assailants. Others went into hiding out of fears for their safety. Two children were killed in grenade and other explosions in the run-up to the presidential elections; no one claimed responsibility for these attacks. In addition, numerous arson attacks were carried out against electoral and party offices. Violence by self-described political partisans continued throughout the year. Sometimes the police failed to intervene and on a few occasions appeared to collude in the violence. In some instances the police were attacked when they intervened to stop violent demonstrators.

Jean Dominique, a prominent radio journalist and advocate of human rights principles, was shot dead by unknown assailants outside his radio station, *Radio Haiti Inter*, on 3 April. The station guard, Jean Claude Louissaint, was also killed. A march of several hundred people calling for those responsible to be brought to justice was disrupted by self-described FL supporters, as was his funeral. They subsequently burned down the headquarters of an opposition party and threatened to attack the premises of a private radio station known to broadcast opinions critical of their party. That station subsequently stopped broadcasting temporarily because of security concerns and *Radio Haiti Inter* suspended broadcasts for one month after Jean Dominique's death. Investigations were continuing at the end of 2000, although one senator refused to comply with a judicial summons to testify, claiming parliamentary immunity.

Emergence of illegal security forces

Some of the local and regional officials elected in May and subsequent run-off elections established illegal security forces, which were responsible for a significant number of human rights violations. There is no legal basis or mechanism of control for these forces, and their members are generally supporters of the FL party to which most elected officials belong. In some instances officials claimed they were creating the forces to combat crime and bolster the Haitian National Police, which they accused of being ineffective; in others, their motivation was overtly political.

On 2 November, three participants and two passers-by were wounded by gunfire when a meeting of the opposition coalition *Convergence Démocratique*, and the grassroots organization *Mouvman Peyizan de Papaye*, in the town of Hinche was attacked by supporters of two local FL-affiliated mayors. The same evening, the house of the regional coordinator of the political party *Espace de Concertation* was set alight by armed attackers who forced their way in and stole radio equipment before setting fire to the building. The mayors themselves were reportedly present and active in some of these incidents. Members of the same group had reportedly closed a local court and threatened several judges whom they accused of belonging to opposing political parties. AI raised the incident with the Minister of Justice and Public Security, the President of the Senate and other high-ranking officials, all of whom expressed concern. The Prime Minister condemned the violence and pledged to dismantle such illegal forces.

The Haitian National Police

There were several reports of unlawful killings by police. Most of the victims were criminal suspects. Reports of ill-treatment of juvenile suspects following arrest were frequent.

A group of 25 children and adult men, illegally and arbitrarily detained in Petionville in mid-September by unofficial agents of the mayor's office, were reportedly beaten when they were seized. They were then handed over to the local police lockup, where they were held in such overcrowded conditions that several had to be hospitalized. When they protested against these conditions, they were reportedly beaten by police officers before eventually being transferred to the National Penitentiary.

The police were repeatedly accused of inaction in the face of politically motivated violence, and at times of complicity with partisans. In one October incident in which police tried to intervene during a political demonstration, a municipal police commissioner in Port-au-Prince attempted to disarm a well-known FL activist. The police commissioner and three accompanying police officers narrowly escaped lynching. Shortly thereafter, five police commissioners fled the country, fearing for their safety in the light of rumours, apparently unfounded, that they had been involved in a coup plot.

A rural police presence was under discussion to supplement the functioning of the Haitian National Police in the countryside. Human rights activists were concerned that its independence and impartiality should be guaranteed in light of the repressive tactics of the rural security system under previous governments, especially given the emergence of illegal and partisan security forces acting in conjunction with local officials.

In late April, the head of the internal affairs division responsible for investigating violations by police was removed; a permanent replacement had not been named by the end of 2000.

Overcoming impunity
Some steps were taken to bring to justice those responsible for human rights violations.

▭ The May 1999 extrajudicial execution of 11 people in Carrefour-Feuilles was the most serious human rights violation committed by members of the Haitian National Police since its inception in 1994. Several arrests were made and for the first time, police officers were brought to trial for human rights violations. Six of those arrested were released for lack of evidence before the trial began. Four police officers, including police commissioner Coles Rameau, were convicted and sentenced to the minimum penalty of three years' imprisonment and fined. Two others were acquitted.

▭ In October the trial began of those accused of participating in the 24 April 1994 Raboteau massacre. Raboteau, a heavily populated coastal neighbourhood outside the town of Gonaives, was targeted for repression under the *de facto* military government because of its activist past and its residents' allegiance to ousted president Jean-Bertrand Aristide. Sixteen defendants were convicted and six acquitted. Among 37 others tried in their absence were former military ruler Raoul Cedras, former police chief Michel François, former paramilitary leader Emmanuel "Toto" Constant and former military leader Philippe Biamby.

Judicial concerns
The judiciary continued to be largely dysfunctional. Lack of progress in investigating and trying suspects contributed to severe prison overcrowding, with an estimated 80 per cent of detainees awaiting trial. In February Claude Raymond, a notorious supporter of the former government of Jean-Claude Duvalier, died in hospital after spending six years in prison without trial. Numerous judicial orders for his release had been ignored.

The Ministry of Justice and Public Security, with input from human rights and other groups, developed seven draft bills on crucial issues such as judicial reform, independence of the judiciary and the administration of justice.

AI country report and visits
Report
- Haiti: Unfinished business – justice and liberties at risk (AI Index: AMR 36/001/2000)

Visits
In May AI met contacts in the Haitian diaspora community in Miami, USA. In October and November AI delegates visited Haiti and met government officials, other authorities and members of different sectors of civil society.

HONDURAS

REPUBLIC OF HONDURAS
Head of state and government: Carlos Flores Facussé
Capital: Tegucigalpa
Population: 6.5 million
Official language: Spanish
Death penalty: abolitionist for all crimes

Indigenous peoples staged renewed demonstrations to promote long-standing demands for land, justice and improved services, but despite an agreement signed with authorities, most of the issues of concern remained unresolved. The National Police employed excessive force against demonstrators. Human rights defenders were again subjected to attacks and threats. Children were victims of grave human rights violations. Despite an important Supreme Court ruling, impunity was still prevalent in cases of past human rights violations.

Background
Among measures taken to deal with a reported rise in crime was a decision to allow the army to join the police force in law enforcement. The police force itself was often accused of involvement in criminal activities from drug-related offences to abuse of authority. A process to purge the force took place during 2000.

The government reduced the budget of the Office of the National Commissioner for the Protection of Human Rights. At least five regional offices had to be closed and staff were reduced in others. This followed an ultimately unsuccessful attempt in 1999 to amend the law regulating the Office, which would have reduced its scope for action and the period in office of the current Commissioner. The Office has played a crucial role in the protection of human rights and in exposing corruption since its inception in 1992.

In November the government finally provided compensation to families of victims of human rights violations in the 1980s. Relatives of 17 "disappeared" people, out of 184 officially acknowledged, received financial compensation following proceedings before the Inter-American Commission on Human Rights. Some of the beneficiaries, however, stated that this action did not absolve the state from its responsibility to properly investigate the violations and bring those responsible to justice.

Indigenous groups
Indigenous groups organized further demonstrations calling on the authorities to tackle the impunity surrounding the murders of indigenous leaders, to find solutions to land disputes and to improve health and education services. In September they organized a hunger strike to protest against the dismissal of Gilberto Sánchez Chandías, Special Prosecutor for Ethnic Affairs in the Public Ministry. His dismissal raised concern that the representation of indigenous

people at an official level would be diminished. On 6 September both sides came to an agreement in which the authorities made a number of commitments, including the defence of the interests of indigenous groups, the creation of a Special Programme of Investigation into the killings of indigenous leaders and others, and the formation of a commission to guarantee the follow-up of previous agreements. However, by the end of 2000, there had been little, if any, progress.

There were further death threats, harassment and intimidation of indigenous leaders. In March, three leaders of the Coordinating Body of Popular Organizations of Aguán (COPA) received death threats, allegedly from armed groups with links to the authorities. One of them had been shot at three times in April and September 1999 and his house was set on fire. COPA works to promote the rights of peasant farmers, environmental protection and participation in elections.

In June Salvador Zúñiga and Berta Cáceres were harassed and intimidated, reportedly because of their work with the Civil Council of Popular and Indigenous Organizations (COPIN) in defence of indigenous people. Their house was broken into twice, and they were subjected to intimidatory surveillance. They opposed the building of the El Tigre dam, which would displace indigenous people and flood their ancestral lands.
Update
In October 1999, 45 members of different indigenous groups were injured in demonstrations. On 12 October 2000, the victims finally received compensation from the state. Among the beneficiaries was 61-year-old Domingo Gómez, a Lenca peasant, who lost his right eye as a result of a wound from a bullet fired by the police.

Human rights defenders
Human rights defenders continued their efforts to protect human rights despite attacks and threats against them.

Julio César Pineda Alvarado, an outspoken journalist and human rights defender, received anonymous threatening calls at his home. In April he was shot at outside his house. His wife and two children were with him when two men got out of a car and, without speaking, one of them put a gun to his head and shot. He was wounded but the fact that he was wearing his motorbike helmet saved his life. In May his wife was approached and threatened by two men on a bus. An investigation into the shooting was initiated only after pressure from the National Commissioner for the Protection of Human Rights, but moved extremely slowly and by the end of 2000 had reported no findings. AI called on the authorities to investigate the threats, to bring those responsible to justice and to guarantee Julio Pineda's safety.

Children
In January, 17-year-old Edy Nahum Donaire Ortega was killed by a police officer. He had been detained for alleged theft and held in the police station in San Juan Antonio de la Cuesta, municipality of San Jerónimo, department of Comayagua. This was in violation of the law which prohibits the detention of minors in adult detention centres such as police stations. He escaped on his way back from being taken before a local judge. An officer of the National Preventative Police fired what he claimed to have been a "warning shot" into the air, but the bullet severed an artery in Edy Nahum Donaire Ortega's leg and he died from loss of blood. The officer was arrested on a charge of murder.

Also in January Francisco Javier Espinoza, a 17-year-old street child, died in custody after the police failed to provide medical attention following a severe beating by a bus driver and conductor in Tegucigalpa. They suspected Francisco Javier Espinoza had stolen some earrings from a passenger and beat him over the head with a metal tube. Police officers took him into custody but he died after receiving no medical attention for eight hours, despite profuse bleeding.
Update
In the case of Alexander Obando Reyes, shot dead by a police officer in April 1999, a warrant was issued in October for the arrest of the police officer suspected of being responsible.

The National Police
The police force was responsible for human rights violations. In March, around 100 people whose houses had been destroyed by natural disasters staged a demonstration against an order to evict them from a housing project. At least 10 demonstrators were injured when they were violently ejected by the police. Others, including children, were overwhelmed by tear gas.

The Special Human Rights Prosecutor in the Attorney General's Office reported allegations against the police for human rights violations including torture, unlawful arrest, abuse of authority and murders. The Office stated that it had initiated court proceedings against police officers.

Amnesty decrees declared unconstitutional
In June the Supreme Court of Justice issued a judgment declaring two amnesty decrees unconstitutional. The appeal against the amnesty decrees had been filed by the Attorney General's Office in January 1999. They related to the case of six university students – three women and three men – who were arrested without warrant in 1982 by armed men in civilian clothes. The students were taken to a police station and then on to an unidentified location where they "disappeared" for four days during which time they were tortured. Four of the students were released on the fourth day, and two were charged, but the case was thrown out by the court after 18 months. The Supreme Court's decision ordered the case against those responsible for the "disappearance" and torture to be returned to the First Criminal Court for further proceedings but no progress had been made by the end of 2000.

In July the Attorney General's Office requested clarification, as it considered that the decision should be applicable to all military personnel suspected of human rights violations in the 1980s, especially 184 "disappearance" cases, and not just one specific case.

In 1995, 10 military officers were charged with attempted murder and illegal detention. The accused argued that amnesty decrees 199/87 and 87/91, which granted "full, unconditional amnesty", protected them. When arrest warrants were issued against them, the officers went "underground" and some were still in hiding at the end of 2000.

AI country report
- Honduras: Human rights violations against children (update) (AI Index: AMR 37/002/2000)

HUNGARY

REPUBLIC OF HUNGARY
Head of state: Ferenc Mádl (replaced Árpád Göncz in August)
Head of government: Viktor Orbán
Capital: Budapest
Population: 10.1 million
Official language: Hungarian
Death penalty: abolitionist for all crimes
2000 treaty ratifications/signatures: Optional Protocol to the UN Women's Convention

Detention of large numbers of asylum-seekers continued; many were reportedly ill-treated. Although widely criticized for tolerating racist discrimination, particularly against Roma, the authorities rejected all appeals for the introduction of anti-discrimination legislation. A former police officer who publicly criticized his superior was threatened with imprisonment.

Ill-treatment of asylum-seekers
Asylum-seekers continued to be detained, although in smaller numbers than in early 1999. There were numerous reports of beatings and the arbitrary use of CS gas by guards in detention centres. Detainees who were ill-treated had little opportunity to file a complaint because the detainee population was transient and because of fears that lodging a complaint could harm their chances of being granted asylum or of being transferred from detention to a refugee reception centre. Former detainees alleged that guards frequently hit them with batons if they did not stand in a straight queue for dinner. They also alleged that guards had sprayed CS gas into detainees' faces and into toilets when detainees needed to use them.

▫ A.O., a Kosovan asylum-seeker, was allegedly beaten by guards with batons after he climbed a fence within the territory of the Nyirbátor detention centre to recover a football.

▫ V.I., a Sri-Lankan asylum-seeker who had longstanding injuries to his leg and arm, was allegedly beaten on the head by a guard in the Nyirbátor detention centre after he tried to explain that he could not comply with an order to take out and clean a dustbin because of his injuries.

▫ In April Sudanese and Liberian asylum-seekers were reportedly ill-treated by guards in the Balassagyarmat detention centre.

Roma
In June the Council of Europe's European Commission against Racism and Intolerance noted that "severe problems of racism and intolerance continue in Hungary". It noted that the incidence of discrimination towards the Roma continued in all fields of life and expressed concern particularly about police ill-treatment. However, at a conference where this report was discussed by local non-governmental organizations, a Ministry of Justice official stated that the government did not support proposals for a separate anti-discrimination act on the grounds that existing legislation provided sufficient protection.

Police investigations into reported cases of ill-treatment of Roma did not appear to be conducted promptly and impartially.

▫ In March, in response to concerns about reports of ill-treatment of six young Roma in September 1999 during a raid on their apartment in Budapest, the Minister of the Interior claimed that detailed police inquiries at the apartment block on the morning of the raid resulted in "a well-grounded suspicion of assault" allegedly committed by the young Roma. However, he failed to explicitly acknowledge that the report upon which the entire police operation had been based was a complete fabrication. In November the Minister conceded that the execution of the police action had been "to our present knowledge, an infraction of the law". An investigation into the case by the Budapest Prosecutor's Office of Investigations was continuing at the end of 2000.

Tibor Karancsi
Tibor Karancsi, a former police captain from Szeghalom, Békés county, who made public statements alleging corruption among the former leadership of Szeghalom police, was threatened with up to three years' imprisonment. He had been indicted in December 1999 by the Szeged Military Prosecutor, accused of defaming his superior in a newspaper article, and sentenced in November to "being stripped of his rank", a decision against which he appealed. In a separate case for defamation of the same superior officer, Tibor Karancsi's trial was suspended pending the outcome of the trial of the complainant who was accused of abusing his powers by impeding investigations into oil smuggling.

AI country visits
In March an AI delegate visited the Nyirbátor and Szombathely detention centres where ill-treatment of asylum-seekers had been reported in 1999.

INDIA

REPUBLIC OF INDIA
Head of state: Kocheril Raman Narayanan
Head of government: A.B. Vajpayee
Capital: New Delhi
Population: over 1 billion
Official language: Hindi
Death penalty: retentionist

Human rights violations occurred throughout India, with socially and economically disadvantaged sections of society continuing to be particularly vulnerable. Inter-caste, communal, inter-religious and political violence claimed many lives in several states including Assam, Bihar, Gujarat, Jammu and Kashmir, Tamil Nadu and West Bengal. The government's continuing preoccupation with national security led it to pursue several initiatives for tackling "terrorism" throughout the country, including giving increased powers to a police force which continued to be identified with torture, corruption and other abuses.

Background

The *Bharatiya Janata* Party (BJP)-led National Democratic Alliance continued in office throughout 2000 with A.B. Vajpayee as Prime Minister. Armed conflicts continued to claim hundreds of lives in Jammu and Kashmir and states of the northeast, despite apparent moves towards cease-fires and peace talks in several states. A cease-fire was announced by the armed opposition *Hizbul Mujahideen* in Jammu and Kashmir at the end of July but collapsed 15 days later. A further cease-fire for the month of Ramzan was announced by the government in November. Killings of civilians in the state continued at an alarmingly high level despite this and other political initiatives towards an end to the conflict. Three new states were established in northern India during the course of the year: Chattisgarh, Jharkhand and Uttaranchal.

Torture/ill-treatment

Torture by police and security forces remained endemic in states throughout India. The National Human Rights Commission (NHRC) expressed concern about the widespread use of torture. In August it disclosed that between 1999 and 2000 it had recorded 1,143 deaths in police and judicial custody. Figures for the number of complaints of torture are not made public, although the Chair of the NHRC reportedly indicated that the majority of complaints received relate to police excesses.

A number of official studies which reported during 2000 acknowledged the widespread use of torture and ill-treatment and pointed to political influence, broad powers of arrest, public approval and inadequate methods of investigation as reasons for the continuing practice of torture. During consideration of India's initial report to the UN Committee on the Rights of the Child, concern was expressed by the Committee about reports of routine ill-treatment, corporal punishment, torture, and sexual abuse of children in detention facilities. By the end of 2000 India had not yet ratified the UN Convention against Torture which it signed in October 1997, nor had it invited the UN Special Rapporteur on torture to visit the country.

In discussions with officials of the government of India about measures needed to end torture, AI recommended initiatives including police reform, enactment of new legislation and comprehensive monitoring mechanisms.

In Kurnool district of Andhra Pradesh in October, a 23-year-old *dalit* (member of a disadvantaged community), Peddinti Tirupalu, was found dead near a police station where he had been detained for questioning about gambling offences 48 hours earlier. Police denied a role in his death but relatives claimed that he had been severely beaten. Three police officers were transferred to other areas and a magisterial inquiry was ordered but had not concluded by the end of 2000.

Impunity

While in a few cases individual members of the security forces were brought to justice for human rights violations, most violations were committed with impunity. Lack of political will, compromise and coercion allowed law enforcement officials to escape censure for violating the rights of people who were mostly members of underprivileged sections of society.

In areas of armed conflict, special legislation continued to shield perpetrators from prosecution. A cautious welcome was given to an announcement by the government of Jammu and Kashmir in October that it was establishing judicial inquiries into a series of incidents which took place in March and April in which scores of civilians were killed by security forces and unidentified gunmen. By the end of 2000 no inquiries had begun. Numerous other incidents remained uninvestigated. In Punjab the establishment of a "Peoples Commission", which sought to document evidence of widespread human rights violations in the face of the failure of the state to investigate past human rights violations, was halted by the High Court on the basis that it was establishing a parallel judicial system. The decision was upheld by the Supreme Court in May.

A new one-man Commission of Inquiry was established in May to investigate the 1984 riots in Delhi which claimed the lives of more than 2,500 people, mainly Sikhs. In October the retired judge presiding over the inquiry was reported to have already received over 10,000 affidavits. An earlier inquiry held between 1985 and 1986 had found 147 police officers guilty of dereliction of duty but proceedings were initiated in only around 20 cases. Of more than 700 criminal cases filed in connection with the riots, only 10 per cent had resulted in conviction.

In Mumbai, recommendations made by the Srikrishna Commission of Inquiry into riots which took place in the city in 1992-1993 remained unimplemented.

Discrimination

Despite safeguards in the Constitution and in law, certain groups remained particularly vulnerable to human rights abuses based on discrimination. Access to justice for women, *dalits* and others who suffer from social and economic discrimination remained problematic.

In January, India's initial report under the UN Women's Convention was heard by the Committee which monitors adherence of states parties to the Convention. Concern at the level of gender-based violence in the country was expressed by the Committee, whose recommendations included the need for rigorous implementation of existing legislation prohibiting such practices as dowry and caste-based discrimination.

International attention continued to focus on violence against Christian minorities but victims of apparently state-backed violence in several areas included Muslims, *dalits* and *adivasis* (tribal people). Concerns about discrimination based on religion, particularly directed at members of the Christian community, were heightened by statements made by members of right-wing Hindu groups which appeared to encourage the use of violence. Attacks on members of Christian communities and church property continued.

Human rights defenders

Harassment of human rights defenders in many parts of India continued. In April, AI hosted a meeting of human rights defenders from throughout the country which concluded by drawing up a set of recommendations for the better protection of human rights defenders. The recommendations included calls for a review of preventive detention provisions used to detain human rights defenders taking part in peaceful activities. They also called for unhindered access for human rights defenders to victims of human rights violations in all areas of India, and to international forums outside India in order to report on human rights concerns or to undergo training.

⊡ In Gujarat in August, several hundred people were arrested under preventive detention provisions to stop them from going to a public hearing organized by a peoples' organization, the *Narmada Bachao Andolan*, about the human rights impact of the construction of dams on the Narmada river. Those detained included individuals facing displacement and senior human rights activists. They were released after the public hearing had taken place.

⊡ In November T. Puroshottam, Joint Secretary of the Andhra Pradesh Civil Liberties Committee, was killed and other human rights defenders in the state received threats. These attacks were believed to be the work of former members of an armed group operating with the tacit and often active support of state authorities. The state government refused to carry out a judicial inquiry into these incidents.

Special legislation

In April the Law Commission of India submitted the draft Prevention of Terrorism Bill 2000 to the government prior to its introduction to parliament. Provisions of the Bill reflected many of those found in the Terrorist and Disruptive Activities (Prevention) Act, 1987 (TADA), which lapsed in 1995. In July the NHRC indicated its opposition to the Bill on several grounds, stating that it would violate international human rights standards and lead to human rights violations. Although it was not introduced to parliament by the end of 2000, state governments were reported as having given it unanimous approval.

In April AI raised concerns with the authorities about the use of the Jammu and Kashmir Public Safety Act. The Indian government dismissed clear evidence of its abuse and maintained that provisions of the Act provide sufficient safeguards for detainees. Leaders of the All Parties Hurriet Conference arrested under the Act between late August and early November 1999 were released in April and May. The Indian government also dismissed claims that TADA was still being used in Jammu and Kashmir to detain people retrospectively, despite clear evidence to the contrary.

⊡ The fate of 50 people, including 12 women, detained under TADA in Karnataka, some since 1993, received national attention after a notorious sandalwood smuggler kidnapped a veteran film star and listed the release of these detainees as one of his demands. While the state governments of Karnataka and Tamil Nadu expressed their willingness to drop charges against them, the Supreme Court stayed their acquittal despite their detention without trial for up to seven years and evidence that almost all had been illegally detained and tortured after arrest.

Human rights commissions

The NHRC submitted recommendations to the government of India for amendments to its statute — the Protection of Human Rights Act 1993. These were based on the recommendations of the Advisory Committee established in 1998. The NHRC's recommendations were not made public and by the end of 2000 the government had given no indication that it was considering amendments to the Act. The NHRC continued to indicate its frustration at statutory limitations on its powers, particularly in relation to investigation of allegations of human rights violations by armed and paramilitary forces, and the investigation of incidents which took place more than a year before a complaint was made.

In Rajasthan the Chair of the State Human Rights Commission established in early 2000 resigned after four months, complaining that no resources had been provided by the government for it to operate. In Uttar Pradesh the government had still not set up a Human Rights Commission by the end of 2000 despite a High Court order to do so.

Death penalty

At least 30 people were sentenced to death in 2000. It was not known if any executions were carried out. The government of India does not publish statistical information about the implementation of the death penalty.

government and GAM was implemented in June. Initially it resulted in a decrease in violations, but within weeks the number of reported incidents rose again. The situation deteriorated further towards the end of the year including in the run-up to a pro-independence rally in Banda Aceh in November. Operations by the security forces to prevent people from attending the rally were believed to have resulted in the extrajudicial execution of at least 20 and possibly many more people. A number of people involved in organizing the rally were detained. One political activist, Muhammad Nazar, head of the Information Centre for a Referendum on Aceh (SIRA), remained in detention at the end of 2000. He was a prisoner of conscience.

Papua
Attempts to respond to mounting demands for independence in Papua (formerly Irian Jaya) through political dialogue were undermined by the actions of the security forces. Dialogue continued and conciliatory measures were introduced, such as changing the name of the province and permitting the raising of the Papuan flag, regarded locally as a symbol of independence. However, these did not prevent flag-raising and other pro-independence protests from being forcibly broken up by the security forces. At least 21 people were killed and dozens injured in the course of these operations. Detainees, including people held for the peaceful expression of their views, were tortured and ill-treated. Pro-independence and pro-integration militia groups were established and there were reports that they had committed human rights abuses.

▫ Three people were shot dead and 12 injured when police forcibly dispersed a crowd which had gathered to raise the Papuan flag outside a church in Sorong on 22 August. Around 30 others were arrested and charged with attempting to separate the state and possessing firearms.

▫ About 100 people, including children, were arbitrarily detained during police raids on student hostels in Jayapura, apparently in retaliation for the killing of two police officers and one security guard on 7 December. Elkius Suhuniab was killed during a raid, and Johny Karrunggu and Orry Doronggi died as a result of torture in police custody. Human rights activists and journalists were subsequently harassed by the police for publicizing the violations.

Refugees and militia
More than 100,000 East Timorese refugees were still in Indonesia at the end of 2000, mostly in West Timor. They had fled or were forcibly expelled to Indonesia by pro-Indonesian militia and the Indonesian security forces in September 1999. Efforts to repatriate the refugees were hampered by threats, intimidation and physical attacks on refugees by militia in West Timor. Frequent threats and attacks by militia on representatives of the UN High Commissioner for Refugees (UNHCR) also disrupted the repatriation program. The program was suspended and all international and many local humanitarian agencies left West Timor after three UNHCR staff were killed by militia in Atambua, West Timor, on 6 September.

In response to international condemnation of the attack, the Indonesian authorities set up an investigation into the killings. Although six suspects were arrested, no one had been brought to trial by the end of 2000. A process to disarm the militias was also established, but some refugees who made their own way back to East Timor later in the year reported that armed militia were still active in West Timor. UNHCR had not returned by the end of 2000.

Death penalty
Eight people were sentenced to death, bringing the total number under sentence of death to at least 34. No executions took place during 2000. The death penalty was introduced as a maximum sentence for a number of crimes under new legislation on Human Rights Courts.

International initiatives
The report of the International Commission of Inquiry (ICOI) on East Timor, established by the UN Secretary-General, was published in January. The ICOI, which had visited East Timor and Indonesia in late 1999, concluded that gross violations of human rights and breaches of humanitarian law were perpetrated by pro-Indonesian militias with the support of the Indonesian military during 1999. It recommended that an international tribunal on East Timor should be established. It also recommended that the voluntary return of East Timorese refugees in Indonesia should be facilitated and that pro-Indonesian militia should be disarmed.

Following the killing of three UNHCR staff in West Timor in September, the UN Security Council adopted Resolution 1319 (2000), in which it insisted that the Indonesian government should immediately disarm and disband the militia, ensure safety and security in refugee camps for humanitarian workers and take measures to ensure the safe return of refugees to East Timor. A UN Security Council delegation visited Indonesia in November to review the progress of the authorities in implementing the resolution.

AI country reports and visits
Reports
- Indonesia: Impunity persists in Papua as militia groups take root (AI Index: ASA 21/034/2000)
- Indonesia: Comments on the draft law on Human Rights Tribunals (AI Index: ASA 21/025/2000)
- Indonesia: The Consultative Group on Indonesia (CGI) – A briefing for government members and donor agencies (AI Index: ASA 21/051/2000)
- Indonesia: A cycle of violence for Aceh's children (AI Index: ASA 21/059/2000)
- Indonesia: The impact of impunity on women in Aceh (AI Index: ASA 21/060/2000)
- Indonesia: Activists at risk in Aceh (AI Index: ASA 21/061/2000)

Visits
AI delegates visited Indonesia, including Jakarta and Aceh.

IRAN

ISLAMIC REPUBLIC OF IRAN
Leader of the Islamic Republic of Iran: Ayatollah Sayed 'Ali Khamenei
President: Hojjatoleslam val Moslemin Sayed Mohammad Khatami
Capital: Tehran
Population: 67.7 million
Official language: Farsi (Persian)
Death penalty: retentionist
2000 treaty ratifications/signatures: Rome Statute of the International Criminal Court

Scores of political prisoners continued to be held; among them were prisoners of conscience and others sentenced in previous years after unfair trials. A clamp-down on freedom of expression resulted in the arbitrary arrest and imprisonment of scores of journalists. Reports of torture and ill-treatment continued. At least 75 people were executed during 2000; the true number may have been considerably higher.

Background

Parliamentary elections held in two stages in February and April formed the background to the struggle concerning freedom of expression and association. The elections were decisively won by supporters of President Mohammad Khatami. The new authorities set out with an ambitious program of social and political reform although only a few such laws had been passed and implemented by the end of the year.

New parliamentary commissions visited prisons and critically evaluated prison conditions, dealt with judicial reform and addressed implementation of constitutional guarantees concerning freedom of expression.

The Press Law, passed in April by the previous parliament, introduced harsh measures that were used to limit freedom of expression. In August, new deputies introduced legislation to reform the Press Law, but the reform was halted by an unprecedented intervention into parliamentary affairs by the Leader.

Scores of people were arrested and injured in provincial centres thoughout the year during civil unrest over social conditions, policing and the allocation of resources.

Student demonstrations occurred throughout the year. In Tehran, Tabriz and elsewhere, scores of students commemorated the anniversary of the July 1999 demonstrations in Tehran, while in Khorramabad, Lorestan, in August, two well-known reformist theologians were prevented from addressing a conference organized by a student group. Dozens of people were reportedly injured and arrested in the disturbances which followed. Many investigations ensued, including by parliament and the National Security Council, which indicated that actions by Revolutionary Guard officials and *Basij* (Mobilization) forces, among others, precipitated the unrest and injuries.

The People's Mujahideen of Iran (PMOI) continued to undertake military operations against the authorities, including a mortar attack in February targeting offices of the security forces in Tehran which reportedly injured a number of civilians.

Freedom of expression

In an unprecedented clampdown on freedom of expression and association, at least 34 journalists, writers and human rights defenders were questioned, detained and tried; some were tortured. At least 12 were imprisoned, usually after unfair trials. These abuses occurred as a result of complaints filed by individuals and state bodies, often under the control of the Leader, which frequently led to legal action against journalists and commentators. These and other people were tried on the basis of vaguely worded laws before Revolutionary Courts and the Special Court for the Clergy, where procedures often fall far short of international standards for fair trial. They were prisoners of conscience. At least 30 publications, the majority supportive of reformist groups, were closed or suspended by judicial order.

Newspaper articles about the use of the death penalty resulted in the imprisonment of two people. Latif Safari, publisher of *Neshat* (Happiness), was sentenced to two-and-a-half years' imprisonment in April. In October, the sentence of Emaddodin Baqi of the newspaper *Fath* (Victory), was reduced from seven to three years on appeal. He had been detained in May and was not freed during his appeal.

Writers who addressed political and social reform or who were critical of the actions of political leaders were often detained, tried and imprisoned, frequently on vaguely worded charges.

◻ In August, journalists Ahmad Zeydabadi of *Hamshahri* (Citizen), Mohammad Quchani of *Asr-e Azadegan* (Era of the Free), and Massoud Behnoud of *Gunagun* (Variety) were detained by the State Employees Court. Mohammad Quchani was released on bail in September pending trial, and Massoud Behnoud was released on bail in December. Ahmad Zeydabadi continued to be held. By the end of the year their trials had not taken place.

◻ In November, the managing editors of *Abrar* (The Righteous) were tried for "spreading lies" and other charges. In December the managing editor of *Ya Lesarat al-Hossein* was tried in the Press Court. The outcome of these trials was not known at the end of the year.

◻ Mahmud Salehi, a trade union leader, was reportedly imprisoned in Saqqez for six months in August in connection with trade union activities.

The Berlin Conference

An academic conference held in Berlin in April, in which 17 Iranian intellectuals participated, was disrupted by exiled Iranian political groups. The conference was filmed by Iran's state broadcasting company and shown in Iran, where it caused controversy. On return to Iran, the participants were summoned for questioning, some were detained, often for prolonged periods, and in October and November participants and translators of conference papers were put on trial for their involvement with the conference. They faced serious but vaguely worded charges concerning "national security", "propaganda against the state" and "insulting Islam". By the end of the year, no verdicts had been announced, but the evidence used in the trials included discourses they had delivered in Berlin, which were legally published and available in Iran.

☐ Journalist Akbar Ganji was detained on 22 April. He was held in solitary confinement for much of the approximately 190 days he was held prior to his trial in November, when he stated he was beaten in prison.

☐ Lawyer Mehrangiz Kar and publisher Shahla Lahiji — both defenders of women's rights — and Ali Afshari, a student leader, were all detained without charge for over two months. In November Mehrangiz Kar was denied permission to seek medical treatment abroad for cancer.

☐ Researcher Hojjatoleslam Hasan Yousefi Eshkevari was arrested after his return from Europe on 5 August. In October he was convicted after an unfair trial by the Special Court for the Clergy. He faced vague charges relating to "national security", defamation, heresy, and being at war with God and corrupt on earth, which are punishable by death. By the end of the year, his sentence had not been made known.

☐ In December Ali Afshari and Ezzatollah Sahabi were rearrested. Still in detention at the end of the year, they were denied the opportunity to see their family and lawyers.

Unfair trials

Deeply flawed trial procedures, especially in Revolutionary Courts and the Special Court for the Clergy, continued.

☐ On 1 July, the Shiraz Revolutionary Court sentenced 10 Iranian Jews to between three and 13 years' imprisonment on charges relating to spying. Three men were acquitted. Despite repeated public assurances by the authorities that they would be given a fair trial, proceedings took place in secret and fell far short of international standards for fair trial. The prison sentences for the 10 were reduced to between two and nine years on appeal.

There were continued reports that scores, possibly hundreds, of political prisoners, including prisoners of conscience sentenced after unfair trials in previous years, continued to be held. Scores of students detained following demonstrations in July 1999, including those associated with banned or tolerated secular political parties, continued to be held throughout the country.

☐ In December, prisoner of conscience and former Deputy Prime Minister 'Abbas Amir Entezam, aged 68, was rearrested and ordered to sign a confession. His refusal to do so resulted in his renewed imprisonment.

Torture/ill-treatment

Torture and ill-treatment, including the judicial punishments of flogging and amputation, continued.

☐ Akbar Mohammadi and Ahmad Batebi were tortured in the *Towhid* detention centre. *Towhid*, administered by the Ministry of Intelligence, was closed in August 2000 by order of the judiciary. Akbar Mohammadi stated that his feet were whipped with metal cables and that he was suspended by his limbs and repeatedly beaten. Ahmad Batebi stated that he had been beaten while blindfolded and bound, and ordered to sign a confession. He reportedly wrote that his head was plunged into a drain full of excrement and held under, forcing him to inhale excrement through his nose and into his mouth. The two men were sentenced to 15 and 10 years' imprisonment respectively.

There were continued reports of psychological torture including death threats. No investigation into any allegations of torture — such as those made by journalist Akbar Ganji, who stated in court in November that he had been tortured by prison officials at Evin — was known to have been undertaken.

At least 49 floggings were reported, many for "depraved dancing", and 10 amputations, often in connection with theft. However, the true number may have been considerably higher.

Human rights defenders

Following a closed trial that ended in September, Shirin Ebadi and Mohsen Rahami, human rights defenders and lawyers, received suspended sentences and five years' suspension from practising law in connection with the production and distribution of the videotaped "confessions" of Amir Farshad Ebrahimi. His videotaped testimony included statements concerning his former group, *Ansar-e Hezbollah* (Partisans of the Party of God), and how the group was instructed to break up public meetings and beat up reformist activists. He was sentenced to two years' imprisonment for spreading lies and was believed to be held in conditions amounting to cruel and inhuman punishment.

The 'Serial Murders' and impunity

In December, the trial began of 18 individuals, including former senior Ministry of Intelligence officials, charged in connection with their alleged involvement with the murder of two politicians and two writers in 1998. These cases, which form part of the "Serial Murders" cases, were tried in the Tehran Military Court behind closed doors, allegedly for "security reasons". The specific charges against the accused were not known. At the start of the trial, only five defendants, said to be the main perpetrators of the killings, were in custody, while others, suspected accomplices, were free on bail. By 31 December, one of the defendants, Mostafa Kazemi, had reportedly confessed to having ordered the killings. It was not known where and under what circumstances this confession was made. Shirin Ebadi (see above), a lawyer representing one of the victims' families, had earlier stated that the judiciary had not given her access to the case files and in December, a lawyer for the families of the two writers, Nasser Zarafshan, was detained for suggesting that other unsolved murders formed part of the case and should be investigated and tried simultaneously. The verdicts were expected in January.

In July, Brigadier General Farhad Nazari and 18 officials of the Law Enforcement Forces were acquitted by a military court of disobeying Ministry of the Interior orders in connection with a raid on student dormitories during the July 1999 student demonstrations. Students injured in the raid, represented by Mohsen Rahami (see above), were, however, compensated by the same court.

Death penalty

At least 75 executions were reported and 16 death sentences imposed, often in connection with murder charges. However, the true number may have been considerably higher. Death sentences passed after the unfair trials of Akbar Mohammadi, Ahmad Batebi and two other students detained following the student demonstrations in July 1999 — Mehrdad Sohrabi and Abbas Deldar — were commuted on 30 April.

Intergovernmental organizations

In February, the UN General Assembly expressed its concern that since 1996 no invitation to visit the country had been extended by the authorities to the Special Representative on the human rights situation in Iran. The General Assembly also expressed serious concern at the "apparent absence of respect for internationally recognized safeguards, the use of national security laws as a basis for derogating from the rights of the individual, cases of torture and cruel, inhuman or degrading treatment or punishment as well as the failure to meet international standards in the administration of justice", along with the restrictions on freedom of expression, opinion, thought and the press.

In May, in its concluding observations to Iran's report on implementation of the UN Children's Convention, the monitoring committee expressed concern at Iran's reservations to the Convention and recommended that Iran review legislation concerning the age of majority to bring it in line with the Convention. It expressed serious concern that the right to life of a person under 18 is not guaranteed and that children can be subjected to a variety of types of cruel, inhuman and degrading treatment and punishment.

AI country statement

- Iran: Open letter from Amnesty International to members of the Sixth *Majles-e Shoura-ye Eslami* (parliament) (AI Index: MDE 13/018/2000)

IRAQ

REPUBLIC OF IRAQ
Head of state and government: Saddam Hussain
Capital: Baghdad
Population: 23.1 million
Official language: Arabic
Death penalty: retentionist

Hundreds of people, among them political prisoners including possible prisoners of conscience, were executed. Hundreds of suspected political opponents, including army officers suspected of planning to overthrow the government, were arrested and their fate and whereabouts remained unknown. Torture and ill-treatment were widespread and new punishments, including beheading and the amputation of the tongue, were reportedly introduced. Non-Arabs, mostly Kurds, continued to be forcibly expelled from their homes in the Kirkuk area to Iraqi Kurdistan.

Background

Continuing economic sanctions, imposed by UN Security Council resolutions following Iraq's invasion of Kuwait in 1990, contributed to a deteriorating economic and humanitarian situation. Many governments and non-governmental organizations criticized the sanctions. In February, two senior UN officials, the head of the humanitarian program in Iraq and the head of the World Food Programme in Iraq, resigned over concerns about their impact. From August until the end of the year many countries, including France and the Russian Federation, sent flights carrying humanitarian aid to Iraq, in most cases with the approval of the UN Security Council Sanctions Committee.

The government of Iraq continued to reject UN Resolution 1284, adopted in December 1999. This established a new arms inspection body, the UN Monitoring, Verification and Inspection Commission (UNMOVIC), and provided for the lifting of sanctions if the government allowed arms inspections to be renewed.

Air strikes by US and United Kingdom (UK) forces against Iraqi targets continued, reportedly resulting in further civilian deaths. According to Iraqi government figures, around 300 people have been killed since the air strikes began in December 1998.

In March a new parliament was elected. All 165 candidates of the ruling Ba'ath Party were elected, including 'Uday Saddam Hussain, the President's eldest son. The remaining 55 seats were won by pro-government independent candidates and a further 30 deputies were appointed by the government to represent Iraqi Kurdistan, two provinces in northern Iraq ruled by Kurdish political parties and which are not under central government control.

In April the UN Commission on Human Rights adopted a resolution condemning the "systematic, widespread and extremely grave violations of human rights and international humanitarian law by the Government of Iraq" and extended for a further year the mandate of the UN Special Rapporteur on Iraq.

Death penalty

The large-scale application of the death penalty continued. Hundreds of people, including possible prisoners of conscience, were executed. The victims included army officers suspected of having links with the Iraqi opposition abroad or plotting to overthrow the government and Shi'a Muslims suspected of anti-government activities. In many cases it was impossible to determine whether the executions were judicial or extrajudicial, given the secrecy surrounding them.

◻ In February, 38 Republican Guard officers were executed. They were arrested in January, reportedly after a failed attempt to assassinate the President. Those executed included General 'Abd al-Karim Hussain al-Dulaimi, head of the Republican Guard's second brigade.

◻ A Jordanian national, Dawud Salman al-Dallu, was executed in Abu Ghraib Prison in Baghdad in June after being convicted of espionage. He had been detained since 1993. The date and details of his trial were not known.

◻ Seven employees at the government's Central Computer Department were executed in July on charges of treason. They reportedly imported a computer system that could be used to send data abroad.

◻ 'Ali Hassan, 'Ali Kamal, Hamid Na'im, all officers in the Republican Guard and originally from southern Iraq, were arrested in Baghdad in January, reportedly on suspicion of contact with an Iraqi opposition group abroad. They were sentenced to death and executed by firing squad in September.

Extrajudicial executions

In October dozens of women accused of prostitution were beheaded without any judicial process in Baghdad and other cities. Men suspected of procurement were also beheaded. The killings were reportedly carried out in the presence of representatives of the Ba'ath Party and the Iraqi Women's General Union. Members of *Feda'iyye Saddam*, a militia created in 1994 by 'Uday Saddam Hussain, used swords to execute the victims in front of their homes. Some victims were reportedly killed for political reasons.

◻ Dr Najat Mohammad Haydar, an obstetrician in Baghdad, was beheaded in October after being accused of prostitution. However, she was reportedly arrested before the introduction of the policy to behead prostitutes and was said to have been critical of corruption within the health services.

◻ In October several women were beheaded in Mosul in northern Iraq. They included Fatima 'Abdallah 'Abd al-Rahman, Shadya Shaker Mahmoud and Iman Qassem Ahmad.

Torture/ill-treatment

Political prisoners and detainees were subjected to brutal forms of torture. The bodies of many of those executed had visible signs of torture, including the gouging out of the eyes, when they were returned to their families. Common methods of physical torture included electric shocks or cigarette burns to various parts of the body, pulling out of fingernails, rape, long periods of suspension by the limbs, beating with cables, *falaqa* (beating on the soles of the feet) and piercing of hands with an electric drill. Psychological torture included threats to arrest and harm relatives of the detainee or to rape a female relative in front of the detainee, mock executions and long periods in solitary confinement.

◻ In June Najib al-Salihi, a former army general who fled Iraq in 1995 and joined the Iraqi opposition, was sent a videotape showing the rape of a female relative. Shortly afterwards he reportedly received a telephone call from the Iraqi intelligence service, asking him whether he had received the gift and informing him that his relative was in their custody.

Amputation of the tongue was reportedly approved by the authorities in mid-2000 as a new penalty for slander or abusive remarks about the President or his family.

◻ In September a man reportedly had his tongue amputated by members of *Feda'iyye Saddam* in Baghdad for slandering the President. He was said to have been driven around after the punishment while information about his alleged offence was broadcast through a loudspeaker.

Arrests of suspected political opponents

During the year hundreds of people were arrested; their fate and whereabouts remained unknown. Those targeted included Shi'a Muslims suspected of anti-government activities and army officers accused of links with opposition groups abroad or planning to overthrow the government.

◻ At least 42 Republican Guard officers were arrested in April, reportedly in connection with an attempt to overthrow the government. Among them were Colonel Hashim Jassem Majid, Colonel Falah al-Din Yusuf and Lieutenant-Colonel 'Ali Soltan Mohammad.

◻ In October scores of Shi'a Muslim religious activists were arrested in Baghdad. They included al-Shaikh Khaled Hassan al-Dulaimi, al-Shaikh Mas'ud Hamam 'Abdallah and Sa'ad Mahmoud al-'Ani.

Forcible expulsion of non-Arabs

Non-Arabs in the Kirkuk region, mainly Kurds but also Turkmen and Assyrians, continued to be expelled to Iraqi Kurdistan. Thousands have been deported in recent years because of their ethnic origin and Kirkuk's strategic location and oil resources. The government encouraged Arabs living in government-controlled areas to move to Kirkuk, and allocated land confiscated from deportees to security personnel.

◻ In October, 78 members of 10 families were expelled to the area controlled by the Patriotic Union of Kurdistan (PUK). One member of each family was detained until the deportation was completed.

Iraqi Kurdistan

At the end of 1999 a new regional government in the area controlled by the Kurdistan Democratic Party

(KDP) included members of four other political parties. In February, in the area controlled by the PUK, the PUK contested municipal elections with 12 other political groups, winning control of 53 out of 58 councils while the remaining five were taken by Islamist parties.

The 1997 cease-fire between the KDP and the PUK remained in force. In February the two parties recommitted themselves to the implementation of the 1998 Washington peace agreement. The KDP released 11 PUK prisoners of war in February and allowed 30 pro-PUK families to return to PUK-controlled Kurdistan. In September the KDP agreed to withdraw its militias from towns under its control. In November both parties agreed to allow the free movement of citizens and the free circulation of printed materials.

However, dissidents were believed responsible for at least a dozen bomb attacks on civilian targets during the year in both areas of Kurdistan. In June, 20 people were reportedly injured when a car bomb exploded in Sulaymania. In November, six people were killed and 17 injured in an explosion in Arbil.

Clashes between forces of the two ruling parties and members of the Kurdish Workers' Party (PKK) left scores dead, including between KDP forces and PKK rebels in July and between PUK and PKK forces in September and October when dozens reportedly died.

In March thousands of Turkish government troops entered Iraqi Kurdistan in pursuit of PKK forces. In August air strikes targeting the PKK resulted in 38 civilians killed and 11 injured. The Turkish authorities reportedly launched an investigation and paid compensation to the victims.

Arrests of political opponents

Politically motivated arrests continued.

☐ Students who set up an independent union, the Free Students and Youth Union, in 1999 were reportedly targeted for arrest in the area controlled by the PUK. Of 11 students arrested in January, nine were released days or weeks afterwards. It was not known whether the remaining two, Hussain Alek Ahmad and Khaled Khidir Babeker, were still held at the end of 2000.

☐ In March, five people reportedly appeared on television in the KDP-controlled area and confessed to their involvement in bomb attacks and killings since 1997. Four of them were said to be members of the Islamic Movement in Iraqi Kurdistan. Their fate was unknown.

☐ In July the authorities in PUK-controlled Sulaymania briefly detained scores of people, including supporters of the Iraqi Workers' Communist Party (IWCP) and the Independent Women's Organization (IWO). They had protested against orders to cease their activities and the cutting of their electricity and water supplies. The PUK informed AI that political party headquarters were moved out of residential areas as a safety measure against their becoming targets of armed opposition groups.

☐ Also in July, PUK security forces arrested women sheltering at an IWO refuge in Sulaymania for women abused by their relatives and closed the refuge. Most were released in the days following but the whereabouts of 12 women and five children, who had been at the refuge and were feared arrested, remained unknown at the end of the year.

☐ In October Hiwa Ahmad, a leading IWCP member, was arrested in Sulaymania by members of the PUK security service, *Dezgay Zanyari*. At the end of 2000 his whereabouts were still unknown.

Political killings

Reports of political killings continued to be received.

☐ In Arbil, in KDP-controlled Iraqi Kurdistan, Sirbit Mahmud, leader of the Democratic Nationalist Union of Kurdistan, and Osman Hassan, a parliamentary deputy, were killed by unidentified gunmen in June and July respectively.

☐ Four IWCP members — 'Abdul Basit Muhsin, Mohammad Mustafa, Ibrahim Mohammad Rostam and Hawri Latif — and Omid Nikbin, a member of the opposition Iranian Workers' Communist Party, were killed by PUK security forces in July. The PUK said that their car had failed to stop at a checkpoint, that they had shot and injured two people, and that they were shot dead when the security forces returned fire. No information about an investigation announced by the PUK was available at the end of 2000.

Communications with the government and the Kurdish authorities

AI raised specific concerns with the Iraqi government and leaders of the KDP and PUK. In January the Iraqi government criticized AI's position on sanctions and for not condemning US and UK air strikes strongly enough, but did not address specifically AI's concerns detailed in a 1999 report. In a letter to AI in September, the government said it could identify only one individual from the victims cited in the *Amnesty International Report 2000* and that the person was living in Syria.

IRELAND

IRELAND
Head of state: Mary McAleese
Head of government: Bertie Ahern
Capital: Dublin
Population: 3.7 million
Official languages: Irish, English
Death penalty: abolitionist for all crimes
2000 treaty ratifications/signatures: UN Convention against Racism; Optional Protocol to the UN Children's Convention on the involvement of children in armed conflict; Optional Protocol to the UN Women's Convention

There were delays in implementing some undertakings arising from the 1998 Multi-Party Agreement. The amended Refugee Act undermines the fundamental right of people fleeing serious human rights violations to seek asylum.

Human rights aspects of the Multi-Party Agreement

On 31 May the President signed the Human Rights Commission Bill into law, and shortly afterwards the President of the Commission was appointed. By the end of 2000 the Commission had not yet started to function. The Commission will have powers to scrutinize upcoming legislation, to conduct inquiries into human rights abuses and to take cases to court on behalf of individuals and groups.

The Irish government failed to produce legislation which would bring into effect its commitment under the 1998 Multi-Party Agreement to incorporate the European Convention on Human Rights into Irish law and to "ensure at least equivalent level of protection of human rights as will pertain in Northern Ireland". AI was concerned that in favouring an "interpretative" incorporation of the Convention, the Irish government fell short of meeting its requirements under the Agreement, as this would not provide people with full access to the rights in the Convention.

The Review of the Offences Against the State Act(s), which was set up by the government as part of its undertakings under the Multi-Party Agreement, had still not reported its findings by the end of 2000. AI had presented a detailed submission about its concerns to the Review group in October 1999.

Shootings by the security forces

Investigations into disputed killings, which consist of police officers investigating actions taken by other police officers, cannot be considered independent. In addition, the current inquest procedure does not satisfy international standards which require a mechanism for public scrutiny of the legality of actions by government agents. The victims' families are severely disadvantaged: their lawyers are not provided with full autopsy statements, full forensic evidence or complete witness statements before the inquest. This hampers the families from effectively challenging the official version. All these documents are available to the *Garda* (police). Furthermore, legal aid is not available to the victims' families to pay for legal assistance and independent expert advice.

▫ John Carthy was shot dead in April 2000 after he had barricaded himself for 25 hours in his home, which was surrounded by dozens of police officers. John Carthy was reportedly suffering from depression and questions were raised concerning the police handling of the incident, including why his request to speak to his solicitor was not met and whether the force used by the police was excessive in the circumstances. John Carthy was the third person to be killed in recent years by police officers from the Emergency Response Unit (ERU), a specially trained and heavily armed response unit. An inquest into his death took place in October. The jury limited itself to a finding of death caused by being shot, having declined to issue a verdict on the circumstances, or any riders. AI believes that only an independent public inquiry could answer the questions that remained unanswered after the inquest.

▫ A Supreme Court ruling concerning the inquest into the killing by the ERU of John Morris (who was killed in June 1997) upheld in July the coroner's decision to allow officers from the ERU to testify anonymously and from behind a screen, and to deny the family's lawyer access to the full forensic evidence, including information concerning the identity of the firearm(s) used in the fatal shooting.

▫ Officers from the ERU were also involved in the shooting of Rónán MacLochlainn in May 1998. His inquest had not taken place by the end of 2000.

Ill-treatment

There were continued reports of ill-treatment by police. AI was concerned that the government did not ensure adequate safeguards against ill-treatment, including provisions against incommunicado detention, for effective legal assistance, and for an effective complaints mechanism. Many people alleging ill-treatment stated that they had no confidence in the complaints procedure, in particular if the investigating officers came from the same police force allegedly involved in the misconduct. AI was also concerned that people detained for criminal matters were not entitled to access to legal counsel during police questioning, and that there was no provision for legal aid for lawyers to attend police stations. AI called for audio- and video-recording of police interviews with detainees to be introduced.

The UN Human Rights Committee

In July the UN Human Rights Committee examined Ireland's second periodic report under the International Covenant on Civil and Political Rights. The Committee expressed concerns about the continued operation of the Special Criminal Court, the lack of independent investigations of complaints against the *Garda* and the treatment of prisoners. AI had raised a number of these issues in its briefing to the Committee.

Refugees and discrimination

The Refugee Act of 1996 finally came into force in November. However, its amended version denies fundamental rights to people fleeing torture. AI expressed concern that the legislation was flawed because of inadequate legal safeguards, including an ineffective appeal system in accelerated asylum procedures. This concern was heightened by the dramatic increase in the number of asylum claims being rushed through such procedures. AI was also concerned about the provision for detention of asylum-seekers in the Refugee Act. Increased powers of detention were introduced by the Illegal Immigrants (Trafficking) Bill 2000.

The Equal Status Act, which was brought into force in October, outlaws discrimination by those providing both public and private services and is designed to combat discrimination on nine grounds: gender, race, religion, age, sexuality, disability, membership of the Traveller community and family and marital status.

AI country report

- Ireland: Briefing to the UN Human Rights Committee on human rights concerns (AI Index: EUR 29/001/2000)

ISRAEL AND THE OCCUPIED TERRITORIES

STATE OF ISRAEL
Head of state: Moshe Katzav (replaced Ezer Weizman in July)
Head of government: Ehud Barak
Official languages: Hebrew, Arabic
Death penalty: abolitionist for ordinary crimes
2000 treaty ratifications/signatures: Rome Statute of the International Criminal Court

More than 300 Palestinians were killed by the Israeli security forces; most were unlawfully killed during the new *Intifada* (uprising). More than 2,500 Palestinians and Israelis were arrested for political reasons. Scores of detainees were ill-treated. At least 25 Palestinians were held in administrative detention during 2000. All Lebanese nationals held in the Khiam detention centre in southern Lebanon under Israeli occupation were released. Hundreds of Palestinians from the Occupied Territories were tried before military courts in trials whose procedures fell short of international standards. Houses in the Occupied Territories continued to be demolished as a result of a discriminatory policy which denied most Palestinians building permits.

Background

The military conflict in Lebanon between the Israel Defence Forces (IDF) and its proxy militia the South Lebanon Army (SLA) on the one hand and *Hizbullah* on the other continued until May when Israel withdrew its forces from south Lebanon.

Palestinians in the Occupied Territories continued to be almost invariably barred from travel to Jerusalem or elsewhere outside area A, which was under security and civil control of the Palestinian Authority (PA), and Area B, which was under security control of Israel and civil control of the PA. During periods of tension Israeli barriers were consistently erected separating Area C from Areas A and B and also between Area A and Area B.

Negotiations between Israel and the Palestine Liberation Organization (PLO) resumed in July at Camp David in the USA, broke down in October following the outbreak of the *Intifada* and resumed in December (see also Palestinian Authority entry).

The *Intifada*

On 29 September Israeli police using excessive force killed five Palestinians and injured more than 200 others at the al-Aqsa Mosque precinct in Jerusalem. The shooting sparked daily demonstrations and riots in Israel and the Occupied Territories which were continuing at the end of the year.

Israeli security services killed at least 300 and wounded more than 10,000 Palestinians. The majority of those killed and wounded were demonstrators throwing stones or using slings; at least 100 of those killed were children under 18. The Israeli police, border police, special patrol force and IDF used excessive lethal force, firing rubber-coated metal bullets and live ammunition including high-velocity bullets at demonstrators. Some Palestinians were deliberately targeted and extrajudicially executed. The Israeli airforce and the navy used heavy weaponry, including helicopter gunships, tanks and naval vessels, to shell randomly Palestinian areas from where armed Palestinians had opened fire. They also used heavy weaponry to conduct punitive raids against PA facilities.

Armed Palestinians, including members of the *tanzimat* — Palestinian paramilitary groups linked to *Fatah*, the predominant group in the PLO — carried out attacks on Israeli soldiers and civilians in the Occupied Territories. A number of gunbattles took place between the IDF and Palestinian security services or paramilitary groups. Palestinian armed opposition groups such as Islamic *Jihad* also placed bombs which killed six Israeli civilians. Israeli settlers were reported to have killed six Palestinian civilians.

☐ Eleven-year-old Sami Abu Jazzar was shot dead during a stone-throwing demonstration in Rafah, Gaza Strip, in October by Israeli soldiers who were based in a blockhouse 100 metres away and who were not in danger at the time.

☐ Hussein 'Abayat, a local leader of the *tanzimat*, was extrajudicially executed in Beit Sahur in the West Bank by a shell launched from an Israeli helicopter gunship which killed two women standing near his van and injured nine others. An IDF spokesperson admitted that Hussein 'Abayat had been targeted, allegedly because he was going to launch an attack on Gilo settlement.

☐ Two Israeli civilians were killed in a bomb attack near Jerusalem's Mahan Yehuda market on 2 November. Islamic *Jihad* claimed responsibility for the attack.

At a summit in Sharm al-Shaikh in October, Israel and the PA agreed that a fact-finding commission should study the causes of the violence and report back to the US government. The commission started work in November. At a special session in October the UN Commission on Human Rights set up a Commission of Inquiry into the violations of human rights in Israel and the Occupied Territories. In November the Israeli government set up a judicial Commission of Inquiry to investigate "clashes with the security forces in which Arab and Jewish Israeli citizens were killed and wounded".

Arrests

More than 2,000 people, the vast majority Palestinians, were arrested during the year, mostly on charges involving political violence. At least 900 Palestinians from Israel or East Jerusalem and 300 Jewish citizens of Israel were arrested during the *Intifada* and charged with offences such as stone-throwing; many were minors. Arrests were often carried out at night by large numbers of armed security force personnel. Some of those arrested reported that they were beaten or kicked immediately after arrest.

Following a Supreme Court decision in October, bail was consistently refused to those arrested; in November the decision was modified allowing some detainees to be released on bail.

Scores of Palestinians from East Jerusalem with residency rights in Israel arrested after 29 September were charged under Military Order 378, previously only applied to Palestinians living in the West Bank and Gaza Strip.

Scores of Palestinians from the West Bank and Gaza were arrested during the year at Israeli blockades. At least 600 Palestinians were arrested during the last three months of the year from Areas B and C and held in prolonged incommunicado detention for days or weeks before being charged under Emergency Regulations dating from the British mandate or Israeli Military Orders.

Administrative detention

The number of Palestinian administrative detainees, which had decreased to four by September, rose to 12 by the end of the year. They were held without charge or trial or any right to full appeal.

In April the High Court of Justice ruled that the state could not hold a suspect in administrative detention unless the detainee personally posed a security threat. Appeals against the ruling were rejected and 13 Lebanese nationals who had been held for up to 12 years as bargaining chips without charge or trial or after the expiry of their sentences were released. All were returned to Lebanon.

A draft law allowing the detention without trial of "illegal combatants" passed its first reading in the *Knesset* (parliament) in July, but had not become law by the end of 2000.

☐ Two Lebanese nationals, Shaikh 'Abd al-Rahman 'Ubayd and Mustafa al-Dirani, continued to be held incommunicado in a secret place of detention as hostages. The High Court of Justice dismissed an appeal against their continued administrative detention in September.

Torture/ ill-treatment

Draft bills submitted to the *Knesset* by individual members which would allow the General Security Service (GSS) to use "special means" to interrogate detainees were dropped in February.

Palestinian detainees under interrogation were frequently held incommunicado for up to 20 days, and some for as long as 90 days. Many detainees reported that they were beaten immediately after arrest by members of the security forces who almost invariably benefited from impunity.

☐ Nidal Daghlas was arrested during an unsuccessful attempt by Israeli undercover units to capture Mahmud Abu Hanud (see Palestinian Authority entry). He stated that he was tortured for four hours in the village by members of the IDF and the GSS before being taken to Petah Tikvah police station. He said that officers stuffed his mouth with stones, poured water over his face, kicked him in the genitals and smashed his head into a steering wheel. He was held incommunicado for 14 days before being allowed access to a lawyer.

☐ Qadr al-Wa'el from Sha'b, Galilee, stated that police officers beat him with the butts of their rifles while he was being transferred to Misgav police station after his arrest in October and that two police officers also beat him in the police station. Five other police officers, who were either in or near the cell, reportedly witnessed the beating. In court he informed a judge that he had been beaten and was later released on bail.

Unfair trials

Hundreds of Palestinians were tried by military courts in trials which did not meet international standards for fair trials.

Conscientious objectors

At least five conscientious objectors who refused to perform military service or to serve in the Occupied Territories were sentenced to terms of imprisonment. They were prisoners of conscience.

Political prisoners

Israel continued to detain 1,600 Palestinians from the Occupied Territories and 29 Palestinians from Israel sentenced in previous years by military courts for offences such as attacks on Israelis. About 120 were released during the year. A number of foreign nationals including 16 Lebanese and four Jordanian nationals sentenced by military courts in previous years continued to be held. Some had reportedly been tortured and received unfair trials.

Mordechai Vanunu continued to serve an 18-year sentence for revealing information about Israel's nuclear weapons capability imposed in a secret trial in 1987.

South Lebanon
At least nine Lebanese, one Syrian and two Palestinian civilians were killed, most as a result of deliberate or indiscriminate attacks on civilians by Israeli forces. Before Israel's withdrawal from south Lebanon in May, *Hizbullah* launched rocket attacks against civilian areas in northern Israel.

Prior to the Israeli withdrawal, Lebanese nationals continued to be detained outside any legal framework in Khiam detention centre where conditions were cruel, inhuman and degrading and torture was systematic. After the Israeli withdrawal, residents of Khiam village stormed the detention centre and released all remaining 144 detainees.

   Sulayman Ramadan was arrested in September 1985. One of his legs was amputated as a result of lack of medical care after his arrest. During his interrogation he was beaten and given electric shocks. He was detained without charge or trial until his release in May 2000.

In October *Hizbullah* announced the capture of three Israeli soldiers and one Israeli businessman and said that they would be exchanged for Lebanese and other Arab prisoners held in Israel. None had had access to the International Committee of the Red Cross (ICRC) by the end of the year.

During the Israeli withdrawal about 6,000 Lebanese nationals, including about 2,000 former members of the SLA and their relatives, fled to Israel where they were given the right to reside and work.

House demolitions
At least eight houses in the West Bank and 23 houses in East Jerusalem were demolished because their owners had failed to obtain building permits from the Israeli authorities. In a discriminatory policy apparently aimed at stopping Palestinians building in East Jerusalem or in areas of the West Bank under Israeli control, building permits were consistently refused to Palestinians.

Human rights abuses against trafficked women
Women trafficked from the countries of the former Soviet Union to work in the sex industry in Israel continued to be subjected to human rights abuses such as violent assaults and enslavement. The *Knesset* established a special committee to investigate the situation of trafficked women. In July the *Knesset* passed an amendment to the Penal Code, making the buying and selling of human beings for the purposes of prostitution a criminal offence punishable by up to 16 years' imprisonment.

United Nations
AI made oral statements at the UN Commission on Human Rights in March, calling on the Israeli government to end torture in Khiam, and during the Fifth Special Session of the UN Commission on Human Rights in October calling on the Israeli government to end excessive use of lethal force.

AI country reports and visits
Reports
- Israel: Human rights abuses of women trafficked from countries of the former Soviet Union into Israel's sex industry (AI Index: MDE 15/017/2000)
- Israel/Lebanon: Attacks on Lebanese civilians in south Lebanon by Israeli forces (AI Index: MDE 02/006/2000)
- Israel and the Occupied Territories: Excessive use of lethal force (AI Index: MDE 15/041/2000)
- Israel and the Occupied Territories: Mass arrests and police brutality (AI Index: MDE 15/058/2000)

Visits
AI delegates visited Israel and the Occupied Territories in April, October and November and met IDF and other officials.

ITALY

ITALIAN REPUBLIC
Head of state: Carlo Azeglio Ciampi
Head of government: Giuliano Amato (replaced Massimo D'Alema in April)
Capital: Rome
Population: 57.2 million
Official language: Italian
Death penalty: abolitionist for all crimes
2000 treaty ratifications/signatures: Optional Protocol to the UN Children's Convention on the involvement of children in armed conflict; Optional Protocol to the UN Women's Convention

There were numerous allegations of ill-treatment by law enforcement and prison officers, some of them relating to previous years. There were reports of detainee and prisoner deaths in disputed circumstances. Criminal investigations were opened or continued into many such incidents. Two paratroopers were convicted in connection with human rights violations committed by Italian troops participating in a multinational peace-keeping operation in Somalia in the 1990s. Seven former members of the Argentine armed forces were sentenced *in absentia* in connection with the abduction and murder of Italian citizens during the years of military rule in Argentina, while another Argentine military officer, detained in connection with the abduction and torture of a French citizen, was released and allowed to return home, amid international protest. A controversial verdict of 1995, which had found three men guilty of participation in a politically motivated murder in 1972, was confirmed following judicial review, thus ending judicial proceedings which had lasted 12 years and whose fairness had been repeatedly called into question. The government pressed on with a program of reforms in the justice system, including measures aimed at strengthening fair trial guarantees for defendants in criminal proceedings, and in the prison system, aimed at the eventual improvement of conditions.

Ill-treatment and shootings by law enforcement officers

There were frequent allegations of law enforcement officers physically assaulting detainees. Although the allegations related to both Italian and foreign nationals, many of the victims were of African origin or Roma. Criminal investigations were under way into a number of complaints of ill-treatment, and into several fatal shootings of unarmed suspects by police and *carabinieri* officers, including those of two 17-year-old youths — Mourad Fikri, a Moroccan national, shot dead by Rome police in May, and Mario Castellano, shot dead by Naples police in July.

☐ In September the Salerno Public Prosecutor's Office requested that a *carabiniere* corporal be charged with the murder of Mohammed Ahdiddou, a 24-year-old unarmed Moroccan shot in January, and that six other *carabinieri* be charged with perjury for lying about the circumstances of the shooting.

☐ The Palermo Chief of Police apologized to Leontine Koadjo, from Côte d'Ivoire, for her treatment inside the Aliens Bureau attached to Palermo police headquarters in April. Criminal and disciplinary proceedings were opened against an officer who apparently subjected her to an unprovoked physical assault after she asked for information. She required hospital treatment for a facial fracture.

Torture/ill-treatment in prisons

Tension was high in prisons and detention centres for aliens with frequent and widespread protests prompted largely by unsatisfactory conditions, in some instances amounting to cruel, inhuman and degrading treatment. Severe overcrowding persisted, together with reports of inadequate medical assistance, poor sanitation and other connected problems, including high rates of suicide, attempted suicide and self-inflicted injuries. Numerous allegations of ill-treatment by prison officers emerged, in some cases amounting to torture, along with reports of a number of prisoner deaths in disputed circumstances. Criminal investigations were opened or continued into many such incidents. Fears expressed in previous years — that the failure to carry out thorough investigations into alleged torture and ill-treatment by prison officers, and to bring those responsible swiftly to justice, might be creating a climate of impunity — appeared justified.

☐ In April, the European Court of Human Rights found Italy guilty of failing to carry out a "thorough and effective investigation into the credible allegations" of ill-treatment by Pianosa prison officers made by Benedetto Labita in October 1993. Benedetto Labita alleged that he and other prisoners had suffered systematic physical and mental ill-treatment, mainly between July and September 1992.

☐ Following complaints made to the judicial authorities by Bolzano prison inmates, 25 prison officers and a doctor were put under investigation in connection with allegations that between 1994 and 1999 prisoners were regularly taken to an isolation cell and severely beaten.

☐ The Public Prosecutor asked for 12 prison officers to be charged with murder and another 12 charged with aiding and abetting in connection with the death of Francesco Romeo in Reggio Calabria prison in 1997. Autopsy and forensic tests concluded that his extensive injuries were not consistent with a fall from a perimeter wall during an escape attempt, as claimed by the prison administration, but that he died as a result of a fractured skull caused by blows with batons or truncheons. The prison's duty records for the time of the incidents apparently displayed clear signs of tampering.

☐ Luigi Acquaviva died in the Sardinian prison of Bad'e Carros in January, within 24 hours of taking a prison officer hostage for some four hours and placing a noose around his neck. Administrative and criminal investigations, involving six prison officers and the prison director, were opened into his death following claims that his death was not the result of suicide as the prison administration maintained. Autopsy and forensic tests found that his body, found hanging in a cell, had suffered extensive traumatic injuries before death as well as neck injuries consistent with suicide.

☐ In December, the Public Prosecutor requested that 96 people be committed for trial following a criminal investigation into allegations that on 3 April more than 40 inmates of Sassari district prison, Sardinia, were subjected to cruel, inhuman and degrading treatment, in some cases amounting to torture, by dozens of prison officers employed in various Sardinian penal institutions and in the presence of the prison director and the regional director of Sardinian prisons.

Human rights violations by the Italian armed forces in Somalia

In January, in response to an AI request of March 1999, the Ministry of Justice provided information about developments in criminal proceedings opened in connection with alleged human rights violations committed by members of the armed forces participating in a multinational peace-keeping operation in Somalia in 1993 and 1994. The Ministry stated that a request by the Milan Public Prosecutor for investigations concerning the alleged rape and murder of a Somali boy in March 1994 to be closed without further action was awaiting decision by a judge of preliminary investigation.

The Ministry also indicated that, although a judicial investigation had established that a Somali woman had been gang-raped at the Demonio checkpoint in Mogadishu, it had not been possible to identify the perpetrators or the victim and thus the Livorno judge of preliminary investigation had ordered the closure of those proceedings. Proceedings against an officer accused of raping a Somali woman inside the former Italian embassy in Mogadishu and proceedings regarding allegations that in June 1993 soldiers had unlawfully shot and killed three Somali citizens on board a vehicle were also closed owing to lack of concrete evidence. The Ministry said that the outcome of three further proceedings, including those concerning Aden Abukar Ali, photographed while Italian soldiers were attaching electrodes to his body, were still awaited.

In April, Livorno Tribunal tried and sentenced a former paratrooper to 18 months' suspended imprisonment for abusing his authority and, pending the outcome of connected civil proceedings, made him provisionally liable to the payment of 30 million lire (US$14,000) to Aden Abukar Ali. A second officer apparently received a lower sentence after plea-bargaining.

Universal jurisdiction over crimes against humanity

In December, Rome Court of Assizes sentenced two Argentine generals to life imprisonment and five other former members of the Argentine armed forces to 24 years' imprisonment, following their trial *in absentia* in connection with the abduction and murder of seven Italian citizens and the kidnapping of the child of one them during the years of military rule in Argentina (1976-1983). The trial was the result of investigations opened by the Italian judiciary in 1983, following complaints lodged by relatives of "disappeared" Italian citizens.

Several other criminal proceedings, at various stages of investigation, were under way into complaints of human rights violations committed against Italian citizens by the Argentine security forces and as a result of past collaboration between the Argentine security forces and those of several other South American countries.

In August, former Argentine military officer Jorge Olivera was arrested in Rome on an international warrant issued by France for the abduction and torture of a French citizen in Argentina in 1976. However, in September, while full examination of a French extradition request was still pending, the Rome Appeal Court ordered his release, on the grounds that the crimes of which he was accused were subject to a statute of limitations. He immediately returned to Argentina. The Procurator General appealed against the Court's decision, the Minister of Justice announced an internal disciplinary investigation into the conduct of the Appeal Court judges and the Public Prosecutor opened an investigation into apparently false information presented to the Court by Jorge Olivera.

AI expressed extreme concern at the court's decision, pointing out that, under international law, the scale and magnitude of human rights violations committed under military rule in Argentina constitute crimes against humanity and, therefore, cannot be subject to statutes of limitation.

Adriano Sofri, Giorgio Pietrostefani and Ovidio Bompressi

In January, Venice Appeal Court confirmed a 1995 verdict by the Milan Appeal Court which had sentenced Adriano Sofri, Giorgio Pietrostefani and Ovidio Bompressi — three leading members of the former extra-parliamentary left-wing group *Lotta Continua* — to 22-year prison sentences for participation in the killing of police commissioner Luigi Calabresi in Milan in 1972. The 1995 sentence had resulted in their imprisonment in January 1997, after nine years of judicial proceedings and seven trials.

AI had repeatedly expressed concern at the excessive length and complexity of the proceedings, as well as serious doubts about their fairness, including the extent to which the final verdict relied on the uncorroborated evidence of a *pentito* (a person benefiting from remission of sentence in return for collaboration with the judicial authorities), whose testimony contained contradictions and inaccuracies.

The court ordered the reimprisonment of the defendants whose sentences had been suspended following an August 1999 ruling that their application for a judicial review of the January 1995 sentence was admissible. Adriano Sofri was reimprisoned immediately while Giorgio Pietrostefani and Ovidio Bompressi went into hiding. In March Ovidio Bompressi surrendered voluntarily to the judicial authorities and, after brief reimprisonment, was granted a suspension of his sentence on health grounds. Giorgio Pietrostefani re-emerged in France where he had right of legal residence.

In October, when the Supreme Court examined an appeal lodged against the January judgment, the Procurator General's Office asked it to annul the Venice judgment and order new review proceedings. However, the court rejected the appeal.

At the end of the year the three men were pursuing a petition against Italy with the European Commission of Human Rights, claiming violations of the European Convention on Human Rights.

AI country reports

- Concerns in Europe, January-June 2000: Italy (AI Index: EUR 01/003/2000)
- *L'Italia e i diritti umani* (Italy and Human Rights)

JAMAICA

JAMAICA
Head of state: Queen Elizabeth II, represented by Howard Felix Cooke
Head of government: Percival James Patterson
Capital: Kingston
Population: 2.5 million
Official language: English
Death penalty: retentionist
2000 treaty ratifications/signatures: Optional Protocol to the UN Children's Convention on the involvement of children in armed conflict; Rome Statute of the International Criminal Court

Reports of police brutality and excessive use of force continued. At least 140 people were killed by the police, often in disputed circumstances. At least 45 people were on death row. The Judicial Committee of the Privy Council (the final court of appeal for Jamaica) commuted the death sentences of six prisoners in a ruling that will also be binding on many other nations using the death penalty in the English-speaking Caribbean.

Background

The economic situation remained dire with large sections of society living below the poverty level, and economic development continued to be hindered by the high level of external debt. Jamaican society continued to suffer from an extremely high level of violence. More than 850 people were reportedly murdered in 2000, including 12 police officers.

In May, the Court of Appeal ruled that the indefinite detention of children at the Governor General's pleasure was unconstitutional.

A legal aid scheme for people unable to pay for legal counsel was established, and police officers were given training in the legal aid regulations, including the rights of all detained or arrested people to legal aid and representation.

Brutality by the security forces

There were at least 140 killings by the security forces, especially the police, many of which resulted in disturbances and tension in communities. There were several apparent extrajudicial executions.

In August the government of the United Kingdom withheld an export licence for the sale of 500 hand guns to the Jamaican police, citing concern about human rights violations by the police, including the very high incidence of fatal police shootings. The government of the USA also withheld the transfer of equipment, citing similar concerns.

Shootings

In several cases, witnesses and relatives of victims of police shootings were reportedly subjected to intimidation and death threats. In September, following protests about escalating crime levels, the Prime Minister established a new police anti-crime unit. By November there were several reports that the unit had committed extrajudicial executions.

☐ On 19 September, Williams Richards, a criminal suspect, was shot and killed in Kingston by members of the police unit, in an apparent extrajudicial execution. When AI delegates visited the site several hours after the shooting, forensic evidence had been disturbed and removed. Family members were subsequently denied permission to view the body. The Bureau of Special Investigations (BSI) stated that it had initiated an investigation, but there had been no ruling on whether charges should be filed at the end of 2000.

Torture/ill-treatment

Arbitrary and illegal arrests, searches and detention were reported, often in the context of curfews which continued to be imposed in some areas. Ill-treatment in police custody remained widespread and incidents of torture were documented. Conditions in police custody remained harsh and in many cases amounted to cruel, inhuman and degrading treatment. Access to medical attention, relatives and legal aid was frequently denied. In August, government officials told AI that children were no longer being detained in police lock-ups. However, in September, AI interviewed a 17-year-old in Hunts Bay police lock-up. There were a number of reported deaths in police custody.

☐ In November, a man was reportedly arbitrarily detained and tortured for a week. During this time he was subjected to a mock execution, was continually kept in handcuffs and was beaten until his eardrums burst.

Prisons

In February, soldiers replaced the majority of prison officers, who were removed and indicted after strike action in protest at the reappointment of the Commissioner of Corrections. The Commissioner of Corrections recommended the release of prisoners serving sentences of six months or less to relieve severe overcrowding. The authorities failed to prevent violence between inmates and at least 13 prisoners were killed. One was reportedly beheaded by fellow prisoners.

☐ In May, a mass beating of a reported 300 prisoners over several days by soldiers and prison wardens in St Catherine's District Prison resulted in injuries including hand, ribs, feet and skull fractures, and broken teeth. Reports indicated that the prisoners were beaten with batons and baseball bats, rifles and irons and that some were strangled with cord and rubber belts. At least 100 injured prisoners were reportedly denied medical attention until the Head of Medical Services in the prison publicly condemned the incident. In September, he was transferred to another prison by the Commissioner of Corrections, who cited concerns for his safety as justification. In June, the authorities established a Commission of Inquiry whose terms of reference included investigating the May events. There were reports of retaliatory beatings against at least three prisoners who testified at the Inquiry. None of the officials allegedly involved were removed from duty. In

September, the Commissioner of Corrections told AI that 80 prison personnel had since been transferred. The Commission had not reported its findings at the end of 2000.

Investigations
By September, the BSI had completed 86 investigations into police shootings since its inception in 1999. In 10 cases, there were subsequent rulings that police officers involved in shootings should face criminal charges.

In March the Director of Public Prosecutions declined to file charges against police or army officers involved in the killing of Michael Gayle in August 1999, on the grounds that the evidence failed to identify the individuals responsible. The Minister for National Security and Justice ordered that the investigation be reopened. No charges had been filed by the end of 2000.

In February, the Prime Minister appointed a Commission of Inquiry to investigate the forced removal and ill-treatment of homeless people in Montego Bay in July 1999 and ordered the reopening of police investigations. In May a police officer was granted immunity from prosecution in exchange for his testimony before the Commission of Inquiry. The Commission's recommendations, published in September, included compensation for 18 of the victims and the amendment of legislation regulating Commissions of Inquiry to strengthen their powers. The Commission identified six police officers involved in the removal but was unable to identify other officials. The findings omitted reference to evidence that two homeless people had disappeared, presumed dead, after the incident. By the end of the year compensation had not been paid and no criminal charges had been filed.

No charges had been brought at the end of 2000 against any of those involved in the 1997 killings of 16 inmates in St Catherine's District Prison. The Commissioner of Corrections informed AI that no disciplinary action had been taken against any prison officers in connection with this event.

Death penalty
At least 45 prisoners remained on death row and the courts continued to impose death sentences.

In September, the Judicial Committee of the Privy Council (JCPC) in the United Kingdom – the final court of appeal for Jamaica – commuted the death sentences of six prisoners in the case of Neville Lewis and others. The JCPC ruled that the procedures for deciding whether prisoners should be granted clemency should be opened to legal scrutiny; that executions cannot occur while the prisoner has an appeal pending before the Inter-American Court of Human Rights; and that the issue of whether prison conditions have a bearing upon executions being carried out should be investigated further. The decision will be binding on other Caribbean states that have the JCPC as their final court of appeal.

Threats to human rights defenders
Human rights defenders were threatened.

In August attorney Dahlia Allen fled the country after receiving telephone death threats. She had previously represented homeless people ill-treated by the police in Montego Bay and prisoners beaten in May at St Catherine's District Prison. Dahlia Allen also alleged that her telephone had been tapped. The Prime Minister strongly refuted these allegations in a meeting with AI in September.

In May and June, two members of the organization Jamaicans for Justice received death threats in a series of anonymous phone calls.

AI country report and visits
Report
- Jamaica: The killing of Michael Gayle – authorities yet to hold police and army officers accountable (AI Index: AMR 38/002/2000)

Visits
AI visited Jamaica in February and August to conduct research. In September AI's Secretary General held talks with the Prime Minister and members of the Cabinet, the Commissioner of Police, the Director of Public Prosecutions and the Commissioner of Corrections. AI's Secretary General visited several places of detention, including death row.

JAPAN

JAPAN
Head of state: Emperor Akihito
Head of government: Mori Yoshiro (replaced Obuchi Keizo in June)
Capital: Tokyo
Population: 126.1 million
Official language: Japanese
Death penalty: retentionist

Three people were executed in 2000 and more than 100 prisoners remained under sentence of death. There were no reforms in the *Daiyo Kangoku* system of pre-trial detention. There were further reports of ill-treatment by immigration officials during interrogation of foreign nationals, and reports of ill-treatment and extortion by private security staff attached to a detention facility known as the Landing Prevention Facility at Narita Airport. The refugee recognition system remained secretive, arbitrary and harsh.

Background
The death of Prime Minister Obuchi Keizo in May led to general elections in June, which saw the return to power of the ruling coalition of the Liberal Democratic Party (LDP), the Komeito Party and the Conservative Party, but with a reduced majority. The vulnerable position of Prime Minister Mori Yoshiro of the LDP was

further weakened by the resignation of his closest aide, Chief Cabinet Secretary Nakagawa Hidenao, in October, and by a no-confidence motion initiated by one of the LDP factions in November, which the government narrowly survived. In early December there was a cabinet reshuffle.

In May and in December, the National Assembly passed a number of anti-crime laws, including a bill (in December) that lowered the age of criminal responsibility from 16 to 14.

The July G-8 summit held in Okinawa was dominated by the improvement in North-South Korean relations. Talks between Japanese and North Korean officials resumed for the first time since 1998. Japan gave food aid to North Korea, ignoring domestic protests over alleged abductions of Japanese nationals by North Koreans.

Death penalty

There were three executions on 30 November 2000. About 15 death sentences were passed, including five on members of the religious cult formerly known as *Aum Shinrikyo*. Execution is by hanging. The prisoner is informed that the execution will take place just hours in advance, denying the prisoner the chance to inform relatives or lawyers.

At the end of December, more than 100 prisoners were under sentence of death and about 52 of them had had their sentence of death confirmed by the Supreme Court. Prison conditions on death row amounted to cruel, inhuman and degrading treatment. Many prisoners had been held in solitary confinement for a decade or more. They had limited contact with the outside world and no contact with other prisoners.

☐ Govinda Prasad Mainali, a Nepalese national who was charged with murder in March 1997, was acquitted in April 2000 by the Tokyo District Court. He continued to be detained after being acquitted. The acquittal was overturned by the Tokyo High Court following appeals from the prosecution, and he was sentenced to life imprisonment on 22 December. AI publicly expressed concern at his continued detention after acquittal and at the trend of prosecution appeals to the High Court against acquittals by lower courts, particularly in death penalty cases.

Torture/ill-treatment

The *Daiyo Kangoku* system of pre-trial detention continued despite criticisms from the UN Human Rights Committee. Suspects may be held for up to 23 days in police detention cells during which time they are closely monitored, and are questioned for long periods by several police interrogators. There are no legal regulations governing police interrogation procedures and no provision for court-appointed lawyers for criminal suspects prior to indictment. Interrogations are not recorded or videotaped nor are defence lawyers allowed to be present during the interrogations. Many detainees confess during this initial detention period. Some have reportedly been beaten and many have alleged that they were tricked into believing that if they confessed the detention would end. The forced confessions have been used in court as evidence.

☐ It was reported in December that a suspect detained on charges of rape and murder had been held under the *Daiyo Kangoku* system repeatedly for more than two months. This prolonged period of detention, surveillance and interrogation was made possible by police charging him with different, allegedly unrelated crimes. There were allegations that the suspect was being coerced to confess to an unrelated crime.

Abuses, including beatings, were reportedly committed by private security staff attached to a detention centre, the Landing Prevention Facility at Narita International Airport, against individuals refused entry to Japan. Money was reportedly extorted from detainees to pay for "room and board" at the detention centre, and those who did comply were strip-searched or beaten. Despite being under the jurisdiction of the immigration authorities, there was no reported action against the guards responsible or the private company that employed them.

☐ In June, two Tunisian men, Thameur Mouez and Thameur Hichm, were reportedly hit on the face, held down, kicked and denied medical attention at the Landing Prevention Facility.

☐ A Chinese national was reportedly beaten until his skull was fractured by an immigration official, during interrogation in August. The official, who spoke no Chinese, conducted the interrogation alone, although the Chinese man did not speak Japanese.

Requirements under the UN Convention against Torture
Japan was due to submit its initial report to the UN Committee against Torture in July 2000, having acceded to the UN Convention against Torture in 1999. However, the report had not been submitted by the end of 2000.

Asylum-seekers

Some 216 asylum-seekers applied for refugee status in 2000. About 138 were rejected and about 22 asylum-seekers were recognized as refugees. The process is very secretive, and rejections are never fully explained and do not take into account the risk the asylum-seeker could face if deported. Many asylum-seekers were detained in immigration detention centres for long periods. There were reports of ill-treatment of detainees in immigration detention centres, including inadequate medical facilities.

There were fears that tens of potential asylum-seekers were deported after being detained in facilities where they were denied access to lawyers and to information about refugee detemination procedures.

Revisions to Juvenile Law

A Juvenile Revision Bill was passed by the *Diet* (Parliament) which includes provisions to lower the minimum age at which suspects can be held criminally responsible for their actions from 16 to 14. These revisions constitute the first major amendment to the Juvenile Law since it came into effect in 1949. Under the amendments, family courts would have the option of sending children as young as 14 to face criminal trials as adults. Already, juvenile offenders have to undergo long hours of questioning for up to 23 days under the *Daiyo Kangoku* system with limited access to family members and lawyers.

AI visits
An AI delegation visited Japan in March. In early December a high-level AI delegation visited Japan and discussed AI's long-standing concerns with government ministers and representatives of leading political parties.

JORDAN

HASHEMITE KINGDOM OF JORDAN
Head of state: King 'Abdallah bin Hussein
Head of government: 'Ali Abu Ragheb (replaced 'Abd al-Ra'uf Rawabdeh in June)
Capital: Amman
Population: 4.7 million
Official language: Arabic
Death penalty: retentionist
2000 treaty ratifications/signatures: Optional Protocol to the UN Children's Convention on the involvement of children in armed conflict

Hundreds of people, including prisoners of conscience, were arrested for political reasons. Trials of most of those charged with political offences continued to be heard before a State Security Court where procedures did not meet international fair trial standards. Reports continued of torture or ill-treatment of detainees by members of the security services. There were reports of the *refoulement* (forcible return) of asylum-seekers at risk of serious human rights violations. At least 10 people were executed and at least 12 people were sentenced to death. Four people were unlawfully killed by public security police. There were at least 21 cases of family killings (also known as "honour" killings).

Background
In March a Royal Human Rights Commission headed by Queen Rania was established. In June 'Ali Abu Ragheb became Prime Minister and Minister of Defence. AI wrote to the new government and the Human Rights Commission about its concerns.

A bill to allow the opening of private radio and television stations, ending the state's media monopoly, was endorsed by the House of Representatives and Parliament in September.

Arrests and incommunicado detention
More than 1,700 people were arrested during 2000 for political reasons. Many were held in prolonged incommunicado detention by the General Intelligence Department (GID). Some were later released without charge and others brought to trial.

▫ At the end of 1999 and beginning of 2000, 15 members of the outlawed Islamist *Hizb al-Tahrir fi'l-Urdun*, Liberation Party in Jordan, were arrested. They were charged with membership of an illegal party and distribution of seditious leaflets, and sentenced to up to 18 months' imprisonment. They were prisoners of conscience.

▫ Sixteen people from Irbid who were arrested at the end of 1999 by the GID, apparently suspected of links with Islamist groups, were held for between 35 and 50 days with no access to lawyers or family before being released without charge.

▫ Around 700 people were arrested between October and December after demonstrations in support of the Palestinian *intifada*. Most were released after a few days or weeks of incommunicado detention. Others were brought before the State Security Court and charged with offences such as inciting riots.

Torture/ill-treatment
Reports of torture and ill-treatment at the hands of security and prison services continued to be received. Most of the victims were held incommunicado in the GID's Wadi Sir detention centre.

▫ Sixteen people arrested in connection with the group *al-Qa'eda* (the base) were held in prolonged incommunicado detention of up to three months at the GID detention centre and reportedly beaten. At least three were moved into solitary confinement for up to two months, apparently as a punishment. Relatives and lawyers reported that they saw marks of torture on the prisoners' bodies when they were finally allowed to visit them. During their trials, the defendants stated they had been subjected to torture, including *shabeh* (suspending the victim by the feet with arms tied behind the back) and beatings which included *falaqa* (beatings on the soles of the feet). They alleged that confessions were extracted from them under duress. No investigation of their allegations was apparently carried out.

Death in custody
▫ Amjad Salem Ahmad Smadi died in police custody in July in circumstances that suggested that torture or ill-treatment may have caused or hastened his death. Although a Commission of Inquiry was set up to investigate the circumstances surrounding his death, the findings had not been made public by the end of the year.

Unfair trials
Trials of political detainees continued before the State Security Court, a court which almost invariably used panels of military judges and failed to provide adequate safeguards for fair trials.

▫ In September, 16 people were convicted for alleged involvement with *al-Qa'eda*. They were found guilty of, among other things, plotting to carry out bomb attacks in Jordan, manufacturing explosives and recruiting people to carry out attacks on Jewish and American targets. Death sentences were passed on Khader Abu

Hosher and Usama Husni Kamel Sammar. They claimed that their confessions had been extracted under duress. Throughout the trial period serious restrictions were imposed on communication between the defendants and their lawyers, allowing them to meet only in the presence of the security forces.

Refugees
AI received reports of the *refoulement* (forcible return) of Libyan and Iraqi asylum-seekers to countries where they were at risk of human rights violations.

☐ In March up to eight Libyans resident in Jordan were removed from Jordan to Libya where there were grave concerns about their safety. In May, AI received reports that 'Abd al-Nasir Ahmad Tlaimon, a Libyan asylum-seeker, had been forcibly returned to Libya. He had been detained in Jordan in April, possibly in connection with the eight Libyans, after his application for asylum had been refused. AI has been unable to confirm his fate.

Death penalty
Ten executions were carried out during 2000 and at least 12 death sentences were passed.

☐ In December Bilal Musa was hanged in Swaqa prison. He had been sentenced to death in April for 11 murders. In July the Court of Cassation upheld the conviction and death sentence. Bilal Musa had admitted to one of the murders and claimed to have been tortured to confess to the others.

Unlawful killings
During the year police carried out at least four unlawful killings.

☐ In March Public Security police killed three members of the *Bedul* tribe in Umm Sayhun (and wounded four others) during clashes between the *Bedul* and the police over the bulldozing of a house built some years ago, allegedly on state land. AI received reports that all but one of the demonstrators killed and wounded were children under the age of 16.

The Ministry of the Interior issued statements of concern at the killings and immediately set up a Commission of Inquiry into the deaths. However, AI remained concerned that the Inquiry was to consist of government officials and would be headed by a member of the Public Security police. By the end of 2000 no findings had been made public.

Family or 'honour' killings
There were at least 21 family or "honour" killings during the year. The Upper House voted to repeal Article 340 of the Penal Code (which exempts from penalty males who murder wives or female relatives on grounds of adultery or reduces the penalty if the victim is found in an "adulterous situation"). However, the repeal was later rejected by the Lower House.

☐ In February, 34-year-old Samir Ayed was sentenced to one year in prison by the Amman Court for killing his 32-year-old sister, Hanan, in 1999. The court ruled that he should benefit from Article 98 of the Penal Code which diminishes the sentence for crimes committed in a "fit of rage" caused by an unlawful or dangerous act on the part of the victim. The prison term was immediately reduced to half because the victim's family dropped charges against their son.

Forcible exile
Four leaders of *Hamas* who were forcibly exiled by Jordan to Qatar during 1999 remained in exile.

KAZAKSTAN

REPUBLIC OF KAZAKSTAN
Head of state: Nursultan Nazarbayev
Head of government: Kasymzhomart Tokayev
Capital: Astana
Population: 16.2 million
Official language: Kazak
Death penalty: retentionist
2000 treaty ratifications/signatures: Optional Protocol to the UN Children's Convention on the involvement of children in armed conflict; Optional Protocol to the UN Women's Convention

Reports of torture and ill-treatment in police custody and pre-trial detention continued unabated, despite official initiatives to combat corruption and to reform the judicial and penal systems. Kazakstan continued to come under pressure from China to forcibly return ethnic Uighurs from Xinjiang Uighur Autonomous Region (XUAR).

Torture/ill-treatment
In April President Nursultan Nazarbayev publicly admitted that the torture or ill-treatment of suspects and detainees by law enforcement officers was widespread and routine. He reportedly accused law enforcement officers of using torture methods that "can surprise the most out-and-out sadists" such as scalding detainees with a hot iron and pouring ice-cold water over them in freezing weather.

The Kazakstan International Bureau for Human Rights and Rule of Law (KIBHR), an independent non-governmental human rights organization, publicized a number of cases of alleged torture in police custody. Most of the detainees claimed that they were severely beaten, choked, handcuffed to radiators, or had plastic bags or gas masks placed over their heads to force them to divulge information. According to KIBHR, at the beginning of the year three police officers were convicted of beating detainees in order to extract confessions from them.

☐ Irina Cherkasova alleged that she was tortured by some 12 police officers at the Abaysk District Office of Internal Affairs in the city of Chimkent in southern Kazakstan in order to force her to confess to murder.

Irina Cherkasova was reportedly beaten with sticks, books, keys and a plastic bottle filled with water; sexually assaulted with a stick; beaten with an instrument that was connected to an electric current which caused excruciating head pains; handcuffed to a radiator overnight; deprived of sleep for three nights; and raped. She was convicted of murder after the court failed to take her allegations of torture into consideration. She reportedly continued to suffer from recurring headaches, a stammer and badly diminished eyesight as a result of torture.

Forcible deportations

The murder of two policemen and a subsequent shoot-out in Almaty in September between Kazak police and alleged ethnic Uighur separatists heightened concerns that China was increasing its pressure on the Kazak authorities to forcibly return ethnic Uighurs to China, where they were at risk of human rights violations.

It was feared that Hemit Memet and Ilyas Zordun were at imminent risk of execution. They had been deported from Kazakstan to China in February 1999 and imprisoned in XUAR. Reports were received that they had been executed in August 1999. However, unofficial sources reported in late 1999 that Hemit Memet and Ilyas Zordun were believed to be still in secret detention.

AI country report

- Concerns in Europe, January – June 2000: Kazakstan (AI Index: EUR 01/003/2000)

KENYA

REPUBLIC OF KENYA
Head of state and government: Daniel arap Moi
Capital: Nairobi
Population: 28.7 million
Official languages: English, Swahili
Death penalty: retentionist
2000 treaty ratifications/signatures: Optional Protocol to the UN Children's Convention on the involvement of children in armed conflict; African Charter on the Rights and Welfare of the Child

Scores of prisoners of conscience were arrested and held for short periods after police stopped public meetings, theatre performances and peaceful demonstrations by human rights groups, politicians and others, sometimes violently. One human rights defender was killed in suspicious circumstances. Torture of criminal suspects by security officials continued, resulting in a number of deaths in custody, including six prisoners on death row. Scores of killings by security officials in circumstances suggesting possible extrajudicial executions were reported. Prison conditions remained harsh. At least 25 people were sentenced to death and more than 1,000 people were reported to be under sentence of death at the end of 2000.

Background

The report of the UN Special Rapporteur on torture on his 1999 mission to Kenya stated that the use of torture by law enforcement officials was widespread and systematic, primarily to obtain information or confessions, but also as means of carrying out extrajudicial punishments. Recommendations by the Special Rapporteur included not allowing confessions to the police to be admissible evidence in court and the abolition of corporal punishment.

The government announced that all the recommendations in the report would be implemented. In October the Criminal Law Amendment Bill was published, which included the above recommendations, together with a bill to establish an independent Human Rights Commission with the power to investigate human rights violations and visit prisons and other places of detention. However, concern was expressed that members of the Commission would be appointed by the President. A Domestic Violence (Family Protection) Bill was also published, which would strengthen the legal protection of women and children. While these proposed legislative reforms were welcomed, human rights organizations questioned whether, without appropriate resources and training, they would result in any real changes in practice, especially in poor rural areas where human rights groups engaging in civic education programs are harassed.

In July the International Monetary Fund (IMF) renewed loans to Kenya that had been suspended since

1997. Conditions imposed by the IMF included reforms to the judiciary and anti-corruption measures.

There was continued heated debate over what form the process of constitutional reform should take. In July the Constitution of Kenya (Amendment) Bill was passed, to enable the appointment of 15 Commissioners to review the Constitution. Opposition members of parliament opposed the Bill and supported the parallel review process set up in 1999 by religious leaders and others to challenge parliament's control of constitutional reform.

Severe drought in parts of Kenya resulted in tensions between different communities searching for grazing and water for their animals. In May fighting between the Somali and Borana communities led to scores of killings. The Kenyan army was accused of indiscriminate use of force when an army helicopter shot at raiders in an operation to stop the fighting.

More than 25,000 people were forced to leave their homes in the Wajir area near the Ethiopian border after armed cross-border clashes in December.

Torture/ill-treatment

Reports of torture by police officers remained widespread during 2000, although the number of police officers arrested for human rights violations increased. There were also reports of torture by vigilante groups permitted by some Provincial Commissioners to arrest, detain and interrogate criminal suspects.

◻ In October a 16-year-old girl who was being held for alleged possession of illicit alcohol in Eshirakwe Chiefs' camp, Kakamega district, Western Province, was reportedly raped by an administrative police officer who removed her from the cells and took her to his house overnight. The girl alleged that he threatened to kill her if she reported the rape. Relatives complained of harassment by officials from the Chiefs' camp after they reported the alleged torture to the police.

Shootings

Scores of people including several children were shot and injured by police officers during police attempts to arrest criminal suspects.

◻ In January, seven-year-old Chesoritich Kalomermoi was reportedly shot and seriously injured by police officers who fired into her family's home in Baringo, Rift Valley Province, in an attempt to arrest her father.

◻ In April, 18-year-old Muslima Abdi Owl was shot and injured by police officers who opened fire on women and children protesting about the allocation of land in Garissa town, North Eastern province. The authorities accused the women of throwing stones at the police.

Deaths in custody

At least 15 people died in custody during 2000 as a result of torture by police and prison officers.

◻ In April Sophia Nyaguthii Mbogo, who was four months pregnant, reportedly died from torture after she had been detained for three days by police. She was held initially at Kagio police post and then at Baricho police station on suspicion of theft. A post-mortem reportedly indicated that she died of internal bleeding and that almost half her body was covered in bruises. Under Kenyan law she should have been charged within 24 hours or released. A police officer was subsequently arrested.

◻ In September, six prisoners on death row at King'ong'o prison, Nyeri, Central Province, died during an escape attempt. The initial police report stated that they had been shot by prison officers to prevent their escape. Prison officers alleged that they had died as a result of falling from the eight-metre high perimeter fence. A post-mortem revealed that none of the bodies had bullet wounds and gave the cause of death as falling from a height. The Attorney General ordered an inquest, which opened in December. Human rights groups and others alleged that the prisoners had been beaten to death and that the authorities were attempting a cover-up. A second independent post-mortem indicated that the bodies had been subject to repeated blunt trauma, injuries that were not consistent with a fall. The body parts of at least one other prisoner with similar injuries were discovered in the same grave. The body of one of the prisoners, James Irungu Ndugo, was not found. A report by the Commissioner of Prisons was not made public during 2000 and no prison officers were suspended from duty pending investigations.

Caning

In June the government announced that corporal punishment in schools was banned following repeated reports of children being injured or killed as a result of caning. An earlier ban in 1996 had not been enforced.

◻ In September Edwin Mogire, an 11-year-old boy, died after reportedly being caned by a teacher at Nyamasakia Primary School, Nyanza Province. The teacher was arrested a month later after the boy's body was exhumed and a post-mortem performed.

Killings by police

Police officers killed scores of people during 2000 in what appeared to be extrajudicial executions or indiscriminate use of force by police officers randomly opening fire when chasing criminal suspects. Although several police officers were arrested, investigations into a number of killings appeared to be summary, with senior police officers frequently justifying them on the grounds that the victims were criminals.

◻ In May a police unit attached to the Criminal Investigation Department, established in 1997 to combat violent crime, was disbanded and officers were transferred to other police stations. Members of the squad were reported to have engaged in torture, extrajudicial executions and violent crime. The authorities denied this. In June, two former members were arrested and charged with the murder of Joseph ole Pirei, after an inquest in August 1999 found he had been shot 10 times while unarmed.

Human rights defenders

Scores of prisoners of conscience were arrested during 2000 for short periods after public meetings, theatre performances and peaceful demonstrations organized by human rights, religious, environmental and other groups were broken up by the police, sometimes violently. In November the President accused some non-governmental organizations of being agents of subversion ostensibly promoting democracy. At least 11 people faced charges of unlawful assembly at the end of the year. One human rights defender was killed in suspicious circumstances.

◻ In March, 11 human rights defenders were arrested while performing a play as part of a civic education program for the Ogiek, an indigenous people living in Tinet forest, Rift Valley Province. They were charged with "holding an illegal meeting" and held for six days before being released. The charges were dropped in May. More than 5,000 people face eviction in Tinet, which is the focus of a land dispute between the government and the Ogiek.

◻ In April, 63 people including nuns, students and human rights defenders were arrested during a peaceful demonstration calling for the cancellation of Kenya's foreign debt, organized by the Kenya Debt Relief Network Jubilee 2000 Campaign. They were charged with unlawful assembly and released on bail. The charges were dropped in May.

◻ In August Father Kaiser, a US Roman Catholic priest, was killed in suspicious circumstances. An outspoken advocate for human rights, in 1998 he had given evidence which reportedly implicated several Cabinet ministers to a judicial inquiry set up to investigate the causes of political violence in Kenya since 1992. At the time of his death he had been assisting an alleged rape victim to bring charges against a senior government minister.

Political rallies

Rallies organized by politicians were violently disrupted by the police.

◻ In August, one person was killed and many others were injured when police and security forces broke up a peaceful pro-democracy rally in Nairobi. Several members of the opposition were prevented from addressing the rally and were forcibly confined to the Parliament buildings by armed youths who attacked them when they attempted to leave. Armed police surrounding the building took no action to prevent the attacks.

◻ In October President Moi banned rallies by a new pro-democracy movement, *Muungano wa Mageuzi*, People's Movement for Change, set up by opposition and government politicians and others. The Movement refused to accept the ban. In November a rally in Eldoret town, Rift Valley Province, was stopped by the police who tear gassed more than 2,000 people, including 10 members of parliament, in an attempt to prevent them reaching the rally venue.

◻ On 26 November at the Tumsifu Centre, Kisumu, western Kenya, about 50 youths violently disrupted a public hearing on the Kenyan Constitution, organized by the Ufungamano Initiative which is challenging Parliament's control of Constitutional reform. The youths, who were armed with clubs, axes and stones, attacked participants while a police patrol reportedly stood by and watched. A petrol bomb was thrown at Dr Oki Ombaka, chairperson of the People's Commission of Kenya (PCK). The injured included members of the PCK and a journalist. Not only was no attempt made by the police to stop the violence, but when Dr Oki Ombaka later attempted to lodge an official complaint, the local head of police refused to take his statement and physically removed him from the police station.

Press freedom

Restrictions on freedom of expression continued. Journalists were arrested, and some were beaten. Private radio stations broadcasting in local languages were threatened with closure, and proposed amendments to the Books and Newspaper Act targeted the independent press by significantly increasing the licence bond required to start a publication.

◻ In January Vitalis Musebe and Mukalo wa Kwayera, the managing and news editors of *The People*, an independent daily newspaper, were arrested and charged under the Official Secrets Act following an article on low morale in the army. The case was still pending at the end of 2000.

Refugees

There continued to be reports of harassment of refugees by the police. In July over 300 people, mostly from Somalia, were arrested in Mombassa and accused of being illegal immigrants.

Death penalty

At least 25 people were sentenced to death during 2000, including a 70-year-old man and one man whose sentence was increased by the Court of Appeal from six years to death. More than 1,000 people were believed to be under sentence of death. The death sentence on one woman was repealed. In October a motion in parliament to abolish the death penalty failed. Only 66 members of parliament attended the debate.

Prison conditions

Prison conditions in many prisons amounted to cruel, inhuman and degrading treatment. Severe overcrowding, food and medical shortages and lack of clean drinking water resulted in scores of deaths. Some prisoners have reportedly been held for over five years, awaiting trial. The President released 10,623 prisoners on Independence Day in December.

◻ In May, two members of the *Mungiki* religious group on remand were forcibly removed by prison officers from Nyeri Provincial General hospital, Central Province, after they had been admitted by the duty doctor because of the seriousness of their injuries. They were taken to the dispensary in King'ong'o prison, Nyeri, which reportedly had no drugs or facilities to treat their injuries.

AI country report and visits
Report
- Kenya: Prisons — Deaths due to torture and cruel, inhuman and degrading conditions (AI Index: AFR 32/010/2000)

Visits
AI visited Kenya in April to attend meetings with non-governmental human rights organizations and in November to attend a post-mortem. In October a launch meeting for AI's worldwide campaign against torture was held in Nairobi.

KOREA
(DEMOCRATIC PEOPLE'S REPUBLIC OF)

DEMOCRATIC PEOPLE'S REPUBLIC OF KOREA
Head of state: Kim Jong Il
Head of government: Hong Song Nam
Capital: Pyongyang
Population: 23.3 million
Official language: Korean
Death penalty: retentionist

The government of the Democratic People's Republic of Korea (North Korea) stepped up its diplomatic and trade initiatives with the outside world. Although the food crisis was reported to have eased slightly, North Korea remained dependent on massive humanitarian aid. Lack of access and government restrictions on the flow of information continued to hamper independent research, giving rise to concern that patterns of serious human rights violations remained hidden.

Intensified diplomatic and trade links
The North Korean government's diplomatic efforts were intensified in 2000, as the country became more engaged in regional and international affairs. In January, Italy became the first of the Group of Seven (G7) nations to establish full diplomatic ties with North Korea. Diplomatic links were also established with Australia and with the Philippines. The government showed interest in improving ties with the USA, Japan, Canada and several European countries. In July, North Korea joined the Association of South-East Asian Nations (ASEAN).

North Korea and Japan resumed talks to normalize relations in April. However, the two countries remained far apart on most key issues, including Japanese compensation for its occupation of the Korean peninsula between 1910 and 1945, and the 10 missing Japanese nationals who Japan believes were abducted by North Korean agents in the 1970s and 1980s.

Contacts between North Korea and the USA accelerated. Foreign Ministers from both countries held a meeting during the ASEAN Regional Forum in Bangkok in July. In October North Korea's Vice-Chairman of the National Defence Commission met President Bill Clinton. The two countries later issued a joint communiqué on improving relations. In October, US Secretary of State Madeleine Albright visited North Korea and held talks with Kim Jong Il and other high-ranking officials. The USA again eased sanctions against North Korea, allowing reciprocal commercial activity, and announced in June that it would donate more food aid through the World Food Program. In response, North Korea returned the remains of 26 US servicemen lost in action during the Korean war and promised to freeze its missile-testing program.

In May, Kim Jong Il made an unprecedented state visit to China; his first official trip abroad since he came to power in 1994.

Inter-Korean summit
In a ground-breaking political move, the North Korean leader held a summit in mid-June in Pyongyang with the South Korean President, Kim Dae-jung. The outcome of the summit was a declaration seeking eventual reunification. A series of meetings between North and South Korean officials followed and both sides agreed to ease military tension and guarantee peace on the Korean peninsula. Three channels of dialogue were established between the two Koreas, on economic, military and family reunion issues. In August, 100 separated families from both countries were briefly reunited in Seoul. A second reunion was held at the end of November in Seoul and Pyongyang.

Humanitarian crisis
Although some slight improvement in the humanitarian situation was reported, the food crisis remained severe, with the country facing grave food shortages for the sixth consecutive year. Uncertainty still prevailed as to the distribution of food aid and the monitoring of needs. In March, the French aid agency *Action contre la faim*, Action against Hunger, pulled out of North Korea on the grounds that "free and direct access to famine victims is denied".

Restrictions on information
Reports suggested the existence of serious and hidden patterns of human rights violations, including public executions, torture, detention of political prisoners and inhumane prison conditions. However, information and access to the country remained tightly restricted, and AI was unable to verify these reports.

Refugees
The food crisis led hundreds, possibly thousands, of people to cross the border into China where their situation was very precarious. Some were reported to have been apprehended by Chinese and North Korean security forces and forcibly returned to North Korea. Little was known about what happened to the returnees but a number of sources reported that they often faced long interrogation sessions and torture. Some returnees were sent to prison or labour camps where conditions were reported to be extremely harsh.

☐ In January, seven North Korean refugees, including a 13-year-old boy, were forcibly returned from China. The seven refugees left North Korea for Russia via China and were recognized as refugees by the UN High Commissioner for Refugees (UNHCR). However, the Russian authorities forcibly returned them to China, which sent them back to North Korea. In June, it was reported that six of the seven refugees were serving "short-term prison sentences" and that the 13-year-old-boy had been released, although AI was not able to verify this information.

Intergovernmental organization
In 1997, North Korea had announced its "withdrawal" from the International Covenant on Civil and Political Rights (ICCPR). However, in March, the government submitted its second periodic report on its

implementation of the ICCPR to the UN Human Rights Committee. Its first report was submitted in 1984.

AI country report
- Democratic People's Republic of Korea: *Persecuting the starving – the plight of North Koreans fleeing to China* (AI Index: ASA 24/003/2000)

KOREA
(REPUBLIC OF)

REPUBLIC OF KOREA
Head of state: Kim Dae-jung
Head of government: Lee Han-dong
Capital: Seoul
Population: 47.4 million
Official language: Korean
Death penalty: retentionist
2000 treaty ratifications/signatures: Optional Protocol to the UN Children's Convention on the involvement of children in armed conflict; Rome Statute of the International Criminal Court

President Kim Dae-jung's promises of domestic political and judicial reforms, including a review of the National Security Law and the enactment of a Human Rights Law, were not realized. Reports suggested that the government had given up plans to form a National Human Rights Commission under the Ministry of Justice, amid continued debate about the proposed Commission's autonomy and powers. The number of political prisoners in long-term detention declined, but a number of political prisoners were arrested and held briefly, mostly students and activists belonging to banned pro-North Korean organizations. Most political prisoners continued to be detained under the vaguely worded provisions of the National Security Law. Excessive force to quell trade union protests continued, and many trade unionists were arrested.

Background
The year was dominated by the thawing of relations between the Republic of Korea (South Korea) and the Democratic People's Republic of Korea (North Korea). President Kim Dae-jung accepted an invitation to a summit with North Korean leader Chairman Kim Jong Il a few days before National Assembly elections in April. President Kim Dae-jung's Millennium Democratic Party (MDP) did not gain a majority and remained a minority government, necessitating the continuation of a coalition with the United Liberal Democratic Party (ULD), whose leader, Lee Han-dong, was appointed Prime Minister in May. The single largest party in the National Assembly was the opposition Grand National Party (GNP).

Despite initial scepticism, the mid-June summit between the leaders of the two Koreas led to an increased impetus to improve inter-Korean relations. Changes included the reunion of 100 separated families from each side in August and December. The South Korean Defence Minister, Cho Seong-tae, and the Defence Minister of North Korea, Kim Il-chol, met for the first time on Cheju island (South Korea). They agreed to work towards reducing tension on the Korean peninsula, and to coordinate efforts on the Military Demarcation Line and the Demilitarized Zone to expedite the construction of a railway and a road connecting North and South Korea. A third round of inter-Korean ministerial talks took place in September and ministers agreed to establish a Committee for the Promotion of Inter-Korean Economic Cooperation. Sixty-three former long-term "unconverted" prisoners were repatriated from South Korea to North Korea in September.

President Kim Dae-jung was awarded the Nobel Peace Prize for his efforts in improving relations between North and South Korea, for fostering democracy and for his role in East Timor and Indonesia.

National Security Law
As of 25 August, of the 99 political prisoners in detention, 54 were detained on charges under the National Security Law. Of these, the majority were arrested under Article 7, which punishes membership of organizations deemed to "benefit the enemy". Improving relations with North Korea prompted debate on reform of the National Security Law. President Kim Dae-jung, apparently encouraged by his award of the Nobel Peace Prize, announced his support for revisions to the National Security Law, but opposition to reform in the National Assembly from both the GNP and the ULD prevented significant revisions.

▫ Park Kyung-soon, who was sentenced to seven years' imprisonment under the National Security Law for reportedly leading the "Youngnam Committee", remained in Pusan prison. He was a prisoner of conscience and was suffering from cirrhosis of the liver.

▫ At least nine members of a university student group, *Hanchongryun*, were detained in August under the National Security Law, accused of belonging to an anti-state organization, praising North Korea and organizing rallies propagating closer relations with "the enemy". They continued to be held at the end of 2000.

▫ Eight men were detained for having organized and participated in an allegedly anti-state organization called *Minhyukdang*, the People's Revolutionary Party. Ha Young-ok, a former student, was sentenced to eight years' imprisonment; Kim Kyung-hwan, a former journalist, was sentenced to four and half years; and Shim Jae-choon, a former lecturer, was sentenced to three and half years. Choi Chin-su, Park Jong-seok, Lee Uei-yeob and Han Yong-jin were held in Seoul Detention Centre and their trials were continuing at the end of 2000. Park Jung-hoon was released on bail.

Security Surveillance Law
The Security Surveillance Law continued to be used to control and supervise the activities of former political

prisoners, including prisoners of conscience. Under the law, former prisoners have to report regularly to the nearest police station, face restrictions on their freedom of movement, and are banned from meeting former political prisoners and participating in demonstrations, especially political demonstrations.

☐ Human rights activist and former prisoner of conscience Suh Jun-shik, who was the first political prisoner to be released without signing the "law-abidance oath", had his appeal against the continued extension of the Security Surveillance Law rejected in September by the Western branch of the Seoul District Court. He lodged an appeal before the Seoul High Court.

Torture/ill-treatment
There were reports that suspects held under the National Security Law were held for interrogation in police detention for up to a month with limited access to relatives and lawyers. There were also reports of detainees being beaten by police. Conditions in prisons continued to be harsh, with prisoners held in unheated cells and denied adequate medical facilities.

☐ Kim Kyong-hwan, who was sentenced to four and a half years' imprisonment for his involvement with *Minhyukdang*, alleged that he had been beaten repeatedly during interrogation.

Trade unions
The police used excessive force to repress strikes and protests by trade unionists. The impact of the 1997 economic crisis continued, and trade unions organized protests against harsh employment conditions, especially in service industries such as hotels and in the financial sector. Labour activists numbered 29 of the 99 political prisoners in August 2000.

☐ In June, police baton-charged a peaceful occupation by union activists at the Lotte Hotel and discharged tear gas in the confined corridors of the seventh floor of the hotel building. They dragged dozens of protesters from a seventh-floor room, many of whom complained of breathing difficulties and panic.

Refugees
Since it signed the UN Refugee Convention in 1992, the South Korean government had not granted refugee status to asylum-seekers from any country other than North Korea. There were fears that asylum-seekers were deported to countries where they risked grave human rights violations, in violation of the principle of non-*refoulement*. Furthermore, the asylum determination process appeared to be weighted against the applicant, with inadequate interpretation facilities during interviews and no support for asylum-seekers while they await the decision.

However, in an unprecedented decision, 28 Burmese asylum-seekers were allowed to submit their applications for consideration.

Death penalty
No executions have been carried out since 1998 when President Kim Dae-jung took charge. A bill to abolish the death penalty was introduced by legislators in the National Assembly, but was not passed during 2000.

AI country visit
AI delegates visited South Korea in March, and met a number of non-governmental organizations.

KUWAIT

STATE OF KUWAIT
Head of state: al-Shaikh Jaber al-Ahmad al-Sabah
Head of government: al-Shaikh Sa'ad al-'Abdallah al-Sabah
Capital: Kuwait City
Population: 1.9 million
Official language: Arabic
Death penalty: retentionist
2000 treaty ratifications/signatures: Rome Statute of the International Criminal Court

At least 42 political prisoners, including prisoners of conscience, convicted in unfair trials since 1991, continued to be held. The fate of more than 70 people who "disappeared" in custody in 1991 remained unknown. At least 21 people were sentenced to death. One man was executed in February. The campaign to secure voting rights for women suffered a setback.

Background
In July the UN Human Rights Committee examined the first report submitted by Kuwait since its accession in 1996 to the International Covenant on Civil and Political Rights (ICCPR). The Committee expressed its concerns about a number of issues, including the number of people still imprisoned following their conviction in 1991 by the Martial Law Court in trials which did not meet minimum international standards of fair trial set by the ICCPR. The concluding observations of the Committee recommended that "[t]he cases of persons still held under such sentences should be reviewed by an independent and impartial body, and compensation should be paid...where appropriate". No steps to implement this recommendation were known to have been taken by the end of the year.

Women's voting rights
Women's rights activists continued their struggle to gain the right to vote and stand for political office. After being turned away by officials from registration centres, which opened in February to update the all-male voters' lists, a number of women filed a complaint against the Minister of the Interior, al-Shaikh

Mohammad Khaled al-Sabah. This challenge to the legitimacy of Kuwait's electoral law, which denies women the right to vote, was heard by the Constitutional Court in June and was rejected. The verdict in another complaint against the electoral law was due to be delivered by the Constitutional Court in January 2001. In a public statement, AI urged the government to withdraw its reservations to the UN Women's Convention and the ICCPR and to give women all human rights.

Bidun (stateless people)
In May the National Assembly passed legislation restricting the number of those who might qualify to apply for citizenship to less than one third of the total number of stateless *Bidun* remaining in Kuwait. The first trial of a *Bidun*, on charges of forgery and illegally staying in Kuwait, began in September. Fifty other people were reported to be under investigation and 13 in detention on similar charges. If found guilty, they could face up to seven years in prison followed by deportation. In effect, thousands of stateless Arabs living in Kuwait for decades could face compulsory deportation if they failed to legalize their status by the end of 2000.

Freedom of expression
Provisions of the Penal Code, along with articles in the Printing and Publications Law (Press Code) were used to limit freedom of expression.

In March the Misdemeanours Appeal Court handed down fines to two women writers — Laila al-'Othman, originally sentenced to two months' imprisonment, and 'Alia Shu'aib — and their publisher, Yahya Rubi'yan. The Appeal Court upheld charges of breaching public decency and using profane and impious language made against Laila al-'Othman; 'Alia Shu'aib was acquitted of all charges except those relating to Press Code violations; charges relating to violations of the Press and Penal Codes against Yahya Rubi'yan were upheld.

Death penalty
At least 21 people were sentenced to death following convictions for murder and drug-related offences. Two others sentenced to death in previous years had their sentences upheld by the Supreme Court. At the end of the year at least 30 people were reported to be on death row, the majority of them having been convicted of drug offences or murder. A Kuwaiti national, Matar al-Mutairi, sentenced to death in 1996 for murder, was hanged in February.

'Collaboration' trial
The death sentence against Ala' Hussein Ali, a former colonel in the Kuwaiti army who led the so-called provisional government of Kuwait during the Iraqi occupation in 1990, was upheld by an appeal court in July. In December the Court of Cassation adjourned its proceedings until January 2001 in response to an appeal by the defence.

AI country visits
AI delegates visited Kuwait in February. They met senior officials, including the Minister of Justice, and attended a session of the writers' trial. Following the visit, the authorities informed AI that Sabiha Rasan Khallati had been granted an amnesty earlier in the year. She had been detained since 1991 after an unfair trial.

KYRGYZSTAN

KYRGYZ REPUBLIC
Head of state: Askar Akayev
Head of government: Kurmanbek Bakiyev (replaced Amangeldy Muraliyev in December)
Capital: Bishkek
Population: 4.6 million
Official languages: Kyrgyz, Russian
Death penalty: retentionist

The clamp-down on suspected supporters of banned Islamist opposition parties continued following new armed incursions into Kyrgyzstan in August by members of the banned Islamic Movement of Uzbekistan (IMU). At least one ethnic Uighur was forcibly deported to China. A leading opposition activist was imprisoned. Human rights groups, the independent media and opposition supporters came under increasing pressure from the authorities.

Background
Law enforcement officers reportedly used excessive force to break up peaceful demonstrations in several regions of the country protesting against irregularities in the February and March rounds of parliamentary elections. Hundreds of demonstrators, including women and the elderly, were reportedly detained and beaten.

Both the February parliamentary and the October presidential elections were heavily criticized by the Organization for Security and Co-operation in Europe (OSCE). Incumbent President Askar Akayev won a third term in office amid claims that a controversial mandatory Kyrgyz-language test for presidential candidates had been aimed at excluding the chairman of the opposition *Ar-Namys* party, Felix Kulov.

In August a military court cleared Felix Kulov of reportedly fabricated and politically motivated charges of abuse of authority while serving as a Minister of National Security. He had spent six months in pre-trial detention.

Arrests of suspected supporters of banned Islamist opposition parties increased following renewed armed incursions by fighters of the IMU who crossed Kyrgyz territory from neighbouring Tajikistan on their way to Uzbekistan in August. Units of IMU fighters also carried out attacks on Uzbek territory.

The President extended the 1998 moratorium on executions until the end of 2001.

Prisoner of conscience

In September former prisoner of conscience and leader of the opposition *Erkindik* party, Topchubek Turgunaliev, was sentenced to 16 years' imprisonment on charges connected with an alleged plot to assassinate the President; seven others were also convicted in the trial. Topchubek Turgunaliev consistently denied the charges and alleged that the case against him was fabricated by the Ministry of National Security (MNS) in order to punish him for his peaceful political opposition activities. Three MNS officers reportedly admitted in court that there was not enough evidence to support the allegations. The charges were based on the testimony of one of the co-accused, Timur Stamkulov, who later confessed that he had carried out MNS instructions to plan a fictitious assassination attempt in order to implicate Topchubek Turgunaliev. In court, Timur Stamkulov reportedly retracted this confession. He was sentenced to four years' imprisonment but was granted an amnesty and released.

The other six co-accused claimed never to have met Topchubek Turgunaliev until the trial. They were sentenced to between 14 and 17 years' imprisonment. Bishkek City Court reduced their sentences on appeal by more than half. On 30 November President Askar Akayev signed a decree granting them amnesties, reportedly because they had admitted their guilt and asked for pardon.

Topchubek Turgunaliev did not qualify for the amnesty because he refused to admit any guilt. On appeal, his term was reduced to six years by Bishkek City Court. A further appeal against his conviction to the Supreme Court was still pending at the end of 2000.

Torture/ill-treatment

In court Topchubek Turgunaliev's co-accused, who were arrested in May 1999, alleged that they had been tortured and ill-treated in pre-trial detention to force them to confess. Mamadyar Orozov, for example, alleged that he was beaten with batons on the soles of his feet, nearly suffocated with a gas mask and handcuffed to a radiator. The court did not take any of these allegations into consideration.

Harassment of human rights defenders

In April human rights activists, including former prisoners of conscience, founded the Guild of Prisoners of Conscience, and applied for registration to the Ministry of Justice. At the end of May the Ministry of Justice explained that it could not proceed with the registration of an organization created to defend the rights of prisoners of conscience since the Kyrgyz Constitution prohibited anyone from being discriminated against because of their political views and the current criminal code did not carry any articles for political crimes.

In July Ramazan Dyryldayev, chairman of the Kyrgyz Committee for Human Rights (KCHR) was forced into exile after the Kyrgyz authorities issued a warrant for his arrest, reportedly detained his son for questioning, and sealed the KCHR's offices. Although the procurator general allegedly ordered the criminal case to be suspended, KCHR's lawyer believed that it was not safe for Ramazan Dyryldayev to return because the criminal investigation had not been officially closed. The criminal charges related to a dispute with a former KCHR member of staff over an unfair dismissal claim.

Restrictions on freedom of the press

In the run-up to the parliamentary and presidential elections, the independent media came under increasing pressure from the authorities for their coverage of opposition parties and candidates. For example, journalists and media organizations were sued for libel and tax evasion or other administrative or criminal offences.

Moldosali Ibrahimov, a freelance correspondent of the Jalal-Abad regional newspaper *Akyikat* and local KCHR activist, was found guilty of defamation and sentenced to two years' imprisonment by Jalal-Abad City Court in June. The defamation charge related to an article he had written in which he reported rumours that a local district court judge had accepted a bribe in a dispute between two rival candidates in the parliamentary elections. He was released on appeal in July.

Forcible deportation

Jelil Turdi, an ethnic Uighur from the Xinjiang Uighur Autonomous Region (XUAR) in the People's Republic of China was reported to have been forcibly deported in April to China where he was at risk of torture and possibly the death penalty for alleged "separatist" activities. He was first detained by Kyrgyz police in early March 2000, reportedly for having an illegal residence permit, then rearrested a few weeks later after the Chinese embassy in Kyrgyzstan claimed that his Chinese documents were false. According to unofficial sources, however, Chinese security officers told their Kyrgyz counterparts that Jelil Turdi was wanted in China for involvement in a nationalist opposition group. The Chinese officers reportedly took part in Jelil Turdi's interrogation, during which he was allegedly tortured. Jelil Turdi was denied the opportunity to challenge the decision to deport him before a court in Kyrgyzstan.

AI country report

- Concerns in Europe, January-June 2000: Kyrgyzstan (AI Index: EUR 01/003/2000)

LAOS

LAO PEOPLE'S DEMOCRATIC REPUBLIC
Head of state: Khamtay Siphandone
Head of government: Sisavat Keobounphanh
Capital: Vientiane
Population: 5.4 million
Official language: Lao
Death penalty: retentionist
2000 treaty ratifications/signatures: International Covenant on Civil and Political Rights; International Covenant on Economic, Social and Cultural Rights

Freedom of expression, association and religion continued to be severely restricted. Tight controls on information prevented adequate international and local monitoring of the human rights situation. At least five people were arrested in connection with a series of bomb attacks. Three prisoners of conscience and two political prisoners continued to be held in cruel, inhuman and degrading conditions. New information suggested that scores of people were detained for their Christian beliefs. The fate of protesters arrested in October 1999 remained unknown.

Background
A bombing campaign began in March, and at least nine bombs were planted during 2000 in busy public locations, mostly in Vientiane, causing one death and dozens of injuries. No group claimed responsibility, but it was reported that the authorities had arrested five people. They were not identified and there was no information on whether they had been charged and tried. In July there was an armed attack on customs and immigration offices in the border village of Vang Tao, Champassak province, by alleged members of an armed opposition group. Six people were killed by Lao security forces, and 28 others were arrested after fleeing to Thailand. There were unconfirmed reports that at least 15 people were arrested in November following a peaceful demonstration in Sanasomboune, Champassak province. As many as 300 demonstrators were reportedly calling for social justice and democracy.

In December Laos hosted the first Ministerial meeting to be held between the European Union and the Association of South East Asian Nations (ASEAN) since 1997.

Political prisoners
Official secrecy about political imprisonment continued. At least five anti-government protesters arrested in October 1999 remained in detention. The authorities did not make public any information about charges against them or their whereabouts, heightening concern for their safety. Thongpaseuth Keuakoun, Khamphouvieng Sisaath, Seng-Aloun Phengphanh, Bouavanh Chanhmanivong and Keochay were all members of the "Lao Students Movement for Democracy of 26 October 1999", who had attempted to publicly call for respect for human rights, the release of political prisoners, a multi-party political system and elections for a new National Assembly. Sinh Sanay and his sister Sinh Keotha were also reportedly arrested in October for involvement in the planned demonstration. The authorities denied that any protest or arrests had taken place, despite eyewitness accounts.

Two political prisoners, Sing Chanthakoumane and Pangtong Chokbengboun, detained for "re-education" without charge or trial since 1975 and then sentenced to life imprisonment after an unfair trial in 1992, continued to be detained at Prison Camp 7 in Houa Phanh Province.

Prisoners of conscience Feng Sakchittaphong and Latsami Khamphoui, both 60 years old, remained in Prison Camp 7, in a remote area of Houa Phanh Province. Both men were arrested in 1990 and sentenced to 14 years' imprisonment in 1992 following an unfair trial. Although they were charged with national security offences, it is believed that they were imprisoned solely for peacefully advocating non-violent political and economic change. The conditions of their detention continued to be harsh, including being held in darkness for almost 24 hours a day and only being allowed to bathe in a river every one or two weeks. Their health was fragile and food and medical care were inadequate. Visiting rights for their families were severely restricted.

Religious persecution
Restrictions on freedom of religious expression continued with the authorities apparently regarding members of small unauthorized Christian churches with suspicion. New information suggested that scores of Christians were arrested in 1999 and remained in detention, and that possibly dozens more were arrested throughout 2000. Christians worshipping in small church groups outside state control were reportedly asked to repent their faith in writing or face imprisonment, confiscation of property and forced relocation of their families. Official closure of unauthorized churches was also reported. Incidents occurred all around the country in the provinces of Attapeu, Champassak, Houa Phanh, Luang Nam Tha, Luang Prabang, Phong Saly, Savannakhet, and Vientiane.

Three pastors arrested in July 1999 in Luang Prabang Province and sentenced to five years' imprisonment were reported to be in poor health. Pastor Boonmee, Pastor Sisamouth and Pastor On Chan were detained with 13 other pastors and village elders. Arrests reported during 2000 included Reverend Savath Heunlith, Pastor Thongla and Pastor Thongsouth in Sayaboury Province in May, and Pastor Ah Lon, reportedly imprisoned in Bolikhamsai Province for three years.

Pa Tood, a rice farmer and local church leader arrested with 15 others in March 1999 in Savannakhet Province remained in detention in Savannakhet City

Prison. He was reportedly held in stocks in solitary confinement because of his refusal to repent his faith.

⬚ Khamtanh Phousy, a prisoner of conscience detained since 1996, remained in detention at Prison Camp 7 in Houa Phanh Province. A former army officer who converted to Christianity, he had been sentenced to seven years' imprisonment for "irresponsibility in his work" and corruption. AI believes that the charges against him were politically motivated.

Torture/ill-treatment
Torture and ill-treatment in police stations were widespread. One person interviewed described it as "normal practice" when a relative detained on criminal charges was beaten, kicked and punched by police in order to make him confess.

Prisoners were commonly held in conditions amounting to cruel, inhuman or degrading treatment. Reports of ill-treatment and torture of prisoners included beatings, being held in stocks for long periods of time, deprivation of light, adequate food, water and medication, and the use of solitary confinement cells. Access to family was also denied.

Official responses
Letters from officials in Lao embassies showed lack of knowledge about individual prisoner cases and dismissed concerns about human rights violations.

AI country report
- Lao People's Democratic Republic: The October protesters – where are they? (AI Index: ASA 26/004/2000)

LATVIA

REPUBLIC OF LATVIA
Head of state: Vaira Vike-Freiberga
Head of government: Andris Berzins (replaced Andris Skele in May)
Capital: Riga
Population: 2.3 million
Official language: Lettish
Death penalty: abolitionist for ordinary crimes

The authorities considered introducing an alternative service to compulsory military service. There was no universal provision for such an alternative service in domestic legislation. Under the Amendment to the Law on Compulsory Military Service, adopted in December 1999, only ordained and trainee clerics who belonged to religious organizations registered by the Ministry of Justice were exempted from military service.

In August the Ministry of Defence issued a statement outlining its position regarding the introduction of an alternative service and stating its wish to convene a round-table discussion of the issue with various non-governmental organizations and religious groups. However, there was concern that the Ministry of Defence's model did not appear to provide for a genuinely civilian alternative service, since conscientious objectors could be forced to perform non-combatant support functions in the armed forces. No decision had been taken by the end of the year.

AI country report
- Latvia: The right to conscientious objection (AI Index: EUR 52/001/2000)

LEBANON

LEBANESE REPUBLIC
Head of state: Emile Lahoud
Head of government: Rafiq al-Hariri (replaced Salim al-Huss in October)
Capital: Beirut
Population: 3.2 million
Official language: Arabic
Death penalty: retentionist
2000 treaty ratifications/signatures: UN Convention against Torture

Hundreds of people, including students and suspected opponents of the government, were arrested on political grounds. Most were arrested after demonstrations or other forms of peaceful protest and held in short-term detention. A dozen of the student demonstrators received unfair trials before the Military Court. Hundreds of former members or supporters of the South Lebanon Army (SLA) received summary trials which fell short of international fair trial standards. There were reports of torture and ill-treatment. At least eight people were sentenced to death, but there were no executions.

Background
Former Prime Minister Rafiq al-Hariri won an overwhelming majority in Beirut Province in the August parliamentary elections and was appointed Prime Minister in October.

Israel withdrew from its self-styled "security zone" in south Lebanon in May. Israel's proxy militia, the SLA, collapsed in the wake of the Israeli withdrawal resulting in the release of the remaining detainees in al-Khiam detention centre. Borders between Lebanon and Israel were redrawn under the auspices of the UN, pursuant to Security Council Resolution 425 of 1978. Shab'a Farms in southeast Lebanon remained a disputed territory between the two countries. The UN Interim Force in Lebanon (UNIFIL) was deployed in the former "security zone" following verification of Israeli withdrawal.

Syria maintained its military presence in Lebanon with the agreement of the Lebanese government. There were discussions in Parliament as well as religious and political circles about reassessing the Syrian presence in Lebanon.

At least 31 people died in armed clashes between an Islamist group and Lebanese security forces in the Dinniyah plateau east of Tripoli in north Lebanon. The dead included 18 Islamist militants, two women hostages, and 11 soldiers. More than 50 members of the Islamist group were arrested following these clashes and referred for trial before the Justice Council.

AI opened a regional office for the Middle East in Beirut in October.

Arrests

Hundreds of people were arrested on political grounds. They included suspected members of an Islamist group; students connected with the Free Patriotic Movement, which supports former exiled army commander General Michel 'Aoun; suspected members of the Lebanese Forces (LF) party; and suspected collaborators with the SLA.

☐ At least 90 suspected members or supporters of the unauthorized LF party were arrested in September and October. These arrests followed a church mass and demonstration organized by the LF in Mount Lebanon to commemorate the death of Bashir al-Gemayel, President-elect and founder of the LF who was killed in 1982. Most of those arrested were detained for a few hours or days and released without charge. Some were reportedly forced to sign an undertaking not to engage in any political activity.

☐ At least four people were arrested in August in Junieh by the security forces for possessing and distributing literature calling for a boycott of the August 2000 parliamentary elections. They were released shortly afterwards without charge.

☐ Two brothers, 'Umar and Samer Mas'ud, were arrested in Qubayat in August, reportedly by a joint Lebanese-Syrian force for writing slogans on the walls calling for a boycott of the elections. They were said to have been taken to the Syrian intelligence headquarters in Halba for interrogation. They were released on the same day.

Unfair trials

More than a thousand political prisoners were tried before the Military Court in summary proceedings. Scores of others were tried before the Justice Council whose verdicts are not subject to judicial review. The proceedings of both courts failed to meet international fair trial standards.

☐ In April, 12 students from the Free Patriotic Movement were tried by the Military Court on charges of assaulting the police and obstructing the highway. The students denied the charges, but were sentenced to between 10 and 45 days' imprisonment.

☐ More than 2,300 former SLA members and alleged "collaborators" with Israel were brought for trial before the Military Court. Most were sentenced to between one month and five years' imprisonment and fines or restriction orders. The longest sentence handed down was 15 years' imprisonment.

In breach of international human rights standards, defendants were detained incommunicado by Lebanese military intelligence for up to 10 days. There was concern that such summary trials, with barely seven minutes spent on each individual, neither allowed the innocent to be acquitted nor ensured that those who committed war crimes, including the systematic torture of detainees in Khiam, would be discovered.

☐ At least 63 defendants were referred for trial before the Justice Council in connection with the Dinniyah clashes. The trial was scheduled to start in January 2001.

Torture/ill-treatment

There were some reports of torture and ill-treatment, including police brutality. Methods of torture reported included sleep deprivation, prolonged standing, psychological torture, beating, electric shocks and *Farruj* (chicken) where the victim is strapped to a revolving wooden bar resembling a roasting spit and beaten.

☐ Those detained in connection with the Dinniyah case were allegedly tortured and ill-treated during incommunicado detention. Khaled Minawi, aged 15, was reportedly beaten by members of the security forces during interrogation at al-Qubbah detention centre in Tripoli.

☐ Hiba Ma'sarani, who was being tried by the Criminal Court of Tripoli, stated that she had been repeatedly subjected to different forms of torture, including *Farruj* and beating during pre-trial detention in 1997 and again in February 2000.

☐ Detained asylum-seekers and refugees were also allegedly tortured and ill-treated. Talib Yassir Sabbah, a recognized Iraqi refugee, stated that he was subjected to various forms of torture including *Farruj* and locked up for hours in a small, crowded and overheated cell while in detention in Furn al-Shiback.

☐ During the trial of former SLA members some of the defendants stated that they had been tortured in pre-trial detention.

In none of the above cases were investigations known to have been carried out.

Khiam detention centre

In the wake of the Israeli withdrawal from south Lebanon, and the collapse of the SLA, people in the surrounding areas broke into the Khiam detention centre and set the detainees free. For years torture and ill-treatment had been routine in Khiam where detainees were held outside any legal framework. At the time of their liberation there were 144 remaining detainees, some of whom had spent up to 14 years in detention without charge or trial. Among the detainees were five women, two of whom, Cosette Ibrahim and Najwa Samhat, were hospitalized in March for illnesses incurred as a result of torture and ill-treatment. Sixteen detainees were believed to have died in Khiam as a result of torture during the previous 15 years.

Human rights defenders
Two human rights defenders — Muhammad Mugraby, a lawyer, and Kamal al-Batal, director of the human rights group *Mirsad* — were subjected to harassment and prosecution before criminal and military courts. In May Muhammad Mugraby was charged with libel, defamation and dishonouring the judiciary in connection with criticisms he had made and his allegations of professional misconduct against five named judges. Kamal al-Batal was first summoned by the police for interrogation concerning an urgent appeal issued by *Mirsad* expressing concern about a raid by the Lebanese vice-squad on an Internet service provider, "Destination", and the interrogation of its manager about a Lebanese gay website. Kamal al-Batal appeared before the Military Court in November on charges of "tarnishing the reputation of the vice-squad". The trials of both men were continuing at the end of the year.

Death penalty
At least eight people were sentenced to death; no one was executed. At the end of the year, 10 people were reported to be on death row.

☐ Hussain 'Ali 'Alyan, a former sergeant in the Lebanese Army, was sentenced to death by the Military Court in January on charges of "collaboration" with Israel.

Three death sentences passed in previous years were upheld by the Criminal Court of Cassation. In March the executions of two men were suspended following the refusal of then Prime Minister Salim al-Huss to sign the death penalty decree.

'Disappearances'
In January the government set up an official Commission of Inquiry into the fate of those missing and kidnapped during the civil war (1975 to 1990). The Commission, which was headed by an army general and composed of four other military and security officers, was created as a result of pressure from the families of the "disappeared". A committee for the Relatives of the Kidnapped and Missing held vigils near the premises of the weekly Cabinet meetings outside the Beirut Museum. In July the Commission made public the conclusions of its report stating that none of the "disappeared" was alive in Lebanon and recommending that those missing for at least four years should be considered dead. A list of 216 people whose families believed they had been taken by Israeli forces or transferred to Israel was sent to the Israeli government through the International Committee of the Red Cross (ICRC). A list of 168 people whose families believed they had been taken by Syrian forces or transferred to Syria was sent to the Syrian government. Both governments denied all knowledge of the whereabouts of those on the lists.

Refugees
Hundreds of refugees and asylum-seekers, especially those from Iraq and Sudan, were periodically detained on charges of illegal entry and residence in Lebanon. Scores of asylum-seekers were deported from Lebanon, some while their cases were still under review by the UN High Commissioner for Refugees (UNHCR). Most claimed that they were tortured or held in conditions amounting to cruel, inhuman or degrading treatment to force them to accept deportation to their countries of origin.

☐ Trabun Ibrahim Laku, a Sudanese national, was arrested in April and detained for six months. He was released in October suffering from partial paralysis and severe back pains. By the end of the year no investigation has been launched into his allegations of torture and ill-treatment.

☐ 'Ammar Kazim Shams, an Iraqi national who had been recognized as a refugee by the UNHCR in May, was deported from Lebanon to an unknown destination. There are fears that he may have been forcibly returned to Iraq where he was at risk of human rights violations.

AI country statements and visits
Statements
- Lebanon: Commission of Inquiry into "disappearance" must be effective and public (AI Index: MDE 18/001/2000)
- Amnesty International calls on all involved in the conflict in south Lebanon to respect international human rights and humanitarian law (AI Index: MDE 15/020/2000)
- Lebanon: Guilt and innocence blurred in summary trials (AI Index: MDE 18/010/2000)

Visits
AI delegates visited Lebanon several times during 2000 for research, trial observation and meetings with government officials, including Prime Minister Salim al-Huss. In March the Lebanese authorities approved a request by AI to open a regional office in Beirut for the promotion of human rights education and awareness.

LESOTHO

KINGDOM OF LESOTHO
Head of state: King Letsie III
Head of government: Pakalitha Bethuel Mosisili
Capital: Maseru
Population: 2.1 million
Official languages: Sesotho, English
Death penalty: retentionist
2000 treaty ratifications/signatures: Optional Protocol to the International Covenant on Civil and Political Rights; Optional Protocol to the UN Children's Convention on the involvement of children in armed conflict; Optional Protocol to the UN Women's Convention; Rome Statute of the International Criminal Court

Political conflict continued during 2000 over the implementation of political reforms necessary for holding elections. Thirty-three soldiers were convicted of mutiny with violence. Concerns remained about the independence and impartiality of the trial proceedings and the appeals process. There were new reports of torture and ill-treatment and of excessive use of force by law enforcement agents.

Background

Political tension continued during 2000, exacerbated by the failure to implement the new electoral system agreed upon by the government and the multi-party Interim Political Authority (IPA) in December 1999. Representatives of intergovernmental organizations, including the Southern African Development Community and the Commonwealth, intervened again to try to resolve the protracted conflict between the government and the IPA.

Under the November 1998 law which established the IPA, the authorities were obliged to hold elections within the following 18 months. However, elections scheduled for May were postponed, and a newly-appointed Independent Electoral Commission announced a provisional timetable for elections in 2001.

The failure to hold elections in May led to some protests. Opposition political leaders distanced themselves from calls by unidentified organizations for a stay-away from work. There were threats of violence against those who ignored the call and many businesses closed out of fear of disturbances. Heavily armed police and soldiers patrolled Maseru and five people were reportedly arrested in connection with the stay-away.

In April the government appointed a commission of inquiry into the political disturbances which occurred between 1 July and 30 November 1998.

Remaining military instructors and forces from South Africa and Botswana withdrew from Lesotho after completing their retraining program for Lesotho Defence Force (LDF) units.

Torture/ill-treatment

There were a number of reports of torture of criminal suspects by police. Allegations included the use during interrogation of suffocation with rubber tubing, being forced to strip, cigarette burns and beatings.

▫ The government settled out of court a claim for damages from Moitheri Katiso who alleged that he had been tortured in Lesotho by members of the South African National Defence Force in September 1998. He alleged that he had been kicked and beaten with gun butts, including on his face.

Excessive use of force

The security forces were involved in killings and injuries in disputed circumstances. There were allegations of excessive use of force.

▫ An LDF soldier, Corporal Monesapula, who was allegedly being sought by the combined police-military Counter Crime Unit (CCU) in connection with criminal investigations, was found dead with gunshot wounds to the head. He had reportedly fled from Ratjamose Barracks where he had been questioned by the Military Police on 16 January. His body was found about two weeks later at Ha Khabisi, lower down the Caledon River. An army spokesman stated that Military Police had searched him for weapons when he reported to Ratjamose Barracks, but claimed also that Corporal Monesapula had pulled a gun when he fled. There were separate reports that two army officers chased him as he fled towards the Caledon River. No inquest into his death had been held by the end of 2000.

▫ CCU members searching for guns opened fire with automatic weapons on Anthony Phafa, a Pitseng resident, after he denied possessing guns. During nearly three months of hospital treatment in Maseru, he was kept under guard and chained by his feet to the hospital bed railings. He was not charged with any offence until his transfer from the hospital to Leribe police station in mid-March.

Political trials

In November, 33 LDF soldiers were convicted of mutiny with violence, an offence carrying the death penalty, for their role in the junior officers' insurrection of September 1998. They were sentenced to between three and 13 years' imprisonment. Four other defendants were acquitted. In August, in a separate but linked court martial, three further LDF soldiers were convicted of mutiny and sentenced to prison terms of between five and 13 years.

Concerns remained that these court martial trials, as well as the appeal processes available to the convicted soldiers, did not meet international standards for independence and impartiality. The accused had been in custody since October 1998.

Twenty-five police officers were acquitted of the capital offence of high treason but convicted of sedition in connection with a February 1997 police mutiny which was suppressed by the army. Thirteen received prison sentences of up to three years, partly suspended. The remainder were fined. The defendants had been in custody since February 1997.

The trial continued of eight police officers in connection with the fatal shootings in Maseru Central Police Station in 1995. The arrest of these officers had sparked the February 1997 mutiny.

Human rights defenders
Benedict Leuta, a campaigner for the rights of communities affected by the Lesotho Highlands Water Project, was harassed by National Security Service members. They seized a number of documents from his home and questioned him about his activities and about his views.

Government communications
In letters to the authorities, AI raised concerns about the harassment of Benedict Leuta. In replies, the National Security Service gave assurances of their respect for the rights of freedom of association, movement and expression. AI also raised with the authorities its concerns about continuing reports of torture and excessive use of force in the context of criminal investigations.

LIBERIA

REPUBLIC OF LIBERIA
Head of state and government: Charles G. Taylor
Capital: Monrovia
Population: 3.1 million
Official language: English
Death penalty: retentionist

Torture, ill-treatment and other human rights violations continued to be carried out by the security forces. Human rights defenders and journalists were arrested, assaulted and forced into exile. Political prisoners were sentenced to prison terms after trials which failed to meet international standards for fair trial. There was no progress in investigating past human rights abuses. The international community continued to accuse the Liberian government of assisting rebel forces responsible for atrocities in neighbouring Sierra Leone.

Fighting in Lofa County
In July armed opposition forces attacked Lofa County, northern Liberia; the government deployed the armed forces, the Anti-Terrorist Unit and war veterans against them. The government accused the Guinean government of allowing attacks on Liberia from bases in neighbouring Guinea. Thousands of people fled upper Lofa County. In December the Liberian authorities reported that about 100 soldiers had been killed in the fighting.

From September hostilities between armed groups along the borders between Liberia, Sierra Leone and Guinea resulted in massive population displacement. The Guinean authorities accused armed groups backed by Liberia and Burkina Faso, the armed opposition in Sierra Leone and Guinean dissidents of killing hundreds of people in attacks on border towns in the Macenta region of Guinea. The attacks resulted in massive displacement of Liberian and Sierra Leonean refugees and of Guinean nationals.

More than a hundred people, mostly belonging to the Mandingo ethnic group, were arrested by government security forces on suspicion of backing the incursion into Lofa County. Most of those arrested were held incommunicado without charge in unofficial detention centres, including the military base in Gbatala, and were tortured. Dozens were allegedly extrajudicially executed. The number of those held incommunicado and summarily executed could be higher. Sierra Leonean refugees, including former child soldiers, were reportedly recruited by the Sierra Leone armed opposition which was supported by the Liberian government. There were also reports of forcible recruitment of Liberian nationals by the Liberian security forces. Insurgents allegedly from Guinea were accused of carrying out abductions of civilians.

Ethnic clashes broke out following the incursion and members of the Mandingo community suspected of backing insurgents came under armed attack by civilians in Lofa and Nimba Counties, allegedly with the acquiescence of local security forces on at least one occasion.

Involvement in the Sierra Leone conflict
The international community continued to accuse the Liberian government of providing arms, ammunition and fighters, in violation of a 1998 UN embargo, to armed opposition forces in neighbouring Sierra Leone which have been responsible for large-scale atrocities against civilians.

The Liberian government continued to deny the allegations, accused the US and United Kingdom (UK) governments of seeking to destabilize Liberia, and called for an independent investigation.

In June the European Union expressed concern about Liberia's role in the illicit diamond trade from Sierra Leone and its failure to stop arms reaching rebel forces in Sierra Leone through Liberian territory, and threatened to suspend aid to Liberia. In July the UN Security Council imposed an embargo on diamond exports from Sierra Leone. In October the US government imposed visa restrictions on senior Liberian officials; the Liberian authorities announced reciprocal measures.

A UN panel of experts, established in August to investigate the link between the diamond trade and the conflict in Sierra Leone, published its report in December. The panel found evidence of the Liberian government's support for rebel forces in Sierra Leone, including military training and weapons transfers, and of trafficking of diamonds through Liberia from rebel-held areas. Other governments were found to have been implicated. The panel made recommendations, including for an embargo on diamonds from Liberia and a travel ban on Liberian officials by UN member states.

Amnesty International called for diamond trading in western Africa to be investigated and regulated in order to stop diamonds from rebel-held areas of Sierra Leone financing the purchase of arms used to kill and mutilate civilians in Sierra Leone.

Impunity

No progress was made by the authorities in bringing to justice the perpetrators of massive human rights abuses carried out during the seven-year civil war which ended in 1996. There were also no independent investigations into political killings and other human rights violations committed by the security forces or armed groups operating in support of the government since the return to constitutional rule in 1997. Those responsible for the killing of Samuel Dokie, a former government minister who was arrested and later found dead with three others in 1997, were not brought to justice.

No independent or thorough investigation was carried out into alleged extrajudicial executions, torture and other human rights violations against members of the Krahn ethnic group and others during fighting in September 1998 between forces loyal to President Taylor and supporters of Roosevelt Johnson, a former faction leader. A 1999 UN investigation into the fighting obtained accounts of extrajudicial executions and other human rights violations by government security forces. They found that the dead and injured numbered several hundred and that ethnic Krahns had been targeted. The government had said 100 people had been killed or injured.

No training in international human rights standards was known to have been provided to the security forces, including special forces such as the Anti-Terrorist Unit which have been accused of serious human rights violations. Former combatants of the armed opposition group formerly headed by Charles Taylor, the National Patriotic Front of Liberia, which was implicated in major human rights violations, were recruited to the security forces without training in human rights.

Extrajudicial executions and torture

There were further reports of extrajudicial executions. The security forces continued to be responsible for torture and ill-treatment of political prisoners and criminal suspects. Liberian human rights organizations called for the closure of the Anti-Terrorist Unit base in Gbatala, central Liberia, where detainees have been tortured. Detention conditions in most police cells and prisons continued to be so harsh as to amount to cruel, inhuman and degrading treatment. Beatings and harassment of civilians by members of the security forces and former combatants continued, especially in rural areas.

☐ In May the bodyguards of a government official reportedly beat and burned three people in Monrovia; they were suspected of stealing from the official. One of them, Gbaela Willie, died as a result of his injuries. Monrovia police reportedly arrested four bodyguards and opened an investigation into the death.

☐ In September an army commander said that he had personally executed Aruna Boakai, an Anti-Terrorist Unit officer, in the town of Voinjama, Lofa County, for killing a soldier in August.

☐ In November a Senate committee investigated allegations that a senator had ordered the security forces to detain illegally, beat and flog civilians in River Gee County, southeastern Liberia. The investigation had not been completed by the end of the year.

Attacks on the news media and human rights defenders

Journalists and human rights defenders were arrested, physically abused and threatened by the Liberian authorities.

☐ In March Suah Deddeh, Chair of the Liberian Press Union, was arrested and questioned by security officers after criticizing the closure of two privately owned radio stations, Star Radio and Radio Veritas, by the authorities. He was released the next day without charge. After protests, Radio Veritas was allowed to reopen but Star Radio remained banned.

☐ In late March James Torh, a prominent human rights activist, fled the country after Anti-Terrorist Unit officers twice came looking for him at his home at night. In December 1999 he had been briefly detained and charged with sedition for allegedly making remarks critical of the government. When he did not appear at a court hearing in April, the authorities ordered his rearrest.

☐ In August, four journalists working for *Channel 4*, a UK television station — Sorious Samura, Gugulakhe Radebe, David Barrie and Timothy John Lambon — were detained for several days in Monrovia and accused of spying. The four were beaten following their arrest and one of them was threatened with death. They were released unconditionally after widespread protests.

☐ In September, staff members of the independent *New Democrat*, including its editor Charles Jackson, fled Liberia following death threats, intimidation and harassment by the security forces.

☐ In November armed men believed to be civil war veterans, who reportedly included a senior armed forces officer, attacked members of a non-governmental organization, the Centre for Democratic Empowerment (CEDE), in Monrovia. They stabbed and wounded Conmany Wesseh, and physically assaulted Amos Sawyer, formerly head of the Liberian interim government during the civil war and CEDE Chairman, and other staff. The armed forces officer and seven others were subsequently charged with aggravated assault and released on bail to await trial. However, others believed to be also responsible for the attack were not known to have been investigated by police. Local human rights activists called for an independent inquiry. Suspects arrested in connection with a 1999 attack on the home of Conmany Wesseh and death threats against his family had been released without charge or trial despite evidence against them.

Sedition and treason trials
One trial ended, another started and an appeal was heard in trials held in connection with the fighting in Monrovia in September 1998 between government forces and forces loyal to opposition leader Roosevelt Johnson.

▫ In February a court martial convicted four army officers of sedition — General Joseph Jarlee, Major Alphonso Dubar, Master Sergeant Alexander Gee and Private Okpakakpu Monger — and sentenced them to 10 years' imprisonment. Five other officers were acquitted. There were concerns that the trial did not meet international standards for fair trial and about the alleged intimidation of defence lawyers. The defendants, who were reportedly beaten following their arrest, continued to be detained in harsh conditions at a military barracks. General Jarlee was reportedly denied adequate food or medical treatment.

▫ In June the treason trial started of five civilians — Jardiah S. Farley, Charles C. Sobue, Kaye Gbagba, Alpha Massaley and Roosevelt Togba — suspected of supporting Roosevelt Johnson's forces. The trial had not concluded by the end of 2000.

▫ In December the Supreme Court heard appeals by 13 people convicted of treason in April 1999 and by the prosecution in the same case which called for longer prison sentences. The Court increased the sentences from 10 to 20 years' imprisonment. In April 1999 the Criminal Court had given as its reason for a lenient sentence the "need for genuine reconciliation in the country". The trial had been marred by irregularities and some of the defendants had been beaten severely following their arrest. Most were former government officials serving 10-year prison sentences in the Central Prison, Monrovia, where they were reportedly harassed and denied adequate medical care.

▫ In August the Liberian government issued an arrest warrant for Ellen Johnson-Sirleaf, an opposition leader in exile, to face treason charges, with 14 others, for allegedly supporting the insurgents. Of those charged, only Raleigh Seekie was arrested and was still in detention awaiting trial at the end of 2000. Several other civilians suspected of supporting the insurgents were reported to have been arrested in Monrovia and in other parts of the country. It was not known whether they had been released by the end of the year.

AI reports
- Liberia: Crackdown on media signals further repression of human rights defenders (AI Index: AFR 34/001/2000)
- Liberia: Attacks on media continue with the arrest of a foreign television crew (AI Index: AFR 34/002/2000)
- Liberia: Fear for safety of Conmany Wesseh and others (AI Index: AFR 34/004/2000)

LIBYA

SOCIALIST PEOPLE'S LIBYAN ARAB JAMAHIRIYA
Head of state: Mu'ammar al-Gaddafi
Capital: Tripoli
Population: 5.6 million
Official language: Arabic
Death penalty: retentionist

Hundreds of political prisoners, including prisoners of conscience and possible prisoners of conscience, remained in detention, many without charge or trial. Libyans forcibly returned to the country, including asylum-seekers, were believed to have been subjected to human rights violations. Torture, especially during incommunicado detention, continued to be reported. The authorities failed to protect hundreds of sub-Saharan Africans from racist attacks, reportedly leading to the killings of dozens of Africans. The death penalty remained in force.

Background
There were two government reshuffles during the year. In March a new government was appointed and the Ministries of Justice and General Security were combined into one ministry. The reshuffles also included the abolition of several ministries, including the Information Ministry, and the allocation of their responsibilities to other bodies.

Diplomatic and economic ties were resumed as part of Libya's re-entry into the international arena, following the suspension of sanctions in April 1999. Colonel Mu'ammar al-Gaddafi continued to call for advances in African unity, including the establishment of an African parliament and political and economic union.

Libya had no independent non-governmental organizations, human rights groups or independent bar association. Libyan law prohibits the formation of political parties and criticism of the political system. The press continued to be strictly controlled by the government.

The Lockerbie trial
In May the trial began of two Libyans, 'Abd al-Basit al-Miqrahi and al-Amin Khalifa Fahima, accused of the 1988 bombing of an airplane over Lockerbie, Scotland, which killed 270 people. The two defendants pleaded not guilty to charges of murder, conspiracy to murder and violation of the Aviation Security Act. The trial was continuing at the end of the year.

The UTA airliner bombing
In October a French Court of Appeals authorized a judicial investigation into charges against Colonel Mu'ammar al-Gaddafi for complicity to murder in connection with the 1989 UTA airliner bombing. The Paris Public Prosecutor's Office subsequently appealed against the ruling.

Racist attacks

In September racist attacks against sub-Saharan Africans, including Chadian, Niger and Sudanese nationals among others, reportedly led to dozens of deaths and scores of injuries. In contrast, at the 28th Ordinary Session of the African Commission on Human and Peoples' Rights in October, a Libyan representative claimed that five people, including one Libyan, had died in the attacks. Disturbances in Tripoli and neighbouring al-Zawiyah soon spread to other parts of the country, leaving many homeless after their homes were burned and looted. As a result, many of the victims were forced to live in special camps, where sanitation was reportedly very poor and where on occasion members of the security forces failed to protect them from further attack.

On at least one occasion, there were allegations of police involvement in the attacks. Large numbers of Chadians, Ghanaians, Nigerians and other sub-Saharan Africans were repatriated after seeking refuge at their embassies. The Libyan authorities announced an investigation and preventive security measures to protect sub-Saharan Africans from further attacks. In November the Minister of General Security and Justice announced that 75 people, the majority of them Libyans, would be tried in connection with the violent incidents.

Prisoners of conscience and political prisoners

Some political prisoners arrested in 1989 were reportedly released in small groups between April and August. In August and September, several prisoners arrested in 1984 were released. Some of the men had been acquitted in a trial in 1995 but had remained in detention.

Political detainees were reportedly held in cruel, inhuman or degrading conditions and denied adequate medical care; several were reported to have died in custody as a result in recent years.

Hundreds of political prisoners arrested in previous years, including possible prisoners of conscience, remained in detention without charge or trial; many had been held for more than a decade. Scores of other political detainees remained held despite having been tried and acquitted. Others continued to serve prison sentences imposed in previous years after grossly unfair trials.

▫ Rashid 'Abd al-Hamid al-'Urfia, a law graduate, remained in Abu Salim Prison in Tripoli. He had reportedly been arrested with 20 others in 1982 on suspicion of founding an Islamist opposition group. All those arrested with him were released following a general amnesty in 1988.

▫ Five prisoners of conscience, who were arrested in 1973 and convicted of membership of the prohibited Islamic Liberation Party, continued to serve life sentences in Abu Salim Prison.

Scores of professionals, including engineers and university lecturers, who were arrested in June and July 1998 on suspicion of supporting or sympathizing with *al-Jama'a al-Islamiya al-Libiya*, the Libyan Islamic Group, a clandestine Islamist movement which was not known to have used or advocated violence, remained held in Abu Salim and 'Ain Zara prisons in Tripoli.

▫ Among those who remained in detention was Mohammad Faraj al-Qallal, an executive in a printing house in Benghazi, who was arrested by plainclothes security men and given no reason for his arrest.

Deaths in custody

At least one person died in police custody; torture reportedly caused or contributed to his death. On 26 April Yusuf Muhammad al-Hour, a Chadian national, was arrested in Tripoli and transported to Sirte. The following day his body was given to his relatives who reported signs of torture on his body.

Forcible return of refugees

Following the suspension of sanctions against Libya in April 1999, refugees and asylum-seekers were at increasing risk of being forcibly returned to Libya. Some of those forcibly returned were detained and there were reports that some had been the victims of serious human rights violations, including torture.

▫ In February, eight Libyan nationals suspected of being Islamist sympathizers were forcibly returned to Libya by the Jordanian authorities.

▫ In July, four Libyans suspected of being Islamist sympathizers were forcibly returned from Pakistan. Youssef Khalifa and 'Abdessalam Musa Muhammad's applications for asylum were still under consideration when they were deported, while the other two men were reportedly residing and working legally in Pakistan. Their whereabouts following their return to Libya were unknown.

Torture/ill-treatment

There were continuing reports that political detainees were routinely tortured while held in incommunicado detention. Reported methods of torture included beatings, hanging by the wrists, being suspended from a pole inserted between the knees and elbows, electric shocks, burning with cigarettes and attacks by aggressive dogs, causing serious injuries.

▫ Defendants in a trial of 16 health professionals, among them five women, stated that they were tortured or ill-treated while in detention. The 16 included foreign nationals, who were kept in incommunicado detention for about 10 months without access to family or legal representation. Some alleged that their confessions had been obtained under duress. Following the formal opening on 7 February, the trial was postponed on several occasions at the request of defence lawyers and had not begun by the end of the year. The defendants were accused of infecting almost 400 children with the HIV-virus in a Libyan hospital, leading to the deaths of children. The charges against them are punishable by death.

Death penalty

Reports continued to be received that people convicted of criminal charges were sentenced to death.

AI correspondence with the authorities
By the end of the year AI had still not received replies to its requests to visit Libya or to the human rights concerns raised in correspondence with the authorities.

MACEDONIA

THE FORMER YUGOSLAV REPUBLIC OF MACEDONIA
Head of state: Boris Trajkovski
Head of government: Ljubčo Georgievski
Capital: Skopje
Population: 2 million
Official language: Macedonian
Death penalty: abolitionist for all crimes
2000 treaty ratifications/signatures: Optional Protocol to the UN Women's Convention

Torture and ill-treatment by police was the principal concern. One man may have been extrajudicially executed and another died in custody allegedly after being beaten by police. Detainees were held incommunicado for prolonged periods. The authorities generally failed to investigate allegations of human rights violations. At least four conscientious objectors were imprisoned.

Background
The shooting of three police officers in Aračinovo village in January raised tensions between the ethnic Albanian minority and Macedonian majority populations early in the year. The situation in Kosovo (see Federal Republic of Yugoslavia entry) remained an important political issue. However, political rivalries did not focus on ethnic divisions as the government was composed of members from a coalition of parties with either Macedonian, ethnic Albanian or mixed membership and support. Local elections held in several rounds from September were accompanied by allegations of widespread irregularities and violent incidents in which one person was killed and 10 others were injured.

Several Macedonian soldiers were injured in a series of clashes on the border with Kosovo with armed gangs from Kosovo. In one incident in April soldiers were detained by ethnic Albanian paramilitaries and held in Kosovo for at least 24 hours. Their release coincided with the release on bail of Xhavit Hasani, an ethnic Albanian and a former commander of the Kosovo Liberation Army (KLA), who was awaiting trial in connection with the wounding of police officers. The incident provoked claims by opposition parties that the soldiers had been held as hostages and that the authorities had given in to the kidnappers' demands by releasing Xhavit Hasani.

There was a noticeable increase in pressure on the media. For example, *Bota Sot,* an Albanian newspaper which was also printed in Macedonia and was openly critical of the Albanian party in the government coalition, was temporarily closed down in Macedonia.

Torture/ill-treatment
Torture and ill-treatment by police occurred in a variety of situations. The victims included Macedonians, Roma and ethnic Albanians. There were also reports that civilians assaulted political opponents but that they were not brought to justice because of their government connections. The response of the authorities to complaints of ill-treatment and other human rights violations was generally inadequate.

☐ On 27 May, five Romani men were detained and beaten with wooden sticks by police and civilians in a forest near Štip. Three of them — Memet Redžepov, Orhan Aliov and Selajdin Mustafov — stated that they were again beaten or kicked at the Štip police station. Each heard the screams of the others as they were beaten one by one in an adjoining room, despite the sound of a radio which was allegedly used to hide their screams.

☐ Eighty-year-old Ordan Jovanovski, a vocal opposition supporter, was seriously assaulted by a government official in a village near Prilep in May after an argument over politics. He suffered facial and other injuries. Although the incident was reported to the police, no charges had been brought by the end of the year.

The Aračinovo incident
Numerous human rights violations were perpetrated during house searches and arrests in the days that followed the killing of three police officers — two Macedonians and an ethnic Turk — in January. The killing of the three officers at a checkpoint in Aračinovo village near Skopje did not appear to be politically motivated, but the ethnicity of the victims and subsequent police actions gave the incident political dimensions.

Dozens of men and at least three minors were beaten in their homes, and women and children were allegedly threatened with firearms. A number of men were taken to police stations and beaten. Some were coerced into making "confessions" under torture. Officers reportedly beat them with truncheons, threatened to burn them with hot metal, made them drink urine, and put plastic bags over their heads. The detainees were held incommunicado, some for as long as 11 days, before being taken before a judge. Relatives and lawyers were denied information about their whereabouts and access to them.

The authorities admitted only that excessive force had resulted in damage to property during the Aračinovo raids and paid some compensation. Recommendations by bodies such as the national Ombudsman that criminal investigations should be initiated into the police actions were not acted upon by the authorities.

◰ Sabri Asani was detained on 18 January by police in connection with the Aračinovo murders. He died on his way to the police station in circumstances suggesting he may have been extrajudicially executed. Officials claimed that he had suffered heart failure because he was intoxicated with drugs. However, pictures of his body indicated that he had been badly beaten and had most likely died of a bullet wound to the head. An autopsy was performed, but the authorities failed to make the report available to his family. No information on any criminal investigation connected with his death had been released by the authorities by the end of the year.

Samedin Guri, whose arrest may also have been connected with the Aračinovo murders, died in prison in May after reportedly having been severely beaten by police several days before.

In July, six ethnic Albanians were charged with the killing of the three police officers; their trial was continuing at the end of the year.

Conscientious objection
No purely civilian alternative to military service was available. A draft defence law incorporating the possibility of civilian service was introduced to parliament but had not been passed by the end of 2000. There was concern that, although the new law provided for alternative civilian service, this would be punitive in length, would not be available to all those liable to military service and would not be under civilian control.

Four conscientious objectors, all of them Jehovah's Witnesses, were known to have been imprisoned during the year for between one and three months; all had expressed their willingness to perform a civilian service in lieu of military service.

Refugees
Some 8,000 refugees were officially registered at the end of 2000. Most were Roma who had fled Kosovo in 1999. The situation in Kosovo (see Federal Republic of Yugoslavia entry) offered little prospect for their safe return and few did so during the year. The government renewed their temporary protection during the year. A draft Law on Asylum to regulate the protection of refugees and ensure that the state met its obligations under the 1951 UN Convention relating to the Status of Refugees was before the legislature at the end of 2000.

AI country reports and visits
Reports
- The former Yugoslav Republic of Macedonia: After the Aračinovo murders – Torture, ill-treatment and possible extrajudicial execution (AI Index: EUR 65/003/2000)
- The former Yugoslav Republic of Macedonia: Joint appeal calling for rights for conscientious objectors (AI Index: EUR 65/012/2000)

Visits
An AI delegate was based in the country from April to gather information about human rights concerns in the region and work with local organizations on the promotion of human rights.

MALAWI

REPUBLIC OF MALAWI
Head of state and government: Bakili Muluzi
Capital: Lilongwe
Population: 10.4 million
Official languages: Chichewa, English
Death penalty: retentionist
2000 treaty ratifications/signatures: Optional Protocol to the UN Children's Convention on the involvement of children in armed conflict; Optional Protocol to the UN Women's Convention

There were reports of torture and ill-treatment by police officers. Prison conditions were harsh. The death penalty continued to be imposed, but no executions were carried out.

Torture/ill-treatment
There were reports of torture and ill-treatment by police during arrest and interrogation. At the end of 2000 local non-governmental organizations were pursuing at least three cases of alleged torture of criminal suspects through the courts.

Prison conditions
Prison conditions were poor and in some cases there were concerns that they could constitute cruel, inhuman or degrading treatment. There were particular concerns about juvenile offenders who were held in youth wings of adult prisons. A report by a non-governmental organization, commissioned in 1999 by the commissioner of prisons, documented cases of sexual violence against juveniles by adult prisoners, sometimes with the involvement of prison wardens.

Death penalty
At least 53 people were sentenced to death in 2000. No prisoners were known to have been executed since 1994. President Bakili Muluzi, who had publicly stated his opposition to the death penalty, had so far commuted all death sentences.

AI country reports
- End sexual violence against children in custody in Malawi (AI Index: ACT 76/007/2000)

MALAYSIA

MALAYSIA
Head of state: Sultan Salahuddin Abdul Aziz Shah Alhaj
Head of government: Mahathir Mohamad
Capital: Kuala Lumpur
Population: 22.2 million
Official language: Bahasa Malaysia
Death penalty: retentionist

The authorities launched politically motivated prosecutions against leading opposition party members. Former deputy Prime Minister Anwar Ibrahim and his co-accused Sukma Darmawan were convicted of sodomy after an unfair trial. Demonstrations in support of Anwar Ibrahim and of political reform (*reformasi*) were violently broken up by police. Reports of ill-treatment of detainees by police were not adequately investigated. Two people were executed and at least 13 people were sentenced to death.

Background

Prime Minister Mahathir Mohamad reaffirmed his dominant political position following the ruling alliance's election victory in November 1999 and the prolonged tensions sparked by the dismissal and charging of Anwar Ibrahim in 1998. Despite this, the authorities continued to apply laws restricting rights to freedom of expression, association and assembly.

Politically motivated prosecutions

In January the authorities launched selective, politically motivated prosecutions under the Sedition Act and the Official Secrets Act (OSA) against leading opposition party members. None of the prosecutions had concluded by the end of 2000.

◻ In a prosecution which had grave implications for the independence of lawyers in Malaysia, Karpal Singh, Anwar Ibrahim's defence lawyer and deputy chairman of the Democratic Action Party (DAP), was charged under the Sedition Act on account of statements he had made in court about the alleged poisoning of his client.

◻ Marina Yusoff, vice-president of the *Parti Keadilan Nasional* (PKN), National Justice Party, was charged with sedition for comments allegedly provoking racial tensions made at an election rally in 1999. PKN Youth leader Mohamad Ezam Mohamad Noor was charged under the OSA for distributing allegedly classified documents about official corruption to journalists.

Press freedom

Using its powers under the Printing Presses and Publications Act, the authorities imposed restrictions on news media regarded as pro-opposition. From March, *Harakah*, newspaper of the *Parti Islam SeMalaysia* (PAS), Islamic Party of Malaysia, was allowed to print only twice a month instead of twice a week. Other pro-reform publications, including the magazines *Detik* and *Eksklusif*, had the renewal of their permits arbitrarily denied.

◻ In January sedition charges were brought against Zulkifli Nordin, editor of *Harakah*, and its publisher, Chia Lim Thye, for publishing an allegedly seditious article which had reportedly been written by an opposition leader. Chia Lim Thye pleaded guilty and was fined, while proceedings against Zulkifli Nordin continued at the end of 2000.

Anwar Ibrahim

After a year-long trial Anwar Ibrahim was convicted in August of sodomy and sentenced to nine years' imprisonment, to be served consecutively with a six-year sentence imposed in April 1999 for alleged abuse of ministerial powers.

Anwar Ibrahim's co-accused, Sukma Darmawan, was also convicted of sodomy and sentenced to six years' imprisonment and four strokes of the cane. He was granted bail pending appeal.

Anwar Ibrahim was a prisoner of conscience as he was prosecuted and imprisoned in order to remove him from public political life. His trial was unfair in several respects: public statements by government leaders undermined the defendant's right to be presumed innocent, detainees were ill-treated to coerce confessions and defence lawyers were intimidated.

In addition, the independence of the court in this case was in doubt, as the prosecution received permission for a series of amendments to the charges in relation to the date of the alleged offence, whereas Anwar Ibrahim was refused permission to call certain witnesses and to present evidence considered crucial by the defence.

The judiciary

Domestic and international legal and human rights groups, including AI, expressed concern about the lack of independence of the judiciary in politically sensitive cases. In politically motivated prosecutions, the courts failed adequately to defend human rights principles enshrined in the Malaysian Constitution and in international human rights law.

◻ In September the Court of Appeal upheld a three-month prison sentence for contempt of court against Zainur Zakaria, one of Anwar Ibrahim's defence lawyers. He had filed an affidavit in 1998 alleging that two public prosecutors had attempted to fabricate evidence against his client. Zainur Zakaria filed a final appeal.

◻ In July the High Court struck out a defamation suit against the UN Special Rapporteur on the independence of judges and lawyers, Param Cumaraswamy, upholding the immunity from prosecution of the Special Rapporteur, as confirmed in 1999 by the International Court of Justice.

In 1995, four defamation suits had been filed against the Special Rapporteur on account of comments he had made in his official capacity.

Freedom of assembly

The authorities responded to periodic, peaceful public demonstrations in support of Anwar Ibrahim and *reformasi* by dispersing them violently, arresting protesters and filing charges of illegal assembly. Senior members of opposition parties were also arrested on suspicion of incitement ahead of planned demonstrations. Police permits for public meetings by opposition parties were issued or refused arbitrarily and selectively.

☐ In November, 125 people were arrested at a demonstration in support of Anwar Ibrahim and at least 26 reported injuries from beatings sustained during and after a violent police dispersal. After five days in remand detention, 124 were released but faced possible charges of illegal assembly.

☐ In November, three PAS activists were jailed for a month for illegal assembly after refusing to pay a fine for participating in a demonstration against a visiting Israeli cricket team in 1997.

Torture/ill-treatment

There were reports of excessive use of force by police in dispersing demonstrations, and of beatings of protesters on arrest and in detention. Investigations into the ill-treatment of detained demonstrators, and of others arrested since 1998 in connection with the Anwar Ibrahim case, remained inadequate. No police officers were reported to have been brought to trial except the former Inspector-General of Police, who, after the original charges were reduced, was convicted in March of assaulting Anwar Ibrahim in custody in 1998. He was sentenced to two months' imprisonment but remained free pending appeal.

Former migrant workers from Bangladesh who testified for the defence in the trial of women's rights activist Irene Fernandez detailed torture and sexual abuse in camps for migrant workers in 1994-1995. Irene Fernandez' trial began in 1996. She was charged with "maliciously publishing false news" in a report describing ill-treatment in camps for detained migrant workers.

There were also reports of ill-treatment and unlawful deaths in police custody of ordinary criminal suspects.

Internal Security Act

Opposition parties and civil society groups repeated calls for the repeal of the Internal Security Act (ISA) which allows indefinite detention without charge or trial. At least five Shi'a Muslims were reportedly detained under the ISA for allegedly posing a threat to Muslim unity. In July at least 27 people suspected of links to the *Al Ma'unah* Islamic martial arts group, which seized arms from a military base and killed two hostages, were detained under the ISA. Twenty-nine *Al Ma'unah* suspects were charged with "waging war against the King" (treason) under the Penal Code. The fairness of their trial was compromised by the Attorney General's application of emergency regulations restricting normal rules of evidence in designated security cases. Six of the accused pleaded guilty to a lesser charge, while 15 faced the death penalty if convicted.

National Human Rights Commission

In April the Human Rights Commission of Malaysia was established. It met representatives of local human rights groups and began to receive complaints, mostly allegations of police brutality against demonstrators.

Although concerns over its effectiveness continued to be expressed, the Commission asserted the right to peaceful assembly, sent monitors to observe demonstrations and held hearings into reports of police brutality. Other issues considered by the Commission included human rights education for police and for youth, and the need for reform of restrictive laws, including the ISA.

Death penalty and corporal punishment

In the first reported executions since 1996, two men accused of drugs trafficking were executed in November. At least 13 people were sentenced to death. Caning, a cruel, inhuman and degrading punishment, was imposed throughout 2000 as an additional punishment to imprisonment.

Communications to government

In January AI issued a series of appeals *Human rights undermined - Appeal cases* (AI Index: ASA 28/013/1999) related to application of the ISA, the torture, ill-treatment and unfair trial of Anwar Ibrahim and his associates, the arrest and ill-treatment of peaceful demonstrators, the trial of Irene Fernandez, and the threatened prosecution of students and teachers. AI also expressed concern at the arrest and charging of Karpal Singh and other opposition leaders and called for reform of the Sedition Act and other restrictive laws. In June AI stated its grave concerns at the verdict in the sodomy trial of Anwar Ibrahim and Sukma Darmawan, reiterated its calls for Anwar Ibrahim's release as a prisoner of conscience and again called for full, independent investigations into credible reports of ill-treatment to coerce confessions.

MALDIVES

REPUBLIC OF MALDIVES
Head of state and government: Maumoon Abdul Gayoom
Capital: Male
Population: 0.3 million
Official language: Maldivian Dhivehi
Death penalty: abolitionist in practice

Prisoners of conscience continued to be held. There were continued allegations of torture and ill-treatment of prisoners.

Background
As in previous years, political parties were not allowed to function. The media and the judiciary remained tightly controlled by the government.

Prisoners of conscience
⊡ Prisoner of conscience Umar Jamal was arrested on 29 October 1999 by plainclothes police. He was held in various detention centres until April 2000 when he was put under house arrest. Umar Jamal was reportedly charged with attempting to discredit the government. A rival candidate closely linked to the government alleged that Umar Jamal had said that "although this is called a democracy it is a kingdom and there is no freedom". Fourteen witnesses reportedly testified to the authorities that Umar Jamal had not made the incriminating statement, with three of them giving statements to that effect to the police, and others writing to the President, the Defence Minister and the Attorney General. The court hearings against Umar Jamal were closed to the public and, in an apparent attempt to conceal the unfair nature of the trial, the court reportedly did not make a record of its own proceedings. The outcome of the proceedings was not known at the end of the year.

⊡ Ismail Saadiq, who had been in detention or under house arrest since June 1996 on politically motivated grounds and had suffered from deteriorating health while denied adequate medical treatment, was allowed to go to Thailand in August 2000 to visit his daughter who was in hospital. He was accompanied by a Maldivian police officer instructed to stay with him at all times, and was not allowed to visit his wife, resident in Thailand, or to obtain medical treatment for himself. In Thailand, Ismail Saadiq applied to a third country for protection and was granted asylum.

Torture/ill-treatment
There were continued allegations of torture of prisoners. Information came to light that at least three parliamentary candidates detained in the run up to the November 1999 parliamentary elections were tortured or ill-treated in custody. Ibrahim Ahmed Maniku and Abdul Rasheed were held in Dhoonidhoo detention centre in early November 1999 where they were deprived of sleep for several days, forced to sit on stools in the rain, and beaten every time they fell asleep.

MALI

REPUBLIC OF MALI
Head of state: Alpha Oumar Konaré
Head of government: Mande Sidibe (replaced Ibrahim Boubacar Keita in February)
Capital: Bamako
Population: 11.2 million
Official language: French
Death penalty: abolitionist in practice
2000 treaty ratifications/signatures: Optional Protocol to the UN Children's Convention on the involvement of children in armed conflict; Optional Protocol to the UN Women's Convention; Rome Statute of the International Criminal Court

At least 14 people were sentenced to death. No executions were carried out. The work of a commission of inquiry set up by the government to investigate allegations of torture and ill-treatment was hampered by lack of funding.

Background
In February, President Alpha Oumar Konaré appointed former presidential adviser Mande Sidibe as Prime Minister following the resignation of his predecessor, Ibrahim Boubacar Keita.

Death penalty
At least 14 people were sentenced to death during the year, most of them following convictions for offences including murder and armed robbery. In July the Assize Court in Bamako convicted Cheick Ibrahim Khalil Kanouté, the founder of a religious group known as the *Pieds nus* (the Barefooted), and two of his supporters of murdering a judge in August 1998.

No executions have been carried out in the last decade. On several occasions, President Konaré has stated his opposition to the death penalty.

Commission of inquiry
In December 1999 the government named a commission of inquiry to investigate allegations by opposition party supporters arrested in Niamakoro in May 1997. They alleged that they had been tortured and ill-treated in the presence of senior police officers. In January 2000 the commission requested financial support to enable it to carry out its work but received no response. A commission of inquiry set up to investigate allegations of torture and ill-treatment was unable to carry out its work because of lack of funding.

AI action
Following meetings with government officials by an AI delegation in December 1999, the organization urged the government in February 2000 to give the commission sufficient resources to enable it to fulfil its functions in accordance with international standards for human rights investigations. No response was received to this appeal.

MAURITANIA

ISLAMIC REPUBLIC OF MAURITANIA
Head of state: Maaouiya Ould Sid 'Ahmed Taya
Head of government: Cheikh El Avia Ould Mohamed Khouna
Capital: Nouakchott
Population: 2.7 million
Official language: Arabic
Death penalty: retentionist

Dozens of political opponents of the government were arbitrarily detained; some were severely beaten by the security forces. Demonstrations were violently suppressed. The media and human rights organizations continued to be subjected to restrictions. No steps were taken by the authorities to investigate massive human rights violations committed during the late 1980s and early 1990s and to bring those responsible to justice.

Background

The government of President Maaouiya Ould Sid'Ahmed Taya, which came to power in December 1984 following a military coup, has consistently prevented investigations into widespread human rights violations, including political killings, "disappearances" and torture, during the late 1980s and early 1990s.

Attempts by the authorities to silence the opposition continued throughout the year. Political repression increased at the beginning of October, after the *Union des Forces Démocratiques-Ere Nouvelle* (UFD-EN), Union of Democratic Forces-New Era, urged the government to break off diplomatic ties with Israel in response to renewed conflict in Israel and the Occupied Territories. Several pro-Palestinian demonstrations were banned and violently suppressed. Scores of political opponents were arrested. Tension increased at the end of October when the government dissolved the UFD-EN.

Mauritanian anti-slavery organizations continued to express concern about the failure of the government to eradicate slavery. Local human rights organizations, including those campaigning against slavery, were forced to operate without government authorization, leaving human rights defenders liable to prosecution and imprisonment under Mauritanian law for "administer[ing] associations which are functioning without authorization". In 1998, four Mauritanian human rights defenders including Boubacar Ould Messaoud, President of the anti-slavery organization *SOS-Esclaves*, were arrested after a television program on slavery featuring an interview with Boubacar Ould Messaoud was broadcast on a French language cable channel.

Arrests of political opponents

Scores of political opponents, including members of the UFD-EN, were arbitrarily detained and held incommunicado before being released without charge.

◻ In April opposition leader Ahmed Ould Daddah, Secretary General of the UFD-EN, was arrested and held incommunicado for five days before being released without charge. He was arrested after calling on the population to join a peaceful mass meeting in Nouakchott, organized by the UFD-EN, to protest against the government's failure to guarantee the rule of law in Mauritania and investigate the widespread political killings, "disappearances" and torture committed during the late 1980s and early 1990s.

◻ Ahmed Ould Lafdal, Ahmed Ould Wediaa, Ahmed Ould Bah and Sidi Ould Salem, all senior members of the UFD-EN, were arrested on 9 and 11 November following the government's decision to dissolve the UFD-EN. They were held incommunicado in a secret place of detention before being released without charge on 25 November.

◻ Mohamed El Hacen Ould Lebatt, Sidi Ould Yessa and Mouvid Ould Taleb, three students close to the UFD-EN, were arrested between 1 and 4 December, charged with "incitement to undermine the security of the state and belonging to a criminal organization", and transferred to Kaédi, in southern Mauritania. They were awaiting trial at the end of the year. Concerns were expressed by their defence lawyers and local human rights organizations about irregularities marring the legal proceedings.

Torture/ill-treatment

There were consistent reports of beatings and ill-treatment of political opponents at the time of arrest and in custody. Scores of demonstrators were injured during attempts by the security forces to disperse protests.

◻ In June, dozens of black Mauritanian villagers belonging to the Haratines group were reportedly tortured by the security forces in Brakna district, southern Mauritania, following protests over land rights issues. The victims, including 29 women at least two of whom were pregnant, were severely beaten and many of them were forced to eat sand.

◻ On 27 April, Mohamed Mahmoud Ould Ematt, a lawyer and leading member of the UFD-EN, Yedali Ould Cheikh, former Justice Minister, and Fatimetou Mint Haydala, were severely beaten by the security forces in front of the UFD-EN headquarters in Nouadhibou while protesting at the detention of opposition leader Ahmed Ould Daddah. The judicial authorities in Nouadhibou did not pursue the complaint lodged by two of the victims, despite evidence of the beatings, including photos and a medical certificate. Appeals filed with higher courts were not allowed to proceed.

◻ On 4 November Aminetou Mint Eleyat died after the security forces used tear gas to suppress a peaceful high-school student demonstration in Nouakchott. The authorities denied reports suggesting that her death was related to the use of tear gas.

◻ In October and November some of those arrested in Nouakchott in the context of pro-Palestinian demonstrations were severely beaten.

On 1 November Mohamed Ould Moloud, a leading member of the UFD-EN, and two other opposition supporters, Cheikh Ould Sidaty and Mohamed Ould Rabah, were arbitrarily detained. The three were hit with batons at the time of their arrest and then beaten while being taken to the regional police headquarters. They were released in the evening after being questioned about their political affiliation.

Impunity
In April, Captain Ely Ould Dah, a Mauritanian officer arrested in France in 1999 on suspicion of torturing at least two people in 1990 and 1991, fled France while on bail. In September 1999 a French court had ordered his provisional release, but required Ely Ould Dah to stay in the country until investigations were completed. Ely Ould Dah returned to Mauritania where he was reportedly allowed to remain in the army. On 7 April a French judge issued an international arrest warrant against him but no attempt to arrest him was known to have been made by the Mauritanian authorities.

The Mauritanian authorities failed to take any steps to investigate massive human rights violations committed during the late 1980s and early 1990s and to bring those responsible to justice.

Restrictions on press freedom
During 2000 several issues of weekly newspapers were seized under Article 11 of the 1991 Press Law which allows the government to censor arbitrarily publications which criticize government actions or policies. In August in one week alone, issues of four newspapers, including *La Tribune*, were seized. In December the weekly *Al Alam* was closed down by the authorities; no reason was given for the closure.

AI country statement
- Mauritania: As an opposition coalition is banned, growing political unrest could lead to further deaths, arbitrary arrests and ill-treatment by the security forces (AI Index: AFR 38/003/2000)

MEXICO

UNITED MEXICAN STATES
Head of state and government: Vicente Fox Quesada (replaced Ernesto Zedillo Ponce de León in December)
Capital: Mexico City
Population: 98.8 million
Official language: Spanish
Death penalty: abolitionist for ordinary crimes
2000 treaty ratifications/signatures: UN Refugee Convention and its 1967 Protocol; Optional Protocol to the UN Children's Convention on the involvement of children in armed conflict; Rome Statute of the International Criminal Court

Torture, death threats and political killings continued to be reported in 2000. Three prisoners of conscience remained in prison. Human rights defenders and journalists were harassed and intimidated. Hundreds of cases of torture, "disappearance" and extrajudicial execution from previous years remained unresolved.

Background
Elections in July resulted in the unprecedented defeat of the candidate for the ruling *Partido Revolucionario Institucional* (PRI), Institutional Revolutionary Party, which lost the presidency for the first time since the party was established in 1929. At his inauguration ceremony on 1 December, President Vicente Fox of the *Partido de Acción Nacional*, National Action Party, told Congress that "Mexico will no longer be held up as a bad example in matters of human rights. We will protect human rights as never before, respecting them as never before and seeking a culture that repudiates any violation and punishes the guilty." He also pledged to reform the economy, tackle poverty, crime and impunity, and bring about a peaceful solution to the conflict with the *Ejército Zapatista de Liberación Nacional* (EZLN), Zapatista National Liberation Army, the Chiapas-based armed opposition group.

President Fox's cabinet included the new post of Special Ambassador for Human Rights and Democracy. Human rights organizations severely criticized the appointment of an army general as Attorney General for the Republic, claiming that it ran counter to the new government's pledge to combat impunity.

Within days of assuming power President Fox ordered the army in Chiapas to return to their barracks and presented Congress with a bill, based on the San Andrés Accord on indigenous rights signed in 1996 by the EZLN and the previous government. The EZLN announced it was prepared to hold talks with the new government. Administrative provisions introduced in 1998 which hindered the access of foreign non-government organizations (NGOs) to freely conduct on-site monitoring of the country's human rights situation were lifted in late December.

MEX

In August Mexico City's legislature approved an addition to the Penal Code for the Federal District allowing for sentences of between 15 and 40 years in prison for public servants found responsible for enforced disappearance. In December, President Fox signed a technical cooperation agreement with the UN High Commissioner for Human Rights, under which the UN is to provide Mexico with assistance to strengthen the protection of human rights. An amnesty law approved by the state of Oaxaca in December led to the release of some 30 political prisoners.

By the end of the year a judge in Mexico had not issued a ruling on an extradition request submitted by Spain in August against an Argentine citizen accused of torture during the military government in Argentina (see Argentina entry).

Arbitrary detention, torture and ill-treatment

The detention of criminal suspects without a judicial order remained widespread. Many of the detainees were allegedly tortured while under criminal investigation. Prison inmates were subjected to ill-treatment.

The joint publication in October of a report by AI Mexico and four other national organizations recommending reforms designed to prevent torture, led the National Commission for Human Rights (CNDH), a federal body, to claim that torture was on the decline in Mexico. The national organizations replied that the CNDH underreported torture cases and that the problem was widespread.

▫ In July, the president of the CNDH informed the Secretary of National Defense that two army officers "had violated [the] Fundamental Rights" of Rodolfo Montiel Flores and Teodoro Cabrera García, including their right not to be subjected to torture or to cruel, inhuman or degrading treatment or punishment as enshrined "in article 5 [...] of the Universal Declaration of Human Rights". The two men had been detained and tortured by the army in May 1999 following their peaceful protests about excessive logging in the forests of Guerrero. A prosecutor who opened an investigation into the allegations of torture concluded that the Public Ministry was not competent to take the investigation forward and had transferred the case to a military prosecutor in December 1999. In April a court sentenced Teodoro Cabrera to 10 years, and Rodolfo Montiel to six years and eight months' imprisonment. The sentences, based on drugs- and firearms-related charges, were upheld on appeal in October. Both men were prisoners of conscience.

▫ In October, a prisoner held in the Topo Chico Prison in Nuevo León state was reportedly ill-treated after human rights activists staged a peaceful protest outside the prison to launch AI's worldwide campaign against torture. A prison official accused inmate Héctor Perez Córdova of being responsible for the protest and added that "we're going to punish you for it". Héctor Perez Córdova was stripped naked, placed in solitary confinement for seven days, and deprived of food and medicine needed to control his symptoms of multiple sclerosis.

▫ In October, Remedios Alonso Vargas and her two adult sons, Irineo and Luciano Mederos Alonso, were reported to have been detained and beaten by the Guerrero State Judicial Police (PJE) and then held incommunicado for seven days. During their incommunicado detention members of the PJE threatened them with suffocation and the brothers had carbonated water forced up their nostrils. All three were forced to sign confessions which they claimed not to have read.

Chiapas and Guerrero states

For most of the year members of indigenous communities in Chiapas continued to suffer acts of intimidation and violence, including death threats. Those responsible were reported to be members of the security forces or so-called "paramilitary" or "armed civilian" groups acting with the support or acquiescence of local and regional authorities. In Guerrero, members of the *Organización Campesina de la Sierra del Sur* (OCSS), a peasant organization, were harassed, threatened or killed in circumstances suggesting they were being targeted for political reasons.

▫ On 1 March, a dispute over land rights in the municipality of Nicolás Ruiz, Chiapas, turned violent when members of the Public Security Police reportedly aided *Alianza Campesina*, an armed civilian group linked to the PRI, to attack peasants affiliated to the opposition *Partido de la Revolución Democrática*, Democratic Revolutionary Party. At least three people received gunshot wounds and a fourth was beaten. In a separate incident on the same day, a group known as *Los Chinchulines*, reportedly accompanied by members of the Federal Judicial Police, attacked villagers in Nuevo Poblado de Nachejev, municipality of Chilón. The villagers were threatened with death if they did not leave the area.

▫ In July, Marco Antonio Abadicio Mayo, an OCSS activist, was ambushed late at night and survived being shot in the chest and arm by a group of men, near Atoyaquillo, municipality of Coyuca de Benítez. The previous January he was allegedly beaten and threatened by members of the security forces and then released without charge. In April OCSS activists José Martínez Ramón and Felipe Nava Gómez were shot dead in Coyuca de Benítez. It was not known whether investigations were conducted into these incidents.

Prisoners of conscience

Three prisoners of conscience, including Rodolfo Montiel Flores and Teodoro Cabrera García (see above) remained in prison.

▫ Brigadier General José Francisco Gallardo served the seventh year of his 28-year sentence. He had been convicted by a military court of a range of military offences after publishing an article calling for the appointment of a military ombudsman in Mexico. In 1996 the Inter-American Commission on Human Rights

Amnesty International Report 2001

recommended to the Mexican government that he be immediately released.

Human right defenders and journalists

Mexican human rights defenders and journalists continued to suffer acts of intimidation, including death threats.

◻ In February an anonymous caller rang the offices of the *Centro de Estudios Fronterizos y Promoción de Derechos Humanos*, Centre for Border Studies and the Promotion of Human Rights, and made death threats against its members. Much of the work of this NGO in Reynosa concerns abuses suffered by would-be illegal migrants wishing to cross from Tamaulipas state into the USA. Arturo Solís, the director of the NGO, was accused by the authorities of defamation after he alleged that officials at Mexico's National Institute of Migration were guilty of extortion and ill-treating illegal migrants and were implicated, together with criminal organizations, in aiding their entry into the USA. In July witnesses for the defence of Arturo Solís were threatened and one received a death threat. As a result two of them retracted statements made in his defence.

◻ Two men claiming to be officers of the Judicial Police reportedly abducted journalist Freddy Secundino Sánchez in mid-June, apparently because of his articles in the political magazine *Época*. When he arrived at his Mexico City home in a taxi, the men shoved him back into the taxi, pushed him to the floor and forced the driver at gunpoint to drive off. Holding a pistol to Freddy Secundino's head, they beat him about the face and chest, and threatened to kill him before releasing him. Three weeks later an anonymous caller told the journalist that he was going to die. Freddy Secundino filed a complaint about both incidents with the authorities.

Impunity

The authorities continued to be accused by Mexican and international NGOs of having failed to break the cycle of impunity which had characterized Mexico's human rights record over the past decades.

The arrest in August of two army generals accused of drug-trafficking reawakened accusations by victims' relatives and human rights defenders that both were implicated in hundreds of "disappearances" during counter-insurgency operations in Guerrero state in the 1970s. A proposal by opposition senators for a commission of inquiry into these "disappearances" was not successful. However, in November a human rights NGO was reported to have filed a complaint before the Office of the Attorney General of the Republic relating to 19 of the "disappearances" and two cases of torture.

The full circumstances surrounding political killings in previous years remained unclear. These included the massacre of dozens of students in Mexico City in 1968; the killing of 26 peasants in Aguas Blancas and El Charco, Guerrero state, in 1995 and 1998 respectively; and the killing of 45 indigenous people in Acteal in 1996 and a further 11 in El Bosque in 1998, in Chiapas state.

AI country reports and visit
Reports
- Mexico: Prisoners of conscience – Environmentalists Rodolfo Montiel and Teodoro Cabrera (AI Index: AMR 41/013/2000)
- Mexico: Mother and two sons tortured (AI Index: AMR 41/058/2000)

Visit
AI delegates visited Mexico in January.

MOLDOVA

REPUBLIC OF MOLDOVA
Head of state: Petru Lucinschi
Head of government: Dumitru Braghiș
Capital: Chișinău
Population: 4.4 million
Official language: Moldovan (Romanian)
Death penalty: abolitionist for all crimes (self-proclaimed Dnestr Moldavian Republic is retentionist)
2000 treaty ratifications/signatures: Rome Statute of the International Criminal Court

Arbitrary detention and ill-treatment by police continued. Conditions in prisons, institutions for compulsory treatment of alcoholics, and orphanages amounted to cruel, inhuman and degrading treatment or punishment. At least four political prisoners remained imprisoned in the self-proclaimed Dnestr Moldavian Republic (DMR).

Background

The power struggle between President Petru Lucinschi and parliament continued throughout 2000. This impeded the adoption of legislation introducing social and economic reforms and affected international aid payments. In July amendments to the Constitution reduced the President's power to veto legislation and replaced direct presidential elections with a parliamentary vote for a head of state.

Talks on regulating the status of the DMR continued inconclusively. Efforts by the Organization for Security and Co-operation in Europe (OSCE) to find a political settlement stalled after DMR representatives failed to take part as planned in the government delegation. There was no tangible progress in the reduction of Russian military stockpiles and forces from the DMR.

The Council of Europe's Commissioner on Human Rights visited Moldova in October. The following month, the Council's Secretary General stated that Moldova had failed to meet a number of requirements to reform its legal system, particularly to adopt a new criminal code, code of criminal procedure, and laws concerning state prosecutors; to lift a series of press restrictions; and to resolve the conflict between the Moldovan and Bessarabian orthodox churches.

Arbitrary detention and ill-treatment
Police officers continued to resort to administrative detention in order to detain suspects arbitrarily. The risk of arbitrary detention and ill-treatment was increased in July when the Constitutional Court reportedly ruled that police could keep suspects in custody for up to 72 hours before bringing them before the courts to decide whether arrest warrants should be issued. Those who are administratively detained for minor offences do not enjoy the rights to a public hearing, to be represented and to present their own defence. Such cases were routinely examined in the absence of the defendants.

☐ In April at least 24 students were detained in Chişinău following protests concerning deteriorating student benefits. They were charged under the Administrative Code with participating in an unauthorized assembly and "shouting abusive words or slogans in public places". Many of the students complained about police ill-treatment at the time of arrest.

Cruel, inhuman or degrading prison conditions
The authorities failed to improve prison conditions which in many instances amounted to cruel, inhuman or degrading treatment. Conditions were especially harsh in pre-trial detention facilities.

☐ Around 1,700 people detained in Prison number 3 in Chişinău awaiting trial were subjected to serious overcrowding and poor sanitary conditions. Iron bars and shutters blocked daylight and air from cells; most prisoners were not allowed to exercise in the one small courtyard available; and around 120 minors were kept in their cells 24 hours a day without access to any educational or recreational activity other than one hour a day in front of the television in a windowless room with no furniture.

People subjected to compulsory treatment for alcoholism and drug addiction were held in similarly deplorable conditions in psychiatric institutions or special facilities where they were compelled to undertake forced labour. Administrative procedures for ordering compulsory treatment lacked adequate judicial supervision and effective safeguards. Particularly poor conditions were reported in the psychiatric hospital in Curchi and in the Leova Rehabilitation Centre.

In January, an official administering European Union aid in Chişinău described the conditions in state institutions for orphans and children with disabilities as critical and "resembling Nazi camps during the Second World War". In addition to appalling standards of care, many children in orphanages in Bender and Tiraspol were subjected to a brutal regime in which they were tied to beds, kept in cages or kept isolated in locked rooms.

Political prisoners in the DMR
Ilie Ilaşcu, Alexandru Leşco, Andrei Ivanţoc and Tudor Petrov-Popa of the so-called "Tiraspol Six", convicted of murder in 1993 by a court in the DMR, remained in prison. Their trial had reportedly failed to meet international standards of fairness and the men had allegedly been prosecuted for political reasons. In June the European Court of Human Rights began considering their application; they claimed that they had not been convicted by a competent court, that the proceedings leading to their conviction were not fair, and that their prison conditions were in breach of the European Convention for the Protection of Human Rights and Fundamental Freedoms. International efforts to organize a retrial in a third country continued.

MOROCCO/ WESTERN SAHARA

KINGDOM OF MOROCCO
Head of state: King Mohammed VI
Head of government: Abderrahmane Youssoufi
Capital: Rabat
Population: 28.3 million
Official language: Arabic
Death penalty: retentionist
2000 treaty ratifications/signatures: Optional Protocol to the UN Children's Convention on the involvement of children in armed conflict; Rome Statute of the International Criminal Court

The arbitration commission, established in 1999 to decide on compensation for the victims of "disappearance" and arbitrary detention and their families, announced that it had examined 148 claims. However, the authorities failed to clarify the cases of several hundred "disappeared", most of them Sahrawis, or to acknowledge the deaths of some 70 Sahrawi who "disappeared" in secret detention between the 1970s and early 1990s. One long-term prisoner of conscience was released from house arrest in May. Four prisoners of conscience were tried and sentenced to prison terms. Hundreds of political arrests were made and more than 60 political prisoners sentenced after unfair trials in previous years continued to be detained. There were continued reports of torture of detainees and demonstrations were often repressed with excessive force. The failure to bring those responsible for human rights violations to justice remained a major concern.

Background
There was no tangible progress in negotiations between Morocco and the *Frente Popular para la Liberación de Saguia el-Hamra y Rio de Oro*, Popular Front for the

Liberation of Saguia el-Hamra and Rio de Oro (known as the Polisario Front), on a proposed referendum on independence for Western Sahara. The UN Mission for the Referendum in Western Sahara (MINURSO) did not begin hearing the around 140,000 appeals concerning the register of people eligible to vote in the referendum and no new date was scheduled for the ballot.

Three national newspapers were banned in December following the publication of an article implicating the political left in a bid to kill the late King Hassan II in 1972. Earlier in the year, seven foreign and national newspapers had been subject to circulation bans, apparently in response to articles published in favour of independence for Western Sahara and criticizing the monarchy. Moroccan journalists were sentenced to suspended prison terms, fined and temporarily banned from journalism after being convicted of libel against a government minister. One foreign journalist was expelled from the country with no explanation.

Morocco's first centre for the rehabilitation of torture victims, a non-governmental initiative, was opened in Casablanca in May.

Redress for past human rights violations

In July the arbitration commission established by King Mohammed VI to decide on compensation for material and psychological damage suffered by the victims of "disappearance" and arbitrary detention and their families announced that it had examined 148 of the 5,819 compensation claims passed to it by the *Conseil consultatif des droits de l'homme* (CCDH), Human Rights Advisory Board, set up by King Hassan II in 1990. The commission awarded compensation totalling 140 million dirhams (US$13 million) relating to 68 cases which had been examined and given priority. Survivors of the secret detention centre of Tazmamert, who were released in 1991 after 18 years' "disappearance", and the families of those who died there made up the majority of the beneficiaries.

However, families of those who died in Tazmamert who submitted compensation claims but refused to sign a declaration that they would abide by the decision made by the commission on their case were not awarded compensation. The commission's internal regulations state clearly that its decisions are final and admit no recourse to appeal. By the end of 2000, the families of "disappeared" people whose deaths had been officially acknowledged by the authorities had not been provided with information concerning the date, place and cause of their relatives' deaths and had not received their relatives' remains for burial or been told where they were.

The mandate of the arbitration commission is limited to the issue of compensation for the victims of "disappearance" and arbitrary detention and their families. In no case was an investigation known to have been carried out to establish responsibility for grave and systematic human rights violations which occurred in the past; the perpetrators, including those responsible for gross violations over long periods of time, were not brought to justice.

By the end of 2000, the cases of several hundred people, the majority of them Sahrawis, who "disappeared" between the mid-1960s and early 1990s, had not been officially clarified. The deaths between 1976 and 1991 of some 70 Sahrawi who "disappeared" in the secret detention centres of Agdz, Qal'at M'gouna and Laayoune had not been acknowledged by the authorities, and their families had not received the remains for burial or been told where they were.

Prisoners of conscience

One long-term prisoner of conscience was released, but four prisoners of conscience were sentenced to prison terms in 2000.

▢ 'Abdessalam Yassine, spiritual leader of the banned Islamist association *al-'Adl wa'l-Ihsan* (Justice and Charity) who had been held under administratively imposed house arrest since December 1989, was released on 15 May 2000.

▢ In June, three Sahrawis were sentenced to terms of imprisonment by the Court of First Instance in Agadir for "threatening state security". Brahim Laghzal and Cheikh Khaya were sentenced to four years' imprisonment and Laarbi Massoudi to three years' imprisonment. In addition, they were fined 10,000 dirhams (US$930) each. The Court of Appeal turned down an appeal against the verdict and increased Laarbi Massoudi's sentence to four years' imprisonment. The three men had been arrested in December 1999 in separate incidents in Tan Tan, Laayoune and Agadir. Two days later they were transported to military barracks where they alleged that they were tortured; these allegations were never investigated. They were interrogated about material they had been carrying linking them to the Polisario Front, including a video cassette of the Polisario's 10th Congress and the Constitution of the Sahrawi Arab Democratic Republic.

▢ On 17 February, Mustapha Adib, a Moroccan Air Force captain, was sentenced to five years' imprisonment by the Military Tribunal of Rabat and dismissed from the armed forces for indiscipline and dishonouring the army. His trial followed the publication of an article in the French newspaper *Le Monde* which quoted him as denouncing corruption in the Moroccan armed forces. The trial violated international standards for fair trial and was held behind closed doors. Following an appeal, the Supreme Court quashed the ruling in June on the grounds that there had been irregularities in the case and ordered a retrial. In October Mustapha Adib was sentenced by the Military Tribunal of Rabat to two and a half years' imprisonment and dismissed from the armed forces.

Torture/ill-treatment

The number of reported cases of torture has significantly decreased in recent years, but information continued to be received that detainees held incommunicado and prison inmates were tortured or ill-treated in order to extract confessions and information, or to punish and intimidate them.

Demonstrations continued to be dispersed with excessive force by the security forces.

▫ In May and June, the authorities used excessive force against several peaceful demonstrations by associations of unemployed graduates. Dozens of unemployed graduates and union leaders, including Amine 'Abdelhamid, Vice-President of the Moroccan Human Rights Association and leader of the Moroccan Union of Workers, were beaten with clubs and dozens more were arrested and held overnight.

Polisario camps

Freedom of expression, association and movement continued to be restricted in the camps controlled by the Polisario Front near Tindouf in southwestern Algeria. Those responsible for human rights abuses in the camps in previous years continued to enjoy impunity. The Polisario authorities failed to hand over perpetrators still resident in the camps to the Algerian authorities to be brought to justice and the Moroccan authorities failed to bring to justice the perpetrators of abuses in the Polisario camps present on its territory.

Communications with the government

In response to a memorandum sent to the Moroccan authorities in April, AI received a set of documents from the Human Rights Ministry later in the year. The Ministry provided a list of 102 detainees under sentence of death, a list of 53 prisoners of war held by Morocco and detailed information on cases of prisoners of conscience, deaths in custody, torture and ill-treatment, and on the issue of "disappearances". The response indicated that judicial proceedings had been initiated against members of the security forces alleged to have been responsible for torture and ill-treatment, but did not provide any details of individual cases.

MOZAMBIQUE

REPUBLIC OF MOZAMBIQUE
Head of state: Joaquim Alberto Chissano
Head of government: Pascoal Mocumbi
Capital: Maputo
Population: 19.7 million
Official language: Portuguese
Death penalty: abolitionist for all crimes
2000 treaty ratifications/signatures: Rome Statute of the International Criminal Court

Reports of human rights violations including torture and killings of suspected criminals by the police increased, while efforts to reform the criminal justice system and to retrain the police continued. At least 41 people were shot dead by the police during demonstrations. There was political unrest during protests against the 1999 election results, which led to arrests. Prisons remained severely overcrowded. At least 80 people died in police custody.

Background

Severe flooding hit Mozambique for several weeks in February and March with devastating effects on the economy and infrastructure. About 700 people died and 330,000 became homeless. Landmines laid during the civil war, which ended in 1992, became dislodged, posing a new threat to the population. Many donor governments cancelled part or all their bilateral debts.

Following parliamentary and presidential elections in December 1999, which were won by the ruling *Frente para a Libertação de Moçambique* (FRELIMO), Mozambique Liberation Front, the government was reappointed in January. In February President Joaquim Chissano was sworn in for a further five-year term. Provincial governors were appointed in July. The opposition coalition, *Resistência Nacional Moçambicana–União Eleitoral* (RENAMO-UE), Mozambican National Resistance–Electoral Union, requested a recount of the vote and an inquiry into allegations of vote-rigging, but this was turned down. In January RENAMO's president, Afonso Dhlakama, threatened to set up a provincial government in the six northern and central provinces where the coalition had won a majority. He also moved the party's headquarters to Beira, Sofala province, despite a law requiring political parties to be based in the capital. Protests against election results led to clashes with the police and the arrest of RENAMO members.

In January skirmishes between FRELIMO and RENAMO-UE in Ilha de Moçambique, Nampula province, resulted in several people being injured and damage to property, as RENAMO members protested against the election results. In May there was a report that RENAMO sympathizers had rioted in Morrumbala, Zambézia province, in protest against the local authorities.

Excessive use of force

In May the police used excessive force to deal with a demonstration. Six people were shot dead and several wounded in Aube, in the Angoche district of Nampula province, as they peacefully demonstrated outside the police station to call for the release of a RENAMO member arrested earlier. Domingos Francisco Damião, Feliciano José Carlos and Nanlissa Alberto died instantly while Mussa Aiuba died later in hospital. The bodies of two other demonstrators who had been shot were later found outside the town. Six people were arrested including Alvaro Chime Chale, RENAMO's representative in Angoche, who was arrested in Maputo several days after the incident and charged with inciting civil disobedience. The six were subsequently released on bail. They had not been tried by the end of 2000, nor had an inquiry into the incident been held.

In early November, 41 people died in clashes with the police during nationwide demonstrations organized by RENAMO to protest against the results of the December 1999 elections. Scores of demonstrators were wounded and hundreds arrested. Dozens of detainees were reportedly tried and some sentenced to prison terms in rapid trials, raising concern about their fairness. Others were still held uncharged at the end of 2000. There had been no inquiry into the killings and woundings by the end of 2000.

Police abuses

The number of allegations of police abuses increased, including in Maputo where there had been an improvement in previous years. There were reports of police officers assaulting street vendors who refused to comply with demands for illegal payments. Some officers were dismissed for abuse of power and misbehaviour.

In July, two police officers in Maputo were arrested and charged with the indecent assault of five women and a security guard during an interrogation in connection with a theft in the restaurant where they worked. The officers had not been tried at the end of the year.

Torture/ill-treatment

Reports of severe beatings or other forms of torture in police stations in order to extract confessions increased, including in Maputo where the number of cases reported in previous years had slightly declined. Many of the incidents were not investigated.

Marcelino Mutolo and his brother-in-law Luciano Homo were tortured in Inhambame city in January by members of the *Polícia de Intervenção Rápida* (PIR), Rapid Intervention Police, who were apparently investigating a vehicle theft. Marcelino Mutolo was held handcuffed to a pillar in a mosquito-infested cell and made to stand for hours before he and Luciano Homo were taken outside the city. The two men were pushed to the ground and severely beaten and had shots fired above their heads. Both men were released uncharged several days later. Marcelino Mutolo reportedly had to pay a large sum of money to the police. No investigation was known to have been initiated.

Suspected extrajudicial executions

There were further reports of extrajudicial executions of suspected criminals by the police, which did not appear to have been investigated by the authorities. The police often claimed that the victims were shot when trying to escape.

Gildo Joaquim Bata, who was accused of possession of a gun, and Tomás Paulo Nhacumba were arrested in Maputo in March. The day after their arrest the police took them in handcuffs to Gildo Joaquim Bata's home and demanded money from relatives for their release. As the families were unable to pay, both men were apparently taken back to the police station and subsequently "disappeared". Three days later their bodies were found in the morgue where they had been registered under different names. The body of Gildo Joaquim Bata had a bullet hole in the forehead while that of Tomás Paulo Nhacumba had one bullet hole in the forehead and one in the heart. The police claimed that both men had been shot while trying to escape. By the end of 2000 no investigation had been carried out.

Deaths in detention

At least 80 people died in suspicious circumstances in custody in Montepuez, in the northern province of Cabo Delgado, in late November. They had been arrested two weeks earlier during nationwide demonstrations called by RENAMO. Many of the deceased were RENAMO members. A team of investigators, including pathologists, concluded that the deaths were caused by suffocation. However, they were only able to perform post-mortem examinations. Survivors told Mozambican human rights organizations that on the night of the incident, at least 96 people were held in a cell at the police station which measures 7m x 3m. Human rights organizations which investigated the deaths claimed that the detainees had also been deprived of food and that guards ignored the detainees' cries for help. By the end of 2000 a commission of inquiry had been set up but was not yet functioning.

Prison conditions

Some attempts were made to improve prison conditions by processing cases more quickly and allowing bail. Nevertheless, prisons remained severely overcrowded. In June the president of the Parliamentary Commission on Justice, Legality and Human Rights stated that prison conditions violated human rights and degraded human life, adding that 65 per cent of the inmates were in pre-trial detention.

MYANMAR

UNION OF MYANMAR
Head of state and government: General Than Shwe
Capital: Yangon
Population: 46.8 million
Official language: Burmese
Death penalty: retentionist

Hundreds of people, including more than 200 members of political parties and young activists, were arrested for political reasons. Ten others were known to have been sentenced to long terms of imprisonment after unfair trials. At least 1,500 political prisoners arrested in previous years, including more than 100 prisoners of conscience and hundreds of possible prisoners of conscience, remained in prison. Daw Aung San Suu Kyi and other leaders of the National League for Democracy (NLD) were placed under *de facto* house arrest after being prevented by the military from travelling outside Yangon to visit other NLD members. Prison conditions constituted cruel, inhuman or degrading treatment, and torture of political prisoners was reported. The military continued to seize ethnic minority civilians for forced labour duties and to kill members of ethnic minorities during counter-insurgency operations in the Shan, Kayah, and Kayin states. Five people were sentenced to death in 2000 for drug trafficking.

Background
As in previous years, the army continued to engage in skirmishes with the Karen National Union (KNU), the Karenni National Progressive Party (KNPP), and the Shan State Army-South (SSA-South). Sixteen cease-fire agreements negotiated in previous years between the State Peace and Development Council (SPDC) and various ethnic minority armed opposition groups were maintained.

Continuing political stalemate
In spite of international and domestic efforts, the military government of the SPDC refused to engage in dialogue with the NLD. In August Daw Aung San Suu Kyi and other NLD leaders left Yangon to visit NLD members. They were detained on the road in Dalah township by the military authorities for 10 days before being forcibly returned to Yangon. They were then held incommunicado under house arrest for 12 days. The NLD headquarters in Yangon were raided and documents reportedly confiscated. In September, when Daw Aung San Suu Kyi and NLD Vice-chairman U Tin Oo attempted to travel by train to Mandalay, they were forcibly removed from the Yangon train station. U Tin Oo was taken to Yemon Military Intelligence Base and detained there; Daw Aung San Suu Kyi and eight other NLD Central Executive Committee members were placed under house arrest where they remained at the end of the year. Almost 100 NLD members were arrested in connection with the two attempted NLD trips, including NLD supporters who had gathered to greet Daw Aung San Suu Kyi at the train station.

Political prisoners
At least 1,700 people remained imprisoned for political reasons, including 37 NLD members of parliament-elect. An additional 45 members of parliament-elect arrested in September 1998, 43 of them members of the NLD, continued to be held without charge in "government guesthouses". They had been arrested in a pre-emptive move to prevent them from convening a parliament after the SPDC's refusal to do so. Saw Naing Naing, an NLD member of parliament-elect from Pazundaung township, Yangon, who had been released in January 1999, was rearrested in September 2000.

Ten political prisoners were known to have been released, including five elderly men released after the Special Envoy of the UN Secretary-General for Myanmar visited the country in October.

In the run-up to the 10th anniversary in May of the NLD election victory, hundreds of NLD supporters were arrested. In press conferences held in May and July, the SPDC accused the NLD of having links with exiled opposition groups which it claimed were involved in "terrorist" acts.

▫ U Than Lwin, an NLD member of parliament-elect from Constituency 2, Madaya township, Mandalay Division, was arrested and sentenced in May to nine years' imprisonment for sending a letter to the local authorities. The letter protested against a demonstration held against him in March, staged by the authorities, who reportedly forced people to attend.

▫ In May scores of NLD members from Taungdwingyi township, Magwe Division, were arrested for attending a party meeting; seven were sentenced to eight years' imprisonment.

▫ U Aye Tha Aung, a prisoner of conscience and leader of the Arakan League for Democracy, was arrested in April and sentenced to 21 years' imprisonment. His health deteriorated significantly following his arrest. He was the Secretary of the 10-member Committee Representing the People's Parliament which the NLD and other opposition parties formed in 1998, and represented four ethnic minority opposition parties, including his own.

▫ Seven Rohingyas, including Serajudin bin Nurislam, were arrested in June for attempting to travel to Yangon. They were later sentenced to between eight and 12 years' imprisonment and were held in Sittwe, capital of the Rakhine State. Rohingyas, who are Muslims living in the Rakhine State, are forbidden from travelling outside their home townships.

Prison conditions
The International Committee of the Red Cross (ICRC) continued visiting prisons, "government guesthouses" where members of parliament-elect were detained, and some labour camps. However they were not known to have had access to Military Intelligence Headquarters where torture was most frequently

reported. In April the ICRC announced that it had identified some 1,500 "security detainees". Conditions in most prisons were extremely poor, owing to lack of adequate food, water, sanitation, and medical care. Myingyan Prison in Mandalay Division and Tharawaddy Prison in Bago Division were known to be particularly harsh.

Daw San San Nweh, prisoner of conscience and well-known writer, suffered from high blood pressure, arthritic rheumatism and kidney problems, but did not receive appropriate medical treatment. Poor prison conditions in Myanmar's largest facility, Insein Prison, further exacerbated her health problems.

Torture/ill-treatment

Torture and ill-treatment of political prisoners continued to be reported. Methods of torture included severe beatings and kicks with boots; an iron bar being rolled repeatedly up and down the shins until the skin peeled off; near-suffocation; and "the airplane", where prisoners are suspended from the ceiling, spun around and beaten.

A Karenni Christian farmer from Loikaw township, Kayah State, reported that he was arrested by the army and accused of working with the KNPP after a battle between the two forces in February. He was beaten with rifle butts, punched in the face and kicked in the head so severely that his hearing was permanently damaged. He was then forced to accompany troops as a guide for one week during which time he was beaten every day with sticks and tied with a rope.

Forced labour

The army continued to seize ethnic minority civilians from the Shan, Karen and Karenni ethnic minorities for forced labour. They were made to work on infrastructure projects and to carry equipment for patrolling troops. Forced labour of criminal prisoners in labour camps, who were made to break rocks or to work as porters for the army, was also reported.

A Shan woman from Laikha township, Shan State, reported that in February she had regularly been forced to cut bamboo, build fences, and maintain military camps and roads.

Extrajudicial executions

Extrajudicial executions of ethnic minority civilians taking no active part in the hostilities continued to be reported. In Kunhing township, Shan State, more than 100 Shan and hill tribe people were believed to have been killed in January, February and May. The SSA-South was reportedly active in Kunhing township.

International responses

The SPDC presented its initial report to the UN Committee on the Elimination of Discrimination against Women. The Committee expressed concern about, among other things, violations against ethnic minority women and the plight of women in custody.

At the International Labour Organisation (ILO) Conference in June, the ILO gave the SPDC until 30 November to enact "concrete and detailed measures" to comply with ILO Convention No. 29 on forced labour, to which Myanmar became a party in 1955. If the SPDC was found not to comply, the ILO recommended, among other things, that ILO members should review "the[ir] relations... to ensure that [the SPDC] cannot take advantage of such relations to perpetuate or extend the system". In November the ILO's governing body met and decided that sufficient concrete measures had not been taken by the SPDC to comply with Convention No. 29 and therefore it upheld the ILO measures adopted in June.

In April the UN Commission on Human Rights adopted by consensus its ninth resolution extending the mandate of the UN Special Rapporteur on Myanmar for another year and deploring "the continuing pattern of gross and systematic violations of human rights in Myanmar". A strongly worded resolution was also adopted by consensus at the UN General Assembly in December. In April the UN Secretary-General appointed a new Special Envoy for Myanmar, whose mandate is to ensure implementation of the 1999 General Assembly Resolution on Myanmar. He visited the country in June and July, and again in October, when he met with General Than Shwe and Daw Aung San Suu Kyi. In November the UN Special Rapporteur on Myanmar resigned; during his four-year tenure he had never been permitted by the SPDC to enter the country.

In May the USA renewed limited economic sanctions. In April the European Union (EU) strengthened its Common Position to include freezing the funds of SPDC members and other government officials in EU countries; this was renewed in October. The SPDC postponed an EU troika visit which was to have taken place in October, but the meeting between the EU and the Association of South-East Asian Nations (ASEAN), which the SPDC attended, took place in Laos in December.

AI country reports

- Unsung heroines: Women of Myanmar (AI Index: ASA 16/004/2000)
- Myanmar: Exodus from the Shan State (AI Index: ASA 16/011/2000)
- The institution of torture in Myanmar (AI Index: ASA 16/024/2000)

NAMIBIA

REPUBLIC OF NAMIBIA
Head of state: Dr Samuel Nujoma
Head of government: Hage Geingob
Capital: Windhoek
Population: 1.6 million
Death penalty: abolitionist for all crimes
2000 treaty ratifications/signatures: Optional Protocol to the UN Children's Convention on the involvement of children in armed conflict; Optional Protocol to the UN Women's Convention

There was a sharp rise in human rights violations in the northeastern Kavango and Caprivi provinces, particularly early in 2000, following Namibian involvement in the Angolan civil war. Human rights violations were reportedly committed by the Angolan and Namibian armies, as well as by the Namibian police's Special Field Forces (SFF), including extrajudicial executions and torture. There were also concerns regarding freedom of expression and association.

Background

From December 1999 onwards, the Namibian government permitted the Angolan army to mount attacks into Angola from Kavango and Caprivi provinces against the forces of the *União Nacional para a Independência Total de Angola* (UNITA), National Union for the Total Independence of Angola.

Kavango and Caprivi provinces

Extrajudicial executions

Human rights violations, including extrajudicial executions, by the Angolan and Namibian armies, as well as by the SFF, were reported throughout 2000.

▢ Angolan soldiers reportedly shot dead Thaddeus Mubili, a villager from western Caprivi, on 22 January, after one of their number was injured by a landmine. Thaddeus Mubili had been helping the soldiers track suspected UNITA members who had attacked a village the previous day.

▢ A group of Angolans and Namibians, apparently members of a family group who live on both sides of the border river, reportedly crossed into Namibia west of the Kavango provincial capital, Rundu, on 10 January. The presence of the group aroused suspicion and Namibian soldiers arrived and started shooting. A six-year-old girl was shot dead and a man was shot in the buttocks.

Torture/ill-treatment

There were reports of torture and excessive use of force by Angolan and Namibian armed forces, as well as the SFF. Early in 2000 there were reports of Angolan soldiers torturing young women by raping them. There were also reports of soldiers based in Angola abducting girls from Namibia and taking them to Angola.

▢ Erkki Fiderato was arrested on 7 January at his home in eastern Kavango by SFF officers. During arrest he was reportedly kicked and beaten with rifle butts. Villagers heard him screaming throughout the night.

▢ Muyeva Thaddeus Munango was shot and wounded in the hand and leg on 4 February. He had been fishing in a river east of Rundu when an SFF officer reportedly ordered him to leave the river, then shot him and left him for dead. He regained consciousness and managed to reach his home, where villagers took him to hospital.

Forcible returns

Some refugees who fled the Angolan conflict after November 1999 were forcibly returned. Accounts of the way the authorities dealt with the population in the northeast suggested a pattern of cooperation between the Namibian police and members of the Angolan army.

Angolan women in Osire refugee camp in January reported that they had been separated from their husbands and that they feared the men may have been handed over to the Angolan army. The missing men were mostly from Angola's central highlands where UNITA drew much of its support. The authorities did not respond to inquiries by the UN High Commissioner for Refugees (UNHCR) about 50 men reported missing in November and December 1999.

Torture/ill-treatment

More than 100 people remained in custody throughout 2000 after an armed secessionist uprising in Katima Mulilo, the provincial capital of Caprivi, in August 1999. About 300 people were initially arrested and others were arrested in the following months. All of those initially arrested were reportedly tortured during their arrests. More than 130 of those released without charge filed complaints of torture during 2000 and sought compensation. Their cases were still pending at the end of the year. Three police officers named by many detainees as perpetrators of torture remained on duty.

Freedom of expression and association

Many of those still detained following the uprising in Katima Mulilo appeared to be possible prisoners of conscience. They were accused of sedition and treason because of their opinions or the organizations they belonged to, even though they did not participate in or advocate any violence.

There was growing criticism by government ministers and government party officials of the press, the judiciary and non-governmental organizations. Officials threatened to withdraw residence permits from foreign judges and encouraged the police to "eliminate gays and lesbians from the face of Namibia".

AI country report and visit

Report
- Namibia: Human rights abuses in the border area (AI Index: AFR 03/001/2000)

Visit
AI delegates visited Namibia in January to investigate the situation in the border area with Angola.

NEPAL

KINGDOM OF NEPAL
Head of state: King Birendra Bir Bikram Shah Dev
Head of government: Girija Prasad Koirala (replaced Krishna Prasad Bhattarai in March)
Capital: Kathmandu
Population: 23.9 million
Official language: Nepali
Death penalty: abolitionist for all crimes
2000 treaty ratifications/signatures: Optional Protocol to the UN Children's Convention on the involvement of children in armed conflict

Grave human rights violations by police, including extrajudicial executions, "disappearances" and torture, were reported in the context of the "people's war" declared by the Communist Party of Nepal (CPN) (Maoist) in 1996. There were also widespread abuses by members of the CPN (Maoist), including deliberate killings, hostage-taking and torture. The National Human Rights Commission (NHRC) was finally set up in May, but had not become fully operational by the end of 2000. Impunity and the lack of independent investigation into human rights violations remained a major concern.

Background

Political instability adversely affected the human rights situation. A power struggle within the leadership of the Nepali Congress Party (NCP), particularly between Girija Prasad Koirala and Krishna Prasad Bhattarai, resulted in the former replacing the latter as Prime Minister in March. However, the power struggle continued and hampered efforts to initiate a dialogue between the government and the CPN (Maoist).

In April, the National Defence Council (NDC), a constitutional body, was activated by Prime Minister Koirala as one of several measures to address the Maoist "people's war". The implementation of a government decision in April to establish a paramilitary force called the Armed Security Force was delayed and it had not been set up by the end of 2000. In October, the NDC decided to station the army in district headquarters.

There were several attempts to initiate talks between the government and representatives of the CPN (Maoist), including by the Consensus Seeking Committee, set up in December 1999 and chaired by former Prime Minister Sher Bahadur Deuba (a political ally of Krishna Prasad Bhattarai). Among the conditions for talks set by the CPN (Maoist) was a demand for an inquiry into the whereabouts of CPN (Maoist) members and supporters who had "disappeared".

The mandate of the Consensus Seeking Committee was not extended when it ended on 16 October. The Committee's final report described the Maoist "people's war" as a political problem arising from the country's socio-economic structure, and urged the government to hold talks with the CPN (Maoist) about their demands, apart from those calling for constitutional changes. It also suggested that the security apparatus be strengthened. In November, the prospects for dialogue worsened after a released Maoist leader alleged that the government had forced him to denounce the CPN (Maoist) at a press conference.

Extrajudicial executions

According to official figures, between November 1999 and October 2000, 221 people were killed by police in the context of the "people's war". The government claimed there were no civilians among them and that all members of the CPN (Maoist) were killed during exchanges of fire. However, there was clear evidence that dozens of civilians and many members of the CPN (Maoist) were unlawfully killed. There were also reports that riot police killed several civilians, including two children, when they opened fire during demonstrations in December.

The UN Special Rapporteur on extrajudicial, summary or arbitrary executions visited Nepal in February. In her report, she stressed the urgent need to put in place strong, independent and credible mechanisms to investigate and prosecute human rights abuses.

◻ Seven civilians and two alleged members of the CPN (Maoist) were killed on 14 January at Thaku, Achham district, when police went on a rampage in the village. Early that day, members of the CPN (Maoist) had coerced villagers into attending a "cultural program". When a police patrol thought to be from Kamal Bazar police station approached the village, the organizers fled. Police started shooting at random. Four villagers were shot dead while taking shelter in a tea shop, three others while running away. Two members of the CPN (Maoist) reportedly surrendered to the police and were interrogated for several hours. Villagers later heard shots. The next morning, police forced villagers to carry nine dead bodies to the river. The bodies were cremated there despite protests from the relatives of the dead villagers.

◻ On 22 February, 15 unarmed civilians were allegedly killed by police in Rukum district, apparently in reprisal for the killing of 15 policemen during an attack by members of the CPN (Maoist) on a police station at Ghartigaun, Rolpa district, three days earlier. Police dragged people outside their houses and shot them. They also burned the houses. All those killed were reportedly supporters of the NCP, including Trivan Wali.

'Disappearances'/unacknowledged detention

There was mounting evidence of secret detention of people arrested on suspicion of being members of the CPN (Maoist). The whereabouts of 13 people arrested during 2000 remained unknown at the end of the year. More than 50 other "disappearances" reported in 1998 and 1999 also remained unclarified.

Several of those released after long periods of unacknowledged detention gave evidence of torture and of cruel, inhuman and degrading conditions of detention.

☐ Tara Prasad Bhusal, a 17-year-old school student, was rearrested by police on 25 June from the premises of the Butwal Appelate Court, immediately after a judge had ordered his release. He was held in secret detention at three different places for one month and kept blindfolded and with his hands tied for most of the time.

Torture/ill-treatment
Torture continued to be reported on a regular basis.
☐ A student from Kailali district who was arrested in May on suspicion of being a Maoist sympathizer was tortured for three days at the district police office. He was subjected to prolonged beatings on his back and legs with a stick and to *falanga* (beating on the soles of the feet).

Arbitrary arrests and detention
An estimated 1,600 people were serving a prison sentence or awaiting trial in relation to crimes allegedly committed in the context of the "people's war" at the end of 2000. The abuse of the Public Security Act, under which political activists were repeatedly rearrested despite court orders for their release, continued. The authorities also increasingly used provisions of the Anti-State Crimes and Penalties Act, 1989, which includes crimes such as insurrection and treason carrying punishments of up to life imprisonment. It appeared that the police were using this law to prevent suspects' release on bail pending trial.

Abuses by the CPN (Maoist)
According to official sources, members of the CPN (Maoist) killed 82 civilians between November 1999 and October 2000. Most of them were members of the NCP. Dozens of people were also taken hostage or abducted. Children as young as 14, including girls, were recruited. There were also reports that those held captive were subjected to cruel punishments.

AI wrote to the leadership of the CPN (Maoist) in June to express concern about abductions of civilians, including children. In a public statement issued on 23 August, the leadership denied that children had been recruited into the "people's army". In a further letter sent in October, AI clarified that it opposed any form of recruitment, training or deployment of children under the age of 18, including for support roles such as messengers or porters. AI also sought clarification about "death sentences" reportedly imposed by Maoist "people's courts" on seven people as announced during a press conference organized by the Rolpa district unit of the CPN (Maoist) on 27 August.

☐ Man Singh Shahi, the President of the Association of Victims of Maoists in Kalikot district, was killed on 1 September.

☐ Shiva Prasad Bhatta, headmaster of the Mandali Primary School in Pandrung, Gorkha district, was killed on 22 August.

☐ Three 14-year-olds and a 15-year-old student from Janapriya High School in Jajarkot district were taken away by members of the CPN (Maoist) from their school hostel in Dashera on 8 and 9 June respectively. They had not returned by the end of 2000.

Impunity
There was a complete lack of accountability for extrajudicial executions. Investigations were internal and conducted by the police or the Ministry of Home Affairs, and in most cases the bodies of victims were disposed of without any inquiry.

Accountability in relation to "disappearances" and torture was also lacking. In August the Ilam district court awarded compensation of Rupees 5,000 (US$70) to Hasta Rai, who had been tortured by police at Aitabari police post in November 1999. This was only the second case in which compensation had been awarded since the Torture Compensation Act came into force in 1996.

National Human Rights Commission
Members of the NHRC were appointed in May, more than three years after the law for the establishment of the Commission was enacted. The institution experienced logistical and financial problems arising from lack of government cooperation. The police also appeared reluctant to cooperate with the NHRC.

AI country report and visits
Report
- Nepal: Human rights and security (AI Index: ASA 31/001/2000)

Visits
A high-level delegation, including AI's Secretary General, visited Nepal in February. During a further visit in November, the Secretary General launched a campaign to eradicate torture in Nepal.

NEW ZEALAND

NEW ZEALAND
Head of state: Queen Elizabeth II, represented by Michael Hardie Boys
Head of government: Helen Clark
Capital: Wellington
Population: 3.8 million
Official language: English
Death penalty: abolitionist for all crimes
2000 treaty ratifications/signatures: Optional Protocol to the UN Children's Convention on the involvement of children in armed conflict; Optional Protocol to the UN Women's Convention; Rome Statute of the International Criminal Court

A man was shot dead by police in disputed circumstances. A number of asylum-seekers were detained.

Background
The government announced a major review of existing systems and legislation for the protection and promotion of human rights. In June, the Ministry of Justice issued a set of guidelines for government policy advisers on the application of the 1993 Human Rights Act and the implications of the prohibition of discrimination due to come into effect from 2002. A parliamentary committee commenced a major inquiry into New Zealand's part in the promotion and implementation of international human rights standards, particularly in the Asia/Pacific region.

Police shooting
In April, a police officer at Waitara, Taranaki, shot dead Steven Wallace, a 23-year-old Maori man, in disputed circumstances. The shooting led to racial tension which was investigated by the national Human Rights Commission. In August, a police inquiry found that the shooting was lawful, and that "race was not an issue". According to the police, Steven Wallace had been acting in an irrational, destructive and threatening manner, and had smashed the windows of a police car and various buildings before being confronted by two armed officers. About one minute later, one of the officers fired four shots at Steven Wallace, allegedly as he came to within six metres of them holding a baseball bat. Police admitted that there had been delays in providing medical attention. Investigations by a coroner and the Police Complaints Authority had not been completed by the end of 2000.

Detention of asylum-seekers
A number of asylum-seekers who arrived without travel documents were detained. In May the High Court in Auckland ruled that such detention may become illegal once it ceases to be reasonable under the circumstances.

In July the Court of Appeal overturned an earlier High Court decision which in 1999 had led to the release from prison of 16 asylum-seekers. The New Zealand Immigration Service had argued that the 1951 UN Refugee Convention and the UN High Commissioner for Refugees Guidelines on the Detention of Asylum-Seekers imposed no obligations on government officials to release detained asylum-seekers.

NICARAGUA

REPUBLIC OF NICARAGUA
Head of state and government: Arnoldo Alemán Lacayo
Capital: Managua
Population: 5 million
Official language: Spanish
Death penalty: abolitionist for all crimes

Human rights defenders were threatened. Police officers injured demonstrators and detainees.

Background
The effects of the agreement signed in 1999 between the two main political parties, the ruling *Partido Liberal Constitucionalista,* Constitutionalist Liberal Party, and the *Frente Sandinista de Liberación Nacional*, Sandinista National Liberation Front, started to emerge. They were criticized by sectors of civil society as a threat to the democratic process and to basic human and civil rights. For example, electoral reforms introduced in January established new rules for the creation of political parties, imposing difficult conditions, and changed the requirements for the registration of candidates. During municipal elections in November, a significant number of parties were left out of the contest and candidates were prevented from running for office.

Human rights defenders
Human rights defenders and non-governmental organizations were threatened. In March government ministers accused Vilma Núñez de Escorcia, President of the *Centro Nicaragüense de Derechos Humanos* (CENIDH), Nicaraguan Centre for Human Rights, of obstructing police work. Pro-government newspapers and radio stations suggested her death might be the answer to the unrest in the northeast of the country. CENIDH had been investigating the killing of three men, former members of an armed group of ex-soldiers, the *Frente Unido Andrés Castro* (FUAC), Andrés Castro United Front. In May an anonymous letter with further threats was delivered to CENIDH's office.

Government authorities, including President Arnoldo Alemán, were reported to have strongly criticized non-governmental organizations, calling them "merchants of poverty" among other things. In some cases these attacks came after the groups had criticized the authorities' handling of aid for victims of natural disasters.

☐ In December, Dorothy Virginia Granada, a 70-year-old US citizen working as a nurse in a cooperative clinic in Mulukuku, North Atlantic Autonomous Region, was harassed and intimidated by police and immigration agents. The clinic had faced allegations of attempting to influence its patients politically; of illegal abortions; of treating members of FUAC; and of not being properly registered to practise. President Arnoldo Alemán had attacked Dorothy Granada in the press, claiming that she was an illegal resident. On 8 December, 15 heavily armed anti-riot police, accompanying immigration officers, entered her house without a warrant to arrest and deport her. She was not at home at the time. She went into hiding in fear of another display of force and her health deteriorated. On 13 December, the Minister of the Interior, José Marenco, announced that her residency had been revoked on 7 December, and that she had 24 hours to leave the country. However, a judge reviewing the case annulled the minister's decision and ruled that she was a legal resident. The minister appealed and a final decision was pending at the end of 2000..

National Police
Police officers reportedly used excessive force, causing injuries to demonstrators, and ill-treated detainees. In March about 20 demonstrators protesting against law reforms were beaten and injured by members of the National Police who used rubber bullets and tear gas against them. Dozens of police officers were expelled from the force for corruption or abuse of authority, including beating people in their custody. In August a police officer was expelled from the force after a photograph appeared in the press showing him kicking two young men.

AI action
AI called on the government to protect human rights defenders and others who were being threatened.

NIGER

REPUBLIC OF THE NIGER
Head of state: Mamadou Tandja
Head of government: Hama Amadou (replaced Ibrahim Assan Mayaki in January)
Capital: Niamey
Population: 9.4 million
Official language: French
Death penalty: abolitionist in practice

The human rights situation improved with the return of civilian rule after elections in November 1999. However, some journalists were targeted and arrested during 2000 and there were several cases of torture in detention.

Background
For the first time since 1996, Niger was ruled throughout 2000 by a civilian head of state, elected at the end of 1999 after fair and transparent elections. The presidential election ended four years of military rule marked by two coups, the second of which led to the killing of President Ibrahim Baré Maïnassara by members of his presidential guard in April 1999. During this period of military rule, the human rights situation had deteriorated.

Impunity
In March, President Mamadou Tandja declared himself ready to "seek out and establish the truth" concerning the killing of President Baré Maïnassara. In July a coalition of 11 opposition parties, the *Coordination des forces démocratiques* (CFD), Coordination of Democratic Forces, called for the truth behind this killing to be established. The European Union and AI also called for investigations into the killing, but no inquiry was opened by the end of 2000.

Detention of journalists
Several journalists were detained during 2000.

☐ In June, Abdoulaye Tchiémogo, publishing director of *Le Canard libéré*, a private weekly, and one of his journalists, Illa Kané, were arrested and held for four days. The newspaper had been highly critical of the military junta which took power in April 1999. The journalists received a two-month suspended sentence in August for publishing an article which described Prime Minister Hama Amadou as a "pyromaniac and coward". In a second case, the two journalists received a six-month suspended sentence in October for publishing several articles which were deemed defamatory, and which allegedly "sapped the morale of the army".

☐ In October, three journalists from the private weekly *L'Enquêteur* were charged with "spreading false news" after the publication of an article about a dispute between Niger and Benin concerning the island of Lété. The three were Soumana Maga, the founder of the weekly; Tahirou Gouro, its managing director; and Salif Dago, a journalist. In November, Soumana Maga was sentenced to eight months' imprisonment. He was a prisoner of conscience. The two other journalists received six-month suspended sentences.

Torture/ill-treatment
Torture and ill-treatment of both criminal and political prisoners were reported during 2000.

In August, three detainees in Diakena prison near the town of Tillabéry in the west of the country were handcuffed and hanged head down from a tree by their feet for more than 10 hours. The three men were suspected of theft. One had to have a leg and an arm amputated as a result. An investigation was opened and three prison warders were arrested.

In June, several soldiers arrested on suspicion of kidnapping Major Djibrilla Hamidou Hima, spokesman of the former military junta, were tortured and ill-treated. The detainees and their lawyer lodged a complaint but no inquiry into these allegations of torture had been opened by the end of 2000.

AI country report
- Niger: The right to justice (AI Index: AFR 43/001/2000)

NIGERIA

FEDERAL REPUBLIC OF NIGERIA
Head of state and government: Olusegun Obasanjo
Capital: Abuja
Population: 111.5 million
Official language: English
Death penalty: retentionist
2000 treaty ratifications/signatures: Optional Protocol to the UN Children's Convention on the involvement of children in armed conflict; Optional Protocol to the UN Women's Convention; Rome Statute of the International Criminal Court

There was no investigation into continuing incidents of alleged extrajudicial executions or excessive use of force by the security forces which have taken place since the restoration of civilian government in May 1999. One amputation and several public floggings were carried out under new laws introducing corporal punishment in some northern states. Evidence was heard in the trial of security officers allegedly involved in an attempted extrajudicial execution in 1996, and hearings started before a commission of inquiry investigating human rights violations committed before May 1999.

Background
There were sporadic outbreaks of civil unrest throughout the year in which hundreds died. As many as 1,000 people were killed in intercommunal violence between Christian and Muslim communities in February over the possible extension of *Sharia* (Islamic law) in Kaduna State, northern Nigeria, and in reprisal killings in eastern Nigeria. In May renewed rioting in Kaduna led to a further 300 deaths. Further unrest over *Sharia* left 10 dead in Gombe State in September and at least nine in Niger State in November. In October more than 100 people died in Lagos, southwest Nigeria, in intercommunal conflict.

There was widespread lack of public confidence in the severely under-resourced police force, and lynchings of criminal suspects by vigilante groups or community militias sometimes provoked intercommunal conflict. The government condemned the emergence of ethnically based militias and, following serious unrest, carried out widespread arrests of those allegedly involved. It increased the size of the police force and deployed troops in support of the police in areas of unrest. Special task forces were posted to the oil-producing Niger Delta area where thefts from fuel pipelines rose, scores of people died in explosions at pipelines ruptured by thieves and oil company personnel continued to be taken hostage for ransom.

In April, the Supreme Court ruled that the African Charter on Human and Peoples' Rights and other international treaties took precedence over domestic law. This overturned a March 1996 ruling by the Federal High Court that international legal obligations were overruled by military decrees which prohibited recourse to the courts. Human rights lawyer Gani Fawehinmi had challenged his detention without charge or trial from January to November 1996 on the grounds that it violated rights guaranteed by Nigeria's Constitution and the African Charter on Human and Peoples' Rights, incorporated into Nigerian law in 1983.

Killings by the security forces
There were reports that the security forces used excessive force in response to protests against oil company activities and thefts from oil pipelines in the Niger Delta, resulting in several reported fatalities. Earlier killings and ill-treatment by the security forces since May 1999 were not subject to independent investigation. Local human rights organizations expressed concern at persistent reports that suspected armed robbers were killed by the police instead of being prosecuted.

In April police shot dead at least one person, 18-year-old Barinaadua Gbaraka, and burned down homes in K-Dere village in Rivers State after residents opposed a road-building project by the Shell oil company. Several residents were detained and reportedly assaulted. Ledum Mitee, lawyer and leader of the Movement for the Survival of the Ogoni People (MOSOP), was among 11 people subsequently released on bail to await trial on charges including arson and attempted murder. His family home was among those burned. The trials were repeatedly adjourned.

☐ A police task force in Abia State reportedly killed at least three people in the Osisioma area suspected of stealing fuel from ruptured pipelines: in May Sunday Benjamin, in June Ikechi Nwogu and in October Egbulefu Ugwuzor. In September and November the task force was alleged to have looted and burned property of relatives or associates of suspected fuel thieves.

☐ House of Assembly representatives in Delta State reported that in September members of a paramilitary police unit had fired indiscriminately at residents of several villages, burned and ransacked homes, and looted property.

☐ In October at least eight youths were reportedly killed when troops guarding an oil facility belonging to the Agip oil company fired on protesters from the nearby town of Olugbobiri, Bayelsa State. About 50 youths in speedboats had reportedly intended to shut down production after disagreements over a road-building project.

☐ The Benue State authorities said that a judicial commission of inquiry would investigate the reported killing of 10 people by members of a federal paramilitary police unit in December. Raids on villages in the Mbalim and Mbasombo districts reportedly took place after community leaders reported pipeline leakages and contamination of farmland and waterways to the Nigerian National Petroleum Corporation.

Cruel, inhuman or degrading punishment

At least one amputation and several floggings were carried out. New laws introduced or announced in 10 northern states during 2000 provided harsh corporal punishments for offences including theft, sexual offences, consumption of alcohol and gambling. Several men and at least one woman were publicly flogged for offences which included smoking marijuana, gambling and carrying women on the back of motorcycle taxis.

The federal government did not challenge the unconstitutionality of some of the new state laws, but advised citizens to seek legal redress in the higher courts, including the Supreme Court. However, sentences were often carried out immediately after conviction and most defendants had no defence lawyer or means to bring an appeal.

☐ In February Sani Mamman, aged 18, was given 100 lashes in Zamfara State for having sexual relations outside marriage.

☐ In March a farmer in Zamfara State, Buba Bello Jangebe, had his right hand amputated after being convicted of stealing a cow. He failed to appeal against the sentence within the allotted 30 days.

☐ In August Sule Sale received 86 lashes for drinking alcohol and stealing cigarettes in Katsina State.

☐ In September, 17-year-old Bariya Ibrahim Magazu was sentenced to 100 lashes for having sex outside marriage. Unable to produce sufficient witnesses to substantiate her allegation that she had been coerced into having sex with three men, one of whom had made her pregnant, she was sentenced to a further 80 lashes for her accusations against the three men, which were judged to be false.

Political imprisonment

Supporters of opposition groups were arrested and charged with offences, sometimes following unrest, in circumstances suggesting that their detentions were politically motivated.

☐ In May, 54 supporters of the Movement for the Actualisation of the Sovereign State of Biafra (MASSOB) were arrested in Aba, Abia State, and charged with treasonable felony and unlawful assembly. They were alleged to have conspired to overthrow the government by declaring an independent state. In August a magistrates' court struck out the charges of treasonable felony on the grounds that the court lacked jurisdiction to try a federal offence and granted them bail on the charges of unlawful assembly.

☐ In early September Alhaji Sule Zurmi, an opposition party leader in Zamfara State, was arrested with 17 supporters and detained for more than two weeks. Charged with responsibility for an attack on the State Governor's convoy in which a number of people were injured, their arrest and prosecution were criticized by federal government officials as arbitrary and politically motivated. They were released pending trial.

☐ In October the authorities arrested scores of suspected supporters of the O'odua People's Congress (OPC), an organization set up to defend the interests of the Yoruba ethnic group. They were charged with offences including murder, arson and illegal possession of arms, in connection with unrest in Lagos and Ilorin, southwest Nigeria, in which more than 100 people, mostly from the Hausa community, died. Dr Frederick Fasehun, a leading OPC member, was released on bail by the Lagos High Court after three weeks. Immediately rearrested to face similar charges in Ilorin, he was again released on bail by a magistrates' court in Ilorin. The Lagos High Court subsequently dismissed the charges against him for lack of evidence.

Death penalty

No death sentences or executions were known to have been imposed during 2000. In January President Olusegun Obasanjo granted an amnesty to prisoners under sentence of death: those who had been awaiting execution for 20 years were to be pardoned and released; those under sentence of death for between 10 and 20 years were to have their sentences commuted to life imprisonment.

In December the government reportedly proposed to reintroduce capital punishment for the sabotage of fuel and power supply networks.

Impunity

Trials

The trial of five former security officials, including former Chief of Army Staff General Ishaya Bamaiyi, continued. They were charged with the attempted murder in February 1996 of Alex Ibru, newspaper publisher and former government minister. The state's main prosecution witness, a former army sergeant, told the High Court in Lagos that he and a senior police officer had fired at Alex Ibru. He said he had been part of a hit squad acting on the orders of superior officers.

No evidence was heard in two cases against former security officers and Mohammed Abacha, son of former head of state General Sani Abacha. They were charged in connection with the shooting dead in June 1996 of Kudirat Abiola, wife of the imprisoned winner of the 1993 presidential elections, Moshood Abiola, and the unexplained death in custody in December 1997 of Shehu Musa Yar'Adua, a former deputy head of state.

Human Rights Violations Investigation Commission
In October the Human Rights Violations Investigation Commission, set up in June 1999, began hearing evidence from witnesses to human rights violations committed between 1966 and the return to civilian rule in May 1999. From more than 11,000 petitions received, it selected about 150 of the most serious cases for public hearing in five sessions in Abuja and other major cities.

Witnesses before the Commission described killings and torture by agents of the military government of General Sani Abacha (1993 to 1998). Former Captain U.S.A. Suleiman described being held in an unventilated and unlit cell and forced to stand all night by being chained hand and foot to a wall. Former Colonel Gabriel Ajayi described being tied up, hung from the ceiling and beaten. Both had been detained in connection with an alleged coup plot in 1995. The family of Alfred Rewane, a 79-year-old opposition supporter murdered in 1995, alleged that senior security officials had told a military investigation in 1998 of a government conspiracy to kill him and that supposed suspects arrested by the police had since died in custody. A former police commissioner told the Commission that security police had planted explosives to incriminate an airport manager killed in a car bomb explosion at Lagos international airport in 1996. This and other bomb blasts were widely believed to have been the work of the security services and were used as a pretext to imprison pro-democracy activists. Security officials denied the most serious accusations or refused to appear before the Commission. In December former head of state General Ibrahim Babangida and former military and police security chiefs obtained a High Court injunction restraining the Commission from compelling them to appear before it, on the grounds that their personal security would be at risk. They had been invited to give evidence about the alleged extrajudicial execution in 1986 of Dele Giwa, editor of *Newswatch* magazine.

AI country report and visit
Report
- Nigeria: Time for justice and accountability (AI Index: AFR 44/014/2000)

Visit
An AI delegation visited Nigeria in July for talks with government officials and for meetings with local AI members and other human rights groups.

PAKISTAN

ISLAMIC REPUBLIC OF PAKISTAN
Head of state: Mohammad Rafiq Tarar
Head of government: General Pervez Musharraf
Capital: Islamabad
Population: 156.5 million
Official languages: English and Urdu
Death penalty: retentionist

Despite the government's stated commitment to human rights protection, human rights violations including torture and deaths in custody increased during 2000. Minorities were not given adequate protection when religiously motivated violence flared up. Violence against women and children continued at a high level. Political activities remained restricted following a ban on public activities in March. Activists contravening the ban were detained and some were charged with sedition. Several people detained at the time of the coup remained in unlawful detention. The death penalty was frequently imposed, but was banned for juveniles.

Background
The military government under Chief Executive Pervez Musharraf presented a comprehensive reform program to fight corruption and prepare for local elections by December, and a human rights agenda that focused on the protection of women, children and minorities. However, various groups, especially Islamist groups, exerted considerable pressure on the government and several initiatives were reversed.

In January, judges of the higher judiciary were asked to take an oath on the Provisional Constitutional Order (PCO) of 1999 which had suspended the Constitution. The Chief Justice and five Supreme Court judges refused to take the oath and seven High Court judges were not asked to take it. The Supreme Court in May declared the military takeover of October 1999 valid under the doctrine of necessity and gave the government three years to complete its declared objectives.

In April, former prime minister Nawaz Sharif was convicted of hijacking a plane and other offences and sentenced to two terms of life imprisonment. His co-accused were acquitted. The trial before an anti-terrorism court did not fully meet standards for fair trial. In July, Nawaz Sharif was sentenced to 14 years' imprisonment and disqualified from holding public office for concealing the purchase of a helicopter. In December Nawaz Sharif was pardoned in both cases and exiled, according to the government on "humanitarian grounds".

Political arrests and detention
Following a ban in March on political activities in public, dozens of political activists were arrested for breaches of the ban. Most were released within a short

time but several politicians of the Pakistan Muslim League were charged with sedition for making speeches criticizing the military government. All were freed on bail.

Some members of the previous government continued to be detained without charge or trial. Former minister for information Mushahid Hussain, who was arrested in October 1999, was held under house arrest, although there were no charges against him. In July, he was cleared of any suspicion of corruption. He was released in December.

The government in September announced a review of the cases of members of the *Muttahida Qaumi Movement* (MQM) who had been held for over five years without trial. Other people charged under previous governments continued to face trial. Rehmat Shah Afridi, editor-in-chief of *The Frontier Post*, arrested in April 1999, continued to be tried on drugs charges although the prosecution failed to produce any compelling evidence against him. Before his arrest, his newspaper had documented official corruption. He appeared to be a prisoner of conscience.

Dozens of activists and others were detained without charge or trial, most often to extract money from them. Many such detainees were tortured.

☐ Two children, 12-year-old Madad Ali and 14-year-old Sanjar, were discovered on 6 October by High Court officials in a police station in Hyderabad. Their brother had filed a petition alleging that they had been held without charge since 14 September and that police had demanded money for their release. Forty other people who had not been charged were found in that police station. No action was known to be taken against the police officers involved.

Anti-corruption trials

The anti-corruption drive did not always uphold the rights of the accused. Corruption charges were brought under the National Accountability Bureau Ordinance (NAB) of 1999 against dozens of bureaucrats, businessmen and former politicians. Several NAB provisions contravene international standards for fair trial, including one allowing detainees to be held for up to 90 days in executive, not judicial, custody; a requirement that detainees prove their innocence; and the denial of bail. Some NAB detainees were held for longer than 90 days, were reportedly detained and interrogated by military personnel, and were denied access to lawyers and family.

Torture/ill-treatment

Torture in police custody and jails, often of people held in unlawful detention, continued to be widespread, leading to at least 25 deaths.

☐ Mushtaque Maseeh was arrested on 31 July by police in Hyderabad because of a property dispute. He was beaten severely and suffered a skull fracture. When his condition deteriorated, he was released on 1 August. Doctors in the Civil Hospital noted marks of beating on his head, neck and torso. He died on 8 August after an operation. A judicial inquiry identified the official responsible and ordered him to be charged with murder, but he had reportedly not been arrested by the end of 2000.

Children

Abuses of children in custody continued to be reported. Members of the Lahore High Court Bar Association who visited Lahore Camp Jail noted sexual abuse of juvenile detainees by staff and inmates. In Hyderabad Central Jail, some 50 juvenile prisoners who had been regularly sexually abused by adult convicts were discovered by a new jail administration in September. They were transferred to the juvenile ward and disciplinary action against prison staff was announced.

Extrajudicial executions

Extrajudicial executions of criminal suspects declined sharply compared to previous years. Eighteen cases were reported. Victims of extrajudicial executions were mostly criminal suspects.

☐ Mumtaz, who was riding a bicycle in the early hours of 30 September in Karachi, was shot dead by police officers on a motorbike when he refused to stop at their signal. They claimed that Mumtaz had opened fire at them. The police officers were arrested for exceeding their powers but it is not known if they were charged.

In October, a Punjab police report detailing hundreds of killings by police during so-called "encounters" since 1990 was presented to the provincial government for further investigation. Between February 1997 and October 1999, 967 criminal suspects were killed by police in "encounters" in Punjab province.

Lack of protection for religious minorities

In April, the Chief Executive announced procedural changes to the blasphemy law, which carries a mandatory death penalty, to prevent its misuse. One month later, following protests by Islamists, the amendment was withdrawn. At least 60 people were charged with religious offences. About half of these were detained as prisoners of conscience.

☐ In August, Yousuf Ali was sentenced to death for blasphemy after a manifestly unfair trial amid media vilification. He denied ever having claimed to be a prophet of Islam as alleged. Several prosecution witnesses admitted that they had not fully understood what the Sufi mystic taught. His appeal was pending.

☐ At least a dozen members of the Ahmadiyya community were killed by people opposing their beliefs. In November, five Ahmadis including two children were killed by a mob in Sargodha district and their bodies mutilated with axes. No one was arrested. Although the police were asked for help as tension built up before the incident, they took no protective or preventive steps. A judicial inquiry was set up.

Women

In August the National Commission on the Status of Women was set up to protect women's rights, but it had no enforcement powers, contrary to earlier government commitments. Its chairperson announced the setting up of a national ombudsperson for women's issues and stated that laws discriminating against women would be amended.

In October, the Interior Minister said that "all discriminatory laws against women should be repealed or amended to remove any discrimination against women". Women's rights activists and a Senate-ordered study published in 1997 had identified the Zina Ordinance as discriminating against women, but no action to amend laws was taken during 2000.

'Honour' killings

The Chief Executive, General Pervez Musharraf, announced in April that "killing in the name of honour is murder and will be treated as such". In August, a governmental legal aid unit was set up in Larkana to ensure that honour killings would be treated as murder. In the absence of public awareness raising, these innovations had no impact on the rising trend of violence against women, including honour crimes. Scores of honour killings were reported from all parts of the country.

☐ In November, a man in Karachi who suspected his 11-year-old daughter of having an illicit affair axed her to death. When her mother and nine-year-old sister tried to protect her, he killed them too. He gave himself up to police stating that he had no regrets as "it was a question of honour".

Children

Children were subjected to abuses in custody and in the community, for instance as child labourers or bonded labourers. Domestic violence against children, including sexual abuse, remained widespread. The state made virtually no attempt to prevent these abuses or to hold the perpetrators to account.

The Juvenile Justice System Ordinance 2000 was promulgated in July, establishing juvenile courts to try juvenile suspects. It bans the death penalty for anyone less than 18 at the time of the alleged offence as well as the use of fetters and corporal punishment. The Ordinance contains no reference to around 50 juveniles already under sentence of death.

☐ Mohammad Saleem, who was around 14 at the time of an alleged murder in June 1998, was sentenced to death in December 1998 by a military court. He was acquitted in January 1999, tried and sentenced to death again in June 1999 — despite the prohibition of double jeopardy. He remained in a death cell with adult convicts as his appeal remained undecided.

Death penalty

At least 52 people were sentenced to death, the majority for murder, many by special courts whose procedures do not fully conform to international standards for fair trial. A verdict in March sentencing Javed Iqbal to be publicly strangled, cut into pieces and thrown into acid for the serial killing and mutilation of dozens of runaway children was opposed by human rights activists. The Council of Islamic Ideology declared it un-Islamic. An appeal was pending.

Three men due to be executed in April in Gujrat, Punjab province, for killing four people in a domestic dispute in 1989 were released when the family of the victims pardoned them and accepted compensation under the qisas and diyat law. Many others who could not offer adequate compensation continued to be held in death cells, sometimes for many years. There were nearly 4,000 people on death row.

At least six people were hanged. In April, Pakistan voted against a UN Commission on Human Rights resolution condemning the death penalty and calling for a reduction in executions.

AI visit

AI delegates were invited by the government to the Convention on Human Rights and Human Dignity in April and met several officials to discuss aspects of the human rights program. The delegates earlier travelled to different parts of Pakistan to research the human rights situation after the military takeover.

PALESTINIAN AUTHORITY

PALESTINIAN AUTHORITY
President: Yasser 'Arafat
Death penalty: retentionist

More than 360 people, including prisoners of conscience, were arrested for political reasons during 2000; most had been released by the end of the year. Torture and ill-treatment were widespread. At least 300 people arrested in previous years were held without charge or trial, including people suspected of "collaborating" with the Israeli authorities and suspected members of Islamist opposition groups. Large numbers of Islamists, some of whom had been held without charge since 1996, were released in September and October. State Security Courts continued to sentence political detainees after unfair trials. Three people were sentenced to death. The Palestinian Authority (PA) failed to bring those responsible for human rights abuses to justice.

Background

Peace negotiations between Israel and the Palestine Liberation Organization (PLO) continued until October. The Camp David summit, involving President Yasser 'Arafat, Israeli Prime Minister Ehud Barak and US President Bill Clinton ended in July without a peace agreement having been achieved. Negotiations between Israel and the PLO broke down following the outbreak in September of a new uprising or Intifada, but resumed in December (see also Israel and the Occupied Territories entry).

Administration of justice

In November Congress passed measures approved in the *Mesa de Diálogo* to restore the functions previously taken away from the National Council of the Magistracy and to abolish the executive commissions of the judiciary and Public Ministry, which had been blatant interference by the executive in the administration of justice. The Attorney General resigned because of her alleged links with Vladimiro Montesinos. Three judges of the Constitutional Tribunal who had been sacked in 1997 were reinstated.

Prisoners of conscience

More than 200 people falsely charged with terrorism-related offences remained in prison at the end of 2000. During President Fujimori's last years in office very few of these prisoners were released despite the findings of the *Ad Hoc* Commission established in 1996. In its final report, published in August, the Commission stated that it considered that 35 prisoners should be pardoned. Two members of the Commission also recommended that a further seven prisoners should be pardoned. However, the Minister of Justice had not made his recommendation by the end of the year. In addition the report stated that the Commission had passed 246 cases to the National Council for Human Rights and that 1,440 cases which had been rejected by the Commission should be reviewed by the Council. The government of Valentín Panigua released 31 prisoners in November and December.

◻ María Montenegro Montenegro, a mother of four, was sentenced to 15 years' imprisonment in 1994 for the terrorism-related crime of "treason". She had already been acquitted twice by two military tribunals. The charges against her were based solely on statements by two *arrepentidos* — members of the armed opposition who supply information leading to the capture of other alleged members in return for exemption from prosecution, or reduction in or remission of their sentences.

Unfair trials

Anti-terrorism legislation continued to allow civilians to be tried by military courts which were neither independent nor impartial. At least 1,800 people had been tried by military courts for the terrorism-related offence of "treason" since 1992. Peru withdrew from the Inter-American Court of Human Rights in 1999, claiming that it could not comply with the Court's ruling that four Chilean citizens convicted of treason by military courts in 1994 had to be retried under international fair trial procedures.

◻ Lori Berenson, a US citizen, was sentenced to life imprisonment in 1996 by a military court. In August 2000, in an unprecedented move and following international pressure, especially from the USA, the military justice system ruled that there had been no evidence to convict her of the terrorism-related offence of "treason" and transferred her case to the ordinary courts. Her trial before a civilian court was continuing at the end of the year.

Intimidation and death threats

Journalists, human rights defenders, members of the opposition and their families were intimidated and threatened. However, there were no signs that the authorities took these threats seriously. It was widely reported that the harassment and intimidation was organized from within the National Intelligence Services (see above).

Torture/ill-treatment

There were reports of torture and ill-treatment and dozens of deaths in custody as a result. Methods of torture reported included beatings, electric shocks, submerging the prisoner's head in water and sexual assault.

Prison conditions remained harsh and in many cases amounted to cruel, inhuman or degrading treatment.
◻ The prison of Challapalca was located at over 4,600 metres above sea level in the department of Puno. Access to lawyers, relatives and medical attention was seriously hindered by the remote location.
◻ Conditions at a prison located in the Callao Naval Base near Lima remained harsh. Leaders of the two armed opposition groups — *Movimiento Revolucionario Túpac Amaru* (MRTA), Túpac Amaru Revolutionary Movement, and *Sendero Luminoso*, Shining Path — were held in solitary confinement in underground cells and had no direct contact with their relatives during the visits which were only allowed once a month.

UN Human Rights Committee

In October, the Human Rights Committee reviewed Peru's fourth periodic report. The Committee recommended that the 1995 amnesty laws be annulled and that the authorities refrain from adopting a new amnesty law in the future. The Committee also urged the Peruvian authorities to ensure the independence and impartiality of judges and to create a mechanism guaranteed by law which would prevent the executive interfering in the judicial system. In addition the Committee urged the government to review all cases of civilians who had been tried by military tribunals and deplored the fact that the military justice system continued to be able to try civilians. The Committee expressed its concern at conditions in Lurigancho prison in Lima and at Yanamayo and Challapalca prisons in Puno department. Finally the Committee urged the Peruvian government, among other things, to respect freedom of expression in all circumstances.

AI country reports and visits
Reports

- Peru: Breaking the circle of impunity and restoring the rule of law in Peru – Tasks which must be undertaken without delay during the transition (joint statement by AI and the International Commission of Jurists) (AI Index: AMR 46/038/2000)
- Peru: UN Human Rights Committee's recommendations must be implemented (AI Index: AMR 46/037/2000)

• Peru: Torture continues unabated (AI Index: AMR 46/40/2000)

Visit
In November, prior to President Alberto Fujimori's dismissal, a joint delegation from AI and the International Commission of Jurists visited Peru. The delegates met with the members of the *Mesa de Diálogo*, the Attorney General, the Ombudsman, and staff of the human rights division of the Ministry of Foreign Affairs. The Minister of the Interior and the Minister of Justice did not agree to a meeting with the delegation.

PHILIPPINES

REPUBLIC OF THE PHILIPPINES
Head of state and government: Joseph Estrada
Capital: Manila
Population: 71.5 million
Official languages: Pilipino, English
Death penalty: retentionist
2000 treaty signatures/ratifications: Optional Protocol to the UN Children's Convention on the involvement of children in armed conflict; Optional Protocol to the UN Women's Convention; Rome Statute of the International Criminal Court

An escalation of armed conflict in central Mindanao led to the displacement of over 400,000 civilians amid reports of indiscriminate bombings and human rights violations by the Armed Forces of the Philippines (AFP). The Moro Islamic Liberation Front (MILF) withdrew from the peace process following the capture of its main bases. Tensions in the region intensified further following a series of kidnappings of civilians by the *Abu Sayyaf* armed group on the Sulu archipelago. After protracted negotiations, military assaults on *Abu Sayyaf* positions on Jolo island led to the displacement of thousands of civilians and reports of human rights violations. One person was executed before President Joseph Estrada announced a temporary moratorium on executions in March. In December President Estrada commuted 13 death sentences after declaring his support for the abolition of the death penalty. There were continued reports of the torture and ill-treatment of criminal suspects, including women, to coerce confessions.

Background
Armed conflict in the Mindanao region, including the protracted *Abu Sayyaf* hostage crisis, increased pressure on President Estrada's administration. Intermittent clashes with units of the communist armed opposition group the New People's Army (NPA), or with NPA breakaway factions including the Alex Boncayao Brigade (ABB), continued in various provinces nationwide. In December, following a local peace agreement with the ABB's political wing, President Estrada pledged to release over 200 political prisoners convicted or being prosecuted for offences allegedly committed within the context of armed insurgency. Political uncertainty intensified in November as allegations of corruption led the House of Representatives to impeach President Estrada. An impeachment trial in the Senate was continuing at the end of 2000. Falls in the value of the currency heightened fears of an economic downturn.

Armed conflict in Mindanao
Moro Islamic Liberation Front
Armed conflict intensified in central Mindanao from April. AFP offensives resulted in the capture of a series of MILF bases, including the group's headquarters in July. Over 400,000 civilians were internally displaced amid reports of indiscriminate aerial and artillery bombardment of civilian areas suspected of containing MILF forces, and of extrajudicial executions, "disappearances" and torture of those thought to have links to the MILF. At least 300 civilians were reportedly killed in the conflict.

In July the MILF announced its withdrawal from the peace process and called for a *jihad* (holy war) against the government. Clashes between the AFP and MILF forces continued throughout 2000. Mobilization of expanded local militia units and of Christian civilian vigilante groups escalated tensions. MILF forces were responsible for breaches of international humanitarian law including bombing civilian targets, deliberate and arbitrary killings of civilians and hostage-taking.

Abu Sayyaf
In March, members of *Abu Sayyaf*, a Muslim separatist armed group involved in kidnapping for ransom, took hostage over 50 civilians, mainly schoolchildren, on Basilan island. In May, more than 25 of the remaining hostages were freed after military assaults during which six hostages were reportedly killed by *Abu Sayyaf*. In May, *Abu Sayyaf* units kidnapped 21 foreign tourists and workers from a resort in Sabah (Malaysia) and held them hostage on Jolo island. After protracted negotiations, the seizure of more hostages and the payment of ransoms, some of the hostages were freed. In September, after the kidnap of three other Malaysians, the AFP launched assaults on *Abu Sayyaf* positions on Jolo, imposing a temporary media and travel ban on the island. At least 80,000 civilians were reported to have fled their homes to escape armed clashes and bombardments, often apparently indiscriminate. Although difficult to corroborate, there were persistent reports of human rights violations by the military, including extrajudicial executions, arbitrary arrests and "disappearances" of suspected *Abu Sayyaf* members. Military operations continued at the end of 2000 as at least two hostages remained in captivity.

Torture/ill-treatment
Reports of torture and ill-treatment of detainees by police and AFP personnel continued. Victims included

both those suspected of links with communist or Muslim armed opposition groups and ordinary criminal suspects, including women and minors. Methods reported included beatings with fists and gun butts, electro-shocks, partial suffocation, rape and sexual abuse. Safeguards such as valid warrants of search and arrest, and the right of detainees to have access to lawyers and relatives during custodial investigation, were not implemented effectively.

□ In May, nine Muslim men who had been arrested, reportedly without valid warrants, on suspicion of links to a series of bombings in shopping malls in Manila alleged that they were kicked and beaten by police in an attempt to coerce confessions.

□ At least seven female detainees reported that they had been raped or sexually abused in custody. In April, two police officers were reportedly arrested for raping an 18-year-old woman detained for alleged vagrancy.

Extrajudicial executions
Criminal suspects were periodically killed by police while allegedly "resisting arrest" or "attempting to escape". Suspected members of the NPA were reported to have been extrajudicially executed, some while wounded, in the aftermath of clashes with AFP units.

□ In June murder charges were filed against 10 members of a police unit who shot dead two Muslim men in Manila during an arrest operation against suspected MILF sympathizers.

Death penalty
In January Alex Bartolome, convicted of raping his daughter, became the seventh person to be executed by lethal injection since the Philippines resumed executions in 1999. Death sentences continued to be imposed throughout the year, and over 1,400 prisoners were reported to be under sentence of death by the end of 2000. Concerns that people were sentenced to death after unfair trials continued, particularly in light of allegations that police tortured and ill-treated criminal suspects in order to coerce confessions or to implicate alleged accomplices.

In March President Estrada declared a temporary moratorium on executions to mark the Christian Jubilee year. In December he announced his intention to commute at least 107 death sentences confirmed by the Supreme Court. Thirteen commutation orders had been signed by the end of 2000. Noting that most of those sentenced to death were poor and underprivileged, President Estrada declared his support for a congressional review and the eventual repeal of the death penalty law.

AI country reports and visits
Report
- Philippines: The Rolando Abadilla murder inquiry – an urgent need for effective investigation of torture (AI Index: ASA 35/008/2000)

AI also issued a series of statements calling on all sides of the Mindanao conflict to respect international humanitarian and human rights law. The organization condemned hostage-taking by armed opposition groups.

Visits
AI delegates visited the Philippines in March and June to research the torture and ill-treatment in detention of political and criminal suspects, including women and children.

POLAND

REPUBLIC OF POLAND
Head of state: Aleksander Kwaśniewski
Head of government: Jerzy Buzek
Capital: Warsaw
Population: 38.7 million
Official language: Polish
Death penalty: abolitionist for all crimes
2000 treaty ratifications/signatures: Second Optional Protocol to the International Covenant on Civil and Political Rights, aiming at the abolition of the death penalty; Protocol No. 6 to the European Convention on Human Rights concerning the abolition of the death penalty

There were reports of arbitrary detention and ill-treatment in "sobering-up" centres. The authorities appeared to condone the ill-treatment of new recruits to the army. Some Roma were inadequately protected from racist violence.

Arbitrary detention and ill-treatment
There was concern that a 1982 law which allows people to be held for up to 24 hours in "sobering-up centres" was used by police officers to detain people arbitrarily. Under this law, detention is not subjected to judicial review. Many of those detained under this law complained that they were ill-treated by officers working in the centres, but investigations appeared to have been conducted only in cases of grave injury or death in custody.

□ In April the European Court of Human Rights ruled that the detention of Witold Litwa had been in violation of the European Convention for the Protection of Human Rights and Fundamental Freedoms. Witold Litwa had been arrested by police officers in a post office in Kraków in May 1994, following a complaint by postal clerks that he was drunk and behaving offensively. He was then taken by police officers to a "sobering-up" centre where he was beaten by police officers and ill-treated by staff.

□ In May, 28-year-old Robert M. was stopped by police at a railway station in Warsaw and taken to the "sobering-up" centre in Kolska Street. According to the police, he was so drunk he could not travel on his own. It later came to light that he had a relatively low level of alcohol in his blood and that during a medical examination he had been conscious, in good physical condition with a normal pulse and blood pressure. In the morning he was taken unconscious to a hospital where he died following an operation in which a haematoma was removed from his brain. The doctor who operated on him reportedly said: "He didn't stand a chance. If he was conscious on entering the 'sobering-up centre', his injuries must have happened there." An investigation into Robert M.'s death was reportedly under way at the end of the year.

Army recruits

The humiliation and abuse of new recruits was believed to be endemic in the army. The Polish Helsinki Foundation for Human Rights expressed concern that military commanders failed to tackle the routine ill-treatment of younger soldiers.

☐ In February Polish television broadcast a documentary film about the 25th Air Cavalry Brigade, based at Tomaszów Mazowiecki. The documentary showed non-commissioned officers tormenting conscripts with verbal abuse, and humiliating them during training. In April, two corporals of this brigade were reportedly convicted by a military court for forcing two conscripts who were caught smoking to perform press-ups while wearing gas masks containing 10 lighted cigarettes.

☐ In February, seven former senior conscripts went on trial before the Szczecin Garrison Court for forcing younger colleagues to "play sheep", which involved crawling around on the floor and hitting their heads against the wall. Junior conscripts were also forced to wear dog collars and walk on a lead, and were undressed and sexually assaulted.

Roma

In June the Council of Europe's European Commission against Racism and Intolerance expressed concern about racially motivated violence against Roma. The Commission noted that according to some reports, the police response to such acts was slow and investigations inadequate. The Commission also expressed concern about allegations of police violence and called on the authorities to investigate all alleged malpractice and to punish offenders.

☐ In August, in Tarnów, two masked men broke into the home of Agata Ciureja, a 32-year-old Romani mother of six, and attacked her with an axe, causing injuries which required hospitalization. Agata Ciureja told a local Romani organization that she believed that the attackers were members of a group of about 20 skinheads who had broken into her apartment about three weeks previously, in an attempt to scare her out of the neighbourhood. At the time the police detained two suspects who were subsequently released. Following the second attack Agata Ciureja went into hiding.

PORTUGAL

PORTUGUESE REPUBLIC
Head of state: Jorge Fernando Branco de Sampaio
Head of government: António Manuel de Oliveira Guterres
Capital: Lisbon
Population: 9.8 million
Official language: Portuguese
Death penalty: abolitionist for all crimes
2000 treaty ratifications/signatures: Optional Protocol to the UN Children's Convention on the involvement of children in armed conflict; Optional Protocol to the UN Women's Convention

Several deaths in, or immediately following, police custody were reported. The arrest of two police officers in connection with a homicide charge prompted angry street protests by police, and a prosecuting magistrate claimed to have been severely intimidated by some officers. Allegations of police ill-treatment and of cruel, inhuman and degrading conditions in prisons persisted. Judicial inquiries continued into previous allegations of police ill-treatment.

Background

In a year marked by serious allegations of police brutality, the UN Committee against Torture urged Portugal to shift "police culture" further towards respect for human rights. A range of legal and regulatory initiatives were undertaken. They included the establishment in May of a working group, coordinated by an inspector of the Interior Ministry's police oversight body, the General Inspectorate of Internal Administration (IGAI), to draw up an ethical code for the Public Security Police (PSP) and National Republican Guard (GNR). Practical measures to combat police violence included plans to install video cameras in all police stations and to close detention cells in police stations, concentrating them in the divisional buildings of the PSP, where detainees could be placed under the surveillance of officers of higher rank. The Justice Ministry confirmed that a new prison inspectorate was being created. This would, among other things, receive and examine complaints from prisoners. Its work was complemented by magistrates who carried out monthly visits to prisons and who were able to receive complaints.

Deaths in or after police custody

At least three judicial investigations were opened into deaths in or after police custody. In January, two men died in separate incidents, on the same night and in the same city, allegedly after being severely beaten by PSP officers. In all three deaths the cause was attributed to a ruptured spleen.

☐ Álvaro Rosa Cardoso, a Rom, was allegedly beaten severely with truncheons and pistol-whipped by police who had been called to a street disturbance in the Aldoar area of Oporto. After being held in custody at Pinheiro Manso police station, he was taken to the Hospital de Santo António, where he died. Varying versions were given of the death. Álvaro Cardoso was said to have been injured in a street fight before the arrival of the police. He was also said to have injured himself in a fall at the station and to have died of one or two heart attacks. After the Commander of the PSP of Oporto endorsed the police version that death was caused by a heart attack, the cause of death was found, on the contrary, to have been a ruptured spleen. Criminal and disciplinary procedures were opened and the Commander replaced. According to the Interior Ministry there was evidence of "violence inflicted by one or more PSP officers". Two officers were provisionally detained and examined in connection with a homicide charge.

In April PSP officers reportedly made death threats against a prosecuting magistrate after a judge's decision not to release the two officers. Because no formal complaint was lodged by the magistrate, no judicial investigation was undertaken. The threats took place against a background of angry street protests by police throughout Portugal, some of whom surrendered their weapons and wept openly.

In October, almost six months after the detentions, the Oporto criminal court (TIC) ordered the closure of the case on grounds of lack of evidence. A relative of Álvaro Cardoso, 17-year-old Franquelim Romão, who had been arrested with him, and had reportedly testified to the beating, remained the sole defendant in the proceeding, accused of assaulting PSP officers. The prosecutor appealed against the court decision, which was reportedly based largely on the testimony of nine witnesses, many of whom were police officers who had originally been suspects, and on a particular interpretation of the opinion of a forensic specialist that the spleen was not a "vital" organ.

☐ On the same night in January Paulo Silva died of internal injuries after complaining to his mother that he had been badly beaten by PSP officers in the Cerco area shortly before. He was taken to the Hospital de São João with a ruptured spleen. Nine officers remained under investigation in connection with the death. A separate internal inquiry was being conducted into an apparent attempt by the officer in command of the police unit involved to falsify paperwork.

☐ Judicial and IGAI inquiries were also being carried out into the death of António Mendes dos Santos, who died about 10 days after being held at a police station at Coimbra in June. He too was reported to have died from injuries to the spleen.

Police ill-treatment

New allegations of police ill-treatment were reported and various judicial investigations continued into previously reported cases of police brutality.

☐ Judicial and disciplinary inquiries were opened into the alleged ill-treatment of Mário João Augusto Rocha, a young black man who claimed that in February he was assaulted by PSP officers who intercepted him while he was walking to his girlfriend's home at Arroja, Odivelas. According to Mário Rocha he was punched and slapped by plainclothes officers both before and after being taken to the police station at Odivelas, where he was also racially abused. He was asked only later for his identity papers. He was subsequently treated at the Hospital de Santa María. He lodged a complaint with the PSP of Santo António dos Cavaleiros, Loures.

☐ In December Mozambican national Cândido Ventura Coelho, who suffers from a mental disability, and his 17-year-old brother, José Carlos Coelho, were taken to the PSP station in Damaia, near Lisbon, to be identified and questioned. Cândido Coelho, who had become a little muddled during questioning, was reportedly taken into a bathroom by an officer who pushed his head against a wall and punched him repeatedly in the face and head until a second officer intervened. Cândido Coelho was subsequently treated in hospital. His complaint was being investigated by the Judicial Police at the end of the year.

Prisons

Ill-treatment by prison guards — mainly beatings — inhuman and degrading conditions, and cases of medical neglect continued to be reported. Many such reports were received about Linhó prison, Sintra. Prisoners suffering from illnesses, often with HIV/AIDS, alleged inadequate access to medical treatment, medical neglect and disregard of their dietary needs. The Justice Ministry informed AI that the rate of overcrowding was diminishing and that out of a total of 1,164 inquiries into complaints during 1998-99, only 117 related to alleged acts of violence by prison staff. Twenty-three prison officers (out of a total of approximately 4,000) were punished with dismissal or compulsorily retired. These punishments did not all relate to assaults on prisoners.

The UN Committee against Torture

In May the UN Committee against Torture examined Portugal's third periodic report on its compliance with the provisions of the Convention against Torture. The Committee expressed concern about continuing reports of deaths in custody and police ill-treatment and persisting reports of inter-prisoner violence. The Committee urged Portugal to ensure in particular that the criminal investigation and prosecution of public officials, such as police officers, were undertaken as a "*matter of course*", where the evidence revealed the commission of torture or cruel, inhuman or degrading treatment or punishment. AI submitted a report to the Committee. It summarized AI's main concerns about death and ill-treatment in police custody and in prisons and about cases of effective impunity and excessive use of force by law enforcement officers between 1997 and the beginning of 2000. AI acknowledged the positive contribution made by IGAI to the monitoring and supervision of the activities of the PSP and GNR. Nevertheless, IGAI could not conduct its own disciplinary investigations, or impose its own penalties, and questions remained over the thoroughness of some of the inquiries carried out.

AI country report
- Portugal: Small problems ...? A summary of concerns (AI Index: EUR 38/001/2000)

QATAR

STATE OF QATAR
Head of state: al-Shaikh Hamad Ibn Khalifa Al-Thani
Head of government: al-Shaikh Abdullah Ibn Khalifa Al-Thani
Capital: Doha
Population: 0.6 million
Official language: Arabic
Death penalty: retentionist
2000 treaty ratifications/signatures: UN Convention against Torture

The trial of more than 100 people charged with involvement in the failed coup attempt of 1996 was concluded. At least 33 defendants received lengthy prison sentences. One political detainee, 'Abd al-Rahman bin 'Amir al-Na'imi, remained held without charge or trial for a third consecutive year. At least three people were executed in the first executions recorded by AI in more than 10 years.

International human rights treaties
In January Qatar acceded to the UN Convention against Torture. This was the third major international human rights instrument to which Qatar has become a party. The others are the UN Children's Convention and the UN Convention against Racism.

Coup trial
At least 33 people were sentenced to life imprisonment for their involvement in the failed coup attempt of 1996. Of the 33 convicted, nine had been tried *in absentia*. A total of 85 other defendants were acquitted. In previous years AI expressed concern that many of the defendants in this trial were allegedly tortured to force them to confess. To AI's knowledge, there was no investigation into these allegations. AI had no details of the evidence on which the defendants were convicted. Both the defence and the prosecution launched appeals against the sentences.

Fahd 'Abdullah Jasim Al-Malki, one of the defendants sentenced to life imprisonment, had been forcibly returned to Qatar from Yemen in August 1998. He was allegedly beaten while under interrogation.

Detention without trial
'Abd al-Rahman bin 'Amir al-Na'imi continued to be held without charge or trial and without the opportunity to challenge the legality of his detention in a court of law. He was arrested in June 1998, after he sent a petition to the members of the Consultative Council (*Majlis al-Shura*), in which he criticized aspects of government policy. The government has failed to respond to AI's repeated requests for clarification of his legal status.

Torture/ill-treatment
AI continued to receive reports of torture and ill-treatment.

Mazen al-Khatib, a United Kingdom national, was allegedly tortured while awaiting trial after his arrest in December 1999. Mazen al-Khatib was alleged to have been forced to lie for seven hours on his back, with his hands handcuffed behind his back, and beaten around the neck and head with a stick. The government failed to respond to AI's request that these allegations be fully investigated.

Executions
Two men, Qader Aktar Hassan and Anis Qassem Dahnassi, and a woman, Fatima Yussef al-Din Sayed, all Indian nationals, were executed on 14 June in Doha prison. According to AI's records, these were the first executions in the country for more than 10 years. The last execution recorded by AI took place in October 1988.

ROMANIA

ROMANIA
Head of state: Ion Iliescu (replaced Emil Constantinescu in December)
Head of government: Arian Năstase (replaced Mugur Isărescu in December)
Capital: Bucharest
Population: 22.5 million
Official language: Romanian
Death penalty: abolitionist for all crimes
2000 treaty ratifications/signatures: Optional Protocol to the UN Children's Convention on the involvement of children in armed conflict; Optional Protocol to the UN Women's Convention

There were numerous reports of torture and ill-treatment by law enforcement officials. The intimidation and harassment of victims and witnesses impeded prompt and impartial investigations. Reforms to improve procedures on the use of force and firearms by police and to establish an independent complaints investigation mechanism had not been initiated by the end of 2000. Reforms to the Penal Code, the Penal Procedure Code, the Law on the Execution of Penal Sentences and legislation governing the police, proposed by the authorities in September 1999, were also not adopted by parliament. Conscientious objectors to military service were threatened with imprisonment.

Background

In November and December, the voters returned to power Ion Iliescu and the *Partidul Democrației Sociale din România* (PDSR), Social Democratic Party of Romania, who had been defeated in elections four years earlier. The ruling coalition had failed to deliver promised reforms and to end widespread corruption, and had presided over instability and a further deterioration in living conditions, with close to 40 per cent of the population below the official poverty line.

During the presidential and parliamentary elections the extremist *Partidul România Mare* (PRM), Greater Romania Party, gained significant support, especially among younger voters. The PRM leader, Corneliu Vadim Tudor, had previously made xenophobic and anti-Semitic remarks and had incited intolerance against the ethnic Hungarian and Roma communities. Leaders of the PDSR claimed that they would not seek to form a coalition with the PRM, a party whose support they had enjoyed in the previous 10 years, and with whom they shared government between 1992 and 1996.

Torture/ill-treatment

Ill-treatment and torture by law enforcement officers continued to be widespread. Many incidents occurred during police investigations into criminal complaints, when force was allegedly used to extract "confessions" from suspects. Police often charged their victims with a misdemeanour such as "insulting a police officer" or "disturbing the peace". In a few incidents the police ill-treated peaceful demonstrators or those who engaged in legitimate political activity.

A number of victims of ill-treatment who filed complaints or whose cases were widely publicized were subsequently intimidated and harassed. As a result, some withdrew their complaints. As in the past, the authorities did not acknowledge that harassment took place, failed to provide adequate protection to the complainants and failed to investigate the incidents.

☐ In July Marian Ionel Pavel was summoned to the police station in Ciochina to answer questions about the theft of a horse. When he refused to confess he was reportedly punched, beaten with truncheons and kicked by three police officers. He was subsequently released without charge.

☐ In January Silviu Roșioru and a friend were drinking at a bar on the Buzău-Ploiești road. Silviu Roșioru reportedly made a flippant remark about officers of the Buzău emergency intervention police sub-unit, who were sitting at a nearby table. On hearing it, they allegedly threw him to the floor, handcuffed him, kicked him and beat him with their batons. When he and his friend tried to escape, the police officers dragged Silviu Roșioru out of the taxi-cab and placed him in their van where they beat him on the way to the police station. He was later fined for allegedly insulting the bar staff and refusing to provide identification. His signature on a confession was allegedly forged. As a result of the beating, Silviu Roșioru suffered multiple bruises on his chest, abdomen, thigh and buttock.

☐ In November the PDSR mayor of Târgușor, Constanța county, apprehended three university students who were putting up election posters for *Convenția Democrată din România–2000* (CDR-2000), Democratic Convention of Romania–2000. They were taken to the mayor's office where one of them was allegedly beaten. After they left the town, they were stopped by a local police officer, who reportedly assaulted them and tried to run them down with his vehicle.

Investigations

Although the authorities reportedly initiated investigations into complaints of torture or ill-treatment, in most instances investigations were not conducted promptly and impartially. Complaints were often dismissed on technicalities.

☐ In September, information was received from the Ministry of Justice concerning the investigation into the 1998 police raid in the village of Merișani when six people had been ill-treated. None of the police officers was charged, on the grounds that the victims "did not lodge complaints ... accompanied by medical papers or other evidence". The Ministry did not comment on the fact that investigations into torture and ill-treatment are legally mandatory and not dependent on the victim's consent or ability to provide evidence. In this case the victims could not obtain a forensic medical certificate because the police had kept their identity cards for 11 days. The Ministry of Justice explained the legal procedures for retaining identity cards, but omitted to state whether these rules had been respected in this case.

☐ Another report from the same ministry, concerning the alleged ill-treatment of Dumitru Auraș Marcu and his wife in 1998, contained copies of 16 witness statements, including some by people who had denied any knowledge of the incident when approached after the event by an AI delegate. The statements contained contradictory views on the manner in which the victim had been restrained by police officers, casting doubts on the veracity of the officers' version of events. The authorities did not make public a full report of the investigation which would have explained how the acting prosecutor assessed the evidence when deciding not to charge the suspected officers with any criminal offence.

Failure to reform the police force

The relative impunity enjoyed by police officers who committed human rights violations was in part perpetuated by the government's failure to reform the Ministry of the Interior. The Law on the Status of Police Officers, which would have demilitarized the Ministry of the Interior, and amendments to the Law on the Police Force were not adopted by the end of 2000.

☐ In April, Adrian Pîtu, a former major in the police force, was tried *in absentia* by the Bucharest Military Tribunal on charges of tampering with or destroying documents. He was sentenced to two years' imprisonment. He was apparently charged in violation of his right to freedom of expression following complaints by colleagues whom he had publicly criticized. The sentence was quashed on appeal in November, a month after his case was featured in a BBC radio program. Adrian Pițu joined the police in 1990, following the democratic changes in the country, but soon became disillusioned with the lack of reforms within the police and the growing corruption among his colleagues. In 1997 he publicly urged the newly elected authorities to investigate police abuses, including cases of torture and ill-treatment, and alleged that police gave protection to people with links to organized crime. Shortly after he met the then Minister of the Interior, Gavril Dejeu, Adrian Pițu and his wife started receiving threats. He was also harassed by colleagues and superiors, some of whom initiated criminal proceedings against him on fabricated evidence. He resigned and left the country in July 1998.

Use of firearms by police

Domestic legislation continued to allow officers to shoot "to apprehend a suspect who is caught in the act and attempts to escape without obeying an order to stay at the scene of the crime", in breach of international human rights standards. In September, the Ministry of the Interior issued new instructions on the use of force and firearms which restricted the above provision to cases of "crime, considered as serious". It remained unclear who would assess whether a crime was serious and on what basis.

◻ In May in Bucharest, a 20-year-old Romani man, Mugurel Soare, and his brother were chasing their former brother-in-law when they were stopped by three plainclothes police officers. Mugurel Soare was shot in the head, as a result of which he was paralysed and unable to speak. The officers later stated that Mugurel Soare had been armed with a knife and had stabbed a police officer in the abdomen, and that the officer shot him in self-defence. The officer reported his wound, a scratch, two hours later, but it required no treatment. Two witnesses reported seeing a man in civilian dress beating Mugurel Soare, hitting his head against a wall and sticking the barrel of a pistol against the back of his head. The witnesses were later taken to Bucharest 10th precinct police station, where they were held overnight and questioned by an investigator and police officers in an intimidating way. One witness was allegedly warned that he risked being accused of "incitement to scandal" if he maintained his version of the shooting incident.

Conscientious objectors

Twenty-nine conscientious objectors to military service refused to carry out alternative service because they had reservations about its length and nature, and on the grounds that the law exempts from military service ordained ministers of recognized churches. All were ministers of the Jehovah's Witnesses. They were tried individually by military tribunals of first instance which acquitted all but three of the defendants, finding that the failure to carry out alternative service was not proscribed by any law in force.

Ruling on appeal, the Bucharest Military Tribunal convicted all 29 objectors and sentenced them to different terms of imprisonment. In July the Military Court of Appeal reviewed the cases of 13 of them and sentenced each to 18 months' imprisonment, suspended for a period of three years, six months. The presiding judge published a separate opinion in which he concurred with the first instance courts which had acquitted the conscientious objectors of the charges. In December, the same court acquitted three conscientious objectors, but convicted another and sentenced him to a suspended sentence of 18 months' imprisonment. The grounds for these apparent inconsistencies were not made clear.

Since the adoption in 1996 of the legislation providing for an alternative service, AI has urged the authorities to amend certain legal provisions which are at variance with internationally recognized principles. These provisions concern the grounds for applying for alternative service, its punitive length and restrictions on when applications for alternative service may be submitted.

RUSSIAN FEDERATION

RUSSIAN FEDERATION
Head of state: Vladimir Putin
Head of government: Mikhail Kasyanov
Capital: Moscow
Population: 146.9 million
Official language: Russian
Death penalty: retentionist
2000 treaty ratifications/signatures: Rome Statute of the International Criminal Court

Serious and widespread human rights violations took place in 2000, including grave crimes against civilians on a massive scale during the renewed armed conflict in the Chechen Republic (Chechnya). Russian federal forces were responsible for gross human rights violations against the civilian population of Chechnya. Thousands of civilians were killed in indiscriminate attacks and there were widespread reports of torture, incommunicado detention and summary executions. Few, if any, investigations into these crimes took place and none of those responsible were known to have been prosecuted in 2000. Throughout the Russian Federation, torture and ill-treatment in police custody, in prisons and in the armed forces continued. Prison conditions were cruel, inhuman and degrading. Former prisoners of conscience faced trials. Refugees, asylum-seekers and internally displaced people were not given adequate protection. Conscientious objectors to military service continued to face imprisonment.

Background

2000 saw continuing political and economic instability and a general disregard for the rule of law. Government pressure to limit civil liberties increased against the background of the ongoing war in Chechnya.

Acting President Vladimir Putin won a decisive victory in the March presidential elections. President Putin divided the 89 regions of the Russian Federation into seven administrative regions and appointed representatives — some of them allegedly close friends and supporters from his time as a KGB officer — responsible only to the President. He also pushed through special legislation stripping regional leaders of their seats in the Federation Council.

The Russian authorities repeatedly made inflammatory statements designed to divert public criticism of the government by heightening anti-Chechen sentiment in the country. For example, the authorities repeatedly blamed Chechen "terrorists" for bomb attacks, such as the bombing in Moscow in August, before investigations had produced any evidence as to who was responsible.

The Chechen conflict

The Russian authorities claimed that the situation in Chechnya had normalized following the scaling down of military activities in the first quarter of 2000. However, the human rights crisis in Chechnya continued. There were frequent reports that Russian forces indiscriminately bombed and shelled civilian areas. Chechen civilians, including medical personnel, continued to be the target of military attacks by Russian forces. Hundreds of Chechen civilians and prisoners of war were extrajudicially executed. Journalists and independent monitors continued to be refused access to Chechnya. According to reports, Chechen fighters frequently threatened, and in some cases killed, members of the Russian-appointed civilian administration and executed Russian captured soldiers.

☐ At least 60 civilians were summarily executed in the Noviye Aldy suburb of the Chechen capital, Grozny, by Russian forces during a "cleansing operation" on 5 February.

☐ In March Russian forces launched an attack on a group of up to 60 civilians, mostly women and children, in the village of Samashki. The villagers had been promised a "safe corridor" for one day to allow them to collect food. Despite these assurances, the group came under artillery attack and at least three women were killed and five were wounded.

☐ Andrey Babitsky, a Russian war correspondent working for *Radio Liberty*, went missing in Chechnya while trying to leave the capital Grozny. It later emerged that he had been arrested by the Russian military authorities and was being held incommunicado. On 3 February the Russian authorities announced that Andrey Babitsky had been handed over to Chechen fighters, reportedly in exchange for Russian soldiers held by Chechen forces. On 25 February Andrey Babitsky was found in detention in the Dagestan capital, Makhachkala, from where he was released and flown to Moscow following the intervention of Vladimir Putin.

Andrey Babitsky stated that he had been detained in the Chernokozovo "filtration camp" where he had been beaten with truncheons by Russian guards and heard the screams of other detainees, including a woman, being tortured. He also said that the Russian authorities had handed him over to unidentified Chechens, whom he believed to be collaborating with the Russian authorities, against his will.

Torture in 'filtration camps'

Russian forces continued to detain people in Chechnya at checkpoints and in the territories under their control. Most people were detained during so-called "cleansing operations" in newly occupied towns or during identity checks on civilian convoys travelling from Chechnya to neighbouring Ingushetia. People apprehended by Russian forces were sent to secret "filtration camps" where they were held without access to their relatives, lawyers or the outside world. Survivors of "filtration camps" stated that torture was routine and systematic. There were numerous reports of detainees being raped, beaten with hammers and clubs, given electric shocks or tear gassed. There were also reports that some detainees had their teeth filed down or were beaten around both ears simultaneously to burst the ear-drums. Senior Russian officials continued to deny the existence of "filtration camps" and to claim that no detainees in Chechnya were tortured.

☐ Witnesses stated that a 14-year-old girl, originally from Urus-Martan, died in detention in Chernokozovo at the beginning of the year, allegedly as a result of torture; she had been repeatedly raped by Russian guards. She had reportedly been detained at a checkpoint while travelling on a bus. According to the witnesses, the girl was among 60 women held together in cell number 25 in Chernokozovo, who were subjected to beatings by the guards.

☐ Musa (not his real name), a former detainee in Chernokozovo, stated that a 16-year-old boy called Albert, originally from the village of Davydenko, was brought to his cell after being gang-raped and severely beaten by prison guards. One of his ears had been cut off. Musa believed that up to 10 men were raped in the camp during his 21-day detention. His other cellmates included a man whose hands had been severely burned by prison guards with cigarette lighters and a 17-year-old youth whose teeth had been filed with a metal file and whose lips were shredded, leaving him unable to eat, drink or speak.

Internally displaced people

An estimated 300,000 civilians remained displaced by the conflict, both inside Chechnya and in neighbouring republics. About half were in Ingushetia living in very poor conditions; many lacked adequate shelter and sanitation. Arbitrary official restrictions prevented most from travelling to other territories of the Russian Federation, placing a major strain on Ingushetia's own population.

Persecution of Chechens

Chechens and other people from the Caucasus continued to be arbitrarily detained, ill-treated and tortured in Moscow and other parts of the Russian Federation. In Moscow, Mayor Yury Luzhkov used unconstitutional measures, including the so-called *propiska* (residence permit) system, to expel thousands of Chechens and to deny registration to internally displaced Chechens who had fled the conflict zone. Reports continued to be received that in some cases police fabricated criminal charges against Chechens and planted drugs or weapons on them. In Moscow alone, more than 50 Chechens were sentenced to prison terms despite compelling evidence that the charges against them had been fabricated.

Abuses by Chechen fighters

Dozens of civilian hostages were reportedly held by armed Chechen groups. Two former hostages said they witnessed the killing in February of Vladimir Yatsina, a Russian news agency photojournalist who had been kidnapped in Ingushetia by a Chechen group in July 1999.

The international community

The Russian authorities refused to allow the UN High Commissioner on Human Rights to visit a number of secret "filtration camps" made public by AI. The reasons given were bad weather and security problems.

In April, the Parliamentary Assembly of the Council of Europe voted to suspend the Russian delegation's voting rights and called on its Committee of Ministers to immediately invoke a procedure for the suspension of Russia's membership.

AI urged the UN Commission on Human Rights to call for an international investigation. However, the Commission called for the establishment of a national, broad-based, independent commission, in accordance with recognized international standards; none of the bodies established by the Russian authorities measured up to these standards.

Former prisoners of conscience

⌼ In November the Supreme Court ordered that the case of Grigory Pasko, a journalist and naval captain arrested in 1997 after exposing the Russian navy's illegal dumping of nuclear waste, be reconsidered.

⌼ In April the Supreme Court upheld the acquittal in December 1999 of human rights defender Aleksandr Nikitin. He had been charged with espionage and revealing state secrets for his writings on the risks of radioactive pollution from Russia's Northern Fleet. An appeal against the acquittal by the Prosecutor General was dismissed in September.

Conscientious objectors

There was no civilian alternative to military service and conscientious objectors continued to face imprisonment. Young men who claimed conscientious objection to military service based on their religious beliefs and membership of banned organizations, such as the Jehovah's Witnesses, were often not considered to be legitimate conscientious objectors by the courts. In some cases judges who ruled in favour of the conscientious objectors risked government pressure and retaliation by the authorities.

⌼ Prominent reformist judge Sergey Pashin was stripped of his post in the Moscow City Court in October because of a scholarly paper in which he questioned the legality of Dmitry Neverovsky's conviction for draft evasion. Dmitry Neverovsky — a student from Kaluga Region and a conscientious objector who refused to serve in the army during the war in Chechnya because of his pacifist beliefs — had been sentenced to two years' imprisonment in November 1999. He claimed that while in pre-trial detention he was systematically ill-treated by the guards. In April 2000 he was released from prison after his conviction was overturned on appeal.

Torture/ill-treatment

Torture and ill-treatment of detainees in police custody, during pre-trial detention and in the armed forces continued to be reported.

⌼ Feodor Avdeev, a 68-year-old retired navy aviation major, was reportedly beaten to death on 28 November 1999 in the local market by a police officer in Podolsk. He was apparently selling chocolates at the market without a licence to trade. After Feodor Avdeev failed to produce a passport during an identity check, a police officer reportedly beat him repeatedly even after he had fallen to the ground. A criminal case against the officer on charges of "abuse of power" opened by the Office of the Procurator was closed in March, apparently for lack of evidence.

⌼ New developments were reported in the case of Sergey Mikhailov who was sentenced to death in April 1995 by the Arkhangelsk Regional Court for the rape and murder of a girl. Sergey Mikhailov claimed that he was subjected to torture and ill-treatment in order to force him to confess to the crime, and maintained his innocence. In April 2000 the Supreme Court of the Russian Federation cancelled the previous court decision to sentence Sergey Mikhailov to death and returned the case for further investigation to the Office of the Procurator of Volgograd Region.

⌼ Masked law enforcement officers reportedly ill-treated staff and visitors during a raid on the Moscow offices of the human rights organization, Glasnost Foundation, in August. Officers reportedly ordered everyone present, including a 10-year-old girl, to lie face down on the floor at gunpoint. Officers allegedly kicked several of those present, including Sergey Grigoryants who was kicked in the head and back for not lying down quickly enough. The activists were kept lying on the floor for about 30 minutes.

Armed forces

Widespread torture and ill-treatment in the armed forces resulted in a number of deaths of soldiers and officers.

◻ In August, four discharged soldiers who served during the war in Chechnya — Vladimir Murashkin, Igor Koshelev, Larisa Klimova and Victor Khmyrov — reported the systematic use of torture and ill-treatment in the 72nd regiment of 42nd army division stationed around Stanitsa Kalinovskaya. They alleged that conscripts were systematically beaten by fellow officers and senior soldiers from the intelligence unit; that soldiers were kept for days in special zoo-like cages in front of the barracks; and that injured soldiers were shot at using automatic rifles. The four soldiers reported that private Vladimir Demakov was forced to spend 15 days in a cage and beaten with belts and a crowbar after writing a complaint to the unit commander about the ill-treatment of fellow soldiers.

Conditions of detention

Conditions in penitentiaries and pre-trial detention centres, which held up to a million people, did not improve and amounted to cruel, inhuman or degrading treatment. Hundreds of thousands of people awaiting trial continued to be held in grossly overcrowded conditions. Thousands had to sleep in shifts, often without bedding. Many cells were filthy and pest-ridden, with inadequate light and ventilation. Food and medical treatment were often inadequate. Tuberculosis and skin diseases were widespread. It was reported that on average more than 10,000 inmates died each year and more than 100,000 suffered from tuberculosis.

In May a new law designed to grant amnesty to detainees and prisoners sentenced for minor crimes was adopted by the State *Duma* (parliament) lower house to mark the 55th anniversary of the end of the Second World War in Europe. It was not clear how many people were freed under the amnesty, although the authorities reported in November that more than 168,000 people were released.

Politically motivated killings

◻ Despite the conviction in November 1999 of three men in the Republic of Kalmykia in connection with the murder in June 1998 of Larisa Yudina, human rights groups in Kalmykia continued to maintain that the journalist was killed on the orders of Kalmykian President Kirsan Ilyumzhinov. According to Russian press reports, criminal investigators had indicated that President Ilyumzhinov's brother had ordered the killing.

◻ In January police in St Petersburg detained Larisa Plaskova in connection with the murder on 20 November 1998 of prominent member of parliament Galina Starovoitova; she was released in February.

The death penalty

No steps were taken to abolish the death penalty in law.

There were several calls during the year by senior officials for the lifting of the *de facto* moratorium on the death penalty. In September some 60 deputies of the State *Duma* appealed to President Putin to lift the *de facto* moratorium on the grounds of rising crime throughout Russia, the series of apartment bombings in 1999, and a number of contract killings.

Refoulement

Legal provisions for asylum-seekers remained inadequate. Many people were at risk of *refoulement* (forcible return) to countries where they could face grave human rights violations.

◻ In December 1999 the Russian authorities forcibly returned seven North Koreans, recognized as refugees by the UN High Commissioner for Refugees, to the People's Republic of China, apparently without giving them access to asylum procedures. At the beginning of 2000 the Chinese authorities forcibly returned the seven refugees to the Democratic People's Republic of Korea where they were at risk of grave human rights abuses.

◻ Polvonnazar Khodzhayev was detained by officers of the Russian Special Services in the town of Samara on 5 April. He was subsequently handed over to Uzbek law enforcement officers and was forcibly returned to Uzbekistan. On 14 May he was sentenced to death by Tashkent Regional Court for attempting to overthrow the constitutional order of Uzbekistan in order to create an Islamic state.

AI country reports and visits

Reports

- Russian Federation: Environmental activist Grigory Pasko faces new imprisonment risk (AI Index: EUR 46/045/2000)
- Russian Federation: Only an international investigation will ensure justice for the victims (AI Index: EUR 46/023/2000)
- Russian Federation: Continuing torture and rape in Chechnya (AI Index: EUR 46/036/2000)
- Russian Federation: What future for Chechens — citizens or subjugated people (AI Index: EUR 46/044/2000)

Visits

Between March and June AI visited the country several times to carry out research on violations of human rights and international humanitarian law and to interview people affected by the Chechen conflict.

RWANDA

RWANDESE REPUBLIC
Head of state: Major-General Paul Kagame (replaced Pasteur Bizimungu in April)
Head of government: Bernard Makuza (replaced Pierre-Célestin Rwigema in March)
Capital: Kigali
Population: 7.7 million
Official languages: Kinyarwanda, French, English
Death penalty: retentionist

Reports of "disappearance", arbitrary arrest, unlawful detention, and torture or ill-treatment of detainees continued throughout 2000. A number of killings of unarmed civilians were also reported. An estimated 125,000 people continued to be held in detention, the overwhelming majority accused of taking part in the 1994 genocide. Many have been held for prolonged periods without charge or trial in conditions amounting to cruel, inhuman and degrading treatment. At least 140 people were sentenced to death for crimes committed during the 1994 genocide, some after unfair trials, but no executions took place. Trials of genocide suspects also continued at the International Criminal Tribunal for Rwanda (ICTR) in Tanzania. In eastern Democratic Republic of the Congo (DRC), Rwandese military and allied forces, as well as Rwandese armed groups opposing them, were responsible for massacres of civilians, torture, including rape, "disappearances" and the systematic harassment of human rights defenders.

Background

The Rwandese Patriotic Front (RPF)-led government retained tight political control of the country. Open political opposition was not tolerated. Despite signs of growing internal dissatisfaction from genocide survivors and from dissident RPF members, no significant political opposition emerged in the country. Both the RPF and the government were criticized for being dominated by members of the Tutsi ethnic group.

Political tension increased following the departure from office of senior political figures perceived as critical of the RPF leadership. Joseph Sebarenzi Kabuye, former Speaker of the National Assembly, fled Rwanda in January. In March the RPF, acting with the National Assembly, forced the resignation of President Pasteur Bizimungu, a Hutu who had been included in the inner circle of power since the early days of the RPF. The Vice-President, Major-General Kagame, took over as President in April.

The government continued with a national policy of "villagization" under which hundreds of thousands of people were required to abandon their homes in order to be housed in new "villages" or settlements known as *imidugudu*. By the end of 2000, the conditions in many of these villages remained extremely poor, with inadequate access to food and water. Insecurity and numerous cases of rape and sexual violence were reported in these villages.

During 2000 a new police force under civilian control replaced the paramilitary gendarmerie, formerly under the control of the Ministry of Defence. Officers of the new police force received basic training in human rights.

Abuses in Democratic Republic of the Congo

The Rwandese Patriotic Army (RPA) and forces of the Rwandese-backed Congolese armed opposition group, the Goma-based *Rassemblement congolais pour la démocratie* (RCD-Goma), Congolese Rally for Democracy, continued to control large areas of eastern DRC. In opposition to the DRC government of Laurent-Désiré Kabila, units of both forces were responsible for widespread human rights abuses, in particular the killing of hundreds of unarmed civilians and torture, including rape. Such abuses were often committed in response to attacks by Rwandese *interahamwe* and ex-FAR (former Rwandese government army) armed groups, or by the *mayi-mayi* Congolese armed group which opposes the RCD-Goma and the Rwandese presence in the DRC. These groups were also responsible for grave human rights abuses. In November and December 2000, the RPA and RCD-Goma undertook a massive recruitment drive in eastern DRC. Among those recruited were children under the age of 18. All forces continued to use child soldiers, some of whom were forcibly recruited and trained in foreign countries before being sent back to fight in the DRC.

Torture and ill-treatment in Rwandese and RCD-Goma detention centres were routine, and numerous cases of "disappearance" were reported. Congolese human rights defenders and civil society activists were singled out by the Rwandese and RCD authorities for harassment or worse: many suffered arbitrary arrest, unlawful detention, ill-treatment or "disappearance". (See Democratic Republic of the Congo entry.)

In addition to fighting between the two sides in the DRC conflict, there were increasing internal divisions within the RCD alliance, including deepening rifts between the Rwandese and the Ugandans. In June, Rwandese and Ugandan forces fought for control of the Congolese city of Kisangani. More than 700 civilians were killed and thousands more forced to flee.

Killings of civilians

The level of killings in Rwanda was lower than in previous years as the activities of armed groups such as the *interahamwe* and counter-insurgency operations by the Rwandese military were increasingly restricted to eastern DRC. However, a number of unarmed civilians were killed, some by members of the Rwandese security forces, others by armed opposition groups, others by unidentified assailants. Members of Local Defence Forces (LDF), an armed but unpaid and poorly trained civilian force recruited to protect local communities, were also responsible for killings of civilians and other abuses. Some detainees who had been acquitted of genocide charges or conditionally released were killed.

◻ In February Aloys Rurangangabo, who had been acquitted by a court of participation in genocide, was shot dead in Gakoni, Murambi commune, Umutara. His wife and four-year-old child were also injured when a grenade was thrown into their house. The attackers reportedly included a serving and a demobilized RPA soldier.

◻ In March Assiel Kabera, adviser to President Bizimungu, was shot dead outside his home in Kigali by three men in military uniform.

◻ In May an armed opposition group killed nine civilians in Rwerere commune, Gisenyi préfecture, and three students in Kiningi, Ruhengeri.

◻ In August, in Kinigi, Ruhengeri, 22-year-old Innocent Manragaba was killed by RPA soldiers, and two other civilian men were wounded. The unarmed men, who had undertaken a village night security patrol, were ordered to sit on the ground by the soldiers who then opened fire on them.

'Disappearances'

A number of "disappearances" continued to be reported. Some victims were arrested in the DRC and subsequently transferred to Rwanda and held in incommunicado detention.

◻ Bruno Bahati, a civil society activist from eastern DRC, was arrested at the Rwanda-Uganda border in April as he returned from a civil society conference in the DRC government-held capital of Kinshasa. His whereabouts were unknown until his release in July. It transpired that he had been held incommunicado in military detention in Kigali before being transferred to a detention centre in Goma, eastern DRC.

Torture/ill-treatment

Torture and ill-treatment were practised routinely in "*cachots communaux*" (local detention centres) and military detention sites, especially in the early stages of detention. An unknown number of civilians continued to be held illegally in military detention centres.

◻ In June, four students from Goma, eastern DRC — Mapendano Bahavu, Eric Sikubwabo-Sibomana, Lazare Lukute Tschonga and Obin Lukute Kiembo — were arrested at the Rwanda-Uganda border and held incommunicado for 16 days at the Kicukiro military detention centre, in Kigali. They were denied food for the first three days. At least two were tortured: one was severely beaten around his head with a piece of wood, and another had a gun held to his head.

Conditions in Rwanda's chronically overcrowded prisons and detention centres continued to be harsh and life-threatening, and in most cases constituted cruel, inhuman and degrading treatment. The authorities failed to provide adequate food or medical treatment to detainees and sanitary conditions remained extremely poor. The death rate in prisons and detention centres remained high. Many child detainees were incarcerated with adults, putting them at additional risk of violence and sexual abuse: only six of Rwanda's 13 central prisons have separate wings for minors. The UN Children's Convention, to which Rwanda is party, states that children should only be detained in prison exceptionally, as a last resort, and should always be separated from adults.

Genocide trials

At least 2,283 people were tried in Rwandese courts on charges of participation in the 1994 genocide. At least 140 people were sentenced to death — an increase over previous years. There were no judicial executions. The number of trials increased, but the quality of trials varied, and some trials were unfair. Some witnesses were intimidated, and some trials were repeatedly postponed. There was also an increase in group trials, which reportedly led to breaches of fair trial procedures.

One of the most prominent genocide trials, that of Augustin Misago, Roman Catholic bishop of Gikongoro, concluded in June when he was acquitted.

Around 125,000 people remained in detention, the overwhelming majority accused of participation in the genocide. Since the launch of genocide trials in 1996, only 4,875 suspects have been tried, less than 4 per cent of the detained population. Detainees included more than 4,400 children under 18 years old, and many elderly people over 70 years old. More than 450 children who would have been less than 12 years old at the time of the genocide, and who had reportedly been cleared of involvement, remained in detention.

In order to accelerate the pace of the trials, the government planned to introduce a new communal system of justice, known as *gacaca*, to try people accused of genocide crimes, with the exception of "Category 1" suspects accused of playing a leading or significant role in the genocide. While the use of the new *gacaca* system might alleviate the huge burden on the courts and prison system, there were concerns that some aspects of this system would not conform to international standards of fairness, particularly regarding the right to legal defence and the lack of professional training for and independence of the lay judges.

International Criminal Tribunal for Rwanda

Trials of leading genocide suspects continued at the ICTR in Arusha, Tanzania. By the end of 2000, 46 were detained in Arusha. The United Kingdom, France, Belgium and Denmark surrendered indicted genocide suspects to the ICTR in the course of 2000.

◻ In June former radio presenter Georges Ruggiu was sentenced to 12 years' imprisonment for crimes relating to incitement to genocide and persecution, as a crime against humanity, after he pleaded guilty. Georges Ruggiu worked for the Hutu extremist radio station *Mille Collines* (Thousand Hills), which incited Hutus to kill Tutsis and Hutus opposed to the atrocities.

Swiss court ruling

◻ In May, a Swiss military appeal court reduced a life sentence imposed on Rwandese ex-mayor Fulgence Niyonteze to 14 years' imprisonment. He had been sentenced to life imprisonment in April 1999 after a lower court found him guilty of murder, incitement to murder and war crimes. This was the first trial of a Rwandese genocide suspect in the national jurisdiction of a foreign country. The appeal court dismissed the charges of murder and incitement to murder on the grounds that it lacked the competence to try such crimes committed by one foreigner against another outside Switzerland, allowing only the war crimes charges to stand.

Arbitrary arrests and detentions
Arbitrary arrests and detentions were reported. Thousands of detainees awaiting trial on genocide charges had been detained for prolonged periods, some without any evidence against them. Several detainees who had been tried and acquitted were rearrested.

Daniel Gahinda, Christophe Kagiraneza, and Eugene Nkulikiyinka, school teachers from Nyamyumba commune, Gisenyi, were arrested in December 1999, accused of being supporters of Rwanda's exiled former king and members of a supposed "Army of the King". They were detained for six months in military and gendarmerie detention centres, despite there being no evidence against them, before being released without charge in July.

Refugee issues
In the course of 2000, hundreds of people, mainly Hutu from Kibungo in eastern Rwanda, fled to Tanzania. The reported reasons for their flight included a prolonged drought and fear of being accused by the forthcoming *gacaca* tribunals of participation in the genocide.

From September, many Congolese refugees from the Masisi region of eastern DRC, who had been living in a camp in Byumba, Rwanda, were returned to the Masisi region. Because of the continued fighting and insecurity in the Masisi region, they were at serious risk of human rights abuses during or after their return.

Intergovernmental organizations
In May the Organization of African Unity's International Panel of Eminent Personalities submitted the report of its investigation into the 1994 genocide and made recommendations to prevent conflict in the region.

Government response to AI report
In June the government published a lengthy response to AI's April report, *Rwanda: The troubled course of justice*, which highlighted the plight of tens of thousands of detainees held on suspicion of genocide as well as the negative impact of long delays in bringing suspects to trial and the process of delivering justice to the victims and survivors of the genocide. The government response, while acknowledging that "some human rights related problems do still exist" in Rwanda and welcoming some of AI's observations, largely sought to refute AI's findings.

AI country report and visit
Report
• Rwanda: The troubled course of justice (AI Index: AFR 47/010/2000)
Visit
AI delegates visited Rwanda and eastern DRC in October to carry out research and meet government officials.

SAINT LUCIA

SAINT LUCIA
Head of state: Queen Elizabeth II, represented by Pearlette Louisy
Head of government: Kenneth Anthony
Capital: Castries
Population: 0.16 million
Official language: English
Death penalty: retentionist

There were reports of severe beatings in prison and of police brutality and excessive use of force. At least two men remained under sentence of death.

Torture/ill-treatment
There were reports of severe beatings in prison, and of conditions that amounted to cruel, inhuman or degrading punishment. Sanitation was poor, with an open pit for all prisoners to use as a latrine. Severe overcrowding was exacerbated by the large number of remand prisoners awaiting trial.

In one case, a mentally ill man on remand was allegedly beaten and punched by prison guards until he became unconscious.

In July, a court ordered that shackles be immediately removed from Alfred Harding, a Bajan national. He had been kept in prison since August 1999 and held continuously in handcuffs and metal ankle restraints chained together, in contravention of the Prison Rules and international standards. He was also kept in solitary confinement and denied visiting rights. Reports indicated that he was detained in the part of the prison reserved for prisoners under sentence of death, although he was on remand, and that he was regularly subjected to punitive cell searches. The court ordered compensation to be paid to Alfred Harding, but this was not paid. By the end of the year the authorities had not responded to calls for an end to the practice of holding prisoners in chains and for an investigation into the torture of Alfred Harding.

Corporal punishment
No reports were received of sentences of judicial corporal punishment being imposed or inflicted. In 1999 the Court of Appeal had ruled that there was no provision in law for such punishments.

Police brutality
There were reports of police brutality and excessive use of force. Unofficial reports claimed that there were at least seven fatal shootings by the police, some in disputed circumstances. No inquests were held into any of these deaths.

In October Paul Hamilton was fatally shot by police officers in Castries. Reports indicated that he was shot in the back following a chase. Media reports stated that an internal police investigation had been announced, but the outcome was not known at the end of the year.

☐ In November, Alfred Harding (see above) was shot dead by police in La Clery after escaping from custody. The circumstances of the killing suggested that he had been extrajudicially executed. Witnesses stated that Alfred Harding was ordered by a police officer to lie down and was subsequently shot twice in the thigh and spine. According to reports, he was denied medical attention. Witnesses were reportedly intimidated by police. Following the shooting, the Minister of Home Affairs announced that an independent investigation would take place into Alfred Harding's death and the circumstances of his escape from custody. The Prime Minister announced an internal investigation. The results of both investigations had not been disclosed by the end of the year.

Death penalty
At least two men remained under sentence of death. No further death sentences were imposed and no executions took place.

Human rights defenders
The Minister of Home Affairs accused human rights lawyers of being "politically motivated". The media was also critical of their work and at least one lawyer was subjected to anonymous death threats, verbal harassment and intimidation from members of the public.

SAMOA

INDEPENDENT STATE OF SAMOA
Head of state: Malietoa Tanumafili II
Head of government: Tuila'epa Sailele Malielegaoi
Capital: Apia
Population: 0.17 million
Official languages: Samoan, English
Death penalty: retentionist

At least 54 villagers on Savai'i island were detained on account of their religious activities. Their imprisonment led to public debate about constitutional guarantees of freedom of religion. Death sentences against two former cabinet ministers convicted of assassinating another government minister were commuted.

Prisoners of conscience
Throughout the year, scores of Christian villagers on Savai'i island were arrested, imprisoned or banished for taking part in religious activities outside mainstream Christian churches.
☐ In May, Tuasivi District Court sentenced 42 people from Falealupo village to four weeks' imprisonment and another 12 villagers to two months' imprisonment for refusing to obey orders by the Land and Titles Court to stop their Bible classes and other religious activities. They were prisoners of conscience. In September, the Land and Titles Court upheld decisions by Falealupo village council to banish the prisoners and 144 other villagers from Falealupo and to prohibit them from forming a new church. Banishment is a recognized form of law enforcement in Samoa.

Following unsuccessful petitions to the village council, the banished group appealed to the Land and Titles Court against the orders. In October police reportedly forced the majority of the banished villagers to leave Falealupo, despite court instructions to suspend their eviction pending the appeal. About 60 members of the group were reportedly taken to the Tuasivi police station, apparently for questioning. Court officials in Apia then intervened to inform Tuasivi police and the Falealupo village council of a decision by the Land and Titles Court President that all banished villagers should remain in Falealupo pending appeal hearings due to take place in 2001.
☐ In September, at least three people from Papa Puleia village were reportedly detained for two days by Tuasivi police in similar circumstances. They were charged with disobeying their village council's prohibition on their religious activities. The case was pending at the end of the year.
☐ In July the Supreme Court upheld constitutional guarantees of religious freedom in a similar case and ruled that the Land and Titles Court and the Saipipi village council had no authority to restrict religious freedom or to limit the number of churches at Saipipi. In response, the National Council of Churches declared its intention to seek amendments to the Constitution in order to allow village councils to limit the number of churches in their jurisdiction.

Death penalty
In April, the Supreme Court sentenced to death former government ministers Leafa Vitale and Toi Aukuso Cain for their role in the assassination in July 1999 of Luagalau Levaula Kamu, another minister, at a reception celebrating the ruling Human Rights Protection Party. Leafa Vitale's eldest son, Alatise Vitale, gave evidence at the trial that his father and Toi Aukuso Cain had arranged the assassination and pleaded guilty to shooting dead Luagalau Levaula Kamu. His own death sentence had been commuted to life imprisonment in 1999 by Malietoa Tanumafili II. In May, Malietoa Tanumafili II visited Leafa Vitale and Toi Aukuso Cain in prison before also commuting their death sentences to life imprisonment.

SAUDI ARABIA

KINGDOM OF SAUDI ARABIA
Head of state and government: King Fahd bin 'Abdul-'Aziz al-Saud
Capital: Riyadh
Population: 19 million
Official language: Arabic
Death penalty: retentionist
2000 treaty ratifications/signatures: UN Women's Convention

Serious human rights violations continued. Women continued to face severe discrimination, and suspected political or religious activists continued to suffer arbitrary arrest and detention or punishment under secretive criminal judicial procedures which deny the most basic rights, such as the right to be defended by a lawyer. At least 123 people were executed and there was an alarming increase in the number of amputations. One person reportedly had his eye surgically removed as judicial punishment. Torture and ill-treatment continued to be reported. The government continued to enforce a ban on political parties and trade unions and to impose restrictions on access to the country by non-governmental human rights organizations.

Background
In an unprecedented move, the government publicly stated its belief in the universality and indivisibility of human rights and announced measures to promote and protect such rights. During the March/April 2000 session of the UN Commission on Human Rights, Saudi Arabia's Deputy Foreign Minister stated that "human rights are a non-negotiable objective for the achievement of which we must all strive together", and that Saudi Arabia was committed to "the protection and promotion of human rights through carefully studied measures within the context of a comprehensive human rights strategy". He informed the Commission of steps already taken or planned by the government to carry forward this strategy, including an invitation to the UN Special Rapporteur on the independence of judges and lawyers to visit the country. The steps also included plans to introduce a new regulation to govern the legal profession and legal counsel, and the creation of mainly governmental structures for the protection of human rights. The establishment of a committee to investigate allegations of torture and other abuses was also announced, in response to the government's obligations under the UN Convention against Torture.

During 2000, the government embarked on a number of legislative initiatives related to human rights. In May, the Minister of Justice announced that statutes had been drafted to form a new professional code of practice for the legal profession. A law on criminal trial procedures was reported to have been proceeding through the legislative process. The Consultative Council was also reported to have begun studying proposals for a comprehensive labour law for women.

In September, Saudi Arabia acceded to the UN Women's Convention, but entered the following reservation: "In the case of contradiction between any form of the Convention and the norms of Islamic law, the Kingdom is not under obligation to observe the contradictory terms of the Convention". The government also entered a reservation so that it would not be bound by provisions on the equal rights of men and women to pass their nationality on to their children.

In July Saudi Arabia appointed a woman to the government post of assistant under-secretary at the Presidency For Girls' Education.

In May Saudi Arabia was one of a number of states voted onto the UN Commission on Human Rights.

Emerging human rights debate
On 31 March, the government issued a response through the news media to AI's report *Saudi Arabia: A secret state of suffering*. The government denied the patterns of human rights violations documented by the organization. Without referring to any individual cases or specific events covered by the report, the response claimed that arbitrary arrest and torture were not allowed in Saudi Arabia and that the courts guaranteed fair trial. It denied that any political prisoners were held and pointed out that Saudi Arabia played an active role in the field of human rights. This statement started a debate on human rights led by Saudi Arabia's national and international press. Government officials were also prompted to make statements on human rights, including the Minister of Interior who reportedly said: "We tell those who level accusations against the Kingdom to present their proof. And we welcome anybody who wants to know the facts as we don't have anything to hide...". The debate was continuing at the end of 2000.

Women's rights
AI welcomed Saudi Arabia's accession to the UN Women's Convention and other developments related to women's rights, but remained concerned at continuing severe forms of discrimination and human rights abuses against women. Discrimination against women included limitations on freedom of movement, allowing for effective imprisonment within the home, and preventing recourse to protection or redress from human rights abuses. Equal educational and vocational opportunities continued to be denied to girls and women. Women were also subjected to human rights violations, including arbitrary arrest and detention, torture and the death penalty. Women abused by private individuals such as husbands or employers continued to be denied access to adequate protection or redress by the government. Female domestic workers remained at particular risk of human rights abuses, including physical abuse, as a result of severe restrictions on their liberty, freedom of movement and association.

Prisoners of conscience and political prisoners

There were continuing arrests on political or religious grounds. People arrested in previous years remained in detention, some of whom were held without charge or trial.

Hundreds of members of the Shi'a Ismaili community of Najran province, including possible prisoners of conscience, were arrested following demonstrations and clashes in April in protest against the forcible closure of their mosque by security forces. Many of those arrested were apparently held incommunicado and their whereabouts were unknown. At least two were reported to have been sentenced to prison terms and lashes (see below). Some were reported to have been killed during the clashes and demonstrations, in circumstances which suggested that they may have been the victims of extrajudicial execution or excessive use of force by the security forces. At least one security officer was reported to have been killed and others were injured.

A number of Christians were also reported to have been arrested during 2000 for the non-violent expression of their religious beliefs. Those known to AI had all been released by the end of the year without charge or trial.

◻ In January, 15 Filipino nationals, including three women and five children, were reported to have been arrested while participating in a Christian service at a private home in Riyadh. All were released without charge after several weeks' incommunicado detention in Malaz prison.

◻ In August, Sheikh 'Ali bin 'Ali al-Ghanim was arrested at the border between Saudi Arabia and Jordan upon his return from a holiday in Syria. The reasons for his arrest may have been related to his Shi'a religious beliefs or political activities. Before his arrest he was reportedly summoned to the headquarters of *al-Mabahith al-'Amma* (General Investigations) and asked to write a detailed report about himself, including the countries he had visited and his associates. He remained held in the *al-Mabahith al-'Amma* prison in Dammam at the end of 2000.

◻ Dr Sa'id bin Zua'ir, head of the Department of Information at Imam Mohamed bin Sa'ud Islamic University, remained in prison throughout 2000. He had been arrested in early 1995 by members of *al-Mabahith al-'Amma*, and remained held without charge or trial in al-Ha'ir prison, having reportedly refused to sign an undertaking to cease political activities in exchange for his release.

◻ Hani al-Sayegh, who was forcibly returned to Saudi Arabia from the USA in 1999 after seeking asylum there, remained held in virtual incommunicado detention in connection with the bombing of a US military complex at al-Khobar in 1996, an offence punishable by death. At the end of 2000 he was held reportedly in al-Ha'ir prison without access to lawyers and with only limited contact with his family. He remained at risk of torture and of being sentenced to death after secret proceedings.

Release

Muhammed al-Faraj, a lecturer arrested in 1999 reportedly on account of a poem he had written, was released in January.

Torture/ill-treatment

AI received fewer allegations of torture than in previous years, but the lack of judicial supervision of arrest and detention continued to facilitate torture and ill-treatment. There were no indications that investigations had been carried out into reports of torture in previous years, including reports of deaths in custody as a result of torture. Political prisoners, including possible prisoners of conscience, held in incommunicado detention remained at risk of torture. Confessions obtained under torture or duress could still be used as the sole evidence for conviction.

◻ George Joseph, an Indian national, was reportedly arrested outside his home in May as he returned from a Catholic service with a religious cassette tape. He was held in incommunicado detention for several months and reportedly beaten before being released without charge and deported back to India.

In August, prisoners in the city of al-Jawf were reported to have protested over their conditions of detention, including poor food. Several people were reported to have been injured during the incident. No details were available to allow assessment of any human rights violations that may have taken place.

Judicial corporal punishments

There were 34 reported cases of amputations during 2000, seven of which were cross amputations (of the right hand and left foot). Flogging continued to be frequently imposed for a wide range of offences.

◻ In August, 'Abdel Mo'ti 'Abdel Rahman Mohammad, an Egyptian national, was reported to have had his left eye surgically removed as punishment ordered by a court in Medina after he had been found guilty of throwing acid in the face of a compatriot and damaging his left eye.

◻ Two teachers, arrested following demonstrations in Najran, were reported to have been sentenced to 1,500 lashes each to be carried out in front of their families, students and other teachers.

Death penalty

In an increase over the previous year, at least 123 people were executed, all after trials about which very little was known. Among those executed were three women. The majority of those executed – 71 – were foreign nationals, from India, Pakistan, Nigeria, Philippines, Yemen, Sudan, Eritrea, Ethiopia, Iraq, Egypt, Bangladesh, Syria, Afghanistan, Indonesia and Thailand. Some were sentenced to death for crimes without lethal consequences such as highway robbery, sodomy, drug smuggling and sorcery.

◻ The body of one of those executed in May, Muhammad Mustafa Kamal 'Abd al-Qadir Jadi, an Egyptian national, was reported to have been crucified following his execution in Jizan on charges of murder.

The number of people under sentence of death was unknown as the government does not divulge such information. However, among those at risk of the death penalty was Sit Zainab binti Duhri Rupa, a 32-year-old Indonesian domestic worker, detained on charges of murdering her employer. She was reported to be psychologically ill and to have "confessed" to the crime during police interrogation.

AI action
Five country reports were issued by AI during the year as part of a campaign against human rights violations in Saudi Arabia, under the slogan "End Secrecy, End Suffering". Each report detailed different patterns of human rights violations together with recommendations to the Saudi Arabian authorities designed to redress such violations.

Lack of government cooperation
During 2000, AI welcomed the commitments to human rights made by the government and requested further details as to the time-frame and terms of reference of the establishment of planned human rights bodies, but received no further information.

AI continued to send communications to government officials regarding issues or individual cases of concern, all of which remained unanswered. AI sought clarification of the reported killings in Najran, together with assurances that those detained in connection with the incidents would be protected against torture and execution, but received no response. AI also repeatedly requested permission to visit the country, but the government continued to deny access.

Intergovernmental organizations
AI submitted updated information on Saudi Arabia for review by the UN Commission on Human Rights under a procedure established by UN Economic and Social Council Resolutions 728F/1503 for confidential consideration of communications about human rights violations. In March, AI made an oral statement to the Commission's 56th session, concentrating on unfair trials, torture in custody, corporal punishment and amputations.

AI country reports
- Saudi Arabia: A secret state of suffering (AI Index: MDE 23/001/2000)
- Saudi Arabia: A justice system without justice (AI Index: MDE 23/002/2000)
- Saudi Arabia: Encouraging human rights debate (AI Index: MDE 23/034/2000)
- Saudi Arabia: Execution of Nigerian men and women (AI Index: MDE 23/049/2000)
- Saudi Arabia: Gross human rights abuses against women (AI Index: MDE 23/057/2000).

SENEGAL

REPUBLIC OF SENEGAL
Head of state: Abdoulaye Wade (replaced Abdou Diouf in March)
Head of government: Moustapha Niasse
Capital: Dakar
Population: 9.4 million
Official language: French
Death penalty: abolitionist in practice
2000 treaty ratifications/signatures: Optional Protocol to the UN Children's Convention on the involvement of children in armed conflict; Optional Protocol to the UN Women's Convention

Despite peace moves, there was continued tension in the disputed region of Casamance between members of the government and the *Mouvement des Forces démocratiques de Casamance* (MFDC), Democratic Forces of Casamance Movement, an armed opposition group claiming independence for Casamance. The number of human rights violations lessened in comparison with previous years, although the security forces in Casamance were responsible for several cases of extrajudicial executions, "disappearances" and torture. About 30 suspected MFDC sympathizers remained in prison without trial at the end of 2000. Most appeared to be prisoners of conscience who had been arrested because they were members of the Diola community. Members of the MFDC also continued to commit human rights abuses against civilians. In July, a Senegalese court dismissed charges of complicity in acts of torture against former Chadian leader Hissein Habré on the grounds that it could not prosecute crimes committed in Chad.

Background
Attempts to find a peaceful solution to the 18-year-old conflict in the Casamance region continued throughout 2000. In February, peace talks which took place in Banjul, Gambia, led to the setting up of a joint mission composed of members of the government and the MFDC to monitor a cease-fire agreement. In December a first formal meeting was held in Ziguinchor between the Senegalese authorities and the leader of the MFDC, Father Diamacoune Senghor. Among the issues on the agenda were the future of army bases, the freeing of prisoners, the return of displaced people and the implementation of development projects in Casamance. Nevertheless, tension remained high in the conflict area throughout 2000, leading to border problems with neighbouring Guinea-Bissau, from where suspected members of the MFDC launched attacks against Senegalese soldiers and civilians in Casamance.

Presidential elections were held in March and for the first time since independence in 1960, the candidate of the ruling Socialist Party, the incumbent President Abdou

Diouf, lost power. Abdoulaye Wade, head of a coalition of opposition parties, became head of state. He immediately announced a constitutional referendum to allow him to dissolve the National Assembly, where the Socialist Party had a majority, and to hold new legislative elections. This referendum was due to take place in November but was postponed until early 2001.

Detention without trial

About 30 suspected MFDC sympathizers remained in prison without trial at the end of 2000 in Dakar and Kolda. Most of these detainees appeared to be prisoners of conscience, arbitrarily arrested because they were members of the Diola community. Most of them were charged with "threatening state security" but no evidence was ever produced as to their individual responsibility for acts of violence.

In Kolda, at least four nationals of Guinea-Bissau remained in detention without trial at the end of 2000. The reasons for their arrest remained unclear. There was serious concern about the conditions in which people were detained in Kolda as no human rights organization — neither the Senegalese *Rencontre africaine pour la défense des droits de l'homme* (RADDHO), African Conference for the Defence of Human Rights, nor the *Liga Guineense Dos Direitos Humanos*, Guinea-Bissau Human Rights League — was allowed access to them, despite repeated requests.

Extrajudicial executions and 'disappearances' in Casamance

The number of human rights violations lessened in comparison with previous years, notably after April 2000, when a new army commander was appointed in Ziguinchor. However, the security forces in Casamance were responsible for several cases of extrajudicial executions, "disappearances" and torture.

☐ Momany Tendeng was reported to have been extrajudicially executed in January by soldiers near a military camp in Nyassia. Two other young people, Daniel Sambou and Denis Sambou, were shot dead in March by soldiers who forced other civilians to bury them.

☐ Several people "disappeared" after being arrested by the security forces, including Jean Dacougna, a 40-year-old mentally ill man arrested in February in Ziguinchor, and Ephène Diatta, arrested in Kabrousse in March. Both remained unaccounted for at the end of 2000.

Abuses by the MFDC

Despite the cease-fire agreement accepted by the MFDC leader, some elements of the armed wing of the MFDC continued to commit human rights abuses against civilians. In February, armed groups shelled the area of Niaguis, apparently to deter the population from voting in the presidential election. Throughout 2000, civilians were attacked while they were in cars or in the fields and their belongings were stolen by alleged members of the MFDC. In April, for the first time, Father Diamacoune Senghor publicly condemned the armed attacks launched by one of the military leaders of the armed wing MFDC, Salif Sadio, and protested against the fact that these armed groups refused to obey him and to respect the cease-fire agreement.

Impunity: the Habré case

In February, Hissein Habré, former President of Chad, who found refuge in Senegal in 1991, was indicted on charges of complicity in acts of torture following a criminal complaint filed in January by Chadian victims and a coalition of non-governmental organizations. Hissein Habré was placed under house arrest while investigations into the charges against him began. In July, a Senegalese court dismissed the charges on the grounds that it could not prosecute crimes committed in Chad. AI was disappointed by the court ruling that Senegal could not exercise universal jursidiction over torture in Chad. The coalition of non-governmental organizations appealed against the decision to the Court of Cassation, which had not given its ruling by the end of 2000.

SIERRA LEONE

REPUBLIC OF SIERRA LEONE
Head of state and government: Ahmad Tejan Kabbah
Capital: Freetown
Population: 4.8 million
Official language: English
Death penalty: retentionist
2000 treaty ratifications: Optional Protocol to the UN Children's Convention on the involvement of children in armed conflict; Optional Protocol to the UN Women's Convention; Rome Statute of the International Criminal Court

The 1999 peace agreement collapsed after rebel forces captured UN peace-keeping troops in May. Killings, mutilations, rape and abduction of civilians, including women and children, by rebel forces increased. Government forces were responsible for extrajudicial executions, torture and ill-treatment. Several hundred alleged government opponents were held without charge or trial. Renewed insecurity added to already large numbers of refugees and internally displaced people. The international community made efforts to resolve the crisis, including by strengthening the UN peace-keeping operation and taking action to halt the diamond trade used to procure arms. In a significant move to end impunity, the UN Security Council resolved to establish a Special Court for Sierra Leone.

Background information

Before its collapse in May, implementation of the July 1999 Lomé peace agreement between the government and the armed opposition Revolutionary United Front (RUF) was limited: attacks on civilians by rebel forces continued and thousands remained held captive; disarmament and demobilization was slow; large areas of the north and east, including diamond-producing areas, remained under rebel control; and up to a million people remained beyond reach of humanitarian assistance.

With the capture by RUF forces of some 500 troops of the UN Mission in Sierra Leone (UNAMSIL), hostilities resumed. Government forces comprised the Sierra Leone Army and a civilian militia, the Civil Defence Forces (CDF). Rebel forces included the RUF and renegade soldiers from both the Armed Forces Revolutionary Council (AFRC) — in power from 1997 to 1998 — and from the army. Some demobilized combatants again took up arms. United Kingdom (UK) troops were deployed until mid-June to defend Freetown and support UNAMSIL. Several hundred UK troops remained to train the Sierra Leone Army. All UNAMSIL captives had been released by July after intervention by Liberian President Charles Taylor.

Following his arrest in May, RUF leader Foday Sankoh, who had been given a government position following the peace agreement, was succeeded by Issa Sesay. There was little contact, however, between him and the authorities and it was unclear whether he controlled all RUF forces. On 10 November the government and the RUF agreed a 30-day cease-fire in Abuja, Nigeria, under the auspices of the Economic Community of West African States (ECOWAS). Although this agreement included deployment by UNAMSIL in rebel-held areas, this had not begun by the end of the year.

From September hostilities between armed groups along Sierra Leone's borders with Liberia and Guinea resulted in further population displacement. Indiscriminate shelling by Guinean security forces of villages close to the border in Kambia District resulted in civilian casualties. Responding to fears of conflict spreading throughout the region, ECOWAS planned to deploy an observer mission along the borders.

Abuses by rebel forces

In early 2000 human rights abuses against civilians — abduction, rape, looting and destruction of villages — by rebel forces occurred almost daily in Northern Province, particularly Port Loko District. From May deliberate and arbitrary killings, mutilation, rape, abduction and forced labour and recruitment increased. Aid workers were attacked and forced to withdraw from rebel-held areas.

Although abuses in and around Makeni and Magburaka, Northern Province, decreased from September, refugees forced to return from Guinea were attacked and pressured to join RUF forces in Kambia District.

A group of renegade soldiers known as the West Side Boys terrorized civilians through killings, rape, torture, abduction and ambushes along major roads in the Occra Hills area east of Freetown until September, when their leader was captured and many surrendered or were arrested.

Deliberate and arbitrary killings

Large numbers of civilians were killed by rebel forces from May, particularly in areas around Port Loko, Lunsar, Makeni and Magburaka.

☐ On 8 May RUF members killed about 20 people and injured dozens of others when they fired on some 30,000 people protesting outside Foday Sankoh's residence in Freetown against RUF attacks on UNAMSIL.

☐ A man was killed and decapitated in June after he tried to prevent the abduction of his 15-year-old daughter as his family fled from Makeni.

☐ A man from the village of Magbile recounted how his sons, aged 11, 21, 23 and 25, were shot and killed in June when they refused to join rebel forces.

☐ In early September rebel forces attacked Guinean villages close to the Sierra Leone border, killing Sierra Leonean refugees.

Torture, including mutilations and rape

Many civilians had limbs deliberately amputated; others had the letters RUF carved into their flesh. Abduction of girls and women, rape and sexual slavery were systematic and widespread. Most victims had contracted sexually transmitted diseases and many became pregnant. Often, abducted women and girls, without adequate support, were unable to leave the combatants who had forced them into abusive relationships when they disarmed and demobilized.

☐ During a rebel attack on Lunsar in late May several people suffered amputations, some of both hands.

☐ Civilians near Mongeri who escaped from six months' captivity in October had been used as forced labour and repeatedly beaten and threatened with death; women had been repeatedly raped.

☐ A woman with a five-month-old baby was stripped and raped by several combatants when rebel forces attacked Masiaka in May; she was then abducted and subjected to further rape.

☐ A 19-year-old woman from Magburaka reported the rape and killing of her sister during an attack in May; her husband was also killed.

☐ Nine women and girls abducted by West Side Boys in August were taken to the village of Makupr where they were beaten, raped and threatened with death.

Hostage-taking

On 25 August, a Sierra Leone Army officer and 11 UK military personnel were taken hostage by West Side Boys in the Occra Hills. Five were released after five days and the rest were rescued on 10 September in an operation in which one UK soldier and at least 26 West Side Boys were killed.

Human rights violations by government forces

Members of the CDF and the Sierra Leone Army were responsible for summary executions, arbitrary detention and torture of captured or suspected rebels and recruitment and use of child combatants. The CDF, operating in Eastern and Southern Provinces, became increasingly undisciplined and usurped police authority. Civilians were also arbitrarily detained at CDF headquarters, including in Bo,

Koribundu and Kenema. Ill-treatment and extortion of money and property at checkpoints were common and several incidents of rape, previously rare, were reported.

◻ In May, five unarmed RUF combatants travelling with civilians were intercepted at a CDF checkpoint at Baiima, north of Bo; one was summarily executed and the others detained.

◻ A detainee captured by the CDF in May and held in Bo lost an ear and suffered cuts to his back after being beaten with a bayonet; others reported being stripped and beaten with sticks until they bled.

◻ In September, two men were killed and a third injured when they resisted recruitment by the CDF.

◻ In September the CDF attacked police headquarters in Kenema, and detained and beat a senior police officer.

◻ Making no attempt to involve the police or investigate, in September the CDF stripped two young boys accused of stealing money and beat them in public in a village near Mile 91.

◻ In October Jia Kangbai, a journalist with the *Standard Times* newspaper, was detained in Freetown for two days by the CDF, and kicked, beaten and pistol-whipped, after publication of an article considered critical of the CDF.

Civilian casualties from aerial attacks

In May and June, attacks by government forces from a helicopter gunship on suspected rebel positions in Northern Province resulted in up to 30 civilian deaths and many other casualties. Attacks often appeared to be indiscriminate and undertaken without adequate measures to safeguard civilians. Although warning leaflets were dropped in Makeni and Magburaka, attacks followed shortly afterwards. Civilians fleeing Makeni, however, said that they were forced out of their homes by rebel forces as the gunship flew overhead. At least 14 civilians were killed in Makeni and at least six were killed in an early afternoon attack on the market in Magburaka.

Child combatants

The resumption of hostilities in May halted demobilization of child combatants, leaving several thousand still to be released by rebel forces, and resulted in further recruitment.

RUF forces continued to abduct and forcibly recruit children in Northern Province. Recruitment of children by the CDF also continued in Southern Province, despite assurances to the contrary given to AI representatives in May by the Deputy Minister of Defence, who is also National Coordinator of the CDF. In May about 25 per cent of combatants fighting with government forces near Masiaka were observed to be under 18, some as young as seven. The government reiterated that 18 was the minimum age for recruitment and instructed the acting Chief of Defence Staff to ensure demobilization of all those under the age of 18.

International and national organizations worked towards ending the use of child soldiers and assisting in their rehabilitation.

Refugees and internal displacement

From May renewed fighting and bombing caused hundreds of thousands of people to flee: about 5,000 to Guinea and 300,000 to other parts of Sierra Leone, bringing the number of internally displaced people to some 500,000. From September, when violence erupted along the Guinean border, 22,000 refugees in Guinea returned to Sierra Leone to escape arrest and harassment by the local population, incited by the Guinean authorities.

Those displaced remained at risk of human rights abuses. Around Port Loko, people venturing from camps to gather food and water were frequently abducted, raped and used for forced labour by rebel forces. Others fleeing areas behind rebel lines were accused by the CDF of being rebels or rebel sympathizers, and were beaten or killed.

Political detention

Several hundred members of the RUF or other perceived opponents were arrested in May, including Foday Sankoh. Some, fearing reprisals by the CDF, gave themselves up. They were held under emergency legislation introduced in 1998, and repeatedly renewed by parliament, which allowed indefinite detention without charge or trial. In June the government published the names of 121 detainees held under emergency powers in Freetown's Central Prison. The legal basis for the detention of others remained unclear. During August at least 200 detainees were released in Freetown and Kenema. Almost 300 detainees, including more than 10 children, however, remained held at the end of the year. Detainees were denied visits from their families and the UNAMSIL human rights section was not granted access to detainees in Freetown until September.

◻ Abdul Kouyateh, publisher of *Wisdom Publications*, was arrested in Freetown in May after publication of an article about the alleged use of mercenaries by the government and was held without charge until October.

Intergovernmental organizations

The crisis precipitated in May forced the international community, in particular the UN, the Organization of African Unity (OAU) and ECOWAS, to reassess the viability of the peace agreement and the performance of UNAMSIL, the largest UN peace-keeping operation.

Although the UN Secretary-General recommended an increase in UNAMSIL troops to respond to continuing instability, meeting the existing complement of 13,000 agreed by the UN Security Council in May was hindered by withdrawal of Indian and Jordanian forces later in the year and reluctance by many countries to contribute troops.

The UNAMSIL force had a mandate to protect civilians under imminent threat of physical violence, within its capabilities and areas of deployment. AI called for all civilians to be protected at all times, including by deployment of UNAMSIL troops in areas where civilians were at greatest risk. It appeared, however, that on several occasions, for example in

Kabala in June and along major roads, they failed to protect civilians from attack.

The UNAMSIL human rights section continued to report abuses and promote protection of human rights, including by providing human rights training for police and prison officers and UNAMSIL troops. With the Office of the UN High Commissioner for Human Rights, it contributed towards establishing a Truth and Reconciliation Commission and a National Human Rights Commission, both provided by the peace agreement.

In October a UN Security Council delegation visited Sierra Leone and recommended that, while maintaining military pressure, priority be given to dialogue with RUF leaders. It also recommended development of a comprehensive and coordinated strategy for Sierra Leone. The UN Secretary-General visited Sierra Leone in early December to assess the peace-keeping operation.

Impunity

The peace agreement had provided a general amnesty for all acts undertaken in pursuit of the conflict but its collapse forced reconsideration of this provision. In June the government requested UN assistance to establish a special court to try leading RUF members.

AI and other human rights organizations insisted that trials focus on those most responsible for grave human rights abuses, whether members of the RUF, AFRC, Sierra Leone Army or CDF, and regardless of current political position or affiliation.

In August the UN Security Council decided to establish a Special Court for Sierra Leone to prosecute those most responsible for crimes against humanity, war crimes and other serious violations of international humanitarian law. Commenting on the Special Court's draft Statute in November, AI called for the Court to have jurisdiction over crimes committed since the conflict began in 1991 rather than, as proposed, from November 1996; for any recruitment of children under the age of 15 years, whether forced or voluntary, to be defined as a crime; and for adequate and sustained funding for the Court.

Since the Court would only try a limited number of cases, AI stressed that its establishment must provide long-term benefits to the national judicial system, which had to be rebuilt and strengthened in order eventually to assume responsibility for trying perpetrators of human rights abuses.

Military assistance to rebel forces

The governments of Liberia and Burkina Faso were consistently cited as violating a UN arms embargo on rebel forces. They were accused of transferring arms and ammunition through their territories and trading diamonds from rebel-held areas. The Liberian government came under growing diplomatic pressure to end its support for the RUF.

International attention focused increasingly on "conflict diamonds". In July the UN Security Council imposed an 18-month prohibition on direct or indirect import of rough diamonds from Sierra Leone, other than those certified by the government. The international diamond industry introduced measures towards regulating trade.

A UN Panel of Experts was established in August to investigate the link between the diamond trade and the conflict in Sierra Leone, including the implication of the governments of Liberia and Burkina Faso. It published a report in December which unequivocally established the involvement of both governments by means of international networks of arms and diamond brokers, dealers and transporters based in many countries. It made recommendations for effective implementation of the bans on illicit diamond trading and arms transfers.

AI public statements, selected country reports and visits
Reports and statements
- Sierra Leone: United Nations Security Council must ensure the protection of civilians (AI Index: AFR 51/015/2000)
- Sierra Leone: Rape and other forms of sexual violence against girls and women (AI Index: AFR 51/035/2000)
- Sierra Leone: Amnesty International calls for fast and effective action on diamonds (AI Index: AFR 51/054/2000)
- Sierra Leone: Ending impunity – an opportunity not to be missed (AI Index: AFR 51/060/2000)
- Sierra Leone: Childhood – a casualty of conflict (AI Index: AFR 51/069/2000)
- Sierra Leone: Recommendations on the draft Statute of the Special Court (AI Index: AFR 51/083/2000)
- Sierra Leone: UN investigation exposes continuing trade in arms and diamonds (AI Index: AFR 51/086/2000)

Visits
AI delegates visited Sierra Leone in March, May, June and July. They met President Ahmad Tejan Kabbah and members of the government, RUF leader Foday Sankoh and UN officials, as well as members of non-governmental organizations and victims of human rights abuses. Research was undertaken in Freetown and Northern and Eastern Provinces.

SINGAPORE

REPUBLIC OF SINGAPORE
Head of state: S.R. Nathan
Head of government: Goh Chok Tong
Capital: Singapore City
Population: 3.1 million
Official languages: Chinese, Malay, Tamil, English
Death penalty: retentionist
2000 treaty ratifications/signatures: Optional Protocol to the UN Children's Convention on the involvement of children in armed conflict

Freedom of expression continued to be curbed by an array of restrictive legislation and by the effects of civil defamation suits against political opponents. At least 29 Jehovah's Witnesses were imprisoned during the year. Death sentences continued to be imposed and 21 people were executed. Criminal offenders, including juveniles, were sentenced to caning.

Background
The ruling People's Action Party (PAP), in power since 1959, continued to dominate the political scene, with 80 out of 83 elected seats in parliament. In May parliament passed the Political Donations Act, which sets tight limits on anonymous donations to political parties and prohibits civil society organizations from receiving foreign funding. Opposition leaders criticized the new legislation, saying it would make it more difficult for Singapore's small opposition parties to raise funds. They also expressed fears that the activities of non-governmental organizations would be adversely affected.

Restrictions on freedom of expression and assembly
Although no new civil defamation suits were filed by government leaders, this practice continued to be misused to curb the right to freedom of expression and the right of political opponents to participate freely in public life. An array of restrictive legislation also remained in place, undermining the rights to freedom of expression and assembly.

In May police refused to issue a permit for a public forum on homosexuality, claiming it would be contrary to the public interest. Under Singapore's Penal Code, homosexual acts between consenting adults may incur lengthy prison terms. In recent years the authorities have also denied a gay and lesbian support group permission to register under the Societies Act.

In September, as part of an apparent attempt to encourage public debate on issues of national concern, the authorities allowed the creation of a new open-air forum, known as the "Speakers' Corner". Opposition leaders voiced their scepticism about the "Speakers' Corner", reiterating concerns that there could be no true freedom of speech without reform of restrictive laws such as the Internal Security Act, which allows for indefinite detention without trial. In December, police refused to issue a permit to the organizers of a marathon run to commemorate international human rights day.

Civil defamation suits
J.B. Jeyaretnam, the 74-year-old leader of the opposition Workers' Party, continued to face bankruptcy and the loss of his parliamentary seat. One set of proceedings stemmed from a defamation payment awarded against him, as the editor of the Workers' Party newsletter, for allegedly defaming a PAP parliamentarian and nine other members of the ethnic Tamil community in an article written by a colleague in 1995. In October, eight of the plaintiffs lodged a bankruptcy petition against J.B. Jeyaretnam, but later agreed to accept payment of the defamation award in instalments.

In December, in a separate case, a court awarded over 66,000 Singapore dollars (approximately US$38,000) to J.B. Jeyaretnam after ruling in his favour against a lawyer who had failed to pay costs previously awarded against him. Immediately following this, the Minister of Foreign Affairs and four others, including three PAP parliamentarians, applied to the courts to seize the 66,000 Singapore dollars awarded to J.B. Jeyaretnam on the grounds that a 1996 defamation award against the Central Council of the Workers' Party had not been paid in full. There were concerns that the timing of this application appeared designed to prevent J.B. Jeyaretnam from paying further instalments of damages in the Workers' Party newsletter case, thereby bankrupting him.

Conscientious objectors
At least 29 conscientious objectors to military service were imprisoned during the year. All were members of the banned Jehovah's Witnesses religious group. There was no alternative civilian service for conscientious objectors to military service.

Death penalty
The death penalty was mandatory for drug trafficking, murder, treason and certain firearms offences. At least five death sentences were reportedly passed during the year and 21 people were executed by hanging, 17 of whom had been convicted of drug trafficking. In reply to a parliamentary question, the Minister of Home Affairs revealed that 340 people were executed between 1991 and 2000, giving Singapore possibly one of the highest execution rates in the world, relative to its population. This was the first time special government statistics relating to the use of the death penalty had been made available.

Cruel judicial punishment
Caning, which constitutes cruel, inhuman or degrading punishment, remained mandatory for some 30 crimes, including attempted murder, rape, armed robbery, drug trafficking, illegal immigration offences and vandalism. Drug addicts also faced a mandatory caning sentence and imprisonment if they had been admitted more than twice to a drug rehabilitation centre.

SLOVAKIA

SLOVAK REPUBLIC
Head of state: Rudolf Schuster
Head of government: Mikuláš Dzurinda
Capital: Bratislava
Population: 5.4 million
Official language: Slovak
Death penalty: abolitionist for all crimes
2000 treaty ratifications/signatures: Optional Protocol to the UN Women's Convention

There were reports of ill-treatment of Roma by police officers, and of the authorities failing to protect Roma from violence by skinhead gangs. Conscientious objectors to military service faced imprisonment.

Violence against Roma

Roma continued to face poverty, social discrimination and racist violence. For example, in March residents of Hlohovec town collected signatures to oppose plans by municipal authorities to move Roma into a house in a predominantly non-Romani neighbourhood. In August Vitazoslav Mórič, a member of the National Council (parliament), stated in a radio broadcast that reservations for Roma should be established. In September the National Council stripped Vitazoslav Mórič of his immunity from prosecution, allowing him to be charged with incitement to racial hatred, but no charges had been brought by the end of 2000.

In August, three men broke into a home in Žilina and beat Anastázia Balážová and her daughters with baseball bats. Anastázia Balážová, mother of eight, died three days later. Two of her children were treated for injuries. Prime Minister Dzurinda promised to ensure "that this criminal act is investigated as soon as possible". In October the police charged four suspects with crimes including racially motivated infliction of bodily harm, resulting in death.

In April a group of around 15 skinheads attacked three Roma in Poprad, hitting one on the head with an iron bar. Two police officers who arrived at the scene physically assaulted Romani witnesses of the skinhead attack. After another police patrol arrived, Emil Mirga and his sons Robert, Maroš and Milan were taken into custody for allegedly assaulting the police. All four were reportedly beaten in the police station. Another man, Ľubomír Šarišský, had been shot and killed in the same police station in August 1999. The police officer responsible for that shooting was sentenced in October to a suspended one-year prison sentence.

Violent police raids

There were further reports of violent police raids on entire Romani communities, ostensibly in order to arrest criminal suspects.

In September, in the Romani neighbourhood of Plavecký Štvrtok, masked police officers broke into houses and reportedly beat and kicked women, children and men. The police were allegedly looking for three Romani men. Nadežda Huberova was awoken by seven masked officers who kicked open the door of her house. Her 10-year-old daughter reportedly suffered an epileptic fit when they pushed her out of her bed.

International organizations

In August, the UN Committee on the Elimination of Racial Discrimination expressed concern at the "persistence of acts of violence by groups, particularly skinheads, directed towards Roma and other ethnic minorities". The Committee recommended that Slovakia should strengthen procedures for timely and thorough investigations and effective prosecutions against racist organizations.

In June the Council of Europe's European Commission against Racism and Intolerance published a report detailing problems facing the Romani community in Slovakia. The report highlighted racial violence and harassment and the apparent lack of police response to such incidents.

Conscientious objection

In July an amended Law on Civilian Service came into force which obliges the military authorities to inform recruits about their right to apply for alternative service. AI expressed concern about the time limits that were retained in the amended law, which effectively disqualify people who develop a conscientious objection to military service after being conscripted.

AI country report

- Slovakia: Conscientious objector Milan Kobolka — a possible prisoner of conscience (AI Index: EUR 71/001/2000)

SLOVENIA

REPUBLIC OF SLOVENIA
Head of state: Milan Kučan
Head of government: Andrej Bajuk
Capital: Ljubljana
Population: 1.99 million
Official language: Slovenian
Death penalty: abolitionist for all crimes
2000 treaty ratifications/signatures: Optional Protocol to the UN Children's Convention on the involvement of children in armed conflict

There were reports of ill-treatment and excessive use of force by police officers. Conditions in reception centres for refugees and asylum-seekers were inadequate and in at least one case reportedly amounted to degrading treatment.

Torture/ill-treatment

In May the UN Committee against Torture reviewed Slovenia's initial report on its implementation of the Convention against Torture. In its Conclusions and Recommendations, the Committee expressed concern that the present Slovenian Criminal Code, adopted in 1994, does not include torture as a criminal offence. Slovenia's report argued that crimes within the Convention's definition of torture — specifically the infliction of aggravated and serious bodily harm and the abuse of power by state officials — were incorporated in the Criminal Code. However, the Committee stated that the Convention definition of torture was more comprehensive than merely inflicting bodily harm and that failure to include torture as defined by the Convention in criminal law led to people guilty of torture not being appropriately punished. The Committee was also concerned about allegations of police ill-treatment and use of excessive force against people in custody, in particular members of the Romani community. In addition, Slovenian legislation on the treatment of aliens allowed, under certain circumstances, for the expulsion of people to countries where they could be at risk of torture, which constitutes a breach of the Convention.

In November the European Court of Human Rights found that Slovenia had breached several provisions of the European Convention on Human Rights in the case of Ernst Rehbock, a German national who had been ill-treated by Slovenian police in September 1995. The Court concluded that the arresting officers had used unwarranted force, as a result of which Ernst Rehbock had his jaw broken and sustained further injuries. In addition, his right to have the legality of his detention reviewed promptly had been violated as it took local courts several months to decide on his complaint against his detention.

Reports of ill-treatment by police officers increased from late 1999 onwards. Police officers resorted to excessive force in several instances against young people and children.

☐ During the night of 21 to 22 April, 16-year-old Goran Razgoršek was reportedly beaten by police in the town of Slovenj Gradec. Goran Razgoršek left a local discotheque around midnight with some friends and then found that his motor cycle had a flat tyre. While he was calling his parents on his mobile phone, two passing police officers accused him and his friends of making a noise and of having damaged a traffic sign. They then ordered Goran Razgoršek to come with them to the police station. One officer reportedly grabbed his arm, twisted it behind his back, punched him in the chest and threw him on the ground. While he was lying on the ground, Goran Razgoršek was reportedly kicked in the back and stomach by both police officers, one of whom also kicked him on the head. He was taken to the police station in Slovenj Gradec, along with three friends who were released after questioning. Goran Razgoršek was refused permission to call his parents or a lawyer and, after being questioned, was locked in a cell. After an hour in the cell he became dizzy and vomited some blood. His parents were finally informed about his whereabouts and came to pick him up around 2am. An examination by the Slovenj Gradec hospital revealed bruising to his chest and back, a tear in his left ear lobe, bruising and swelling on his cheekbone, and a bump on his temple. Goran Razgoršek's parents filed a complaint with the Ministry for Interior Affairs in Ljubljana which was referred back to the Slovenj Gradec police station, which replied that since the complaint had not been sent to them within the legally required period it could not be taken into consideration. However, the complaint was forwarded to the district public prosecutor.

SOLOMON ISLANDS

SOLOMON ISLANDS
Head of state: Queen Elizabeth II, represented by John Ini Lapli
Head of government: Manasseh Sogavare (replaced Bartholomew Ulufa'alu in June)
Capital: Honiara
Population: 0.4 million
Official languages: Solomon Islands Pidgin, English
Death penalty: abolitionist for all crimes

The conflict between rival armed political groups – the Malaita Eagle Force (MEF) and the Isatabu Freedom Movement (IFM) – continued on the country's main island, Guadalcanal. Both sides committed human rights abuses against the civilian population. Scores of civilians, including women, children and other non-combatants, were abducted, ill-treated, raped and killed; these abuses were attributed to the MEF, the IFM or splinter groups. Thousands of villagers were internally displaced and deprived of medical assistance and relief supplies during an MEF blockade. The blockade was lifted following the signing of a peace accord in October.

Armed conflict and coup

The MEF emerged as the main armed political group representing the interests of settlers on Guadalcanal island. The settlers, from Malaita province, had been displaced in 1999 following attacks by the IFM. The MEF declared it was using military force to put pressure on the government to provide compensation for loss of life and property in Malaita during previous attacks by the IFM.

In June Malaitan paramilitary police officers led a coup and joined forces with the MEF. They raided the main police armoury, took Prime Minister Bartholomew Ulufa'alu hostage and forced him to resign. Opposition leader Manasseh Sogavare was elected as the new Prime Minister after the MEF leader threatened "all out war" unless parliament elected a new Prime Minister.

Following the coup, acts of intimidation and reprisals against civilians by both groups escalated. The MEF used captured police weapons to launch a series of major assaults against IFM positions; hundreds of homes in rural areas were destroyed. Perpetrators of human rights abuses continued to enjoy impunity and a climate of lawlessness prevailed on Guadalcanal and Malaita.

Peace talks

South Pacific government ministers and UN disarmament experts visited the country, but their reports were not made public. A series of peace talks and a cease-fire signed in August failed to halt hostilities, but growing pressure from civil society and business groups led to a peace agreement, signed on 15 October in Townsville, Australia, by members of the MEF, the IFM and the government. National and international efforts were made to implement the agreement's priority provisions, including the arrival of unarmed peace monitors from countries in the region. The peace agreement provided for, among other measures, the rehabilitation of members of armed groups, a general amnesty for all parties to the conflict, reform of the police and the reintegration into the police force of officers who had joined the MEF or IFM. The agreement made no provision for an investigation into human rights violations and abuses.

Killings

Dozens of civilians and other non-combatants were killed; the deaths were attributed to the MEF, the IFM or splinter groups. Both parties to the conflict failed to respect the principles of international humanitarian law, which regulate the conduct of armed conflict and protect civilians. Following the coup, MEF fighters indiscriminately shelled villages east of Honiara from a police patrol boat. Displaced civilians in the Marau Sound were reportedly targeted by both the MEF and the IFM.

☐ In May the MEF was linked to the murder of a Guadalcanese man whose headless body was left in Honiara central market, with a note linking the murder to ongoing peace talks. His death triggered the apparently revenge killing of a Malaitan man two days later. His severed head was reportedly displayed at an IFM roadblock.

☐ In July gunmen suspected of belonging to the MEF shot dead two wounded IFM members as they lay in their beds in a surgical ward in the capital's Central Hospital. Days later gunmen in MEF and paramilitary police uniforms attacked a rural medical centre on Guadalcanal and opened fire on staff and patients as they tried to flee, killing an old man and a teenage boy.

Torture/ill-treatment

Both the MEF and the IFM reportedly tortured or ill-treated suspected members of armed political groups. Some captives were believed to have died as a result of torture, or to have been subsequently killed. Malaitans abducted by the IFM were reportedly beaten at an IFM camp where torture was reported to have been routine. Suspected Guadalcanese militants and civilians were reportedly tortured or ill-treated in MEF camps on the outskirts of Honiara and in the former Guadalcanal provincial government offices, temporarily the MEF "headquarters".

☐ In April the MEF reportedly abducted a Guadalcanese man who was later seen at an MEF camp, suspended by wire tied to his hands and ankles, bleeding and bearing the marks of severe beatings. His body was found several days after his abduction in a suburb of Honiara.

☐ In June two Malaitan men were captured by the IFM and then tortured by an IFM splinter group notorious for its use of violence. They were reported to have been paraded through villages with visible injuries before being killed and buried. In what appeared to be a reprisal attack, two Guadalcanese men — John Bosco, an 18-year-old student in a Catholic college who had been evacuated to the capital to escape the fighting, and Walter Tavai — were abducted by MEF members in early July. John Bosco was reportedly beaten at an MEF camp before being killed and secretly buried. According to eyewitnesses, Walter Tavai was beaten unconscious and subsequently died of his injuries.

Other concerns
Hostage-taking
Allan Kemakeza, the brother of the Deputy Prime Minister, was held hostage by the IFM (Western Command) for 10 days in August. An IFM splinter group hijacked a Solomon Airlines aircraft in September and held the pilot hostage for two and a half weeks.

Peace activists and journalists
Academics and other members of civil society who tried to engage in public debate about peace talks were threatened and attacked.

◻ The family of Matthew Wale, a peace activist, was robbed and his relatives were beaten by gunmen linked to the MEF.

◻ Several local journalists and their families were threatened by the MEF for their reports on the conflict.

Displaced people
Between 7,000 and 10,000 people fled their homes in rural Guadalcanal during the year, following threats, abductions, looting and burning of their property by armed political groups. Humanitarian aid for those displaced by the conflict was intermittent. MEF blockades prevented essential supplies reaching Guadalcanese islanders. MEF and IFM members were reported to have beaten, threatened and harassed International Committee of the Red Cross (ICRC) staff, medical professionals and clerical and lay workers trying to carry out humanitarian work or perform their religious duties among displaced people. The leader of the ICRC delegation sustained head injuries when he was attacked by an ethnic Malaitan gunman.

AI country report
- Solomon Islands: A forgotten conflict (AI Index: ASA 43/005/2000)

SOMALIA

SOMALIA
Head of state: Abdiqasim Salad Hassan; Head of Somaliland Republic: Mohamed Ibrahim Egal; Head of Puntland Regional State: Abdullahi Yusuf Ahmed
Head of transitional government: Ali Khalif Gelayadh
Capital: Mogadishu
Population: 6.9 million
Official language: Somali
Death penalty: retentionist

After having no central government since 1991, the collapsed state of Somalia gained a transitional government in July, which started to work for control of the south of the country. Outbreaks of fighting in the south between armed clan-based militias linked to political factions were frequent throughout 2000. There was no central judicial or police system, leaving Islamic courts, which did not follow international standards of fair trial, as the only courts in the south. They condemned several prisoners to death and their militias executed them. Scores of civilians were killed in inter-clan fighting. Human rights abuses also included kidnappings (often for ransom) of civilians and humanitarian agency staff. Prisoners of conscience were held in Somaliland and Puntland for attending or supporting a Somali peace conference in Djibouti, and their trials failed to meet international fair trial standards.

Background
Peace conference and formation of transitional central government
Somalia has had no central government since the state collapsed in 1991. Twelve previous peace conferences in the past decade had failed to resolve the conflict.

In 2000, a major new peace and reconciliation conference was held in Arta, Djibouti, supported by the UN and other donors and intergovernmental organizations including the European Union and Arab League. The conference met between May and August with over 2,000 delegates from Somalia and the worldwide Somali diaspora. Delegates included clan elders, leaders of most of the armed and unarmed political factions, and representatives of civil society including human rights groups, women and minorities. Notable absentees opposing the conference were the self-proclaimed governments of Somaliland and Puntland and four "war-lords" heading armed factions in Mogadishu.

In July the conference agreed on the formation of a transitional national assembly, which in August elected Abdiqasim Salad Hassan, an exile and former Somalia government Minister of the Interior, as President for three years. The assembly comprised 245 members, 44 from each of the four major clans, with 25 seats for women and 24 for the minorities, leaving 20 members to be appointed later by the President of Djibouti. In October President Abdiqasim Salad Hassan appointed a Prime Minister, who formed an interim government based in Mogadishu. It faced opposition from the governments of Somaliland and Puntland, Hussein Mohamed Aideed's Somali National Alliance faction, and other factions which controlled parts of Mogadishu and the south. There were promises of substantially increased international aid and support. The new President made a commitment to protect human rights. He began to form a new national army and police force, to demobilize faction militias, and to seek international recognition as well as support among Somalis for the peace process and for the transitional government.

Somaliland and Puntland

The Somaliland Republic in the northwest continued to seek international recognition. In February its parliament declared that attendance at the peace conference or participation in any resulting transitional government constituted treason. Somaliland continued to consolidate its institutions of government and economic reconstruction, although adherence by courts to international fair trial standards was weak. In early 2000 the Somaliland authorities arrested some Ethiopian and Eritrean refugees, deporting some and raising fears of forcible return of people at risk of human rights violations.

The Puntland Regional State accepted that it could be part of a federal unitary Somali state in the future, but its government boycotted the peace conference, repressing any local support for it. A constitution was drafted for a proposed Puntland constitutional conference in 2001.

Civilian victims of armed conflict

Throughout 2000 there were periodic outbreaks of fighting between clan or faction militias in the south, involving killings of civilians as well as combatants. Weapons were easily available. The greatest areas of tension — the UN-designated "zones of conflict" — were in the Kismayu area, in Mogadishu where different clan-based factions controlled territory, in the Bay and Bakol region and Lower Shebelle where the Rahanwein Resistance Army had Ethiopian army support against Hussein Mohamed Aideed's forces, and in Gedo region bordering Ethiopia which was contested between Ethiopian troops, Islamist militias and local clan forces.

There were killings and reprisal killings of clan opponents, expulsions of members of other clans, cases of kidnapping as well as acknowledged detention, and torture or ill-treatment of prisoners. Women and the minorities were particularly vulnerable to abuses including rape, killing and theft of land and property. The minorities at risk, who had suffered most from militia attacks in the civil wars and social discrimination, included urban coastal peoples (Benadiri or Rer Hamar), Bantu agriculturalists frequently subjected to forced labour, artisan groups (Midgan, Tumal, Yibir) and fishing people (Bajuni).

◻ In June, six unarmed Bantu people were killed by clan gunmen in a land dispute near Jowhar in central Somalia.

Attacks on humanitarian personnel

In February the Somalia Aid Coordination Body complained of increasing attacks on aid staff, premises and relief convoys, and theft of humanitarian supplies. The UN Security Council in June condemned attacks on civilians and humanitarian personnel. In July, two international staff of Action against Hunger were abducted in Mogadishu and held by faction-related gunmen for almost two months.

Freedom of expression

Freedom of expression was very limited, with little tolerance by government authorities or armed factions for criticism by individuals or the media. Political entities in the south included political factions, mostly with armed militias, and unarmed groups including community-based organizations. Human rights groups such as the Dr Ismail Center for Human Rights, and community groups such as members of the Peace and Human Rights Network in Mogadishu, pressed the factions to observe human rights.

There were no political parties allowed in Somaliland or Puntland. In Somaliland there were several cases of people imprisoned as prisoners of conscience during 2000 on account of their peaceful opinions or beliefs, including Abdiqadir Awil Nur, detained in mid-2000 for converting to Christianity. In June the Somaliland parliament passed a law allowing the formation of three political parties to contest elections planned for 2001.

Peace conference supporters

In several areas there were clashes between supporters and opponents of the Djibouti peace conference. There were violent confrontations in Mogadishu. In Somaliland and Puntland the authorities arrested people returning from the conference. In July the UN Independent Expert on Human Rights in Somalia appealed to the Somaliland and Puntland authorities to stop harassing peace conference supporters. Tensions and threats of violence persisted after the inauguration of the new government. In late 2000 a former army general supervising demobilization of militias and a member of the transitional assembly were assassinated in Mogadishu.

◻ In Somaliland, police arrested Abdirahman Osman Alin in March in Hargeisa for attending the peace conference preparatory meeting. He was released by a court after three months.

◻ Garad Abshir Salad, a member of the transitional assembly and also of the Puntland parliament, was arrested in September in Berbera while in transit from Puntland. He was jailed for seven years by a court after a brief, unfair trial. President Egal ordered his pardon and release three weeks later.

Several other dissident Somalilanders, including a Garhajis clan leader, were arrested later in 2000 on the same grounds. They were freed without charge after short periods and President Egal subsequently announced that in future no one would be arrested for supporting the peace conference.

In Puntland, demonstrations in April in support of the peace conference were attacked by police who briefly detained demonstrators, and there were several reported deaths. A Djiboutian television reporter was briefly detained in November on account of his reporting of the peace process.

Journalists arrested
Journalists in Mogadishu were frequently at risk of violence by faction militias. A new Press Law in Puntland imposed restrictions on media freedom.

◻ In March, Mohamed Ali Salad of *Qaran* newspaper was abducted and beaten by gunmen in Mogadishu on account of an article criticizing business leaders for causing environmental degradation.

◻ In Puntland, Mohamed Abdulkadir Ahmed of *Sahan* newspaper was arrested in Bossaso in July for criticizing the official boycott of the peace conference.

Absence of rule of law
There was no central system of administration of justice in the south. In an increasing number of areas, local Islamic courts with their own militias were set up and partially accepted as a means of establishing security and justice, in addition to informal traditional clan mechanisms for conflict resolution. However, they did not follow recognized standards of fair trial and judicial competence. These courts imposed several death sentences, which were immediately carried out, and floggings. No amputations were reported during 2000.

◻ In April an Islamic court near Merca in Lower Shebelle region reportedly convicted a woman of a morality offence and sentenced her to death by stoning, but the execution was suspended as she was pregnant.

In Somaliland and Puntland there were emergent judicial administrations and police forces, but with inconsistent respect for legal rights. Human rights defenders in Somaliland criticized arbitrary detentions, unfair trials, poor prison conditions and cases of torture and unlawful killing by police.

Impunity
In no part of the former state were public officials known to have been prosecuted for human rights violations, past or present. Several held new public office, including some prominent alleged war criminals of the former Siad Barre government (1969-1991) who were nominated by their clans to the transitional national assembly.

SOUTH AFRICA

REPUBLIC OF SOUTH AFRICA
Head of state and government: Thabo Mbeki
Capital: Pretoria
Population: 40.3 million
Official languages: Afrikaans, English, Ndebele, Pedi, Sotho, Swazi, Tsonga, Tswana, Venda, Xhosa, Zulu
Death penalty: abolitionist for all crimes
2000 treaty ratifications/signatures: Rome Statute of the International Criminal Court; African Charter on the Rights and Welfare of the Child

There were reports of ill-treatment, torture and unjustified use of lethal force by police and security forces. Asylum-seekers and suspected illegal immigrants were also victims of official ill-treatment or racially motivated attacks. Further evidence emerged about past human rights violations during trial proceedings against the former head of the Chemical and Biological Warfare program and in hearings held by the Truth and Reconciliation Commission's Amnesty Committee. Human rights defenders were harassed and attacked because of their work.

Background
Local government elections were held nationally in December. They were largely peaceful and the ruling African National Congress (ANC) won an overall majority of votes. However, in several provinces there were incidents of violence, including in KwaZulu Natal where a number of election candidates were killed or injured in the run-up to the elections.

Continuing official and public concern at levels of violent crime, large-scale circulation of illegal weapons and a spate of bombings in the Cape Town area led to a number of high profile joint military and police security operations in different parts of the country. Investigators from the Office of the National Director of Public Prosecutions and the police arrested and charged a number of members of People Against Gangsterism and Drugs (PAGAD) in connection with killings and other violence in the Cape Town area. In October investigators seized from the South African Broadcasting Corporation and other media organizations film footage which was then apparently used as a basis for arresting three PAGAD members in connection with the public killing of gang leader Rashaad Staggie in 1996. Two prosecution witnesses were killed in December.

The South African Law Commission issued an interim report on a proposed anti-terrorism bill, which contained provisions for prolonged detention without charge for interrogation of individuals believed to have information on terrorist acts.

The government and the statutory Human Rights Commission held a number of hearings and a national conference examining patterns of racism in the country, preparatory to the UN World Conference against Racism in 2001. The Human Rights Commission also held hearings into alleged racist practices in media institutions.

The Constitutional Court in September upheld the appeal by an applicant refused employment by South African Airways because of his HIV status. In its ruling the Court drew attention to the stigma attached to the illness and the importance of ensuring that those living with it enjoy special protection from the law.

Human rights violations by the security forces

There were reports of torture, ill-treatment and unjustified use of lethal force by the security forces, including military units based in KwaZulu Natal province, primarily in the context of crime investigation and searches for illegal weapons. Incidents included the cases below.

▫ In April, police tied 16-year-old Siphiwo Zide and another youngster suspected of involvement in a robbery with ropes to a police vehicle which was then driven away. Siphiwo Zide died when his head was crushed under a wheel. In September, three Barkley East police officers were charged with offences including culpable homicide and assault with intent to do grievous bodily harm, following an investigation by the statutory oversight body, the Independent Complaints Directorate (ICD).

▫ In June, 16-year-old Simon Khubeka was arrested without warrant by a police officer investigating animal stock theft. While in custody at Villiers police station he was allegedly assaulted and verbally abused by another, white, officer who forced him to maintain painful physical postures for prolonged periods and repeatedly punched him and banged his head against a wall. Following his release without charge Simon Khubeka required hospital treatment.

▫ In July a woman police officer, Sergeant Nozipho Ntoni, was beaten, kicked, stamped on and threatened with a gun in her home by a senior police officer from Bisho police station in the Eastern Cape, with whom she was involved in a personal relationship. Bleeding from her injuries, she attempted to lay a charge against him at the police station, but was again assaulted by the same officer in the presence of other, junior-ranking, officers. The next day she reported the case to King William's Town police station whose officers attempted to arrest the perpetrator but were prevented by his brother, also a senior police officer. Following ICD investigations, the perpetrator was arrested and charged with assault with intent to do grievous bodily harm.

▫ Six soldiers and a Police Reservist were charged in a magistrates' court with murder in connection with the death of 33-year-old Basil Jaca at Flaxton Farm, near Ixopo. They were accused of beating Basil Jaca at his home on 1 July and assaulting him by repeatedly pushing a rifle into his anus, while demanding to know the whereabouts of a gun. The doctor who later examined him failed to refer him to hospital although Basil Jaca was bleeding, in great pain and barely able to walk. He died on 2 July.

▫ Four police officers were charged with murder and released on bail in connection with the suspected extrajudicial execution of an ANC parliamentarian, Bheki Mhkize, in July. He was shot dead when about a dozen members of the Public Order Police Unit based at Ulundi in KwaZulu Natal raided his home, apparently searching for weapons. Independent forensic and other evidence gathered by the ICD indicated that he was shot intentionally at close range by the police.

Impunity

The trial of the former head of the Chemical and Biological Warfare program, Dr Wouter Basson, for murder and attempted murder of opponents of the apartheid government, and on other charges, continued in the Pretoria High Court. The Court heard evidence from prosecution witnesses of covert operations to eliminate identified enemies of the state, and of the killing of members of the security forces who threatened to expose these operations. Witnesses testified about their involvement in the "dumping" of bodies or of semi-comatose individuals from aircraft into the seas. The victims included imprisoned members of the South West Africa People's Organization (SWAPO). Some of the victims were allegedly injected with toxic chemicals by or under the instruction of the accused and others, including military doctors. Other witnesses told the Court of their involvement, as members of clandestine army units, in attempted killings of government opponents in the 1980s.

Truth and Reconciliation Commission

The Amnesty Committee of the Truth and Reconciliation Commission (TRC) continued its hearings on applications for amnesties. Cases considered included applications from former police commissioner Johan van der Merwe and former Vlakplaas security police commander Eugene de Kock for the raid in December 1985 into Lesotho which led to the killing of six ANC members and three Lesotho nationals; from former security police officers for the death in detention in 1982 of trade unionist Neil Aggett; and from members of a covert military unit for the attempted murder of government opponents, including a current government minister, Dullah Omar, during the 1980s.

The Committee granted amnesty to, among others, former Azanian People's Liberation Army commander Phila Dolo, who admitted to ordering an attack which resulted in the deaths of three white civilians travelling in a vehicle in March 1993. The decision to grant amnesty to former security police member Craig Williamson and explosives expert Jerry Raven, for the killings of exiled apartheid government opponents Ruth First and Jeanette Schoon and six-year-old Katryn Schoon in the early 1980s, was challenged by surviving family members. They lodged an appeal for judicial review of the decision on the grounds that the applicants failed to make full disclosure and meet other requirements of the law, in addition to their failure to show any remorse for the deaths they caused.

In September the Minister of Justice, Penuell Maduna, stated that the government would finalize by the end of 2000 its policy on reparations for the thousands of people whom the TRC had declared in 1998 to be eligible for compensation. The government's apparent reluctance to implement the TRC's recommendations led to public conflict with the TRC and protests by victim support groups.

Human rights defenders

Human rights lawyers and members of investigation bodies were subjected to physical attack, death threats or other forms of harassment as a consequence of their work.

◻ In July an ICD investigator, Velaphi Kwela, was killed on his way to carry out an arrest. He was shot seven times and thrown out of his vehicle. The vehicle and the investigation dockets he had with him were not recovered.

◻ Two police officers were acquitted by a magistrates' court of perjury and of attempting to defeat the course of justice in connection with investigations into the 1998 Richmond tavern massacre. Two of their lawyers were subjected to death threats and damage to their property during the course of the trial. The trial proceedings and the court's ruling revealed evidence of possible complicity of National Intelligence agents in killings in the Richmond area, and conflicts between police, justice and intelligence officials which undermined the effectiveness of subsequent investigations.

◻ In September magistrate Pieter Theron, who was hearing a case against PAGAD members, was killed in a drive-by shooting outside his home in Cape Town.

◻ In October Zackie Achmat, a member of the Treatment Action Campaign, was arrested and charged with importing generic drugs to treat AIDS patients unable to afford patented drugs. This prosecution underlined the human rights dimensions of the conflict between non-governmental organizations, the government and drug companies over the importation or manufacture of cheap life-saving drugs in South Africa.

Refugee concerns

The government ordered the arrest of members of the police East Rand Dog Unit after being shown film footage of police officers deliberately inciting dogs to maul three captive suspected illegal immigrants from Mozambique. The helpless men were attacked by the dogs, as well as being beaten and subjected to racist verbal abuse by the police officers. Although the incident had taken place in 1998, the broadcasting of the footage on state television in November 2000 led to a public outcry and statements by officials and civil society organizations on the need to address persistent problems of racism and xenophobia. Six police officers were later charged in a magistrate's court with abduction and assault with intent to do grievous bodily harm before being released on bail.

In separate reports the Human Rights Commission and the non-governmental Human Rights Committee documented abuses of undocumented migrants and asylum-seekers. These included unlawfully prolonged detentions, poor conditions and beatings of detainees by guards at Lindela Repatriation Centre, assaults by police officers involved in the arrest of suspected illegal immigrants, and arbitrary and verbally abusive conduct towards asylum-seekers by Department of Home Affairs officials.

In March the police launched an anti-crime initiative, Operation Crackdown, with the arrest by police and soldiers of over 7,000 alleged illegal immigrants in the Johannesburg area. The raids were allegedly accompanied by abuses such as beatings and theft, as well as arbitrary arrests of individuals with a legal right of residence.

The 1998 Refugee Act, which was brought into effect in 2000, denies asylum-seekers the right to education and the right to seek employment until they have been granted refugee status.

In December, the High Court ordered the government to release official correspondence relating to the deportation to the USA of a Tanzanian national, Khalfan Khamis Mohammed. He faced a possible death penalty for his alleged involvement in the 1998 bombing of the US Embassy in Nairobi, Kenya, and was allegedly removed from South Africa without an extradition hearing, as required under South African law.

AI country reports and visits
Reports
- South Africa: Amnesty International welcomes Government action against racially motivated violence by police (AI Index: AFR 53/003/2000)
- South Africa: Preserving the gains for human rights in the 'war against crime': Memorandum to the South African Government and South African Law Commission on the draft Anti-Terrorism Bill, 2000 (AI Index: AFR 53/004/2000)
- South Africa: Points of clarification on Amnesty International's comments on torture (AI Index: AFR 53/006/2000)

Visits
AI delegates visited South Africa in October to conduct research and meet officials concerning allegations of police and military complicity in the ill-treatment of individuals in custody. In March AI co-sponsored with several regional non-governmental organizations a workshop in Pretoria on policing and human rights in southern African countries.

SPAIN

KINGDOM OF SPAIN
Head of state: King Juan Carlos I de Borbón
Head of government: José María Aznar López
Capital: Madrid
Population: 39.6 million
Death penalty: abolitionist for all crimes
2000 treaty ratifications/signatures: Optional Protocol to the UN Children's Convention on the involvement of children in armed conflict; Optional Protocol to the UN Women's Convention; Rome Statute of the International Criminal Court

There was unprecedented racist violence against foreign workers, mainly from North Africa, in El Ejido (Almería). Allegations of race-related ill-treatment by police officers increased. A large rise in the numbers of undocumented foreign nationals arriving on southern shores prompted claims that the authorities were failing to provide basic humanitarian care and that detention facilities were inhuman and degrading. A new law came into force that severely restricted the rights of undocumented immigrants, fined companies for transporting them, and provided for an accelerated expulsion procedure. Allegations of ill-treatment in prisons persisted, as did allegations of torture made by suspected members of the Basque armed group *Euskadi Ta Askatasuna* (ETA), Basque Homeland and Freedom. ETA committed numerous human rights abuses in which 23 people, the majority civilian, were shot dead or killed by car bombs and many others, including children, were injured. There was an increase in acts of "street violence" by groups reportedly close to ETA, including arson, bombings and death threats. The government proposed new penal measures, including increased penalties for minors convicted of politically motivated violence.

Torture/ill-treatment

Police brutality continued to be widely reported and there was a rise in allegations relating to ill-treatment of immigrants or others of non-European ethnic origin. Allegations were mainly of beatings with truncheons, punches, kicks, slaps and insults by officers of the local, national and autonomous police forces. A number referred to ill-treatment of immigrants, including minors, in the Spanish North African enclaves of Ceuta and Melilla, and there were criticisms about police passivity in connection with ill-treatment of immigrants in El Ejido where, in February, several days of race riots had forced some foreign workers to flee to the foothills of the mountains.

Allegations of torture made by ETA suspects held in incommunicado detention persisted. In April the European Committee for the Prevention of Torture and Inhuman or Degrading Treatment or Punishment (CPT) described a 1997 visit to ETA prisoner Jesús Arkauz Arana. The CPT commented that his account of ill-treatment by Civil Guards, following expulsion from France and while being held incommunicado, was technically credible and "the manner in which he described the sensation of losing consciousness as a result of asphyxiation was particularly convincing". It recommended a "general investigation of a thorough and independent nature ... into the methods used by members of the Civil Guard when holding and questioning persons" suspected of involvement in armed bands. The CPT subsequently expressed disappointment that the Spanish authorities had still not carried out such an investigation. It also found that examining judges and magistrates "could be more proactive" when they receive allegations of ill-treatment.

▫ A judicial inquiry was opened in October into allegations that municipal police officers severely ill-treated two Algerians, Hassan U. and Said M. The Algerians claimed that they were beaten by truncheons both before and after transfer to a police station in Ceuta. Said M., a 17-year-old minor, reportedly lost consciousness during the beating and was revived with water from a rubber hose, with which, at the same time, he was beaten. While lying on the ground he was also allegedly kicked and insulted. Both Algerians were reportedly stripped to the waist and then taken to a police vehicle, again beaten, and left in the area of Calamocarro, where they had first been detained.

Deaths in custody

▫ António Augusto Fonseca Mendes, a native of Guinea-Bissau resident in Madrid, died in police custody while on holiday in Arrecife (Lanzarote) in May. His family claimed he had been severely beaten by police officers and photographs revealed a number of bruises on the body. A first autopsy found no sign of external ill-treatment but a second concluded unequivocally that a fatal injury was dealt to the right side of the neck by a "blow with a blunt instrument". A forensic opinion ordered by the judge to investigate the two apparently irreconcilable autopsy findings reportedly concluded that António Fonseca had probably died of natural causes. The grounds for this finding were not clear. The police offered a series of different and contradictory explanations for the death. AI was concerned that in September the Interior Minister told Congress that there was no evidence of police ill-treatment, even though the judicial investigation was still under way and a number of serious questions remained unresolved.

▫ In December Abdelhadi Lamhamdi, an undocumented Moroccan reportedly trying to flee after disembarking on the coast of Tarifa (Cádiz), died after being shot by a Civil Guard who was pursuing him with a gun in his hand. Government representatives stated that the shot had been fired accidentally. An Algeciras court opened an inquiry into the death. A disciplinary investigation was ordered by the Director General of the Civil Guard and the officer was suspended.

Ill-treatment of immigrants

The numbers of undocumented African nationals disembarking on the beaches of the Campo de Gibraltar and Canary Islands — including pregnant women, children and babies — rose considerably. More than 14,000 were reported to have been intercepted. Many were from Nigeria, Senegal and Sierra Leone. Particular concern was expressed by some non-governmental organizations about the failure to provide basic humanitarian care for many suffering from malnutrition, hypothermia and physical injuries. Most of these immigrants were allegedly held in overcrowded, inappropriate and insanitary conditions in the cells of Civil Guard barracks and a municipal sports centre before being served with expulsion orders and released. Concern was also expressed about delays in recovering bodies from beaches and a lack of diligence in identifying them.

In October, hundreds of undocumented Moroccans were deported to Ceuta and from there to Morocco, allegedly in conditions that infringed international standards, including maritime regulations on safety at sea. The Moroccans were reportedly held, sometimes handcuffed, inside police vans or buses in the holds of ferries. They were reportedly overcrowded and at risk of injury from the movement of other vehicles in heavy seas, subject to great heat and engine noise, and without access to safe escape routes in time of danger. Some ferry captains alleged that police officers had pressured them to accept the Moroccans as cargo rather than as passengers, in contravention of the International Convention for the Safety of Life at Sea.

Excessive use of force against demonstrators

Several reports alleged excessive use of force by police or Civil Guards at demonstrations. In August an inquiry was opened by the Catalan government, the *Generalitat*, into the action of the Catalan autonomous police, the *Mossos d'Esquadra*, during a demonstration by hundreds of Moroccan workers at Aitona (Lleida). Some alleged they had been beaten and subjected to degrading treatment. In November a demonstration outside Congress by pacifists demanding the abolition of the external debt reportedly resulted in 24 injuries and seven arrests. The Interior Minister told Congress that, while police intervention had been justified, the action of some officers had been "inappropriate" and "excessive". In Galicia too there were reports of excessive use of force by police officers.

Ill-treatment in prisons

A second report published in April by the CPT concerned its 1998 visit to police and Civil Guard headquarters and prisons, including Soto del Real (Madrid) and Salto del Negro (Las Palmas de Gran Canaria). The CPT reported that a number of prisoners at Salto del Negro alleged they had recently been ill-treated by prison staff. They referred to blows with batons while handcuffed to beds in the prison's segregation unit. The delegation found that inmates were handcuffed to beds in the unit on a "fairly regular" basis, sometimes for prolonged periods of time. Allegations of ill-treatment, such as blows with batons, were also received from Soto del Real. The CPT noted that the Spanish authorities had undertaken to address excessive duration of confinement in restraints and the failure to provide the prisoners concerned with mattresses, but added that the above-mentioned use of handcuffs was "unacceptable".

Lasa/Zabala trial

In April the National Court sentenced former General Enrique Rodríguez Galindo and former civil governor Julen Elgorriaga to a total of 71 years' imprisonment each for the illegal detention and murder in 1983 of ETA suspects José António Lasa and José Ignacio Zabala. Three former Civil Guard officers were sentenced to between 67 and 69 years' imprisonment, and two — including a former secretary of state already convicted in another case — were acquitted. However, the court set aside charges of torture on the grounds of insufficient evidence and, more controversially, ruled that there was not enough evidence to prove that the accused had been members of an armed band, the *Grupos Antiterroristas de Liberación* (GAL). General Galindo — who had been promoted to that rank in 1995, after the emergence of evidence that he could be implicated in the murders — and his co-defendants appealed against their convictions to the Supreme Court. However, the National Court ordered the immediate detention of those defendants who were not already in prison, including General Galindo, without awaiting the verdict of the Supreme Court. The case had taken 16 years to come to trial, during which time crucial evidence was undoubtedly lost.

Abuses by armed groups

Following the ending of its cease-fire the previous November, ETA embarked on a new campaign of violence, which killed 23 people in various parts of Spain and injured many others, including children. Many of those who died were civilians, including local councillors, a journalist, an industrialist, a chief prosecutor and a judge. Several murders were attempted. The new ETA campaign was accompanied by an escalation in "street violence" ("*kale borroka*"), aimed at creating an atmosphere of intimidation and fear. In June AI urged ETA to put an immediate end to its campaign of killings of civilians and expressed concern about the "*kale borroka*" attacks. In October AI groups began a campaign to call ETA's attention to fundamental standards of human rights and international humanitarian law.

Abuses were also committed by the armed political group, the *Grupos de Resistencia Antifascista Primero de Octubre* (GRAPO). In November, following the arrest of presumed GRAPO leaders in Paris, France, a police officer was shot dead in Madrid.

The government responded to the ETA killings and "*kale borroka*" attacks with proposed new measures to curb politically motivated violence. These sought to increase the length of detention for minors convicted of terrorist offences and to create a special juvenile court within the National Court in Madrid. In November AI urged the authorities to ensure that any eventual legislation respect in particular the UN Children's Convention. AI also recalled its long-standing opposition to Spanish laws governing incommunicado detention. These remain in force and, in AI's view, facilitate torture.

In October and November, 10 people involved in various Basque political, social or cultural organizations were arrested, on the grounds of alleged links with ETA. They included Sabino Ormazabal Elola, a well-known writer, journalist, ecologist and supporter of non-violent civil disobedience. He and others arrested and subsequently detained denied belonging to, or collaborating with, ETA.

Updates

In January the Provincial Court of Vizcaya acquitted, on grounds of lack of evidence, two national police officers charged with the torture of Rita Margarete Rogerio, a Brazilian national, in 1995. The officers denied the charge and were supported by the public prosecutor, who did not accept that Rita Rogerio had been ill-treated. In an earlier trial in 1998 three officers had been acquitted of raping her. In 1999 the Supreme Court referred to the acquittal for rape as "horrifying" because, while a lower court had found it "luminously clear" that Rita Rogerio had been raped by a uniformed officer in police custody, the police witnesses had conspired to lie and conceal the fact, refusing to identify the person they must have known was the rapist. As a result the Supreme Court had no alternative but to uphold the acquittal. Two officers had subsequently been temporarily suspended from work.

In December a court in Sevilla sentenced a Civil Guard, a shooting instructor, to one year's imprisonment for killing Miriam Gómez Cuadrado in 1999. The Civil Guard shot at the car in which she was travelling after her boyfriend tried to escape a breathalyzer test. The boyfriend was sentenced to one year's imprisonment for reckless driving and disobedience.

AI country reports and visits
Report
- Concerns in Europe, January – June 2000: Spain (AI Index: EUR 01/003/2000)

Visits
An AI delegate visited Spain in October to gather information. In November AI delegates visited Vitoria and Madrid in connection with a campaign against ETA killings. They met the Spanish Secretary of State for Justice to discuss concerns about proposed new legislation aimed at minors involved in politically motivated acts of violence, as well as ETA abuses.

SRI LANKA

DEMOCRATIC SOCIALIST REPUBLIC OF SRI LANKA
Head of state and government: Chandrika Bandaranaike Kumaratunga
Capital: Colombo
Population: 18.8 million
Official languages: Sinhala, Tamil, English
Death penalty: abolitionist in practice
2000 treaty ratifications/signatures: Optional Protocol to the UN Children's Convention on the involvement of children in armed conflict

The continuing armed conflict and a general rise in violence dominated Sri Lanka in 2000. April and May saw particularly ferocious fighting between the security forces and the Liberation Tigers of Tamil Eelam (LTTE), the main armed opposition group fighting for an independent state, Eelam, in the north and east of Sri Lanka. Tens of thousands of people were internally displaced by the fighting. People taking no active part in the hostilities faced gross human rights abuses, including indiscriminate bombing and shelling, killings, "disappearances", torture and the recruitment of child soldiers. Widespread violence took place during parliamentary elections in October. There was also a rise in paramilitary and vigilante activities. The failure to bring to justice those responsible for human rights violations remained a major concern.

Background
A state of emergency remained in force throughout the country. After heavy fighting and the capture of the strategically important Elephant Pass army camp by the LTTE, measures were introduced in May to put the country on a "war footing". New Emergency Regulations (ERs) considerably extended the security forces' powers to detain and included provisions granting powers of arrest to "any other authorized persons". The ERs also provided wide powers of censorship.

In February, the Norwegian government agreed to facilitate a dialogue between the government and the LTTE, but by the end of the year few concrete results were visible. The government's efforts to introduce constitutional reforms aimed at resolving the ethnic conflict were shelved in August after it failed to muster the required two-thirds majority in parliament.

No party won an overall majority in parliamentary elections in October. The People's Alliance formed a new government with the Sri Lanka Muslim Congress and the Eelam People's Democratic Party.

The security forces and LTTE stepped up the procurement of arms.

Killings of civilians
Amid the escalating conflict, the number of internally displaced civilians rose from around 400,000 in January to around 570,000 by the end of June. At least

150 civilians were killed in attacks by both sides. Both the army and the LTTE were responsible for not taking adequate measures to avoid civilian casualties.

▫ In October, at least 24 civilians were killed in two separate attacks on election rallies by LTTE suicide bombers. Scores of civilians were killed in other attacks, apparently carried out by the LTTE, in Colombo.

▫ The army shot dead 17 civilians, including nine children, in Batticaloa town in May, apparently in reprisal for the killing of three policemen by a bomb concealed in a ice cream vendor's freezer box.

▫ On 2 October, seven Tamil civilians were killed by Muslim Home Guards — villagers armed ostensibly for their own protection — at Poonagar, Muttur, Trincomalee district, in apparent reprisal for the killing of two Muslim Home Guards by members of the LTTE earlier that day.

'Disappearances'

At least 20 "disappearances" were reported during 2000. As in previous years, the highest number — 11 — were reported from the Vavuniya area. An internal inquiry ordered by President Chandrika Bandaranaike Kumaratunga into seven cases reported between 10 and 26 August seemed to bring a temporary halt to "disappearances" in that area, but two more cases were reported in early October. Other "disappearances" were reported from Colombo, Batticaloa, Jaffna, Mannar and Trincomalee. Naval personnel were held responsible for two "disappearances" in Trincomalee.

▫ Eight displaced civilians, including a five-year-old boy, "disappeared" after being arrested while visiting their homes on 19 December. Their bodies were recovered from an illegal grave six days later. Thirteen soldiers were arrested in connection with their abduction and murder.

Torture/ ill-treatment

Torture remained common, both in the context of the armed conflict and during routine policing operations. Reports of torture increased following the introduction of ERs in May. However, later in the year reports of torture appeared to decline, possibly partly as a result of a number of measures taken by the government after a visit to the country by the Committee against Torture. These included, among other things, the establishment of an Inter-Ministerial Standing Committee to take action with regard to cases of torture. By the end of 2000 no one had been convicted of offences related to the crime of torture. There were frequent reports of torture involving the Security Coordinating Unit of the Vavuniya police and the army camps at Urelu and Atchelu in Jaffna. There were reports of rape by the army in Jaffna and Batticaloa and by police in Negombo.

▫ Five labourers arrested on suspicion of involvement with the LTTE were tortured by police at Kantalai, Trincomalee, in June. One of them died apparently as a result of torture, although police and other officials claimed that he was shot while trying to escape.

Deaths in custody

Several incidents of violence in prison and other detention facilities were reported.

▫ A Tamil detainee died as a result of injuries sustained during a clash between prison guards and political prisoners in Ward F at Kalutara prison on 6 January. The following day, another detainee was killed in an apparently deliberate attack by prison guards on prisoners in Ward C.

▫ On 25 October, 27 young Tamil men and boys aged between 14 and 23 detained for "rehabilitation" were killed during an attack by a mob of Sinhalese villagers on a rehabilitation camp at Bindunuwewa, Badulla district. There was evidence of collusion by members of the local police and deliberate failure to protect the detainees.

Political prisoners

Thousands of Tamil people were arrested on suspicion of involvement with the LTTE. At least 1,500 were held without charge or trial at the end of the year; some had been detained for more than four years.

Impunity

Impunity for the perpetrators of human rights abuses remained a major concern. Victims who sought justice through the courts received death threats. The report of a Presidential commission of inquiry, set up in 1998 to investigate complaints of past "disappearances" not examined by three earlier commissions, was handed over to the President in late August. The implementation of the recommendations of previous commissions and of the UN Working Group on Enforced or Involuntary Disappearances, which visited the country in 1999, proceeded slowly.

▫ Officers from Tangalle police station standing trial for torturing Mahanama Geeganage Chandrakumara in 1990, attempted to stop him and his parents from giving evidence against them by intimidation and death threats. The trial was continuing at the end of the year.

▫ Four army personnel and a police officer were arrested in March on suspicion of involvement in the "disappearance" in 1996 of 15 people whose bodies were recovered from shallow graves in the Chemmani area of Jaffna district in 1999. The five were released on bail in June. The criminal investigation was continuing at the end of the year.

Death penalty

Scores of people were sentenced to death for murder. No one was executed. In November, the government announced that it would put into practice a decision announced in 1999 to resume executions. AI expressed concern about this major step backwards for human rights.

Violations by vigilante and paramilitary groups

Tamil armed groups working alongside the security forces, and members of the security forces acting outside the normal command and control structures, were allegedly responsible for human rights violations, including against journalists.

◻ Circumstantial evidence put the blame for the killing of Mylvaganam Nimalrajan, Jaffna correspondent for various newspapers and international agencies, on members of the Eelam People's Democratic Party working with the security forces. He was killed in his home in the High Security Zone of Jaffna town during curfew.

◻ Kumar Ponnambalam, President of the All Ceylon Tamil Congress, was killed on 5 January by two gunmen in what appeared to be a carefully planned attack. The motive and the identity of those responsible for ordering the killing were unclear. There were concerns that police investigations into his murder may have been subject to political influence. A reserve police constable was among those arrested in connection with the murder.

Child soldiers
The LTTE stepped up the recruitment of children as combatants after the intense fighting in Jaffna in May. Those recruited included children as young as 12.

AI country report
- Sri Lanka: New Emergency Regulations – erosion of human rights protection (AI Index: 37/019/2000)

SUDAN

REPUBLIC OF THE SUDAN
Head of state and government: Omar Hassan Ahmad al-Bashir
Capital: Khartoum
Population: 29.4 million
Official language: Arabic
Death penalty: retentionist
2000 treaty ratifications/signatures: Rome Statute of the International Criminal Court

The civil war continued to devastate the lives of countless civilians during 2000. Those most affected were people living near oil fields where pro-government forces and armed opposition groups were fighting for control of oil production and territory. All parties to the conflict committed gross human rights abuses against civilians living in the contested areas including indiscriminate bombing, abduction, enslavement, forcible recruitment, torture and killings. Tens of thousands of people were forced to leave their homes. Despite government claims that the human rights situation in areas under its control was improving, lawyers, journalists, students and human rights defenders were harassed and intimidated. Dozens were arrested and tortured. Those responsible for human rights abuses were not brought to justice. Restrictions on the rights to freedom of expression and association in cities under government control persisted.

Background
By the end of 2000, the civil war, which resumed in 1983, had cost the lives of almost 2,000,000 people and resulted in a further 4,500,000 people being internally displaced. In addition, some 500,000 people were believed to have sought asylum abroad.

The main parties to the conflict since 1983 were those supporting the government — including the Sudanese People's Armed Forces (the regular army), the paramilitary Popular Defence Forces, and various militia groups known as the *murahaleen* — and the opposition forces made up of the Sudan People's Liberation Army (SPLA) and various allied militias.

The drive for oil and territorial control over the oil fields was central to the war between the government and armed opposition forces, as well as to the ongoing conflict between the various militia factions. For example, the 1,600km oil pipeline which came into operation in August 1999 continued to be the target of repeated attacks by opposition forces. In addition to the conflict between the regular army and the SPLA, another conflict raged between the various militias allied with the government or the SPLA. These forces frequently changed sides depending on their perceived interests or simply the supply of arms. It was estimated that during the past few years more people had lost their lives as a result of interfactional fighting between militias than in armed encounters with government forces. The government pursued a policy of providing support and weapons to the various militia commanders and encouraging interfactional fighting, which resulted in widespread destruction and destitution for the local civilian population.

The Bahr el-Ghazal humanitarian cease-fire — agreed between the SPLA, the UN and relief agencies operating under the umbrella organization Operation Lifeline Sudan (OLS) — to provide food to civilians affected by the conflict collapsed in July. However, a new agreement was subsequently reached between the OLS and the government which allowed relief supplies to resume. Although the cease-fire was not restored, a 12-day truce was agreed in October to allow the UN Children's Fund (UNICEF) to carry out anti-polio vaccinations. Some non-governmental organizations accused the government of not respecting this truce and bombing towns.

The state of emergency declared in December 1999 remained in place for most of the year.

Presidential and parliamentary elections took place in December. Both UN and European Union monitors turned down invitations to monitor the elections which were widely believed to be seriously flawed. Arrests of journalists, political opponents and human rights activists intensified ahead of the elections and the main opposition parties called for a boycott of the elections; people in areas under rebel control did not take part in the elections. President Omar al-Bashir, in power since 1989, was declared the winner of the elections.

Internal displacement
Tens of thousands of people were terrorized into leaving their homes in oil-rich Upper Nile by aerial bombardments, mass executions and torture. This massive displacement was followed by the deployment of additional weaponry and forces to protect the oil fields. Crops and livestock were burned and looted to prevent people from returning to their homes. Bombings in Northern Bahr el-Ghazal also resulted in mass displacement of the civilian population.

Bombing of civilians
Indiscriminate bombing of civilians in the south of the country continued. International outcry at the bombing of hospitals and schoolchildren in February and March led President al-Bashir to order his forces to stop all air bombardment operations except where these were justified by self-defence or during military operations to "protect lives and property". However, following the collapse of the Bahr el-Ghazal humanitarian cease-fire, the bombings intensified. From September bombardments of civilian targets intensified in other parts of the country including Eastern Equatoria, Upper Nile and south Blue Nile.

☐ In July alone, more than 250 bombs reportedly hit civilian targets in at least 30 separate incidents causing several deaths and disrupting the harvest and humanitarian relief in Bahr el-Ghazal.

Child soldiers
Conscription into the armed forces is compulsory for both men and women and the law stipulates that military training is a precondition for entry into further and higher education or into certain jobs. There was increasing evidence that child soldiers were being used by the various parties to the conflict. There were reports that children were being abducted in the streets of Khartoum and forcibly recruited into the Popular Defence Forces. The parents were not informed and most of the young recruits were sent to the front line. There were reports of ill-treatment of child conscripts.

☐ On 29 May the body of 17-year-old Ghassan Ahmed Al Amin Haroun was transferred to the Khartoum morgue from the Jabal Awlia Compulsory Military Service Joint Camp. He had joined the army unit just two days earlier. A post-mortem examination revealed injuries on his hands, back, right foot and eye and bruising on other parts of the body and confirmed the cause of death to be "respiratory failure". The authorities did not comment on the post-mortem findings, but shortly afterwards placed the family under surveillance by the security forces.

☐ Sixteen-year-old Mohanad Abdelrahman M. Zakana died at the Aljouli military training camp in May. His death was believed to have been caused by the harsh training meted out to young conscripts. It was alleged that he was denied adequate medical treatment after he collapsed with sunstroke.

Children continued to be forcibly recruited by the SPLA, despite the fact that the SPLA had informed UNICEF that it would demobilize all child soldiers in its forces and end the recruitment of children.

Slavery
Although the government continued to deny that slavery existed in Sudan, thousands of people were believed to be held in forced labour or slavery. Estimates varied regarding the number of people held in slavery; some non-governmental organizations put the figure as high as 100,000, while government sources put the figure at 5,000. The sexual slavery of women was widely reported, especially in the areas affected by the armed conflict. Those who escaped described widespread torture, including rape, and forced marriages.

Torture/ill-treatment
Widespread torture and ill-treatment continued to be reported in many government-held towns. There was grave concern that suspected government opponents were particularly at risk. Reports of torture were not investigated and the perpetrators were not brought to justice. Reports of torture were also received from SPLA-held territories.

☐ No investigation was carried out into the deaths in custody of Joseph Adhiang Langlang, Abdallah Col, Hassan Abu Adhan and Gladino Sam Okieny. They reportedly died as a result of torture. The four men had been held with Hillary Boma and 25 others, accused of planting bombs in Khartoum in 1998. After Hillary Boma and his fellow prisoners were pardoned and released in December 1999, no investigation was carried out into their allegations of torture.

☐ In December, eight members of opposition political parties were arrested by the security forces during a meeting with a US diplomat. They were accused of plotting a coup. A few days later, two lawyers – Ghazi Suleiman and Ali Mahmoud Hasanain – were arrested for signing a petition against the arrests. Ghazi Suleiman sustained a head injury and was reportedly hospitalized twice while in detention, raising grave concerns that he was tortured. The 10 detainees were held in a secret location in solitary confinement and without access to their families, medical treatment or lawyers.

Amputation
At least 12 people were sentenced to have limbs amputated during 2000. At least one amputation was carried out.

☐ In March Al Salik Obeid had his right hand and left foot amputated at Kober Prison.

Rape and other violence against women
Violence against women by combatants on all sides, long a feature of the conflict in Sudan, intensified during the year. There were widespread reports of sexual abuse, including sexual slavery, rape and forced pregnancies. Rape was used as a tactic of war by both government and opposition forces to dehumanize and humiliate civilians in the conflict zone. However, because of the taboos and stigma attached to rape, reports were rare and impunity for the rapist was the rule. There were frequent reports of women being abducted while collecting firewood or water and being forced to carry heavy loads of goods looted from ransacked villages. They were also used

as bonded labour and forced to clean, cook and provide domestic services to soldiers in barracks and camps.

Women's rights

Violations of women's rights were widespread. In central Sudan, especially in Khartoum, women faced severe restrictions on their freedom of movement.

▫ In September the Governor of Khartoum issued a decree banning women from working in public places. Days later, 26 women were arrested and three were injured when police used tear gas and batons to break up a peaceful demonstration against the decree.

The decree was challenged on the grounds that it was unconstitutional in the Constitutional Court which in October temporarily suspended the ban. The Court's final decision was still pending at the end of the year. However, the Minister of Justice, while recognizing that the Constitution and international conventions guarantee a woman's right to work, would not condemn the ban as unconstitutional.

Students and human rights defenders

Students and human rights defenders were harassed and intimidated during 2000, particularly in and around Khartoum. The security forces prevented or disrupted student activities and activists were arrested and tortured; one was killed.

▫ In June soldiers opened fire on a student seminar on the crisis in Sudan at the University of Sennar. One participant, 'Mirghami Mahmoud al-Norman, was shot dead and several others were injured. In the days that followed the shooting, several demonstrations in support of the students took place. At least 11 people, including seven students, were arrested and charged with rioting and disturbing public order. All were believed to have been tortured and most were hospitalized as a result.

Lawyers and relatives trying to pursue cases of human rights violations frequently faced harassment and repeated summons to appear at police stations or security force installations. The perpetrators of human rights violations, in contrast, were not pursued through the justice system.

▫ Relatives seeking justice for an 11-year-old girl raped by a police officer in May 1999 were harassed and intimidated. The authorities repeatedly attempted to subject the girl to further intrusive medical examinations. However, instead of pursuing the allegations of rape, the Sudanese authorities chose to view the case as a "security" issue. Family members and lawyers acting on their behalf were required to report to the Federal Criminal Investigation Department and documents were seized from the lawyers' offices by members of the security forces. Neither the relatives nor lawyers were charged with a recognizably criminal offence.

AI country report

- Sudan: The Human Price of Oil (AI Index: AFR 54/001/2000 ERR)

SURINAME

REPUBLIC OF SURINAME
Head of state: Ronald Venetiaan (replaced Jules Wijdenbosch in August)
Head of government: Jules Ajodhia
Capital: Paramaribo
Population: 0.4 million
Official Language: Dutch
Death penalty: abolitionist in practice

Impunity for human rights abuses committed under previous regimes was a major issue for the newly elected government. Conditions in prisons and police detention centres remained poor. Reports of ill-treatment and torture of prisoners continued.

Background

President Ronald Venetiaan took power on 18 August, having won general elections in May at the head of a four-party New Front coalition composed of political groups that were deposed by coups in 1980 and 1990. President Venetiaan had previously held power in 1995 and 1996. He took over from Jules Wijdenbosch of the National Democratic Party.

Impunity

There was little or no action until the change of government to bring to justice those responsible for human rights abuses committed under previous governments. These include a 1986 massacre of civilians at the village of Moiwana, the beating of a prisoner to death by prison guards in 1993, and the so-called "December murders" of 1982.

▫ In 1982, 15 journalists, academics and labour leaders were extrajudicially executed at Fort Zeelandia, an army centre near the Surinamese Cabinet Office, in Paramaribo. On 31 October 2000, after the change of government, the Court of Justice ordered the prosecution of former military leader Desi Bouterse and others in connection with these killings. Dozens of witnesses, including politicians, were questioned by the Public Prosecutor's Office. However, under the country's 18-year statute of limitations, legal proceedings should have been concluded by 8 December 2000. At the end of the year, the Public Prosecutor's Office was working on a summons to start a preliminary judicial investigation. Desi Bouterse denied charges that he presided over the murders, saying that he took responsibility only because he was head of government and the military at the time.

Conditions in prisons and detention centres

Prison conditions were extremely harsh and severely overcrowded, amounting sometimes to cruel, inhuman or degrading treatment. Conditions of hygiene and ventilation were poor, with food, blankets, cleaning equipment, soap and medicines in short supply. Medical care was inadequate. Most prisoners could not afford their own lawyer, and state-funded advisers were scarce.

Pre-trial detainees constituted a large percentage of inmates, many of whom were held in overcrowded detention cells at local police stations. Police officers who had not been trained in prison work served as jailers in local detention centres.

Beatings of detainees and prisoners were also reported.

Ill-treatment
Human rights groups continued to express concern about ill-treatment by law enforcement officials. They documented cases of police ill-treating detainees, particularly during arrests, and abuses of prisoners by guards.

SWAZILAND

KINGDOM OF SWAZILAND
Head of state: King Mswati III
Head of government: Barnabus Sibusiso Dlamini
Capital: Mbabane
Population: 1 million
Official languages: English, Swazi
Death penalty: retentionist
2000 treaty ratifications/signatures: UN Refugee Convention

Rights of association, assembly and expression continued to be denied. Opposition protests led to arbitrary detentions and ill-treatment by the security forces. Government opponents faced arrest and politically motivated charges in the courts. At least 12 death sentences were passed.

Background
The Constitutional Review Commission (CRC), appointed by King Mswati III in 1996, presented its recommendations for a new constitution to the King in November. Its findings and recommendations were not made public. The CRC was criticized for limiting public access to its proceedings.

There were a number of incidents of political violence. They included the petrol bombing in December of magistrates' courts in Mbabane. There was also a bomb explosion at a security force encampment in the Macetjeni area in December.

Violations of freedoms of association, assembly and expression
Journalists faced harassment in reporting political or human rights issues. In February the government closed the state-owned *Swazi Observer* newspaper after journalists refused to disclose the sources of an article about a 1998 bomb explosion. In July a case against journalist Bheki Makhuba for criminal defamation was struck off the court roll when the prosecution failed to appear in court. He had been briefly detained and charged in 1999 in connection with a newspaper article about King Mswati.

Protests over restrictions on fundamental freedoms intensified towards the end of 2000. Members of banned political parties, students and trade union members held demonstrations and meetings. They called for an end to the 1973 suspension of freedoms of association and assembly, the repeal of legal restrictions on trade union rights and a new government.

In October the government banned meetings of the Swaziland Federation of Trade Unions (SFTU) and the Swaziland National Association of Teachers (SNAT), and threatened civil servants with arrest if they participated in strikes and boycotts deemed political. The government obtained an Industrial Court order declaring illegal a proposed strike by the SFTU. Following the visit of a delegation from the International Labour Organisation in November, King Mswati signed into law an amended Industrial Relations Act which restored some trade union freedoms.

Detentions, restrictions and political trials
Opposition leaders were prosecuted on the basis of politically motivated charges. Journalists and other critics were briefly detained without charge or trial. AI appealed to the government to respect the rights of its citizens to non-violent political association and assembly, and to freedom of expression.

◻ A number of local and foreign journalists reporting political protests in October and November were briefly detained and had film footage confiscated. Foreign journalists were ordered to leave the country.
◻ On 7 November SFTU officials were briefly held at a security force roadblock outside Mbabane to prevent them joining protesters seeking to hand a petition calling for political reforms to the Prime Minister. Jan Sithole, SFTU Secretary General, was subsequently held under extra-legal house arrest for several days and his communication with others was restricted by the security forces.
◻ On 7 November members of the banned opposition party, the People's United Democratic Movement (PUDEMO), were prevented by the security forces from delivering a petition to the Prime Minister. Mario Masuku, President of PUDEMO, was arrested by police on 10 November and held incommunicado. On 15 November he was charged in the High Court with sedition for allegedly criticizing the King and released under restrictive bail conditions to await trial. The presiding judge, the Chief Justice, was later questioned by government ministers about his decision to grant bail.

Torture/ill-treatment
The security forces ill-treated and used excessive force against political activists and protesters.

☐ In February delegates to a Swaziland Youth Congress conference required hospital treatment for injuries sustained when police forcibly broke up the gathering.

☐ In October some 200 villagers in Macetjeni and KaMkhweli were evicted from their homes at gunpoint by soldiers, apparently because they refused to accept the King's brother, Prince Maguga, as chief. They were left in the countryside without shelter or other basic necessities. After a petrol bomb attack in December on Prince Maguga's home, Dumisa Ndhlandhla was arrested and charged with arson. He was allegedly beaten and subjected to suffocation torture by police during interrogation.

☐ During protests and strikes in October and November a number of trade union officials and other protesters were assaulted by the security forces. Musa Dlamini, SNAT Secretary General, was allegedly beaten at police regional headquarters in Manzini, and Bongihlanhla Gama, another SNAT official, was shot and wounded by police. They both required treatment in hospital.

Death penalty

At least 12 death sentences were imposed by the High Court in separate murder trials. No executions were known to have taken place.

SWEDEN

KINGDOM OF SWEDEN
Head of state: King Carl XVI Gustaf
Head of government: Goran Persson
Capital: Stockholm
Population: 8.9 million
Official language: Swedish
Death penalty: abolitionist for all crimes
2000 treaty ratifications/signatures: Optional Protocol to the UN Children's Convention on the involvement of children in armed conflict

At least two unarmed people were shot dead by police, and at least two people died in custody in disputed circumstances. More than five years after the death in custody of Osmo Vallo, no one had been held accountable.

Osmo Vallo

More than five years after the death in custody in disputed circumstances of Osmo Vallo, the government established a commission of inquiry into the authorities' handling of the case; no one had been held accountable.

Osmo Vallo died shortly after his arrest on 30 May 1995. A police officer had stamped on his back as he lay face down on the ground. After he appeared to have collapsed, no attempt was made to assist or resuscitate him. Instead, police officers transported him, still handcuffed and lying face downwards, to the hospital.

In closing the investigation into the case on 30 March 2000, the Prosecutor General acknowledged that Osmo Vallo may have died from being stamped on the back by a police officer. The Prosecutor General also acknowledged that there had been flaws in the investigation and urged that a further investigation be carried out into how the authorities had handled the different aspects of the case.

There was concern that Osmo Vallo's death was not an isolated incident; a pattern of similar deaths in custody had been reported in which the manner of restraint or excessive use of force by law enforcement officials may have caused asphyxia. The inadequacy of many of the investigations into these deaths led AI to call for a totally independent body such as a commission of inquiry, possibly including experts from other countries, to investigate the handling of Osmo Vallo's case by the different authorities, as well as other cases of deaths in custody since 1992.

In a letter to AI in June, the Minister of Justice stated that the 21 June report of the Chancellor of Justice was critical of actions taken by various authorities involved in the handling of the Osmo Vallo case and indicated flaws within the criminal justice system. The Chancellor of Justice's report called for further consideration of certain questions.

The Chancellor of Justice's report was immediately followed by a report by the Parliamentary Ombudsperson who stated that the current procedure for dealing with complaints against the police was inadequate and proposed that an independent system be established. The Ombudsperson was particularly critical of the local prosecutors' failure to initiate preliminary investigations into some cases of alleged police misconduct even though such investigations would have been justified. The Minister of Justice established a commission of inquiry in December to look into past deaths in custody in order to propose preventive measures for the future. The commission was scheduled to report in one year's time.

Shootings by police

At least two unarmed people were shot dead by police.

☐ Magnus Carlsson, aged 19, was shot dead in Kalmar on 13 May after a car chase and a struggle with police officers. A police officer was accused of causing the death of another person or breach of duty, but was acquitted in October, after the court accepted that he had acted in self-defence.

☐ Mikael Pettersson, aged 31, was shot dead on 13 March at Vikbolandet near Norrköping after he crashed his car while being chased by the police and then tried to run away. The police officer reportedly fired a warning shot, then shot Mikael Pettersson because he was convinced that he was armed. No weapon was found at the scene. In October the police officer was convicted of breach of duty, aggravated assault and causing the death of another person through grave carelessness and sentenced to 18 months' imprisonment. The officer lodged an appeal which was pending at the end of the year.

Death in prison
In June Bruce Joel Jason Hulthén, a 28-year-old prisoner, died after being restrained by four prison guards. He had attempted to escape from the Storboda Institution in Stockholm. The prison authorities were immediately alerted to his escape and he was chased and caught by four prison guards. The prison guards restrained him, including reportedly by sitting on him as he lay on the ground. It was also reported that one guard grabbed the back of Bruce Joel Jason Hulthén's head and neck, which may have caused his death. When the police arrived on the scene shortly afterwards, the prisoner was apparently already unconscious. The Regional Director of Prison and Probation Services told the media that the prisoner "went blue in the face and stopped breathing". Prison guards reportedly tried to resuscitate him, but he was dead on arrival at the hospital. The prison guards were suspended pending the police investigation into the death. In October, one of the prison guards was charged with manslaughter; he was awaiting trial at the end of the year.

Death in police custody
On 3 November, Peter Andersson, a 35-year-old suspected burglar, died after being arrested and restrained by four police officers in Örebro. The preliminary report of a post-mortem examination indicated signs of violence on his face, arms, legs and body as well as symptoms of death from asphyxia.

Forcible return
In November the UN Committee against Torture concluded that the decisions of the Swedish immigration authorities in connection with the case of an Iranian woman had constituted a violation of Sweden's obligations under the UN Convention against Torture. The woman feared that she might be sentenced to death by stoning for adultery if she was returned to Iran.

AI country report
- Concerns in Europe, January – June 2000: Sweden (AI Index: EUR 01/003/2000)

SWITZERLAND

SWISS CONFEDERATION
Head of state and government: Adolf Ogi
Capital: Bern
Population: 7.3 million
Official languages: German, French, Italian
Death penalty: abolitionist for all crimes
2000 treaty ratifications/signatures: Optional Protocol to the UN Children's Convention on the involvement of children in armed conflict

There were further allegations of ill-treatment of criminal suspects by police and of foreign nationals during forcible deportation. Some official investigations into such allegations were unsatisfactory. A criminal investigation continued into the death of an asylum-seeker during deportation in 1999. A military appeal court confirmed that a Rwandese national was guilty of war crimes.

Background
A new Federal Constitution which came into force in January included specific prohibitions on torture and all other cruel, inhuman or degrading treatment or punishment and on the return of any individual to a state where they would risk such treatment.

In March a national referendum voted in favour of a package of reforms in the justice system, already approved by parliament, including the eventual unification of the existing 26 cantonal codes of penal procedure and three federal laws on penal procedure. The text of a draft bill of unification was expected in 2001. In previous years both the UN Human Rights Committee and the UN Committee against Torture had recommended that Switzerland intensify its efforts to harmonize the cantonal codes, particularly with regard to the granting of certain legal guarantees providing safeguards against ill-treatment in police custody.

Ill-treatment on arrest
There were fresh reports of police ill-treatment of detainees, often accompanied by racist abuse in the case of non-Caucasians. Some criminal and administrative investigations into such allegations were inadequate. In its second report on Switzerland, published in March, the Council of Europe's Commission against Racism and Intolerance noted reports concerning police ill-treatment "particularly of non-citizens and Swiss of foreign origin" and stressed "the importance of setting up an independent body to investigate complaints of police ill-treatment" and of more systematic police training on "the subject of racism and discrimination".

◻ A criminal investigation was opened into a complaint which Rashid Abdul-Ackah, a Swiss citizen of Ghanaian origin, lodged against members of Zurich Municipal Police in December 1999. He said that while walking through central Zurich, police officers subjected him to repeated, unnecessary identity checks, knocked him to the ground, handcuffed him, subjected him to racist abuse and transferred him to a police station where he was forced to strip. Within hours of his release, without charge, a local hospital issued a medical certificate recording bruises on his left arm and head. He maintained that there were no legal grounds for his detention and that the police had taken him to the police station in order to humiliate him.

◻ In January a 17-year-old Angolan schoolboy lodged a criminal complaint against three Geneva police officers. He accused them of kicking and beating him with truncheons until he lost consciousness and subjecting him to racist abuse after detaining him in November 1999 on suspicion of being involved in a street fight. He was held in a police station overnight, then charged with resisting the police, but subsequently acquitted. In April the Geneva Attorney General, who had opened a preliminary inquiry entrusted to the police, ruled that there were no grounds to justify further investigation and closed the inquiry. The boy had never been questioned about his allegations. In August, following an appeal, a Geneva court ruled that an investigating magistrate should carry out a full inquiry into the allegations, including questioning the boy and other relevant witnesses.

Ill-treatment during deportation

There were allegations that police officers subjected some foreign nationals resisting deportation to physical assault, death threats and racist abuse immediately prior to and during forcible deportations from Zurich-Kloten and Geneva airports. There were also unconfirmed reports that on occasion recalcitrant deportees were given sedatives in order to subdue them rather than for purely medical reasons. Some deportees claimed that they were deprived of food, liquid and access to a lavatory for many hours until they reached their destination.

There were also claims that some form of mouth restraint was used in isolated cases involving deportations from Zurich. The use of any materials or methods which could block an individual's airways is highly dangerous and can result in fatalities. It was unclear whether any explicit instruction banning the use of all forms of mouth restraint was in existence and whether an internal service instruction issued to Zurich Cantonal Police in May 1998, explicitly authorizing gagging as a means of restraint during deportation, had been withdrawn. In August 1999 the Zurich cantonal government had announced that adhesive tape would no longer be used to cover deportees' mouths to prevent them shouting. In September 2000, it stated that a specially modified helmet introduced in July 1999, which had a chin-cup attached forcing the jaws closed and a cover which could be placed across the mouth, had not been used since September 1999. The government said that the helmet was no longer necessary because "forseeably difficult" deportations now took place via specially chartered flights and no longer on normal passenger flights. It added that open-faced rubber helmets were in use to prevent recalcitrant deportees injuring themselves.

The Zurich government refused to supply AI or the Zurich parliament with copies of internal service instructions or any written guidelines issued to police officers concerning the treatment of detainees during forcible deportation. In November it stated that officers were authorized to wear masks during deportation operations, for their own protection. There was concern that, if masked officers did not display some form of identification prominently on their uniforms, this could prevent identification of alleged assailants and thus provide them with complete impunity.

◻ Gilbert Kouam Tamo, a Cameroonian, alleged that during his deportation from Zurich in April, masked officers kicked and punched him, beat him with batons, applied such pressure to his neck that he felt he was choking, pressed a pillow over his face and, when he was bound hand and foot and attached to an airline seat by several belts, twice punched him in the face. He also claimed that there was an unsuccessful attempt to inject him and that he was deprived of food and drink during a nine-hour flight. A hospital in Cameroon recorded extensive cuts and bruises to his face and body.

Khaled Abuzarifa

In January the Bülach Public Prosecutor's office investigating the death of Khaled Abuzarifa, a Palestinian, during deportation from Zurich-Kloten airport in March 1999, announced that, in view of the findings of a post-mortem examination, three police officers and a doctor employed by the Canton of Bern, where the deportation operation began, had been put under formal investigation in connection with possible manslaughter charges.

Khaled Abuzarifa was given a sedative tablet, had his mouth sealed with adhesive tape, was bound hand and foot, and strapped into a wheelchair in preparation for deportation. The post-mortem report concluded that he died of suffocation as a result of the restraining measures to which he was subjected. It criticized the escorting police officers for losing valuable time in removing the adhesive tape after observing that he was unwell and noted that they had not received relevant training. The doctor, who assisted at the taping of the mouth and certified it as safe, even though the deportee was only able to breath through one nostril, was criticized for failing to provide them with relevant instructions. A supplementary forensic report was subsequently drawn up at the request of the accused and the criminal investigation remained open at the end of the year.

Universal jurisdiction over war crimes

In May a military appeal court reduced a sentence of life imprisonment passed on Fulgence Niyonteze, a former local government official in Rwanda, to 14 years' imprisonment. In 1999, in the first trial of its kind in the national jurisdiction of a foreign country, a military court had found Fulgence Niyonteze guilty of murder, incitement to murder and war crimes in the context of the 1994 genocide in Rwanda.

The appeal court found him guilty of war crimes and sentenced him for violation of the Geneva Conventions but set aside the charges of murder and incitement to murder, declaring that military jurisdiction was not competent to examine such offences when committed abroad by a civilian. Both Fulgence Niyonteze and the prosecutor lodged appeals against the sentence. As in the first instance trial, there was concern that the anonymity of witnesses was not adequately protected during the appeal hearings.

AI country report
- Concerns in Europe, January – June 2000: Switzerland (AI Index: EUR 01/003/2000)

SYRIA

SYRIAN ARAB REPUBLIC
Head of state: Bashar al-Assad (replaced Hafez al-Assad in July)
Head of government: Muhammad Mustafa Miro (replaced Mahmud al-Zu'bi in March)
Capital: Damascus
Population: 16.1 million
Official language: Arabic
Death penalty: retentionist
2000 treaty ratifications/signatures: Rome Statute of the International Criminal Court

Hundreds of political prisoners including prisoners of conscience were released during 2000, mostly as the result of a presidential amnesty issued in November. Restrictions on freedom of expression were apparently relaxed to some extent. Dozens of people were arrested during 2000 for political reasons. Hundreds of political prisoners, including prisoners of conscience, remained in detention without trial or serving long sentences passed after unfair trials by the Supreme State Security Court (SSSC). At least one political prisoner died in custody and scores of ill political detainees remained held in cruel and inhuman conditions. The fate of hundreds of people who "disappeared" in the late 1970s and 1980s remained unknown. There were continuing reports of torture and ill-treatment of political detainees.

Background
Following the death of President Hafez al-Assad in June, his son Bashar al-Assad was elected President in a general referendum in July. He was nominated as the sole candidate for the presidency by the ruling Ba'th party.

There were calls for political and economic liberalization from people including members of the National Assembly. A public statement issued by 99 Syrian intellectuals, mostly resident in Syria, called for the lifting of the state of emergency, which has been in place since 1963, and the release of political prisoners. This was the first time that such a statement had been issued without those involved being arrested and detained or otherwise harassed. In addition, the Ba'th party leadership approved a resolution allowing junior members of the Progressive National Front, including the two wings of the Syrian Communist Party, to publish their own newspapers.

Human rights defenders
Restrictions imposed on the Committees for the Defence of Democratic Freedoms and Human Rights in Syria (CDF) were relaxed during 2000, allowing a plenary meeting to take place, attended by CDF members and other human rights activists and intellectuals. (In a related development, the restrictions imposed on the movement of Aktham Nu'aysa, a former prisoner of conscience, were lifted). During 2000, four members of the CDF who had been detained in connection with the distribution of a CDF leaflet marking the anniversary of the Universal Declaration of Human Rights were released, although prisoner of conscience Nizar Nayyuf remained in detention. The four released prisoners were 'Afif Muzhir, Muhammad Ali Habib, Bassam al-Shaykh and Thabit Murad.

Human rights defender Nizar Nayyuf remained held despite his ill-health, after being moved to Sednaya Prison following the closure during the year of Mezze Prison. Sentenced to 10 years' imprisonment for his involvement with the CDF, he was held in solitary confinement. Nizar Nayyuf was suffering from, among other things, a disease of the lower spine, apparently caused as a result of torture; weakening of the legs, leaving him unable to walk unaided; and deteriorating eyesight.

Arrests
Sporadic arrest and detention of individuals for political reasons continued during 2000.

Among those detained were individuals critical of the government and nationals of neighbouring Arab countries.

There were reports about the arrest and detention of asylum-seekers forcibly returned to Syria. They included Hussain Daoud, reportedly forcibly returned to Syria from Germany accompanied by German police officers. He was reportedly arrested in December at Damascus airport and transferred to *Far' Falastin*, Palestine Branch, where he was held at the end of 2000. His arrest was believed to be connected to his involvement with the unauthorized Kurdish Popular Union Party in Syria.

The arrest and transfer from Lebanon to Syria of at least five Lebanese soldiers in 1999 came to light. They included sergeants Nimer al-Naddaf and Fuad 'Asaker. They were held incommunicado in detention centres including *Far' Falastin*, Palestine Branch, and *Far 'al-Tahqiq al-'Askari*, Military Interrogation Branch, where torture and ill-treatment were routine.

There were reports of harassment and intimidation of former prisoners of conscience released during the year and of the families of exiled Syrians.

◻ Ra'ad Washil Muhammad al-Shammari, an Iraqi national aged 42, was arrested in June and was reportedly held incommunicado in a detention centre in Damascus. Married with four children, Ra'ad Washil Muhammad al-Shammari was apparently arrested solely for political reasons and there were fears that he may have been tortured. He had in the past been detained for several years in Iraq for his involvement with the unauthorized Iraqi Communist Party.

◻ Relatives of a former prisoner of conscience who sought asylum overseas were repeatedly summoned to the Political Security Department for questioning about his whereabouts. Members of his family, including his wife and children, were held for hours at the security office almost daily and subjected to verbal abuse and beating. Before managing to escape, the former prisoner of conscience used to be summoned regularly to the same department and subjected to torture and ill-treatment.

Releases of political prisoners
Presidential amnesty
Hundreds of political prisoners, including prisoners of conscience, were released in November following an amnesty issued by President Bashar al-Assad marking the 30th anniversary of the military coup which brought the late President Hafez al-Assad to power in 1970. The main beneficiaries were members of the unauthorized *al-Ikhwan al-Muslimun,* Muslim Brotherhood, and their sympathizers. They had been held, mostly incommunicado, in Tadmur Prison. Some had been detained without trial since 1979. Out of a total of around 600 released prisoners, according to the official media, more than 400 had been held in Tadmur Prison.

Among those released were scores of prisoners of conscience, most of whom were detained in connection with their involvement with the unauthorized *Hizb al-'Amal al-Shuyu'i* (PCA), Party for Communist Action, and *al-Hizb al-Shuyu'i al-Maktab al-Siyassi* (CPPB), Communist Party – Political Bureau. All these prisoners of conscience had been sentenced to up to 15 years' imprisonment after unfair trials before the SSSC. They included Faraj Ahmad Birqdar, Jurays Yusuf al-Talli, Nu'man 'Ali 'Abdu and 'Umar al-Hayek.

The presidential amnesty also led to the release of 46 Lebanese political detainees, some of whom who had been imprisoned since the 1980s.

Other releases
A pattern of releases of political prisoners, including prisoners of conscience, after the expiry of their sentences or after long-term detention without trial, continued during 2000. Among those released were prisoners of conscience Fateh Jamus and Aslan 'Abd al-Karim, both leading members of the PCA, who had been held beyond the expiry of their 15-year sentences. Also released were more than 20 Jordanian and Palestinian political prisoners.

Prisoners of conscience
Although the number of prisoners of conscience decreased significantly during 2000 as a result of releases, dozens remained in detention, some of them serving long sentences passed by the SSSC after unfair trials. They included nine members of the PCA serving up to 22 years' imprisonment, and scores of prisoners of conscience or possible prisoners of conscience detained incommunicado since the late 1970s in connection with their involvement with the Muslim Brotherhood, whose fate remained unknown. All the remaining prisoners of conscience who had been sentenced to prison terms of up to 15 years in connection with their membership of the CPPB were released during 2000.

◻ 'Abd al-'Aziz al-Khayyir was arrested in February 1992 by members of *al-Mukhabarat al-'Askariyya,* Military Intelligence, in connection with his involvement with the PCA, along with a dozen other leading members of the PCA. All were reportedly tortured and ill-treated during their initial stage of detention. In August 1995, he was sentenced by the SSSC to 22 years' imprisonment after an unfair trial. 'Abd al-'Aziz al-Khayyir was tried together with Bahjat Sha'bu, 'Abbas Mahmud 'Abbas, Muhammad Hasan Mi'mar and 'Adnan Mahfuz, who also remained in prison serving up to 17 years' imprisonment.

'Disappearances'
The cases of hundreds of people, including suspected members of the Muslim Brotherhood and Lebanese nationals, who "disappeared" in the late 1970s and 1980s remained unresolved. Despite the release of 46 Lebanese political prisoners, the fate of scores of others remained unknown. They included Lebanese soldiers believed to have been taken to Syria in October 1990 following armed clashes between Syrian forces and troops loyal to the former Lebanese Army Commander Michel 'Aoun.

◻ Khadija Yahya Bukhari, a Lebanese woman singer, "disappeared" following her arrest in Syria on 29 April 1992. AI was informed by the authorities during 2000 that she had in fact been sentenced to death and executed on 2 December 1992. The authorities had not informed her family about her execution or handed over her body. The authorities stated that she had been executed on charges of spying for the Israeli intelligence service in Cyprus and recruiting a Syrian officer to cooperate with the Israeli intelligence service. The Syrian officer, who according to AI's information was her husband, was also sentenced to death and executed. The authorities did not provide his name or the date of his execution.

Political prisoners
Hundreds of long-term political prisoners, including members of the Muslim Brotherhood, the Arab Communist Party (ACP) and the Democratic Ba'th Party (DBP), remained held in prisons since being arrested in the 1970s and 1980s. Many were held incommunicado without trial and others were serving long sentences passed after unfair trials.

Reports indicated that members of the ACP were particularly harshly treated while held in Sednaya Prison. They were said to be suffering from serious health and mental problems. They included Haytham Na 'al, a university law student arrested in 1975; Ghayyath Shima, a university science student; and Faris Murad.

Scores of people, including women taken as "hostages" in the early 1980s and in recent years instead of relatives suspected of links with the Muslim Brotherhood, remained detained incommunicado in Tadmur Prison and other detention centres.

◻ Midhat Munir Tayfur, a 46-year-old foreman, was reportedly arrested by the Syrian security forces at Dar'a at the Syrian-Jordanian border on 22 May 1998, despite having permission from the Syrian embassy in Jordan to visit his family. Midhat Munir Tayfur, married with five children, is the brother of a leading member of the Muslim Brotherhood. Since his arrest, he has been held incommunicado, apparently at the Military Interrogation Branch in Damascus. There were serious concerns about his fate and fears that he may have been tortured to extract information about his brother.

Torture/ill-treatment

There were fewer reports of torture during 2000, but the system allowing for its application remained intact and there were apparently no investigations into previous allegations of torture and ill-treatment. Torture and ill-treatment of political detainees continued to be systematically applied in Tadmur Prison and other detention centres, including Palestine Branch and the Military Interrogation Branch in Damascus and other centres operated by the Political Security Department.

◻ One prisoner, held incommunicado for seven days in December in lieu of his exiled relative, was reported to have been tortured by the method known as *dullab*, beating with sticks and cables while hanging from a suspended tyre.

According to reports reaching AI from Tadmur Prison during 2000, torture and ill-treatment, though decreased in intensity, continued to be routine. Political prisoners, including those who were ill, were reported to be held in solitary confinement in underground cells. They were reportedly subjected to *falaqa*, beating on the soles of the feet, and repeated kickings, especially on the back and hips, leading to fractured vertebrae. Political prisoners were also allegedly ordered to beat fellow prisoners, especially those from their own political parties. Political prisoners who refused to obey orders were reportedly tortured.

Deaths in custody

At least one political prisoner died in custody.
◻ 'Attiyah Diab 'Attiyah died in February in Tadmur Prison, apparently as a result of torture and ill-treatment coupled with illness. 'Attiyah Diab 'Attiyah was arrested in Lebanon in 1989 for his involvement with the Fatah Movement and transferred to Syria.

Death penalty

The death penalty remained applicable in law for a wide range of crimes but information on the number of death sentences and executions during 2000 was not available.

Government communications

AI sent several letters to the authorities. Among the issues raised were cases of arbitrary detention.

The authorities responded, addressing some of AI's concerns.

AI actions

AI submitted dozens of cases from Syria to the UN Working Group on Arbitrary Detention and the UN Working Group on Enforced or Involuntary Disappearances.

TAIWAN

TAIWAN
President: Chen Shui-bian (replaced Lee Teng-hui in May)
Head of government: Chang Chen-hsiung (replaced Tang Fei in October, who replaced Vincent Siew in May)
Capital: Taipei
Population: 22.2 million
Official language: Mandarin Chinese
Death penalty: retentionist

The new government of President Chen Shui-bian publicly committed itself to the protection of human rights. However, legislative reforms to ensure improvements in human rights were not enacted during 2000. The death penalty continued to be imposed and at least 17 people were executed.

Background

In the March presidential elections, Chen Shui-bian of the Democratic Progressive Party was elected as the first non-*Kuomintang* President of Taiwan.

The new government included many former political prisoners, including prisoners of conscience and human rights activists. In his inaugural speech on 20 May, President Chen Shui-bian requested the advice of AI in bringing Taiwan's domestic law into conformity with the International Covenant on Civil and Political Rights and in establishing a National Human Rights Committee.

Political and economic instability within Taiwan increased. Prime Minister Tang Fei of the largest party in the Legislative *Yuan*, the *Kuomintang*, resigned in October following disputes over the construction of a nuclear plant. The new Prime Minister, Chang Chen-hsiung, came from the same party as the President, the Democratic Progressive Party, but the President found it difficult to steer legislation through the opposition-controlled legislature. There was also concern that the economy was slowing down and unemployment was rising.

Taiwan planned to commence historic direct contacts with the People's Republic of China by permitting the "three mini links" of direct trade, transportation and postal services between the cities of Kinmen (Quemoy) and Matsu in Taiwan, and Xiamen and Fuzhou in China.

Taiwan gained greater integration within the international community. It was expected to enter the World Trade Organization in 2001 and was represented at the ministerial level at the regional APEC meeting.

Legal reforms

The government stated its intention to introduce structural and legislative changes to improve human rights. Vice-President Annette Liu, a former prisoner of conscience, was appointed chief coordinator of the President's Advisory Group on Human Rights. The Group's mandate included compiling a work of reference on human rights for use in Taiwan; promoting a National Human Rights Bill; considering the formation of a National Human Rights Committee; promoting human rights education; and reviewing Taiwan's human rights conditions.

A preparatory committee led by Annette Liu was formed to consider the mandate and the process of establishment of a National Human Rights Committee. Proposals from non-governmental organizations included the formation of an autonomous commission in line with international standards. The *Kuomintang* party proposed a part-time, *ad hoc* commission.

Conscientious objectors to military service

On 15 January, the military conscription law was revised and a provision was created for civilian service as an alternative to military service.

On 10 December, there was a presidential amnesty for 21 prisoners, including 19 Jehovah's Witnesses who had been convicted of refusing to undergo mandatory military service for religious reasons.

Death penalty

There were at least 17 executions during 2000. There were no reforms to laws providing a mandatory death penalty for a wide range of crimes.

▫ The case of Su Chien-ho, Liu Bin-lang and Chuang Lin-hsun, known as the "Hsichih trio", who were sentenced to death in 1992, was sent to the Taipei High Court for a retrial. The retrial started in November and was broadcast live on television. AI had earlier called on the government to institute a thorough, impartial and independent investigation into reports that the three men were tortured while in police custody and confessed under duress, and had called for a retrial. AI had expressed concern that their earlier trial did not conform to international standards of fairness, and that it appeared that they had been convicted on the basis of confessions extracted under torture.

TAJIKISTAN

REPUBLIC OF TAJIKISTAN
Head of state: Imomali Rakhmonov
Head of government: Akil Akilov
Capital: Dushanbe
Population: 6.1 million
Official language: Tajik
Death penalty: retentionist
2000 treaty ratifications/signatures: Optional Protocol to the UN Women's Convention; Rome Statute of the International Criminal Court

At least 38 people were reportedly sentenced to death during 2000, although the true number was believed to be much higher. One death sentence was known to have been commuted. There were reports of torture and ill-treatment of detainees.

Background

In February the People's Democratic Party won Tajikistan's first multiparty parliamentary elections since the signing of the 1997 peace agreement. However, independent international observers stated that the elections had been tainted by official meddling.

The opening of the bicameral parliament, following elections to the upper chamber in March, officially concluded the peace process. The body responsible for implementing the peace agreement, the National Reconciliation Commission, was dissolved. The mandates of the UN Mission of Observers in Tajikistan (UNMOT) and of the Commonwealth of Independent States peace-keeping force ended in May and September respectively.

The Tajik, Kyrgyz and Uzbek authorities joined forces against the banned Islamic Movement of Uzbekistan (IMU) following incursions by IMU members into Kyrgyzstan and Uzbekistan (see entries on Kyrgyzstan and Uzbekistan).

By the end of December, some 10,000 refugees heading for Tajikistan to escape the fighting in northern Afghanistan were reportedly stranded in very poor conditions along the Panj River which marks the Tajik-Afghan border. Despite Tajikistan's international obligations, the refugees were denied access to Tajik territory.

The level of political violence remained high. Among the victims of assaults and killings were government officials and former commanders of the United Tajik Opposition.

Reportedly at least 200 suspected supporters of the banned Islamist party, *Hizb-ut-Tahrir*, Party of Liberation, faced criminal proceedings. The charges against them included anti-constitutional activity, fuelling religious strife and calling for the overthrow of the existing state system.

Torture/ill-treatment

There were reports of torture and ill-treatment by law enforcement officers in detention facilities. One detainee was allegedly forced to undergo an abortion.

⎕ Dilfuza Numonova, who was held in Dushanbe Prison under sentence of death (see below), stated that she was taken to hospital and forced to have an abortion in late January. Under Tajik law pregnant women cannot be executed. She maintained that she was innocent and had confessed to murder under duress.

Death penalty
Under the criminal code, 15 offences were punishable by death. However, there were no comprehensive statistics on the use of the death penalty, which remained a state secret. One death sentence was known to have been commuted.

⎕ Rustam Baybulatov was sentenced to death by Dushanbe City Court in September. He had been convicted of charges including "banditry" in connection with his alleged membership of a banned armed group. He had been arrested in February after threatening a former UNMOT staff member in order to extort money. The chairman of the court reportedly stated that in passing sentence the court had taken into account the fact that the victim belonged to an international organization and was a foreign national.

⎕ In January, 21-year-old Dilfuza Numonova was convicted of killing her lover in November 1999 and sentenced to death by Dushanbe City Court. Her trial was reportedly unfair. In July, following international pressure, her sentence was commuted to 15 years' imprisonment by the Presidium of the Supreme Court of Tajikistan.

TANZANIA

UNITED REPUBLIC OF TANZANIA
Head of state: Benjamin Mkapa
Head of government: Frederick Sumaye
Capital: Dar es Salaam
Population: 33.5 million
Official languages: Kiswahili, English
Death penalty: retentionist
2000 treaty ratifications/signatures: Rome Statute of the International Criminal Court

Scores of opposition political activists were arrested and ill-treated on the semi-autonomous island of Zanzibar in the context of elections which were widely seen as unfair. Eighteen opposition leaders and their supporters were released after more than two years in jail as prisoners of conscience.

Background
The much-debated Zanzibar constitutional reform agreement of 1999 between the ruling *Chama cha Mapinduzi* (CCM), Party of the Revolution, and the main opposition party, the Civic United Front (CUF), remained unimplemented. Elections were held in October, despite controversy over the independence of the electoral commission, particularly in Zanzibar. Political tension on Zanzibar between the CCM and the CUF escalated as the election drew near. International observers concluded that the poll was fairly conducted on the mainland, but not in Zanzibar. President Benjamin Mkapa was re-elected on the mainland and announced his wish to cooperate with the opposition.

The CUF refused to accept the result in Zanzibar, where the electoral commission ordered a re-run in 16 of the 50 constituencies. The CCM presidential candidate, Amani Abeid Karume, won the second ballot on 5 November. This ballot, along with parliamentary sessions after the election, was boycotted by the opposition. At the end of the year, CUF and CCM leaders were negotiating through intermediaries.

There was no progress on a promised Tanzanian human rights commission.

Zanzibar
Treason trial
In January the trial of 18 CUF leaders and their supporters charged with treason was again adjourned. On 26 January, a new Zanzibar Attorney General was appointed. His predecessor reportedly stated that the CUF trial was a political issue and that the accused "deserved to be hanged".

An appeal, lodged on the basis that Zanzibar did not have a legal right to bring charges of treason as it was not a sovereign state, was finally heard in August, but the court deferred judgment to await further information. The 18 remained in custody until 9 November when charges against them were dropped. The appeal court verdict confirmed that there was no legal basis for the charges. All were prisoners of conscience who had been held for at least two years, and many for more than three.

Arrests and ill-treatment of CUF supporters

The January adjournment in the treason trial provoked mass protests which were brutally broken up by armed police. Some 30 people were injured, including 14 police officers, and 40 arrested. A CUF rally planned for the following day was banned. Some 30 people were held in custody for several weeks; charges against them were still pending at the end of the year.

Widespread arbitrary beatings of some 300 opposition party supporters and the arrest of more than 100 others followed an incident on 2 April when armed police, raiding a CUF office meeting, were disarmed and beaten by CUF guards. One CUF supporter reportedly died as a result of a police beating. Some were released without charge, others were released on bail. Twenty-one others, including CUF secretary general Seif Sharif Hamad, were later arrested, and charged with robbery with violence, but released on bail. Seif Sharif Hamad and his campaign manager also faced charges of taking part in an illegal demonstration for their campaigning activities in late September.

There were further short-term arrests and beatings of prisoners and demonstrators in the run-up to the elections. On 11 October, six people were reportedly injured on Zanzibar when police opened fire to disperse CUF supporters at a campaign rally at their branch office. This appeared to be part of a continuing pattern of intimidation and harassment.

On 30 October police in riot gear opened fire with live ammunition, tear gas and rubber bullets on demonstrators protesting against irregularities in the elections. Scores of people, including bystanders not involved in the protest, were reportedly injured, at least one seriously. Thirty-two people were arrested and charged with "causing a breach of the peace".

Following the elections, there were reports of several explosions, one of which extensively damaged the Zanzibar Electoral Commission office in Pemba on 27 December, and numerous arrests and beatings. The authorities blamed the explosions on the opposition and more than 40 people connected with the opposition were detained; some were formally charged in relation to the explosions. The CUF claimed that the charges were fabricated.

Freedom of expression and assembly

◻ In February, 10 suspected followers of Sheikh Issa Ponda, a Muslim leader in Mwanza, were charged with illegal assembly and inciting Muslims to revolt against the government, after they held a meeting to discuss the February 1998 Mwembechai riots in Dar es Salaam. They were released on bail a few days later, and had not been tried by the end of the year.

◻ In November Ally Saleh, a reporter for the British Broadcasting Corporation (BBC) and human rights activist, was arrested and falsely charged with kidnapping two women. He had persistently reported on the chaotic election period and human rights abuses in Zanzibar. He was released on bail after 12 hours in custody. Charges were later dropped.

Refugees

Implementation of the 1998 Refugees Act, under which all refugees from Burundi and Rwanda were required to go to refugee camps, began in February 2000. However, many refugees were not taken to refugee camps. By May, 80 Rwandese and 580 Burundian refugees who had settled in villages along the border region, some since the 1960s, were forcibly returned to their countries of origin and scores of others were detained awaiting possible *refoulement*. There were some allegations of ill-treatment. Families were separated and refugees given no chance to collect their possessions.

In a separate case, two Rwandese refugees accused of helping the former speaker of the Rwandese National Assembly to flee Rwanda, were arrested in February shortly after their arrival in Tanzania and forcibly returned to Rwanda, although they were clearly under the protection of the UN High Commissioner for Refugees (UNHCR). In Rwanda they were immediately taken into military custody and reportedly tortured before being released.

Despite measures taken by the UNHCR and the Tanzanian government, many women and girl refugees in Tanzania faced sexual and domestic violence both inside and outside the camps. There were frequent reports of women being attacked and raped by local villagers when they left the camps to collect firewood.
◻ In one case dating back to 1999, 11 people charged with assaulting a group of Burundian refugee women and girls and raping at least 10, including one girl, were summarily acquitted in December because the prosecutor was late. In June 2000 this ruling was successfully appealed against and the case has been reopened.

Nearly 200 Burundian refugees, including young children, were arrested during the year on suspicion of links with Burundian armed opposition groups. Most were returned to the camps but some remained in detention in harsh conditions on charges of illegally leaving the camps. There were further reports of recruitment from the camps by all Burundian armed opposition groups.

Extradition

In August Bernard Ntuyahaga, a former Rwandese army officer accused of murdering the Prime Minister and 10 Belgian peace-keepers in 1994, remained in prison while appealing against extradition to Rwanda. AI remained concerned that if extradited he could face an unfair trial and, if convicted, the death penalty.

Other concerns

Courts continued to pass death sentences, but for the sixth successive year no one was executed. Non-governmental organizations, including AI, continued to campaign against female genital mutilation, advocating both legal reform and greater popular awareness.

Witchcraft killings

There were further reported killings of elderly people, mostly women, suspected of witchcraft, particularly in the Shinyanga and Mwanza districts. In June, the Tanzania Media Women's Association launched a video to raise awareness about the issue and stated that over the past 10 years, thousands of people had been lynched by witch-hunting mobs. The government pledged to increase efforts to stem the killings.

AI country reports

- Great Lakes Region: Refugees denied protection (AI Index: AFR 02/002/2000)
- Tanzania: A human rights brief for election observers (AI Index: AFR 56/013/2000)

THAILAND

KINGDOM OF THAILAND
Head of state: King Bhumibol Adulyadej
Head of government: Chuan Leekpai
Capital: Bangkok
Population: 60.6 million
Official language: Thai
Death penalty: retentionist
2000 treaty ratifications/signatures: Optional Protocol to the UN Women's Convention; Rome Statute of the International Criminal Court

In January, 10 Myanmar nationals were shot dead by the security forces after they had taken patients and staff of Raatchaburi Hospital hostage. The same month, one Myanmar national convicted of drugs trafficking was executed. At least one person reportedly died as a result of torture by police. Poor prison conditions, including severe overcrowding, continued to be reported. More than 14,000 asylum-seekers from the Karen and Karenni ethnic minorities in Myanmar entered refugee camps, whose population increased to 115,000. More than 100,000 Shan asylum-seekers from Myanmar continued to be denied access to camps in Thailand. Several Myanmar nationals were forcibly returned to Myanmar where they were at risk of human rights violations. The Prime Minister dissolved parliament in November, and in consultation with the Elections Commission, set the election date for January 2001.

Hostage-taking and extrajudicial executions

In January, 10 heavily armed Myanmar nationals believed to be led by the Vigorous Burmese Student Warriors, who in October 1999 seized the Myanmar embassy in Bangkok, took hundreds of patients and staff hostage at Raatchaburi Hospital. The group reportedly demanded medical assistance for people in Kamaplaw, a settlement in Myanmar near Thailand, which was controlled by God's Army, a Karen armed opposition group. Kamaplaw had been attacked by the Myanmar army and reportedly shelled by the 9th Division of the Thai First Army. Security forces secured Raatchaburi Hospital less than 24 hours after its seizure, shooting dead all 10 men, although no civilian casualties were reported. Some of the 10 were reportedly extrajudicially executed after they had surrendered, but no investigation was known to have been conducted. In October the bodies of nine of the men, which remained unclaimed by relatives, were cremated in Raatchaburi by the authorities. One body had previously been claimed by a Muslim organization for burial.

Refugees and migrant workers

About 1,000 refugees from Myanmar were resettled to third countries from Maneloy camp as part of the Thai authorities' ongoing policy to ensure the resettlement of all Myanmar political opposition activists. In February Myanmar national Saw Tin Oo was forcibly returned by the Thai authorities to Myanmar, where he was arrested, tried and sentenced to death by the Myanmar authorities.

Migrant workers and asylum-seekers from Myanmar continued to be arrested throughout the year, held in poor conditions in Immigration Detention Centres and forcibly returned to the Myanmar-Thai border. In February, in the aftermath of the January hospital siege and in the run-up to an international UN meeting in Bangkok, thousands of Myanmar nationals were arrested in Bangkok alone. Migrant workers and asylum-seekers from countries which do not border Thailand were arrested for "illegal immigration" and were forced to remain in Immigration Detention Centres for long periods.

In January about 1,000 Karen asylum-seekers fled to Thailand after attacks by the Myanmar army on the Me Pia base of the Karen National Union, the main Karen armed opposition group in Myanmar. The asylum-seekers were forcibly returned to Myanmar by the First Army's 9th Division. A few days later, after further attacks by the Myanmar army resulting in civilian casualties, the same group fled again, and were allowed to remain at Bo Wii, Raatchaburi Province. The First Army's 9th Division initially blocked them from entering refugee camps but they were moved to Don Yang refugee camp in February.

In January, after the attack on Kamaplaw, more than 400 Karen asylum-seekers fled to Thailand. Some 50 Karen male asylum-seekers from this group "disappeared" after having been arrested by the 9th Division, reportedly for national security reasons. AI had no further information about their fate.

More than 100,000 Shan asylum-seekers who had fled human rights violations in Myanmar continued to be denied access to refugee camps and were treated by the Thai authorities as "illegal immigrants", liable to arrest and deportation.

Political imprisonment

Sok Yoeun, a Cambodian refugee and prisoner of conscience in Thailand, was arrested in December 1999 for "illegal immigration" and detained throughout the year pending possible extradition to Cambodia. The Cambodian government accused him of involvement in a rocket attack on Prime Minister Hun Sen's motorcade in September 1998, but there was no evidence linking him to the attack.

Ramlek Nilnuan, an adviser to the non-governmental organization Forum of the Poor, was arrested in July for trespassing in a national park and remained held without trial. His arrest was related to a land dispute between the Royal Forestry Department and villagers in Kalasin Province, and he appeared to be a prisoner of conscience.

Torture/ill-treatment

In February Chamlong Khamsunthorn died in police custody in Ayuthaya Province, reportedly as a result of severe beatings and electric shocks. No independent investigation was known to have been conducted.

About 200,000 prisoners nationwide were reportedly held in prisons with a capacity of 80,000. Women's facilities were particularly crowded as increasing numbers of women have been arrested for possession of small amounts of illegal drugs. Conditions in Klong Prem in Nonthaburi province near Bangkok and in Chonburi, Phuket, Songkhla, Surat Thani, and Chiang Mai Prisons were also especially poor. Prisoners on death row were held in iron shackles continuously. Conditions in Immigration Detention Centres, which were supervised by the police, continued to be poor after mass arrests of migrant workers, but in general improved.

Death penalty

A bill banning the death penalty for people under 18 was introduced by the Attorney General's Office to the Cabinet in December in order to bring Thailand's law into compliance with the International Covenant on Civil and Political Rights, which Thailand acceded to in 1997.

Hla Win, a Myanmar national convicted of drug trafficking, was executed in January. Some 130 prisoners were under sentence of death at Bangkwang Prison. At least 45 death sentences were passed during 2000.

Legal developments

In May the government released a censored version of a Ministry of Defence report about the military's violent suppression of pro-democracy demonstrations in Bangkok in May 1992, in which at least 52 people were killed. After protests from the relatives of victims, the government released a largely uncensored version in June, but calls by the relatives to bring those found responsible to justice remained unanswered.

In October the newly-elected Senate elected nine of 11 National Human Rights Commissioners stipulated in the 1997 Constitution. By the end of the year the remaining two Commissioners had still not been elected, making it impossible for the Commission to convene.

AI country reports and visits
Statement
- Kingdom of Thailand: Justice denied eight years after Bangkok massacre (AI Index: ASA 39/002/2000)

Visit
AI delegates visited Thailand in February and March.

TOGO

TOGOLESE REPUBLIC
Head of state: Gnassingbé Eyadéma
Head of government: Gabriel Messan Agbeyome Kodjo (replaced Eugène Koffi Adoboli in October)
Capital: Lomé
Population: 4.6 million
Official language: French
Death penalty: abolitionist in practice

Human rights activists, including trade unionists, student leaders and independent journalists, were arbitrarily arrested, harassed and threatened by the authorities. There were reports of torture and ill-treatment in detention. In June 2000, a joint UN/Organization of African Unity (OAU) Commission of Inquiry was appointed to investigate hundreds of alleged extrajudicial executions in 1998.

Background

The government was criticized by the UN for breaching international sanctions and providing support to an armed opposition group in Angola responsible for widespread human rights abuses against civilians.

In August, the Togolese parliament censured Prime Minister Eugène Adoboli, one year after his appointment, for failing to end the economic crisis by overcoming the country's international isolation. Eugène Adoboli resigned and was replaced by Gabriel Messan Agbeyome Kodjo, the speaker of the National Assembly and a former government minister.

Earlier, in June, Harry Octavianus Olympio was forced to resign as Minister of Human Rights. He was accused of organizing an attack on himself on 5 May with the help of his brother, Antonio Olympio. He denied the allegations. A few days later Antonio Olympio was arrested and accused of driving the car from which his brother was allegedly attacked. He was released on 8 July.

New legislation

A new press bill was passed at the beginning of 2000 which limited press freedom and made defamation of the government an imprisonable offence. AI believed this to be a further measure to silence critics, in particular independent journalists. Detention for press offences such as "spreading false information" has been regularly used by the authorities against independent journalists who play a key role in exposing human rights violations by the security forces.

Political imprisonment

More than a dozen people, including prisoners of conscience, were arrested during 2000. Among them were trade unionists, students and journalists.

Trade unionists

On 28 January, Norbert Gbikpi-Benissan, General Secretary of the *Union nationale des syndicats indépendants du Togo* (UNSIT), National Union of Independent Trade Unions, and Pierre Allaga-Kodegui, General Secretary of the *Fédération des travailleurs de l'enseignement* (FETREN), Teachers' Federation, were arrested on charges of "spreading false information". Both were released one week later after the government withdrew the complaint against them.

Students

Attempts to silence students continued throughout 2000. The authorities arrested leading members of the *Conseil des étudiants de l'Université du Bénin* (CEUB), the Student Council of the University of Benin. In January an international arrest warrant was issued against Alphonse Lawson-Hellu, leader of the CEUB, on a charge of spreading false information. He went into hiding for over a week until the charge was dropped.

In March, student meetings were violently dispersed by pro-government armed militias who beat students and allegedly tried to stab a student leader. As a result of the clashes, a leading member of a pro-government militia died and some students were injured. Also in March, the security forces used tear gas to disperse student demonstrations. Some students were beaten and injured by the security forces. At least 12 students were arrested and charged with gathering illegally. All were tried a week later and were released after being acquitted or given suspended sentences. However, at the same trial, five student leaders of the CEUB, including Lorempo Lamboni, Hanif Tchadjobo and Kokou Segbeaya, were tried in their absence and convicted of "disturbing public order, illegal gathering and administering a fatal blow". They were sentenced to suspended 18-month prison terms.

Hanif Tchadjobo was arrested on 10 April, one week after the arrest of another CEUB leader, Koumoyi Kpelafia. Both were detained in the civil prison of Lomé on criminal charges for more than one month before being released. They were prisoners of conscience. It was not clear whether the charges against them were dropped.

Journalists

The authorities brought suits for defamation against independent journalists, apparently to silence them. On at least five occasions, the authorities confiscated editions of the independent press. On 31 July, the *Combat du peuple* and the *Scorpion* were seized when they published the July report of the *Ligue togolaise des droits de l'homme* (LTDH), Togolese Human Rights League, which was critical of the country's human rights record.

▭ Kpagli Comlan, editor of *L'Aurore*, arrested in December 1999 on charges of "spreading false information" was held until 4 February. After his release, he received death threats and was forced into hiding.

▭ Hippolyte Agboh, director of the independent weekly *L'Exilé*, was arrested on 14 April after mistakenly reporting the death of President Eyadéma's daughter. After being charged with spreading false information, he was sentenced to a three-month prison term and a heavy fine, and his newspaper was suspended for six months. He was released in June after a presidential pardon.

Human rights defenders

Threats against human rights defenders, particularly members of organizations critical of the country's human rights record, became a regular pattern. In May 1999, AI published *Togo: Rule of terror*, describing a persistent pattern of extrajudicial executions, "disappearances", arbitrary arrests and detentions followed by torture and ill-treatment, sometimes leading to death, and harsh conditions of detention. Since then, members of Togolese human rights organizations — including AI members — have been harassed, intimidated, arrested and tortured. Others have been forced into hiding or have fled the country. In November 2000, the Dean of Examining Judges ordered that charges of "false accusation and defamation" against Togolese human rights defenders arrested in relation to AI's May 1999 report should be dropped, including those against Nestor Tengue, director of the *Association togolaise pour la défense et la promotion des droits de l'homme* (ATPDH), Togolese Association for the Defence and Promotion of Human Rights.

▭ On 31 July and 1 August, Koffi Messa Devotsu, chairperson of the LTDH, was questioned by the Minister of the Interior and threatened with arrest after the publication of a critical report by his organization on the human rights situation. The interrogation took place in the presence of a number of independent journalists, who were also questioned and criticized by the Minister for having published articles on the LTDH report.

Torture/ill-treatment

There were continuing reports of torture and ill-treatment in detention, some relating to incidents in previous years.

▭ Nine Togolese refugees, including Lawson Akouete Latévi, Messa Kokou Paul and Seke Koudjo, were handed over to the Togolese authorities by the Ghanaian authorities at the end of 1997. Most were members of the *Comité togolais pour la résistance* (CTR), Togolese Resistance Committee, an opposition party in exile in Ghana. After their arrest, they were detained in the civil prison and at the *Direction de la police judiciare* (DPJ) in Lomé. In July 1998, they were all transferred to a prison in Kara in the north of Togo. It was not clear whether they were charged. On their arrival at the civil prison of Lomé, guards beat, slapped, and kicked them. One prisoner, Nyableji John, was allegedly forced to eat sand and was then refused water. After the beating, it was reported that the prisoners could not walk and had difficulties with breathing. At the DPJ, the prisoners were reportedly kept permanently tied up. They were not given any food by prison authorities, but received food from their families.

In April 1998 Ntsukpui Attiso died, allegedly as a result of the beatings he received, insufficient food and harsh prison conditions. According to a letter from the *Commission nationale des droits de l'homme*, National Commission for Human Rights, to the ATPDH, Ntsukpui Attiso died as a result of tuberculosis.

The eight other prisoners reportedly suffered from malaria and skin diseases, for which they did not receive the necessary medication. In Kara prison, food was inadequate, the prisoners could only wash themselves twice a week, they slept on the floor and were only allowed to wear underwear. The prisoners were permitted to see members of their family only to receive food or medicine. Visitors who saw these prisoners told AI that they looked like skeletons.

Proceedings against AI

After the publication of the May 1999 report, the authorities arrested human rights defenders, including AI members, on suspicion that they were passing information to AI. In September 1999, the Togolese authorities started legal proceedings against Pierre Sané, AI's Secretary General, and summoned him to appear before an investigative magistrate of the High Court in Lomé for "a possible indictment for contempt, incitement to revolt, dissemination of false news and conspiracy against the external security of the state". On 12 March 2000, the government indicated that it would withdraw its complaint against Pierre Sané once the international Commission of Inquiry began its work in Togo. In November, the Dean of Examining Judges ordered that all proceedings against Pierre Sané and four other human rights defenders should be stopped until further notice. However, it remained unclear whether or not the charges had been dropped.

International Commission of Inquiry

In its May 1999 report, AI called on the Togolese authorities to accept national and international investigations into widespread human rights violations, including hundreds of extrajudicial killings committed during the 1998 election period. Reports of extrajudicial killings in that period were later corroborated by investigative reports undertaken by journalists and the *Ligue beninoise des droits de l'homme*, Benin Human Rights League.

In August 1999, the UN Sub-Commission on the Promotion and Protection of Human Rights announced the establishment of a commission of inquiry to investigate allegations of extrajudicial executions in Togo in 1998 and noted the government's undertaking to cooperate fully with it.

On 7 June 2000, the UN and the OAU announced the establishment of a joint Commission of Inquiry into allegations of hundreds of extrajudicial killings in Togo. The Commission was composed of delegates from Chad, Brazil and Niger.

In August and September, an AI delegation met members of the Commission to provide information relevant to the inquiry. AI stressed the need for an effective witness protection program and informed the Commission about ongoing attempts by the Togolese authorities to silence witnesses. The Commission published two public information notes setting out the measures it intended to take to protect witnesses, before it visited Togo and neighbouring countries towards the end of the year.

AI also expressed concern that criminal charges of passing information to AI, which had been brought against Togolese human rights defenders, still stood under Togolese law, even if pursuit of these cases had been suspended when the Commission of Inquiry arrived in Togo.

Impunity

For the past 10 years the Togolese authorities have failed to respond effectively to the public demand for an end to impunity for human rights violations. No steps have been taken to clarify, for example, the extrajudicial execution of Tavio Amorin and the "disappearances" of David Bruce, Kouni Kodjo, Adjisse Essie Djiewone and Edoh Komlan.

TRINIDAD AND TOBAGO

REPUBLIC OF TRINIDAD AND TOBAGO
Head of state: Arthur Napoleon Raymond Robinson
Head of government: Basdeo Panday
Capital: Port-of-Spain
Population: 1.3 million
Official language: English
Death penalty: retentionist
2000 treaty ratifications/signatures: UN Refugee Convention and its 1967 Protocol

Death sentences continued to be imposed but no executions were carried out. In an attempt to increase the number of executions, Trinidad and Tobago withdrew from the (first) Optional Protocol to the International Covenant on Civil and Political Rights (ICCPR). Sentences of corporal punishment were imposed but not carried out. Reports of ill-treatment by police persisted and conditions of detention continued to cause grave concern.

Background

The government ignored repeated requests to meet with AI. In September, following a visit by AI's Secretary General, the Prime Minister and Attorney General accused AI "and its internal agents" of demonstrating "scant regard for the sovereignty" of Caribbean nations. In October, the Attorney General read out a nine-page statement to the House of Representatives accusing AI of being inaccurate and "an instrument of persecution, oppression and subversion" of small Caribbean countries. The Attorney General also published a lengthy criticism of the entry on Trinidad and Tobago in the *Amnesty International Report 2000*.

Elections were held in December. The ruling United National Congress party was returned to power with an increased majority.

Death penalty

There were at least 63 men and four women on death row at the end of the year. There were no executions or death warrants issued. In October the Offences Against the Person (Amendment) Act became law, making the death penalty for murder mandatory for one out of three categories of murder, or for those who had committed more than one murder.

On 27 March Trinidad and Tobago withdrew from the (first) Optional Protocol to the ICCPR, denying individuals the right to petition the UN Human Rights Committee. The government justified the withdrawal on the grounds that the UN Human Rights Committee was preventing executions, despite the execution of 10 men in 1999.

The government sought to increase the number of executions through the Constitution Amendment (No. 3) Bill, commonly known as the "Hanging Bill", which limited the issues upon which condemned prisoners could lodge legal appeals and stipulated that once a death warrant had been signed by the President, the High Court would have "no jurisdiction". However, the government failed to have this Bill passed into law.

In June the Judicial Committee of the Privy Council (JCPC) in the United Kingdom — the final court of appeal of Trinidad and Tobago — overturned the conviction of death row inmate Desmond Baptiste. He had signed a written confession despite having no lawyer present and having difficulty reading and writing, and had not been advised of his right to have a lawyer present during interrogation. The ruling also found significant fault with the judge's directions to the jury. Desmond Baptiste was released from prison.

The JCPC's ruling commuting the death sentences of six Jamaican prisoners in the case of Neville Lewis and others had implications for Trinidad and Tobago's administration of the death penalty (see Jamaica entry).

Corporal punishment

Sentences of flogging or whipping continued to be imposed by the courts. In October, the government informed the UN Human Rights Committee that no prisoners had been subjected to corporal punishment in 2000, but that 17 prisoners were whipped in 1999.

Abuses by police

There continued to be reports of ill-treatment and excessive force by the police. In January the Prime Minister announced that another inquiry would take place into the police service and convened an advisory committee to undertake this. Critics noted that no previous recommendations arising out of reviews of the police service had ever been implemented.

In February the National Security Minister stated that a total of 769 complaints had been submitted and recorded by the Police Complaints Authority for 1999.

In July the Police Commissioner was criticized by members of the Commission of Inquiry into the independence of the judiciary for his vehement public refutation of allegations made by a religious foundation regarding the ill-treatment of homeless children by police.

☐ On 4 February a *TNT Mirror* reporter, Nylnd Dwarika, was allegedly beaten by police in San Fernando, after he stopped to check a man lying on the ground who appeared to be unconscious. He received injuries to his chest and knee as a result of beatings with police batons and was subsequently denied access to medical attention and legal assistance. He was later charged with obstructing the police.

Police shootings

There were allegations that police used excessive force.
☐ A 17-year-old girl, Anisha Neptune, was shot dead by a Special Reserve Policeman in Diego Martin on 1 May outside the Four Roads Police Station, where she had gone following the arrest of her brother earlier that day. The police officer involved allegedly told police investigators that the girl and her mother had attacked him with stones, and that his gun had been fired during

this fight. Anisha Neptune's mother denied that such a fight took place, and claimed that she was gunned down in cold blood.

Detention conditions
In October police officers at the Belmont Police Station threatened to close their station because of deplorable and inhuman conditions. They were protesting against overcrowded and insanitary conditions, where detainees spent most of or all day locked in overcrowded cells without bedding, sleeping on the concrete floor, with buckets for sanitation.

Intimidation and abuse of journalists
The government continued to criticize the press and to make comments that could incite politically motivated violence. In January journalists were attacked by political activists attending a rally after a speaker told the crowd the media should be "chased away" and "humiliated". In February the Prime Minister told a rally of his supporters to "do them before they do us" and declared "virtual war" on the government's opponents. In May, two men entered the home of government critic and journalist Professor Selwyn Cudjoe and assaulted his family in what appeared to be a politically motivated attack.

Gay men and lesbians
Sexual acts between consenting adults of the same sex remained illegal and gay and lesbian people were regularly subjected to discrimination and intimidation. The government continued to attempt to pass the Equal Opportunities Bill with a clause excluding discrimination on the basis of sexual orientation. The Bill failed to become law. In September, the Minister for Trade accused AI of wanting to turn the population of Trinidad and Tobago "into homosexuals".

AI country visits
AI visited Trinidad and Tobago in February and September.

TUNISIA

REPUBLIC OF TUNISIA
Head of state: Zine El 'Abidine Ben 'Ali
Head of government: Mohamed Ghannouchi
Capital: Tunis
Population: 9.5 million
Official language: Arabic
Death penalty: retentionist

Repression of human rights defenders escalated and journalists and political activists were targeted by the police, but responded with an unprecedented level of protest against harassment and intimidation. Torture and ill-treatment in police stations and prisons remained widespread and at least two detainees died in police custody. Three prisoners of conscience were released but dozens of others were arrested. Up to 1,000 political prisoners, most of them prisoners of conscience, remained detained. Trials of political detainees continued to violate international standards for fair trial. Thousands of former prisoners of conscience and their relatives, and the families of prisoners and exiled government opponents, were subjected to harassment and intimidation. Scores of prisoners undertook lengthy hunger strikes to demand their release and to protest at ill-treatment and poor conditions of detention.

Background
In February and April high-school students and unemployed youths demonstrated in several towns against price rises and changes in examination procedures.

In April the authorities' decision not to hold a state funeral for former President Habib Bourguiba prompted widespread protests.

In May people demonstrated in Bou Salem to protest at the floods and damage following the authorities' decision to open a dam without warning the local population.

In all cases, the demonstrations were forcibly broken up by police. In some cases demonstrators burned or damaged cars and public property. Scores were arrested, including people who had not participated in violent acts, and dozens were sentenced to prison terms. In October police beat women's rights activists and others who demonstrated peacefully in support of the Palestinian people.

The authorities often blocked Internet access to the websites of human rights organizations and the foreign media, and human rights defenders were often unable to access their own e-mail addresses.

In May, days after criticizing the authorities in a French newspaper, former journalist Riad Ben Fadhel was shot and injured outside his home, next to the presidential palace, in what may have been an attempted extrajudicial execution.

Human rights defenders and civil society activists

The targeting of human rights defenders escalated to an unprecedented level. Many were prosecuted or threatened with prosecution, some were beaten or ill-treated and others had their telephone and fax lines cut.

In December Nejib Hosni, a human rights lawyer and leading member of the *Conseil national pour les libertés en Tunisie* (CNLT), National Council for Liberties in Tunisia, was imprisoned for failing to comply with an arbitrarily imposed five-year ban on practising law. Earlier in the year the Tunisian Bar Council, the only institution competent to suspend or disbar a lawyer, had confirmed that he was never suspended or disbarred and was fully entitled to practise law. He remained detained at the end of the year and was notified that he would also have to serve the remaining five and a half years of an eight-year prison sentence imposed in 1996 on trumped-up charges of forgery.

In December, Moncef Marzouki, a doctor and CNLT spokesman, was sentenced to one year's imprisonment for his human rights activities on behalf of the CNLT. In July he was arbitrarily dismissed from his post at Sousse University.

In November the authorities suspended all activities of the *Ligue tunisienne des droits de l'homme* (LTDH), Tunisian Human Rights League, shortly after the organization's general assembly had elected to its board a majority of outspoken human rights activists. In December the authorities initiated legal proceedings against LTDH vice-president Slaheddine Jourchi for a statement he had signed on behalf of the LTDH after its suspension.

In June Fathi Chamkhi, President of the *Rassemblement pour une Alternative Internationale de Développement* (RAID), Rally for an International Alternative for Development, and RAID member Mohamed Chourabi were sentenced to one month's imprisonment for possessing reports by the RAID and the CNLT, both of which organizations had been refused registration by the authorities.

Following national and international protests, the authorities returned the passports of some human rights defenders and former prisoners of conscience. However, throughout the year human rights defenders were subjected to harassment and intimidation and their activities and meetings were often broken up or prevented by the police. On several occasions police ill-treated human rights activists, including CNLT members Sihem Ben Sedrine, 'Ali Ben Salem, 'Omar Mestiri, and members of the *Association tunisienne des femmes démocrates* (ATDF), Tunisian Association of Democratic Women.

In December LTDH and CNLT members were prevented from holding meetings and some were ill-treated by police who blocked access to the meeting places.

CNLT spokesperson Moncef Marzouki remained banned from leaving the country at the end of the year, as were CNLT and RAID members 'Ali Ben Salem, Sadri Khiari and Mohamed Chourabi, and lawyer 'Ameur Rouani.

AI's Tunisian Section also remained under surveillance and in March its members were prevented from holding a number of public events by police who manhandled some of its leading members.

Torture/ill-treatment

Torture and ill-treatment continued to be widely used by police to extract confessions in both criminal and political cases and by prison guards to punish detainees. A new law, adopted in 1999, making torture a crime punishable by eight years' imprisonment was disregarded, and no member of the security forces was prosecuted for acts of torture committed during 2000 or in previous years. The six-day legal maximum limit on incommunicado detention also continued to be breached.

☐ Lotfi Ferhati, a Tunisian living in France, was arrested in August, when he arrived in Tunisia with his wife for a family visit. He was held in the Ministry of the Interior for 18 days, where he said he was suspended by his feet from a pulley and his head was repeatedly plunged in a bucket of dirty water, causing near-asphyxiation (known as the *baño* method); kept in constrained positions; allowed only about one hour's rest a day; and threatened that his wife would be tortured. He was allegedly forced to sign an unread confession admitting to links with an unauthorized Islamist group. He was awaiting trial at the end of the year.

☐ Ridha Jeddi was arrested in September and reportedly tortured in Menzel Bourguiba police station, where he died later the same day. Police claimed he committed suicide by hanging but the forensic report ruled out death by strangulation. At his burial his family noted bruises on his face and chest. An investigation was reportedly opened but no information could be obtained by the end of the year.

Conditions in prisons remained very poor, especially for political prisoners, who were held in overcrowded cells, where scant hygienic facilities resulted in the spread of scabies and other skin diseases. Political detainees were often denied medical care; forced to sleep on concrete floors; beaten and ill-treated; placed in solitary confinement, at times chained; and denied access to their families and lawyers.

☐ 'Abdellatif Bouhajila, Yassine Benzerti and scores of other Islamist sympathizers on prolonged hunger strike to protest against the length and unfairness of judicial proceedings and against ill-treatment and poor conditions of detention, were prevented from receiving visits from their families and lawyers for several weeks at a time. 'Abdellatif Bouhajila was placed in solitary confinement in October; he was kept in chains for five days and had to sleep on a concrete floor. He and scores of others were also beaten and verbally abused.

Prisoners of conscience

Three prisoners of conscience were released but dozens of others were arrested. At least three Tunisians resident abroad were arrested when they went to Tunisia for family visits.

☐ In June 'Abdelmoumen Belanes and Fahem Boukaddous, supporters of the *Parti communiste des ouvriers tunisiens* (PCOT), Tunisian Workers' Communist Party, were released before completion of their sentences.

☐ In August Taoufik Chaeb, an Islamist sympathizer, was released by presidential pardon after a 52-day hunger strike. He had been tried and sentenced three times on the same charges.

☐ In August, Mehdi Zougah, a French-Tunisian national, and 'Abderraouf Messa'oudi, resident in Austria, were arrested on arrival in Tunisia. They had previously been sentenced *in absentia* on charges of links with the unauthorized Islamist group *al-Nahda* (Renaissance). They remained in detention awaiting retrial at the end of the year.

Several former prisoners of conscience were arrested and sentenced to prison terms on charges of non-compliance with the administrative control requirements to report to the police daily or, in some cases, several times a day. Such measures, at times part of the sentence and in other cases arbitrarily imposed, continued to prevent former prisoners from working and resuming a normal life.

☐ In June, former prisoner of conscience 'Ali Ben Salem Sghaier symbolically offered his children for sale at the local market in Douz to protest at the administrative control measure which prevented him from working and earning a living to feed his seven children. He was arrested, threatened with imprisonment and released, but was rearrested in August and sentenced to six months' imprisonment on charges of non-compliance with administrative control measures. His sentence was upheld on appeal in September and he continued to serve his sentence at the end of the year.

Unfair trials

Trial proceedings began against scores of people arrested in previous years on political grounds. Many had been held longer than the 14-month maximum limit for pre-trial detention. Some detainees were tried in two or more cases on similar charges and in relation to the same events, in breach of the rule against double jeopardy. Lawyers were often prevented from visiting their clients or were refused access to their clients' files, and some prisoners were summarily tried without their lawyers having been notified of the date of the hearing.

☐ Ahmed 'Amari was deported from Libya in 1997 with dozens of other Islamist supporters, tortured in secret detention, and sentenced to two and five years' imprisonment respectively in June 1998 and June 1999. His lawyers were refused access to the documents relating to these trials. In 2000, he was being tried in three different cases in which the main charge was "membership of a criminal gang", a charge widely used against political opponents of the government.

☐ In September the trial began of 'Abdellatif Bouhajila, Yassine Benzerti and at least seven other Islamist supporters arrested in September 1998 and accused of having links with an unauthorized association and intelligence with a foreign power, reported to be Iran. No evidence was produced to support these charges and it was believed that they were tried for their links with exiled Tunisian government opponents. In November they were sentenced to up to 17 years' imprisonment, after the defence lawyers withdrew from the trial in protest at the unfairness of the procedings. 'Abdellatif Bouhajila and Yassine Benzerti, who had been on hunger strike for more than 80 days, could not stand, sit up or speak.

Intergovernmental organizations

The UN Special Rapporteur on the promotion and protection of the right to freedom of opinion and expression issued a report following his visit to Tunisia in December 1999 and strongly condemned the restrictions imposed by the authorities on such liberties.

In June and December, the European Parliament adopted two resolutions condemning the lack of freedom of association and expression, calling on the Tunisian government to end human rights violations and allow political pluralism, and calling on the European Commission to present a report on Tunisia.

AI country reports and visits

Reports

- The administration of justice in Tunisia: Torture, trumped-up charges and a tainted trial (AI Index: MDE 30/004/2000), issued jointly by AI, Human Rights Watch and the *Fédération internationale des ligues des droits de l'homme* (FIDH), International Federation of Human Rights

Visits

In July the authorities refused entry to Tunisia to a joint AI-FIDH delegation; both the AI researcher and the FIDH President had been banned from Tunisia since 1994 and 1995 respectively. The government did not respond to any of AI's communications seeking information and raising concerns about specific cases.

TURKEY

REPUBLIC OF TURKEY
Head of state: Ahmet Necdet Sezer (replaced Süleyman Demirel in May)
Head of government: Bülent Ecevit
Capital: Ankara
Population: 66.6 million
Official language: Turkish
Death penalty: abolitionist in practice
2000 treaty ratifications/signatures: International Covenant on Civil and Political Rights; International Covenant on Economic, Social and Cultural Rights; Optional Procotol to the UN Children's Convention on the involvement of children in armed conflict; Optional Protocol to the UN Women's Convention

Human rights defenders continued to face harassment and intimidation; branches of human rights associations were temporarily closed and board members put on trial. Writers, politicians, religious leaders, human rights defenders and many others were tried and imprisoned for exercising their right to freedom of expression, particularly when they expressed opinions on the Kurdish question or the role of Islam. Torture remained widespread and the perpetrators were rarely brought to justice. Prisoners were killed and seriously wounded when protests against the replacing of dormitories with smaller cells were ended with force. There were concerns that conditions in the new smaller cells could amount to cruel, inhuman or degrading treatment. Some 2,000 suspected members of the militant Islamist organization *Hizbullah* were arrested; some were held in prolonged police detention. The bodies of dozens of people were exhumed; the killings were attributed to *Hizbullah*. A number of political killings were reported. The *de facto* moratorium on executions was upheld.

Background
Although the conditions set out in December 1999 for accepting Turkey as a candidate for membership of the European Union (EU) included an improvement in the country's human rights record, no substantive reforms or improvements were recorded in 2000. The government committed itself to a schedule for reforms, but major legal changes were envisaged only for 2001 or 2002. The Chairman of the High Coordination Board for Human Rights drafted a proposal for steps to be taken to meet the Copenhagen political criteria, a precondition for the start of accession negotiations with the EU. A revised version of this report was adopted in September.

The former head of the Constitutional Court, Ahmet Necdet Sezer, was elected President in early May and made several speeches in which he stressed the importance of human rights, the rule of law and democracy.

The armed conflict between government forces and the Kurdistan Workers' Party (PKK) effectively came to an end in 1999 and only a few clashes between the Turkish army and dissident PKK groups were reported. Nevertheless, repression of political parties and organizations in southeastern Turkey, which has a mainly Kurdish population, continued unabated. Representatives of the pro-Kurdish People's Democracy Party (HADEP) were arrested and put on trial. Numerous associations and media companies were closed and demonstrations, meetings and other public events were banned.

Torture/ill-treatment
Torture was widespread. There were numerous reports of torture and ill-treatment of men, women and children, mainly from western cities, the southeast and the region around Adana in the south. Many of the victims were political activists, including supporters of leftist, pro-Kurdish and Islamist groups. Despite intimidation and fear of reprisals, dozens of allegations of torture were received from people arrested on criminal charges. Other victims of torture and ill-treatment included Kurdish villagers, relatives of political activists, students and women's groups. Allegations were also received from police officers and leading figures in organized crime.

Torture and ill-treatment occurred mainly in police and gendarmerie stations during the first days after arrest. The most frequently reported methods included severe beatings, prolonged blindfolding, suspension by the arms or wrists, electric shocks, sexual abuse, and food and sleep deprivation.

▫ Ramazan Tekin, Deputy Mayor of Diyarbakır, was arrested in January and held for 10 days at Diyarbakır Gendarmerie where he was reportedly beaten, suspended by the arms, sexually abused and given electric shocks. Doctors from the Forensic Institute who examined him reportedly confirmed that his ribs were broken and his kidneys damaged. His lawyer filed a formal complaint against the security officers suspected of being responsible, but the governor of Diyarbakır did not give permission for the two gendarmes to be prosecuted.

Rape in custody
Rape and sexual assault by members of the security forces continued to be reported. During incommunicado detention in police or gendarmerie custody, women and men were routinely stripped naked. Methods of sexual abuse reported included electric shocks and beating on the genitals and women's breasts and rape.

▫ Azime Arzu Torun was reportedly raped by gendarmes and prison guards with a truncheon when security officers ended the inmates' protest in Burdur prison on 5 July. She was also said to have been exposed to sexual harassment while giving her testimony to an inspector.

Suspected Islamists
Some 2,000 alleged members of *Hizbullah* were arrested following the launch of an extensive operation against the organization by the security

forces in January. Subsequently, the bodies of some 67 people were exhumed; their abduction and murder were attributed to *Hizbullah*. Some observers claimed that *Hizbullah* had been acting in collusion with parts of the Turkish security forces during the armed conflict. Some of those detained in the raid against *Hizbullah* were held in police detention for prolonged periods during which they were at risk of torture and ill-treatment. The maximum period for police and gendarmerie detention is seven days and, in the provinces under State of Emergency, 10 days. However, several of these detainees were held for much longer periods.

▫ Fahrettin Özdemir was detained in February and later indicted in the main *Hizbullah* trial in which he and 14 others were charged with some 150 murders and in which the death sentence was sought. On 10 July, in the first trial session, he stated that he had been held in police custody for a total of 59 days and that he was given electric shocks and suspended by the arms, and his testicles were squeezed and beaten at the Police Headquarters in Gaziantep.

Parliamentary Human Rights Commission

The Parliamentary Human Rights Commission published nine reports on their investigations into torture and ill-treatment. They had interviewed prison inmates in various provinces and subsequently carried out unannounced on-the-spot visits to detention centres where there had been frequent allegations of torture and ill-treatment. For example, in Istanbul the Commission found equipment used for suspending detainees by the arms. The reports, which contained pictures of detention places, interrogation rooms and torture equipment, as well as the transcripts of interviews, represented an extraordinary step forward in official circles in documenting and acknowledging torture.

Prisons

There were reports of poor medical care in prisons and beatings during transfers to and from prison. Most prisoners were housed in large dormitories holding 60 or more prisoners, but wings based on a cell system were added to many prisons and 11 new prisons with small cells were being built. There was concern that regimes of isolation already practised in Kartal and Imralı prisons might be extended to the new prisons.

From October, more than 1,000 prisoners participated in a hunger strike against the new prisons. On 19 December the security forces conducted an operation in 20 prisons in which dozens of prisoners died. Hundreds of prisoners were beaten before, during and after their transfer to three new prisons where they were subjected to solitary confinement and small-group isolation.

▫ On 5 July political prisoners in Burdur prison barricaded themselves in dormitories. According to the prisoners, the security forces threw smoke bombs, tear gas and nerve gas into the dormitories and started to break down the walls with bulldozers. The prisoners said the security forces attacked them with iron poles, truncheons, roof tiles and stones, dragging unconscious prisoners out of the dormitories with long-handled hooks. Lawyers permitted to meet some of the prisoners on 8 July noted that all had signs of severe injuries on the visible parts of their bodies, and had difficulty breathing and speaking.

Impunity

The authorities remained reluctant to investigate allegations of torture. Officers accused of torture were rarely suspended from duty, and in some cases received promotions. It was difficult to establish who was responsible as detainees were almost invariably blindfolded during interrogation and custody records were often poorly maintained or non-existent. Medical evidence of torture was frequently suppressed. Medical officers who falsified reports were promoted while doctors who carried out their duties scrupulously were harassed, put on trial or imprisoned. The intimidation of witnesses and a generalized climate of fear also contributed to impunity, as did prosecutors' reluctance to investigate the work of security force officers. Judges often refused to investigate allegations of torture and accepted confessions extracted under torture as evidence, in violation of the UN Convention against Torture. Under the 1999 Law on the Prosecution of Civil Servants the permission of a senior official is required for the prosecution of suspected human rights abusers.

▫ In July 1999 Cevat Soysal was reportedly abducted in Moldova, taken to Turkey and held for 10 days in incommunicado detention. He reported that at the Turkish Secret Service (MIT) headquarters he was given electric shocks, hung by the arms, forced to lie naked on ice, sprayed with pressurized water, deprived of sleep, beaten and forced to swallow a drug. At their meeting Cevat Soysal's lawyer noted needle marks, bruising and other signs consistent with his client's allegations of torture. In November 1999, the prosecutor decided not to open a trial against the alleged torturers; the Office of the Prime Minister had informed him that a prosecution would not be appropriate. In January and February 2000 the appeals of Cevat Soysal and his lawyers against the decision not to prosecute the suspected torturers were rejected. At the end of 2000 Cevat Soysal remained imprisoned on charges of separatism and being a leading member of the PKK.

No justice for women raped in custody

By November, 132 women — 97 of them Kurds — had sought help from a legal aid project in Istanbul set up to bring perpetrators to justice. Forty-five of the women alleged that they had been raped and 87 reported other forms of sexual abuse. The suspected perpetrators — overwhelmingly police officers, although allegations were also made against gendarmes, soldiers, and village guards — were rarely brought to justice.

▫ In November 1996, a young Kurdish woman, Zeynep Avcı, arrested during an operation against the PKK, was subjected to sexual harassment, rape and electric shocks at Izmir Police Headquarters. The authorities not only failed to initiate prompt, comprehensive and impartial investigations into these allegations, but also exposed Zeynep Avcı to additional gender-based discrimination. In an apparent attempt to discredit her, allegations of a previous abortion were submitted to the European Court of Human Rights to which she had meanwhile filed an application.

Prisoners of conscience

Writers, publishers, researchers, environmentalists, trade unionists, local and national politicians, religious leaders, human rights defenders and many others continued to be imprisoned or tried for exercising their right to freedom of expression, particularly on issues related to the Kurdish question or the role of Islam in politics.

▫ In July the Appeal Court upheld a sentence of one year's imprisonment against Necmettin Erbakan, the former leader of the banned Islamist Welfare Party. Necmettin Erbakan had been sentenced in March 2000, for a speech he delivered in February 1994 during local elections. In his speech Necmettin Erbakan had criticized the representatives of other parties for "false beliefs" and being dependent on the West. He had also referred explicitly to a Kurdish electorate. There was no incitement to violence in his speech.

Human rights defenders

Human rights defenders continued to face harassment and intimidation. Human Rights Association (IHD) branches in Van, Gaziantep and Malatya were closed indefinitely and those in Diyarbakır and Konya were closed temporarily. The Urfa branch of the Islamic-oriented human rights organization *Mazlum Der* was reopened in April, but the Malatya branch remained closed. Doctors and other staff of the Human Rights Foundation in Turkey (TIHV) working on the documentation and treatment of torture in Izmir were put on trial. Doctors in Istanbul who certified torture were also harassed. Trials were continuing against a number of lawyers as well as representatives of IHD and *Mazlum Der*.

▫ Akın Birdal, former President of the IHD, was imprisoned between March and September to serve the remainder of two one-year sentences imposed for speeches in connection with World Peace Day in 1995 and 1996. He had been temporarily released from prison on 25 September 1999 to enable him to receive proper medical treatment, but was banned from leaving the country and thus prevented from taking advantage of offers of specialized medical treatment abroad. In March 2000 the prosecutor rejected his application for the postponement of his sentence on medical grounds.

Death penalty

With the decision in January to halt the procedures related to Abdullah Öcalan's death sentence, the *de facto* moratorium on executions was upheld. However, at least 80 death sentences were passed in the first 11 months of the year, 28 of which were later commuted to prison terms. By the end of the year the death sentences of 71 other people had been upheld by the Appeal Court and submitted to parliament for final confirmation.

Other concerns

A number of possible extrajudicial executions were reported.

▫ Three villagers were killed on 19 October in the southeastern province of Hakkari. A fourth villager was wounded and subsequently taken into gendarmerie custody. The circumstances of the killings were disputed.

Numerous deliberate and arbitrary killings were attributed to armed opposition groups.

More than a hundred "disappearances" from previous years remained unresolved. Some new cases were reported.

AI country reports and visits
Reports
- Turkey: Torture – a major concern in 1999 (AI Index: EUR 44/018/2000)
- Turkey: Amnesty International's recommendations to the government (AI Index: EUR 44/019/2000)
- Turkey: The alleged torture of Cevat Soysal at National Intelligence Agency Headquarters, Ankara (AI Index: EUR 44/036/2000)
- Turkey: New law on the prosecution of civil servants – not a major step towards ending impunity for torturers (AI Index: EUR 44/038/2000)
- Turkey: Torturers of mother and infant go free (AI Index: EUR 44/061/2000)
- Turkey: Amnesty International's continuing concerns and the EU Accession Partnership with Turkey (AI Index: EUR 44/068/2000)

Visits
AI delegates visited Turkey in April and November to research human rights violations. AI trial observers visited Turkey in February, March, May, June and August.

TURKMENISTAN

TURKMENISTAN
Head of state and government: Saparmurad Niyazov
Capital: Ashgabat
Population: 4.4 million
Official language: Turkmen
Death penalty: abolitionist for all crimes
2000 treaty ratifications/signatures: Second Optional Protocol to the International Covenant on Civil and Political Rights, aiming at the abolition of the death penalty

A prominent opposition activist was sentenced to imprisonment. Members of unregistered religious denominations and their families continued to report frequent harassment by the authorities, including deportation and internal exile. There was concern for the health of political prisoners.

Prisoner of conscience

In February Nurberdi Nurmamedov, co-chair of the opposition movement *Agzybirlik* and one of the few opposition figures to openly criticize President Niyazov's policies, was sentenced to five years' imprisonment. At the same trial Nurberdi Nurmamedov's 25-year-old son, Murad Nurmamedov, was sentenced to a suspended two-year prison sentence and confined to live in Ashgabat for five years. Despite an official invitation to send trial observers, representatives of foreign embassies and of the Organization for Security and Co-operation in Europe (OSCE) were refused access to the court. AI believes that the charges of "hooliganism" brought against Nurberdi Nurmamedov were fabricated, that he was imprisoned for his peaceful opposition activities, and that his son was put on trial in order to put pressure on him.

Appeals against their sentences were turned down in March. The two lawyers representing Nurberdi Nurmamedov at the appeal reportedly left the courtroom before the end of the hearing in protest at violations of international fair trial standards. At the end of March Nurberdi Nurmamedov was reportedly forced to publicly confess his guilt on television. In September unofficial sources reported that Nurberdi Nurmamedov had been transferred from Turkmenbashi maximum security prison to a prison near Kyzylkaya in the south of Turkmenistan. As a result of poor prison conditions his health had apparently deteriorated sharply and he was reported to be suffering from an acute stomach ulcer. Nurberdi Nurmamedov was released on 23 December under a presidential amnesty. Earlier in December he reportedly had to repent on state television and swear an oath of loyalty to President Niyazov.

Political prisoners

Following an official visit in May, the OSCE Chairman-in-Office said she was deeply disappointed at President Niyazov's unwillingness to release political prisoners as requested by the OSCE.

☐ There was concern that the lives of political prisoners Mukhametkuli Aymuradov and Pirimkuli Tangrykuliev were in danger following reports that their health had deteriorated sharply as a result of poor prison conditions and the absence of medical care. According to reports, Pirimkuli Tangrykuliev was beaten repeatedly by prison guards. He was released under the December presidential amnesty. He was reportedly forced to repent on state television and swear an oath of loyalty to President Niyazov.

Repression of religious minorities

Human rights violations by law enforcement officials against religious believers continued to be reported. Peaceful religious meetings in private homes were broken up and the participants fined or detained for short periods; religious materials were confiscated and places of worship destroyed; religious believers were physically and verbally abused and some were imprisoned because of their religion. A number of foreign missionaries were deported.

Internal exile

Some religious activists had their freedom of movement within Turkmenistan restricted through the use of residence permits.

☐ Artygul Atakova, the wife of Shagildy Atakov, and their five children were deported to the village of Kaakhka in February and put under "village arrest". Shagildy Atakov, an ethnic Turkmen member of a Baptist congregation in Turkmenbashi, continued to serve a four-year prison sentence in a corrective labour camp. His supporters believed that the true reason for his imprisonment was his religious affiliation. Shagildy Atakov's brother, Chariyar, was administratively detained for 15 days; the reason for his detention was not clear. In February a younger brother of Shagildy Atakov was found hanged. The circumstances surrounding his death remained unclear.

☐ In February, 72-year-old Khodzha Akhmed Orazgylych, a Muslim cleric, was arrested and charged with "swindling". In a radio interview, he had reportedly criticized an invitation by President Niyazov at the end of 1999 for children to celebrate the new year by dancing around a Christmas tree chanting a prayer to the President. Around a month later Khodzha Akhmed Orazgylych was said to have been among a group of prisoners taken to meet President Niyazov. The cleric reportedly asked for forgiveness, and President Niyazov replaced a possible prison term with internal exile in a village in Khodzha Akhmed Orazgylych's home region.

Conscientious objectors

Information came to light that conscientious objectors Roman Sidelnikov, Oleg Voronin and Roman Karimov had been released under a presidential amnesty in 1999. However, conscientious objectors to military service continued to be sentenced to prison terms.

⮡ Two Jehovah's Witnesses were imprisoned for their conscientious objection to military service. Nuryagdy Gairov was serving a one-year prison sentence, imposed in January, in the Tedzhen corrective labour colony. He reportedly did not benefit from the 1999 amnesty because he refused to swear the oath of allegiance to President Niyazov. Igor Nazarov, who was also detained in the Tedzhen corrective labour colony, was serving a second prison term imposed in March; he had previously been sentenced to a suspended two-year term.

AI country report
- Turkmenistan: Harassment and imprisonment of religious believers (AI Index: EUR 61/007/2000)

UGANDA

REPUBLIC OF UGANDA
Head of state: Yoweri Museveni
Head of government: Apollo Nsibambi
Capital: Kampala
Population: 21.7 million
Official language: English
Death penalty: retentionist

Gross human rights abuses by armed opposition groups, including killings and abductions, continued throughout 2000. Torture and possible extrajudicial executions by the security forces were reported. The Ugandan army was accused of human rights violations including torture in the Democratic Republic of the Congo (DRC). Meetings by political parties and others, peaceful demonstrations and strikes were disrupted by the security forces, sometimes violently. Scores of political prisoners, some of whom may have been prisoners of conscience, were arrested. Prison conditions were harsh. At least 10 people were sentenced to death, but no one was executed.

Background
Human rights abuses by armed opposition groups increased during 2000. The Amnesty Act, which came into force in December 1999 and offered an amnesty to all rebel fighters who gave themselves up, was extended in July to the end of the year. The Commission to implement the Act was not set up until June and was hampered by under-funding. Under an agreement between Uganda and Sudan, Uganda returned more than 70 Sudanese prisoners of war, but large numbers of abducted children held in Sudan in camps run by the Lord's Resistance Army (LRA) were not returned. Of the 10,000 children estimated by the UN Children's Fund (UNICEF) to have been abducted by the LRA since 1994, more than 5,000 remained unaccounted for. Although the government of Sudan had stated that the people it returned would be primarily abducted children still held in LRA camps, these appeared to be less than half of those returned.

In June a referendum was held to choose a political system in preparation for the 2001 presidential and parliamentary elections. The referendum approved President Yoweri Museveni's "Movement" system, which does not allow political parties to contest elections. In August the Referendum and Other Provisions Act was annulled by the Constitutional Court, following a petition by the opposition Democratic Party, on the grounds that it had been passed into law without a quorum. In response, the government enacted the Constitutional Amendments Act in September, which increased the power of parliament, barred courts from inquiring into parliamentary proceedings, and reduced the requirement for a parliamentary quorum.

In September the Ugandan Human Rights Commission opened an office in Soroti district and the army set up a human rights desk in Luwero district.

Abuses by armed opposition groups
Lord's Resistance Army
There was an increase in abuses by the LRA in 2000, primarily against civilian targets. Killings, torture, including rape, and abductions, particularly of children, were reported throughout the year, mainly in the northern districts of Gulu and Kitgum. Abducted children were forced to become child soldiers, and girls were used by LRA commanders as sexual slaves. Nearly 80 per cent of LRA combatants were abducted children, according to estimates.

⮡ In May, 16 children between the ages of nine and 18 were reportedly abducted by the LRA in Gulu district.
⮡ In October a two-year-old child was among five civilians abducted in Alero sub-county.
⮡ In October Father Rafaelle Di Bari, an Italian priest who had lived in Uganda for over 30 years, was killed by the LRA on the road to his home in Kitgum district. His death was followed by a grenade attack by the LRA on Opit Travellers Inn disco hall in Gulu town, which left nine people killed and scores injured. Both attacks appeared to be in response to a renewal of the agreement between Sudan and Uganda in September in which the Sudanese government agreed to force the LRA to move its bases 1,000km from the border.

Allied Democratic Front
Abuses in western Uganda by the Allied Democratic Front (ADF), based in the DRC, continued throughout 2000. They included killings, maimings and abductions of civilians, including children, to become soldiers. Although security in Kasese, Kabarole and Bundibugyo districts improved a little, attacks by the ADF spread to Bushenyi, Hoima, Kibaale and Mbarara districts during the year.

⮡ In August, seven people were killed in one attack by the ADF in Bushenyi district.

Human rights violations by security forces

Reports of human rights violations by the security forces, including possible extrajudicial executions, torture and detention without trial, continued. There were reports of human rights violations by the army, the Ugandan People's Defence Forces (UPDF), fighting in support of rebel forces in the DRC.

In April Ugandan troops were reportedly involved in deliberate and arbitrary killings of members of the Lendu ethnic group in Kibali-Ituri province, and in other abuses. At least 700 unarmed civilians were reportedly killed when Ugandan and Rwandese troops fought for control of Kisangani in June and July. In August over 100 children were reportedly taken from the DRC to Jinja in Uganda by government forces for military training. More than 4,000 members of the UPDF were withdrawn from the DRC by September.

Political prisoners

Scores of people, including some possible prisoners of conscience, were briefly detained without charge or trial, often in military barracks. The majority of detainees were suspected members or supporters of armed opposition groups.

In February, two men were reportedly arrested by the army and held in incommunicado detention in military barracks in Mbarara district for more than three months before being released without charge.

In June Azia Turigye was reportedly arrested by the police in Bushenyi district and handed over to the UPDF in Mbarara. She was held illegally in incommunicado detention at an undisclosed location for two months before being charged with treason and held on remand in Luzira prison.

At least 75 prisoners were pardoned under the Amnesty Act, some of whom had been held without trial on treason charges for more than three years. The Amnesty Commission reported that it had received over 300 applications from prisoners detained in Luzira prison, the majority of whom were held on treason charges. More than 2,000 refugees in Nairobi, Kenya, mainly former members of the LRA, were still waiting for their applications to be processed by the end of 2000.

Torture and killings

There were reports of torture and possible extrajudicial executions by members of the UPDF, members of Local Defence Units (LDU) and the police.

In August Hafusa Muzamili was reportedly raped and killed by UPDF soldiers from the army headquarters at Bombo, Luwero district.

In September, 18 LDU members reportedly forced more than 15,000 villagers in Kapchorwa district to flee their homes. The LDU members attacked local home guards at the sub-county prison who were holding three LDU members accused of beating Simon Kitiyo, an alleged thief, into a coma. One civilian and two LDU members were injured and three killed.

Freedom of assembly and association

Despite legislative changes in preparation for the referendum on the political system, restrictions to prevent political parties contesting elections remained. Scores of prisoners of conscience were arrested for short periods after public meetings and peaceful demonstrations organized by political parties, human rights groups and others were broken up by the police, sometimes violently.

In May in Mbale district, police officers dispersed a crowd and arrested participants at a seminar on the referendum organized by the Uganda Young Congress, youth wing of the opposition Uganda People's Congress.

In June, 11 students were arrested in Kampala and charged with "misconduct and alarming the President", which carries a life sentence, after they attempted to disrupt a rally by the President at Makerere University. They were reportedly carrying anti-Movement placards and shouting slogans.

In September several people were injured when police violently dispersed a meeting in Gulu district to celebrate the fifth anniversary of the Uganda Young Democrats.

Freedom of expression

Journalists continued to face harassment and arbitrary arrest.

In February, two journalists, Frank Bagonza Kimome and Joseph Kasimbazi, were detained by the army for a week and subsequently charged with publishing false news after *Voice of Toro* radio falsely reported that over 30 people had been killed by the ADF. The station retracted the report shortly after it was broadcast. The case had not come to court by the end of 2000.

The case against the three senior editors of the independent daily *The Monitor* — Charles Onyango-Obbo, David Ouma Balikowa and Wafula Oguttu — began in September. They had been charged in May 1999 with sedition and publishing a false statement following the publication of a photograph allegedly showing members of the UPDF assaulting a woman.

Prison conditions

Prison conditions remained harsh and life threatening. Both civilian and military prisons had high mortality rates from overcrowding, malnutrition, diseases spread by insanitary conditions, and HIV/AIDS. Pre-trial detainees comprised nearly three quarters of the prison population. The average time in pre-trial detention was two to three years. Because of lack of space in juvenile facilities, juveniles were often imprisoned with adults.

Death penalty

At least 10 people were sentenced to death, including one woman. At least 11 members of the UPDF had their sentences quashed on appeal, including two who had been in prison awaiting appeal for more than 11 years. In July President Museveni commuted the death sentences of 16 prisoners to life imprisonment and pardoned over 500 other prisoners. There were more than 260 prisoners under sentence of death at the end of 2000.

AI visit

AI delegates visited Uganda in April. They met journalists, human rights organizations and others.

UKRAINE

UKRAINE
Head of state: Leonid Kuchma
Head of government: Viktor Yushchenko
Capital: Kiev
Population: 50.7 million
Official language: Ukrainian
Death penalty: abolitionist for all crimes
2000 treaty ratifications/signatures: Optional Protocol to the UN Children's Convention on the involvement of children in armed conflict; Optional Protocol to the UN Women's Convention; Rome Statute of the International Criminal Court; Protocol No. 6 to the European Convention on Human Rights concerning the abolition of the death penalty

Ukraine removed the death penalty from its criminal code. There were a significant number of allegations of police ill-treatment and torture of detainees. Allegations that military conscripts were subjected to violent treatment known as "hazing" were also received. An independent journalist apparently "disappeared". The Ukrainian coastguard reportedly used excessive force against Turkish fishermen in the Black Sea, resulting in one death. Ukraine lacked a genuine civilian alternative service to military service.

Death penalty

The Constitutional Court ruled on 30 December 1999 that articles in the criminal code providing for the death penalty were unconstitutional. Following the Court's decision, on 22 February 2000 the Ukrainian parliament, *Verkhovna Rada*, removed the death penalty from the criminal code. It also ratified Protocol No. 6 to the European Convention on Human Rights in line with Ukraine's commitments to the Council of Europe, which it had joined in 1995.

Torture/ill-treatment

Ill-treatment and torture of detainees by law enforcement officials appeared to be relatively widespread. A delegation of the European Committee for the Prevention of Torture and Inhuman or Degrading Treatment or Punishment undertook a 16-day visit to Ukraine in September, after having visited the country in 1999 and 1998. Reports of the visits had not been made public by the end of 2000.

▫ Anatoly Voskoboinikov was allegedly forced to sign a confession at the Ministry of the Interior in Enakievo in November 1998. According to the Kharkov Group for Human Rights Protection, police officers handcuffed his wrists under his knees and slotted a length of wood between his arms and chest, then lifted him up by the piece of wood and hung him between two tables. The police officers allegedly then punched and kicked him while he was suspended in this painful position.

There were reports of ill-treatment and torture of young conscripts in the Ukrainian army. Each year a number are reportedly driven to suicide and desertion as a result of hazing at the hands of other soldiers and officers.

▫ Between May 1998 and September 1999, 18 recruits who had deserted from their units appealed for help from the Kharkov Union of Soldiers' Mothers. Sixteen of them stated that they had deserted because they had been subjected to hazing.

Possible 'disappearance'

Georgiy Gongadze, a 31-year-old investigative journalist, failed to return home on the evening of 16 September. He was editor of the Internet newspaper *Ukrayinskaya Pravda* and an independent radio journalist, and had criticized members of the government and their allegedly corrupt relationship with powerful interest groups. In June he reportedly wrote an open letter to the Procurator General after being forced into hiding by police harassment. AI called for an immediate and impartial investigation into his apparent "disappearance".

On 3 November a decapitated body was found in a shallow grave in woodland in the Tarashcha Rayon area, near the capital, Kiev. The body was later reportedly identified as the missing journalist. Later in November the former presidential candidate and leader of the Socialist Party of Ukraine, Olexandr Moroz, claimed to have in his possession an audiotape recording of President Kuchma, allegedly made by a former officer of the Ukrainian State Security Service, in conversation with the Minister of the Interior, Yury Kravchenko, and the Chairman of the Presidential Administration, Volodymyr Lytvy. The recording allegedly implicated them in the "disappearance" of Georgiy Gongadze. President Kuchma and his colleagues vociferously denied the allegations and threatened Olexandr Moroz with libel action.

Excessive use of force

In March the Ukrainian coastguard fired shells at Turkish fishing vessels in the Black Sea in two separate incidents. AI expressed concern that the use of shells by the coastguard to stop fishing vessels may have represented unreasonable and excessive use of force.

▫ On 22 March a Turkish fisherman, Gûrmiz Çinar, was killed and one of his colleagues was injured by a shell fired by the Ukrainian coastguard. The Turkish vessel was fishing illegally in Ukrainian waters around 200km from Odessa.

Harsh prison conditions

Conditions in prisons and pre-trial detention centres continued to fall below international minimum standards, and amounted to cruel, inhuman or degrading treatment. Prisoners were poorly fed, received inadequate medical care and were held in poorly heated and ventilated conditions in overcrowded cells.

Conscientious objectors

The alternative civilian service to military service in Ukraine extends only to those who object to military service on religious grounds and belong to religious organizations registered with the state. At 36 months, it is also twice as long as military service.

☐ On 12 July Andrij Tvardijevych, an 18-year-old conscientious objector, was given a suspended one-year prison sentence and fined by a court in Kiev for refusing to serve in the army for reasons of conscience.

AI country report
- Concerns in Europe, January – June 2000: Ukraine (AI Index: EUR 01/003/2000)

UNITED ARAB EMIRATES

UNITED ARAB EMIRATES
Head of state: Al-Sheikh Zayed bin Sultan Al-Nahyan
Head of government: Al-Sheikh Maktum bin Rashid al-Maktum
Capital: Abu Dhabi
Population: 2.6 million
Official language: Arabic
Death penalty: retentionist
2000 treaty ratifications/signatures: Rome Statute of the International Criminal Court

At least 15 death sentences and 18 flogging sentences were reportedly handed down during 2000, although the true figures may have been higher. At least two death sentences were commuted, while five others were upheld on appeal. There were no reported executions.

Background
The authorities announced a crack-down on drug offenders, following a reported 60 per cent rise in drug-related offences during 1999. Twelve of the 15 death sentences handed down in 2000 were for drug-related offences.

Death sentences
At least 15 people, all foreign nationals, were sentenced to death during the year. Among them was Kartini bint Karim, an Indonesian national, who was sentenced in February by a *Shari'a* (Islamic) court in the Emirate of Fujairah to be stoned to death, reportedly after she had confessed to adultery (see below).

During the year, appeal courts in Dubai upheld five death sentences. In March, the death sentences against two men, originally handed down in 1997 for drug-related offences, were upheld. In April the death sentence against an Afghan national, originally handed down in January for drug-related offences, was also upheld. In June, the death sentence against a Pakistan national, originally handed down in February for drug-related offences, was upheld. In July, the death sentence previously passed on an Indian national for murder was also upheld.

Commutation of death sentences
The sentence of stoning to death against Kartini bint Karim was commuted on appeal in April to one year's imprisonment and deportation. During her appeal, Kartini bint Karim reportedly denied confessing to the offence of adultery. As she had already spent 10 months in prison when her sentence was commuted, under United Arab Emirates law this time was deducted from her one-year sentence, after which she was deported. The court also sentenced *in absentia* the man involved in the case, an Indian national who had fled the country, to one year's imprisonment.

In April there were reports that Khalid Al-Malla, a Pakistan national reportedly sentenced to death for murder at the age of 14, was pardoned after having spent 10 years in detention in Ras al-Khaimah. His release and deportation reportedly followed the payment of blood money (*diya*) of approximately US$45,000 to the murder victim's family.

Cruel judicial punishments
At least 18 sentences of cruel, inhuman or degrading punishments such as flogging were passed during the year; 11 of them were handed down in the Emirate of Fujairah. Ten of the 18 sentences were allegedly for adultery and 11 of those sentenced were foreign nationals.

☐ In June a *Shari'a* court in Ras al-Khaimah reportedly sentenced Pakistan nationals Jamilah Rasul and Mohammad Ish'ar to 150 lashes and 90 lashes respectively, to be followed by prison terms and deportation, for adultery.

☐ In November, a *Shari'a* court in Fujairah reportedly sentenced Pifatool Karima, an Indonesian national, to 120 lashes and 14 months' imprisonment, to be followed by deportation, for adultery.

Freedom of expression
In September there were unconfirmed reports that the Ministry of Information had made a number of rulings resulting in several academics and journalists being banned from writing or publishing materials in the media. The rulings also reportedly required newspaper publishers to obtain ministerial permission before they could employ columnists to write for their newspapers. Several radio and television programs were also reportedly suspended in Abu Dhabi.

UNITED KINGDOM

UNITED KINGDOM OF GREAT BRITAIN AND NORTHERN IRELAND
Head of state: Queen Elizabeth II
Head of government: Tony Blair
Capital: London
Population: 58.8 million
Official language: English
Death penalty: abolitionist for all crimes
2000 treaty ratifications/signatures: Optional Protocol to the UN Children's Convention on the involvement of children in armed conflict

The Human Rights Act came into force in October, incorporating most of the European Convention on Human Rights into domestic law. Negotiations concerning the implementation of the Multi-Party Agreement in Northern Ireland continued, but killings, bombings and beatings persisted. In the United Kingdom (UK), the government introduced more sweeping powers for the security forces in anti-terrorist and surveillance legislation. Detainees and prisoners were reportedly subjected to ill-treatment and racist abuse.

Background

Negotiations over the implementation of the Multi-Party Agreement in Northern Ireland continued throughout 2000. In February the peace process broke down when the government dissolved the Northern Ireland Assembly and reinstated direct rule. However, the Assembly was re-established in May.

Northern Ireland

In November, the Police (Northern Ireland) Act 2000 renamed the Royal Ulster Constabulary (RUC) the "Police Service of Northern Ireland (incorporating the RUC)" and introduced measures to encourage the recruitment of Catholics and women. The Act failed to highlight the centrality of human rights protection and to include all the measures for increased police accountability recommended by the Independent Commission on Policing for Northern Ireland in October 1999. These included increasing the effective powers of the Policing Board and of the Police Ombudsperson to initiate inquiries. In June Nuala O'Loan became the first Northern Ireland Police Ombudsperson, leading a team of independent investigators into complaints against the police.

In March, the Review of the Criminal Justice System in Northern Ireland set up under the Multi-Party Agreement was published by a group of experts. It made 294 recommendations, including the creation of a new prosecution service and an Independent Judicial Appointments Commission.

The cases of Patrick Finucane and Rosemary Nelson

The Stevens police investigation continued into the killing of Patrick Finucane in February 1989 by Loyalist paramilitaries in collusion with intelligence agents. The only person charged was William Stobie, arrested in June 1999, whose trial was still pending. AI published a report which called on the government to establish a judicial public inquiry into this killing, in line with international standards. The government stated that it would make its decision once criminal proceedings had been completed.

Rosemary Nelson, also a lawyer, was killed by a Loyalist car bomb in March 1999. In January 2000, it was announced that the Director of Public Prosecutions (DPP) had decided that the RUC officers accused of issuing death threats against her would not be prosecuted. In May it was announced that no disciplinary action would be taken against the officers. After 20 months of police investigation, no one had been charged in connection with her murder.

Freedom of expression

Charges under the Official Secrets Act were dropped in November against a former military intelligence officer, using the name of Martin Ingram, and a *Sunday Times* journalist. The two had revealed information about the operations of a secret military intelligence unit, the Force Research Unit (FRU), in the late 1980s and 1990 in Northern Ireland. Martin Ingram alleged that the FRU had used a Loyalist agent to target suspected Republicans for killing. Injunctions had been issued against two newspapers to stop publication of further revelations.

'Bloody Sunday' inquiry

The public judicial inquiry into the events of "Bloody Sunday", in which 13 people were killed and hundreds injured by soldiers in January 1972, opened on 27 March. It was expected to last at least two years.

Investigations into killings by the security forces

Four cases, involving 12 killings of Catholics in Northern Ireland, were declared admissible by the European Court of Human Rights in April. It was alleged that RUC officers had operated a policy of killing rather than arresting suspected opponents, or had colluded with Loyalist paramilitaries.

At the end of 2000, there were at least 15 inquests outstanding into disputed killings and deaths in custody. AI was concerned about delays in holding such inquests, including in the cases of Sam Marshall and Roseanne Mallon.

Robert Hamill

The coroner leading the inquest into the death of Robert Hamill, who was kicked to death by a Loyalist crowd in Portadown in 1997, decided that he was unable to hold an inquest because he could not guarantee the safety of a key witness. Investigation of the conduct of the police officers at the scene of the attack continued.

Abuses by armed political groups

Sectarian killings and attacks continued during 2000, as well as "punishment" killings and beatings by members of armed Loyalist and Republican groups. During 2000 there were 18 killings, 15 by Loyalists and three by Republicans. A feud between different Loyalist armed groups led to the killing of seven people, including two teenagers.

There were dozens of "punishment" shootings and beatings by both Republicans and Loyalists. So-called "punishments" were also meted out to children. In April, a 15-year-old and a 17-year-old were shot and injured by Loyalists in Belfast and a 16-year-old suffered head injuries after being beaten by Republicans wielding iron bars in Belfast.

Legislation

The Human Rights Act came into force in October, incorporating most of the European Convention on Human Rights into domestic law.

The Terrorism Act, enacted in July, made temporary or emergency measures into permanent ones. AI expressed concern that some measures contravened international human rights standards or could result in human rights violations.

The Regulation of Investigatory Powers Act, enacted in July, legalized a variety of intrusive surveillance techniques, covert use of informants and agents, and the interception of communications. AI was concerned that the Act failed to provide sufficient safeguards, including judicial oversight, to ensure accountability and protection of fundamental human rights.

In November, Parliament lowered the age of consent for homosexual acts from 18 to 16, thereby equalizing it with the age of consent for heterosexuals, for England, Scotland and Wales. The age was equalized at 17 for Northern Ireland.

Deaths in custody/disputed killings

In May the government began a consultation process on mechanisms to investigate misconduct by police officers. AI published a report on deaths in custody in the context of the consultation. In December the government announced that it would introduce a new, independent investigation system for serious misconduct cases, including deaths in custody.

At least one person died in police custody in disputed circumstances: Asif Dad died in police custody in January.

Updates

☐ In May an inquest jury returned a verdict of "accidental death" in the case of Glenn Howard, but added that the police officers had used excessive restraint and had subsequently failed to provide medical care. He died in January 1999 after being in a coma since December 1997. There were no prosecutions or disciplinary action.

☐ In June an inquest jury returned a verdict of unlawful killing in the case of Christopher Alder, a black former paratrooper who died in April 1998 in Hull police station. A videotape showed how officers ignored him as he lay on the police station floor for 10 minutes before they realized he was unconscious. The Crown Prosecution Service (CPS) was considering whether to bring prosecutions against five officers.

☐ In June the High Court instructed the prosecution authorities to re-examine their decision not to prosecute seven prison officers involved in the death in prison of Alton Manning, who died in 1995 after being restrained.

☐ In November the CPS decided that no criminal charges would be brought against eight police officers reportedly involved in the restraint of Roger Sylvester in January 1999. The exact cause of his death remained disputed; an inquest was pending.

☐ In December the CPS decided that no criminal charges would be brought against the police officers who shot dead Harry Stanley in September 1999. Harry Stanley was walking home carrying a repaired table leg in a bag. He had stopped in a pub, where another customer mistook his Scottish accent for Irish and the table leg for a shotgun and alerted the police. Armed police officers approached Harry Stanley from behind and reportedly shouted a warning. Harry Stanley did not stop, and when he turned around, reportedly after another police shout, he was shot dead.

☐ In February, a coroner's jury issued a verdict which effectively rendered the killing of unarmed IRA member Diarmuid O'Neill lawful. Diarmuid O'Neill was shot dead during a police raid in west London in September 1996.

Police handling of racist killings

There were renewed allegations that police forces were not investigating the deaths of black people, which could have been racially motivated, with the same rigour as in other cases.

☐ Harold McGowan and his nephew Jason were found hanged in Telford in July 1999 and January 2000 respectively. The family alleged that police had assumed suicide and had neglected warnings that they were under threat of racist attacks. The Metropolitan Police's Racial and Violent Crimes Task Force assisted the local police investigation.

☐ In March, a fresh inquiry was announced into the police handling of the death of Ricky Reel following complaints from his family. Ricky Reel drowned in the River Thames in October 1997. His family alleged that he died as a result of a racist attack. The Police Complaints Authority's inquiry resulted in finding three officers guilty of neglect of duty. An inquest jury in November 1999 returned an open verdict on the cause of death.

Ill-treatment in prisons

Reports of racist abuse and cruel, inhuman or degrading treatment were received from prisons including Wandsworth, Frankland, Swaleside, Durham, Wormwood Scrubs and Brixton. Reports were also received of ill-treatment of teenagers in Medway Secure Training Centre, in Portland, and in Lisnevin, Northern Ireland. The government announced in November that Lisnevin Juvenile Justice Centre would be closed down.

☐ In November Robert Stewart, aged 20, was convicted of murdering his cellmate, Zahid Mubarek, aged 19, in March at Feltham Young Offender Institution and Remand Centre. Zahid Mubarek, of Pakistani origin, was put in the same cell as Robert Stewart, although Robert Stewart's racial prejudices and violent behaviour were known. AI called for a public inquiry into the killing and the failures of Feltham, as well as the compatibility with international standards of detention policies and treatment of children and young offenders.

Ill-treatment by police
There were continued allegations of ill-treatment by police officers throughout the UK.

◻ In March, Stuart Melchor, a black warehouse manager, was reportedly bitten by a police dog and hit with truncheons by police who mistakenly presumed he was breaking into a building.

◻ In May, two Northern Ireland police officers were sentenced to one and two years' imprisonment respectively in connection with the ill-treatment of Bernard Griffin in 1998.

◻ In June the Northern Ireland High Court upheld a decision not to prosecute RUC officers alleged to have ill-treated David Adams during his arrest in 1994.

Impunity: Augusto Pinochet
In January Home Secretary Jack Straw announced that he was considering refusing Augusto Pinochet's extradition to Spain because of his ill-health. He based his decision on a secret medical report by four doctors. The Home Secretary refused to disclose the report to the four countries seeking extradition until a High Court ruling that it had been wrong to keep it secret. On 3 March, after 17 months' detention in the UK pending extradition, Augusto Pinochet was allowed to return to Chile. (See Chile entry.)

Child soldiers
In November AI called on the UK to stop its policy of deploying under-18s in armed conflicts. Children can be recruited into the armed forces from the age of 16 and can be deployed in the battlefield from the age of 17. In September the UK signed the Optional Protocol to the UN Children's Convention on the involvement of children in armed conflict, but added a declaration which AI believes undermines the spirit of the Optional Protocol. AI urged the UK to ratify the Optional Protocol without reservation.

Samar Alami and Jawad Botmeh
The appeal hearing held in October in the case of Samar Alami and Jawad Botmeh was adjourned to 2001. They had been sentenced to 20 years' imprisonment after being convicted of conspiracy to cause explosions in 1994 in London at the Israeli embassy and Balfour House. AI was concerned that both during and after the trial they had been denied full access to crucial evidence, in breach of fair trial standards.

Freedom of expression
In May, the UN Special Rapporteur on the promotion and protection of the right to freedom of opinion and expression issued a report criticizing provisions and practices which limit freedom of expression in the UK.

Charges under the Official Secrets Act were brought against David Shayler, a former MI5 (intelligence) officer, who had made a series of allegations about misconduct by security and intelligence agencies. David Shayler returned to the UK in August from France in order to face the charges. The editor of *The Observer* newspaper and a journalist were also investigated under the Official Secrets Act for publishing David Shayler's disclosures.

Charges under the Official Secrets Act were also brought against a former army general, Nigel Wylde, and journalist Tony Geraghty for the book, *The Irish War.* Charges were dropped against the journalist and in November Nigel Wylde was acquitted after the prosecution offered no evidence. The book included information about computer-assisted surveillance in Northern Ireland.

Refugees
In April, a system giving new asylum applicants assistance in the form of vouchers rather than cash came into force, as did dispersal of asylum-seekers. These measures immediately ran into difficulties. As predicted by AI, there was an alarming shortfall in access to legal advice for dispersed asylum-seekers, many of whom were sent to areas where people had no experience of living with asylum-seekers. There was some very negative media coverage which pandered to racial prejudice and created a hostile environment for many asylum-seekers. After substantial pressure, at the end of September the government announced a full review of the voucher and support system as a whole.

Although the majority of asylum-seekers were granted temporary admission pending the determination of their claim, about 1,000 asylum seekers were held in detention at any given time.

AI country reports and visits
Reports
- Northern Ireland: The Killing of Patrick Finucane – Official collusion and cover-up (AI Index: EUR 45/026/2000)
- United Kingdom: Questions remain after the inquest into the killing of Diarmuid O'Neill (AI Index: EUR 45/041/2000)
- United Kingdom: Deaths in custody – lack of police accountability (AI Index: EUR 45/042/2000)
- United Kingdom: Briefing on the Terrorism Bill (AI Index: EUR 45/043/2000)
- United Kingdom: The Regulation of Investigatory Powers Bill (AI Index: EUR 45/049/2000)
- United Kingdom: Policing in Northern Ireland – A New Beginning? (AI Index: EUR 45/048/2000)
- United Kingdom: U-18s – Child soldiers at risk (AI Index: EUR 45/056/2000)
- United Kingdom: U-18s – Report on the recruitment and deployment of child soldiers (AI Index: EUR 45/057/2000)

Visits
AI delegates visited Northern Ireland in May and October. An AI delegate attended the inquest in February into the disputed killing of Diarmuid O'Neill, and an AI delegate observed the appeal hearing in October in the case of Samar Alami and Jawad Botmeh.

UNITED STATES OF AMERICA

UNITED STATES OF AMERICA
Head of state and government: William Jefferson Clinton
Capital: Washington D.C.
Population: 278.3 million
Official language: English
Death penalty: retentionist
2000 treaty signatures/ratifications: Optional Protocol to the UN Children's Convention on the involvement of children in armed conflict; Rome Statute of the International Criminal Court

Police brutality, disputed shootings and ill-treatment in prisons and jails were reported. In May the UN Committee against Torture considered the initial report of the USA on implementation of the UN Convention against Torture. Eighty-five prisoners were executed in 14 states bringing to 683 the total number of people executed since 1976. Those executed included individuals who were children under 18 at the time of their crimes, and the mentally impaired. In December it was announced that George W. Bush had won the November presidential elections.

UN Committee against Torture

In May the UN Committee against Torture considered the initial report of the USA. In its conclusions and recommendations the Committee welcomed "the extensive legal protection" against torture and ill-treatment in the USA but found failings in important areas, many of which had been raised by AI.

Areas of concern highlighted by the Committee included torture and ill-treatment by police and prison guards — much of it racially motivated; the sexual abuse of female prisoners by male guards; prisoner chain gangs; and the "excessively harsh regime" of supermaximum security (isolation) units. The Committee urged the USA to abolish electro-shock stun belts and restraint chairs, stating that their use "almost invariably" led to breaches of the Convention; and to cease holding juveniles and adult prisoners together.

The Committee also recommended that the USA withdraw all "reservations, interpretations and understandings" registered on its acceptance of the Convention against Torture. These included a reservation to Article 16 in which the USA agreed to be bound by the Convention only to the extent that it matched the ban on cruel punishment contained in the US Constitution.

Racial discrimination

In September the USA submitted its initial report on compliance with the Convention on the Elimination of All Forms of Racial Discrimination. The report described the protections against racial discrimination under US laws and the Constitution, but acknowledged that discrimination persisted in certain areas, including in the criminal justice system.

Race was a factor in many of the issues cited below, for example in police ill-treatment and "racial profiling" in police stops and searches, in sentencing, and in the juvenile justice system.

Police brutality

Police brutality and disputed police shootings of unarmed suspects were reported; a disproportionate number of the victims were from racial minorities. Many incidents of alleged abuse occurred at the end of vehicle pursuits, during traffic stops, or during police street patrols. Several suspects died after being placed in dangerous restraint holds or subdued with pepper spray.

During the year, the US Justice Department investigated several police departments for patterns of abuses and civil rights violations, including racism, ill-treatment and excessive force.

▫ In February, four New York Police Department (NYPD) officers were acquitted of all criminal charges in the killing in 1999 of Amadou Diallo, an unarmed West African immigrant who was shot 41 times outside his home.

During 2000, a federal Justice Department investigation found that the NYPD's Street Crime Unit, to which the officers belonged, engaged in racial profiling — a practice in which blacks and Hispanics were disproportionately targeted in street stops and searches. The Justice Department was reported to be negotiating with the authorities on the implementation of a range of reforms to the NYPD, including improvements to the disciplinary system.

▫ In November the Los Angeles city authorities and the federal government reached an agreement (known as a consent decree) to reform the Los Angeles Police Department (LAPD), following a lengthy federal investigation into systemic problems including racism and excessive force. The decree mandated a range of measures, including a requirement that the LAPD collect data on the ethnicity and gender of people subjected to traffic and pedestrian stops and the establishment of an independent monitor to oversee reforms.

An investigation continued into the scandal arising from the LAPD's Rampart division, in which officers were accused of having beaten, shot, robbed and framed people. More than 70 current or former police officers were under investigation and more than 100 criminal convictions had been thrown out, with scores more under review. In November, three officers were convicted of conspiracy and other offences involving framed gang members.

▫ Two New Jersey state troopers faced trial in connection with the 1998 shooting and wounding of three unarmed black and Hispanic men during a traffic stop on the New Jersey Turnpike. The troopers had fired 11 shots at the van in which the youths were travelling to college basketball trials.

Earlier studies, showing that state troopers practised racial profiling, had forced the department to reform its practices and to monitor stops and searches for racial and ethnic bias.

☐ In November the US Justice Department announced that it was investigating an alleged pattern of abuses involving the Prince George's County Police Department, Maryland, following a spate of police shootings and complaints of brutality in recent years, including complaints filed by more than two dozen people who said they had been maimed by police dogs.

Ruling on pepper spray

In May a federal appeals court reinstated a lawsuit filed against law enforcement agencies in Humboldt County, California, for swabbing liquid pepper spray into the eyes of non-violent environmentalists during protests in 1997, action which AI had said at the time was "tantamount to torture". The appeals court ruled there was evidence that the protesters had suffered "excruciating pain" and that use of pepper spray could in some circumstances constitute an "unreasonable use of force". The case was remanded to a jury for further proceedings.

Torture/ill-treatment in prisons and jails

Torture and ill-treatment were reported in prisons, jails and juvenile detention facilities. Abuses included beatings and excessive force; sexual misconduct; the misuse of electro-shock weapons and chemical sprays; and the cruel use of mechanical restraints, including holding prisoners for prolonged periods in four-point restraint as punishment. Many reported abuses took place in isolation units or during forced removal of prisoners from cells ("cell extractions").

Cruel conditions in supermaximum security (supermax) prisons, where prisoners are held in prolonged isolation, continued to be reported. AI's requests to tour such facilities in Illinois and Virginia were turned down by the authorities.

☐ Up to 30 guards were alleged to have been involved in the systematic ill-treatment of five prisoners in a high security wing of Cook County Jail, Illinois, in July. It was alleged that guards kicked and punched the prisoners without provocation during cell searches and subjected them to racist abuse in retaliation for having reported earlier ill-treatment of jail inmates. The prisoners — who were also reportedly beaten after they were shackled — sustained lacerations, bruising and bone fractures. A civil lawsuit in the case was pending at the end of the year.

In July, three Cook County sheriff's deputies were indicted on first degree murder charges for the beating of inmate Louis Schmude in a holding cell in another detention facility in May; he died hours later of a ruptured spleen.

☐ In September the US Justice Department opened a civil rights investigation into Red Onion State Prison, one of two supermax prisons in Virginia where there had been persistent allegations of excessive use of force by guards, including misuse of firearms, restraints and electro-shock weapons. AI renewed its call for the suspension of the use of all electro-shock weapons in Virginia prisons following the death in Wallens Ridge Prison, the state's other supermax prison, of a diabetic prisoner shocked with a stun weapon in July (see below). The Department of Corrections refused to ban the equipment and turned down a request by AI to tour Wallens Ridge Prison.

Abuse of incarcerated children

Children in detention were subjected to ill-treatment which included the cruel use of restraints and prolonged isolation as punishment. Many children continued to be prosecuted as adults and sent to adult prisons where, in some states, they were not separated from adults and were held in inhumane or inappropriate conditions.

A study of the juvenile justice system published in April, sponsored by the US Justice Department and six of the country's leading foundations, found that youths from ethnic minority groups, especially African Americans, were more likely to be imprisoned and to serve longer sentences than white youths charged with similar offences.

☐ In February a lawsuit was filed alleging widespread abuse at the State Training School in Plankinton, South Dakota, a juvenile detention facility. Children were reportedly placed in punitive handcuffs and shackles; forced to lie spread-eagled in four-point restraints for hours at a time, including overnight; and girls were forcibly stripped by male staff while held in four-point restraint. It was also alleged that children, some of them mentally ill, were routinely held in isolation for 23 hours a day, sometimes for months at a time.

In December a federal judge approved a settlement which placed strict limits on the use of force and punishment at Plankinton. This included a ban on restraints as punishment and the removal of four-point rings used to tie inmates to beds, and the setting of limits on the length of time children could be confined to cells.

Ill-treatment of women prisoners

Male guards continued to have unsupervised access to women prisoners or detainees in women's prisons and local jails. There were allegations of sexual abuse of female prisoners by male staff in states including California, Connecticut, New York, South Carolina and West Virginia. Draft legislation was introduced in New York to ban pat-down searches of women prisoners by male staff.

☐ Reports of ill-treatment of inmates at Wayne County Jail, West Virginia, included claims that women prisoners were made to parade partially naked in front of male inmates, forced to undergo strip searches by male guards, fondled by male officers or watched while dressing. One prisoner said she was coerced into a sexual relationship with a guard who later resigned. There were also allegations of assaults by guards against both male and female inmates and the abusive use of pepper spray. The results of a Justice Department investigation into allegations of federal criminal civil rights violations by guards at the jail were not known by the end of the year.

☐ In October a state legislative committee held hearings on ill-treatment in two California prisons, Valley State Prison for Women and the California Institute for Women. Women prisoners testified about medical neglect and sexual abuse by male staff.

Deaths in prison

☐ Lawrence Frazier, a diabetic, died in July after being restrained by guards and zapped with a 45,000 volt electro-shock stun gun after becoming delirious and "combative" in the Wallens Ridge Prison infirmary where he had been taken for hypoglycemia. Although the prison authorities said afterwards that a doctor had ruled out the stun weapon as a cause of death, this was discounted by many observers as the doctor had had no access to the autopsy results. Inquiries into the death were still pending at the end of the year.

☐ In October a state jury acquitted a former prison guard on a charge of aggravated battery and coercion to falsify reports in the case of Frank Valdez who died in Florida State Prison in July 1999. The guard was accused of beating Valdez and breaking his jaw after he was handcuffed. Frank Valdez died the next day after an altercation with four other guards whose trial on second-degree murder charges was still pending at the end of 2000.

☐ In June, eight prison guards accused of staging "gladiator style" fights among prisoners at Corcoran State Prison, California, between 1989 and 1995, were acquitted of criminal charges after a jury trial. Guards had shot 31 prisoners, seven of them fatally, while breaking up the fights. Although the guards were acquitted, the state had earlier been forced to change its policies after an independent panel found that 80 per cent of the shootings had been unjustified. State legislative hearings in 1998 had found a pattern of brutality at the prison.

Death penalty

In 2000, 85 prisoners were executed in 14 states, bringing to 683 the total number executed since the US Supreme Court lifted a moratorium on executions in 1976. The USA continued to violate international standards by using the death penalty against the mentally impaired, individuals who were under 18 at the time of the crime, and defendants who received inadequate legal representation.

In January, the Governor of Illinois declared a moratorium on executions in his state owing to its "shameful" record of wrongful convictions in capital cases. His decision fuelled calls for executions to be halted elsewhere in the country, as concern about the fairness and reliability of the capital justice system grew. The New Hampshire legislature voted to abolish the death penalty, but the state governor vetoed the bill. Amidst a wave of national and international appeals, the Governor of Maryland commuted the death sentence of Eugene Colvin-El shortly before he was due to be executed in June, because of lingering doubts about his guilt. In November, the Governor of North Carolina commuted the death sentence of Marcus Carter hours before his execution, after 11 years on death row. The governor cited concern about the fairness of Marcus Carter's trial.

A Justice Department review of federal death sentences, made public in September 2000, found widespread geographic and racial disparities in the application of the federal death penalty nationwide. The first federal execution since 1963, scheduled to take place on 12 December, was stayed for six months by President Clinton pending more analysis of the Justice Department review.

Texas executed 40 prisoners during the year, a record in any one year. In December, the 150th prisoner was executed under the five-year governorship of president-elect George W. Bush.

Execution of child offenders

☐ Chris Thomas, Steve Roach, Glen McGinnis and Gary Graham were executed for crimes committed when they were 17. Gary Graham was put to death in Texas in the face of widespread national and international protest and serious doubts about his guilt. More than 80 prisoners remained on death row in 16 states at the end of the year for crimes committed when they were 16 or 17.

Execution of the mentally impaired

☐ Thomas Provenzano, who was executed in Florida in June, suffered from paranoid schizophrenia. A judge found him competent for execution despite agreeing that the prisoner believed he was being killed because he was Jesus Christ. On 20 June, Thomas Provenzano was already strapped down for execution, with the lethal injection needles inserted, when a court issued a stay. Twenty-four hours later, Thomas Provenzano was put through the same ordeal and executed.

Ineffective legal assistance

☐ On 27 October, the US Court of Appeals for the Fifth Circuit vacated a lower court ruling that death-row inmate Calvin Burdine should get a new trial because his lawyer had slept during the original proceedings. The State of Texas argued that it had not been proved that the lawyer's sleeping had rendered him ineffective, and the Fifth Circuit court agreed. A dissenting judge described the case as one which "shocks the conscience".

Violation of the Vienna Convention

☐ A Mexican national, Miguel Angel Flores, was executed in Texas on 9 November, despite appeals for clemency from the Mexican and other governments. He was denied his treaty-based consular rights, as were most of the 90 foreign nationals on death row in the USA. In November, the International Court of Justice in The Hague heard arguments in a case brought against the USA by Germany following the execution of two German nationals in Arizona in 1999. The Court had not issued a ruling by the end of 2000.

Other concerns

In June the parole board denied parole in the case of Leonard Peltier, imprisoned since 1977 for the murder of two FBI agents. There were concerns about the fairness of the proceedings leading to his conviction. In December President Clinton announced that he was reviewing the case for a possible pardon. AI had repeatedly called on President Clinton to grant clemency in the case.

Mazen Al-Najjar, a Palestinian immigrant jailed for more than three years on the basis of secret government evidence, was released in December after a court ruled that a summary of that evidence, which purported to show his links with a terrorist group, was insufficient to justify his detention. New proceedings had been ordered into the case by a court in May which found that his due process rights had been violated. AI called for a ban on the use of secret evidence to detain people during deportation proceedings.

In August AI wrote to the government to express concern about the treatment of Dr Wen Ho Lee, who was shackled and held in solitary confinement in federal detention pending his trial on charges of leaking nuclear secrets to China. Dr Wen Ho Lee was released in September after pleading guilty to one of the charges against him; the other charges were dropped.

AI country reports and visits
Reports
- USA: A Life in the Balance – The case of Mumia Abu-Jamal (AI Index: AMR 51/001/2000)
- USA: Failing the Future – Death penalty developments April 1998-March 2000 (AI Index: AMR 51/003/2000)
- USA: A Briefing for the UN Committee against Torture (AI Index: AMR 51/056/2000)
- USA: A call to action by the UN Committee against Torture (AI Index: AMR 51/107/2000
- USA: Worlds Apart: Violations of the rights of foreign nationals on death row – Cases of Europeans (AI Index: AMR 51/101/2000)
- USA: Memorandum to President Clinton – An appeal for human rights leadership as the first federal execution looms (AI Index: AMR 51/158/2000)

Visits
AI delegates attended a conference on supermaximum security prisons in Washington D.C. in February, and the "Committing to Conscience" Conference on the abolition of the death penalty in San Francisco in November.

URUGUAY

EASTERN REPUBLIC OF URUGUAY
Head of state and government: Jorge Batlle (replaced Julio María Sanguinetti in March)
Capital: Montevideo
Population: 3.3 million
Death penalty: abolitionist for all crimes
2000 treaty ratifications/treaties: Optional Protocol to the UN Children's Convention on the involvement of children in armed conflict; Optional Protocol to the UN Women's Convention; Rome Statute of the International Criminal Court

Steps were taken to establish the fate of people who "disappeared" under military governments between 1973 and 1985. There were reports of torture and ill-treatment.

Background
President Jorge Batlle took office at the beginning of March. His first months in office were marked by a willingness to clarify the fate of those who "disappeared" in Uruguay between 1973 and 1985. Some 34 people "disappeared" in Uruguay and at least 100 Uruguayans "disappeared" in Argentina during this period. Thousands of people were tortured and ill-treated under the military government in Uruguay.

In August the government established a special commission, the *Comisión para la Paz*, Peace Commission, to clarify the fate of all those who "disappeared" during those years. However, the 1986 Expiry Law, which granted exemption from punishment to all police and military personnel who committed human rights violations for political motives or to fulfil orders before 1 March 1985, prevented the perpetrators being brought to justice. The Inter-American Commission on Human Rights has stated that the Expiry Law violates the American Convention on Human Rights.

Developments in 'disappearance' cases
◻ In May a civil court ruled that the mother of Elena Quinteros had the right to find out the whereabouts and circumstances in which her daughter "disappeared". Elena Quinteros "disappeared" in 1976 in Montevideo after being detained by the security forces inside the Venezuelan embassy where she had hidden. In addition, in November, a court ruled that those civilians who were allegedly involved in Elena Quinteros' "disappearance", including the then Minister of Foreign Affairs, who were not covered by the 1986 Expiry Law, should be brought to justice.
◻ The fate of Juan Gelman's granddaughter was established. Juan Gelman's son, Marcelo Gelman, and his pregnant wife, María Claudia García Irureta Goyena, both Argentine citizens, "disappeared" in Argentina in August 1976. Marcelo Gelman's body was discovered in 1989. In 1999 it emerged that María

Claudia García had given birth to her baby at the Military Hospital in Montevideo.

Torture/ill-treatment
There were continued reports that detainees were ill-treated and tortured by police and prison guards.

◻ Reports came to light that in July 1999, four men and a 17-year-old boy, who had been detained by police on suspicion of theft, were tortured and ill-treated in order to force them to sign confessions. The four men were also reported to have been tortured and ill-treated at the Santiago Vázquez prison.

AI country report
- Uruguay: The "Disappeared" – One step closer to truth and justice (AI Index: AMR 52/002/2000)

UZBEKISTAN

REPUBLIC OF UZBEKISTAN
Head of state: Islam Karimov
Head of government: Otkir Sultanov
Capital: Tashkent
Population: 24.3 million
Official language: Uzbek
Death penalty: retentionist
2000 treaty ratifications/signatures: Rome Statute of the International Criminal Court

Reports of ill-treatment and torture by law enforcement officials of members of independent Islamic congregations or followers of independent imams (Islamic leaders) continued unabated. Hundreds of suspected members of the banned Islamic party *Hizb-ut-Tahrir*, including women, were reportedly arbitrarily arrested and sentenced to long terms of imprisonment after unfair trials. Several prisoners died in custody, allegedly as a result of torture. There were at least 13 death sentences and eight executions, reportedly imposed after unfair trials.

Background
In January Islam Karimov consolidated his power after being re-elected President with nearly 92 per cent of the vote. The Organization for Security and Co-operation in Europe (OSCE) refused to send an observation mission because there was no democratic competition. The only other candidate, a member of the pro-government People's Democratic Party, admitted to having voted for Islam Karimov.

In August violent clashes broke out between the Uzbek armed forces and armed units of the banned opposition Islamic Movement of Uzbekistan (IMU) when they tried to enter southeastern Uzbekistan from neighbouring Afghanistan, Tajikistan and Kyrgyzstan. In November the Supreme Court of Uzbekistan sentenced Takhir Yuldash and Juma Namangani, the alleged leaders of the IMU, to death in their absence. They were convicted of terrorism and treason and of causing the death of 73 people in armed incursions and in the February 1999 bombings in Tashkent. Muhammad Salih, the exiled leader of the banned Erk Democratic Party, was sentenced to 15 years' imprisonment on the same charges, also in his absence.

On 28 August President Karimov granted an amnesty to more than 10,000 prisoners in order to mark the country's ninth anniversary of independence. According to the chairman of the Supreme Court, there were no political or religious prisoners in Uzbekistan and the more than 2,000 prisoners convicted of anti-state crimes or membership of illegal organizations, mostly suspected members of *Hizb-ut-Tahrir* who did not qualify for the amnesty, were criminals.

Torture/ill-treatment
Reports of ill-treatment and torture by law enforcement officials of members of independent Islamic congregations or followers of independent imams continued. Hundreds of suspected members of *Hizb-ut-Tahrir*, including women, were reportedly arbitrarily arrested and sentenced to long terms of imprisonment after trials that fell far short of international fair trial standards. The courts were reported to have systematically failed to investigate or take into account allegations of torture.

Defendants accused of non-political criminal activities were also reported to have been tortured and ill-treated in detention in order to make them confess.

◻ In July the presiding judge at Tashkent Regional Court reportedly dismissed allegations of torture by 15 members of *Hizb-ut-Tahrir* charged with distributing leaflets and calling for the overthrow of the constitutional order, even after one of the accused took off his shirt to show the court the injuries and bruises he had suffered. He was also said to have shown a hole in his foot which he had received as a result of being beaten with a nail fixed to a plank of wood. Other co-accused claimed to have been raped, tortured with electric shocks, violently beaten and threatened with murder in order to force them to confess.

Deaths in custody
Human rights groups reported several cases of deaths in custody as a result of torture or ill-treatment by law enforcement personnel.

◻ In March, the family of 33-year-old Nemat Karimov, who was serving a 20-year sentence in Navoy prison camp in connection with the February 1999 Tashkent bombings, was informed of his death. The prison authorities reportedly did not disclose the cause of death. When the body was prepared for burial, it was allegedly discovered that the left-hand side of Nemat Karimov's face was disfigured, his nose twisted, his upper lip broken, and there was a hole in the middle of his skull. There were reportedly also injuries to his legs.

Prisoner of conscience Makhbuba Kasymova

Makhbuba Kasymova, a member of the Independent Human Rights Organization of Uzbekistan (NOPCHU), was sentenced to five years' imprisonment in July 1999 for "concealing a crime" and "misappropriation of funds" after a grossly unfair three-hour trial described by human rights monitors as a "farce". In August 1999 Tashkent City Court turned down Makhbuba Kasymova's appeal against her sentence after a hearing lasting 14 minutes, at which she was not present. An appeal lodged by her lawyer with the Supreme Court was still pending at the end of 2000.

Makhbuba Kasymova, who was held in Tashkent City Prison, was reported to be suffering from heart problems. In August NOPCHU reported that she qualified for release under the presidential independence anniversary amnesty, and would probably be released at the end of September. On 6 October Makhbuba Kasymova's daughter was told by the director of Tashkent Women's Colony that her mother had committed three offences against prison rules which was enough to disqualify her from the amnesty. Makhbuba Kasymova claimed that the offences had been fabricated in order to prevent her from being released. On 22 December Makhbuba Kasymova was unexpectedly released from prison.

Possible prisoners of conscience

Mamadali Makhmudov, a writer, and Muhammad Bekzhon, a brother of Erk Democratic Party leader Muhammad Salih, were reported to have been secretly transferred to Yaslik prison in April. AI had previously expressed concern at reports of prison camps in remote areas of Uzbekistan where the overwhelming majority of prisoners were members of independent Islamic congregations accused of supporting the banned Islamic opposition. The existence of one of these prison camps — Yaslik — located in former Soviet army barracks in the Karakalpakstan Autonomous Republic (a desert area southwest of the Aral Sea), was independently confirmed in 1999. Conditions were said to be cruel, inhuman and degrading, with prisoners being denied adequate drinking water while doing forced labour. The camp may also be situated in a chemically or biologically contaminated area. Unofficial sources estimated that at least 20 , and possibly as many as 38, prisoners died in Yaslik in 1999 and 2000 as a result of torture and poor conditions.

Mamadali Makhmudov was reported to have faced punitive treatment, including being forced to sit crouching for extended periods with his hands behind his head. He was said to have lost a lot of weight and to be suffering from pain in his chest, sides and back. He had apparently not been given access to appropriate food or medical care and had fainted on several occasions. In early July the Ministry of Internal Affairs denied that Mamadali Makhmudov had suffered ill-treatment and that his health was deteriorating. However, later that month he was reportedly urgently transferred to the medical wing of Tashkent prison. His relatives were not informed of his whereabouts until September. He was reported to be in a critical condition.

On 18 August 1999, after a trial which fell far short of international standards, Tashkent Regional Court sentenced Muhammad Bekzhon, Mamadali Makhmudov and their co-accused, Yusif Ruzimuradov, Rashid Bekzhon, Kobil Diyarov and Negmat Sharipov, to prison terms of between eight and 15 years. All six men were reportedly tortured in pre-trial detention, in order to force them to confess to fabricated charges and to incriminate Muhammad Salih.

The death penalty

AI learned of at least 13 death sentences and eight executions during 2000, but believed the actual number to be much higher. Many of these sentences were handed down in connection with the February 1999 bomb explosions in Tashkent and subsequent armed clashes between law enforcement forces and alleged members of the IMU. AI was concerned at the number of allegations that international fair trial standards were violated in capital punishment cases. In particular, victims claimed that they were convicted on the basis of confessions made as a result of torture.

In July the general procuracy confirmed that 19 death sentences handed down in 1999 for alleged involvement in the Tashkent bombings had been carried out.

In 2000 at least four death sentences were commuted. The death sentences passed in November 1999 on two young musicians, Arsen Arutyunyan and Danis Sirazhev, were commuted to 15 years' imprisonment on 31 March by the Presidium of the Supreme Court of Uzbekistan.

New death sentences

◻ In June AI learned that the Supreme Court of Uzbekistan had upheld the death sentences of Oybek and Uygun Ruzmetov, Shikhnozor Yakubov, Sardor Allayarov and Utkir Yusupov. The five men had been sentenced to death by Tashkent Regional Court in July 1999 for planning to blow up a water reservoir, attempting to overthrow the constitutional order and setting up an Islamic state. According to the mother of Oybek and Uygun Ruzmetov, law enforcement officers planted cartridges in Oybek Ruzmetov's room the day before they arrested the brothers in December 1998. In February 1999 the police were reported to have briefly detained their mother and father and humiliated them by forcing them to undress and taking them handcuffed and in their underwear to see their sons. Oybek and Uygun Ruzmetov reportedly told their parents that they had been tortured in detention and that law enforcement officers had threatened to arrest their parents and rape Uygun Ruzmetov's wife. AI also received unconfirmed reports that Shikhnozor Yakubov had died of beatings in prison in October 1999.

◻ On 14 May Polvonnazar Khodzhayev was sentenced to death by Tashkent Regional Court for attempting to overthrow the constitutional order of Uzbekistan in order to create an Islamic state. According to the non-governmental international organization Human Rights Watch, his trial did not meet international fair trial standards. The co-accused were sentenced to prison terms ranging from

14 to 24 years' imprisonment. In September the Supreme Court turned down his appeal against his death sentence. A petition for clemency was believed to be still pending with the President at the end of the year. Polvonnazar Khodzhayev had been detained in the Russian town of Samara on 5 April by Russian officials and handed over to Uzbek law enforcement officers.

Reportedly, in the first quarter of 1999 officers of the Khorezm Internal Affairs Department had frequently questioned Polvonnazar Khodzhayev's parents about the whereabouts of their sons, who were suspected of links with Islamist armed groups. In April 1999 Polvonnazar Khodzhayev's father, Azimboy Khodzhayev, was arrested, allegedly in place of his sons. Three days earlier President Karimov had reportedly said that he would issue a decree allowing for the arrest of a suspect's father if a son involved in "religious extremism" could not be found. In June 1999 Azimboy Khodzhayev was sentenced to eight years' imprisonment on reportedly fabricated charges of "illegal possession of narcotics". Only two weeks after the trial he was said to have died in custody in Yaslik prison camp. The family reportedly received a death certificate but was not allowed to see his body.

Executions

☐ Dmitry Chikunov was sentenced to death for premeditated, aggravated murder by Tashkent Regional Court on 11 November 1999. He alleged that in pre-trial detention he had been beaten unconscious, nearly asphyxiated with a gas mask over his head and that police had threatened to rape his mother unless he confessed. AI was not aware of any investigation of these allegations. His appeal against his death sentence was rejected by the Supreme Court on 24 January and he was executed on 10 July. The news was given to his mother when she went to visit him in Tashkent prison on 12 July.

☐ Six men sentenced to death by the Supreme Court on 28 June 1999 for their part in the February 1999 bombings in Tashkent were reportedly executed at the beginning of January. The defendants had been accused of belonging to extremist religious organizations which advocated a *jihad* (holy war) to overthrow the constitutional order in Uzbekistan and the assassination of President Karimov. There were reports that the defendants had been beaten or otherwise ill-treated in pre-trial detention and forced under duress to give false evidence. Human rights monitors had expressed concern that fair trial standards, although promised by the authorities, had not been respected. The defendants had reportedly been denied the right to a lawyer of their own choice and there were allegations that the defence lawyers did not represent the defendants' interests. According to Human Rights Watch, there was no presumption of innocence and the prosecution failed to present any solid evidence to prove the defendants guilty. The European Union condemned the executions and urged Uzbekistan to introduce a moratorium on the death penalty.

AI country reports

- Uzbekistan: Ismail Adylov – Human rights defender and prisoner of conscience (AI Index: EUR 62/002/2000)
- Uzbekistan: Makhbuba Kasymova – Human rights defender and prisoner of conscience (AI Index: EUR 62/004/2000)

VENEZUELA

BOLIVARIAN REPUBLIC OF VENEZUELA
Head of state and government: Hugo Chávez Frías
Capital: Caracas
Population: 24.1 million
Official language: Spanish
Death penalty: abolitionist for all crimes
2000 treaty ratifications/signatures: Optional Protocol to the UN Children's Convention on the involvement of children in armed conflict; Optional Protocol to the UN Women's Convention; Rome Statute of the International Criminal Court

Several people were reported to have "disappeared" or been extrajudicially executed by the security forces during rescue operations following catastrophic floods in December 1999. Scores of cases of torture and ill-treatment were reported. Chronic prison overcrowding was eased by the release of prisoners awaiting trial, but prison conditions remained poor. Hundreds of prisoners were killed during the year, the majority by fellow inmates. Hundreds of refugees fleeing political violence in Colombia were denied a proper hearing to determine if they would be at risk if returned to their country.

Background

In July, Hugo Chávez Frías of the *Movimiento de la V República* (MVR), Movement of the Fifth Republic, was re-elected President. The MVR also won an outright majority in congress. High crime rates continued to generate debate. In June the Ministry of the Interior and Justice proposed a bill reforming the Criminal Code of Criminal Procedures (COPP), which would give the police wider powers to detain criminal suspects without a judicial order. Critics of the bill argued that it was unconstitutional and violated international human rights standards. In November the National Assembly approved a law allowing President Chávez to govern by decree for a period of 12 months. The law included matters affecting the administration of criminal justice.

Human rights and the Vargas floods

In late December 1999, the state of Vargas suffered torrential rain and floods in which up to 50,000 people died. In the aftermath of the disaster, journalist Vanessa Davies and the human rights organization Provea published reports claiming that several people had "disappeared" or been extrajudicially executed by members of the security forces in Vargas. President Hugo Chávez reacted by calling on witnesses to come forward, but accused Provea of publishing a "suspicious and superficial" report. Within a week the Offices of the Attorney General and of the Ombudsman announced that they had opened investigations into the allegations. By the end of the year only one person had been brought to justice and convicted for these violations.

▭ Marco Antonio Monasterio and Oscar José Blanco Romero "disappeared" on 21 December 1999, during the flood rescue operations. They were reportedly detained by the army in the neighbourhood of Valle del Pino and transferred into the custody of the Directorate of Intelligence and Criminal Prevention Services (DISIP). By the end of the year their whereabouts had not been established. José Francisco Rivas Fernández and Roberto Hernández apparently suffered a similar fate. Luis Rafael Bastardo was extrajudicially executed on 25 December. A National Guard corporal admitted to shooting him deliberately and was sentenced in September to 10 years in prison.

Torture/ill-treatment

Torture and ill-treatment continued to be reported; most cases involved police officers beating victims.
▭ In August Ronny Yosmar Aquino and Alexis Medina, two transgendered friends, were detained without a judicial order in the city of Valencia, Carabobo state. They were reportedly forced to undress in the street and severely beaten. They were then held in incommunicado detention without access to a lawyer, doctor or their families. The detentions took place in the context of a campaign of intimidation directed at the transgendered community, during which José Luis Nieves was fatally shot on 29 July while recovering from wounds inflicted in an earlier shooting by a state police officer.

Prison conditions

The authorities claimed that the perennial crisis of overcrowding in Venezuela's prisons had been ameliorated as a result of the implementation of the COPP in July 1999 which allowed for the conditional release of prisoners awaiting trial.

In March the vice-president of the government's Commission on the Functioning and Restructuring of the Judicial System claimed that the prison population had been reduced from 25,000 to some 14,000 inmates, and that inmate killings had diminished. However, 460 prisoners were reported to have been killed by guards or fellow prisoners between October 1999 and September 2000, a small reduction compared to the previous 12 months.

In April, following a visit to several prisons, a European Union delegation was reported to have expressed concern about prison conditions, describing them as "very hard and limited, because the inmates control them...as it is the only way they can survive the violence".

Refugees

Scores of people fleeing political violence in Colombia were forcibly returned. The Venezuelan authorities failed to provide them with access to a full and fair asylum procedure to identify those at risk of human rights violations. The authorities argued that those fleeing the violence were not refugees, but "displaced people in transit", and therefore did not fall within the terms of the UN Refugee Convention. However, many of those fleeing the violence stressed that their lives would be at risk if they were to return home. The UN High Commisioner for Refugees stated that there was a need for an official refugee service and that it was collaborating with the authorities to implement one.

Impunity

In March, a friendly settlement was reached between the government and relatives of 41 people killed by the security forces in November 1992 in the Retén de Catia. The case had been referred to the Inter-American Commission on Human Rights. Of some 300 cases of human rights abuses registered by local non-governmental organizations between 1985 and 1999, only 40 had been resolved as a result of judicial proceedings. Of at least 200 cases of torture reported since 1995, in none had those responsible been brought to justice. The authorities failed to open a prompt judicial investigation into allegations that Peru's Ambassador to Venezuela, army general Julio Salazar Monroe, had been responsible for crimes against humanity. He returned to Peru, claiming to be suffering from ill health.

AI country report

- Venezuela: Protecting human rights – the task is not yet over (AI Index: AMR 53/008/2000)

VIET NAM

SOCIALIST REPUBLIC OF VIET NAM
Head of state: Tran Duc Luong
Head of government: Phan Van Khai
Capital: Ha Noi
Population: 75.1 million
Official language: Vietnamese
Death penalty: retentionist
2000 treaty ratifications/signatures: Optional Protocol to the UN Children's Convention on the involvement of children in armed conflict

Dozens of prisoners of conscience and possible prisoners of conscience remained in prison throughout 2000, and restrictions on released prisoners continued to be harsh. Political dissidents and religious critics of the government were subjected to surveillance, harassment and denial of basic freedoms, including freedom of expression. At least five possible prisoners of conscience were sentenced to prison terms. The government continued to prevent independent human rights monitors from visiting the country. More than 110 people were sentenced to death and at least 12 executions were carried out.

Background

A reported total of 22,597 prisoners were released under a special amnesty to mark two important anniversaries, and thousands of others had sentences reduced. No information was made public about whether political prisoners were included. Only two prisoners of conscience were known to have been released in the April amnesty commemorating the 25th anniversary of South Liberation Day. A self criticism campaign launched by the Communist Party in 1999 continued throughout the year, as did campaigns against official corruption and crime. A revised Criminal Code came into effect in July. In the latter part of the year the country suffered the worst flooding in decades, resulting in the deaths of more than 500 people. In November President Bill Clinton became the first US president to visit the country since the Viet Nam war.

Death penalty

Twenty-nine offences ranging from national security to economic crimes remained punishable by death. One hundred and twelve death sentences and 12 executions were recorded. However, the true figures were believed to be much higher; the authorities did not make public full information on the death penalty. Most of the reported death sentences were imposed for drug trafficking. Seven death sentences were recorded for economic offences such as fraud and forgery. Executions are carried out by firing squad, sometimes in public. It was common for relatives not to be informed of executions beforehand, but to be asked to collect belongings a few days after execution.

In July changes to the Code of Criminal Procedure came into effect which allowed death sentences on pregnant women or breast-feeding mothers of children aged up to 36 months to be changed to life imprisonment.

◻ Nguyen Thi Hiep, a 42-year-old Canadian national of Vietnamese origin, was executed in April. She had been sentenced to death in April 1997 on charges of drug trafficking. Her 73-year-old mother, arrested with her in 1996, was sentenced to life imprisonment. The Canadian authorities called for a review of the sentence to take into account evidence gathered by Canadian police authorities that both women had been unwittingly used as couriers by a major drugs ring. Despite indications that the Vietnamese authorities would review the evidence, Nguyen Thi Hiep was executed without any advance notice. Her mother was subsequently granted an amnesty.

Prisoners of conscience

Dozens of prisoners of conscience and possible prisoners of conscience continued to be detained for their political beliefs and religious affiliations. Many were elderly and in poor health.

◻ Sixty-eight-year-old Professor Nguyen Dinh Huy, the founder and president of the "Movement to Unite the People and Build Democracy", continued to be held in prison camp Z30A, in Dong Nai province, for his peaceful political activities. He had been arrested in November 1993 and sentenced to 15 years' imprisonment in August 1995 after trying to organize a conference about human rights and democracy in Ho Chi Minh City. He had previously spent 17 years in detention without charge or trial.

◻ Reverend Pham Ngoc Lien (Tri), a 59-year-old Roman Catholic monk, was one of three members of the banned Congregation of the Mother Coredemptrix who remained in detention. He was arrested in May 1987 and sentenced to 20 years' imprisonment in connection with his religious activities. He was reportedly in poor health.

Trials

At least five possible prisoners of conscience were tried and sentenced for activities relating to the practice of their religion. Trials routinely fell short of international standards.

◻ In September, five members of the Hoa Hao Buddhist Church were sentenced to between one and three years' imprisonment for "using religion to abuse democratic rights and freedoms". Truong Van Thuc, Nguyen Chau Lang, Tran Van Be Cao, Tran Nguyen Huon and Le Van Nhuom were arrested in March in An Giang province after reportedly complaining to the central authorities about abuses by local authorities.

Harassment of government critics

Political and religious dissidents, including former prisoners of conscience, continued to face harassment and restrictions on their peaceful activities by the authorities.

◻ Thich Quang Do, a 73-year-old former prisoner of conscience and Secretary General of the unofficial

Unified Buddhist Church of Viet Nam (UBCV), remained under surveillance at his monastery in Ho Chi Minh City with harsh restrictions on his activities and movements. In October he and several other UBCV members attempted to deliver relief to victims of the severe floods in the Mekong Delta. They were stopped by the authorities on arrival in An Giang province and prevented from carrying out the relief distribution, which the authorities stated should only be done through official channels. However, a second attempt to carry out an aid mission in November was allowed to go ahead. In 1995 Thich Quang Do had been sentenced to five years' imprisonment after protesting about the arrest of UBCV members who attempted to carry out a similar relief mission to flood victims in 1994. He had been released under an amnesty in 1998.

Denial of access
AI continued to receive no response from the government to correspondence about human rights violations. Domestic human rights monitoring was not permitted and no access was given to independent human rights monitors.

AI country report
- Socialist Republic of Viet Nam: The death penalty — recent developments (AI Index: ASA 41/001/2000)

YEMEN

REPUBLIC OF YEMEN
Head of state: 'Ali 'Abdullah Saleh
Head of government: 'Abd al-Karim 'Ali al-Iryani
Capital: Sana'a
Population: 18.1 million
Official language: Arabic
Death penalty: retentionist
2000 treaty ratifications/signatures: Rome Statute of the International Criminal Court

Political activists, including prisoners of conscience, were detained and court proceedings continued against several journalists in an apparent attempt to harass them for criticizing the government. Torture and deaths in custody were reported. The judicial punishment of flogging continued to be imposed. At least 13 people were executed and scores, possibly hundreds, were under sentence of death at the end of 2000.

Background
In August the government submitted to parliament a proposal to amend the Constitution. The proposed amendments included extending the term of office of the president from five to seven years and of parliament from four to six years. The government also proposed the establishment of a consultative council (*Majlis al-Shura*) of 111 members appointed by the president. The proposed amendments were approved by the parliament in November and were expected to be the subject of a referendum in early 2001.

In al-Dala' two people, a soldier and a child, were reportedly killed in February and May respectively. The killings occurred amid ongoing tensions and protests calling for the demilitarization of the area, the integration of former South Yemeni soldiers into the army, and the release of detainees.

Scores of people were reportedly killed in clashes between armed tribes, and between tribes and the security forces in different parts of the country. In July and August, 39 people were reportedly killed during clashes between the Wailah and Dalim tribes near the border with Saudi Arabia. At least three people, including a child, were killed in July during clashes between the Al Zayidi tribe and the military in Mareb governorate. The clashes followed the kidnapping of military officers by tribesmen. Scores of residents fled their homes, reportedly after the area was bombarded by the Yemeni army. The village of Misrakh, in Ta'iz governorate, was also reportedly shelled by the Yemeni army in July following clashes between residents and army units arising from a land dispute. Confrontations with the military also occurred in Kud Qru, near Aden, in September, after local people prevented a contractor from digging stones from a mountain, the ownership of which was claimed by the Kud Qru tribe. More than 200 people were reported to have fled the area in fear of their lives. Reports suggested that some people may have died as a result of excessive use of force by members of the security forces.

In October, 17 US sailors were killed and 35 wounded when a bomb exploded on a US destroyer in the port of Aden. Around 100 people were detained by the Yemeni authorities for questioning; most were released after a brief period in detention. Members of the US Federal Bureau of Investigation (FBI) travelled to Yemen to take part in the investigation but it was not known whether they were involved in the interrogation of the detainees. No information was available as to how many people remained held by the end of the year.

A total of 17 people were reported to have been abducted by tribesmen in seven incidents. In most cases the abductors demanded that the government improve local services and amenities.

Political prisoners and prisoners of conscience
Hundreds of people were arrested and detained on political grounds in different parts of the country but particularly in the southern regions. Some arrests took place after clashes with the security forces, others after what appeared to have been peaceful protests against government policies. Some of those detained were prisoners of conscience.

In July Mohamed 'Omar Haji, a 27-year-old Somali national, was put on trial for converting to Christianity from Islam, an offence which is punishable by death. He was arrested and detained several times by police officers who allegedly beat him and threatened to kill him to force him to repent. In September the Yemeni authorities stated that Mohamed 'Omar Haji had left Yemen, but did not specify for which country.

☐ Up to 150 people were reportedly detained in the al-Dala' governorate at the beginning of 2000 following protests and clashes between residents and the security forces. The detainees were said to have included children as young as seven. It was not known if the detainees remained held at the end of the year.

☐ On 26 August, four members of the Yemen Socialist Party (YSP) — 'Ali Munser Muhammad, Yassine Ahmad Saleh, Ahmad Belghaith 'Othman and Ahmad Muhammad Ana'am — were reportedly arrested in Aden for participating in a YSP meeting. They were detained for several days and then released without charge.

☐ At least 100 people, including children, were reportedly detained following armed clashes in Kud Qru in September. Among the children who were detained were 10-year-old Mehdi Fadhl Hadi and eight-year-old Muhammad Fadhl Hadi. It was not known how many of those detained remained held at the end of the year.

☐ At least 13 political prisoners, suspected members of the former *al-Jabha al-Wataniya al-Dimuqratiya*, National Democratic Front, an opposition organization in the former Yemen Arab Republic, remained in prison. They had been arrested in the 1980s and most had been under sentence of death since 1986.

☐ At the beginning of April, the Supreme Court upheld the jail sentences of five United Kingdom (UK) nationals who were part of a group of 10 individuals, including two Algerian nationals, convicted of forming an armed gang and possessing weapons. The defendants alleged that they had signed their confessions under torture, but it was not clear whether the Supreme Court took this into account when considering the case. No investigation into their allegations of torture was known to have been carried out.

☐ 'Omar Ibrahim Dagah was released without charge at the beginning of January. He had been arrested in August 1999 in connection with an explosion in Aden and held in incommunicado detention for several months. His family was never allowed to visit him in prison and his case never went to court.

Harassment of journalists
Legal proceedings continued against several leading journalists and newspaper editors for articles they had written or published.

☐ In May Hisham Basharahil, editor-in-chief of the newspaper *al-Ayyam*, was accused of having caused "damage to national unity" following an interview with UK-based Islamist activist Abu Hamza al-Masri. Days later, in the second case to be brought against him within a week, Hisham Basharahil was charged with provoking tribal and religious strife by publishing an article that criticized the demolition of an old synagogue in Aden. In June he was also summoned for questioning, for a third time, by the General Prosecution Office in Aden for publishing a news item entitled "Prisoner attempts to commit suicide". Legal proceedings against him were continuing at the end of the year.

Torture/ill-treatment
Torture and ill-treatment were reported. One prisoner reportedly died in custody as a result of torture.

☐ In August Sabah Seif Salem, a pregnant Yemeni woman, reportedly died while detained in the al-'Udain district of Ibb. She had allegedly been tortured in order to force her to confess to adultery. No investigation into the circumstances surrounding her death was known to have taken place.

Death penalty
Scores, possibly hundreds, of people were believed to be under sentence of death or facing trial for capital offences at the end of 2000. At least 13 people were executed.

☐ Salih 'Ali Ahmad al-Kabdi, who had been convicted of murder, was reportedly executed in October in a public square in al-Hawtah in front of a large crowd. Some local residents were said to have protested against the use of the square for executions because of the psychological effect on patients in a nearby hospital and children.

☐ At the end of the year, a response from the Yemeni government informed AI that the Supreme Court had referred the case of Fuad 'Ali Mohsen al-Shahari to the appeal court in Ta'iz. His case was pending before the Supreme Court; the death sentence against him had been upheld by the court of appeal. Fuad 'Ali Mohsen al-Shahari had been convicted of the murder of a captain in the Political Security Department. He had been sentenced to death by the Court of First Instance in Ta'iz on 12 November 1996 after an unfair trial. He had been held incommunicado for about a month and allegedly tortured and ill-treated in order to force him to confess to the murder. Key defence witnesses were reportedly intimidated to prevent them from testifying in the case.

Flogging
People continued to be sentenced to flogging for offences of a sexual nature, for the consumption of alcohol and for slander.

☐ In May, Yemen's Supreme Court reportedly upheld the sentence of 80 lashes imposed on journalist 'Abd al-Jabbar Sa'ad. He had been sentenced for accusing Sheikh 'Abdel Majid Zendani, president of the central committee of the main Islamist opposition party, *al-Islah*, of adultery in an article published in the weekly newspaper *al-Shura*. The court also banned him from working as a journalist for a year, ordered the closure of *al-Shura* for six months, and ordered him to pay damages to Sheikh Zendani. It was not known if the flogging was carried out during the year.

'Disappearances'
The fate of hundreds of people who had "disappeared" in Yemen since the late 1960s remained unknown. Undertakings made by the government to investigate the cases of those who had "disappeared" since 1994 were apparently not implemented.

YUGOSLAVIA
(FEDERAL REPUBLIC OF)

FEDERAL REPUBLIC OF YUGOSLAVIA
Head of state: Vojislav Koštunica (replaced Slobodan Milošević in October)
Head of government: Zoran Žižić (replaced Momir Bulatović in October)
Capital: Belgrade
Population: 10.6 million
Official language: Serbian
Death penalty: retentionist
2000 treaty ratifications/signatures: Rome Statute of the International Criminal Court

The period preceding the election of a new president and the establishment of a new government from October saw an increase in the frequency and severity of reported human rights violations within the Federal Republic of Yugoslavia (FRY). The majority of these violations were directed at opposition activists, independent journalists and conscientious objectors to military service. They included arbitrary detention, ill-treatment, unfair trials and prosecutions on political grounds. Hundreds of ethnic Albanian prisoners transferred from Kosovo when Serbian and Yugoslav forces withdrew were sentenced to prison terms after unfair trials. Some may have been prisoners of conscience. Many reported ill-treatment or torture during detention. The frequency of such violations was reduced dramatically following the advent of a new government, but cases of police ill-treatment continued to be reported. All four prisoners of conscience identified by AI had been released by the end of 2000. At least three death sentences were passed although no executions were carried out.
In Kosovo, the UN Interim Administration in Kosovo (UNMIK) and NATO-led peace-keeping force (KFOR) continued to grapple with enormous problems in fulfilling their missions. UNMIK was headed by a Special Representative of the UN Secretary-General who had executive authority in Kosovo. Some progress was made during 2000, but the human rights situation remained very unsatisfactory. At least 3,300 people remained unaccounted for in Kosovo. Many had been the victims of "disappearances" after detention by the Serbian police or had been abducted by armed ethnic Albanians.

Torture/ill-treatment
Members of opposition parties and of the "*Otpor*" ("Resistance") movement, a loosely organized opposition group with a largely student and youth membership, were frequently detained by police officers and questioned about their activities. Some were beaten or otherwise ill-treated during their detention. During demonstrations in Belgrade on 17 and 18 May against the extension of state control to the independent *Studio B* television station, police used batons and tear gas to break up the crowd. Dozens of protesters were injured. Opposition demonstrations throughout the country calling for the resignation of President Slobodan Milošević were generally held peacefully and without police intervention, but on several occasions police beat and injured demonstrators.
Following the change of government, a number of police officers accused of involvement in incidents of ill-treatment were transferred to other duties, but no independent investigations into the majority of these incidents had taken place by the end of 2000. Police ill-treatment of detainees continued to be reported following the change of government, but to a lesser degree.

◻ On 23 March Nenad Simonović was beaten unconscious by police and private security guards during an *Otpor* demonstration in the provincial town of Kragujevac. He returned home after medical treatment and was visited by men in civilian clothes who threatened to kill him if he did not stop his activities.

◻ On 8 September Miloš Kitanović and five others who had been called to the police station in Vladičin Han for informal questioning were prevented from leaving by three drunken police officers. The six men were beaten on the head, body and soles of the feet, strangled with a rope, and forced to remain in a squatting position and beaten if they moved. They were released the following day. The police officers involved were reportedly transferred to other duties.

Ethnic Albanian prisoners
Trials of ethnic Albanian prisoners transferred to Serbia from jails in Kosovo when Serb and Yugoslav forces withdrew from the province in 1999 continued. Many were convicted of "terrorism" although the evidence against them was inadequate and circumstantial, or consisted solely of confessions which they repudiated during trial because they had been extracted under torture. Many remained in jail at the end of 2000, along with others previously convicted of similar offences, although some were released having served their sentences or after being sentenced to a period equivalent to time already held. Some had their sentences reduced to time served, following appeal.
At the end of 2000, around 800 remained in prison, of whom around 600 had been tried for political offences. Others, including minors, had been held in detention for up to 18 months without a judicial order, in contravention of the Code of Criminal Procedure, before being released without charge following the change of government.

◻ Prisoner of conscience Flora Brovina, serving a sentence of 12 years' imprisonment on charges of "terrorism", was released on 1 November.

◻ On 22 May, 143 ethnic Albanians were sentenced to between seven and 13 years' imprisonment on terrorism charges by the Niš district court after a grossly unfair trial which violated both FRY law and international standards. Irregularities in the pre-trial procedures were followed by a hearing in which the main evidence was the results of a test for gunpowder traces. This test is widely regarded as unreliable. Reportedly, no evidence was presented to suggest that the defendants had been involved in the particular incidents for which they were sentenced.

Freedom of expression

Independent media companies and journalists were heavily fined for libel under the law of public information, which fails to meet international standards on freedom of expression. On 29 December key articles of the law were pronounced unconstitutional.

On 17 May the government took control of the independent Belgrade television station *Studio B* and installed a new editorial team. A number of other independent radio and television stations were closed on the grounds that they had failed to obtain broadcasting licences. *Studio B* was returned to the control of its owners following the November elections.

▫ Prisoner of conscience Nebojša Ristić was released on 17 March, 26 days before the end of his one-year sentence for disseminating false information.

▫ Journalist Zoran Luković was imprisoned on 15 August on charges of disseminating false information, and was adopted by AI as a prisoner of conscience. He was released after being pardoned on 21 October.

▫ Journalist Miroslav Filipović was sentenced to seven years' imprisonment on 26 July, on charges of espionage and disseminating false information, apparently for publishing articles on the Internet about the conflict in Kosovo, one of which contained eye-witness accounts of human rights violations committed by Serbian and FRY forces. Much of the trial, which allegedly involved "state secrets", was held behind closed doors. No details of the charges and evidence against Miroslav Filipović were made public. He was transferred to hospital, suffering from heart problems, in August but returned to jail in September despite the risk to his health. The sentence was overturned by the Supreme Military Court in Belgrade on 10 October, and he was released. The case was returned to the Military Court in Niš for a retrial.

Conscientious objectors and deserters

During the early part of 2000, prosecutions of conscientious objectors and those who had evaded military service continued. By the end of November all those serving sentences for refusing or evading military service had been released. Those who had fled the country or gone into hiding remained at risk of prosecution. Although the introduction of an amnesty law covering such cases was announced, it was not brought before parliament. Provisions for alternative civilian service failed to meet international standards.

War crimes

The Serbian and federal governments failed to cooperate with the International Criminal Tribunal for the former Yugoslavia in arresting and handing over to the custody of the Tribunal individuals indicted for violations of international humanitarian law. These included former Federal President Slobodan Milošević and four members or former members of the Serbian and federal governments.

The death penalty

The death penalty remained in force for aggravated murder in both the Serbian and Montenegrin Criminal Codes, although it was finally abolished in the federal criminal code in 1993. At least three men were sentenced to death during 2000. No executions have been carried out since 1992, but more than 20 people remained in jail under sentence of death.

Kosovo

Violence continued to plague Kosovo; many murders or other violent incidents had ethnic or political motivations. Members of minority groups were frequently the victims of violence, mainly Serbs, Roma or Muslim Slavs, but also ethnic Albanians in areas with a sizeable Serb population. There were also political killings of prominent ethnic Albanians representing moderate political positions. It was rare for the perpetrators of killings to be apprehended, or for responsibility for killings to be admitted by any organization.

Security, particularly for minorities, depended largely on the presence of KFOR troops. Police investigations were carried out by an international police force under UNMIK.

International officials, international police officers and soldiers operating under UNMIK and KFOR were responsible for violations of the rights of pre-trial detainees, and there were also some allegations of ill-treatment. KFOR allegedly shot and killed men on several occasions; in at least one case there were questions about the lawfulness of the killing.

The killing of Avni Hajredini

Ethnic violence erupted in and around the town of Mitrovica in the north of Kosovo in February. About 13 people were killed, 50 injured and 1,500 forced to flee their homes in a series of incidents. KFOR soldiers struggled to maintain law and order. In one incident during the violence, KFOR troops were shot and injured. Avni Hajredini, an ethnic Albanian, was shot and killed, reportedly by KFOR soldiers responding to the attack. Initial claims by KFOR that he had been shooting at the soldiers from a balcony were withdrawn, but no other explanation which might justify his killing was provided. No independent investigation into his killing was completed in the immediate aftermath of the incident. UNMIK later informed AI that an investigation into incident was under way, but no results had been made public by the end of 2000.

The criminal justice system

The importance of protecting and promoting human rights was emphasized by the UN in the creation of the international presence in Kosovo. However, the international presence failed to ensure that international human rights standards were consistently respected in the actions of the international police, KFOR soldiers and courts in the new judicial system.

In November the office of the Ombudsperson, an international appointee with deputies from the Albanian and Serb communities, began to receive complaints. The Ombudsperson's mandate includes investigating allegations of human rights violations perpetrated by the international civil administration or new local institutions. However, allegations of human rights violations by KFOR were not included in the initial mandate and no agreement to include KFOR had been reached by the end of 2000.

Pre-trial detainees
UNMIK police and KFOR soldiers frequently ignored the requirements of the applicable law and of international human rights standards to bring detainees promptly before a judicial authority. For example, during the violence in Mitrovica in February, some 49 people were detained for several days by KFOR soldiers without judicial review. Fourteen of them were held for five days. It was not explained to the detainees why they were being detained, or who was detaining them (KFOR or UNMIK police). Families of the detainees were not notified of their detention, nor were the detainees able to contact their families or defence counsel. Some detainees were detained for weeks on the orders of the KFOR Commander or the Special Representative of the UN Secretary-General. Since the applicable law and international standards permit detention only on the orders of a judicial authority, such detentions were arbitrary and unlawful.

One such detainee, Afrim Zeqiri, was held from 26 July to 14 September by order of the UN Special Representative. He was subsequently held for four weeks on the basis of a judicial order. His release was ordered by the district court on 31 October, but he remained in custody on the order of the Special Representative until the end of 2000.

The 'disappeared' and missing
More than 3,300 people from Kosovo were unaccounted for at the end of 2000. Most were ethnic Albanians who were believed to have "disappeared" in the custody of Serbian police or paramilitaries between early 1998 and June 1999. Serbs, Roma, people of other nationalities and ethnic Albanians of moderate political views or those regarded as "collaborators" with the Serbian authorities had also gone missing in circumstances which implicated armed ethnic Albanians in many cases. Most of these incidents occurred during or after June 1999 but there were new cases during 2000.

◻ Marian Melonasi, a journalist of mixed Albanian and Serbian parentage, was reportedly abducted in Pristina on 9 September. He had been reporting in the Serbian language for the state media under UNMIK control. No information about his whereabouts emerged before the end of 2000.

Exhumations of grave sites led to the identification of around 260 mortal remains during 2000, but some 1260 bodies which were exhumed in 1999 and 2000 remained unidentified. Not all grave sites had been examined by the end of the year.

Refugees and displaced persons
Some 82,000 ethnic Albanian refugees had returned to Kosovo by September 2000, about 9,000 of whom were forcibly returned by foreign governments. About 222,800 Kosovo Serbs, Roma or members of other minorities remained displaced within Serbia or Montenegro. Return to their own homes was for the most part dangerous and few tried to do so.

◻ On 7 November, three men and a boy from the Ashkali community (an Albanian-speaking minority perceived as Roma by ethnic Albanians) who had been displaced within Kosovo returned to their homes in Dašovac/Dashovc village in central Kosovo. The men hoped to repair their damaged homes to enable their families to return. The men themselves and international organizations negotiated with ethnic Albanian leaders before their return, seeking guarantees for their safety. However, the four were found murdered two days later. Offers to provide a KFOR guard had reportedly been refused by the men who feared that it would make them conspicuous. Local people appeared frightened or unwilling to give information about the killings.

AI country reports and visits
Reports
- Federal Republic of Yugoslavia (Kosovo): Update from the field – January 2000 (AI Index: EUR 70/002/2000)
- Federal Republic of Yugoslavia (Kosovo): Amnesty International's recommendations to UNMIK on the judicial system, February 2000 (AI Index: EUR 70/006/2000)
- Federal Republic of Yugoslavia: *Otpor* – Students and academics in the Federal Republic of Yugoslavia (AI Index: EUR 70/012/2000)
- Federal Republic of Yugoslavia (Kosovo): Setting the standard? UNMIK and KFOR's response to the violence in Mitrovica (AI Index: EUR 70/013/2000)
- Federal Republic of Yugoslavia: "Collateral damage" or unlawful killings? Violations of the Laws of War by NATO during Operation Allied Force (AI Index: EUR 70/018/2000)
- Federal Republic of Yugoslavia: Still forgotten – an update on conscientious objectors after the Kosovo conflict (AI Index: EUR 70/028/2000)
- Federal Republic of Yugoslavia (Kosovo): Amnesty International's recommendations on the return of refugees to Kosovo (AI Index: EUR 70/031/2000)
- Federal Republic of Yugoslavia: Continuing Concerns (AI Index: EUR 70/057/2000)

Visits
AI delegates visited the FRY including Kosovo regularly during 2000 to carry out research and human rights education activities. Two AI researchers were based in Kosovo until March 2000; an AI researcher was based in Skopje, Macedonia, until the end of the year.

ZAMBIA

REPUBLIC OF ZAMBIA
Head of state and government: Frederick Chiluba
Capital: Lusaka
Population: 9.1 million
Official language: English
Death penalty: retentionist

Torture and ill-treatment by police during the arrest and interrogation of suspects was widespread. At least three people reportedly died as a result of torture. At least 11 men were sentenced to death, but no executions were reported.

Background
When Zambia transformed itself in 1991 from a one-party state to a multi-party system, the first country in southern Africa to do so, expectations were raised regarding improvements of human rights. However, in the run-up to the second multi-party elections in 1996, the government used various tactics to prevent opposition politicians from standing, including calling their citizenship into question. Among those stripped of citizenship was former president Kenneth Kaunda. Several members of his party were deported to Malawi. Government restrictions on the rights to freedom of expression and assembly intensified ahead of elections due in 2001.

Torture/ill-treatment
The police continued to torture arrested suspects as a routine part of criminal investigations. In at least three incidents the torture allegedly resulted in death. Some police stations were reported to have specially adapted rooms where torture of suspects regularly took place.

◻ On 25 December Dave Muyembe died in police custody, reportedly after being tortured in connection with the theft of a vehicle.

◻ A 20-year-old man accused of stealing money from his employer was reportedly handed over to Siavonga police on 2 September. While in custody he was reportedly tortured to extract a confession. On 5 September the employer discovered that one of his relatives had stolen the money and the man was released. The man filed charges against the police officer and police station, but later withdrew his charges allegedly after intimidation by local police.

◻ On 11 January Shadreck Selemani was arrested at his house accused of theft. He was reportedly tortured for two days in a police station before being charged, and sustained a deep cut in his left leg. After his acquittal he filed charges against the police. The case was still pending at the end of 2000.

Human rights defenders
The government appeared to be taking steps to inhibit the work of human rights defenders. In rural areas, agents from the Special Branch of the police attended meetings of non-governmental organizations and opposition parties. In some cases they threatened people teaching human rights. In urban areas the Public Order Act, which requires those planning demonstrations to notify police in advance, was used to deny the right to hold peaceful demonstrations.

◻ Several non-governmental organizations staged a demonstration on 17 January outside the main police station in Lusaka to protest against the failure of the police to investigate the rape and killing of several young girls. The organizers had applied for a licence well in advance and believed they had permission from the police. When the demonstration started the police dispersed the crowd violently and arrested 39 women, who were held overnight before being released without charge.

Freedom of expression
Zambia has a vibrant independent press. *The Post*, a leading independent newspaper, has been repeatedly targeted by the government. The editor, Fred M'membe, and several of its journalists, who were arrested in 1999, faced charges of espionage in connection with an article commenting on Zambia's lack of military capacity. They were freed on bail pending judgment. On 21 December 2000 the High Court acquitted the last of the accused, Fred M'membe.

Forcible exile
The government continued to use deportation as a method of suppressing dissent despite a ruling against it by the African Commission on Human and Peoples' Rights in 1999. Human rights defenders and opposition politicians were threatened with deportation during 2000.

◻ Despite the ruling of the African Commission on Human and Peoples' Rights that the deportation of William Banda in 1994 to Malawi violated his human rights, the government refused to allow him to return.

◻ On 30 October the Supreme Court ruled that Kenneth Kaunda, the former president who had been stripped of his citizenship to prevent him standing in elections, is a Zambian citizen.

◻ On 4 January Abdul Majid Tickley, a United Kingdom (UK) citizen who had lived in Zambia for more than 54 years, was deported to the UK. The deportation followed a letter he published in *The Post* which challenged the Asian community in Zambia to be more active in politics.

Death penalty
During 2000 at least 11 prisoners were sentenced to death, bringing the number under sentence of death to more than 230. There have been no executions since 1997.

There was increased debate over the use of the death penalty during 2000. In September the Minister for Legal Affairs addressed an abolitionist conference, arranged by the Catholic Commission for Justice and Peace.

◻ Benjamin Banda and Cephas Kufa Miti, who were sentenced to death on 13 October 1999, appealed against their sentence in the first legal challenge to the constitutionality of the death penalty in Zambia. The case had a first hearing 14 December in the High Court, but no judgment had been passed by the end of 2000.

AI country visit
AI delegates visited Zambia in February and met members of AI and other human rights organizations.

ZIMBABWE

REPUBLIC OF ZIMBABWE
Head of state and government: Robert Mugabe
Capital: Harare
Population: 11.6 million
Official language: English
Death penalty: retentionist

The election campaign leading up to June parliamentary elections saw what appeared to be a deliberate and well-thought-out plan of systematic human rights violations by forces allied to the government. Violations included more than 30 political killings and widespread torture and ill-treatment throughout the country. Violations continued after the elections, albeit on a smaller scale. In an apparent attempt to intimidate the population, a strong military presence was deployed immediately after the elections in those areas where the opposition had won a substantial number of votes. Incidents of torture, ill-treatment and political killings continued throughout the year, particularly in the run-up to two parliamentary by-elections.

Background
The Zimbabwe African National Union-Patriotic Front (ZANU-PF), which had ruled Zimbabwe since independence in 1980 without any serious challenge under a Constitution negotiated in the United Kingdom at the time of independence, remained in power. A government-dominated constitutional commission had presented a draft new constitution to the President in November 1999. The National Constitutional Assembly, consisting of most of Zimbabwe's non-governmental organizations (NGOs) and opposition parties, refused to participate in the commission and campaigned against its recommendations.

The government put forward a slightly amended version of the proposal from the constitutional commission for a referendum in February. The campaign for the referendum was marked by some violence against voter education officials and those campaigning for a "no" vote, some of whom were arrested. However, the proposal was rejected in the referendum. This was the first time ZANU-PF had been defeated in a popular vote since independence. Shortly after the referendum, a violent campaign against real or suspected opponents of the government started. Government supporters and people paid by ZANU-PF invaded farms and harassed supposed government opponents. By the end of March the situation had degenerated into political violence and killings which continued until the elections. The opposition was involved in some of the violence, but the vast majority of human rights violations were committed by ZANU-PF supporters. As a result, most international observers declared that the elections were not free and fair. The main opposition party, the Movement for Democratic Change (MDC), challenged the election results in 38 constituencies. The cases were still pending at the end of the year.

Political killings
More than 30 people were killed during the election campaign; most were reported to be supporters of opposition parties. There were allegations that the state intelligence police, the Central Intelligence Organisation (CIO), was involved in several of the killings.

◻ On 15 April, two MDC activists, Tichaona Chiminya and Talent Mabika, were killed when a petrol bomb was thrown into their car. Police in the area reportedly failed to take appropriate action, even though they were given the names of two suspects, believed to be members of the CIO.

◻ On 15 April, David Stevens, a commercial farmer in the Macheke area and MDC supporter, was abducted from his farm and killed, allegedly by ZANU-PF supporters. A witness, who rushed to the local police station to report the abduction, reported that he was himself abducted from inside the police station and taken to the office of the local "war veterans" in Murehwa where he and David Stevens were severely beaten. They were then driven away, taken out of the car, and forced to march up a hill. The witness explained that, after they complained that they could walk no further, they started walking back towards the car. On their way back to the car, the captors shot David Stevens, in the presence of the witness, but left the witness after one of the captors pleaded for his life.

Torture/ill-treatment
At the end of April reports began to emerge that torture centres were operating in different parts of the country in which ZANU-PF supporters, particularly the "war veterans", were torturing actual or suspected supporters of the opposition with impunity.

One such centre was in a doctor's surgery in the Budiriro suburb of Harare, where a large number of people were reportedly tortured in the first two weeks of May.

◻ On 13 May a man was abducted 50 metres from the surgery as he was returning home from work by five people, all allegedly ZANU-PF supporters. He said the attackers beat and kicked him and squeezed his testicles. He alleged that inside the surgery he was beaten until his mouth and nose bled, deprived of sleep for three days, subjected to death threats, and had his head forced into a toilet while his captors were urinating in it. The injuries sustained were clearly visible to AI delegates who met him more than two weeks after his release. He was believed to have been abducted because his brother was the chair of a local branch of MDC's youth league.

◻ On 8 May an MDC youth league activist was abducted from a nearby shopping centre and taken to the surgery. He alleged that groups of six people took turns to torture him and that some 90 people were involved. He reported that the torture included electric shocks applied to his armpits and genital area, beatings on the soles of his feet, and piercing of the skin with bottletops. Forensic experts confirmed that his physical scars were consistent with his allegations.

Witnesses stated that they informed the police of the activities at the surgery and that the police freed some of the victims upon request, but it was only when a victim was killed while fleeing from the surgery on 17 May that the police moved in and arrested those torturing people at the surgery. The surgery was owned by a leader of the "war veterans" who was elected to parliament in June. To AI's knowledge he had not been questioned about the use of his surgery as a torture centre by the end of the year.

The torture centres appeared to have closed down after the elections. However, reports of beatings and threats continued throughout the year, although they appeared to be more targeted and to be focused around the by-elections.

◻ On 17 October, Justin Mutendadzamera, a recently elected MDC member of parliament, and his wife were beaten at their home, allegedly by police officers who accused him of having instigated protests against food prices.

Prior to the June elections, groups, mostly made up of young people, travelled from village to village identifying opposition party supporters and beating them or forcing them to attend *pungwes* (party rallies) for ZANU-PF where they were made to chant slogans and denounce the opposition.

◻ On 3 April, alleged ZANU-PF supporters attacked game warden Farai Sandikonda near Mvurwi, breaking his arm and cutting his head.

◻ On 10 April, ZANU-PF youth league members in the Mount Darwin area publicly stripped and assaulted six farm workers, four men and two women, and made them dance and sing ZANU-PF songs.

Army involvement

During July the army was actively involved in intimidating people in many of the areas where the opposition had made a strong showing in the elections. There were reports of random beatings in the streets and in beer houses. There were numerous reports of people in the suburbs of Harare and Kwekwe being assaulted by soldiers in what appeared to be targeted reprisals for voting for opposition parties.

Breakdown in the rule of law

The independence of the judiciary was under constant threat during the year. There were a number of strong verbal attacks on the judiciary in general as well as on individual judges. These culminated on 24 November in an invasion of the Supreme Court by a group of "war veterans" who disrupted the court hearing and threatened to kill the judges.

The government complied with court rulings in a selective way during the year. There was no evidence that police took any action to comply with a 30 March Supreme Court order to investigate the abduction and torture of two journalists in January 1999. Court rulings ordering the police to evict those who invaded farms were routinely ignored. The government did not act to comply with court rulings which declared their land reform scheme unconstitutional. In some cases the authorities openly stated that they would not comply with court decisions. For example, the police commissioner publicly stated that his force would not act in what he called "political matters", regardless of court rulings.

Internally displaced people

During the course of the election campaign more than 10,000 people fled the campaign of violence and intimidation in the countryside to seek refuge in the cities.

In May and June the Harare headquarters of opposition parties, such as the MDC and the United Parties, provided shelter for injured party members arriving in large numbers from the countryside. In addition, people with no apparent party affiliation fled the countryside following the threats and violence.

Freedom of expression and human rights defenders

Journalists were prevented from carrying out their work in a number of ways. They were arrested, beaten and threatened. A request from the Zimbabwe Union of Journalists for police protection of journalists travelling into dangerous areas in April received no response.

Zimbabwe's strong NGO community was under constant threat. Any criticism of government policy was perceived as opposition activity. NGO members and activists were threatened with human rights violations, including death and torture. Voter education workers, many of whom were drawn from human rights organizations, were targeted. On numerous occasions they had their T-shirts torn off and were chased away, especially in the Mashonaland provinces, but also in rural areas of the rest of the country.

NGOs reported that individuals, who they suspected were from the CIO, visited their headquarters, and that their telephone calls and e-mail were regularly tapped.

◻ On 30 March human rights activist Mr Mahoso, a headmaster, was assaulted by armed men, near Machete, during a school function. He was beaten with stones, sticks, boots and fists. The armed men also berated school staff, pupils, parents and guests for neglecting their national duty by not invading farms.

◻ Pius Ncube, the Roman Catholic Archbishop in Bulawayo, reportedly received several death threats during the year. In his post-election speech, broadcast on national television, the President named

Archbishop Ncube as one of the key figures contributing to the opposition vote.

Freedom of assembly and association

Throughout the country, political meetings were violently disrupted. The MDC called off all their rallies in the last week of campaigning ahead of the by-election in Marondera in November, after several of their members and supporters had been severely injured.

People who were unable to produce the correct party membership card were beaten. When prominent politicians were holding rallies people were forced to participate. People who refused were in many instances beaten.

Impunity

Impunity for human rights violations remained an entrenched problem. Wide-ranging amnesties had been granted for human rights violations committed during the war of independence and after large-scale atrocities in Matabeleland in the 1980s. In February, a Supreme Court order granted two human rights organizations the right to sue the President's office to obtain the release of two official reports produced on the atrocities in Matabeleland in the 1980s. The ruling stated that "no impunity was accorded to the office of the President". At the end of the year the two human rights organizations were preparing an application to the Supreme Court to secure the publication of the reports.

Amnesty for politically motived crimes

On 6 October President Mugabe announced a clemency order granting amnesty for all politically motivated crimes committed between 1 January and 31 July, during the two campaign periods and immediately after the elections. Although some offences, such as murder, rape and possession of arms, were excluded from the amnesty, other serious human rights violations, such as torture and abductions, were not.

AI country reports and visits

Reports

- Zimbabwe: Constitutional reform — an opportunity to strengthen human rights protection (AI Index: AFR 46/001/2000)
- Zimbabwe: Open letter to President Mugabe on the 20th Anniversary of Independence (AI Index: AFR 46/015/2000)
- Zimbabwe: A human rights brief for election observers (AI Index: AFR 46/012/2000)
- Zimbabwe: A human rights agenda for political parties (AI Index: AFR 46/018/2000)
- Zimbabwe: Terror tactics in the run-up to parliamentary elections (AI Index: AFR 46/014/2000)

Visits

AI delegates visited Zimbabwe in February, May and June.

AI REPORT 2001
PART 3

WHAT IS AI?

Amnesty International (AI) is a worldwide voluntary activist movement working for human rights. It is independent of any government, political persuasion or religious creed. It does not support or oppose any government or political system, nor does it support or oppose the views of the victims whose rights it seeks to protect. It is concerned solely with the impartial protection of human rights.

AI mobilizes volunteer activists — people who give freely of their time and energy in solidarity with the victims of human rights violations. There are more than 1,000,000 AI members and subscribers in over 140 countries and territories. AI members come from many different backgrounds, with widely different political and religious beliefs, united by a determination to work for a world where everyone enjoys human rights.

Many AI members are organized into groups: there are more than 7,500 local groups, youth and student groups and other specialist groups in more than 100 countries and territories. Thousands of other members are involved in networks working on particular countries or themes. In 56 countries and territories, the work of AI members is coordinated by sections, whose addresses are given below. In another 23 countries and territories, AI has pre-section coordinating structures, which are also listed below.

What does AI do?
AI works independently and impartially to promote respect for all the human rights set out in the Universal Declaration of Human Rights. AI believes that human rights are interdependent and indivisible — all human rights should be enjoyed by all people at all times, and no one set of rights can be enjoyed at the expense of other rights.

AI contributes to building respect for the Universal Declaration of Human Rights by promoting knowledge and understanding of all human rights and by taking action against specific violations of people's fundamental civil and political rights. The main focus of its campaigning is to:
- free all prisoners of conscience. According to AI's Statute, these are people detained for their political, religious or other conscientiously held beliefs or because of their ethnic origin, sex, colour, language, national or social origin, economic status, birth or other status — who have not used or advocated violence;
- ensure fair and prompt trials for all political prisoners;
- abolish the death penalty, torture and other ill-treatment of prisoners;
- end political killings and "disappearances";
- ensure that governments refrain from unlawful killings in armed conflict.

AI also works to:
- oppose abuses by armed political groups such as the detention of prisoners of conscience, hostage-taking, torture and unlawful killings;
- assist asylum-seekers who are at risk of being returned to a country where they might suffer violations of their fundamental human rights;
- cooperate with other non-governmental organizations, the UN and regional intergovernmental organizations to further human rights;
- ensure control of international military, security and police relations in order to protect human rights;
- organize human rights education and awareness raising programs.

AI: a democratic movement
AI is a democratic, self-governing movement. Major policy decisions are taken by an International Council made up of representatives from all national sections. The Council meets every two years, and has the power to amend the Statute which governs AI's work and methods. Copies of the Statute are available from the International Secretariat.

The Council elects an International Executive Committee of volunteers which carries out its decisions and appoints the movement's Secretary General, who also heads up the International Secretariat.

The movement's Secretary General is Pierre Sané (Senegal), and the members of its International Executive Committee are Samuel Zan Akologo (Ghana), Margaret Bedggood (New Zealand), Mahmoud Ben Romdhane (Tunisia), Mary Gray (USA), Paul Hoffman (USA), Hans Landolt (Peru), Jaap Rosen Jacobson (Netherlands), Colm Ó Cuanacháin (Ireland) and Angelika Pathak (International Secretariat).

Finances
AI's national sections and local volunteer groups and networks are primarily responsible for funding the movement. No funds are sought or accepted from governments for AI's work investigating and campaigning against human rights violations. The donations that sustain this work come from the organization's members and the public. The international budget adopted by AI for the financial year April 2000 to March 2001 was £19,510,000. This sum represents approximately one quarter of the estimated income likely to be raised during the year by the movement's national sections to finance their campaigning and other activities.

AI's ultimate goal is to end human rights violations, but so long as they continue AI tries to provide practical help to the victims. Relief (financial assistance) is an important aspect of this work. Sometimes AI provides financial assistance directly to individuals. At other times, it works through local bodies such as local and national human rights organizations so as to ensure that resources are used as effectively as possible for those in most need.

During the financial year April 2000 to March 2001, the International Secretariat of AI distributed an estimated £125,000 in relief to victims of human rights violations such as prisoners of conscience and recently released prisoners of conscience and their dependants,

WHAT IS AI?

and for the medical treatment of torture victims. In addition, the organization's sections and groups distributed a further substantial amount, much of it in the form of modest payments by local groups to their adopted prisoners of conscience and dependent families.

Information about AI is available from national section offices and from: International Secretariat, 1 Easton Street, London WC1X 0DW, United Kingdom.

AI Online

AI Online is dedicated to providing AI's human rights resources on the web in English (http://www.amnesty.org). It contains more than 10,000 files and receives over six million hits a month. It holds most AI reports published since 1996 and all the latest news releases detailing AI's concerns about human rights issues around the world. Additionally, there is information on the latest campaigns and appeals for action to help protect human rights (http://www.stoptorture.org). You will also find contact details for AI's offices around the world and links to hundreds of websites with a human rights theme.

There are also AI international sites in French (http://www.efai.org/), Spanish (http://www.edai.org/), and Arabic (http://www.amnesty-arabic.org/).

AI sections

Algeria Amnesty International, BP 377, Alger, RP 16004
E-mail: amnestyalgeria@hotmail.com
Argentina Amnistía Internacional, Av. Rivadavia 2206 - P4A, C1032ACO Ciudad de Buenos Aires
E-mail: info@amnesty.org.ar
http://www.amnesty.org.ar
Australia Amnesty International, Private Bag 23, Broadway, New South Wales 2007
E-mail: adminaia@amnesty.org.au
http://www.amnesty.org.au
Austria amnesty international austria, Moeringgasse 10, A-1150 Wien
E-mail: info@amnesty.at
http://www.amnesty.at
Bangladesh Amnesty International, 28 Kabi Jasimuddin Road, 1st Floor, North Kamalapur, Dhaka - 1217
E-mail: admin-bd@amnesty.org
Belgium Amnesty International (AI Vlaanderen), Kerkstraat 156, 2060 Antwerpen
E-mail: amnesty@aivl.be
http://www.aivl.be
Belgium Amnesty International (francophone), rue Berckmans 9, 1060 Bruxelles
E-mail: aibf@aibf.be
http://www.aibf.be
Benin Amnesty International, 01 BP 3536, Cotonou
E-mail: aibenin@nakayo.leland.bj
Bermuda Amnesty International, PO Box HM 2136, Hamilton HM JX
E-mail: aibda@ibl.bm

Brazil Anistia Internacional, Caixa Postal 5013, CEP 90041 -970 Porto Alegre, Rio Grande do Sul
E-mail: anistia@anistia.org.br
Canada Amnesty International, 214 Montreal Road, 4th Floor, Vanier, Ontario, K1L 1A4
E-mail: info@amnesty.ca
http://www.amnesty.ca
Canada Amnistie Internationale (francophone), 6250 boulevard Monk, Montréal, Québec H4E 3H7
E-mail: info@amnistie.qc.ca
http://www.amnistie.qc.ca
Chile Señores, Casilla 4062, Santiago
E-mail: admin-cl@amnesty.org
Costa Rica Amnistía Internacional, 75 metros al norte de la Iglesia de Fatima, los Yoses, San Pedro, San José
Côte d'Ivoire Amnesty International, 04 BP 895, Abidjan 04
E-mail: aicotedivoire@globeaccess.net
Denmark Amnesty International, Dyrkoeb 3, 1166 Copenhagen K
E-mail: amnesty@amnesty.dk
Ecuador Amnistía Internacional, Casilla 17-15-240-C, Quito
Faroe Islands Amnesty International, PO Box 1075, FR-110, Tórshavn
E-mail: amnesty@amnesty.fo
http://www.amnesty.fo
Finland Amnesty International, Ruoholahdenkatu 24, D 00180 Helsinki
E-mail: amnesty@amnesty.fi
http://www.amnesty.fi
France Amnesty International, 76 blvd. de La Villette, 75940 Paris cedex 19
E-mail: admin-fr@amnesty.asso.fr
http://www.amnesty.asso.fr
Germany Amnesty International, 53108 Bonn
E-mail: admin-de@amnesty.de
http://www.amnesty.de
Ghana Amnesty International, Private Mail Bag, Kokomlemle, Accra - North
E-mail: amnesty@ighmail.com
Greece Amnesty International, 30 Sina Street, 106 72 Athens
E-mail: info@amnesty.gr
http://www.amnesty.gr
Guyana Amnesty International, c/o Palm Court Building, 35 Main Street, PO Box 10653, Georgetown
Hong Kong Amnesty International, Unit B, 3/F, Best-O-Best Commercial Centre, 32-36 Ferry Street, Kowloon
E-mail: admin-hk@amnesty.org
Iceland Amnesty International, PO Box 618, 121 Reykjavík
E-mail: amnesty@rhi.hi.is
http://www.amnesty.is
Ireland Amnesty International, Sean MacBride House, 48 Fleet Street, Dublin 2
E-mail: info@amnesty.iol.ie
http://www.amnesty.ie
Israel Amnesty International, PO Box 14179, Tel Aviv 61141
E-mail: amnesty@netvision.net.il
http://www.amnesty.org.il

WHAT IS AI?

Italy Amnesty International, Via Giovanni Battista De Rossi 10, 00161 Roma
E-mail: info@amnesty.it
http://www.amnesty.it

Japan Amnesty International, Sky Esta 2F, 2-18-23 Nishi Waseda, Shinjuku-ku, Tokyo 169
E-mail: amnesty@mri.biglobe.ne.jp
http://www.amnesty.or.jp

Korea (Republic of) Amnesty International, Kyeong Buk RCO Box 36, Daegu 706-600
E-mail: admin-ko@amnesty.org
http://www.amnesty.or.kr

Luxembourg Amnesty International, Boîte Postale 1914, 1019 Luxembourg
E-mail: e-mail@amnesty.lu
http://www.amnesty.lu

Mauritius Amnesty International, BP 69, Rose-Hill
E-mail: amnesty@intnet.mu

Mexico Amnistía Internacional, Calle Patricio Sanz No. 1104, Depto. 8, Col. del Valle, CP 03100, México DF

Morocco Amnesty International, Place d'Angleterre, Rue Souissra, Immeuble No. 11, Appt No. 1, Rabat - l'Océan
E-mail: admin-ma@amnesty.org

Nepal Amnesty International, PO Box 135, Bagbazar, Kathmandu
E-mail: ain@ccsl.com.np

Netherlands Amnesty International, PO Box 1968, 1000 BZ, Amsterdam
E-mail: amnesty@amnesty.nl
http://www.amnesty.nl

New Zealand Amnesty International, PO Box 793, Wellington
E-mail: campaign@amnesty.org.nz
http://www.amnesty.org.nz

Nigeria Amnesty International, PMB 3061, Suru Lere, Lagos
E-mail: amnestynig@alpha.linkserve.com

Norway Amnesty International, PO Box 702 Sentrum, 0106 Oslo
E-mail: info@amnesty.no
http://www.amnesty.no

Peru Señores, Casilla 659, Lima 18
E-mail: admin-pe@amnesty.org

Philippines Amnesty International, Room 305 CRM Building II, 116 Kamia Road, 1101 Quezon City
E-mail: amnesty@info.com.ph

Portugal Amnistia Internacional, Rua Fialho de Almeida 13-1, PT-1070-128 Lisboa
E-mail: aisp@ip.pt
http://www.amnistia-internacional.pt

Puerto Rico Amnistía Internacional, Calle El Roble No. 54-Altos, Oficina 11, Río Piedras, Puerto Rico 00925

Senegal Amnesty International, BP 21910, Dakar
E-mail: aisenegal@sentoo.sn

Sierra Leone Amnesty International, PMB 1021, Freetown
E-mail: ai_sl@hotmail.com

Slovenia Amnesty International, Komenskega 7, 1000 Ljubljana
E-mail: amnesty.slo@guest.arnes.si
http://www.ljudmila.org/ai-slo

Spain Amnistía Internacional, Apdo 50318, 28080 Madrid
E-mail: amnistia.internacional@a-i.es
http://www.a-i.es

Sweden Amnesty International, PO Box 23400, SE-10435 Stockholm
E-mail: info@amnesty.se
http://www.amnesty.se

Switzerland Amnesty International, Postfach CH-3001, Bern
E-mail: info@amnesty.ch
http://www.amnesty.ch

Taiwan Amnesty International, Room 525, No.2, Section 1, Chung-shan North Road, 100 Taipei
E-mail: aitaiwan@transend.com.tw
http://www.transend.com.tw/~aitaiwan/

Tanzania Amnesty International, Luther House, 3rd Floor, PO Box 4331, Dar es Salaam
E-mail: aitanz@intafrica.com

Togo CCNP, BP 20013, Lomé
E-mail: aitogo@cafe.tg

Tunisia Amnesty International, 67 rue Oum Kalthoum, 3ème étage, Escalier B, 1000 Tunis
E-mail: admin-tn@amnesty.org

United Kingdom Amnesty International, 99-119 Rosebery Avenue, London EC1R 4RE
E-mail: info@amnesty.org.uk
http://www.amnesty.org.uk

United States of America Amnesty International, 322 8th Ave, New York, NY 10001
E-mail: admin-us@aiusa.org
http://www.amnestyusa.org

Uruguay Amnistía Internacional, Tristan Narvaja 1624, Ap 1, CP 11200, Montevideo

Venezuela Amnistía Internacional, Apartado Postal 5110, Carmelitas, 1010 A Caracas
E-mail: admin-ve@amnesty.org
http://www.amnistia.int.ve

AI coordinating structures

Bolivia Amnistía Internacional, Casilla 10607, La Paz

Burkina Faso Amnesty International, 08 BP 11344, Ouagadougou
E-mail: Contact.buro@cenatrin.bf

Caribbean Regional Office Amnesty International C.R.O., PO Box 1912, Grenada, West Indies
E-mail: amnestycro@caribsurf.com

Croatia Amnesty International, Martičeva 24, 10000 Zagreb
E-mail: admin@amnesty.hr

Curaçao Amnesty International, PO Box 3676, Curaçao, Netherlands Antilles

Cyprus Amnesty International, 81 Onasagorou str., PO Box 2497, 1011 Nicosia
E-mail: amnesty@logosnet.com.cy

Czech Republic Amnesty International, Palackého 9, 110 00 Praha 1
E-mail: amnesty@amnesty.cz
http://www.amnesty.cz

WHAT IS AI?

Gambia Amnesty International, PO Box 1935, Banjul
E-mail: amnesty@gamtel.gm

Hungary Amnesty International, 1399 Budapest, PF 701/343
E-mail: amnesty.hun@mail.matav.hu

Malaysia Amnesty International, Pro-tem Committee, 43A, Jalan SS 15/4, 47500 Subang Jaya Selangor Darul Ehsan
E-mail: amnesty@tm.net.my
http://www.crosswinds.net/~aimalaysia

Mali Amnesty International, BP E 3885, Bamako
E-mail: amnesty-mli@spider.toolnet.org

Mongolia Amnesty International, Ulaanbaatar 21 0648, PO Box 180
E-mail: aimncc@magicnet.mn

Pakistan Amnesty International, NEC, B-12, Shelozon Centre, Gulsan-E-Iqbal, Block 15, University Road, Karachi - 75300
E-mail: amnesty@cyber.net.pk

Palestinian Authority Amnesty International, PO Box 543, Khalaf Building, Racheed Street, Gaza City, South Remal via Israel
E-mail: admin-pa@amnesty.org

Paraguay Amnistía Internacional, Calle Juan de Salazar 488 casi Boquerón, Asunción
E-mail: ai-info@amnistia.org.py
http://www.amnistia.org.py

Poland Amnesty International, ul. Jaśkowa Dolina 4, 80-252 Gdańsk
E-mail: amnesty@amnesty.org.pl
http://www.amnesty.org.pl

Slovakia Amnesty International, Staromestská 6, 811 03 Bratislava
E-mail: amnesty@internet.sk
http://www.internet.sk/amnesty

South Africa Amnesty International, PO Box 29083, Sunnyside 0132, Pretoria, Gauteng
E-mail: info@amnesty.org.za

Thailand Amnesty International, 61/9 Park Ploenchit Tower, Soi Sukhumvit 1, Sukhumvit Road, Klongtoey, Wattana, Bangkok 10110
E-mail: admin-th@amnesty.org
http://www.thailand.amnesty.com

Uganda Amnesty International groups, PO Box 23966, Kampala
E-mail: augamnesty@yahoo.com

Ukraine Amnesty International, Maydan Rynok 6, Drohobych, 293 720 Lvivska obl
E-mail: officeai@dr.lv.ukrtel.net

Zambia Amnesty International, Private Bag 3, Kitwe Main PO, Kitwe
E-mail: zebbiesmm@hotmail.com

Zimbabwe Amnesty International, 25 E Bible House, 99 Mbuya Nehanda Street, Harare
E-mail: gertrudena@natfood.co.zw (attn AI Zim)

AI groups
There are also AI groups in:
Albania, Angola, Aruba, Azerbaijan, Bahamas, Barbados, Belarus, Bosnia-Herzegovina, Botswana, Cameroon, Chad, Dominican Republic, Egypt, Estonia, Georgia, Grenada, Jamaica, Jordan, Kazakstan, Kenya, Kuwait, Kyrgyzstan, Lebanon, Liberia, Lithuania, Macao, Macedonia, Malta, Moldova, Romania, Russian Federation, Turkey, Yemen, Yugoslavia (Federal Republic of)

AI IN ACTION

"The success of the 1961 Amnesty Campaign depends on how sharply and powerfully it is possible to rally public opinion. It depends, too, upon the campaign being all-embracing in its composition, international in character and politically impartial in direction."

So wrote Peter Benenson in his 1961 article in the London *Observer* which founded Amnesty International (AI). From that call for a year-long campaign on behalf of prisoners of conscience has grown a worldwide organization of more than a million members whose activities now extend far beyond those originally envisaged. It is important to remind ourselves that the present reputation and international standing of AI are based on the essential characteristics which were laid out 40 years ago and which still underpin our work.

AI's strength reflects the quality of the materials it produces and the meticulous research on which its campaigning activities are based. During 2000, AI delegates visited more than 70 countries and territories to meet victims of human rights violations, observe trials, and interview local human rights activists and officials.

The facts are gathered in order to generate action. AI members, supporters and staff around the world mobilize public pressure on governments and others with influence to stop human rights abuses. AI makes it possible for any interested person to send messages of concern directly to those who can change the situation.

Activities range from public demonstrations to letter-writing, from human rights education to fundraising concerts, from targeted appeals on behalf of a single individual to global campaigns on a specific country or issue, from approaches to local authorities to lobbying intergovernmental organizations.

AI confronts governments with its findings, by issuing detailed reports and by publicizing its concerns in leaflets, posters, advertisements, newsletters and on the Internet; AI information is available on countless websites worldwide.

AI campaigns to change government attitudes and unjust laws. One of the ways it does this is by feeding a constant stream of information to the media, to governments and to the UN, urging them to take action.

AI also strives to promote awareness and strengthen the protection of human rights. It appeals to international organizations to intervene when a crisis appears likely to develop. It seeks the protection of refugees fleeing persecution and it works with local human rights workers who are subjected to harassment or who are under threat of attack.

Long and medium-term actions

Actions by AI's local groups and networks – based in more than 100 countries – continued to grow steadily during the year. Members took part in actions involving 3,685 named individuals, including prisoners of conscience and other victims of human rights violations, in countries across the world. A total of 993 long-term Action Files were active and running and assigned to 2,732 groups who used a variety of campaigning techniques on behalf of the cases, including letter-writing and public events. A total of 108 new Action Files were produced and allocated during the year while 230 were closed in the same period.

The year saw an increasing number of innovative Action Files being produced for work by AI activists. These included one to provide protection to activists from the Yugoslav group OTPOR (see Youth and students below), as well as a demand to change legislation discriminating against the gay and lesbian community in Uganda and an Action File on Guatemala in support of HIJOS, a youth-based organization in defence of the rights of children of the "disappeared".

Local groups were also involved in Regional Action Networks (RANs), medium-term actions which require campaigning for between one and 12 months. A variety of campaigning techniques were also used in RAN actions. During the year a total of 1,776 groups were assigned to 23 RANs and they took part in 208 actions.

Youth and students

Youth and student groups make up approximately half of the AI membership worldwide and are organized into about 3,500 groups. In 2000 they campaigned vigorously on all AI concerns, including focusing on human rights abuses faced by the Serbian student pro-democracy group OTPOR ("Resistance"). Members of OTPOR travelled to Slovenia, the Palestinian Authority and the United Kingdom (UK) to speak to AI youth and to work with them on creating strategies for addressing human rights abuses in Serbia. AI youth and students sent postcards, e-mails and letters to the Yugoslav and Serbian authorities, created websites about OTPOR, and raised awareness in universities with information stalls, posters and press conferences. The second International Youth Meeting was held in Slovenia where 35 representatives of the youth and students network from all regions of the world came together to create an action plan. Youth camps took place in South Africa (attended by young people from 15 African countries), the Palestinian Authority and the Philippines, and brought together young people to discuss human rights and take practical action.

Urgent Actions

If urgent action is needed on behalf of people in imminent danger of gross human rights violations, volunteers around the world are alerted, and thousands of letters, faxes and e-mails are sent within days.

During 2000 AI initiated 481 such appeals for the Urgent Action network. There were also 347 updates issued to urgent action appeals; 171 of these asked for further appeals to be sent. These actions were issued on behalf of people in 85 countries and territories, who were either at risk or had been the victims of, for example, torture or ill-treatment; "disappearances"; political killings and death threats; judicial executions;

AI IN ACTION

deaths in custody; or *refoulement* (forcible return) of asylum-seekers to a country where they would be in danger of human rights violations.

Health professionals

Among those long recognized as having an important role to play in defending human rights are health professionals. The AI health professional network continued to act in cases of prisoners suffering ill health because of torture, poor prison conditions and deprivation of medical care, and campaigned on some 50 medical actions issued on such cases during 2000. The network, which has members in more than 30 countries, also acted on behalf of many doctors and other health workers whose rights were abused. In May, AI published *Harming the healers: Violations of the human rights of health professionals* (AI Index: ACT 75/002/2000), a report on more than 20 health workers who had been imprisoned, ill-treated or had "disappeared" in recent years. It documented the problems faced by health workers in the context of human rights violations and in the exercise of their profession.

AI health professional groups participated in a number of AI campaigns throughout the year as well as organizing meetings, undertaking human rights education activities and maintaining contacts with national professional bodies and non-governmental organizations (NGOs).

AI health professionals contributed to important initiatives within the medical profession internationally, which included the publication of the Istanbul Protocol on the medical documentation of torture. This was the product of three years' work by a coalition of human rights, legal and medical experts, and was handed to the UN High Commissioner for Human Rights, Mary Robinson, in August. The Principles on the Effective Documentation of Torture — drawn from the Istanbul Protocol — were included in an AI compilation: *Ethical codes and declarations relevant to the health professions* (AI Index: ACT 75/005/2000), issued in December.

Crisis response: Sierra Leone

In early May, the capture of around 500 UN peace-keeping troops by rebel forces of the Revolutionary United Front (RUF) and the resumption of hostilities heightened the risk of further mass human rights abuses against civilians. AI responded by stepping up its ongoing work and increasing its research capacity in the country, as well as exploring new areas of campaigning. The intense campaigning by AI members over subsequent months has already contributed to dramatic changes in the international community's approach to resolving the conflict in Sierra Leone.

AI lobbied governments and intergovernmental organizations (IGOs), in particular the UN, to take immediate action to prevent human rights abuses and to ensure that all efforts to resolve the crisis placed human rights protection as a priority. Specifically, AI emphasized the obligation of the international community to ensure that UN peace-keeping forces in Sierra Leone fulfilled their mandate to protect civilians under imminent threat of physical danger. AI delegates in Freetown, including AI's Secretary General Pierre Sané, held meetings with the Sierra Leone President and other senior government officials, UN representatives, foreign officials and members of Sierra Leone NGOs to discuss AI's concerns and recommendations.

AI researchers in Sierra Leone interviewed many children who had been abducted and forced to fight or "serve" during the conflict, as well as women and girls who had been subjected to rape and forced into sexual slavery. Their testimonies and the children's drawings have been used by AI members worldwide, including women's, youth and student groups, to publicize the plight of women and children in Sierra Leone and to lobby their own governments as well as the government of Sierra Leone to ensure that the needs of victims of the conflict are met.

AI had consistently campaigned against the blanket amnesty granted in the July 1999 peace agreement, believing that there can be no lasting peace unless the perpetrators of human rights abuses are brought to justice. The events of May 2000 forced the international community to acknowledge this. AI made specific proposals on steps to be taken to address impunity which helped to move forward the international debate and contributed to discussions taking place within Sierra Leone civil society. In August the UN Security Council decided to establish a Special Court for Sierra Leone to prosecute those most responsible for the gravest human rights abuses.

AI and other NGOs from around the world joined together to campaign for immediate action to end the trade in diamonds from rebel-held areas which finances military assistance to the RUF, enabling it to continue to commit widespread abuses against civilians. There was unprecedented lobbying of the diamond industry itself, as well as of governments in major diamond-importing countries, the UN and other IGOs. AI's unique contribution to the NGO campaign was its capacity to generate pressure from members around the world directed at all levels of the diamond trade, from jewellery shops to the Diamond High Council. AI's campaigning with other NGOs also aimed to ensure that the UN arms embargo was enforced and that no further military assistance reached RUF forces.

Israel/Occupied Territories/Palestinian Authority

On 29 September at least five people died in Jerusalem and more than 200 were wounded after being shot by Israeli security forces. The days and weeks that followed saw almost daily confrontations between stone-throwing Palestinians and Israeli troops. By the end of 2000, Israeli security forces had killed at least 300 and wounded more than 10,000 Palestinians, many of whom were children under 18.

AI mobilized its membership to take action to stop the killings. AI sections all over the world initiated public events as well as lobbying and mass letter-writing activities. As deaths of children mounted, AI issued a children's action, followed soon after by a report based on its mission in October. The report criticized Israeli security services for using military methods against demonstrators who were not endangering lives; for using ammunition and weapons that were suitable for combat situations, not for policing demonstrations; and for the rapid escalation to lethal force and the frequent impeding of medical assistance.

AI members responded to the escalating situation by sending thousands of letters not only to the Israeli government and officials but also to the Palestinian Authority reinforcing the need to protect children. A UN Commission of Inquiry was set up, though without the hoped-for support of all members. However, massive AI pressure may have helped to influence the Israeli government to agree to set up a judicial commission of inquiry to investigate the circumstances of the killing of Palestinian citizens of Israel.

AI sections were sent regularly a list of Palestinian and Israeli dead, and a poster was produced in Arabic, English and French. Members began to organize increasingly visible actions, from reading the names of the dead out loud at street corners in the USA to organizing the ringing of all the church bells in Switzerland for the dead on 16 December.

Human rights defenders

Human rights defenders play a vital role in holding states to account in respect of their promises and obligations to protect the rights of their citizens. In many countries around the world human rights defenders face constant persecution, in particular in Colombia, Indonesia, Togo, Tunisia and Turkey, on account of their efforts to support the victims of human rights violations and to expose the abuses committed by state agents. Work to strengthen and protect human rights defenders continued to be one of AI's priorities.

In Latin America, AI's special program of protection mechanisms for human rights defenders at risk worked closely with local and international organizations to develop and apply national programs of protection. This work included supporting national and international internships, as well as initiatives to enable mainly foreign nationals to accompany human rights defenders — including witnesses — facing imminent danger. Members of the electronic Human Rights Defenders Network for Latin America took special action on behalf of Brazilian human rights defenders, including AI members. Other actions included Guatemalan defenders threatened and attacked because of their work on impunity, the "disappearance" of Colombian human rights activist Jairo Bedoya Hoyos, and activists campaigning for land rights and against police violence in Pará, Brazil.

In May AI published a report, *Colombia: Protection of human rights defenders — one step forward, three steps back* (AI Index: AMR 23/022/2000) and launched a one-year campaign on Colombian human rights defenders who continue to work despite the alarming dangers. The report emphasizes that while security measures offered by the authorities for human rights defenders at risk — such as bullet-proof vests and reinforcements for office premises — are welcome, they fail to address the root causes or complexity of the problem of military and paramilitary threats and attacks.

In May AI conducted a workshop in Mexico to discuss the application of the UN Declaration on the Right and Responsibility of Individuals, Groups and Organs of Society to Promote and Protect Universally Recognized Human Rights and Fundamental Freedoms. The workshop, attended by 40 defenders, was one part of a long-term strategy to build a national program on the protection of defenders.

Following regional and sub-regional consultations during 1998 and 1999, a coordinator was appointed in April for a one-year campaign on human rights defenders in Western Africa. Collaborative discussions with human rights NGOs in a number of countries in the region resulted in a small international consultative meeting in June organized by AI Ghana. This meeting discussed the development of plans for materials and the organization of a launch event, and led to the establishment of coalitions of networks of human rights defenders, including AI members.

Worldwide campaigns
Take a step to stamp out torture

In October the movement began a major new worldwide campaign, *Take a step to stamp out torture*, focusing on three key themes: the means of preventing torture; the role of discrimination in supporting the torture inflicted on certain groups in the population; and putting an end to the impunity which has shielded so many people responsible for torture. The campaign was launched with a rolling program of media events in Tokyo, Beirut, Nairobi, London and Buenos Aires and in most of the countries where AI has a section. A website was set up, **www.stoptorture.org**, giving visitors and subscribers the opportunity to take immediate action on urgent cases with a risk of torture. For the first time, AI offered notices of urgent cases sent to subscribers' mobile telephones using "SMS" text messages.

AI sections organized scores of publicity events and press briefings to raise public awareness about torture. These ranged from a marathon run in Peru to a motorbike tour in Nepal, a student march in Canada and visits to police stations in South Africa. Government officials and prime ministers publicly signed commitments to end torture. The campaign attracted extensive media coverage and members' protest actions swiftly began to draw responses from governments.

Saudi Arabia

Human rights are no longer a taboo subject in Saudi Arabia. Within days of AI's first-ever campaign against human rights violations in the country being launched in March, the government, in an unprecedented step, announced its belief in the universality and indivisibility of human rights. The authorities also gave undertakings to introduce new legislation with more human rights guarantees and acceded to the UN Women's Convention. A dynamic and unprecedented debate on human rights began in the media.

AI IN ACTION

Throughout the campaign AI activists demonstrated their concern and outrage at the secrecy surrounding human rights violations and at the suffering of countless victims, left with no safeguards and no form of redress.

AI members in Europe and North America focused their campaigning on economic relations and the role of the business community. They lobbied their governments to voice their concerns about human rights in meetings with Saudi Arabian government officials. Asian members of AI focused on the plight of migrant workers, particularly women domestic workers suffering abuse at the hands of their employers, and organized meetings with trade unions and migrant workers' organizations, as well as their own governments, to raise awareness and discuss solutions. Members in the Middle East and North Africa emphasized the urgency of addressing women's rights, particularly in terms of personal status, freedom of movement and equal opportunities in employment.

An important breakthrough with this campaign was to end the silence of the international community about grave human rights violations in Saudi Arabia. For the first time statements by many governments raised concerns about the situation, in particular the lack of protection given to their own citizens caught up in the criminal justice system, or in some cases demanding proper redress for their lack of protection. AI members campaigned in the streets throughout the world, and thousands of signatures were collected in countries as diverse as the Netherlands and Nepal, Morocco, Venezuela and Nigeria, united in their concern to end the secrecy and end the suffering in Saudi Arabia.

Other campaigns

Other campaigns during the year covered human rights abuses in Algeria, Belarus, Democratic Republic of the Congo, Haiti, India, Indonesia, Russian Federation and Sudan. AI members also mobilized support for human rights defenders in Colombia, India and Western Africa, continued to develop initiatives on economic relations and approaches to companies, and the transfer of military, security and police equipment, as well as undertaking pioneering work on human rights violations linked to identity-based discrimination. In addition, AI members mounted lobbying operations at many of the worldwide and regional intergovernmental organizations' meetings that took place, and participated actively in meetings including the fifth-year review of the Beijing Platform for Action (Beijing plus Five) and preparations for the World Conference against Racism.

Children's rights

For the 2000 Children's Rights Action and as part of AI's Campaign against Torture, AI launched a report on the torture and ill-treatment of children, *Hidden scandal, secret shame* (AI Index: ACT 40/038/2000). Drawing on AI's field research and other evidence, the report examines the contexts in which children are tortured, looks at the international legal framework that defines and prohibits torture, and makes numerous recommendations for ending the torture and ill-treatment of children. The report reveals that children are tortured because they are caught up in wars and political conflict; children suspected of criminal activity are most at risk of torture at the hands of the state; children are often detained in conditions that pose a threat to their health and safety; and many children face being beaten or sexually abused by the very adults who are supposed to protect them. AI is calling on governments to fulfil their obligations under the Convention on the Rights of the Child (UN Children's Convention) to ensure that children are protected from torture and ill-treatment. AI members around the world undertook a variety of initiatives such as a painting competition for children; distributing postcards urging governments to "stop the torture of children now"; taking action on appeal cases of children who had been tortured; and organizing school activities including essay competitions.

AI's activists have continued to lobby on the Optional Protocol to the UN Children's Convention on the involvement of children in armed conflict. On 25 May the UN General Assembly adopted the Optional Protocol by consensus. The focus of AI's lobbying, in close cooperation with the International Coalition to Stop the Use of Child Soldiers, has now moved on to encourage all states to ratify it, without reservations, to implement it in national law, and to make declarations endorsing 18 as the minimum age at which voluntary recruitment will be permitted. The aim of the campaign is for a minimum of 100 signatures and 50 ratifications of the Optional Protocol by the UN Special Summit on Children in September 2001.

AI's members also took action for the rights of children who found themselves in the firing line in Sierra Leone and in Israel and the Occupied Territories.

AI's work for juvenile justice is ongoing. In 2000 AI's activists continued to investigate cases of people who were facing the death penalty in the USA for crimes they were convicted of committing when they were under 18. The use of the death penalty on child offenders violates numerous international agreements, including the International Covenant on Civil and Political Rights and the UN Children's Convention.

Many children who come into contact with the justice system encounter torture, ill-treatment and cruel, inhuman and degrading conditions of detention. AI members continued to campaign on the juvenile detention system, Foundation for the Well-Being of Minors (FEBEM) in São Paulo state, Brazil, which collapsed into crisis in October 1999 when years of overcrowding and ill-treatment led to a series of violent riots in one of FEBEM's detention centres. Since then the reforms undertaken have fallen far short of those required to tackle the crisis. AI called on the São Paulo government to take immediate steps to address the human rights crisis in FEBEM.

Women's Rights

In 2000 AI's Women's Rights Action highlighted the ongoing struggle for women's rights. Central to this was AI's lobbying for the ratification of the Optional Protocol to the UN Convention on the Elimination of All Forms of Discrimination against Women (UN Women's Convention) and work at the review of the 1995 UN World Conference on Women, held in Beijing.

The year 1999 ended with the adoption of the new Optional Protocol to the UN Women's Convention by the UN General Assembly which will provide an effective tool to fight discrimination against women. It creates a mechanism whereby individual women in countries which have ratified the Protocol have the right to bring complaints to the Committee on the Elimination of Discrimination against Women (CEDAW) alleging a violation of the rights in the Convention. Under the Protocol the Committee will also be able to carry out an inquiry if it receives reliable information indicating grave or systematic violations by a state party to the Convention.

In June, an AI delegation attended, along with UN member states, a special session of the UN General Assembly to review the delivery of commitments to promote women's equality, peace and development drawn up during the Beijing Conference. Delegates from the Middle East, including AI's Moroccan delegate, managed to stage a lightning picket at the main gate of the UN building although they were threatened with arrest. Three days before the end of the UN meeting, the AI delegates mounted a silent protest. Within 24 hours, AI activists produced hundreds of white T-shirts emblazoned with the slogan "No Going Back – Women's Rights are Human Rights" in different languages, which were distributed to women NGO delegates. The message, visible during the final two days of the UN session, was simple and yet powerful.

Reactions to the outcome of the session were mixed. There was a reaffirmation of the universality and indivisibility of women's rights and human rights, but some governments deliberately avoided repeating the phrase "women's rights are human rights" which appeared in previous UN documents including the Beijing Platform for Action. However, new commitments to combat domestic violence against women and girls were added with specific references to marital rape; crimes committed in the name of honour and passion; and racism and racially motivated violence.

Many AI members around the world took part in the Women's World March 2000 against Poverty and all Forms of Violence against Women. Organized by the *Fédération des Femmes du Québec* of Canada, the event was supported by international and grass-roots women's organizations worldwide. Women's rights activists all over the world marched to raise awareness about poverty and all forms of violence against women as obstacles to women's attainment of equality, development and peace; to demand greater accountability by governments and the international trade and financial institutions for changes required to improve the status of women and women's quality of life; and to forge global solidarity with grass-roots women's movements around the issues of poverty and violence against women.

As part of the program of action on Saudi Arabia, AI's women's rights activists campaigned against abuses of women. They organized appeal cases, petitions, demonstrations, meetings, workshops and letter-writing actions, as well as approaching Saudi Arabian embassies and foreign ministries in the activists' countries. They also participated in the response to the Sierra Leone crisis, campaigning on the issue of rape and other forms of sexual violence against girls and women. In addition, AI members responded to an action on the trafficking of women from countries of the former Soviet Union to work in the sex industry in Israel.

The rights of lesbian, gay, bisexual and transgendered people

The year was marked by an increasing activism and outreach to the gay rights community by AI led by its own growing network of gay rights advocates and activists in more than 40 countries.

In July, AI took part in World Pride in Rome. This was an important and high-profile event at which gay rights were openly stated as a legitimate human rights issue. Despite efforts to disrupt the event, the mood was very positive with activists from around the world marching to proclaim gay pride. AI's presence highlighting discrimination against the gay community as a human rights issue provided a strong human rights dimension to the media and public perception of the event. AI held a press conference and mounted a rally, which was well covered by local and international media. Human rights defenders from the gay community were present, including one on whose behalf AI members have campaigned.

A leading human rights defender in Zimbabwe, Poliyana Mangwiro, of Gays and Lesbians of Zimbabwe (GALZ), took part in an AI speaker's tour in February and March, visiting nine AI sections. She was met by an enthusiastic and engaged audience at all her speaking engagements and the tour provided wide media coverage to GALZ and the situation of lesbian and gay human rights defenders in Zimbabwe. The tour also gave GALZ contacts with lesbian, gay, bisexual and transgender (LGBT) organizations internationally and with the wider human rights movement.

AI's LGBT activists were mobilized to campaign on behalf of prisoner of conscience Anwar Ibrahim, former Deputy Prime Minister and Finance Minister of Malaysia, who was sentenced on charges of sodomy, and on behalf of members of the transgendered community in Valencia, Carabobo State, Venezuela, who continue to be harassed and jailed in conditions which may amount to ill-treatment.

AI's work on the USA has continued with actions on prisons in California and Mississippi in response to reports of attacks against gay prisoners and the inadequate care of prisoners with HIV/AIDS. LGBT activists also responded to Urgent Actions on Argentina, Brazil and Saudi Arabia.

AI IN ACTION

Military, security and police transfers

In 2000 the AI Military, Security and Police (MSP) network grew to include coordinators in over 60 countries worldwide. This was matched by a significant increase in campaigning and research undertaken by AI and partner NGOs. Such MSP campaigning and research has become a key focus of AI's work in increasing the pressure on those directly responsible for human rights violations and highlighting the responsibility of supplier governments.

International advocacy and campaigning actions were produced and carried out on a wide range of AI's concerns on MSP issues. This included the international trade in weapons, equipment and training fuelling the conflict in the Democratic Republic of the Congo, and calls for tougher controls on brokers and greater transparency in MSP export legislation. An action on MSP was produced as part of the program of action on Saudi Arabia.

During 2000, AI activists around the world campaigned with great skill and commitment on a range of MSP issues. During the French Presidency of the European Union, the French World Cup-winning football team called for tough small arms controls, gaining wide media coverage and raising the profile of the debate in France. This was followed by an international conference on small arms at the French Senate, attended by government and civil society representatives from across Europe and West Africa. In Italy the launch of the campaign on small arms engaged decision makers and journalists, and generated mass popular support. South Africa saw the first ever Africa Youth Camp attended by young people from over 25 nations focusing on MSP issues. In the USA, the call for the government to halt transfers of attack helicopters to Israel during the recent conflict had a significant impact on institutional and public opinion, and in the UK the joint AI/Oxfam "tough arms controls" campaign gained the support of top politicians, trade unionists and the public leading to the government proposing new legislation.

AI's crisis work in Sierra Leone and in Israel and the Occupied Territories had a strong focus on MSP issues. During the response to the Sierra Leone crisis, the AI movement campaigned to end continuing military assistance to rebel forces, including by calling for effective controls on arms brokers and an end to the illicit trade in diamonds from Sierra Leone. Linking the sale of conflict diamonds to the flow of weapons into Sierra Leone was a successful issue, stimulating excellent AI activity around the world including in Belgium, Côte d'Ivoire, Israel and the USA. In December AI called for determined action to halt the arms-for-diamonds trade following the publication of the results of a UN investigation.

Companies

More than 20 AI sections worked on approaches to companies in 2000. Training seminars were held in London and New York for AI activists which discussed practical ways in which AI can influence corporate behaviour. AI business groups continued to develop their contacts with companies based in their countries through discussions, smaller bilateral meetings, and direct talks with companies active in countries facing human rights crises. In meetings with officials of the diamond industry during the Sierra Leone crisis AI stressed the importance of effective international regulation of the diamond trade in ending human rights abuses. The organization also made representations to the diplomatic community and the UN.

As part of its ongoing work, AI promoted the responsibility of companies to adhere to human rights principles. AI also participated in discussions to develop practical components of the Global Compact, an initiative of the Office of the UN Secretary-General. AI representatives spoke at national and international conferences on issues related to corporate conduct, reporting of business activities, and human rights.

As part of the campaign on Saudi Arabia, AI issued a booklet, *Saudi Arabia: Open for business* (AI Index: MDE 23/082/2000). This presented an overview of the Saudi Arabian business world and demonstrated how companies can apply internationally recognized standards on human rights despite difficult operating environments. The business community received it with considerable interest.

Human rights education

AI structures around the world continued to reflect the importance of human rights education (HRE) by implementing a varied range of innovative and effective programs.

In many countries, AI leads the way in lobbying for human rights to be included in the curriculum for primary, secondary and tertiary education. In some cases this is successful, but there are still too many governments in all regions who are unwilling to make the commitment to officially integrate education on human rights into curricula.

A number of AI sections integrated human rights education into their plans for the campaign against torture. For example, AI Belgium, AI Italy and AI Spain worked with schools on developing projects and materials. AI Canada produced materials for youth and students and AI Ecuador organized a schools painting competition on the theme "Stop Torture". AI Mongolia targeted the training of law enforcement personnel and held seminars specifically on torture. AI Nepal initiated a range of activities aimed at children including a regular children's column in the section's newsletter. AI developed a package of materials that teachers can adapt for use in schools.

An HRE strategy is being followed in Africa that demonstrates the long-term planning needed for sustainable HRE programs. The strategy first aims to develop the skills and knowledge required to plan, manage and implement HRE programs. Regional workshops conducted for Côte d'Ivoire, Senegal and Togo as well as for Ghana, Gambia, Nigeria and Sierra Leone have covered such topics as strategic planning, interactive methodologies, evaluation and fundraising. These will be followed up on a national basis with more specific capacity-building programs and the implementation of planned HRE programs.

A small workshop for section activists was held in London to discuss the role HRE can play in developing a better understanding of women's rights. The workshop identified that including women's rights in HRE programs can play a major role in strengthening AI structures. AI Morocco has developed strong links with a number of NGOs that work for women's rights and will include them as target groups in their HRE program.

AI representatives attended the UN Decade of Human Rights Education mid-term review in Geneva. They supported the recommendations that ask countries to reaffirm their commitment to HRE by developing and implementing national HRE strategies and committees and providing more resources and initiatives for HRE structures and programs. The review identified that there were too many *ad hoc* activities and not sufficient attention given to a long-term approach that can ensure human rights are integrated into all parts of society.

Refugees

AI continued to campaign and take action on behalf of asylum-seekers and refugees at risk of being forcibly returned to countries where they might face human rights violations. AI sections and structures across the world provided decision-makers and asylum-seekers with information about human rights abuses in countries of origin, and also took action to try to stop the forcible return of hundreds of individual refugees.

AI Canada intervened with the Canadian Minister of Citizenship and Immigration to prevent the deportation of several Libyans whose asylum claims were not successful, fearing that they would be at serious risk of human rights violations after return. In November, two Egyptian families were granted refugee status in Germany after AI had issued a worldwide public appeal; their initial asylum applications had been rejected as manifestly unfounded in an accelerated procedure. Other appeals issued included the forcible return of Libyans from Jordan, and the ill-treatment and forcible return from Lebanon of Sudanese asylum-seekers and refugees.

AI continued its work to ensure that states fulfil their obligations under international law and scrupulously observe the principle of *non-refoulement* by not closing their borders in situations of mass influx of refugees. AI continued to stress this principle in international forums in connection with the evaluation of the response to the Kosovo crisis in 1999. The same concerns were also reiterated in connection with the closure of the border with Sierra Leone by Guinea and the closure of borders with Afghanistan by Tajikistan and Pakistan.

AI urged that countries still hosting Bosnian refugees observe voluntary repatriation standards, and that those Bosnian refugees who cannot yet exercise their right to return in safety and with dignity to their homes in eastern Republika Srpska should not be forcibly returned to other parts of Bosnia-Herzegovina.

AI also continued to campaign and lobby against restrictive legislative and other measures which would deny asylum-seekers and refugees access to fair and satisfactory asylum procedures. On a regional level, AI participated in the joint UN High Commissioner for Refugees (UNHCR) and Organization of African Unity (OAU) meeting of Government and Non-Government Technical Experts on the 30th Anniversary of the 1969 OAU Convention on the Specific Aspects of Refugee Problems in Africa. This resulted in a Platform for Action which provides further guidance to governments in the region hosting refugees. AI's European Union (EU) Association commented on EU proposals on "temporary protection", minimum standards for asylum procedures, revision of the Dublin Convention (which currently decides which member state is responsible for considering an application for asylum), reception conditions and carrier sanctions which fall short of international refugee and human rights law and standards. AI's EU Association also successfully campaigned for the inclusion of a provision on the right to asylum and prohibition of *refoulement* and collective expulsion in the non-binding Charter of Fundamental Rights of the European Union which was endorsed at the EU summit in Nice in December.

Numerous initiatives were taken by AI sections. AI Senegal raised concerns about the quality of decision-making in the National Refugee Commission, the decision-making authority for asylum claims. AI Ghana worked to ensure the rights of refugees from various African countries who had sought protection in Ghana. They had arrived in Ghana claiming that they had been denied effective refugee protection in Burkina Faso. AI Australia reacted against the Australian government's claims that victims of specific forms of gender-based persecution (such as "honour" killings and trafficking) were not deserving of protection under the UN Refugee Convention. AI Sweden successfully participated in a campaign together with other NGOs against a Swedish government proposal on the establishment of a new temporary protection regime in situations of mass flight which would effectively deprive refugees of rights they otherwise would be guaranteed under Swedish law. The proposal was withdrawn before it was voted on in parliament. AI Ireland voiced its concerns about the coming into force of the Irish Refugee Act 1996, mainly on issues of shortcomings in provisions on detention, accelerated procedures, and the short time limits within which representations can be made on behalf of asylum-seekers.

INTERNATIONAL AND REGIONAL ORGANIZATIONS

Intergovernmental organizations play an important role in the protection and promotion of human rights worldwide. Throughout 2000, AI continued its efforts to further its human rights work by seeking to influence international and regional organizations both in terms of campaigning against ongoing human rights abuses and in promoting international standards for the protection of human rights. Below are some of the highlights of AI's work with these organizations.

UN Headquarters, New York

AI continued to encourage the **Security Council** to consider the human rights situation of countries they were deliberating as well as the impact of armed conflict on specific groups of people, such as women, children, refugees and the internally displaced. Where the UN has established peace-keeping operations, such as in Kosovo, Sierra Leone and East Timor, AI called for the Security Council to ensure that all UN personnel involved be adequately trained in human rights standards and that there be a system for holding peace-keeping troops accountable for any human rights violations committed, including a complaints mechanism. In the case of East Timor, where the UN is the *de facto* government and custodian of the human rights of the citizens, AI reviewed the role of the United Nations Transitional Authority for East Timor (UNTAET), making specific recommendations in the areas of the creation of a human rights culture; ending impunity and assisting reconciliation; creating human rights institutions; and enacting legislation and mechanisms for the protection of the rights of women, children and minority groups (see *East Timor: Building a new country based on human rights*, AI Index: ASA 57/005/2000). In the case of Sierra Leone, AI provided a detailed analysis of the draft statute of the Special Court for Sierra Leone and encouraged the Council to ensure that the jurisdiction of the Court and the provisions of its statute would enable it to be a just, fair and effective tool towards ending impunity in Sierra Leone (see *Sierra Leone: Recommendations on the draft statute of the Special Court*, AI Index: AFR 51/083/2000).

Working with other non-governmental organizations (NGOs) and in collaboration with the United Nations Development Fund for Women (UNIFEM), AI urged the Security Council to address the impact of armed conflict on women and the fact that women are not adequately represented in decision-making on negotiating, building or consolidating peace. In October 2000, under the Presidency of Namibia, the Security Council held a debate on **women and peace and security** and was briefed by women and NGOs. Following these discussions, the Security Council unanimously adopted an historic resolution that reaffirmed the important role of women in conflict resolution and peace-building, emphasized the need for a gender-sensitive approach to peace-keeping and invited the UN Secretary-General to report on these matters.

AI participated in the **UN Special Session "Women 2000: Gender Equality, Development and Peace for the 21st Century"** (the Beijing plus Five Review). AI lobbied to ensure that there would be no going back on what had been achieved in the Beijing Declaration and Program of Action, particularly on women's human rights. In addition, AI lobbied strongly for the Outcome Document of the plus Five Review to reflect important developments on women's rights, such as the adoption of the Optional Protocol to the Convention on the Elimination of All Forms of Discrimination against Women; the inclusion in the Rome Statute of the International Criminal Court of all forms of sexual violence as a war crime and, in certain instances, as a crime against humanity or genocide; and the need for governments to make new commitments regarding the responsibility of the state for particular issues, such as "honour crimes" and abuses by non-state actors. To coincide with the plus Five Review, AI published a report, *Respect, protect, fulfil women's human rights: State responsibility for abuses by "non-state actors"* (AI Index: IOR 30/002/2000).

As part of AI's ongoing work to abolish the death penalty, and with the cooperation of the UN Staff Union, AI arranged for the premier screening of *The Hurricane* in the UN General Assembly Hall. The film illustrates how racism can infect criminal trials, an issue of major relevance in the USA where, for example, race, ethnic origin and economic status appear to be key determinants in who will receive a death sentence and who will not. In December 2000, UN Secretary-General Kofi Annan received a petition of more than three million signatures from all over the world calling for a universal moratorium on the death penalty from representatives of AI, Moratorium 2000 and the Sant'Egidio Community.

UN Geneva

In 1998 the Commission on Human Rights initiated a **review of its thematic and country specific special procedures** with a view to enhancing the effectiveness of those mechanisms. An inter-sessional working group established by the Commission produced a report which was adopted by the Commission in April 2000 but which failed to address adequately the serious problems faced by these bodies. While the number of new mandates created by the Commission has risen by over a third since 1995, resources from the UN regular budget have shrunk and consequently the UN servicing of these mandates has diminished. AI urged the Commission to call upon all states to extend open invitations to the UN special mechanisms, to schedule more time for discussion and follow-up of reports from the special procedures and their recommendations, and to urge member states attending the General Assembly to vote for the necessary funds from the regular budget.

As part of its work in relation to UN **thematic mechanisms,** AI briefed the Special Rapporteur on

INTERNATIONAL AND REGIONAL ORGANIZATIONS

torture prior to his visit to Brazil and the Special Rapporteur on extrajudicial, summary or arbitrary executions in preparation for a possible visit to the Occupied Palestinian Territories. In cooperation with the Law Society of England and Wales, AI produced a document entitled *The United Nations Thematic Mechanisms – Update 2000: An overview of their work and mandates* (AI Index: IOR 40/020/2000), available in English, French, Spanish, Arabic and Turkish. During the annual meeting of the Commission on Human Rights mechanisms dealing with specific themes or countries, AI encouraged the systematic inclusion of an in-depth analysis of states' performances as well as an assessment of governments' responses in the reports of the mechanisms to the Commission. AI also expressed concern that the limits placed on the length of reports presented to the Commission could result in less satisfactory reports.

At the fifth special session of the Commission on Human Rights concerning the human rights situation in Israel and the Occupied Territories, AI called for the creation of a **standing body of international investigators**. Experiences in Algeria, East Timor, Togo, and most recently the Occupied Territories demonstrate that the UN is ill-equipped to investigate complex human rights violations. Members of the standing body would have proven expertise in international criminal justice and in conducting criminal investigations, including forensic science and ballistics. These highly qualified professionals would be selected by the UN Secretary-General on the basis of nominations from member states or sought out by the Secretary-General. They would undertake to be available for a fixed period of time to form rapid response investigative teams when required. To ensure independence and impartiality, no member of a team would be a national of the country or territory under investigation. The UN would provide training to the experts in international human rights and humanitarian law.

Against a backdrop of initiatives from Australia and the United Kingdom to restrict refugee protection, the UN High Commissioner for Refugees (UNHCR) launched a **Global Consultation on International Refugee Protection**. The consultation, which coincided with the 50th Anniversary of the 1951 Convention relating to the Status of Refugees, is intended to clarify the scope of refugee protection, but AI fears that it might go beyond the UNHCR mandate to protect refugees, as governments seek out new ways to manage migration flows. AI called on the UNHCR and governments to allow NGOs full participation in the process and not to deviate from the issue of refugee protection.

In September 2000, AI sent an **Open Letter to Australian Prime Minister John Howard**, after his government's threat to review its cooperation with the UN treaty bodies and only to cooperate with UN thematic special rapporteurs and working groups if there are "compelling reasons to do so". In the letter, AI stated that the measures announced would undermine the UN human rights protection machinery and set a bad example for other countries that wish to avoid international scrutiny of their human rights record. AI called on the Prime Minister to abide by treaty obligations to extend full cooperation to the UN thematic and other human rights experts wishing to visit Australia. AI continues to monitor initiatives by states to "rationalize" the treaty-body system.

As in previous years, AI sent a representative to observe the Committee on the Application of Standards of the **International Labour Conference** on governments' effective implementation of international labour standards. AI raised concerns about the situation in Myanmar under the International Labour Organisation Convention 29 on forced labour; in Pakistan under Convention 105 on the abolition of forced labour; and in Colombia and Swaziland under Convention 87 on freedom of association and protection of the right to organize.

Regional intergovernmental organizations

AI made recommendations to the **Organization of African Unity** (OAU) on the establishment of the African Committee of Experts on the Rights and Welfare of the Child. In particular, AI called for the full integration of the work of this Committee into the OAU and urged member states to nominate independent experts for election to the Committee. AI continues to campaign for OAU member states to ratify the African Charter on the Rights and Welfare of the Child, which came into force on 29 November 1999. At the sessions of the **African Commission on Human and Peoples' Rights**, AI raised concerns about the human rights situation in Zimbabwe and human rights defenders in Africa.

Throughout the year, AI sought to influence the **European Union** (EU) to act more vigorously and coherently to implement its growing human rights mandate. Through the Brussels office of its EU Association, AI provided information to the Council, the Commission and the European Parliament on the many countries with which the EU has relations. In doing so, AI consistently urged that more substance be given to the human rights clause that constitutes an "essential element" of the agreements the EU concludes with other countries.

AI issued numerous appeals and briefings in efforts to influence the EU **Common Foreign and Security Policy**. AI made special efforts in connection with certain priority countries, including lobbying the EU institutions in Brussels and in the member states' capitals through the AI sections. Some of those countries featured prominently in the EU joint positioning at the 2000 session of the UN Commission on Human Rights – notably Chechnya, subject of an EU-initiated resolution, and China with which the EU is conducting a special human rights dialogue, of which AI has been increasingly critical. AI also submitted information on human rights in the countries in Central and Eastern Europe and the Mediterranean, including Turkey, that are candidates to join the EU.

AI drew attention to human rights abuses within EU member states, especially torture and ill-treatment, and called for monitoring and accountability at national and EU level. In proposals made at the start of AI's campaign against torture in October, the EU was urged to declare the eradication and prevention of

INTERNATIONAL AND REGIONAL ORGANIZATIONS

torture a key objective of EU human rights policy. AI's suggestion that guidelines on torture be developed for use in relations with non-EU countries (modelled on those the EU had operated successfully on the death penalty since 1998) met with positive interest.

The **European Charter of Fundamental Rights** adopted at the Nice summit in December 2000 prompted AI to reiterate its call for the EU to accede to international human rights treaties, including the European Convention on Human Rights.

An important focus for AI's work at the EU were the comprehensive memoranda drawn up by the respective AI sections and AI's Brussels office and submitted to the incoming presidency government. In 2000 AI thus addressed the Portuguese and French presidencies, and prepared for the 2001 presidencies by Sweden and Belgium.

AI ensured a high profile for the campaign against torture at the Warsaw Human Dimension Implementation Meeting of the **Organization for Security and Co-operation in Europe** (OSCE) on "Human Rights and Inhuman Treatment or Punishment" in March. In addition to presenting a statement to the meeting on AI's concerns about torture and ill-treatment in Europe today, the organization held a special interest meeting to introduce the new global campaign to interested members of government delegations and NGO representatives.

AI also undertook training on international standards for fair trial for OSCE trial monitors in Kosovo and distributed AI's *Fair trials manual* (AI Index: POL 30/002/1998). To mark the 50th anniversary of the European Convention on Human Rights, AI published a report and launched an action on the issue of impunity for torture and ill-treatment in member states of the **Council of Europe**. An AI representative attended the Council of Europe intergovernmental conference in Rome. AI also attended a meeting of international human rights NGOs with the Council of Europe Commissioner of Human Rights in Paris.

AI, in cooperation with other NGOs, continued to encourage the Inter-American Commission on Human Rights to develop its work on human rights defenders, including carrying out a close study of their situation. At the General Assembly of the **Organization of American States**, NGOs pushed for the adoption of a stronger resolution on human rights defenders, for action on the use of child soldiers and the situation in Peru, and for public support for the creation of the International Criminal Court (ICC). In the context of discussions on strengthening the inter-American system for human rights, AI continued to raise concerns on retrograde steps taken by Trinidad and Tobago and Peru, and encouraged states to show their commitment to upholding human rights by ratifying the regional standards.

Developing international human rights law

AI was active in the negotiations on the **Optional Protocol to the Convention on the Rights of the Child on the involvement of children in armed conflict** to raise to 18 years the age at which children can be recruited into armed forces or groups and participate in hostilities. A founder member of the International Coalition to Stop the Use of Child Soldiers, AI worked closely with Coalition partners in campaigning and lobbying activities to strengthen articles during the drafting of the Protocol. In May 2000, the Protocol was adopted by the UN General Assembly. AI is campaigning for a minimum of 100 signatures and 50 ratifications of the Protocol by the UN General Assembly Special Session on Children in September 2001.

AI continued to participate in the elaboration of other international standards, including the draft optional protocol to the Convention against Torture and Other Cruel, Inhuman or Degrading Treatment or Punishment and the draft international convention on "disappearances".

International Criminal Court

AI continued its work as one of more than 1,000 NGO members of the Coalition for an International Criminal Court, campaigning for states to sign and ratify the Rome Statute of the International Criminal Court and enact effective implementing legislation. The ICC will be established after 60 states have ratified the Rome Statute. There were 27 ratifications and 139 signatures at the end of the year.

All AI sections and non-section structures have been requested, as a priority, to lobby their own governments and governments in other countries to ratify the Rome Statute. To this end, AI produced an ICC "ratification kit" which provides advice on lobbying, model letters and draft press releases as well as a series of fact sheets containing summaries and explanations of important aspects of the ICC and a "Checklist for effective implementation". The fact sheets cover such topics as prosecuting crimes against humanity, ensuring justice for women, and fair trial guarantees.

As part of its continued work to establish a just, fair and effective ICC, AI participated in all sessions of the Preparatory Commissions for the International Criminal Court and lobbied government delegations to draft effective Rules of Procedure and Evidence as well as the Elements of Crimes, a supplementary instrument designed to aid the Court in interpreting the Statute.

Selected AI reports

- The United Nations Thematic Mechanisms – Update 2000: An overview of their work and mandates (AI Index: IOR 40/020/2000)
- 2001 UN Commission on Human Rights: Bridging the gap between rights and realities (AI Index: IOR 41/014/2000)
- Respect, protect, fulfil – Women's human rights: State responsibility for abuses by 'non-state actors' (AI Index: IOR 50/001/2000)
- Child Soldiers: Criminals or victims? (AI Index: IOR 50/002/2000)
- Sierra Leone: Recommendations on the draft Statute of the Special Court (AI Index: AFR 51/083/2000)
- International Criminal Court: Checklist for effective implementation (AI Index: IOR 40/011/2000)
- Ratification Kit: Lobbying for effective ratification of the Rome Statute of the International Criminal Court (Available as a ratification kit)

INTERNATIONAL AND REGIONAL ORGANIZATIONS

Rome Statute of the International Criminal Court

As at 1 January 2001, 139 states had signed the Rome Statute of the International Criminal Court and 27 of them had ratified it. On 31 December 2000, the deadline for signing the Statute expired. States which had not signed the Statute by that date will have to accede to the Statute in a single step.
*Indicates ratifications or signatures that took place in 2000.

Countries that have signed and ratified

Austria*
Belgium*
Belize*
Botswana*
Canada*
Fiji
Finland*
France*
Gabon*
Germany*
Ghana
Iceland*
Italy
Lesotho*
Luxembourg*
Mali*
Marshall Islands*
New Zealand*
Norway*
San Marino
Senegal
Sierra Leone*
South Africa*
Spain*
Tajikistan*
Trinidad and Tobago
Venezuela*

Countries that have signed

Albania
Algeria*
Andorra
Angola
Antigua and Barbuda
Argentina
Armenia
Australia
Bahamas*
Bahrain*
Bangladesh
Barbados*
Benin
Bolivia
Bosnia and Herzegovina*
Brazil*
Bulgaria
Burkina Faso
Burundi
Cambodia*
Cameroon
Cape Verde*
Central African Republic
Chad
Chile
Colombia
Comoros*
Congo (Republic of the)
Congo (Democratic Republic of the)*
Costa Rica
Côte d'Ivoire
Croatia
Cyprus
Czech Republic
Denmark
Djibouti
Dominican Republic*
Ecuador
Egypt*
Eritrea
Estonia
Gambia
Georgia
Greece
Guinea*
Guinea-Bissau*
Guyana*
Haiti
Honduras
Hungary
Iran*
Ireland
Israel*
Jamaica*
Jordan
Kenya
Korea (Republic of)*
Kuwait*
Kyrgyzstan
Latvia
Liberia
Liechtenstein
Lithuania
Macedonia (Former Yugoslav Republic of)
Madagascar
Malawi
Malta
Mauritius
Mexico*
Moldova*
Monaco
Mongolia*
Morocco*
Mozambique*
Namibia
Nauru*
Netherlands
Niger
Nigeria*
Oman
Panama
Paraguay
Peru*
Philippines*
Poland
Portugal
Romania
Russian Federation*
St Lucia
Samoa
Sao Tome and Principe*
Seychelles*
Slovakia
Slovenia
Solomon Islands
Sudan*
Sweden
Switzerland
Syria*
Tanzania*
Thailand*
Uganda
Ukraine*
United Arab Emirates*
United Kingdom
United States of America*
Uruguay*
Uzbekistan*
Yemen*
Yugoslavia (Federal Republic of)*
Zambia
Zimbabwe

INTERNATIONAL AND REGIONAL ORGANIZATIONS

Optional Protocol to the Convention on the Rights of the Child on the involvement of children in armed conflict

The Optional Protocol to the Convention on the Rights of the Child (UN Children's Convention) requires 10 ratifications to enter into force. By the end of 2000, 75 states had signed the Protocol and three of them had ratified it. (All signatures and ratifications took place in 2000.) This information is taken from: www.untreaty.un.org.

Ratifications
Bangladesh
Canada
Sri Lanka

Signatures
Andorra
Argentina
Austria
Azerbaijan
Belgium
Belize
Bosnia and Herzegovina
Brazil
Cambodia
Colombia
Congo (Democratic Republic of the)
Costa Rica
Cuba
Czech Republic
Denmark
Ecuador
El Salvador
Finland
France
Gabon
Gambia
Germany
Greece
Guatemala
Guinea-Bissau
Holy See
Iceland
Ireland
Italy
Jamaica
Jordan
Kazakstan
Kenya
Korea (Republic of)
Lesotho
Liechtenstein
Luxembourg
Madagascar
Malawi
Mali
Malta
Mexico
Monaco
Morocco
Namibia
Nauru
Nepal
Netherlands
New Zealand
Nigeria
Norway
Panama
Paraguay
Peru
Philippines
Portugal
Romania
San Marino
Senegal
Sierra Leone
Singapore
Slovenia
Spain
Sweden
Switzerland
Turkey
Ukraine
United Kingdom
United States of America
Uruguay
Venezuela
Viet Nam

Optional Protocol to the Convention on the Elimination of All Forms of Discrimination against Women

The Optional Protocol to the Convention on the Elimination of All Forms of Discrimination against Women (UN Women's Convention) entered into force on 22 December 2000. By the end of 2000, 13 states had ratified, two had acceded to it, and another 50 had signed it. This information is taken from www.untreaty.un.org. * Indicates ratifications, accessions or signatures that took place 2000.

Ratifications/ Accessions
Austria*
Bangladesh*
Bolivia*
Denmark*
Finland*
France*
Hungary (accession)*
Ireland*
Italy*
Mali (accession)*
Namibia*
New Zealand*
Senegal*
Slovakia*
Thailand*

Signatures
Argentina*
Azerbaijan*
Belgium
Benin*
Bosnia and Herzegovina*
Bulgaria*
Chile
Colombia
Costa Rica
Croatia*
Cuba*
Czech Republic
Dominican Republic*
Ecuador
Germany
Ghana*
Greece
Guatemala*
Guinea-Bissau*
Iceland
Indonesia*
Kazakstan*
Lesotho*
Liechtenstein
Lithuania*
Luxembourg
Macedonia (Former Yugoslav Republic of)*
Madagascar*
Malawi*
Mexico
Mongolia*
Netherlands
Nigeria*
Norway
Panama*
Paraguay
Peru*
Philippines*
Portugal*
Romania*
Sao Tome and Principe*
Sierra Leone*
Slovenia
Spain*
Sweden
Tajikistan*
Turkey*
Ukraine*
Uruguay*
Venezuela*

Selected international human rights treaties
(AT 31 DECEMBER 2000)

States which have ratified or acceded to a convention are party to the treaty and are bound to observe its provisions. States which have signed but not yet ratified have expressed their intention to become a party at some future date; meanwhile they are obliged to refrain from acts which would defeat the object and purpose of the treaty.

The **UN Convention on the Rights of the Child** has been ratified by all UN member states with the exceptions of Somalia (which has no functioning government) and the United States of America.

- ● became a state party in 2000
- ○ state is a party
- ◗ signed in 2000
- D signed but not yet ratified
- 22 Countries making a declaration under Article 22 recognize the competence of the Committee against Torture to consider individual complaints
- 28 Countries making a reservation under Article 28 do not recognize the competence of the Committee against Torture to undertake confidential inquiries into allegations of systematic torture if warranted

	International Covenant on Civil and Political Rights (ICCPR)	(first) Optional Protocol to the ICCPR	Second Optional Protocol to the ICCPR, aiming at the abolition of the death penalty	International Covenant on Economic, Social and Cultural Rights	Convention on the Elimination of All Forms of Discrimination against Women	International Convention on the Elimination of All Forms of Racial Discrimination	Convention relating to the Status of Refugees (1951)	Protocol relating to the Status of Refugees	Convention against Torture and Other Cruel, Inhuman or Degrading Treatment or Punishment
Afghanistan	○			○	D	○			○ 28
Albania	○			○	○	○	○	○	○
Algeria	○	○		○	○	○	○	○	22 ○
Andorra					○				
Angola	○	○		○	○		○	○	
Antigua and Barbuda					○	○	○	○	○
Argentina	○	○		○	○	○	○	○	22 ○
Armenia	○	○		○	○	○	○	○	○
Australia	○	○	○	○	○	○	○	○	22 ○
Austria	○	○	○	○	○	○	○	○	22 ○
Azerbaijan	○		○	○	○	○	○	○	○
Bahamas					○	○	○	○	
Bahrain						○			○
Bangladesh	●			○	○	○			○
Barbados	○	○		○	○	○			
Belarus	○	○		○	○	○			○ 28
Belgium	○	○	○	○	○	○	○	○	22 ○
Belize	○			◗	○	◗	○	○	○
Benin	○	○		○	○	D	○	○	○
Bhutan					○	D			
Bolivia	○	○		○	○	○	○	○	○
Bosnia and Herzegovina	○	○	◗	○	○	○	○	○	○
Botswana	●				○	○	○	○	●
Brazil	○			○	○	○	○	○	○
Brunei Darussalam									
Bulgaria	○	○	○	○	○	○	○	○	22 ○
Burkina Faso	○	○		○	○	○	○	○	○
Burundi	○			○	○	○	○	○	○
Cambodia	○			○	○	○	○	○	○
Cameroon	○	○		○	○	○	○	○	22 ○
Canada	○	○		○	○	○	○	○	22 ○
Cape Verde	○	●	●	○	○	○			○
Central African Republic	○	○		○	○	○	○	○	
Chad	○	○		○	○	○	○	○	○
Chile	○	○		○	○	○	○	○	○
China	D			D	○	○	○	○	○ 28
Colombia	○	○	○	○	○	○	○	○	○
Comoros					○	◗			◗
Congo (Democratic Republic of the)	○	○		○	○	○	○	○	○
Congo (Republic of the)	○	○		○	○	D	○	○	
Costa Rica	○	○	○	○	○	○	○	○	○
Côte d' Ivoire	○	○		○	○	○	○	○	○

Amnesty International Report 2001

SELECTED INTERNATIONAL HUMAN RIGHTS TREATIES

	International Covenant on Civil and Political Rights (ICCPR)	(first) Optional Protocol to the ICCPR	Second Optional Protocol to the ICCPR, aiming at the abolition of the death penalty	International Covenant on Economic, Social and Cultural Rights	Convention on the Elimination of All Forms of Discrimination against Women	International Convention on the Elimination of All Forms of Racial Discrimination	Convention relating to the Status of Refugees (1951)	Protocol relating to the Status of Refugees	Convention against Torture and Other Cruel, Inhuman or Degrading Treatment or Punishment
Croatia	○	○	○	○	○	○	○	○	22 ○
Cuba					○	○			○
Cyprus	○	○	○	○	○	○	○	○	22 ○
Czech Republic	○	○		○	○	○	○	○	22 ○
Denmark	○	○	○	○	○	○	○	○	22 ○
Djibouti					○	○	○	○	
Dominica	○			○	○		○	○	
Dominican Republic	○	○		○	○	○	○	○	D
Ecuador	○	○	○	○	○	○	○	○	22 ○
Egypt	○			○	○	○	○	○	○
El Salvador	○	○		○	○	○	○	○	○
Equatorial Guinea	○	○		○	○	○			
Eritrea					○				
Estonia	○			○	○	○	○	○	○
Ethiopia	○			○	○	○	○	○	○
Fiji					○	○	○	○	
Finland	○	○	○	○	○	○	○	○	22 ○
France	○	○		○	○	○	○	○	22 ○
Gabon	○			○	○	○	○	○	●
Gambia	○	○		○	○	○	○	○	D
Georgia	○	○		○	○	○	○	○	○
Germany	○	○	○	○	○	○	○	○	○
Ghana	●	●		●	○	○	○	○	22 ●
Greece	○	○	○	○	○	○	○	○	22 ○
Grenada	○			○	○	D			
Guatemala	○	●		○	○	○	○	○	○
Guinea	○	○		○	○	○	○	○	○
Guinea-Bissau	▶	▶	▶	○	○	▶	○	○	▶
Guyana	○	○		○	○	○			○
Haiti	○				○	○	○	○	
Holy See							○	○	○
Honduras	○	D	D	○	○		○	○	○
Hungary	○	○	○	○	○	○	○	○	22 ○
Iceland	○	○	○	○	○	○	○	○	22 ○
India	○			○	○	○			D
Indonesia					○	○			○
Iran (Islamic Republic of)	○			○		○	○	○	
Iraq	○			○	○	○			
Ireland	○	○	○	○	○	●	○	○	D
Israel	○			○	○	○	○	○	○ 28
Italy	○	○	○	○	○	○	○	○	22 ○
Jamaica	○	○		○	○	○	○	○	
Japan	○			○	○	○	○	○	○
Jordan	○			○	○	○			○
Kazakhstan					○	○			○
Kenya	○			○	○		○	○	○
Kiribati									
Korea (Democratic People's Republic of)	○			○					
Korea (Republic of)	○	○		○	○	○	○	○	○
Kuwait	○			○	○	○			○ 28
Kyrgyzstan	○	○		○	○	○			○
Lao People's Democratic Republic	▶			▶	○	○			

● became a state party in 2000
○ state is a party
▶ signed in 2000
D signed but not yet ratified
22 Countries making a declaration under Article 22 recognize the competence of the Committee against Torture to consider individual complaints
28 Countries making a reservation under Article 28 do not recognize the competence of the Committee against Torture to undertake confidential inquiries into allegations of systematic torture if warranted

Amnesty International Report 2001

SELECTED INTERNATIONAL HUMAN RIGHTS TREATIES

Legend		
●	became a state party in 2000	
○	state is a party	
▶	signed in 2000	
D	signed but not yet ratified	
22	Countries making a declaration under Article 22 recognize the competence of the Committee against Torture to consider individual complaints	
28	Countries making a reservation under Article 28 do not recognize the competence of the Committee against Torture to undertake confidential inquiries into allegations of systematic torture if warranted	

Country	International Covenant on Civil and Political Rights (ICCPR)	(first) Optional Protocol to the ICCPR	Second Optional Protocol to the ICCPR, aiming at the abolition of the death penalty	International Covenant on Economic, Social and Cultural Rights	Convention on the Elimination of All Forms of Discrimination against Women	International Convention on the Elimination of All Forms of Racial Discrimination	Convention relating to the Status of Refugees (1951)	Protocol relating to the Status of Refugees	Convention against Torture and Other Cruel, Inhuman or Degrading Treatment or Punishment
Latvia	○	○		○	○	○	○	○	○
Lebanon	○			○	○	○			●
Lesotho	○	●		○	○	○	○	○	
Liberia	D			D	○	○	○	○	
Libyan Arab Jamahiriya	○	○		○	○	○			○
Liechtenstein	○	○	○	○	○	●	○	○	22 ○
Lithuania	○	○	▶	○	○	○	○	○	
Luxembourg	○	○	○	○	○	○	○	○	22 ○
Macedonia (former Yugoslav Republic of)	○	○	○	○	○	○	○	○	○
Madagascar	○	○		○	○	○	○	○	
Malawi	○	○		○	○	○	○	○	○
Malaysia					○				
Maldives					○	○			
Mali	○			○	○	○	○	○	○
Malta	○	○	○	○	○	○	○	○	22 ○
Marshall Islands									
Mauritania					○	○	○		
Mauritius	○	○		○	○	○			○
Mexico	○			○	○	○	●	●	○
Micronesia (Federated States of)									
Moldova	○			○	○	○			○
Monaco	○		●	○	○	○	○		22 ○
Mongolia	○	○		○	○	○			
Morocco	○			○	○	○	○	○	○ 28
Mozambique	○		○		○	○	○	○	○
Myanmar					○				
Namibia	○	○	○	○	○	○	○		○
Nauru									
Nepal	○	○		○	○	○			○
Netherlands	○	○	○	○	○	○	○	○	22 ○
New Zealand	○	○	○	○	○	○	○	○	22 ○
Nicaragua	○	○	D	○	○	○	○	○	D
Niger	○	○		○	○	○	○	○	
Nigeria	○			○	○	○	○	○	D
Norway	○	○	○	○	○	○	○	○	22 ○
Oman									
Pakistan					○	○			
Palau									
Panama	○	○	○	○	○	○	○	○	○
Papua New Guinea					○	○	○	○	
Paraguay	○	○		○	○	▶			○
Peru	○	○		○	○	○	○	○	○
Philippines	○	○		○	○	○			○
Poland	○	○	▶	○	○	○	○	○	22 ○ 28
Portugal	○	○	○	○	○	○	○	○	22 ○
Qatar						○			●
Romania	○	○	○	○	○	○	○	○	○
Russian Federation	○	○		○	○	○	○	○	22 ○
Rwanda	○			○	○	○	○	○	
Saint Kitts and Nevis					○				
Saint Lucia					○	○			
Saint Vincent and the Grenadines	○	○		○	○	○	○		

Amnesty International Report 2001

SELECTED INTERNATIONAL HUMAN RIGHTS TREATIES

	International Covenant on Civil and Political Rights (ICCPR)	(first) Optional Protocol to the ICCPR	Second Optional Protocol to the ICCPR, aiming at the abolition of the death penalty	International Covenant on Economic, Social and Cultural Rights	Convention on the Elimination of All Forms of Discrimination against Women	International Convention on the Elimination of All Forms of Racial Discrimination	Convention relating to the Status of Refugees (1951)	Protocol relating to the Status of Refugees	Convention against Torture and Other Cruel, Inhuman or Degrading Treatment or Punishment
Samoa					○		○	○	
San Marino	○	○		○					
Sao Tome and Principe	D	▶	▶	D	○	▶	○	○	▶
Saudi Arabia					●	○			○[28]
Senegal	○	○		○	○	○	○	○	[22]○
Seychelles	○	○	○	○	○	○	○	○	○
Sierra Leone	○	○		○	○	D	○	○	D
Singapore					○				
Slovakia	○	○	○	○	○	○	○	○	[22]○
Slovenia	○	○	○	○	○	○	○	○	[22]○
Solomon Islands				○		○	○	○	
Somalia	○	○		○		○	○	○	○
South Africa	○			D	○	○	○	○	[22]○
Spain	○	○	○	○	○	○	○	○	[22]○
Sri Lanka	○	○		○	○	○			○
Sudan	○			○		○	○	○	D
Suriname	○	○		○	○	○	○	○	
Swaziland							○	●	○
Sweden	○	○	○	○	○	○	○	○	[22]○
Switzerland	○		○		○	○	○	○	[22]○
Syrian Arab Republic	○			○		○			
Tajikistan	○	○		○	○	○	○	○	○
Tanzania	○			○	○	○	○	○	
Thailand	○			○	○				
Togo	○	○		○	○	○	○	○	[22]○
Tonga						○			
Trinidad and Tobago	○	○		○	○	○	●	●	
Tunisia	○			○	○	D	○	○	[22]○
Turkey	▶			▶	○	D	○	○	[22]○
Turkmenistan	○	○	●	○	○	○	○	○	○
Tuvalu					○		○	○	
Uganda	○	○		○	○	○	○	○	○
Ukraine	○	○		○	○	○			○[28]
United Arab Emirates						○			
United Kingdom	○		○	○	○	○	○	○	○
United States of America	○			D	D	○		○	○
Uruguay	○	○	○	○	○	○	○	○	[22]○
Uzbekistan	○	○		○	○	○			○
Vanuatu					○				
Venezuela	○	○	○	○	○	○		○	[22]○
Viet Nam	○			○	○	○			
Yemen	○			○	○	○			○
Yugoslavia (Federal Republic of)	○	D		○	○	○	○	○	[22]○
Zambia	○	○		○	○	○	○	○	○
Zimbabwe	○			○	○	○	○	○	

● became a state party in 2000

○ state is a party

▶ signed in 2000

D signed but not yet ratified

[22] Countries making a declaration under Article 22 recognize the competence of the Committee against Torture to consider individual complaints

[28] Countries making a reservation under Article 28 do not recognize the competence of the Committee against Torture to undertake confidential inquiries into allegations of systematic torture if warranted

SELECTED REGIONAL HUMAN RIGHTS TREATIES

Selected regional human rights treaties
(AT 31 DECEMBER 2000)

Organization of African Unity (OAU)

States which have ratified or acceded to a convention are party to the treaty and are bound to observe its provisions. States which have signed but not yet ratified have expressed their intention to become a party at some future date; meanwhile they are obliged to refrain from acts which would defeat the object and purpose of the treaty.

This chart lists countries which were members of the OAU at the end of 2000.

- ● became a state party in 2000
- ○ state is a party
- ▶ signed in 2000
- D signed but not yet ratified

	African Charter on Human and Peoples' Rights (1981)	African Charter on the Rights and Welfare of the Child
Algeria	○	D
Angola	○	○
Benin	○	○
Botswana	○	
Burkina Faso	○	○
Burundi	○	
Cameroon	○	○
Cape Verde	○	○
Central African Republic	○	
Chad	○	●
Comoros	○	
Congo (Democratic Republic of the)	○	
Congo (Republic of the)	○	D
Côte d'Ivoire	○	
Djibouti	○	D
Egypt	○	D
Equatorial Guinea	○	
Eritrea	○	●
Ethiopia	○	
Gabon	○	D
Gambia	○	
Ghana	○	D
Guinea	○	●
Guinea-Bissau	○	
Kenya	○	●
Lesotho	○	○
Liberia	○	D
Libya	○	D
Madagascar	○	D
Malawi	○	○
Mali	○	○
Mauritania	○	
Mauritius	○	○
Mozambique	○	○
Namibia	○	D
Niger	○	○
Nigeria	○	
Rwanda	○	D
Sahrawi Arab Democratic Republic	○	D
Sao Tome and Principe	○	
Senegal	○	○

SELECTED REGIONAL HUMAN RIGHTS TREATIES

	African Charter on Human and Peoples' Rights (1981)	African Charter on the Rights and Welfare of the Child
Seychelles	○	○
Sierra Leone	○	D
Somalia	○	D
South Africa	○	●
Sudan	○	
Swaziland	○	D
Tanzania	○	D
Togo	○	○
Tunisia	○	D
Uganda	○	○
Zambia	○	D
Zimbabwe	○	○

● became a state party in 2000
○ state is a party
▶ signed in 2000
D signed but not yet ratified

SELECTED REGIONAL HUMAN RIGHTS TREATIES

Organization of American States (OAS)

States which have ratified or acceded to a convention are party to the treaty and are bound to observe its provisions. States which have signed but not yet ratified have expressed their intention to become a party at some future date; meanwhile they are obliged to refrain from acts which would defeat the object and purpose of the treaty.

This chart lists countries which were members of the OAS at the end of 2000.

Legend:
- ● became a state party in 2000
- ○ state is a party
- ▶ signed in 2000
- D signed but not yet ratified
- 62 Countries making a Declaration under Article 62 recognize as binding the jurisdiction of the Inter-American Court of Human Rights (on all matters relating to the interpretation or application of the American Convention)

Country	American Convention on Human Rights (1969)	Protocol to the American Convention on Human Rights to Abolish the Death Penalty	Inter-American Convention to Prevent and Punish Torture (1985)	Inter-American Convention on Forced Disappearance of Persons (1994)
Antigua and Barbuda				
Argentina	○ 62		○	○
Bahamas				
Barbados	○			
Belize				
Bolivia	○ 62		D	○
Brazil	○ 62	○	○	D
Canada				
Chile	○ 62		○	D
Colombia	○ 62		○	D
Costa Rica	○ 62	○	●	○
Cuba*				
Dominica	○			
Dominican Republic	○ 62		○	
Ecuador	○ 62	○	○	▶
El Salvador	○ 62		○	
Grenada	○			
Guatemala	○ 62		○	●
Guyana				
Haiti	○ 62		D	
Honduras	○ 62		D	D
Jamaica	○			
Mexico	○ 62		○	
Nicaragua	○ 62	○	D	D
Panama	○ 62	○	○	○
Paraguay	○ 62	○	○	○
Peru	○ 62		○	
Saint Kitts and Nevis				
Saint Lucia				
Saint Vincent and the Grenadines				
Suriname	○ 62		○	
Trinidad and Tobago				
United States of America	D			
Uruguay	○ 62	○	○	○
Venezuela	○ 62	○	○	○

* In 1962 the VIII Meeting of Consultation of Ministers of Foreign Affairs decided to exclude Cuba from participating in the Inter-American system

SELECTED REGIONAL HUMAN RIGHTS TREATIES

Council of Europe

States which have ratified or acceded to a convention are party to the treaty and are bound to observe its provisions. States which have signed but not yet ratified have expressed their intention to become a party at some future date; meanwhile they are obliged to refrain from acts which would defeat the object and purpose of the treaty.

This chart lists countries which were members of the Council of Europe at the end of 2000.

Country	European Convention for the Protection of Human Rights and Fundamental Freedoms (1950)	Protocol No. 6*	European Convention for the Prevention of Torture and Inhuman or Degrading Treatment or Punishment (1987)
Albania	○	●	○
Andorra	○	○	○
Austria	○	○	○
Belgium	○	○	○
Bulgaria	○	○	○
Croatia	○	○	○
Cyprus	○	●	○
Czech Republic	○	○	○
Denmark	○	○	○
Estonia	○	○	○
Finland	○	○	○
France	○	○	○
Georgia	○	●	●
Germany	○	○	○
Greece	○	○	○
Hungary	○	○	○
Iceland	○	○	○
Ireland	○	○	○
Italy	○	○	○
Latvia	○	○	○
Liechtenstein	○	○	○
Lithuania	○	○	○
Luxembourg	○	○	○
Macedonia	○	○	○
Malta	○	○	○
Moldova	○	○	○
Netherlands	○	○	○
Norway	○	○	○
Poland	○	●	○
Portugal	○	○	○
Romania	○	○	○
Russian Federation	○	D	○
San Marino	○	○	○
Slovakia	○	○	○
Slovenia	○	○	○
Spain	○	○	○
Sweden	○	○	○
Switzerland	○	○	○
Turkey	○		○
Ukraine	○	●	○
United Kingdom	○	○	○

- ● became a state party in 2000
- ○ state is a party
- ▶ signed in 2000
- D signed but not yet ratified
- * Protocol No. 6 to the European Convention for the Protection of Human Rights and Fundamental Freedoms concerning the abolition of the death penalty (1983)